CONTEMPLATING MUSIC
Source Readings in the
Aesthetics of Music

CONTEMPLATING MUSIC

Source Readings in the Aesthetics of Music

SELECTED AND EDITED

WITH INTRODUCTIONS BY

Ruth Katz and Carl Dahlhaus

Volume III: Essence

AESTHETICS IN MUSIC NO. 5

PENDRAGON PRESS
STUYVESANT

Aesthetics in Music Series

No. 1   *Analysis and Value Judgment* by Carl Dahlhaus, Translated by Siegmund Levarie (1983) ISBN 0-918728-20-7

No. 2   *Arts, Sciences/Alloys:* The thesis defense for *his doctorat d'Etat* by Iannis Xenakis, Translated by Sharon Kanach (1985) ISBN 0-918728-22-3

No. 3   *Divining the Powers of Music: Aesthetic theory and the origins of opera* by Ruth Katz (1986) ISBN 0-918728-48-7

No. 4   *Musical Aesthetics: A historical reader* edited by Edward A. Lippman (1986) Volume I: *From antiquity to the eighteenth century* ISBN 0-918728-41-X

   Volume II: *The nineteenth century* (1988) ISBN 0-918728-90-8

   Volume III: *The twentieth century* (1990) ISBN 0-945193-10-6

No. 5   *Contemplating Music: Source readings in musical aesthetics* Vol. I, Substance, selected and edited by Carl Dahlhaus and Ruth Katz (1987) ISBN 0-918728-60-6

   Vol. II: Import

Library of Congress Cataloging-in-Publication Data
Main entry under title:

Contemplating Music.

   (Aesthetics in music ; no. 5-   )
   Bibliography: p.
   Includes indexes.
   Contents: v. 1. Substance — v. 2. Import — v. 3. Essence
   1. Music — Philosophy and aesthetics — Addresses,
essays, lectures. I. Dahlhaus, Carl, 1928-1990
II. Katz, Ruth. III. Series: Aesthetics in music series ; no. 5-
ML3345.C66   1986   780'.1   85-28416
ISBN 0-918728-60-6 (v. 1)
ISBN 0-918728-68-1 (v. 2)
ISBN 0-945193-04-1 (v. 3)

Copyright 1992 Pendragon Press New York

ML
3845
·C66
1987
v.3

CONTENTS

VOLUME 3

ESSENCE

PART SEVEN
CONCEPTION AND PERCEPTION

CONTENTS

VOLUME 1

SUBSTANCE

PART TWO
ESSENCE AND DISTINCTNESS

VOLUME 2

IMPORT

Introduction to Volume 2

xiii

VOLUME 4

COMMUNITY OF DISCOURSE

INTRODUCTION

"Essence" is generally understood as referring to an indispensable quality or element of a thing, or, more broadly, to the nature of a thing. What seems commonplace in daily usage, however, constitutes a major philosophical problem, intimately linked to a host of important issues. To begin with, there are critical constraints on what may be said to exist, and how we come to know about that to which we refer. This is further complicated by the fact that alternative descriptions sometimes refer to identical things, creating problems concerning their identity. Certain characteristics, on the other hand, may persist through change. Identity and individuation are thus closely related to the question of essence, presenting problems that are particularly salient as far as music is concerned. To be sure, identities retained through different performances are not abstract qualities but, rather, qualities embodied in physical ways. Do abstract entities also have an existence independent of their physical embodiment?

Our knowledge of geometrical truths lent support to a theory that claimed such an existence, not least because such abstract entities can also be shown to refer to properties of real things. Moreover, such abstract universals have been thought of as especially suitable for the explanation of necessary truths. Yet, while that to which we refer is perceptual, the abstract universal quality is not, for it is neither in time nor in space. Is it then a purely intellectual apprehension? Do particular sound combinations have a relation to some universal that makes us refer to them as music?

Though general words for qualities and relationships are indispensable to discourse, it is not at all clear how we apply such universals to things we have never encountered before. Are our abstract ideas based on an awareness that the thing to which they have been applied have a

xvii

property or properties in common, or are they based on resemblances and partial identities?

In what respect do things resemble? Are resemblances arbitrary, obvious or hidden? Altogether, how do we classify totalities: Do we recognize some things as music because they have a common property, or do we recognize them as such because they are all music, or do we recognize that these sounds have certain properties because they have them in common? These questions and many more are not easily settled, but they all relate to essence, and apply to music as much as they do to other phenomena.

Problems concerning definitions, which constantly recur in philosophical discourse, also relate to essence and likewise loom large in discussions about music. In music, too, definitions are not evaluated in the same ways as empirical descriptions, whether they do or do not provide an explanation of the thing defined. Altogether, are definitions things or names? Are the names accidental or do they refer to a real, but unknown, constitution of a thing's insensible parts? Can the nominal and the real be entirely divorced one from the other?

If the problem of universals has a long history, so does the problem of definitions. Both involve theories that range from essentialism, conceptualism, and nominalism through formalism, linguistic theories, and resemblance theories. It should be stressed, however, that essences or abstract universals were mostly thought of as going beyond their application to perceptible objects. They thus became closely linked to questions concerning meaning, contingent knowledge and timeless truths.

Most of the questions related to essence are "essentials" of contemplating music. They are, in fact, echoed in the various deliberations about music under many different headings. Although these discussions often lack the rigorous characteristics of pure philosophical explication, they reflect similar concerns, questions and answers.

PERMISSIONS

Pendragon Press gratefully acknowledges permission to reprint sections of this collection as follows:

Cooke
: Copyright Oxford University Press 1959. Reprinted from *The Language of Music* by Deryck Cooke (1959) by permission of Oxford University Press.

d'Arezzo
: From "Micrologus" in *Hucbald, Guido, and John on Music* by Claude V. Palisca (1979). Reprinted by permission of Yale University Press.

Helmholtz
: From *On the Sensations of Tones* (1954). Reprinted by permission of Dover Publications, Inc.

Mattheson
: From *Mattheson Johann's der Volkomme Capellmeister*, trans. Ernst C. Harris (1981) reprinted by permission of UMI Research Press, Ann Arbor, Michigan.

Rameau
: From *Treatise on Harmony*, trans. Ph. Gossett (1971). Reprinted by permission of Dover Publications, Inc.

Schenker
: From Sylvan Sol Kalib, *Thirteen Essays from the Three Yearbooks "Das Meisterwerk in der Musik" by Heinrich Schenker: An Annotated Translation (Volumes I–III)*. Reprinted by permission of University Microfilms.

Schoenberg
: From *Fundamentals of Musical Composition*, ed. by Gerald Strang with the collaboration of Leonard Stein; and *Style and Idea*, ed. by Leonard Stein with translations by Leo Black (1975). Reprinted by permission of Faber and Faber Publishers, London.

  From *Structural Functions of Harmony*, rev. edition (1969). Reprinted by permission of W. W. Norton (U.S.A., the Philippines, and Open Market), and A & C Black (Publishers) Ltd. (British Empire).

Winckel
: *Music, Sound and Sensation* (1967). Reprinted by permission of Dover Publications Inc.

Wittgenstein
: From *Philosophical Investigations* (1958), and *Zettel* (1981). Reprinted by permission of Basil Blackwell Limited.

Wolterstorff
: Copyright Nicholas Wolterstorff 1980. Reprinted from *Works and Worlds of Art* by Nicholas Wolterstorff (1980) by permission of Oxford University Press.

Zuckerkandl
: From *Sound and Symbol*, Bollingen Series XLIV. Vol 1: *Music and the External World*, trans. Willard R. Trask. Copyright 1956 by Princeton University Press. Excerpts reprinted with permission of Princeton University Press.

PART SIX

Linguistic Metaphor and Symbolic Language

Introduction to Part Six

One of the decisive watersheds of music history was the process whereby, instead of merely illustrating language, music both laid and realized the claim to be a language itself: a "tone language" or "sound discourse," as Johann Mattheson put it in 1739 in *Der Vollkommene Cappelmeister*. The capacity to be a language, which instrumental music had asserted, formed the precondition for its managing to emancipate itself aesthetically—and not only pragmatically—from vocal music. Since E.T.A. Hoffmann and Eduard Hanslick, instrumental music has been the paradigm of music proper.

The musical aesthetics of the sixteenth to the eighteenth century (which until the early eighteenth century was, strictly speaking, not "aesthetics" but is only called this for the sake of expendiency) was oriented exclusively towards the madrigal and later towards opera and the sacred cantata. (Musical aesthetics proper has, in general, nearly always been an aesthetics of individual genres—a fact that, if taken into account, reveals many controversies to be fruitless dialogues in which the disputants talk at cross purposes about different things.) The efforts of humanism to reconstruct the "meravigliosi effetti" of ancient music and also musical rhetoric and the Doctrine of Affections are theories of vocal music whose concept of music, following the Platonic definition, also embraces—apart from *harmonia* and *rhythmos* —the *logos* (language). (It is inappropriate to separate music and language before the eighteenth century, since the term "music"—apart from the speculations on celestial mechanics—itself implies language.)

The relation to language is characterized, roughly speaking, by the fact that musical symbols and forms of expression, although they heighten the intensity of the aesthetic effect, owe their differentiation to the texts they illustrate—a differentiation whereby they come to make up a richly developed system of signs as opposed to an initially rudimentary one. The elementary musically symbolic contrasts between high and low, rise and fall, rest and motion are comprehensible in themselves, and the association of high and low with bright and dark is so old that one can almost describe it as "given by nature." Whether, however, a canon symbolizes the "law" or a "succession," or whether the figure once called "circulus," although more closely resembling a

3

sine curve, represents an "undulation" or a globe, simply cannot be determined without a text that provides a commentary on the music.

Once language provided a point of reference and the lacking for musical symbolism and the representation of affects, it also constituted, through its structure and punctuation, the model towards which musical syntax and the theory of form were oriented and from which they derived a large part of their terminology. (It was imperative, above all with regard to instrumental music, to develop a syntax and theory of form. The accusation that instrumental music was an empty, albeit pleasant, noise could only be refuted by its "hanging on" to the substance and basic structure of language, though outwardly parted from it, or at least by attempting such a separation.) The caesuras that divide and subdivide speech—comma, colon, semicolon and period—form a graded system whose structure one believed could be recognized in the differentiation among cadences with which musical sections end. In the eighteenth century, the relations between whole, half and interrupted closes and between octave, fifth and third cadences were conceived as syntactic ways of expressing the gradations of emphasis that exist between the component parts of a melody.

Apart from syntax, the form of complete movements was explained or described on the basis of models taken from language. In 1826, Antoine Reicha, teacher of composition at the Paris Conservatoire, interpreted sonata form, whose dramatic character probably occurred to him in works by Beethoven, as the mirror of a tragedy, with "exposition," "tying of the knot" and "dénouement." Moreover, the dialectic of main and second theme was seen, in nineteenth-century aesthetics, as the contrast between a protagonist and an antagonist (whereby the nomenclature caused damage by distorting the significance of the second subject, which can also be an episode).

Even harmony, albeit not explicitly, was interpreted with the aid of language theory. The distinction between substance and function, on which Hugo Riemann's functional theory is based—the thesis, namely, that two chords that, in the extreme, do not have a single note in common can nonetheless represent the same function [e-a-c the *Leittonwechselklang* ("changed leading-note sonority") of the sub-dominant major and f-a flat-d flat as the *Leittonwechselklang* of the subdominant minor in C major]—recalls, not by chance, the difference between the "sound" of a word and its "meaning." According to Riemann, the functions of chords represent their meaning in a sense thoroughly analogous to language.

4

One of the most difficult problems of a musical aesthetics oriented towards language theory is the relationship between the content an individual musical element offers in itself and the refinement or modification of this content through its context. In the first movement of Beethoven's Piano Sonata in F minor, op. 2 no. 1, the character of the themes is partially but unmistakably founded on their being related to each other by "contrasting derivation" (Arnold Schmitz). Against the general expressive content, derived from tradition, of a rising broken triad played staccato and a falling, chromatically infiltrated broken seventh chord played legato, it is the relation between the themes that represents the individualizing factor. For an analysis which goes beyond this general assertion, however, we lack at present the categories and methods.

The straightforward grammatical interpretations of the relationship between music and language developed in the eighteenth century were opposed in the Romantic period by an effusively metaphysical conception: the language of music was elevated above the verbal, becoming the expression of something words could neither reach nor utter. The "language of a distant realm of spirits," which E.T.A. Hoffmann enthused about, is absolute instrumental music, freed from texts, programmes and even from the expression of clearly outlined effects, whose separation from language was justified by its being interpreted as a "metaphysical" language as distinct from the "empirical" one. Music, according to Arthur Schopenhauer, represents the essence of things (the *Ding an sich*) and not—as verbal language does—their mere manifestation.

The transition from vocal music to instrumental music as the paradigm of music proper was a far-reaching watershed; yet it did not alter the fact that problems of musical aesthetics, before and since, were discussed in the context of the relationship between music and language. Thus, one could say that it was this context in thinking about music that guaranteed continuity between the beginning of the modern age and the present, which appears as the end of the age.

5

GUIDO OF AREZZO

Guido of Arezzo (*c* 992–1050) was an important figure not only in the history of musical education but also in the history of musical thought, owing to his invention of staff notation with lines a third apart and his method of solmization. With the fifteenth chapter of his *chef d'oeuvre*, the *Micrologus* (1025–6), he was invoked as a witness in a controversy between chant theoreticians of the nineteenth and twentieth century. If he appears to provide contradictory answers, it is because the questions imposed on his text are at variance with the intentions he himself pursued.

In the dispute between the "equalists" and the "mensuralists," concerning the rhythmical interpretation of the chant, Guido is a poor witness, indeed. In contrast to the "equalists," he presupposes a differentiation of note values and, unlike the "mensuralists," he demands a continual change of "metres." What is conceptually grasped, accordingly, albeit in a makeshift way, is the mere fact that some "longs" in a series of tones tend to stand out. (A series of note values in which, as Guido describes, a Trochee is followed by an Iambus and then by a Dactyl, is certainly not a "metre" in the strict sense of the word.)

According to Guido, it is also possible to produce satisfying ratios between tone groups via either the number of rhythmically equal tones or through a differentiation in their values ("ratio tenorum"). For Guido it was unmistakably the division of melodic parts that mattered, and not the choice of the appropriate rhythmic means, over which the equalists and the mensuralists quarrelled.

Guido's premise concerning the comparison between music and language may be linguistically questionable. Although one may readily draw an analogy between a speech sound and a tone, between a syllable and a tone group, the central linguistic unit, i.e. the word as the bearer of

7

meaning and not just as a conglomeration of syllables, has no musical equivalent. (Neither the earlier neumes nor the later motifs constituted "words" in the "language" of music in anything but a vague, metaphorical sense.)

What is decisive, however, is not the systematic inconsistencies but the historical significance of the Guidonian comparison—a comparison, inspired by the writings of Odo, which demonstrates that the starting-point of our musical conception is not the continuous movement of tones, which is symbolized by a neume, but the distinct individual tone, whose adequate sign is a note. It is quite secondary whether a tone is designated by a letter, as with Guido, or by a point in geometry or the figure one, as with Remy of Auxerre ("... vox enim materies vel initium est musicae et eam vim obtinet vox in musica quam punctus in geometria, monas in arithmetica, littera in grammatica"). The orientation towards grammatical terminology was just one of several possible ways to elucidate by analogy the perception of an individual tone.

Compared to Chapter 15, the theory of the melodic figure (*motus*), which Guido develops in Chapter 16 of the *Micrologus*, appears both as a counterpart and compensation for the otherwise exclusive dwelling on individual tones and the "compositio" of melodies thereof. If the term *motus* suggests, to begin with, the older idea that of a continuous movement of tones which, historically, preceded the assembling of melodies from individual tones, then the movement of tones grasped analytically reveals that—under the premise of listening to individual tones—such a concept was not self-evident. It became an object of theory because it was no longer as readily apparent from musical notation—the mirror of musical concepts—as in the system of neumes.

The method with which Guido presents the *motus* in written form is not primarily characterized through an association with movement in the ancient (Aristoxenos) or modern sense (Ernst Kurth), but via analytical thought which is never very far from blocking access to the very phenomenon that it is supposed to reveal.

Guido takes as his starting-point the six intervals that are melodically admissible ("emmelic"), yet he does not describe the *motus*, as one might expect, as a movement from tone to tone but as an analogue to the construction of syllables from letters. (As a point of comparison, the large number of possible combinations seem to emerge from a small number of elements.) A chance was thereby missed which was quite within the grasp of the music theory of the age: namely, of distinguishing between the speaking voice and the singing voice, between the

8

continuous movement of the former and the discreetly progressing, tone-by-tone or jumping movement of the latter, wherein continuum is contained only latently.

In Guido's systematic description of the relations between intervals that have been joined together, the spatial element of the movement of tones is given its due. But not a single mention is made of music's temporality. The definition of time as the measurement of movement established itself in the minds of intellectuals only with the reception of Aristotle in the thirteenth century, with the result that concepts such as time, measurement and movement could no longer be discussed independently of each other. Only then, it would seem, were the philosophical conditions created for explicit contemplation of music's temporal structure.

from the Micrologus[1]

[80]   Gone from school are the Muses; there may I hope to induce them,
Unknown yet to adults, to unveil their light to the young ones!
Ill will's indiscriminate rage let charity frustrate;
Dire indeed are the blights that else will ravage our planet,
Opening letters of these five lines will spell you the author.

[81]   [Guido's Epistle to Bishop Theodaldus]

To the most kind father and most revered lord Theodaldus, most radiant with the light of godliness and of all wisdom and worthiest of priests and bishops, from Guido, the salutations of a servant and son—would that he were the least of your monks.

Though I desire at least a modicum of solitary life, Your Gracious Eminence wished to associate my littleness with yourself in the study of the Holy Word. Not that Your Excellency lacks many outstandingly [82] spiritual men, most plentifully fortified by the practice of the virtues and most abundantly distinguished by their pursuit of wisdom, who together with you instruct properly the people entrusted to you and apply themselves assiduously and fervently to meditation on holy things; but that you took pity on the helplessness of my insignificant mind and body, and sheltered and sustained me by the protection of your fatherly goodness; so that if by God's will anything useful should come of me, God will impute it to your merit.

Since it was a matter of usefulness to the church, your authority decreed that this way of training in the art of music—for which I am mindful that with God's help I have toiled not in vain—be published. Just as [83] you created by an exceedingly marvelous plan the church of St. Donatus, the bishop and martyr, over which you preside by the will of God and as his lawful vicar, so likewise by a most honorable and appropriate distinction you would make the ministers of that church cynosures for all churchmen throughout almost the whole world. In very truth it is sufficiently marvelous and desirable that even boys of your church should surpass in the practice of music the fully trained

[1]Text: *Huchbald, Guido and John on Music, Three Medieval Treatises*, ed. C.V. Palisca, tr. Warren Babb (New Haven: Yale University Press, 1979), pp. 57-83 (including notes).

veterans of all other places; and the height of your honor and merit will be very greatly increased because, though subsequent to the early fathers, such great and distinguished renown for learning has come to this church through you.

[84] Therefore, since I neither would nor could go against your command, fitting as it is, I offer to your most sagacious and fatherly self the precepts of the science of music, explained, so far as I could, much more clearly and briefly than has been done by philosophers, neither in the same way, for the most part, nor following in the same tracks, but endeavoring only that it should help both the cause of the church and our little ones. The reason that this study has remained obscure up to now is that, being truly difficult, it has been explained in simpler terms by no one. How it came about that I first undertook this explanation, and with what profit and what effort, I shall set forth in a few words.

[85]   Prologue

Since both my natural disposition and my emulation of good men made me eager to work for the general benefit, I undertook, among other things, to teach music to boys. Presently Divine Grace favored me, and some of them, trained by imitating the [steps of the mono]chord, with the practice of our notation, were within the space of a month singing so securely at first sight chants they had not seen or heard, that it was the greatest wonder to many people. But if someone cannot do that, I do not know with what face he can venture to call himself a musician or a singer.

[86] I was extremely sorry for our singers who, though they should persevere a hundred years in the study of singing, can never perform even the tiniest antiphon on their own—always learning, as the apostle says, and never arriving at knowledge of the truth.[2] Desiring therefore to set forth my own so useful method of study for the general benefit, I summarized as briefly as I could, out of the copious musical theorizing which with God's help I have at various times collected, certain things that I believed would help singers. But I judged those musical matters not worth mention which are of little benefit for singing, as well as any of the things that are said but cannot be understood—not [87] worrying

---

[2] 2 Tim. 3:7.

11

about any who might turn livid with ill will so long as the training of others made progress.

Here ends the prologue. The chapters begin. [88]

Chapter 1

What one should do to prepare himself to study music

[91] Let him who seeks our training learn some chants copied in our notation, let him train his hand in the use of the monochord, [92] and let him frequently ponder these rules, until, having learned the effect and character of the notes, he can smoothly sing unfamiliar music as well as familiar. Since we learn the notes, which are the primary foundation of

this art, more easily at the monochord, let us first see how science, imitating nature, has given them their separate places thereon.

Chapter 2

What the notes are, of what nature, and how many

[93] The notes on the monochord are these. First is placed Greek Γ, added by the moderns. There follow seven letters of the alphabet as the *graves* [low], and therefore written in larger letters, thus: A B C D E F G. [94] After these the same seven letters are repeated as the *acutae* [high], but they are indicated by smaller letters. Among them, between a and ♭ [i.e. b^a] we put another b which we made round, whereas we made the former one square, thus: a b d e f g. We add by means of these same letters, but differently written, the tetrachord of the *superacutae* [above the *acutae*], in which we likewise have the two forms of b and ♭, thus: $^{abbcd}_{abbcd}$. The *superacutae* are considered superfluous by many, but we had rather have too much than too little. [95] So in all there are twenty-one, namely Γ A B C D E F G a b ♭ c d e f g $^{abbcd}_{abbcd}$. Their location, which the learned either are silent about or confuse by excessive obscurity, is here explained briefly, yet fully enough even for boys.

Chapter 3

On the location of notes on the monochord

[96] After marking Γ at the beginning, divide the space beneath the string from there to the other end into nine parts, and at the end of the first ninth put the letter A, with which all the ancients began. [97] When you have likewise measured a ninth part [of the length] from A to the far end of the string, in the same way place the letter B. After this, going back to Γ, divide the string from there to the other end by four, and at the end of the first quarter you will find C. By a similar division into quarters, just as C was found from Γ, in the same way you will find successively D from A, E from B, F from C, G from D, a from E, and b-flat from F. The following notes [98] are all easily obtained one after the other as halfway points of notes similar in sound and the same in letter: so, halfway from B to the far end of the string, you put another ♭.

13

Likewise C will point out another c, D will point out another d, E another e, F another f, G another g, and the rest of the notes in the same way. You could continue up or down thus ad infinitum, did not the precept of art restrain you by its authority. Of the many and various systems of dividing the monochord, I have given one, because when one's [99] attention is turned from many things to one, that one is grasped without trouble. It is particularly useful too, since it is both easily learned and, once learned, rarely forgotten.

Here follows another method of dividing the monochord, which is harder to memorize, but by it the monochord is more quickly divided. You make nine steps, that is [equal] segments, from Γ to the other end. The first step will end at A, the second will have no letter, the third will end at D, the fourth will be unlettered, the fifth will end at a, the sixth at d, the seventh at $\frac{a}{a}$, and the others will be unlettered. [100] Likewise, when you divide [the length] from A to the other end into nine parts, the first step will end at B, the second will be unlettered, the third will end at E, the fourth will be unlettered, the fifth will end at ♭, the sixth at e, the seventh at $\frac{♭}{♮}$, and the rest will be unlettered.[3] When you divide [the length] from Γ to the other end into quarters, the first step will end on C, the second on G, the third on g, the fourth at the end of the string. Of the four similar steps from C to the other end of the string, the first will end on F, the second on c, the third on $\frac{c}{c}$, the fourth at the end of the string. Of the quarter-length steps from F, the first will end on b-flat, the second on f.

[101] For laying out the notes on the monochord let these two systems of measurements suffice, [102] of which the former is the easiest to memorize, while the latter is the quickest to apply. Next, all the intervals arising out of the divisions [of the string] will be briefly set forth.

Chapter 4

That notes should be joined to each other by six intervals

[103] With the notes laid out in this way, sometimes a greater distance is noticed between one note and another, as between Γ and A and

---

[3]As the *Commentarius anonymus* noted (Vivell ed., p. 10, van Waesberghe, *Expositiones*, p. 104), this monochord is incomplete, for Guido failed to derive $\frac{♭}{♭}$ and $\frac{d}{d}$ (the commentator said ♭ was missing, but he must have had a faulty text).

between A and B, and sometimes a lesser, as between B and C, and so forth.

The greater distance is called a tone, and the smaller a semitone, from *semis* [a half], that is, not a full tone.

[104] Between any note and the third from it there is sometimes a ditone, that is two tones, as from C to E, and sometimes a semiditone, which has only a tone and a semitone, as from D to F, and so forth. A diatessaron is formed when between two notes there are two tones and a semitone in any order, as from A to D and from B to E, and so forth. A diapente is a tone larger, and occurs whenever between notes there are three tones and one semitone, as from A [105] to E and from C to G, and so forth.

Thus you have six melodic intervals [*consonantiae*], namely, tone, semitone, ditone, semiditone, diatessaron, and diapente. In no chant is one note joined to another by any other intervals, going either up or down. Since [106] all melody [*harmonia*] is formed by so few formulas [*clausulae*], it is most helpful to commit them firmly to memory, and, until they are completely perceived and recognized in singing, never to stop practicing them, since when you hold these as keys, you can command skill in singing—intelligently, and therefore more easily.

Chapter 5

On the diapason and why there are only seven notes

[107] The diapason is the interval in which a diapente and a diatessaron are combined; for while from A to D is a diatessaron and from that same D to acute a is a diapente, from A to the other a is a diapason.

[108] Its property is to have the same letter on both ends, as from B to ♭, from C to c, from D to d, and so forth. Just as both sounds are notated by the same letter, so both are held and believed to be in all respects of the same nature and the most absolute likeness.

Just as when seven days have elapsed we repeat the same ones, so that we always name the first and eighth the same; so we always represent and name the first and eighth notes the same way, because we perceive that they sound together with a natural concord, [109] as D and d. For from each of them you descend by a tone, a semitone, and two tones, and ascend by a tone, a semitone, and two tones. Thus, in singing, if two or three or more singers, as may be feasible, begin and

15

sing through the same antiphon, whichever it be, with the various notes at different pitches [*loci*] but with a minimal difference of sound, and that the same melody resounds in the *graves, acutae,* and *superacutae* as if a single thing, thus [110]:

Example 1

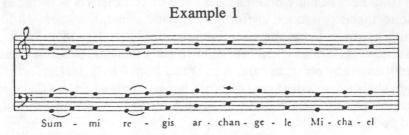

[111] Likewise if you should sing the same antiphon partly in a low and partly in a high register, or however else you transpose it at the interval of a diapason, the same unity of notes [112] will be apparent. Therefore the poet spoke very rightly of "the seven notes,"[4] because even if more occur it is not an addition of other ones, but a renewal and repetition of the same ones. For this reason, we, like Boethius[5] and the musicians of old, indicate all musical sounds by seven letters. However some people nowadays [113] incautiously employ only four symbols. They indicate every fifth sound always by the same symbol, though it is true beyond a doubt that some notes disagree completely with those a fifth away, and that no note agrees perfectly with its fifth. For no note agrees perfectly with any other except its octave.

Chapter 6

Also on the divisions of the monochord and their meaning

[114] To compress many things about the division of the monochord into a few words: the diapason always moves in two steps to the other end of the string, the diapente in three, the diatessaron in four, and the tone in nine; and the more steps they have, the shorter the distance of these. But you can find no other divisions than these four.

[115] "Diapason" means "through all," either because it includes all the notes, or because citharas in antiquity had eight strings extending

---

[4]" . . . septem discrimina vocum," Vergil, *Aenid* 6. 646.
[5]Guido may have had a copy annotated by a modern author, for Boethius did not limit himself to seven letters.

through a diapason. In this interval the lower note has two units of length; the upper one, as A and a. "Diapente" derives from "five," for there are five notes in its span, as from D to a. Its lower note has three units of length; its upper, two.

"Diatessaron" derives from "four," both because it includes four notes and because its lower note has four units of length while its upper has three, as from D to G.

[116] You should remember that these three intervals are called "symphonies,"[6] that is, smooth unions of notes, because in the diapason the different notes sound as one and because the diapente and the diatessaron are the basis [iura possident] of diaphony, that is, organum,[7] and produce notes similar in every case.

The tone gets its name from *intonandus*, that is "to be sounded," and gives nine units of length to its lower note compared with eight to its higher. The semitone, however, the ditone, and the semiditone, although they connect notes in singing, get no dividing point.[8]

Chapter 7

On the affinities of notes through the four modes

[117] Since there are just seven notes—seeing that the others, as we have said, are repetitions—it suffices to explain the seven that are of different modes and different qualities. The first mode of notes arises when from a note one descends by a tone and [118] ascends by a tone, a semitone, and two tones, as from A and D. The second mode arises when from a note one descends by two tones and ascends by a semitone and two tones, as from B and E. The third is that in which one descends by a semitone and two tones but ascends by two tones, as from C and F. The fourth goes down by a tone but rises by two tones and a semitone, like G.[9]

[6]*Symphonia* is the standard term, from Cassiodorus (*Institutiones*. 2. 5. 7) up to Guido.
[7]See below, chap. 18.
[8]Since in Pythagorean tuning their ratios involve terms that are numerically large, for example 32:27 for the semiditone, 81:64 for the ditone, the number of string divisions required to produce them would be impractical on a monochord.
[9]While the other modes have pairs of notes, the fourth, on G, lacks a pair, because it has no affinity, as proved in Fig. 1.

Notice that they follow each other in order. Thus, the first [mode] on A, the second [119] on B, the third on C; and also the first on D, the second on E, the third on F, and the fourth on G. Notice too that these affinities of notes are made through the diatessaron and the diapente, for A is joined to D, and B to E, and C to F by the lower diatessaron, but by the upper diapente, [as in Fig. 1].

Figure 1

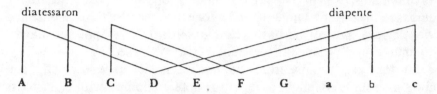

Chapter 8

On other affinities and on b and b

[122] Whatever other affinities there are, they are produced likewise by the diatessaron and the diapente. For since the diapason contains in itself a diatessaron plus a diapente and has the same letters on each end, there is always in the middle of its [123] length a letter which is so related to either end of the diapason that with whatever letter in the low register it gives a diatessaron, with that same one in the high register it makes a diapente, as is notated in the diagram above; and with whatever letter in the low register it made a diapente, with that same one in the upper register it will give a diatessaron, as A, E, a. Now a and E agree in that one descends from them by two tones and a semitone. Also, since G sounds with C and D by these same intervals, it has taken over the descent of the one and the ascent of the other; for C and G rise [124] similarly by two tones and a semitone, and D and G descend similarly by a tone and a semitone.

Moreover b-flat, which is less regular and which is called "added" or "soft," has a concord with F, and is added because F cannot make a concord with b a fourth away, since it is a tritone distant. You should not join b and b in the same neume.

We use b-flat mostly in that chant in which F or f [125] recurs rather extensively, either low or high. Here b-flat seems to create a certain confusion and transformation, so that G sounds as protus and a as deuterus, whereas b[-flat] itself sounds as tritus. Many therefore have never mentioned b[-flat], whereas the other b has been acceptable to all. But if you wish not to have b-flat at all, alter the neumes in which it occurs, so that instead of F G a and b-flat you have G a b c. If it is the kind of neume that, going up after D E F, [126] wants two tones and a semitone—which causes this f [-flat]—or going down after D E F wants two whole tones, then instead of D E F use a b c, which are of the same mode and have the perfectly regular descents and ascents that were just mentioned. For it best avoids a sad confusion if one apportions such ascents and descents clear-sightedly between D E F and a b c.

We have confined ourselves to just a few things about the similarities between notes, because, insofar as similarity is sought out between different things, to this extent is lessened that diversity which [127] can prolong the labor of the confused mind, for organized material is always more easily grasped than unorganized.

All the modes and the "distinctions" of the modes are connected with these three notes [C, D, E]. Now I call "distinctions" what many call "differences." But the term "difference" is used because something distinguishes or [128] divides plagal modes from authentic; otherwise, it is misused. All other notes have some concordance with these three, either below or above; but no notes shown themselves similar to other notes in both directions, except at the diapason. Anyone who seeks can find a representation of all this in the chart [Fig. 2] [129].

Figure 2

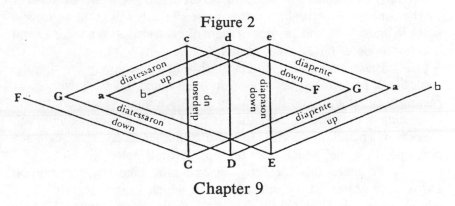

Chapter 9

Also on the resemblance of notes, which is perfect only at the diapason

[130] Insofar as the above-mentioned notes are alike—some in

descent, some in ascent, some in both—they will make neumes sound alike. [131] Thus the knowledge of one makes another clear to you. As for those notes in which no resemblance is evident, or which are of different modes, no one of them will accept the neume or chant of another; or, if you force it to receive one, it will change its sound.

Thus if one should wish to begin on E or F, which are notes of other modes, an antiphon that should begin on D, one would soon tell by ear how great a change was taking place. But on D and a, which are of the same mode, we can most often begin or end the same piece. [132] I say "most often," and not "always," because likeness is not complete except at the octave.

For where there is a difference in the arrangement of the tones and semitones, there is bound to be one also in [the sound of] the neumes. And even among the notes just mentioned, which are assigned to the same mode, dissimilarities are found. For from D you can go down only one whole tone, but from a, two; and so also elsewhere.

Chapter 10

Also on the modes and on recognizing and correcting a wrong melody

[133] Here are [described] the four modes or tropes, which are improperly called "tones." They are do differentiated from one another by their inherent dissimilarity, that none of them will grant another a place in its domain, and any one of them either transforms a neume from another mode or never even admits it.

[134] False notes also creep in through inaccuracy in singing; sometimes performers deviate from well-tuned notes, lowering or raising them slightly, as is done by untrue human voices. Also, by ascending or descending more than is right for the prescribed interval, we pervert a neume of a certain mode into another mode or we begin at a place [in the scale] which does not admit [that] note.

[137] To make this clear by an example, take the communion *Diffusa est gratia*. Many put *propterea*, which should begin on F, a whole tone down, although there is not a whole tone just below F. As a result the end of this communion comes where there is no note. The place and mode where [138] each neume begins should be left to the judgment of the singer, so that if it needs to be transposed [*si motione*

opus est], he may search out related [*affines*] notes. These modes or tropes we name, from the Greek, protus, deuterus, tritus, and tetrardus.

Chapter 11

What note should hold the chief place in a chant and why

[139] Though any chant is made up of all the notes and intervals, the note that ends it holds the chief place, for it sounds both longer and more lasting. The previous notes, as is evident to trained musicians only, [140] are so adjusted to the last one that in an amazing way they seem to draw a certain semblance of color from it.

The other notes should have a harmonious relationship with the note that ends a neume by means of the aforesaid six melodic intervals. The beginning of a chant and the end of all its phrases and even their beginnings need to cling close to the note that ends the chant. An exception is that when a chant ends on E it often [141] begins on c, which is a diapente plus a semitone away, as the antiphon:

Example 2

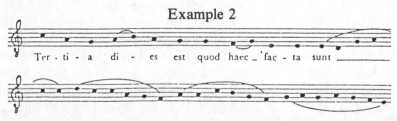

Ter - ti - a   di - es   est   quod haec _ 'fac - ta   sunt

[144] Furthermore, when we hear someone sing, we do not know what mode his first note is in, since we do not know whether tones, semitones, or other intervals will follow. But when the chant has ended, we know clearly from the preceding notes the mode of the last one. For at the start of a chant you do not know what will follow, but at its end you realize what has gone before. Thus the last note is the one we are better aware of. So if you wish to add to your chant either a verse or a psalm or anything else, [145] you should adjust it most of all to the final note of the former, not go back and consider the first note or any of the others. This too we may add, that carefully composed chants end their phrases chiefly on the final note [of the chant].

It is no wonder that music bases its rules on the last note, since in the elements of language, too, we almost everywhere see the real force of

21

the meaning in the final letters or syllables, in regard to cases, numbers, persons, and tenses. Therefore, since all praise, too, is sung at the end, we rightly say that every chant is subject to, and takes its rules from, that mode which it sounds last.

[146] In any chant it is right to go down [as far as] a fifth from the final note and up [as far as] an octave, though it often happens that, contrary to the rule, we go up to a ninth or tenth. Hence D E F G have been established as the final notes, because their location on the monochord fits in preeminently with the upward and downward progress just mentioned. For they have one tetrachord of the *graves* below and two of the *acutae* above.

Chapter 12

On the division of the four modes into eight

[147] Some chants in a certain mode, say the protus, with respect to their final notes are low and level, others high and raised. Therefore, when verses or psalms or whatever else, as we said, had to be fitted to their endings, although they continued in one and the same mode, [148] they could still not be adjusted to these different ranges. For what was added on, if it was low-pitched, did not go well with the high notes; but if it was high, it was at odds with the low notes. So the plan was that each mode should be divided into two, namely a high and a low, and, according to regulations assigned, high notes should go with high and low with low; and each high mode should be called authentic, that is original and principal, while the low mode should be called plagal, that is, collateral and lesser. For he who is said to stand at my side is lower [*minor*] than I; otherwise, if he were higher [*major*], I should be said rather to stand at his side.

Since therefore one says authentic protus [*autentus protus*] and plagal of the protus [*plagis proti*], and likewise with the rest, these modes, which naturally were four according to their notes, have been made [149] eight in chants. A mistaken usage transmitted by the Latins is to say first and second instead of authentic protus and the plagal of the protus, third and fourth instead of authentic deuterus and the plagal of the deuterus, fifth and sixth instead of authentic tritus and plagal of the tritus, and seventh and eight instead of authentic tetrardus and plagal of the tetrardus.

Chapter 13

On the recognition of the eight modes by their height and depth

[150] Thus there are eight modes, as there are eight parts of speech[10] and eight kinds of beatitude;[11] and every melodic line, as it moves to and fro among these, is diversified by eight dissimilar qualities.[12] For ascertaining these modes in chants, certain neumes have been [151] composed,[13] so that we learn the mode of the chant from the way it fits these, just as we often discover from the way it fits the body which tunic is whose. For example,

Example 3

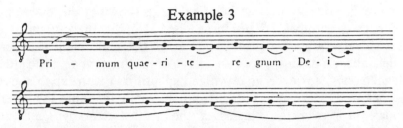

Pri - mum quae - ri - te — re - gnum De - i —

[154] as soon as we have seen that this neume [Example 3] accords with the end of an antiphon, there is no need to doubt that it is authentic protus; and similarly with the other modes. Most helpful for this are the verses of the responsories of nocturns, the psalms of the offices, and all the chants that are prescribed in the formulas of the modes.[14] It is a

[10]Grammatically speaking, a word is either a noun, verb, pronoun, adjective, adverb, preposition, conjunction, or interjection.

[11]The blessed qualities enumerated in the Sermon on the Mount, Matt. 5:3-11.

[12]These must be the eight modes.

[13]Guido refers here to either the *Noeane* formulas (see above pp. 6-8), or the Latin formulas of the modes, which begin with the melody "Primum quaerite regnum Dei" for the first mode, as in Berno, *Tonarius*, GS 2:79. See Antoine Auda, *Les modes et les tons de la musique*, pp. 176ff. and the references given in the Introduction to Hucbald, above, n. 14 to 18.

[14]" . . . in modorum formulis"—here Guido may be referring once again to the series of melodic specimens for each mode that begins with "Primum quaerite regnum Dei" (see n. 4 above), or, as Huglo believes ("L'auteur du 'Dialogue,' " p. 166), to a tonary, since the term *tonarius* was not yet current in Italy, and possibly the tonary of Abbot Odo, the Prologue of which is in *GS* 1:248-249a, the tonary itself in *CS* 2:117-49. Compare the usage in Guido's *Epistola, GS* 2:48a: "Nota autem, quomodo modos dicimus eos, qui in formulis tonorum non proprie sed abusive nominantur toni, cum modi vel tropi proprie dicantur." And later on the same page: "Ideoque habes in formulis modorum duas formulas in unoquoque modo." See also the references in the translation of John, chap. 11, n. 7, p. 120.

wonder if someone who does not know these understands any part of what is being said here. For there one can foresee on what notes of the particular modes chants less often or more often begin, and on what notes they do so least. Thus in plagal modes it is least permissible to rise either in beginnings or endings of phrases [155] to the fifth degree [above the final], although one may very rarely rise to the fourth [degree]. In authentic modes, however, except the deuterus, it is most unsuitable to rise in these beginnings and endings of phrases to the sixth degree. Yet those of the plagal of the protus and the plagal of the tritus go as high as the third, and those of the plagal of the deuterus and the plagal of the tetrardus go as high as the fourth.

You should remember, furthermore, that authentic modes scarcely go more than one note below their finals, as is shown by the testimony of the chants generally used. For these it is evident that the authentic tritus does so very rarely because of the flaw of the semitone just beneath. [The authentic modes] go up an octave or ninth or even a [156] tenth. Plagal modes, however, go down and up a fifth. Yet the sixth above is also allowed by the authorities, as are the ninth and tenth in authentic modes. Moreover the plagals of the protus, deuterus, and tritus sometimes end by necessity on high a, ♭, and c respectively.

The above-mentioned rules are observed very particularly in antiphons and responsories, whose chants [157] should be based on the customary rules so that they will join well with psalms and verses. However, you will find a number of chants in which the low and the high are so intermingled that one cannot make out whether they should be assigned to authentic or plagal. Furthermore, in studying chants new to us, we are helped chiefly by juxtaposing the aforesaid neumes and appendages [*subiunctiones*], since from the way these fit we come to see the particular character of each note through the effect of the "tropes." "Trope" is the aspect of chant which is also called "mode," and we shall now discuss it.

Chapter 14

On the tropes and on the power of music

[158] Some men who are well trained in the particular characters and, so to say, the individual features of these tropes recognize them the instant they hear them, as one who is familiar with the different peoples,

when many men are placed before him, can observe their appearance and say, "This is [159] a Greek, that one a Spaniard, this is a Latin, that one a German, and that other is a Frenchman." The diversity in the tropes so fits in with the diversity in people's minds that one man is attracted by the intermittent leaps of the authentic deuterus, another chooses the delightfulness of the plagal of the tritus, one is more pleased by the volubility of the authentic tetrardus, another esteems the sweetness of the plagal tetrardus, and so forth.

Nor is it any wonder if the hearing is charmed by a variety of sounds, since the sight rejoices in a variety of colors, the sense of smell is gratified by a variety of odors, and the palate delights in changing flavors. For thus through the windows of the body [160] the sweetness of apt things enters wondrously into the recesses of the heart. Hence it is that the well-being of both heart and body is lessened or increased, as it were, by particular tastes and smells and even by the sight of certain colors. So it is said that of old a certain madman was recalled from insanity by the music of the physician Asclepiades.[15] Also that another man was roused by the sound of the cithara to such lust that, in his madness, he sought to break into the bedchamber of a girl, but, when the cithara player quickly changed the mode, was brought to feel remorse for his libidinousness and to retreat abashed. [161] So, too, David soothed with the cithara the evil spirit of Saul and tamed the savage demon with the potent force and sweetness of this art.[16] Yet this effect is fully clear only to Divine Wisdom, thanks to which, indeed, we have gained some insight into obscure things. Since we have poured forth not a few words on the power of this art, let us now see what is requisite for shaping good melodic lines.

Chapter 15

On grateful melodic lines and composing them[17]

[162] Just as in verse there are letters and syllables, "parts" and feet and lines, so in music there are phthongi, that is, sounds, of which one,

---

[15]This story about the Greek physician Asclepiades is told by Censorinus, *De In die natali* 12; Martianus Capella, *Satyricon* 9; and Cassiodorus, *Inst.* 5. 9, from whom Guido probably got it.

[16]1 Sam. 16:23. This story too is told by Cassiodorus, *Inst.* 5. 9.

[17]For a listing of some of the commentaries and translations of this chapter, see the Introduction to this treatise, n. 39.

[163] two, or three are grouped in "syllables"; one or two of the latter make a neume, which is the "part" of music; and one or more "parts" make a "distinction," that is, a suitable place to breathe. Regarding these units it must be noted that every "part" should be written and performed connectedly, and a musical "syllable" even more so.

A "hold" [*tenor*]—that is, a pause on the last note—which is very small for a "syllable," [164] larger for a "part," and longest for a phrase [*distinctio*], is in these cases a sign of division. It is good to beat time to a song as though by metrical feet. Some notes have separating them from others a brief delay [*morula*] twice as long or twice as short, or a trembling [*tremula*], that is, a "hold" of varying length, which sometimes is shown to be long by a horizontal dash added to a letter. [165] Special care should be taken that neumes, whether made by repeating one note or joining two or more, be always arranged to correspond to each other either in the number of notes or in the relationship of the durations [*tenores*]. At some times let equal neumes be answered by equal; at others let "simple" neumes be answered by those two or three times [as long]; and at still others let neumes be juxtaposed with others three-halves or four-thirds [their size] [see Fig. 3].

Figure 3

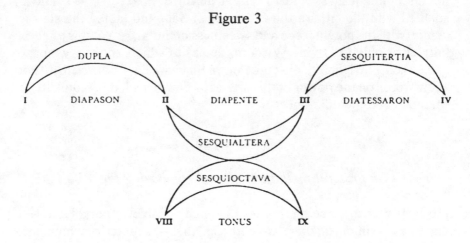

[167] Let the musician consider with which of these proportions [*divisiones*] he will construct the chant that is under way, as the versifier considers with which feet he will make the verse. However, the musician does not restrict himself by such stringency of rule, since in every way this art keeps transforming itself through a reasonable

variety in the ordering of notes. Even though we often may not grasp this reasonableness, still that is thought to be reasonable which pleases a mind in which reason resides. Yet these and other such things are better demonstrated in speaking than can well be done in writing.

[168] The musician should also plan that the phrases be of the same length, like lines of verse, and be sometimes repeated, either the same or modified by some change, even though slight, and, if they are particularly beautiful, be duplicated, with their "parts" not too diverse; and let those occasional phrases that are the same be varied as to intervals [per modos], or, if they retain the same intervals, let them be heard transposed higher or lower.

Also a neume, turning back on itself, may return the same way it came and by the same steps.

[169] Also note that when a neume traverses a certain range or contour by leaping down from high notes, another neume may respond similarly in an opposite direction from low notes, as happens when we look for our likeness confronting us in a well.

Sometimes, too, let one syllable have one or more neumes, and at other times let one neume be divided among more than one syllable. [170] These—indeed all neumes—will be varied, in that in some places they will begin from the same note, in other places from a different one, according to the various qualities of low or high pitch.

Also let almost all phrases proceed to the principal note [of the mode], that is, the final, or some note related to it [affinis] if such be chosen instead of the final. Just as the same note may sometimes end all the neumes or the great majority of the phrases, sometimes, too, let it begin them, as can be found in Ambrosian [chant], if you are interested. [171] But there are, as it were, prose chants that follow these [practices] less, in which no care is taken as to whether some of the "parts" are longer and some shorter and whether the phrase endings [distinctiones] are found in indiscriminate locations in the manner of prosae.

I speak of chants as metrical because we often sing in such a way that we appear almost to scan verses by feet, as happens when we sing actual meters—in which one must take care lest neumes of two syllables persist excessively without an admixture of some of three or four syllables. For just as lyric [172] poets join now one kind of foot, now another, so composers reasonably juxtapose different and various neumes. Diversity is reasonable if it creates a measured variety of neumes and phrases, yet in such a way that neumes answer harmoniously to neumes and phrases to phrases, with always a certain resemblance.

27

That is, let the likeness be incomplete, in the manner of the outstandingly lovely chant of St. Ambrose.

The parallel between verse and chant is no slight one, since neumes [173] correspond to feet and phrases to lines of verse. Thus one neume proceeds like a dactyl, another like a spondee, and a third in iambic manner; and you see a phrase now like a tetrameter, now like a pentameter, and again like a hexameter, and many other such parallels.

Let the subdivisions [*partes*] and phrases of both the neumes and the words end at the same time, [174] and do not let a long stay [*tenor*] on any short syllables or a short stay on long ones create an impropriety, though this will rarely demand attention.

Let the effect of the song express what is going on in the text, so that for sad things the neumes are grave, for serene ones they are cheerful, and for auspicious texts exultant, and so forth.

We often place an acute or grave accent above [the vowels in the text for] the notes, [175] because we often utter them with more or less stress, so much so that the repetition of the same note often seems to be a raising or lowering.

Towards the ends of phrases the notes should always be more widely spaced as they approach the breathing place, like a galloping horse, so that they arrive at the pause, as it were, weary and heavily. Spacing notes close together or widely apart, as befits, is a good way to indicate this effect [in writing].

At many points notes "liquesce," like the liquid letters, so that [176] the interval from one note to another is begun with a smooth glide and does not appear to have a stopping place en route. We put a dot like a blot beneath the liquescent note,[18] thus:

Example 4

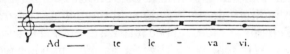

Ad — te le - va - vi.

---

[18]The liquescent clivis appears in *LU* 318 at the syllable "Ad":

Ad te le - va - vi

[177] If you wish to perform the note more fully and not make it liquesce, no harm is done; indeed, it is often more pleasing.

Do everything that we have said neither too rarely nor too unremittingly, but with taste.

Chapter 16

On the manifold variety of sounds and neumes

[178] It should not seem surprising that such an abundance of such different chants is created from so few notes—notes that are joined, as we said, by only six intervals either up or down. But from the letters, likewise few, not so very many syllables are made, [179] for the number of syllables can be estimated. Yet a boundless multitude of words [*partes*] has grown out of these syllables, and in verse how numerous are the kinds of meters from a few feet! One kind of meter, like the hexameter, is found varied in many ways. Let the grammarians investigate how this is done; let us, if we can, see in what ways we can make neumes that are different from each other.

Now melodic motion—which, we said, was made up of six intervals—consists of arsis and thesis, [180] that is, ascent and descent. Of this twofold motion, arsis and thesis, every neume is composed, except for repeated notes and single notes. Next, arsis and thesis are combined, either with themselves, as arsis to arsis and thesis to thesis, or each with the other, as arsis to thesis and thesis to arsis; and this combination is made now of like, now of unlike [elements].

Unlikeness arises if of the aforesaid melodic movements one has more [181] or fewer notes than the other, or closer together or farther apart. Furthermore, when a combination is made of either similar or dissimilar elements, one melodic figure [*motus*] will either be placed above another, that is, placed among higher notes; or placed below it; or placed beside, that is, so that the end of one and the beginning of the other are at the same pitch; or placed within, that is, so that one melodic figure is placed with the span of the other and is less low and less high; or mixed, that is, placed partly within and partly below or above or beside. Again, these [182] configurations can be classified according to various qualities: of lowness or height of pitch; of more or fewer notes; and of the intervals. The neumes, too, can be varied in all these ways, and occasionally the phrases.

29

We have appended a diagram of this topic, so that one can more easily get the picture of it [Fig. 4]. [184]

Figure 4

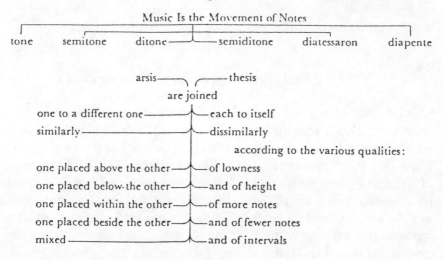

Chapter 17

That anything that is spoken can be made into music[19]

[186] Having briefly discussed the foregoing, we shall present to you another very simple matter, most profitable to consider through hitherto unheard of. While by it a basis [*causa*] for all [187] melodies will become perfectly clear, you will be able to retain for your use whatever you find appropriate and still reject whatever appears objectionable.

Consider, then, that just as everything that is spoken can be written, so everything that is written can be made into song. Thus, everything that is spoken can be sung, for writing is depicted by letters.

Not to draw out our method to great length, let us take from these letters only the five vowels. Without them, manifestly, no other letter or syllable [188] can sound, and it is for the most part due to them whenever an agreeable blending is found in the different units [*partes*]. Thus, in verse we often see such concordant and mutually congruous

[19]See the commentary in van Waesberghe, "Guido of Arezzo and Musical Improvisation," *Musica disciplina* 5 (1951):55-63.

lines that you wonder, as it were, at a certain harmony of language. And if music be added to this, with a similar interrelationship, you will be doubly charmed by a twofold melody.

Let us take then these five vowels. Perhaps, since they bring such euphony to words, they will offer no less harmony to the neumes. Let them be placed in succession beneath the letters of the monochord, and, since they are only five, let them be repeated until beneath each note its particular vowel is written [see Ex. 5].

Example 5

Γ	A	B	C	D	E	F	G	a	b	c	d	e	f	g	a
a	e	i	o	u	a	e	i	o	u	a	e	i	o	u	a

[189] Reflect about this arrangement. Since all speech is activated by these five letters, it should not be denied that five notes also may be set in motion among one another, as we have said. Since this is so, let us take any phrase, adding to its syllables those tones which are indicated by the vowels of these same syllables and sing them, as written beneath [Fig. 5, Ex. 6].

Figure 5

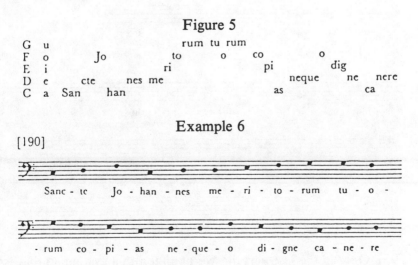

G	u			rum	tu	rum			
F	o		Jo	to		o	co		o
E	i			ri			pi		dig
D	e	cte	nes	me				neque	ne	nere
C	a	San	han				as		ca

Example 6

[190]

Sanc - te Jo - han - nes me - ri - to - rum tu - o -

- rum co - pi - as ne - que - o di - gne ca - ne - re

What has been done with this text can indubitably be done with any.

By this system scarcely any tune [*symphonia*] would get less than five notes, and there would be no way to get beyond these five, as you

31

may often wish. So that thus no onerous compulsion be laid on you and so that you can range about a little more freely, add another row of vowels beneath the first, but varied so that it begins from the third place of the earlier row, in this way [Ex. 7]. [191]

Example 7

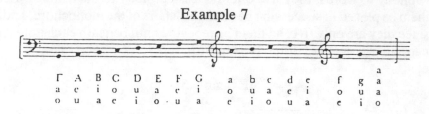

Here, with two vowels beneath each sound—the five vowels being present—since beneath each sound there is not just one vowel but a second also, you have sufficiently freer scope to proceed at will with more extended or more confined melodic movement. So now, with this arrangement, let us see what kind of musical setting [*symphonia*] for this verse its own vowels will provide [Ex. 8]. [192]

Example 8

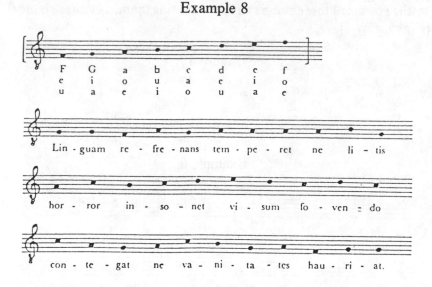

[193] Only in the last part did we abandon this system so that we could lead the melody back properly to its tetrardus. Since certain texts command a suitable vocal setting simply from their own vowels, there is no doubt that the vocal setting will be most suitable if, after practice in

many such, you select from the numerous possibilities only the most effective and those that fit together better. If you then fill in gaps, space out the constricted places, draw together the overextended, and broaden the overcondensed, you will make a unified, [194] polished work. This, too, I wish you to know, that, in the manner of pure silver, all chant gains in color the more it is used, and whatever displeases at first, after being polished through use as by a file, is extolled; and, in accordance with the diversity of people and minds, what displeases one is cherished by another; and, anon, things that blend together delight this man, whereas that one prefers variety; one seeks a homogeneity and blandness in keeping with his pleasure-loving mind; another, since he is serious-minded, is pleased by staider strains; while another, as if distracted, feeds on studied and [195] intricate contortions; and each proclaims that music as much the better sounding which suits the innate character of his own mind.

If you absorb all these things from our teaching with unremitting practice, you cannot remain ignorant. Certainly, such expositions must be employed as long as we know only a part, so that we arrive at the fullness of knowledge. But since the brevity here aimed at demands that we not pursue these matters at length, although indeed there are many things worth garnering from them, let this suffice on setting words to music [*canendum*]. Now let us briefly examine the principles of diaphony.

Chapter 18

On diaphony, that is the principles of organum

[196] Diaphony sounds as a separateness of [simultaneous] sounds, which we also call organum, [197] in which notes distinct from each other make dissonance harmoniously and harmonize in their dissonance. Some practice diaphony in such a way that the fourth step down always accompanies the singer, as A with D; and if you double this organum by acute a, so that you have A D a, then A will sound a diatessaron with D and a diapason with a, whereas D will sound a diatessaron and a diapente with A and a respectively, and acute a with the lower two notes a diapente [198] and a diapason. These three intervals blend in organum congenially and smoothly just as it has been shown above that they caused a resemblance of notes. Hence they are called "symphonies,"

that is, compatible unions of notes, although the term symphony is also applied to all chant. Here is an example of this diaphony [Ex. 9].

Example 9

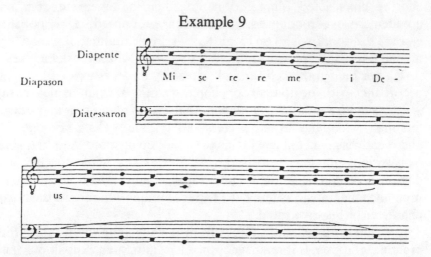

[201] You can both double the chant by an organal voice [*organum*] and the latter by its diapason as much as you like; for wherever there is the concord of the diapason, the aforementioned compatibility of the symphonies will not fail.

Since the doubling of notes has now been made sufficiently clear, let us explain the low voice added beneath the singer of the original line in the way that we employ. For the above manner of diaphony is hard [sounding] [*durus*], but ours is smooth [*mollis*]. In it we do not admit the semitone or the diapente, but we do allow the tone, the ditone, the semiditone, and the diatessaron; and of these the semiditone holds the lowest rank and the diatessaron [202] the chief one. With these four concords the diaphony accompanies the chant.

Of the tropes, some are serviceable, others more serviceable, and still others most serviceable. Those are serviceable that provide organum only at the diatessaron, with the notes a fourth from each other, like the deuterus on B and E; more serviceable are those that harmonize [*respondent*] not only with fourths but also with thirds and seconds,[20] by a tone and, though only rarely, a semiditone, like the protus on A and D. Most serviceable are those that make organum most frequently and

[20]The usage "non solum quartis, sed tertiis et secundis" for fourths, thirds, and seconds is rare in this period.

more smoothly, namely, the tetrardus and tritus on C and F and G; for
these harmonize at the distance of a tone, a ditone, and a diatessaron.

[203] The accompanying voice [*subsecutor*] should never descend
below the tritus either when phrases end thereon or when the tritus is
next below such an ending, unless the singer [*cantor*: singer of the
original line] employs notes lower than that tritus. For the organal voice
[*organum*] must never be taken below a tritus that is the lowest note [of
the original voice] or that is situated next below this. But when [the
original voice] employs notes lower than the tritus at a suitable place,
the organal voice should also descend below it at the diatessaron; and as
soon as that low region of the phrase is left so that [204] one does not
expect it to recur, the accompanying voice should return to the place it
previously had, so that it may remain on the final, if it has arrive there,
or, if the final is above it, that the accompanying voice may proceed to it
properly from nearby.

This convergence on the final [*occursus*] is preferably by a tone, less
so by a ditone, and never by a semiditone. The occursus is scarcely
made from a diatessaron, since a voice accompanying below [*succentus*] is
more satisfactory in such a place; yet one should take care that this last
does not happen at the final phrase-end of the piece.

[205] Often, however, when the singer [of the original line] employs
notes below the tritus, we keep the organal voice fixed on the tritus.
Then the main singer should not end a phrase on these lower notes, but,
while the notes are moving quickly to and fro, go back up to the waiting
tritus and avoid trouble for himself and the other part by making a
phrase ending on higher notes.

When the cadential convergence [*occursus*] is made by a whole tone,
there is a prolongation [*diutinus tenor*] of the final tone, so that it is
accompanied partly from below and partly at the unison. In the case of a
ditone this [prolongation] is still longer, so that often, when the
accompanying voice is pitched, even though briefly, on the note in
between [the ditone], [206] the occursus of a whole tone is not lacking.
This is the close for the deuterus, because it takes place there
harmoniously. If the cantus is not expected to descend beyond, to the
tritus, it will then be useful for the organal voice to sound the protus
[*proto vim organi occupare*], to accompany with the following [notes],
and to converge properly on the ending via a whole tone.

Furthermore, the two voices must not be separated by more than a
diatessaron; therefore, when the singer of the main part goes farther up,

35

the accompanying part must ascend, as, for instance, C should accompany F; and D, G; and E, a; and so on.

Lastly, there is a diatessaron beneath each note except b-natural, so that in phrases where this appears, G will sound in the organan voice [*G vim organi possidebit*]. [207] When this happens, if the original chant either descends to F or ends a phrase on G, then F in the added voice accompanies G and a at suitable places; but if the original chant does not end on G, then F in the chant is not accompanied by F in the organal voice [*F cum cantu vim organi amittit*].

But when b-flat is used in the chant, F will be in the organal voice. Since therefore F and C [tritus] hold the chief place in diaphony to such a degree that they take precedence over the others as the most serviceable, we see that not undeservedly is the tritus beloved by Gregory more than the other notes. He assigns to it the beginnings of many melodies and most of [208] the repeated notes, so that often, if you take away the C's and F's of the tritus from his chant, it will seem that you have removed almost half of it.

The precepts of diaphony have now been given, and if you test them by the following examples, you will understand them perfectly.

Chapter 19

Testing this diaphony through examples

[209] We do not take the organal voice below the tritus if there is a close on it [here] or in the following notes. Here is a close on the tritus C:

Example 10

[210] Here is another phrase-ending on the tritus F, in which we accompany the chant at the diatessaron with the notes a fourth apart. At the end here an accompaniment a diatessaron below is more pleasing than an occursus.

Example 11

Here is another of the same mode:

Example 12

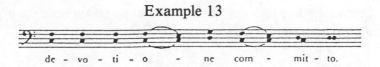

Here is another phrase in the protus D, in which an occursus of a tone appears at the end:

Example 13

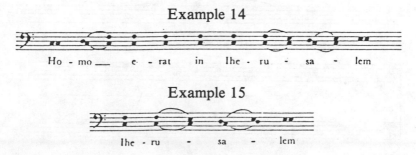

[211] Here are [examples of the] phrase-ending on the deuterus E, showing an occursus of a ditone, either simple [Ex. 14] or with intervening notes [*intermissae*] [Ex. 15]:

Example 14

Example 15

Here is a phrase-ending on the protus A:

Example 16

37

In this phrase-ending, notes below the tritus C, which [212] is next below the final D, are permitted, and after the low passage the earlier pitch [C] is resumed. Similarly in the following one, note how the organal voice rises, avoiding going below the main chant at the end of the final phrase.

Example 17

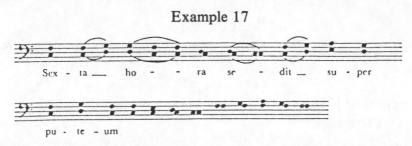

See how when the singer employs low notes we [may] keep the organal voice suspended on the tritus F:

Example 18

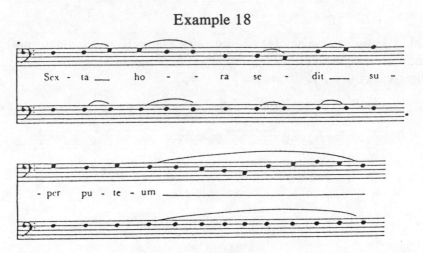

[213] See how toward the end F in the lower voice accompanies G and a in the chant:

Example 19

In the plagal tritus too you will find this practiced, so that b accompanies c and d, just as F accompanies G and a. Thus:

Example 20

Ve - ni - te   ad   -   -   o - /re - mus

[214] Take pains, then, and turn the foregoing to use by practice; for if you have a melody [*symphonia*], these rules will suffice to give you diaphony.

At the outset we were silent about the origin of the science of music, since we realized that the reader was a novice. But now that he is trained and knows more, we impart it to him in conclusion.

Chapter 20

How the nature of music was discovered from the sound of hammers

[228] In ancient times there were instruments that we are not clear about and also a multitude of singers who were, however, in the dark, for no man could by any train of thought reason out the differences between notes or a description of music. Nor could anyone ever [229] have learned anything certain about this science had not Divine Goodness of its own will at length arranged the following event.

When a certain great philosopher, Pythagoras, happened to be taking a walk, he came to a workshop in which five hammers were beating on one anvil. Amazed at their sweet concord, the philosopher drew near and, expecting at first that the basis of the variety of sound and its harmony [*modulatio*] lay in the differences of the hands of the workmen, he exchanged the hammers among them. But after this was done, the quality of sound [*vis*] followed each hammer. So he removed from the others one that was discordant and weighed the rest, and, in wondrous manner, by God's [230] will, they weighed the first with twelve, the second with nine, the third with eight, and the fourth with six, of I know not what units of weight.

Thus he learned that the science of music depended upon numerical ratios and comparisons; for there was precisely the interrelationship among the four hammers that there is among the four notes A, D, E, and

a. For if A has twelve units and D nine, there being four groups of three divisions [on the monochord], A with its twelve units will have four groups of three; [231] and D with its nine, three groups of three. And thus you have the diatessaron. Further, since A has twelve units if E has eight, then A will have three fourfold steps, whereas E will have two, and the diapente appears. Also, if there are twelve units in A and six in the other a, the group of six is half that of twelve, just as acute a is obtained as the midpoint of the other A. Therefore the diapason is present. So from that same A to D gives the diatessaron, from A to E the diapente, and to the other a the diapason. Moreover, from D to E [232] sounds a tone, and from D to A and a, a diatessaron and a diapente respectively. And from E to D also provides a tone, and E to A and a, a diapente and a diatessaron respectively; whereas acute a sounds a diapason with A, a diapente with D, and a diatessaron with E. All these things the careful investigator will find in the aforementioned numbers.

[233] Beginning at this point, Boethius, the expositor of this science, has set forth the extensive, marvelous, and very difficult concordance of this science with numerical ratios.

What more? The renowned Pythagoras first arranged the monochord, ordering the notes by means of the aforesaid intervals. Since this monochord constitutes not a trivial but a diligently revealed knowledge of our art, it has pleased wise men in general. Up to this day our science has gradually increased and grown in strength, with that same Teacher bringing light to the darkness of human affairs whose supreme wisdom flourishes through all the ages. Amen.

[234] End of the Micrologus, that is, the short treatise on music.

CHRISTOPH BERNHARD

The *Tractatus compositionis augmentatus* by *Christoph Bernhard* (1628-1692), probably written in 1660, belongs to the basic texts on the Doctrine of Musical-Rhetorical Figures (*Figurenlehre*), which was the first comprehensive and systematic account of a musical vocabulary. And however inadequate it would be in historical investigations to adopt unquestioningly the terminology of the seventeenth century, it is nonetheless necessary to analyze it thoroughly as a document of musical thought in the Baroque age.

Following the humanistic educational tradition, what one understood by a figure in seventeenth- and eighteenth-century music theory was a deviation from a grammatical norm of strict counterpoint (as codified in 1558 by Gioseffo Zarlino), that was justified by a rhetorical purpose. The grammatical "vitium" (vitiation), insofar as it seemed apt to illustrate a text set to music, was explained as rhetorical "color." (The interruption of a sentence is a rhetorical figure whenever it serves the emotional effect of a speech, like the feigned consternation of the speaker who is left speechless in view of some fatal matter.)

At the stage of development represented by Christoph Bernhard, the Doctrine of Figures was an attempt at a theoretical appropriation of Monteverdi's seconda prattica. (Joachim Burmeister, from whom the first comprehensive account comes, still referred to Orlando di Lasso.) It may at first seem confusing that the Doctrine of Figures was formulated in Germany and not in Italy, the country in which the phenomena under consideration originated. The seconda prattica, it seems, needed an interpretation, above all, where it was foreign. Moreover, the German composers, who as cantors also served as Latin teachers, sound (thanks to Cicero and Quintilian) an available categorical apparatus with the help of which they could come to terms with the

41

irksome musical phenomena they imported from Italy or adopted from Italians working in Germany.

The foundation of Bernhard's Doctrine of Figures constitutes a theory of style: in the church style (stylus gravis) figures are rare, in the chamber style (stylus luxurians communis) more frequent, and in the theatrical style (stylus theatralis) most numerous of all. The style most abundant in figures naturally includes the means of the styles with fewer figures.

Bernhard's strict counterpoint forms the foundation of free composition as was the seconda prattica, proclaimed by Monteverdi, to be a style existing alongside rather than superseding the prima prattica. Counterpoint is not undermined by the Doctrine of Figures but continues to exist as an underlying basis founded in the nature of music.

The eight figures of the stylus theatralis that Bernhard discusses and illustrates are all violations of the rules of strict counterpoint or of its underlying tonal system. Dissonances with irregular preparations prolongations and resolutions are tolerated, even sought after, in the theatrical style because of their affective impact. Interestingly, the figure technically known as "anticipation" was still called by Hans Joachim Moser, due to the character it acquired in the seventeenth century, "pathetic anticipation" and Bernhard's method, confronting a figure with the basic form from which it deviates, was viewed by followers of Heinrich Schenker as a forerunner of the latter's reductive procedures.

Bernhard's "extensio" is a prolonged dissonance encompassing a strong beat together with a weak one. The examples of "ellipsis," the absence of a consonance of resolution, can sometimes also be explained as "heterolepsis," as the transference of a consonance of resolution to another voice (a fact challenging the practice of interpreting names of figures allegorically). "Abruptio" is the suppression of a consonance of resolution or its delay by means of a rest. Bernhard's examples of "mora"—literally "delay"—are partly problematic: the first can be interpreted as a paraphrased resolution into the octave (not the twelfth), the second as a "heterolepsis" (with a sharp as an irregular and c sharp as a regular note of resolution transferred into another, imaginary voice). A "transitus inversus" is a passing dissonance on a strong beat which becomes a figure in the stylus theatralis by being split up into "tone repetitions," in the manner of a recitative. (The question nevertheless remains how, in a recitative in which "no bar is used," a dissonance can exist in the wrong place in the bar.) A "heterolepsis" is a leap into a dissonance whereby its regular resolution is complemented by another voice, whether in the listener's imagination or, in reality, in the figured bass. The diminished third and the augmented sixth violate the mi-contra-fa taboo of strict counterpoint and by going against the norm of diatonic melody and harmony thus come to express painful affections.

Some music historians, who seek support for their hermeneutic intentions in the nomenclature of the seventeenth century, interpret the names of figures symbolically or allegorically, without justification to be found for this in the sources of the Doctrine of Figures. Apart from the musical matter at hand, they also relate its name to the meaning, manifest or implicit, of the text being set. (At the words "through Adam's fall," the heterolepsis, the aberration into something different or strange, becomes the musical symbol of sin.) Whether, however, terms coined in Germany for phenomena of Italian origin convey the latter's authentic significance is as uncertain as an exegesis believing to have grasped in the name of a figure the hidden meaning of a textual passage as understood by the composer. True, allegorization in the seventeenth century could come to grips with virtually any phenomenon between heaven and earth; for this very reason, musical figures and names of figures were not privileged objects of this mode of thought, even if it so appears to some historians.

from the Tractatus compositionis augmentatus[1]

Chapter 35
Of Stylus Theatralis

1. The other subdivision of what I have called *stylus luxurians* is *stylus theatralis.** It derives its name from the place where it is used the most.

2. It is also at times called *stylus recitativus* or *oratorius*, since it was devised to represent speech in music, and indeed not too many years ago. Although it was at first (as everything else) rather rough, today it has been admirably refined and polished through the efforts of considerable talents, so that I hardly believe that the ancient Greeks possessed this species of music (to which they applied themselves most of all) in better form.

3. And since language is the absolute master of music in this genre,† just as music is the master of language in *stylus gravis*, and language and music are both masters in *stylus luxurians communis*, therefore this general rule follows: that one should represent speech in the most natural way possible.[2]

4. Thus one should render joyful things joyful, sorrowful things sorrowful, swift things swift, slow things slow [etc.].

---

[1]Text: "The Treatises of Christoph Bernhard", tr. Walter Hilse, *The Music Forum*, Vol. III (1973), pp. 110-125. All notes are of the translator; those under signs other than numbers present the original in German. Together with the *Tractatus* the translator also brings relevant sections (changing the order of the original) from another treatise— *Ausführlicher Bericht vom Gebrauche der Con- und Dissonantien*—for the sake of comparison, reflecting interesting changes in Bernhard's thought.
Whenever "M-B" is used in the notes it refers to Müller-Blattaw's edition of the German text.
*Cf. *Bericht*, ch. XIII, paras. 2–6, given on pp. 90–91; also *Bericht*, ch. XXII, N.B., given on p. 116.
† "Und weil in diesem *Genere* die *Oratio Harmoniae Domina absolutissima* . . . ist."
[2]"dass man die Rede aufs natürlichste *exprimieren* solle." It is interesting to compare the account given in the subsequent paragraphs with that in paras. 30–34 and 40 of the *Art of Singing*.

5. In particular, that which is heightened in ordinary speech should be set high, that which passes unemphasized set low.

6. Similar observations should be made in connection with texts wherein Heaven, Earth, and Hell are mentioned.

7. Questions, according to common usage, are ended a step higher than the penultimate syllable, as the examples will show.*

8. Textual repetition should be employed either not at all, or just in those places where elegance permits.[3]

9. Musical repetition[†] occurs when two successive utterances are similar in subject matter.

10. Musical repetition a step higher occurs in connection with two or more successive questions, when their words correspond in subject matter,[‡] and when the last seem to be more forceful than the first.

11. *Omnium rerum satietas.* Thus one should observe how an aria is sentences.[§] Hence a poet should bring many songs[¶] into his theatrical work.

12. The figures belonging to *stylus theatralis*, over and above those mentioned before, might be designated as follows: a) *extensio*; b) *ellipsis*; c) *mora*; d) *abruptio*; e) *transitus inversus*; f) *heterolepsis*; g) *tertia deficiens*; h) *sexta superflua*.

13. I do not make special mention of leaps otherwise forbidden but permitted here, since I have already dealt with these sufficiently from time to time.

---

*There are none to be found in this treatise.

[3]This paragraph reads as follows in M-B.: "Die Wiederhohlung des Textes soll entweder garnicht, oder nur an den Orten, wo es die Zierligkeit zulässt im *Unisono* gebraucht werden." According to the *Revisionsbericht*, however, the phrase "im *Unisono*" is only found in one manuscript source; and I feel that the sentence makes more sense when it is left out.

†"Die Widerhohlung der Noten." Obviously the repetition of entire musical phrases is meant.

‡"in . . . Gleichheit der Worte an der *Materie*."

§"als in *Sententiis* bey Schlüssen der *Periodorum*."

¶"viel Lieder," i.e., many portions of text regular and song-like enough to be set as arias.

Chapter 36
Of Extension

1. *Extension* is the rather sizable lengthening of a dissonance.#
2. It is generally combined with *multiplication*.
3. Whenever this figure (for the following ones) is encountered, the organist should play middle or upper voices with it which accompany the dissonances with nothing but consonances. For a voice above the bass* is written [to it] with this in mind: that it should not accord itself, as regards consonances, solely with the bass, but also often with the upper voice. Let this be recalled here once and for all. Examples of *extension*.[4] [Example 223]

Example 223

#"einer *Dissonanz* ziemlich lange während Veränderung." Cf. *prolongation*, in ch. 27.

*"die Stimme über den Bass."

[4]In a variant reading mentioned in M-B.'s *Revisionsbericht*, the tenor has the following note values in the second-last measure of the upcoming example: ♩ ♩ ♩. ♪.
This version may be deemed more "correct" from the standpoint of dissonance treatment, but is certainly less attractive. The flat signature is missing from the lower system throughout this example in M-B. As a consequence the tenor has a B♮ in the second-last measure. While the resulting cross-relation is pleasing in its own way, it is highly doubtful that it was intended here.

Chapter 37
Of Ellipsis

1. *Ellipsis* is the suppression of a normally required consonance.

2. It arrises through the alteration of either *syncopation* or *transitus*.

3. *Ellipsis* arising from *syncopation* occurs quite commonly when a fourth should be resolved through a subsequent third in cadences, but either the third is left out altogether or another consonance is taken in its place. [Example 225]

Example 225

It should stand thus:

4. *Ellipsis* arising from *transitus* is the omission of the consonance which is normally required in *transitus* before a dissonance. [Example 227]

Example 227

Chapter XVIII
Of Ellipsis

1. *Ellipsis* means omission, and is the suppression of a consonance.

2. It occurs in two ways: first, when a rest replaces the consonance and is followed by a dissonance. [Example 224]

Example 224

It should stand thus:

It should stand thus:

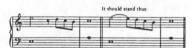

3. Also, when a fourth is not resolved through a third at a cadence, rather standing still, as: [Example 226].

Example 226

N.B. This derives from *cercar della nota*, discussed in Rule 24 of the *Manier.*[5] For the singer must resolve it below.*

[5]The reference is to para. 24 of the *Art of Singing*. This confirms that the *Bericht*, at any rate, was written after that treatise.

*"Den der Sänger muss es unten *resolviren*." The connection between the thought of this last sentence and that of the previous one is unclear.

EXAMPLE 227 *(continued)*

It should stand thus:

Chapter 38
Of Mora

1. *Mora* is an inverted *syncopation*, in that the consonance following the driving dissonance does not fall a second, but rises one instead.

2. Example of a second resolved through *mora*. [Example 228]

Example 228

3. Example of a seventh resolved through *mora*.* [Example 230]

Example 230

4. Example of a diminished fifth. [Example 231]

Example 231

Chapter XIX
Of Retardation

1. *Retardation* is a lingering, when a note should climb a second but waits too long before climbing.

2. It was invented, however, in imitation of *syncopation*, with this difference: that whereas *syncopation* resolves itself downwards, *retardation* does this upwards. [Example 229]

Example 229

---

*The second bass note in the example is indeed F ♮ in M-B. While somewhat unlikely, especially in view of the parallel example in the *Bericht*, it is nonetheless a possible and stimulating reading.

Chapter 39
Of Abruptio

Chapter XXII
Of Abruptio

1. *Abruptio* occurs when, in place of a con-sonance anticipated as a necessary resolution, the vocal line is either ruptured or broken off altogether.

2. Ruptured in the middle of a phrase, if a rest is written down instead of a dot. [Example 232]

Example 232

instead of:

3. Broken off altogether at a cadence, indeed in such a way that the upper voice ends on a fourth before the bass grasps the last note of the cadence, for example: [Example 233].

Example 233

which should stand thus:

1. *Abruptio* means tearing off. It occurs when one ends on the fourth of a cadence, which should first be resolved through the third before the bass finishes the cadence, as: [Example 234].

Example 234

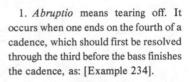

It should be thus:

N.B. The above-mentioned superficial figures, such as *ellipsis, retardation, heterolepsis, quasitransitus,* and *abrup-tio,* are admitted almost exclusively in recitative style, and are not to be em-ployed otherwise.*

*Bernhard mentions precisely those five superficial figures here that are classified under *stylus theatralis* in the *Tractatus*. See also *Tractatus*, ch. 35, para. 12.

Chapter 40
Of Transitus Inversus

1. *Transitus inversus* occurs when the first part of a measure in *transitus* is bad, the second part good.‡

2. This is permitted in recitative style, since the measure is not kept there§ and one therefore does not perceive where its first half is, or its second.

3. Nevertheless, this figure is never encountered without *multiplication*. [Example 236]

Chapter XXI
Of Quasitransitus

1. *Quasitransitus*† occurs when a dissonance is struck on a strong beat, counter to the rule of *transitus*. It is allowed only in recitative style, since no beat is observed there,§ as: [Example 235].

Example 235

Example 236

†Cf. *quasi-transitus* as defined in the *Tractatus*, ch. 18.

‡Bad = dissonant; good = consonant.

§"weil darinnen kein *Tact* gebraucht wird," in the *Tractatus*; "weil daselbst kein *Tact observiret* wird," in the *Bericht*.

*Actually, both of these "correct" versions still feature a dissonance in the first half of the measure, and so leave something to be desired. Cf. the next two progressions and the following footnote.

† Only the second of these "correct" versions actually eliminates the dissonance in the first half of the measure. Bernhard is, typically, peeling off successive layers of figuration in these two versions.

EXAMPLE 236 (continued)

This would correctly stand: †

Chapter 41
Of Heterolepsis

1. *Heterolepsis* is the seizure of a second voice, and is of two kinds.

2. First, when I leap or step into a dissonance after a consonance, if this* could have been done in *transitus* by another voice.

3. Example of *heterolepsis* of the second in *transitus*. [Example 237]

Example 237

The other voices would stand thus: ‡

4. Example of *heterolepsis* of the seventh in *transitus*. [Example 239]

Chapter XX
Of Heterolepsis

1. *Heterolepsis* means taking hold of another voice, and occurs, first, if I move from a consonance [into a dissonance], if this * could have been done in *transitus* by another voice, as: † [Example 238].

Example 238

*Moving to the dissonance.

† The middle system of the example shows both of the voices implied in the top line: the "original" voice and the voice whose domain is suddenly taken over.

‡ That is, the B is understood to come from either the A or the C.

Example 239

The other voices would stand thus:

5. Example of *heterolepsis* of the fourth in *transitus*. [Example 240]

Example 240

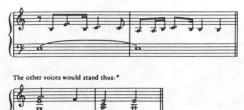

The other voices would stand thus:*

6. Second, when the lower voice is syncopated and the one above, having grasped a fourth, does not rise a second, but rather falls a third. [Example 241]

2. Second, such a seizure occurs in connection with a syncopated fourth, when the lowest voice is resolved but the upper one falls a third instead of climbing a second. [Example 242]

Example 241

[ve - de - te | mi mo - ri - · · · · · re]

It should be thus:

Example 242

§ I give this progression exactly as it appears in M-B.
*In M-B., G appears instead of A in the first chord of the second measure, an obvious misprint. The material in the first measure also bears strikingly little relationship to the ornamented version, but I give it as found in M-B.

7. N.B. The kinds of *syncopatio catachrestica* illustrated in chapter 28, paragraph 4, could also be regarded as *heterolepsis* arising from *syncopation*, especially when these examples are combined with *multiplication.*†

[Example 243] The last two are examples of syncopated *heterolepsis* with the upper voice [driving], just as the first was an example of syncopated *heterolepsis* with the lower voice driving.*

Example 243

Chapter 42
Of the Augmented Second
[and the Diminished Seventh]

1. The augmented second is an interval which is not quite a minor third,[6] and which stands in the following degrees: [Example 244].

Example 244

†The lower voice in the second progression is written a third higher in M-B. Comparison with the related progression in ch. 28, para. 4 shows this to be an error.
*"Dass also die letzteren beyden Emempel *Heterolepseos syncopatae parte superiore* [*ligata*] wären, wie das erste *Heterolepseos syncopatae inferiore parte ligata*." By the "last two" examples Bernhard means the two progressions given in the present paragraph; by the "first," the one given in ch. 41, para. 6 above.
[6]Throughout this chapter the augmented second is referred to as "tertia deficiens," the diminished seventh as "sexta superflua." (See note 45.) Bernhard's statement that the "*tertia deficiens*" is "not quite" a minor third is correct, for a major third minus a diatonic semitone is less than a minor third. ($5/4 \times 15/16 = 75/64 < 6/5$.)

2. Examples of how it is used. [Example 245]

Example 245

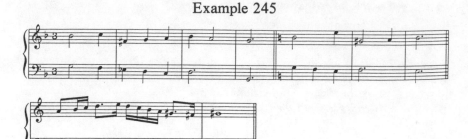

3. The diminished seventh is a minor sixth with a major semitone added, and stands in these degrees: [Example 246].

Example 246

4. Example. [Example 247]

Example 247

Chapter 43
Concerning Emulation

1. Until now we have talked about the use of consonances, both when these are encountered by themselves in *stylus aequalis*, and also when they are encountered in *stylus inaequalis* next to dissonances; and about the various figures which have been invented to mitigate dissonances* in *stylus gravis* as well as *luxurians*, and in the two subdivisions of the latter, namely, *stylus communis* and *theatralis*.

*"zur *Temperirung* der *Dissonantzen*."

2. If an industrious student of composition should find something else, beyond the above-mentioned, in the works of good composers, this will either be easily reducible to the figures described above, or it will be left to his judgment whether he should imitate it or not.

3. For the emulation of the most distinguished composers is no less profitable—indeed necessary—in this profession than in any other art, as a part of one's practice, without which all precepts are useless.

4. But since an aspiring composer might easily err in his choice of models, and seeing that it is impossible and, beyond that, fruitless [to set] them all down in score,* he who would heed my counsel should avail himself of the following eminent people.[†] Nevertheless, I do not want thereby to take anything away from the reputation merited by other people who are not mentioned here, but on the contrary am well aware that many other excellent composers are more worthy of being emulated. But I have desired to propose these few, whose works are easily accessible, without doing prejudice to others. Beyond that, I leave it to the opportunity of each person, what composers he can set down in score, or wishes to.

5. In *stylus gravis*, the man from Praeneste,[‡] whom the Italians call Palestrina after the present name of his birthplace, is especially to be imitated, in my judgment. After him Soriano,[7] his pupil, and Morales, whose Magnificats are particularly esteemed. Among earlier composers, Adrian Willaert; Josquin; and Gombert, Kappelmeister for Charles V; yet since the text is somewhat more difficult to apply in the works of these men,[8] they might lead astray more than aright. Among more recent composers, especially in pieces sung by more than one chorus, the two Gabrielis, Prioli, Orazio Benevoli, Lorenzo Ratti, etc., are worthy of emulation.

6. In *stylus luxurians communis* we have the following: Monteverdi, who indeed invented and elevated this style (praise is not denied others

---

*"alle *in Partitura* [zu setzen]." See note 40.

[†] See note 56 for brief biographies (in alphabetical order) of those composers listed in paras. 5, 6, and 7, whose names are printed in small capitals.

[‡] *"Praenestinus."*

[7] The following are brief biographical sketches (in alphabetical order) of the lesser-known composers mentioned in ch. 43, paras. 5, 6, and 7.

[8] "doch weil bey ihnen der *Text* etwas schwerer zu *appliciren*." Bernhard is probably referring to the fact that the text-underlay was often not very accurate in that earlier period.

Footnote number 7 continued on page 59.

who attempted something similar before him); his successor, Rovetta; Cavalli; Bertali; Stefano Fabri; Francesco Porta; Turini; Rigatti; Cassati; Carissimi; Vincenzo Albrici; Marco Scacchi; Bontempi; Peranda; etc.; and among the Germans, Herr Schütz, Caspar Kerll; Herr Förster; and a few more.

7. In *stylus* [*luxurians*] *theatralis*, the following have shown themselves to great advantage: Monteverdi, Rovetta, Cavalli, Carissimi, Tenaglia, Vincenzo Albrici, Bontempi, Luigi (Rossi); and contemporary Roman musicians would well-nigh take the prize from the others. We Germans up to now have been sorely lacking in charming poems such as are suitable for this genre. Therefore I, in my humble station, also have tried my hand at it, in prose and in verse.[9]

Chapter 44
Of the Musical Modes in General

1. Above, in chapter 2, paragraph 7, it was mentioned that every composition should conform to one of the twelve modes.

2. "Mode," called "tone" by most and "trope" by a few, refers in this context (for in other places these words [occasionally] mean something else,[10] to a certain form and mold of harmony,* viewed in one of the seven species of octave, after this has been divided through the fifth or fourth.†

---

[9]"*in prosa et ligata.*" Three poems by Bernhard are included in Christian Dedekind's song anthology, *Aelbianische Musenlust* (Dresden, 1657). This same poet wrote of Bernhard, after the latter had died, that he was an artist "to whom words and music were one and the same" ("dem Text und Ton war einerlei"). See Gerhard Bittrich's dissertation *Ein deutsches Opernballett des siebzehnten Jahrhunderts; ein Beitrag zur Frühgeschichte der deutschen Oper* (Leipzig, Frommhold and Wendler, 1931) for an attempt to establish Bernhard as the author of a French-style opera-ballet entitled "Die sieben Planeten," which was produced in Dresden ca. 1680.

[10]"Modus" denoted one of the proportional relationships in mensural notation. "Tonus" can mean a specific recitation formula for a psalm, Magnificat, etc., and, of course, the major second. "Tropus," while most often used to mean a textual or musical addition to a pre-existent chant, can also denote one of the various alternative endings of a psalm tone (otherwise called "differentiae").

*"eine gewisse *Forme* under Beschaffenheit einer *Harmonie.*"

†What is meant here is made clear in ch. 45, para. 2.

3. Thus it is the octave and the sounds comprehended therein which form the basis of a mode; and such an octave, with its member sounds, is called *ambitus* by the *musici*.

4. This *ambitus* is of two kinds. Either it may span the octave exactly; or it may not reach an octave, or indeed overstep it. From the first kind arise the *proper tones*,[11] from the second the *improper*, called *deficient* and *superfluous*, respectively. For example:

5. A mode said to be proper in this sense is illustrated in these hymns:

> *Nun lob, mein' Seel', den Herren*
> *Vom Himmel hoch da komm' ich her*
> *O Herre Gott, dein göttlich Wort*
> *Helft mir Gott's Güte preisen*

6. A mode said to be improper and indeed defective‡ appears in the following hymns:

> *Nun komm, der Heiden Heiland*
> *Allein Gott in her Höh' sei Ehr'*
> *Jesus Christus unser Heiland, der den Tod überwand*
> *Erstanden ist der heilige Christ*
> *Komm, Gott Schöpfer, heiliger Geist*
> *Der Du bist Drei in Einigkeit*
> *Nun lasst uns Gott dem Herren*

7. A superfluous mode occurs when the octave is overstepped—that is, when a second or even a third is found either above or below the same, as in the following hymns:

> *Vater unser im Himmelreich*
> *Wir glauben all' an einen Gott*
> *Gelobet seist Du, Jesu Christ*
> *Der Tag, der ist so freudenreich*
> *Christus der uns selig macht*

---

[11]"*Toni proprii.*" The subsequent three kinds are called, respectively, "*improprii*," "*deficientes*," and "*superflui*" by Berhnard. "*Tonus*" and "*Modus*" both appear time and again in the upcoming discussion, seemingly interchangeably. I will, wherever possible, translate each on with its English cognate.

‡"*defectivus.*" Clearly the same as "deficient" (*deficiens*).

Christ ist erstanden
Christ lag in Todesbanden
Nun freut euch, Gottes Kinder all'
Komm, heiliger Geist

8. To the superfluous modes belong also the *mixed modes*, which occur when a tenor not only overshoots the octave by a second or third,[12] but indeed goes as far as a fourth beneath it, or as far as a fifth above it. I indeed do not remember encountering this in our hymns,[13] in figural music, however, it does occur occasionally. They are called mixed because the authentic and plagal modes, which will be defined shortly, may both be perceived therein.

9. As far as the sounds comprehended in the octave are concerned, they are either *principal* or *subordinate.** The principal sounds are the fourths and fifths, as well as the semitones, whose differing location forms the basis of distinction between the modes. The remaining sounds are subordinate and demand no special consideration.

10. The fifth has as its basis the finalis,† its lower limit. Its other limit lies above.

11. There are four species of fifth, ut-sol, re-la, mi-mi, and fa-fa, as is clear from the location of the semitones.

12. The fourth has as its basis either the upper or lower limit of the fifth.

13. And has three species, ut-fa, re-sol, and mi-la, as again is clear from the location of the semitones.

14. From the different ways of joining fourths and fifths arises the distinction between authentic and plagal modes.

---

[12]Here and in the sequel, the exact meaning of "tenor" is not always clear, and in any case seems to vary somewhat. Sometimes the word appears to refer to a principal melody line, be it a *cantus firmus* or a freshly composed line; sometime to a voice with tenor range. In view of the importance of the tenor voice as a frequent carrier of *cantus firmi* in German Renaissance polyphony—whose traditions and precepts remained alive throughout the Baroque—the word may also on occasion denote both these things at once. (In connection with this point, see the quote from Folengo given in *Art of Singing*, note 16.) As used here, it seems to carry the first meaning; in ch. 52, para. 1 and ch. 53, para. 1, the second meaning seems paramount; in ch. 46, para. 5, both may well be intended.

[13]There are clear examples of mixed modes in plainchant, however—e.g., the Easter sequence, *Victimae paschali laudes*.

*"*dominantes* oder *servientes*."

†"*clavem finalem*."

15. A mode is *authentic* if the fourth is found above the upper limit of the fifth. [Example 248]

Example 248

16. A mode is *plagal* if the fourth is found below the lower limit of the fifth. [Example 249]

Example 249

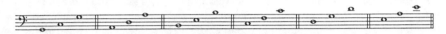

17. Since the semitones are found to be different in any one mode than in all the others, they can best be shown during our demonstration of individual modes.

Footnote number 7 continued from page 55.

VINCENZO ALBRICI was born in Rome in 1631 and died in Prague in 1696. He took up residence at the Swedish court in 1650, as director of the queen's Italian opera house; then he entered the Dresden chapel in 1654. With his brother Bartolomeo, he went to London in 1664, where the two were chapel composers until 1667. That year he was appointed Kapellmeister back at Dresden, a position which he held through 1680, except for a stay in Paris from 1672 to 1676. He was organist at St. Thomas Church, Leipzig, in 1681–82, then became church Kapellmeister at Prague. Albrici's compositions include three Te Deums for chorus and orchestra, and numerous Masses, cantatas, and instrumental works. An item of special interest in his works is a setting of the Lord's Prayer in Swedish, "which is the first important vocal composition with words in that language" (*Grove's Dictionary of Music and Musicians*, 5th ed., I, 98).

ANTONIO BERTALI was born in Verona in 1605 and died in Vienna in 1669. He was Viennese court violinist starting in 1637, and in 1649 was made Kapellmeister there. His compositions, numbering over 600 in all, include twelve operas, two oratorios, and much church and chamber music. A dissertation on his dramatic works was written by Christopher Laroche (Vienna, 1919, unpublished).

GIOVANNI ANDREA BONTEMPI (real name Angelini) was born in Perugia in 1624 and died there in 1705. A castrato, he was in the choir at St. Mark's, Venice, in 1643, then held posts as *maestro di cappella* in various Roman and Venetian churches. He came to Dresden to head the court chapel in 1651, and during his tenure there published a treatise, *Nova quatuor vocibus componendi methodus* (1660), and produced *Paride* (1662), the first Italian opera to be performed in that city. Two German operas followed, both produced there in collaboration with Peranda (*q.v.*), as well as an oratorio. He returned to Italy in 1680, writing two more treatises, one of them a history of music. Bontempi was celebrated for his mastery of both the *stile antico* and the *stile moderno*, and also acquired fame as a theatrical architect.

GASPARO CASSATI (Casati) was born in Pavia early in the seventeenth century. A Franciscan monk, he was named *maestro di cappella* at the cathedral of Novara in 1635, then died there prematurely in 1641. He wrote Masses, psalms, and motets in one to four voices, under the influence of the monodists.

STEFANO FABRI was born in Rome in 1606 and died there in 1658. A pupil of Bernardino Nanini, he was *maestro di cappella* at various churches in his native city, and wrote Magnificats, motets, and concerted psalms.

KASPAR FÖRSTER, the younger, was born in Danzig in 1616 and died in Oliva (near Danzig) in 1673. A pupil of his father, Kaspar Förster, the elder, who was cantor at St. Mary's in Danzig, and later of Marcho Scacchi at Warsaw, he was employed as a baritone and as choral director at the court chapel in Warsaw, then traveled to Venice and Copenhagen between 1652 and 1655 to fulfill similar roles. In 1655 he came back to Danzig to become cantor at St. Mary's himself, retaining that post until 1657. In 1660–61 he again went to Copenhagen, later in 1661 to Dresden, still later to Hamburg. He spent his last years in the monastery of Oliva. His works include six trio sonatas and numerous cantatas and concerted church works.

The elder Förster was a celebrated defender of the *stile moderno*, although we know of no works of his in that style. He engaged in constant polemics over the matter with Paul Siefert, the organist at St. Mary's, who stood against the newer ways. For more on this controversy, see my preface, pp. 2–5.

JOHANN CASPAR KERLL ("Kerl" in M-B.) was born in Adorf, Saxony, in 1627 and died in Munich in 1693. He studied organ with Valentini at Vienna, then went to Rome to study with Carissimi (and possibly Frescobaldi). During these student years he was thoroughly converted to the Italian vocal style, both new and old, and also was struck by the bold, expressive instrumental idiom of Frescobaldi and his followers. Entering the service of the Bavarian elector in 1656, he soon gained a reputation as an outstanding organist; in 1674 he moved to Vienna, where he became organist of St. Stephen's in 1677 and court organist in 1680. He returned to Munich in 1684. Kerll produced at least ten Italian operas during his earlier stay at Munich, plus numerous sacred works. He is best known, however, for his keyboard works, which, like those of his contemporary, Froberger, are remarkable for their daring use of dissonance, and which won the attention of both Bach and Handel years after his death.

MARCO GIUSEPPE PERANDA was born in Rome ca. 1625 and died in Dresden in 1675. Bernhard brought him to Dresden for his alto voice between 1651 and 1656. He then became Vice-Kapellmeister there in 1663, Kapellmeister in 1666. His compositions include concerted Masses, motets and madrigals, a Christmas story, and a Passion according to St. Mark; also instrumental music. With Bontempi (*q.v.*) he produced *Dafne*—"eine Deutsche Musicalische Opera"—at Dresden in 1671, and *Jupiter und Jo* in 1673.

FRANCESCO DELLA PORTA was born in Monza around the start of the seventeenth century and died in Milan in 1666. He held posts as *maestro di cappella* and organist at various churches in the latter city. Three books of his motets, for two to five voices, were published in Venice and Antwerp between 1645 and 1654, and some of his psalms appeared in Venice in 1656 and 1657. He wrote a number of *ricercari* for organ.

GIOVANNI PRIOLI (Priuli) was born in Venice between 1575 and 1580 and died in Vienna in 1629. A composer-organist, he was a pupil of Giovanni Gabrieli and worked at St. Mark's between 1607 and 1612, assisting his aging teacher. In 1615 he became Hofkapellmeister at Graz, and in 1619 went to the imperial court at Vienna. His works include three books of madrigals (the last book partly in concerted style), as well as canzonas, sonatas, motets, psalms, and Masses (again, some of these concerted). Two secular concerted works are found in *Denkmäler der Tonkunst in Österreich*, Bd. 77, 87 ff.; a *Domine labia me* appears in *Caecilia* (1843), p. 128.

LORENZO RATTI ("Laurentius Rattus" in M-B.) was born in Perugia in 1590 and died in Loreto in 1630. He was a boy-singer in the Cappella Giulia in Rome between 1599 and 1601, and was organist at Perugia between 1614 and 1616. Later he held the position of *maestro di cappella* at various religious establishments at Rome. He wrote two books of madrigals, and many motets, most of them a cappella. His *Sacrae Modulationes* (1628), a collection of works on texts from the Proper, were very popular in the smaller Roman churches during the seventeenth century. An opera of his, *Il Ciclope*, was produced in Rome in 1628.

GIOVANNI ANTONIO RIGATTI (Rigati) was born in Venice in 1615 and died there in 1649. A priest, he was appointed *maestro di cappella* at Udine in 1635, and *maestro del coro* at the Venetian Conservatorio degli Incurabili in 1646. He works include concerted Masses, psalms, and motets, and also works for solo voice with basso continuo, both sacred and secular.

GIOVANNI ROVETTA was born ca. 1596 (site unknown) and died in Venice in 1668. The son of an instrumentalist at St. Mark's, he himself was employed there for most of his life: first as a choirboy; then as a bass, starting in 1623; then as vice-*maestro di cappella*, starting in 1627; and finally as *maestro di cappella*, succeeding Monteverdi at that position in 1644. Two operas by him, as well as several books of psalms, concerted madrigals, motets, and Masses are known. Bukofzer (p. 35) mentions him as having excelled in his continuo madrigals.

MARCO SCACCHI was born in Gallese (near Rome) in 1602 and died there ca. 1685. A pupil of G.F. Anerio, he was Kapellmeister and court composer at Warsaw between 1628 and 1648. He wrote five operas, an oratorio, a twelve-part Mass, four-part Masses, and five-part concerted madrigals; also a treatise, *Breve discorso sopra la musica moderna* (Warsaw, 1649), and several important letters and tracts dealing with the features and relative merits of the old style and the new. For more information concerning these letters and tracts, as well as his alleged influence on Bernhard, see my preface.

FRANCESCO SORIANO (Suriano) was born in Viterbo (Suriano) in 1549 and died there in 1621. He was *maestro di cappella* at various churches in Rome, including St. John Lateran, Santa Maria Maggiore, and St. Peter's, and for a time was also in Mantua, a master of the duke's private chapel. His works include three books of madrigals, and much sacred music; an eight-voiced *Ecce sacerdos magnus* is found in *Musica Sacra*, Vol. XXV, ed. by F. Commer (Berlin, 1884); two Masses are found in *Selectus novus Missarum*, ed. by C. Proske (Regensburg, 1855–61); a Passion is given by Fr. X. Haberl in *Kirchenmusikalisches Jahrbuch* X (1895); various sacred works appear in *Musica Divina* III, ed. by C. Proske (Regensburg, 1859). With Felice Anerio he took part in preparing the "Editio Medicaea" of the Gradual (1614).

ANTONIO (or Giovanni) FRANCESCO TENAGLIA was born in Florence early in the seventeenth century and died after 1661 in Rome. He had two operas produced at Rome, in 1656 and 1661, and wrote over fifty cantatas, as well as numerous madrigals and arias.

FRANCESCO TURINI was born in Prague in 1589, the son of an Italian musician there, and died in Brescia in 1656. The pupil of his father, Turini became court organist at Prague at the age of twelve. After holding various other posts, he was named organist at the cathedral of Brescia in 1624, a post which he retained for the rest of his life. He wrote solo madrigals and motets under the influence of Monteverdi and the monodists, as well as many other concerted vocal works, both sacred and secular, and also trio sonatas. Bukofzer (p. 70) says that he was highly skilled in the *stile antico* as well as in the new style. An example of his skill in the former is a four-part Mass, written wholly in canon.

JOHANN MATTHESON

Johann Mattheson (1681–1764) belonged to the same generation as Johann Sebastian Bach. However, as both a theorist and journalist, he avidly championed the change in style during the years 1720–30 which forced Bach onto the periphery of the compositional scene and into a state of resignation, it would seem, which hangs like a shadow over his esoteric late works, removed as they are from musical practice.

In *Der Vollkommene Capellmeister* (Hamburg, 1739), his theoretical *chef d'oeuvre*, Mattheson proceeded, in a form that was characteristic for the epoch, to combine aesthetic premises with those concerned with technical aspects of composition. From the maxim that it is within the very nature of music to have a "stirring and moving" (*rührend und bewegend*) effect, it follows, according to Mattheson, that a theory of composition worthy of its name should have at its core a theory of melody, for only in melody and not in "harmony"—polyphonic writing being the traditional object of compositional theory—could music manifest itself as a language of the emotions (*Empfindungssprache*). (That a book about the tasks of a Capellmeister should primarily deal with a theory of composition rests on the fact that in the eighteenth century the function of the conductor was not separated from that of the composer. A Capellmeister largely wrote works he performed himself.)

The theory concerning the priority of melody over harmony conceals within it the dichotomy between nature and art—the postulate, going back to the Renaissance, that art must conceal its artistry and appear like nature in order to be true. (The same topos crops up in Kant's *Critique of Judgment*.)

Mattheson was believed to have discovered the musically natural, in "noble simplicity" (*edle Einfalt*). (The formula was in circulation, it seems, decades before Winckelmann, who merely supplemented "noble simplicity" with "quiet grandeur"—*stille Größe*). Though one easily overlooks this today, the concept of "noble simplicity" in the eighteenth century contained a polemical element directed against Baroque tradition. According to Baroque criteria, the formula would have been considered a paradox. In the age of Louis XIV, noblesse—royalty and power—presented itself together with ostentatious pomp, in musical terms, with an abundance of figures and ornaments—the very opposite of "simplicity." By contrast, the call for *outer* simplicity was that of a bourgeois opposition, which laid a claim on *"inner* nobility." Notwithstanding, Mattheson had to defend this theory of melody against the sceptics who, conceding that melody contained the "moving and stirring nature" of music, did not believe that one could clearly codify it. Indeed, although it is supposed to refute the prejudice about the irrationality of the melodic, Mattheson's theory of melody consists less of technical instructions than of aesthetic postulates.

His intention is, nevertheless, unmistakable: to discover criteria that would mediate stringently between the general aim of "moving and stirring" through music and the compositional means appropriate for that purpose. Categories like "effortless ease," "clarity," "flowing nature," and "charm" are supposed to guarantee, to a certain extent, the translatability of music, the "language of the emotions," into techically demonstrable and useful rules. Yet the attempt to solve the problem of translation was only partially successful.

The rules concerning "effortless ease"—a facility which Mattheson interpreted for the middle classes as "comprehensibility"—are basically nothing other than paraphrases on the demand for "noble simplicity." "Noble simplicity" however, first appeared under the heading of "clarity," without providing a reason for placing it in one rather than in another category. (The convergence and overlap suffered by aesthetic concepts is not restricted to Mattheson.)

The instructions on "clarity," cast in terms of compositional technique, are unusually explicit, yet they relate to music's "moving and stirring nature" only because "simplicity"—from which the rules of clarity are derived—counts as a requisite for expressivity.

The "flowing nature," suggesting an avoidance or linking up of cadences, contradicts "clarity," which, conversely, demands distinct breaks at regular intervals. The conflict, obviously, has its basis in Mattheson's own position, stylistically speaking, between the late Baroque, in which he grew up, and the Empfindsamkeit, which he later adopted. Using Heinrich Besseler's terminology one could say: Mattheson found it difficult to decide unequivocally between the "uniformity of movement" of the late-Baroque and the pre-classical "correspondences melody," i.e. between the ideal of continuity and that of symmetry.

The fact that the rules concerning "charm" are partly the repetition of instructions already given under other aesthetic headings is an indication of the difficulties standing in the way of stringently deriving the technical from the aesthetic. It is immaterial whether the instruction at the beginning of a piece, for the unambiguous execution of its key, is headed "facility," "clarity," or "charm," nor is it surprising to find such an instruction appearing twice. (The same goes for the demand to use ornaments reservedly and not in excess: a demand that, as already mentioned, corresponds to the anti-Baroque ideal of "noble simplicity.")

Mattheson's theory of melody, the core of his theory of composition, is a theory of *Klangrede* (literally: "sound discourse or rhetoric") or *Tonsprache* ("tone language"). And the comparison with verbal language, which openly or implicitly runs through the whole book, serves the purposes both of demarcation and of drawing analogies. As a "language of the emotions," music is totally different from "conceptual language"; the fact that conceptual language always contains tinges of emotion and, conversely, that the language of emotions contains cognitive elements does not alter the fundamental view of the eighteenth century. According to that view, the hypothetical "primordial language," in which Rousseau and Herder assumed a unity of word and tone, had been irreparably divided by historical developments into a language of concepts and one of emotions—that is, into verbal language and music.

On the other hand, because of its syntax, for the description of which Mattheson borrows from grammar such concepts as comma, colon and period, the language of emotions is an analogue to conceptual and verbal language. (Heinrich Christoph Koch even spoke of a musical "subject and predicate," without, however, stating precisely what he understood thereby.) Mattheson, going beyond the relatively harmless theory of syntax, even made the attempt—albeit partly unsuccessful— to establish a theory of musical form by transferring to the area the categories of legal rhetoric: exordium, narratio, propositio, confutatio, confirmatio and conclusio.

Despite the continual danger of coming to grief, it is difficult to talk about music other than in concepts that have their origin in language theory. Yet the extent to which the terminologies are "true" or "untrue" does not only depend on general, systematically ascertainable facts and structures, but also on the changing philosophical implications contained in the historically variable categories "metaphor," "analogy," "image," or "simile." Where a past epoch believed in an *analogia entis*, a historian does not have the right, with his logical or logically informed critique, as it were, to spoil that epoch's concept.

from der Volkommene Capellmeister[1]

—43—

Nonetheless, it is astonishing that there is no writer on music who has given us proper, concise definition of melody before the writing of *Kern melodischer Wissenschaft*. There is a great difference between generally understanding a thing, and thoroughly describing it in detail. Nothing will be accomplished in pedagogy by our thinking that: **One need not tell a musician what melody is.**

—44—

And even when something on this may have appeared, it has either not been systematically correct as regards substance, form, and purpose, since it is sometimes lacking in this and sometimes in that; or such lengthy statements have been made that one can scarcely measure them with long yardsticks, and yet they say very little in many words, indeed nothing specific at all, but things that apply to more than one thing.

—46—

A good foundation for useful rules for melody can thus be gleaned from the above accurate definition and its explanation alone, and the imagined impossibilities here can very easily be eliminated. For, if first of all one only considers rightly the four characteristics: **facile, clear, flowing, and lovely,** and investigates further, then four classes or classifications of such rules follow.

---

[1]Text: *Mattheson Johann's der volkommene Capellmeister*, tr. Ernst C. Harris (Ann Arbor: UMI Research Press, 1981 [list of paragraphs is included in the text]).

–47–

If we consider secondly, the **moving or stirring nature,** as wherein true melodic beauty first exists, and for which the four above-mentioned qualities are only expedient and useful; then we have the entire theory on natural affections before us, and no lack in good rules will be perceived; but perhaps there will be a deficiency in their intelligent application. This is not the place to enlarge on this last matter, which belongs specifically to philosophy as well as natural science, but only to examine diligently the four mentioned characteristics.

–48–

Accordingly, the following can produce a good foundation for the rules flowing from: a **facile** quality:
We cannot have pleasure in a thing in which we do not participate.
One derives seven rules from this in a natural way:
1. There must be something in all melodies with which almost everyone is familiar.
2. Everything of a forced, farfetched, and difficult nature must be avoided.
3. One must follow nature for the most part, practice to some degree.
4. One should avoid great artifice, or hide it well.
5. In this the French are more to be imitated than the Italians.
6. Melody must have certain limits which everyone can attain.
7. Brevity is preferred to prolixity.

–50–

Much is said of **clarity**, and it also requires more rules than the other characteristics. We want to cite only ten as examples.
1. The caesuras and divisions should be observed precisely: not just in vocal but also in instrumental pieces.
2. One must always aim at one specific passion.

68

3. A meter must not be altered without reason, without need, nor without intermission.
4. The number of beats should be proportionate.
5. No cadence should appear contrary to the usual division of the beat.
6. The accent of the words should be closely observed.
7. One must very carefully avoid embellishment.
8. One must aim at a noble simplicity in expression.
9. One must precisely examine and differentiate the writing style.
10. One must not base the aim on words, but on their sense and meaning: not look to sparkling notes, but to expressive sounds.

–51–

The recognition of the compass of each key is indispensible to the flowing quality. What this word **compass** means here is shown in the *Orchestre*. The cadences, pauses, and caesuras, which are not incorrectly called clauses, are very important in this. For if a melody must lose its flowing character because of frequent stops, then it is easy to see that one has reason not to use such interruptions frequently. Eight rules serve for this:

1. One should pay careful attention to the uniformity of the meters or rhythms.
2. Also, preserve precisely the geometrical proportion of certain similar phrases, namely the *numerum musicum*, i.e., the measurement of melody by numbers.
3. The fewer formal cadences which a melody has, the more flowing it most certainly is.
4. Cadences must be selected and the voices for these managed well before one proceeds to the pauses.
5. In the course of melody, the little intervening resting places must have a certain connection with that which follows.
6. The overly staccato style is to be avoided in singing; unless a special circumstance requires it.
7. Do not take the passages through many sharp jolts, through little chromatic steps.
8. A theme must not impede or interrupt the melody in its natural course.

–52–

Now as far as **charm** is concerned, one could come to its aid with these eight rules:
1. In this case, steps and small intervals are preferred to large leaps.
2. One should cleverly vary such small steps.
3. Collect all sorts of unsingable phrases, in order to avoid them.
4. On the other hand, select and amass ones which sound good as models.
5. Observe well the relationship of all parts, members and limbs:
6. Employ good repetitions, yet not too often.
7. Begin with sounds which are pure, related to the key.
8. Employ reasonable runs or colorful figures.

–55–

Regarding this, the assumption is: That there must be a certain something in a good melody, an *I know not what*, which so to speak the whole world knows: which does not at all imply that one might quite artfully use many worn-out things and spent little formulae; not at all. We mean rather that one would not go too far with his newfangled inventions, would not become an eccentric, and besides would not just make his melody strange, but also heavy and unpleasant.

–56–

The ear always desires something which is familiar to some degree, however trifling; otherwise nothing can appear **facile** to it, much less pleasing. Meanwhile, the more seldom one follows the same familiar paths, and the more one knows how to mix them with other different yet appropriate things, the better the work will succeed.

–57–

The second rule on the **facile** arises from the first: For, on the one hand, one must not completely discard everything familiar; on the other hand, **everything of a forced, pretentious, and too-farfetched nature must be diligently avoided**. What is said here one can better see and hear from the works of mannered composers than describe with words. The examples of this are very detestable: besides many could be produced.

–58–

Frequently when the good people are lacking in fine inventions and in intelligence, yet do not want to copy or steal blatantly from other composers, they tend to become pure eccentrics and take their refuge in nothing but stubborn caprices: so that they strive to replace the loss of natural fertility with wondrous curiosities. As clumsy as this may be to composers, it is equally unpleasant to auditors: excepting some few dandies who want to appear as if they understood something about it.

–59–

The third rule, **that one should follow nature for the most part, and accepted pratice only to a certain degree**, likewise flows from the stated principles, and is closely related with them. The natural babbling of one inexperienced in the science will yield the best melody, and indeed the more so because it is remote from all artificial constraints and is only somewhat related to practice; though such a person must have heard much that was good in his day and must possess an innate talent.

–60–

Nothing can be more facile and more comfortable than that which nature itself makes available, and nothing will be ponderous which practice and custom call good. Hence the composer must occasionally, when constructing his melodies, if they are to be facile, act as a mere dilettante, and with the latter imitate the natural quality which he seeks in vain in great art.

–61–

Fourth, if we **reject artifice**, then **true** art should not be confused with it; however, to produce the latter skillfully and to mask or drape it modestly, that is precisely the very difficult point. My advise would be that the most accomplished composer would rely just as little on the embellishment as the practiced fencer on his feints.

–64–

Overly pretentious and constrained art (I cannot say too much on this) is unpleasant artificially, and deprives nature of its noble simplicity. If nature seems to produce many deformed things, then this alleged ugliness relates only to the superficial appearance; not the inner essence. Nature never lacks beauty, naked beauty, only sometimes it buries it under a discreet disguise or a theatrical mask. Our gem cutters can polish the diamond; but they cannot give it any other luster or purity than that which nature has already given it. The art being employed thus does not give nature any beauty, also it does not increase it by even a hair; but through its efforts, merely places it in its true light: which must certainly be more darkened than brightened, where a despotic art gives the orders.

–65–

The **facile** is aided a great deal if one, following the sixth rule, **sets certain limits** to his melody which every normal voice can reach comfortably. For, if a song goes either too high or too low, then this makes it **difficult** for people, and it must be transposed sometimes one way, sometimes the other, which causes nothing but inconvenience. Those who are good singers will at least find no difficulty in reaching an octave; yet I do not know what special advantage is to be found if one make these bounds even narrower, perhaps at a seventh or sixth: for the more a composer insists on this, the more he accustoms himself to modulations which are simply stuck together, detached and disjointed. Then one proceeds aimlessly, with a presumed freedom, and produces nothing which enters pleasantly or *concinne* into the mind.

–66–

I am not here speaking of those skilled composers who are masters of melody, who have performers at hand capable of performing their melodies, and who know how to use liberties at the proper place, one cannot set such precise limits for them; however, I would advise that a beginning composer of melody choose as a limit the compass of the sixth or octave; but in such a way that even the peasant would not notice it. Certainly, it will help a great deal to make his melodies facile and suitable. For what special benefit is it to me if that this or that person is skilled in performing an aria which for example encompasses over two octaves? I might want to sing along, though only mentally, for therein consists the greatest pleasure; yet I am not allowed to do it: the piece is too wide-ranging for me.

–67–

The last rule of this classification is not the least, namely: **that one should prefer brevity to prolixity**. This needs even less explanation, the more we can understand that a concise and not too widespread melody is easier to retain than a long and extended one.

–68–

Nevertheless, this does not mean that composing a short aria would be a facile task: for with brevity we also include quality. **Facility** here concerns only the hearer, not the composer: though to the former a thing will seldom **seem** facile which has been quite difficult to the latter, in a certain toilsome or laborious sense.

–69–

I say: **seem**. For there are certain composers whose work, toil, and improving actually only serve that they eliminate everything which does not **show common facileness**, or has the appearance of such: and the more they examine and review their works with a view toward such, the more often they bring naturalness and facility into play in them. However, these geniuses are seldom encountered, and they may quite properly use the Italian saying regarding their works: *Questo facile quanto è difficile!* **How very difficult this apparently facile thing is!** We must do it cleverly as if it were only play; although often we secretly break out in a sweat therewith, which moreover no one must perceive; otherwise he sweats in empathy, like that Sybarite who encountered a bungler in hard and unnecessary work.

–72–

The second main characteristic of a well-composed melody is **clarity**: here the first rule is, **that one should observe precisely the caesuras in the text**, which few words say a great deal. It is almost unbelievable how even the greatest masters often violate this: inasmuch as they commonly use all of their powers bringing the hearing to rebellion with noisy and thundering figures; so that the mind is not pleased at all, even less so can the heart be moved.

–73–

The most amazing thing is that everyone is of the opinion that no such remarks would be needed for instrumental music; however, it shall be shown brightly and clearly below that all, long as well as short, instrumental melodies must have their proper *Commata, Cola,* periods, etc., no differently, but in the very same way as the song with the human voice: because otherwise it is impossible to find clarity therein.

–74–

One also never really attains such clarity if the following guiding principle is not observed, through which **we must set as our primary goal** one affection (where not more than one) **with each melody**.

74

–75–

Just as a clever painter always provides only the one or the other of his figures (where there are many of them) with especially prominent colors, so that it would stand out among the other images; thus the composer must also set his sights perpetually and **primarily** toward one or another passion in his melodic phrases, and so arrange or express it that it would have far more significance than all the other secondary details.

–76–

We might consider, with regard to painting, that the purpose of a skilled artist would perhaps not merely be to paint a couple of black or blue eyes, a prominent nose, and a little red mouth; but he always endeavors to present in such features one or another inner emotion, and employs all his best ideas so that the spectator may say, for example: there is something of love in his eyes; something generous in his nose, and something malicious in his mouth.

–78–

However, if nothing like this is expressed in a melody, then it has little or almost nothing of clarity, and the most attentive listener cannot make anything of it but idle singing and playing. Now this rule only prescribes the essential need for presenting such a passion, and indicates why this is so urgent; how one should approach this belongs in another place.

–79–

Yet it is amazing that pieces which are merely composed for instruction are particularly praised for earnestness, for the greatest impact and for the most precise expression of words, the harmony, art and concertizing, and that the desire is rather to amplify these theories and powerful ideas than deal with the affections and passions.

–80–

The greatest expressiveness, the most powerful ideas, and the most precise performance of the words, i.e., of the meaning that is in the words, indeed stems from the affections and passions, and without these they can no more stand than a carriage without wheels: if these are not present, then it is no more than a sledge or a dray. If one would make the application from good and long experience, then it will become evident.

–84–

When the French vary the pulse in almost every line of their recitatives, very often in their airs also, then they go to a lot of trouble for nothing, and could with less effort imitate the Italians in this, if their dissimilar speech would allow it: in as much as the Italians together with us do not observe a measured pulse in vocal recitative at all; except in a poetic phrase. Morever it is almost the same to have no meter as to have a new one every moment.

–85–

Since, however, recitative cannot actually be called melody; while on the other hand melodic phrases, in so far as they are to be clear, should avoid too frequent variation of the pulse: it thus becomes apparent that the **soul of melody**, namely the meter, **simply must be uniform**. And that is the third rule for advancement of clarity. But if the rhyme-scheme or an unexpected affect requires the alteration of the pulse, then necessity does not abide by rules; yet, in my opinion, the poet should not lightly alter his meter in an aria significantly, unless he simultaneously wants to awaken a different passion in a sudden way (*ex abrupto*).

–86–

The fourth rule of clarity is based upon the **number of divisions in the beat**, otherwise called mensuration. Although this relationship cannot be so easily recognized by everyone in great and long phrases, its convenient and intelligible construction will give the song not a little **clarity**, in spite of the fact that many do not understand whence it comes; on the other hand such foresight is always necessary in short and lively melodies (*airs de mouvement*), because otherwise a lively vocal line makes no more sense than perhaps having two arms, one with two hands but the other with three or more hands.

–87–

Now it is in fact not difficult to ascertain to some degree the actual numeration of this mensuration in certain styles of writing, as for example in the hyporchematic and the choraic; but in other styles this is so much more difficult. Where there is much movement, the melos must display the greatest correctness of division in this regard; but, on the other hand, when things are slow and sluggish, or even only slow and serious, one can make more exceptions contrary to the uniformity, because its absence is not so noticeable.

–88–

Usually one does best, even in the greatest *Adagio*, in choosing the even number of pulses rather than the odd. This much is certain, that a fast song should never have an uneven number on the mensuration; and we could even take a the foundation here all these *airs de mouvement* and consider them as model: for they are, as stated, the most correct and the clearest among all types of melodies in this regard.

—89—

The observation of the orderly division of every tactus, namely the so-called caesura, gives us the fifth rule of clarity. Such a division always occurs on either the downbeat or upbeat when the measure is even, never on the second and last quarter. But in the uneven pulse this division occurs only on the downbeat: or better said, there is rather no division at all because the caesura is merely at the first note of the segment.

–94–

Just as the **accent** in pronunciation of the words can make an oration clear or unclear, according to whether it is employed at the proper or improper place; thus also the sound can make the melody clear or unclear, according to whether it is accented correctly or incorrectly: and that is the sixth rule of clarity.

–95–

A composer must have complete mastery of both type of accent, oratorical as well as musical, so that in vocal pieces he would not impinge upon the length and brevity of the syllables, nor in the instrumental pieces upon the musical prosody. However, the significance of this, and the usefulness of the clever application of it, can be learned more thoroughly at the cited place in the *Critica*.

–96–

Here it is also proper to discuss the actual **stress** or the **emphasis**: because the word which is provided with such always requires a certain type of musical accent. Only what matters here is that one should know how to judge properly just which words are actually to be stressed. And here there is no better advice than that one should examine all sorts of utterances, especially in prose, and should endeavor to find the right word, perhaps through the following means.

–97–

If I for example would want to know where the word-stress would be in this sentence: *Unser Leben ist eine Wanderschafft*; then I would only need to present the proposition in question and answer form, namely: *Was ist unser Leben? Eine Wanderschafft*. Thus this reveals that the emphasis would rest upon the word *Wanderschafft*: and if the composer makes such a word prominent in one or another unconstrained way with his tones, he will be **clear**.

78

–101–

The seventh rule of **clarity** teaches us, **to use all embellishments and figures with great discretion**. Daily experience shows us what kind of terrible patchworks are pasted together from neglecting this commandment of melodic beauty. One anonymous person recently wrote the following on this: "The arias are so varied and intricate that one becomes impatient before the end comes. The composer is satisfied if he writes only nonsensical notes, which the singers, through thousands of contortions, make even more absurd. They laugh during the saddest performance, and their Italian excesses always appear at the wrong place. The arias, which the excellent T. has composed, are much too orderly: their passages are always augmented with ravings which are suited for droll throats, but not fit for the intellect."

–103–

These are precisely the pernicious pomposities about which **Quinctilianus** knew how to sing a little song even in his time, since he explicitly asserted that he could not at all approve of what was undertaken with music on the stage at that time, namely where everywhere the **effeminate and obscene style of singing** contributed not a little to thoroughly suppressing and stifling that of the masculine or virtuous which was perhaps still present in some minds.

–104–

Now we come to sensible simplicity, with which the eighth rule of clarity deals: which however must not be understood as something stupid, absurd, or vulgar; but rather as something noble, unembellished and quite singular. Simplicity constitutes the most important point in writing and reading as well as in singing and playing, indeed in the whole of human affairs: and if ever innate characteristics were to occur, this certainly would be the right place.

–105–

This much is beyond dispute, that men, some more than others, also excel in this matter according to how the physique and the orderly or disorderly mixing of the humors are fit or unfit for sensation. Noble thoughts always have a certain simplicity, something of the unaffected, and only a single aim. Whoever presents such without any constraint, according to the simple laws of nature, will best succeed.

–107–

Now we have two rules on **clarity** left to explain: the ninth, which requires **differentiating the styles of writing from one another well**. This says in a few words that one should not mix together vocal and instrumental styles in the church, on the stage and in the chamber; should not place a prayer where a sermon should be; should not require the voice to do things which are appropriate for violins; should not set military pieces for lutes, and many more such things on which more has already been said above.

–108–

The tenth rule of **clarity** is quite accidentally the last here; but in content almost the most important. For if we, according to it, **want to set our main objective not on the words: but on the meaning and on the thoughts contained therein**, then it is appropriate here to have no small impression of the affect which resides in such words, which matter will have to be dealt with in detail in another place.

–109–

Moreover, this rule has two branches, one concerns the human voice, the other concerns instruments, and emphatically commends to us more **clarity** and expressive sounds, not variegated masses of notes. For, the fact that not a single melody should be without meaning, without aim, or without affection, even though without words, is

80

established by this, and through the laws of nature. So much for the second classification in the explanation of our melodic ground rules.

–110–

The third characteristic of a good melody was then that it must be flowing. For this is helps first, that one constantly observe rhythmic conformity and the proper variation of the arithmetic relationship of certain rhythms. This is not to say that one must retain one sort of *rhythmum*, as this would cause an impropriety and disgust; rather one must necessarily alternate various rhythms with one another, just as such occurs in Latin poety, in its way. However these same *rhythmi* must appear in the melody just the same at one place as at another, so that they as it were answer one another and make the melody flowing.

–111–

The ordering which is observed in such a presentation and alternation of the rhythms is called a geometric relationship: for, just as in the arithmetic ratio, wherein the melody moves along, considered in and for itself; the geometric relationship shows how they are united and how their divisions must be properly indicated. For example:

a, is a certain rhythm of three notes which vary in content. *b*, is however of just the same number but of uniform value: Then in each of these is a special arithmetic quality; *c* and *d* on the other hand, both taken together, exhibit the orderly alternation of the preceding rhythms, and make from them one entire geometric phrase.

–113–

The third rule as well as the fourth for the furtherance of the **flowing** character in the melody concerns the cadences or closes: For as it is of course certain that many closes and pauses obstruct the course of the song; thus it is easy to see that a properly flowing melos would have to have very, very few full cadences.

–115–

The worst here is when contrary to the fourth rule such cadences are very badly chosen and the song proceeds to an untimely repose before it even completes the shortest phrase or can have some reason for fatigue. It is good, pleasing, and beautiful, if at the very beginning a full cadence on the tonic is heard. E.g.

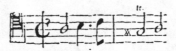

For in this way the hearer forthwith receives information on the entire key, and on the way in which the composer plans to proceed; if he has first gained such a secure foothold: that is nice. However the untimely cadence-makers do not have such an intention at all; in minor keys they immediately cadence on the third, and with the major keys cadence on the fifth: since these are easiest for them to do. This is the end of it, afterwards they simply no longer know what to do.

–116–

One can also add to this explanation the gain which a melody obtains in its **flowing** quality when right at the beginning the arpeggiated triad is heard in a clever way: for from this the listener obtains a still greater capability for judging where his hearing will be led. Everyone likes having advance knowledge and judgment: for this reason such a passage is pleasing.

−117−

Connecting or skillful joining in melody helps a flowing quality a great deal: fifth, one therefore has to take care, especially at certain pauses or cadences, so as not to blurt out something, but to combine and join everything together without a long pause, by means of appropriate approaches and progressions, as occurs in a good speech *per transitiones*. The French carry this almost too far in their music, and thereby make their phrases very monotonous. Thus moderation must also be maintained in this: for what is all-too-flowing becomes slippery and easily slips away.

−118−

Also if an overly staccato quality, especially in vocal pieces, can possess little or nothing **flowing** within itself, here the sixth rule commends us to avoid such. One must not be so punctilious in preludes and fantasies, where a regularly-flowing melody is not required; nor, generally, in the whole of instrumental music; indeed in entrées and similar elevated dances, and occasionally in overtures, it will be explicitly essential to produce much that is detached: this sounds very fresh and lively, expresses quite well various, gay affections, as well as some violent ones; but it is never **flowing**.

−119−

The perpetual drawing and dragging through the half tones and dissonances, with which so many are truly enamoured, has its time and place, as the circumstances permit or require it; but whoever wants to compose something **flowing**, must not seek such crooked, chromatic paths. But where such is not the intent, everyone has a free hand. I do not want to restrain anyone.

–120–

Now as a good, unforced interface, whereby one does not act too timidly, makes a phrase very **flowing** with that which follows: a great obstacle to this quality results when one interrupts the natural course of the song with inept pauses, for the sake of one or another theme, and retards the progress of the melody: for this indeed cannot possibly be **flowing**.

–121–

Here however, we understand the theme to be a primary or secondary voice; not a subject in a fugal piece: that is to say, if perhaps the bass or the violins would not be so prominent in an aria so that the most important or vocal part would have to suffer and be overshadowed merely in order that the former might also seize the theme (be it created as it may); such runs against all reason, and yet occurs daily.

–122–

The classification of charm is more important than the three preceding: although they by contrast are more necessary. In so far as the eight rules on this require a little explanation, the first has as its aim that one must employ more degrees or steps and generally more small intervals than large leaps, if it is to sound **charming**.

–124–

Now if we observe the above rules and for the advancement of **charm** of a melody proceed more through steps than leaps then the following basic principle requires: **that one would cleverly vary** such **steps and small intervals**, this means, that one should not use only steps, only thirds, much less only fourths, nor use the same type in strict sequence; but instead divert the hearing with frequent variation, so that the song will become **most charming**.

–125–

For example, three or four half tones in succession, especially the minor ones, will be too many if otherwise there is no ulterior motive. Five to six steps, especially diatonic ones, are also somewhat unpleasant; unless the words or circumstances, or as stated, a special intent, a theme, a passage, and the like, explicitly would require more. Here we only speak of the charm of a melody in general; not of special cases, where every rule has its exception.

–126–

One can have two to three thirds in sequence and no more of one type without destroying the charm: but one can seldom have more than two fourths, if they are stressed. The downbeat and upbeat of the measure create some hesitation here; yet this is not of the importance to weaken or cancel the rule in and for itself. Whoever will go to the trouble to examine music thoughtfully in this regard will find the truth. E.g.

These 3 fourths would not sound charming:

These two do sound well, however:

–127–

Herewith we are subtly led to the third rule of **charm**, by virtue of which one **should diligently seek out unmelodic or unsingable examples**, bringing these into certain chapters; observing their bad sound, wherein it consists; discovering the causes of this, and carefully avoiding the like.

–128–

One indeed need not search far for such things, because the evil is usually encountered more frequently than the good: however, with those who make a trade of counterpoint one more often encounters a more curious accumulation of crude and unpleasant passages: this becomes rather clear from their failures.

–129–

If for example someone were to write the following:

anyone who had any concept of charming melody would have to readily acknowledge that such an ascending minor third, *b* to *d*, followed by an ascending, accented half tone could not sound natural, much less pleasant.

–130–

Now if someone might say: I hear this; but I do not know why: it is useful to tell them that the two extremities, *b* to *e flat*, constitute a harsh dissonance, namely, a diminished fourth; that they both are accented, and sound even worse with the intervening *d* than otherwise, due to the clumsy separation. This is the reason.

–131–

For if the intervening note, *d*, were omitted, and if the *b* were a half beat, one would not perceive the dissonance nearly as strongly, since the *b* would then receive a pause or rest, and could therefore be the more easily forgotten. Also, the combination of said ascending diminished fourth would not have so bad an effect if it were to appear in shorter notes of equal value; if only both ends had no musical accent; but one of them were on the fourth part of the measure. E.g.

Yet here the execution would also require for camouflage a certain ornament, the *Schleufer*, which we have indicated with dots; one would not need this if the diminished fourth were descending instead of ascending.

–144–

The fifth rule of **charm** consists in the precise **observation of the proper relationship of all parts of a melody with one another**. Our previous concern only related to the relationship of the intervals, which one must distinguish well from this last, where the parts themselves are compared.

–145–

This rule not only refers, for example, to the fact that the second main part of an aria would so to speak be related to or on good terms with the first; but also to the fact that the smaller subdivisions would exhibit their required uniformity. Whereas most galant composers now do this in such a manner that one would often think that one part of their melody would belong in Japan, the other in Morocco.

–146–

One in fact must not be so precise that he would take up the compass and the ruler; however, great dissimilarity and the adverse relationship in the sections are just as detrimental to charm, indeed occasionally to the requisite clarity itself, as a large head and short legs to the beauty of the body. If for example the first part of the melody were:

Then it would have to sound nice if in the second part perhaps the following would answer, which would sustain good comprehensibility and thus would sustain the relationship of the two parts:

–147–

The sixth rule of charm requires that one would employ pleasant repetitions and imitations, yet not too frequently. True repetitions occur more frequently in the beginning of a melody than in its continuation: for there they often follow one another literally, and also without transposition; here however there is always something intervening.

88

–154–

The seventh rule of **charm** requires **that every beginning of a good melody would be made with such sounds which either present the key** itself **or are very closely related** to it. Again we need not search far for examples; but need only observe the immediately preceding, in which the full chord of the key can be heard right in the first four notes, and with one left over.

–155–

This occurs in the indicated place in nothing but leaps, and does not sound as proper as when it is accomplished in steps; yet, on account of the material, such cannot always be done, and one must not only excuse much to love of ornamentation but must also distinguish whether the meaning of the words would be fresh and lively, or passive and quiet. The following gives us an example of this last, where the significance of suffering in patience is expressed very naturally, through nothing but steps and very small intervals; nonetheless the key is therewith adequately revealed.

Adagio.

Soffro in pace

–156–

Nowadays, the effervescent, playful, and exuberant character often meets with the greatest approval in melodic composition, and also mine, so much so, I would not lightly advise anyone to swim against the stream. Now whoever simply desires to please the greatest number of people, and nothing else, must occasionally discard gracefulness and other essential qualities of song to a certain measure. I know some who seem to know how to temporize in this regard: yet they always eventually swing again into the saddle, and conform with the good taste.

The last of our rules on melody will be that for the advancement of charm one should only use moderate melismas or running figures. Here we do not inquire into the places or the words for which such ornaments are well or poorly suited: for that is the most essential part of intelligibility or clarity, which has already been discussed. Here we are only dealing with the form of the melody in observing such embellishments, without special regard to a different aspect of it, and consequently say that the melismas, if they are used immoderately or are extended too far, hinder charm and arouse disgust. This example is good:

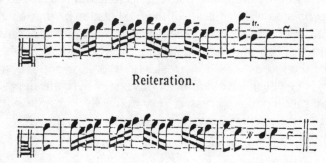

Reiteration.

DANIEL WEBB

Author of several treatises, *Daniel Webb* (1719–1798, b. Maidstown, Limerick, d. Bath?) portrays the typical eighteenth-century man of letters, though his contribution, especially to the deliberation about music, reaches far beyond his age. As a member of the gentry, he received a classical education at Oxford. Like most of his intellectual contemporaries, he acquired the knowledge pertaining to current intellectual queries on his own. Passionately reading each other's treatises, these "intellectuals" formed a 'community of discourse,' for whom Aristotle and Horace, Shaftesbury and Locke, and many others, constituted venerable authorities whom they, nevertheless, often challenged. "Imitation" and "imagination," "genius" and "taste," as well as certain linguistic matters, were continuously discussed throughout the century, oscillating between practical approaches and investigations of a more philosophical nature. Webb's *Inquiry into the Beauties of Painting* (1760), for example, was supposed to contribute to the cultivation of the taste of young travellers, yet the book was considerably more than a regular guide book. Though he treated Antiquity with great reverence in this book—a Renaissance bias which still prevailed in his days—it would be a mistake to draw conclusions, regarding Webb, based on that alone, since in his *Observations on the Correspondences between Poetry and Music* (1769) he challenged the traditional "ut pictura poesis," arguing in favour of what was later to become known as "ut musica poesis."

Webb's new approach stressed the benefits to be gained from defining the limits, correspondences and possible "exchanges" between poetry and music. Taking issue with classical as well as seventeenth-century authorities—whom he enlisted for the task he set for himself—Webb seemed to continue the discussion begun by Harris and Avison, trying, however, to ground his intuitions in philosophical contentions.

His arguments, which had considerable vogue in England as well as in Germany, paved the way for people like Beattie, Twining, Bayly and Smith, on the one hand, and Sulzer and Engel, on the other. These, together with a few others, were responsible for a new trend, the influence and implications of which have yet to be explored systematically. It is no doubt, however, that Webb's "comparisons" and those attempted by his followers, entailed the kind of philosophical-cognitive aspects which contributed, eventually, to both epistemology and psychology. Old questions were approached from a novel point of view; trying to avoid biases and prejudices, Webb wished, for example, to form "*a clear idea* of any natural relation between sound and sentiment." Seeking a way between those who ascribed "naturalness" to one of the components (like the adherers of the *Affektenlehre*) and those who stressed the association between them, he called not only for a deeper understanding of the subject-object relationship but for a clearer idea of its aesthetic function.

Preferring the Horatian maxim of "lucido ordo," as a common denominator of the arts, to the more strict Aristotelian "imitation," Webb was free to look for a "morphological" connection between music, poetry and the passions. His premises were few but solid; they rested, in part, on well-established empirical observations. Firstly, he assumed that passions are to be known only through their manifestations, i.e. through "motions" which they produce in the body. Secondly, he maintained that music, as a "succession of impressions" is likewise perceived as movement. Thirdly, he entertained that the mind relates to symbols via "operations" or "modes of Imitation" and that different symbols may entail different kinds of mental processes. "Exciting certain vibrations in the nerves impresses certain movement on the animal spirits," argues Webb, summing up a psychological heritage of more than two centuries. Hence, if passions are regularly "produced by the mind under certain affects," it is through a reversal of order that the mind connects the movements it perceives to affections. By metaphorically "possessing" the essential properties of passions, Webb claims (anticipating Goodman by almost two hundred years) that "music is said to be in unison with passions," namely to "express" them.

It is, however, a limited number of particular passions and not general sentiments (cf. Scheibe) which are at the heart of Webb's theory. Using these "basic" passions he endeavors to show how music "exemplifies" (to use Goodman's term) each of the various emotions. To begin with, explains Webb, music is at one and the same time less specific than language, and more accurate than language, insofar as the expression of 'innermost feelings' are concerned. Rejecting the neo-classical notion of categorically different "*Affekten*," he argues for the existence of but four basic types, the difference among which is, in the final analysis, quantitative. Vibrations, we are told, are either "impetuous" or "placid," either "ascending" or "descending." Using two axis, as it were, that of intensity and speed, enables Webb not only to classify "pride," "glory" and "emulation," for example, under one and the same passion, but also to circumscribe the various sub-types which result from different combinations. Moreover, it suggests, perhaps for the first time, the notion of "isomorphism" between some aspects inherent to music and to the emotions ("coincidence" in Webb's words) about which Langer, among others, will have much to say. For the "labeling" of specific emotions within a type, music is indeed in need of words. No words, however, can communicate, as well as music is able to, the "softness" insinuated by a particular lover.

Indeed, while music is "flexible" and lends itself to endless nuances and variations, words are "stubborn," "unapt to fall into that order and succession to which the affection leads us." The difference in their communicative ability, Webb argues, can be attributed to the different course of their development. Reminiscent more of a Condillac than a Rousseau, language, speculates Webb, must have resulted from "reiter-ated attempts to excite conceptions" in the hearer. In this venerable attempt music played an important part—that of "enforcing emotions." It was, however, the denotative powers of language, which were empha-sized in the course of its development, signs were conventionalized while their emotive content abraded. Language, Webb concedes, is not only an important achievement, but indispensable for scientific and philosophical discourse. Poetic messages, however, argues Webb, reminiscent of Baumgarten, are "off-springs of sensations." Thus, music is highly recommended in order to regain that "paradise" which language has lost, for music, throughout its development, highlighted those very properties which primitive utterance entailed.

The musical aspects of language, in conjunction with poetry, were seriously discussed throughout the century. Webb's important contri-bution, however, is in distinguishing between the inherent 'musical param-eters' of language and those which are connected to its 'musicalization,' a subject which occupied him already in his *Remarks on the Beauties of Poetry* (1762). Alliteration, onomatopoeia, rhyme and other musical devices are of no interest to Webb; he is not interested in *literal* manifestations but in *imaginative* cognitive operations leading to metaphorical relations.

Having argued the special case of music, Webb does not exclude painting from "the lower cognitive faculty" (see Baumgarten), since "keeping our sense in suspense through maximum gradations" is central for art in general. Still, painting, though the most natural of arts "both in its means and effects" cannot approach music, which, though bound with conventions, becomes "the things it imitates." Poetry, concludes Webb, stands in between, for it deals with images as well as affects. In a successful combination between poetry and music "music borrows sentiments from poetry and lends her (poetry) movements" and with it an "instantaneous feeling."

from Observations on the Correspondence between Poetry and Music[1]

To his GRACE
The DUKE OF GRAFTON,
First Lord of the Treasury, &c. &c.

My Lord,

The beauty of order in the disposition of visible objects, the powerful effects of arrangement in the succession of our ideas, of measure and proportion in the successions of sounds, are but different modifications of one common principle. The *lucidus ordo* or Horace marks how much he thought the second connected with the first; the design of the following essay is to prove, how intimately the third is connected with both: to point out the origin, and to lay open the advantages of a musical elocution. We who have no other merit than to feel these advantages are under a natural subjection to those who exert them: the Critic, my Lord Duke, is but a dependent on the Orator. It is under the sanction of this dependence, that I presume to engage your Grace's attention; and to claim a part of that time which you so happily employ to the noblest purposes.

I have the honour to be
Your GRACE's
Most humble, and
Obedient Servant,

DANIEL WEBB.

---

[1]Text: Daniel Webb, *Observations on the Correspondence between Poetry and Music*, (London, J. Dodsley) 1769, pp. v–vii; 1–41; 47; 50–52; 53–56; 60–69; 72–76; 79–83; 87–90; 91–94; 100–104; 111–113; 117–119; 128–141; 142–145; 147–151.

The Latin sections were not translated because they served to illustrate the arguments rather than elaborate upon them. However, we left them intact for those who may benefit from them.

OBSERVATIONS ON THE CORRESPONDENCE
BETWEEN POETRY and MUSIC

Though the influence of music over our passions is very generally felt and acknowledged; though its laws are universally the same, its effects in many instances constant and uniform; yet we find ourselves embarrassed in our attempts to reason on this subject, by the difficulty which attends the forming a clear idea of any natural relation between sound and sentiment.

Some have though to elude this difficulty, by supposing, that the influence of sound on passion may arise from the habit of associating certain ideas with certain sounds. It cannot be necessary to enter into a formal examination of such a principle as this, since it must fall of course on the discovery of a better.

I have observed a child to cry violently on hearing the sound of a trumpet, who, some minutes after, hath fallen asleep to the soft notes of a lute. Here we have evident marks of the spirits being thrown into opposite movements, independently of any possible association of ideas. This striking opposition in the effects of musical impressions seems to indicate the regular operation of a general and powerful principle.

All musical sounds are divided into acute and grave: the acute spring from strong, the grave from weaker vibrations. No sound, therefore, can act as a single impression, since we cannot have a feeling of it but in consequence of a succession of impressions: should it appear, that our passions act in like manner by successive impressions, or, that they affect us on a principle similar to that which is deducted from the analysis of sounds, we might then hope to become masters of the desired secret, and to discover, so far as such things are discoverable, the nature of the relation between sound and sentiment.

As we have no direct nor immediate knowledge of the mechanical operations of the passions, we endeavour to form some conception of them from the manner in which we find ourselves affected by them: thus we say, that love softens, melts, insinuates; anger quickens, stimulates, inflames; pride expands, exalts; sorrow dejects, relaxes: of all which ideas we are to observe, that they are different modifications of motion, so applied, as best to correspond with out feelings of each particular passion. From whence, as well as from their known, and visible effects there is just reason to presume, that the passions according to their

96

several natures, do produce certain proper and distinctive motions in the most refined and subtle parts of the human body. What these parts are, where placed, or how fitted to receive and propagate these motions, are points which I shall not inquire into. It is sufficient for my purpose to have it admitted, that some such parts must exist in the human machine: however, as in our pursuits after knowledge, it is discouraging to be reminded every moment of our ignorance, I shall take advantage of the received opinion touching this matter, and assign the functions in question to the nerves and spirits. We are then to take it for granted, that the mind, under particular affections, excites certain vibrations in the nerves, and impresses certain movements on the animal spirits.

I shall suppose, that it is in the nature of music to excite similar vibrations, to communicate similar movements to the nerves and spirits. For, if music owes its being to motion, and, if passion cannot well be conceived to exist without it, we have a right to conclude, that the agreement of music with passion can have no other origin than a coincidence of movements.[2]

When, therefore, musical sounds produce in us the same sensations which accompany the impressions of any one particular passion, the the music is said to be in unison with that passion; and the mind must, from a similitude in the effects, have a lively feeling of an affinity in their operations.

In my Remarks on the Beauties of Poetry, I have observed,

That, in music, we are *transported* by sudden transitions, by an impetuous reiteration of impressions.

That we are *delighted* by a placid succession of lengthened tones, which dwell on the sense, and insinuate themselves into our inmost feelings.

That a growth or climax in sounds *exalts* and *dilates* the spirits, and is therefore a constant source of the *sublime*.

If an ascent of notes be in accord with the sublime, then their descent must be in unison with those passions which *depress* the spirits.

---

[2]Whether we account for the imitations of music in this manner, or call them, after Aristotle the ιμννμαια τυιχιυιχαι ϖαθωτ simulacra morum et affectionum we have alike in view a principle of assimilation; with this difference, that, by establishing a mode of operation, whether real or imaginary, we are enabled to convey our ideas with greater clearness touching the several modes of *imitation*.

All musical impressions, which have any correspondence with the passions, may, I think, be reduced under one or other of these four classes.

If they agitate the nerves with violence, the spirits are hurried into the movements of anger, courage, indignation, and the like.

The more gentle and placid vibrations shall be in unison with love, friendship, and benevolence.

If the spirits are exalted or dilated, they rise into accord with pride, glory, and emulation.

If the nerves are relaxed, the spirits subside into the languid movements of sorrow.

From these observations it is evident, that music cannot, of itself, specify any particular passion, since the movements of every class must be in accord with all the passions of that class.—For instance, the tender and melting tones, which may be expressive of the passion of love, will be equally in unison with the collateral feelings of benevolence, friendship, and pity; and so on through the other classes.

On hearing an overture by Iomelli, or a concerto by Geminiani, we are, in turn, transported, exalted, delighted; the impetuous, the sublime, the tender, take possession of the sense at the will of the composer. In these moments, it must be confessed, we have no determinate idea of any agreement or imitation; and the reason of this is, that we have no fixed idea of the passion to which this agreement is to be referred. But, let eloquence co-operate with music, and specify the motive of each particular impression, while we feel an agreement in the sound and motion with the sentiment, song takes possession of the soul, and general impressions become specific indications of the manners and the passions.

It is imagined by some, that verse hath no other object than to please the ear. If by this they understand, that verse cannot excite or imitate passion, they would do well to reflect on the nature of pleasure: at least, through this medium, were there no other, verse must have an influence over all those passions which are founded in pleasure. But verse is motion, and verse produceth pleasure, which is likewise motion.

How then? hath nature struck out a correspondence between external and mental motion in one instance, to the exclusion of all others: provident, industrious, in establishng laws for an inferior purpose, would she stop short at the first opening of advantage, and contract her system at the very point where it called for enlargement? I do not wish to set out upon better ground than in direct opposition to such ideas as these.

It has been supposed, that the correspondence of music with passion springs from a coincidence of movements; and that these movements are reducible to four classes, distinguished by their accords with the passions of pride, sorrow, anger, and love. Should these principles hold good in verse, which is the music of language, we shall have little reason to doubt of their extending to music in general.

The passion of love is soft and insinuating; it dwells with a fond delight upon its object:

—Iilum abfens abfentem auditque, videque.

O fairest of creation, last and best
Of all God's works. Creature in whom excell'd
Whatever can to sight or thought be form'd
Holy, divine, good, amiable, or sweet.[3]

And again:

                    Awake,
My fairest, my espous'd, my latest found,
Heav'n's last best gift, my ever-new delight,
Awake.

The expansion of pride is constant in its influence, and compels the measures into a corresponding movement. In the following lines, we have at once a description of the passion, and a proof of the effect:

            Op'ner mine eyes,
Dim erst, dilated spirits, ampler heart
And growing up to godhead.[4]

Ast ego, quae divum incedo regina, Jovisque
Et soror, et conjux.[5]

[3]Paradise Lost.
[4]Paradise Lost.
[5]Aeneid. 1. I.

But I, who move supreme, heav'n's queen, of Jove
The sister, the espous'd.

It seems to me, that the pleasure which we receive from great and sublime images arises from their being productive of sensations similar to those which are excited by pride. Whether the sensation springs from a consciousness of superiority in ourselves, or from the contemplation of greatness in external objects, we feel the same enlargement of heart; our emotions are congenial, and their accords consonant:

Thus far these beyond
Compare of mortal prowess, yet observ'd
Their dread commander: he above the rest
In shape and gesture proudly eminent,
Stood like a tow'r.[6]

The movement the most opposed to pride must be in accord with sorrow. A descent of notes, if I mistake not, prevails through the following passage:

Me miserable! which way shall I fly
Infinite wrath, and infinite despair?
Which way I fly is hell; myself am hell;
And in the lowest deep a lower deep
Still threat'ning to devour me opens wide.
O then at last relent; is there no place
Left for repentance; none for pardon left?[6]

In general, a protracted sound, joined to a kind of languor or weakness in the movement, will be happily expressive of sorrow:

Longas in flectum ducere noves.

Earth felt the wound, and nature from her seat
Sighing, through all her works gave signs of woe
That all was lost.[7]

[6]Paradise Lost.
[7]Paradise Lost.

On comparing this passage with the following, we shall observe the difference between an imitation by movement and an imitation by *sound*:

> Tellus et pronuba Juno
> Dant signum, sulfere ignes et conscius Aether
> Connubii, summoque *ululabunt* vertice nymphae.[8]

In this second instance, the agreement depends on the force of a particular word or sound, as being imitative of a particular idea. In the former, the accord springs from an agreement of syllables or sounds no otherwise imitative than as they determine by their succession the nature of the movement. A distinction which must be carefully observed in the application of that general maxim,

> The sound must seem an echo to the sense.[9]

It cannot be expected, that the principles of imitation should operate in all similar cases with an equal happiness. There is a stubbornness in the nature of language, which often renders it unapt to fall into that order and succession to which the affection leads us. But the indulgence which the poet may claim from this consideration must not be extended so far as to encourage him to a total violation of the laws of harmony. When our passions are strongly engaged, we are impatient of opposition; and, in every such case, a counter-movement in measure hath much the same effect with a discord in music. Under the impression of these ideas, I cannot reconcile to my feelings that passage with which the Roman poet closes his mournful tale of the death of Priam:

> Jacet ingens litore truncus,
> Avulsumque humeris caput, ac sine nomine corpus.[10]

There is a vigor in this movement that is at variance with the idea: it counter-acts our feelings, renders the nerves elastic, and sets the spirits on the spring.

[8]Aeneid. 1. IV.
[9]Pope's Essay on Criticism.
[10]Aeneid. 1. II.

In the next example, a movement of *dejection* follows, and thereby marks more strongly the character of anger:

> Ite,
> Ferte citi flammas, date vela, impellite remos.
> —*Infelix Dido!*[11]

> Fly,
> Catch the quick flames, spring forward, crowd the sails—
> *Lost, lost Eliza!*

When anger hath for its object a studied and distant revenge, its impetuosity gives place to a deliberate vehemence:

> No, let us rather chuse,
> Arm'd with hell-flames and fury, all at once
> O'er heav'n's high tow'rs to force resistless way,
> Turning our tortures into horrid arms
> Against the torturer; when to meet the noise
> Of his Almighty engine he shall hear
> Infernal thunder; and for lightning, see
> Black fire and horror shot with equal rage
> Among his angels.[12]

In the preceding arrangement of the passions and their accords, anger, pride, sorrow, and love, have been made to preside over, and govern, as it were, the simple movements of music; but as our passions in general are derived from these, or partake, in some degree, of their nature, it should seem that we may, by the various combinations of these primary movements, attain to the expression of *almost* every passion. Thus, pity will find its accord in an union of the movements of sorrow and love; for there cannot be pity without benevolence; and benevolence directed to a particular object is a mode of love:

> How art thou lost, how on a sudden lost,
> Defac'd, deflower'd, and now to death devote?[13]

[11]Aeneid. 1. IV.
[12]Paradise Lost.
[13]Paradise Lost.

Joy is a lively motion of the spirits in ascent, as partaking of the nature of pride. For pleasure, according to the Stoics, is a *sublatio animi*, a lifting-up of the mind. The affinity between pleasure and pride is thus happily marked by the poet:

> That now,
> As with new wine intoxicated both,
> They swim in mirth, and fancy that they feel
> Divinity within them breeding wings
> Wherewith to scorn the earth.[14]

But the explanation of joy differs from that of pride, as being apt to break forth in prompt and lively sallies, flying in giddy rapture from one object to another:

> All Heav'n
> And happy constellations on that hour
> Shed their selectest influence; the earth
> Gave sign of gratulation, and each hill—
> Joyous the birds, fresh gales and gentle airs
> Whisper'd it to the woods, and from their wings
> Flung rose, flung odours.[15]

Terror is a perturbation of the spirits, connected with the sublime by the enlargement of its images, and the vehemence of its impressions:

> What if the breath that kindled those grim fires
> Awak'd should blow them into sev'nfold rage
> And plunge us in the flames? or from above
> Should intermitted vengeance arm again
> His red right hand to plague us? what if all
> Her stores were open'd, and this firmament
> Of hell should spout her cataracts of fire
> Impendent horrors?[15]

In the following passages, the agitations of terror subside into movements of dejection: for fear hath its foundation in sorrow, and, as such, must have a tendency to conform with its principle:

[14]Paradise Lost.
[15]Paradise Lost.

103

While we perhaps,
Caught in a fiery tempest, shall be hurl'd
Each on his rock transfix'd, the sport and prey
Of wracking whirlwinds, or for ever sunk
Under yon boiling ocean, wrapt in chains;
"There to converse with everlasting groans,
"Unrespited, unpitied, unrepriev'd,
"Ages of hopeless end."[16]

Indignation is a mixed affection, uniting the vehemence of anger with the expansion of pride:

Heu furiis incensa ferror, nunc augur Apollo,
Nunc Lyciae fortes, nunc et Jove miflus ab ipso
Interpres divum fert horrida juffa per ausas.

Fury distracts my brain; now Phoebus warns,
Now dreams, now oracles, now winged gods
Bring the curs'd mandate.

From these we pass to movements of pure and unmixed pride:

Scilicet is superis labor est, ea cura quietos
Sollicitat! neque te teneo, neque dicta refello.[17]

Think we such toils, such cares, disturb the peace
Of heav'n's blest habitants! alike I scorn
Thy person and imposture.

How sudden is the return to anger?

Fly, be gone,
Rush through the billows, brave the storm—

If there are passions which come not within the reach of musical expression, they must be such as are totally painful. Painting and sculpture, on whatever subjects employed, act simply, as imitative arts; they have no other means of affecting us than by their imitations. But music acts in the double character of an art of impression as well as of

---

[16]Paradise Lost.
[17]Aeneid. 1. IV.

imitation: and if its impressions are necessarily, and, in all cases pleasing, I do not see how they can, by any modification, be brought to unite with ideas of absolute pain. I am confirmed in this opinion by observing, that shame, which is a sorrowful reflection on our own unworthiness, and therefore intirely painful, hath no unisons in music. But pity, which is a sorrow flowing from sympathy, and tempered with love, hath a tincture of pleasure. Hence the poet:

> Dimn sadness did not spare,
> That time, celestial visages; yet,mix'd
> With pity, violated not their bliss.[18]

Pity, therefore, hath its unisons in music; so hath emulation, which is noble and animating, to the exclusion of envy, which is base and tormenting. The same distinction must extend to anger and hatred; for anger hath a mixture of pleasure, in that it stimulates to revenge; but hatred, having no such hope, works inward and preys upon itself.

The number of the passions thus excluded from becoming the subjects of musical expression will not be very considerable, since, on a strict inquiry into those passions which are generally esteemed painful, we shall find that this very often depends on their motives and degrees. Thus terror, though in reality it be founded in pain, is yet in several of its modes attended with pleasure, as is evident in every instance where the means employed to excite it, either by the idea or the movement, have any connexion with the sublime. But terror, like many other passions, though it be not absolutely painful in its nature, may become so from its excess; for horror, as I conceive, is nothing more than fear worked up to an extremity:

> I could a tale unfold, whose lightest word
> Would *harrow up* thy soul.[19]

It is on this same principle, that certain passions are found to add beauty or deformity to the countenance, according to the different degrees of force with which they act. A truth so well understood by capital painters, that they throw the extremes of passion into strong and charged features, while they reserve the finer expressions for the height-

[18]Paradise Lost.
[19]Hamlet.

enings of beauty. Shakespear has touched on this last circumstance with his usual happiness:

> O what a deal of scorn looks beautiful
> In the contempt of anger on his lip.[20]

Mr. Locke, considering the passions as modes of pleasure or pain, divides them into such as are absolutely pleasing, or absolutely painful, to the entire exclusion of all mixed affections. This division is too vague and general; it may save us the trouble of a minute investigation, but it will never lead us into a knowledge of the human heart. Thus, desire, according to this philosopher, is founded in uneasiness; but Aristotle will have its foundation to be in pleasure: whereas, in truth, it is a compound of both: of uneasiness through the want of an absent good; of pleasure from the hope of obtaining that good. I am tempted to convey my idea of this subject by an illustration borrowed from painting. Let us suppose the painful passions to be *shades*, the pleasing *lights*; we shall then find that many of our passions are composed of mid-tints, running more or less into light or shade, pleasure or pain, according to the nature, motive, or degree of the passion. For instance, if grief arises from the sufferings of others, it becomes pity, and is pleasing by its nature. If grief, proceeding from our own sufferings, be hopeless, and therefore excessive, it becomes misery or despair, and is painful from its degree.

Let grief be tempered with hope, it hath a tincture of pleasure:

> All these and more came flocking; but with looks
> Down-cast and damp, yet such wherein appear'd
> Obscure, some glimpse of joys, t'have found their chief
> Not in despair.[21]

The resemblance of that which was dear to us, though it causes grief, yet it gives to our sorrow a cast of pleasure, as it produces in the soul the movements of love. It is in this situation, particularly, that we are said to *indulge* our grief:

[20]Twelfth Night.
[21]Paradise Lost.

> Ask the faithful youth,
> Why the cold urn of her whom long he lov'd
> So often fills his arms.[22]

If grief should spring from a consciousness of guilt, it is shame, and is painful from its motive; if attended with innocence, it may come within that beautiful description,

> She sat like patience on a monument,
> Smiling at grief.[23]

In order to treat of the passions with precision, we should determine their several modes, and fix an unalienable sign on each particular feeling. To this end we should have a perfect intelligence of our own natures, and a consummate knowledge of every thing by which we can be affected: in short, we should have conceptions in all points adequate to their objects. Such knowledge would be intuitive. We should, in this case, want no comparisons of our ideas and sentiments; no illustration of one thing by its resemblance to another: thus every proposition would be reduced to a simple affirmation, the operations of the understanding would cease, and the beauties of the imagination could have no existence. Providence has judged better for us, and by limiting our powers has multiplied our enjoyments.

The wisdom so conspicuous in the abridgement of our perceptions, appears with equal evidence in the bounds prescribed to those arts which were destined for our delight and improvement. It has been observed, that music can have no connexion with those passions which are painful by their nature; neither can it unite with our other passions when they become painful by their excess; so that the movements of music being in a continued opposition to all those impressions which tend either to disorder or disgrace our nature, may we not reasonably presume, that they were destined to act in aid of the moral sense, to regulate the measures and proportions of our affections; and, by counter-acting the passions in their extremities, to render them the instruments of virtue, and the embellishments of character.

I need not profess, that, in forming my ideas of the passions, I have trusted much more to poets than to philosophers: among the latter, there

[22]Akenside, Pleasure of Imagination.
[23]Twelfth Night.

have been some who would by no means have admitted the distinction just now established between emulation and envy. Hobbes hath, after his manner, given us the portraits of these passions, but with such sister-like features, that it is no easy matter to distinguish the one from the other. He has, with equal industry, and for the same purpose, excluded from pity and the sympathetic affections every idea of benevolence or of natural beauty; conceiving them, contrary to all true feelings, to be nothing more than the different workings of one and the same narrow and selfish principle. It may be considered as a happiness in our subject, that it exempts us from a dependence on the systems of the philosophers, or the refinements by which they are supported. The process in which we are engaged obliges us to trace the passions by their internal movements, or their external signs; in the first, we have the musician for our guide; in the second, the painter; and the poet in both: it is the province of music to catch the movements of passion as they spring from the soul; painting waits until they rise into action, or determine in character; but poetry, as she possesses the advantages of both, so she enters at will into the province of either, and her imitations embrace at once the movement and the effect. How delightful, in this point of view, to contemplate the imitative arts; those sister-graces, distinguished yet depending on a social influence; the inspirers of elegant manners and affections; the favourites of that Venus, or nature, whose beauties it is their office to cultivate, and on whose steps it is their joy to attend!

Among the opinions which have prevailed touching the union of music with passion, the most general seems to be this—That as melody is a thing pleasing in itself, it must naturally unite with those passions which are productive of pleasing sensations; in like manner as graceful action accords with a generous sentiment, or as a beautiful countenance gives advantage to an amiable idea. The proposition taken singly is vague and superficial; but the illustrations by which it is supported penetrate deeper, and give us an insight into the relation between the cause and the effect: for in what manner can action become the representative of sentiment, unless it strikes us as springing from some analogous movement in the soul? it is the same thing with regard to beauty, which can give no advantage to sentiment, without being thrown into motion; nor can this motion have any meaning or effect, unless it carries with it the idea of a corresponding agitation in the mind . . .

. . .

... pleasure is not, as some have imagined, the result of any fixed or permanent condition of the nerves and spirits, but springs from a succession of impressions, and is greatly augmented by sudden or gradual transitions from one kind or strain of vibrations to another ... It is contrary to the nature of passions to rest at any fixed point: there may be, perhaps, an exception from this rule in the case of extreme horror; but it must be of horror unutterable—Vox faucibus haesit.— From the moment that a passion falls within the compass of expression, we cannot even conceive it, much less can we represent it, so as to separate from it the idea of increase or diminution. That action therefore which brings the mind to a full stop cannot be the representative of a mind in motion. The tortures of the Laocoon are most happily expressed by the efforts which he makes to support them, or by the degrees of action which the artist hath wisely kept in reserve.

I have remarked on a former occasion, that in the sublime, "such images as are in motion, and which, by a gradual enlargement, keep our senses in suspense, are more interesting than those which owe their power to a single impression, and are perfect at their first appearance." Where there can be no gradation in an object, its influence on the mind is too suddenly determined. Is it not from the force of progressive sensations that the vivacity of our conceptions seems, at times, to exalt us above ourselves? hence the enthusiastic raptures, the boasted inspiration of poets, when the imagination, hurried through a train of glowing impressions, kindles in her course, and wonders at a splendor of her own creating ...

If we have discovered any one common principle by which our feelings are connected, our next care must be to observe how far the arts can affect us in virtue of this principle, and what relation they bear one to the other in their several operations. How extensive might be the influence of these ideas, were they to be enlarged into system, and traced by men of genius through all their consequences! Infinite are the advantages which may be derived from a diligent attention to the mechanical effects of passion; from an accurate investigation of the correspondent movements of music, and from the consequent application of the powers of verse to the support and enforcement of the pathos.

As to the last of these advantages, I am persuaded that our general neglect of it has been owing, for the most part, to the mean opinion we are taught to entertain of our native language. We cannot, it must be confessed, pretend to equal the sweetnesss of sound or dignity of motion in the Greek measures; but I do not think the comparison so much against us with regard to our musical accords in general; and the reason is this: What we lose through the poverty of our measures, is in some degree restored by the simplicity in the construction of our language, in which every idea is so distinct, unmixed, and complete in itself, that it not only suggests, but often creates its own accord: whereas the arbitrary transpositions in the Greek and Latin make such breaks in the thoughts, and throw them so much out of that order in which they rise up in the mind, that the correspondence between the movement and the idea must become less frequent than would naturally be the case were the construction more simple. We shall generally find, that wherever there is a striking beauty in the ancient poetry, there is at the same time a remarkable simplicity in the succession of the ideas. In the communication of a thought, our aim is to produce in the minds of others an image of what passes in our own: in proportion, therefore, as our feelings are thrown out of their natural order, the image is unfaithful, and the operations of our minds must lose a part of their influence.

. . .

Having thus tried the foundation of our hypothesis by a variety of experiments, let us now proceed to examine how far these same principles may be found to agree with the history of Poetry and Music.

In the first ages of the world, men's thoughts were altogether employed on their feelings; prompted by nature to the communication of those feelings, their words followed the motion of their sensations, and became rather the imitative than the arbitrary signs of their ideas. Hence it is, that original languages, or, which is the same thing, the original parts of mixed languages, are always the most expressive. Plato, after having suggested that language owed its origin to the deepest reflection, and the most consummate wisdom, was notwithstanding forced to acknowledge, that words expressive of their ideas abounded most in the barbarous, or, as he otherwise calls them, the most ancient languages;[24] an inconsistency into which he was betrayed in consequence of his having set out on the investigation of language at the wrong end; for though compounds, in many instances, carry in them the marks of mature reflection, and great ingenuity, yet the signs of simple ideas, which were the first in order, and with which of course he should have begun, are of a very different character: these, most undoubtedly, like the ideas which they represent, were the off-spring of

[24]In Cratylo.

110

sensation; they were the result of reiterated attempts, by men of lively feelings, to excite conceptions in others by the happiest indications of their own.

Words are modifications of sound and motion; consequently they may become imitative of all those ideas which have any natural relation to either.

Imitations of sounds operate by a direct similitude in the words—groan, sigh, whine, hiss, shriek, howl, and the like. The imitations of motion are of the same kind in the words—cling, climb, swing, wind, glide, drive. These, tho' monosyllables, and therefore usually considered as single impressions, yet being composed of several distinct elementary sounds, possess, in effect, the advantage of a succession of impressions: of this we shall be more sensible by comparing them with their opposites —slit, spring, skip, start, drop. In order to account for this remarkable difference, we should inquire into the mechanical formation of letters, or of the elementary sounds of which words are composed; but as this would be a dry and tedious discussion, I shall refer those who may desire to trace this subject minutely, to the philosophers and grammarians who have enlarged upon it.

Some imitations act with the united powers of sound and motion, as—sob, gulp, clap, thump, bounce, burst; in others, the organs of speech seem to undergo the very operation specified, as may be experienced in some of the examples already given, and still more forcible, perhaps, in the words—grind, screw, lisp, yawn: nor is it at all an argument against the aim of imitation in these, that similar articulations are employed without any view to imitation in other instances; because the signs of all simple ideas which have no relation either to sound or motion must have been altogether arbitrary, and, as no attention to similitude could take place in their formation, might as well have been comprehended in one combination of sounds as another.

I have called the preceding imitations direct, to distinguish them from such as do not seem to have an immediate connexion with their object: thus we often borrow ideas from the touch or taste, and apply them metaphorically to sounds, as—soft, hard, smooth, rough, sweet, harsh, and their similars. In like manner the words—sharp, flat, so universally applied to musical sounds, owe the fitness of their application to their conveying different ideas of motion, the one being expressive of a quick, the other of a dull, or languid impression.

The last class of imitations is very extensive; it includes all those articulations, which, though they do not amount to a direct designation of the idea, are yet so constructed as to favour, in some degree, the imitation of the action intended, as in—simile, grin, frown, stare: Under this class likewise may be ranked all such approaches to the idea as seem formed to coincide with the changes in inflexions of the voice, to which we are prompted by a spirit of imitation, as in the following-contrasts—rise, fall; fret, sooth; cut, melt; and infinite others.

The imitations of sounds depend for the most part on vowels; they are obvious, simple, and accurate in their similitude. With regard to these, therefore, all primitive languages should resemble one another, allowance being made for the differences which might have arisen from organization, from the temperature of the air, or the degrees of sensibility in the first inventers.

The imitations of motion depend mostly on consonants; these are far more numerous than the former, less perfect in their similitude, but more powerful by their impressions, because passion and sentiment find their accords in motion. Hence it is, that original languages abound in consonants.

The representation of a sound is the echo of that sound; such signs can no otherwise differ throughout the primitive languages than in their degrees of similitude. But the same modifications of motion may be represented by various articulations, or by sounds totally different: because the similitude is determined by the quality of the movement, and not by the nature of the sound. In this case, therefore, the representative, tho' it hath its origin in imitation, must owe its establishment, *in part*, to consent or agreement. Hence it follows, that a diversity in original languages, with regard to signs of this kind, cannot be brought as an argument against a common principle of imitation.

[. . .]

As the Greek language hath been the channel through which the knowledge of antiquity hath descended to us, it was natural that we should adopt the ideas, and proceed on the authority, of the Greek writers. And yet, a very little reflection might have taught us, that, with regard to the origin of language, they were, of all people, the least fitted to be our instructors. They wrote at a time when their language had been improved to a high degree of refinement; when it retained few or no traces of its primitive character, or of affinity with its rude original, the Phenician. Without examples or materials in their own language, they were too proud to borrow them from any other; destitute of true principles, they took up with the first that presented themselves to their imagination: thus, attributing to single letters or sounds what could only refute from their combinations, they supposed the α to be expressive of greatness, the η of length: they went farther, and confounding the ideas of figure and sound, they conceived the O to be an audible representation of roundness: notions altogether fantastical, I had almost said, puerile; but trifles become venerable from certain characters, and we respect even the slumbers of the divine Plato.[25]

If imitation had so great a share in the formation of language, it must have acted with equal force in the government of modulation. Music, in its original purity, was used as a mode of conveying or enforcing sentiment; it was either the substitute or the support of language . . .

Were this idea to be reduced within the terms of a simple proposition, it would amount to no more than this:—That natural preceded artificial language, or, that sounds must have been imitative before they were made the signs of our ideas by compact.

[. . .]

In our attempts to express our feelings by words significative of those feelings, we should find ourselves limited to a certain number of ideas; all those being necessarily excluded which have no relation to sound or motion: add to this, that a complex idea cannot be represented by any single image or impression. Where imitation fails, compact must take place. But the improvement of language by the multiplication of arbitrary signs, though necessary to the purposes of speculation, would ill correspond with the vivacity of our sensations, with that imitative spirit which had given being to language, and with the early and constant influence of an expressive modulation: We should therefore strike into collateral resources, and fall upon new sounds and movements, springing from certain arrangements of words, and successions of syllables: the process is easily comprehended; with an imitative articulation would co-operate imitation by accent; accents determine the times in which successive syllables are pronounced; syllables of unequal quantities must, in the course of their successions, fall into metrical proportions: and the ear, prompt to cultivate its own pleasure, would seize on every approach to a musical rythmus.

At this period, and under these circumstances, no man could be distinguished by his genius, without an ear for music, and a talent for versification; and, the principle of imitation being in both the same, the

[25]In Cratylo.

characters of poet and musician would of course be united in the same person. This unison, with the principles which produced it, properly considered, we shall have no difficulty in conceiving, that the first improvements of eloquence should appear in verse, and the earliest efforts of genius be conveyed in song.

But, if every original language consisted for the most part of mono-syllables; and, if measure, as hath been supposed, was the genuine and immediate result of feeling, it should seem, that there must have been some one simple and primitive mode of versification antecedent to all others, and similar in its mechanism throughout the several languages.

[...]

The simplest measures are those in which each foot, or metrical division, consists but of two syllables. If the accent rises on the first syllable, and subsides in the second, the weaker vibration will produce a sound of shorter duration, and there will be a transition in the sounds from acute to grave:

Sing, my / harp, of / God on / high.

If the accent[26] is thrown on the second syllable, and the voice touches lightly on the first, the duration of the sounds will be as the force of the vibrations, and the passage from grave to acute:

And on the wings of mighty winds.

By this it appears, that men fell upon the use of measures on the very same principle by which they struck into a musical succession of notes. The learned Kircher hath even gone so far, as to suppose music to have been the off-spring of accentuation . . .

And, in fact, what is music in its simplest form, in recitative for instance, but a happy accommodation of the powers of accent and movement to the tones and proportions of our feelings? We have seen that the quantities of syllables are but the variations of accent; and that primitive measures were nothing more than transitions from acute

---

[26]Let it be remembered, that, throughout this discourse, the word *accent* is made to denote an acute, or grave, sound; or, which is the same thing, an enforcement, or relaxation of the voice, on a single syllable.

sounds to grave, or from grave to acute. How is this? have the Greek and Teutonic poetry one common origin? do the cedar and the bramble spring from the same root? . . .

As the most ingenious compounds, in language, are but artificial combinations of simple ideas, increasing with the improvements of the understanding; in like manner, the most artificial measures, so poetry, are nothing more than ingenious variations of the simple proportions of sounds, keeping pace with the refinements of taste and feeling: for the dactyle does but repeat the second stroke of the trochee, the anapaest the first of the iambic . . .

This principle is not confined to regular and established measures; it governs the succession of our monosyllables even in common discourse, but much more when the occasion calls for a spirited and impassioned articulation. As to our words of two, three, or four syllables, we have borrowed them for the most part from other languages; but, in ours, they disown their vernacular accents; and, complying with the genius of our national pronunciation, fall with great regularity into iambic and trochaic movements. Upon the whole, the laws of musical and therefore of metrical proportions, however varied they may be in their modes, are universal in their influence; they obtain in all languages, and extend through every branch of elocution. Hence it is, that prose hath its rhythmus, as well as verse; that expression so much depends on the music of the voice; and that the finest strains of eloquence fall short of their effects, when delivered in equal tones, or with a lifeless and unaccented pronunciation.

[. . .]

We have seen, that the first enlargement of our verse grew out of the reciprocal dependence of successive movements. But as a continual succession of equivalent impressions must fatigue the ear, a relief was sought to the monotony by diverting the movements from an immediate into an alternate dependence:

> To drive the deer with hound and horn
>   Early Piercy took his way;
> The child may rue that is unborn
>   The hunting of that day.[27]

[27]Chevy Chase.

The responses of the stanza set the genius of our rhythmus in the clearest light; and it is probable that rhimes were first employed as the marks of these responses. But an unvaried and uniform alternation was ill fitted to correct a monotonous harmony: it became expedient therefore to extend the scale of the rhythmus, to give it a more liberal flow, and, by introducing with greater freedom into the movements measures of unequal and even opposite effects, to throw them into new modes and degrees of dependence. Let us examine whether our pentameter be formed for the attainment of these ends, and how far it may be intitled to the flattering distinction of heroic verse.

The genuine measures of this verse are the trochee, the iambic, and the spondee,[28] but it runs with the greatest promptness and constancy into the iambic. From this very difference it is, that we derive the principal means of varying our measures; as in the passage from the trochee to the iambic, a movement, the most spirited and elastic:

Arms and the man I sing[29]
Stood like a tow'r.

When an enforced or ascending accent strikes on a monosyllable, the vibrations continue, as in the chord of a musical instrument, after the impression or articulation hath ceased; especially when the stroke is succeeded by a pause, as in the last example. It has been before observed, that the structure of a monosyllable may be such as to render it equivalent to a succession of impressions. Where accent and structure cooperate, they may give a degree of duration to a single syllable, which it would be difficult to equal by a succession of syllables:

And, fled from monarchs, St. John, *dwells* with thee.[30]

[. . .]

[28]Some are of opinion, that the dactyle may take place in the pentameter. This verse consists of five feet, or ten syllables; if, therefore, we appropriate three syllables to any one foot, then there must be in that verse a foot of one syllable: for instance,

And vindicate the ways of God to man.

If the word vindicate be considered as a dactyle, then the monosyllable *and* must be a compleat measure, which is absurd, and contrary to the nature of measure.
[29]Dryden's Trans. of the Aen.
[30]Pope's Essay on Man.

I have supposed that the rhythmus of our verse depends on the relative effects of successive movements; thus, should movements of equal force be divided by the pause into equal time, the balance will be exact, and the rhythmus perfect:

Or seek to ruin—whom I seemed to raise.[31]

On the contrary, should the structure of the verse be such, as that the ear cannot with facility make a division of the movements, nor reduce into any proportion their successive effects, then the rhythmus will be dissolved, and the movements become prosaic.

And with a pale and yellow melancholy.[32]

The constant and even tenor of the couplet secures it from falling into such relaxations; a security, however, in which the poet hath little reason to triumph, while the perpetual returns of similar impressions lie like weights upon our spirits, and oppress the imagination. Strong passions, the warm effusions of the soul, were never destined to creep through monotonous parallels; they call for a more liberal rhythmus; for movements, not balanced by rule, but measured by sentiment, and flowing in ever new yet musical proportions.

[...]

It cannot be imagined that the Greeks could create any new mode of imitation: their great object seems to have been, by a gradual reformation of their language, to vary their measures, and multiply the resources of sound and motion; not so much in the view of improving the means of imitation, as of preserving to the ear the continual enjoyment of a regular dignity and sweetness of versification. It was in consequence of this general intention, that they bestowed the utmost dignity of sound and motion on the most familiar ideas, though they hereby deprived the more important of their just distinction and pre-eminence.

The music of the hexameter is noble, vigorous, sublime; but in this, as in our modern counterpoint, the specific impressions are sunk in the

[31]Ben. Johnson, Verses addressed to Shakespear.
[32]Twelfth Night.

117

general effect.[33] All refinements have a tendency to efface the principles of the art into which they are introduced. Were the counterpoint to take intire possession of our music, we should lose every idea of its original destination, and the sole object of the art would be to flatter the ear.

[...]

If from musical quantities we pass to the consideration of an artificial prosody, it will be difficult to conceive, that this change could have been made with a view, as some have imagined, to a more intimate and perfect union of Music with Poetry: since, should music observe the quantities by institution, she must abandon her own; should she neglect those quantities, the musical rhythmus would be at variance with the poetic.

The artifice of contracted measures, and the variety resulting from these contracts, are most unfavorable to music, because they disturb her in the government of her accents, and thwart her in the exertion of her natural powers. It is for this reason, that, from our simple measures, music ever selects the most simple. But the ancient lyric poesy abounds with the most varied measures, and embraces every mode of versification: true; it abounds likewise with the most picturesque images, and the boldest metaphors: are we therefore to conclude that these are the true objects of musical imitation? How long are we to be amused with inferences drawn from an union which we do not comprehend, and from a practice of which we have not one decisive example?

Vossius asserts with great confidence, that the music of the ancients derived its excellence from the force of their poetic rhythmus: this force he makes to consist in the power of conveying just and lively images of the things represented. It seems intirely to have escaped him, that these images are confined to objects of sound or motion; and that, in the imitation of such, music must, from its nature, be superior to verse; so that the more powerful imitation must have borrowed its advantages from the more imperfect. From this notable proposition he concludes, that modern language and poetry are totally unqualified to unite with music. And yet, where measure flows from the laws of musical

---

[33]Il contrappunto, essendo composito di varie parti, l'una acuta, l'altera grave, questa di andamento presto, quella di tardo, che hanno tutte a trovarsi in sieme, e ferir l'orecchie ad un tempo, comme potrebbe egli muovere nell' animo nostro: una tal determinata passioné, la quale di sua natura rechiede un determinato moto, e un determinato tuono. Algarotti, Saggio sopra l'Opera in Musica, p. 285.

pronunciation, Poetry and Music have one common rhythmus: and, if sentiment takes a part in determining the measure, their union becomes still more happy and intimate: for music hath no expression but in virtue of her accents; nor have her accents any imitative force but what they derive from sentiment. The truth is, music borrows sentiments from poetry, and lends her movements, and consequently must prefer that mode of versification which leaves her most at liberty to consult her own genius.

After what hath been already observed of the nature and origin of these sister-arts, it cannot be thought necessary, in this place, to prove, that a dramatic spirit must be the common principle of their union. This spirit is not confined to the regular drama; it inspires the lover's address, the conqueror's triumph, the captive's lamentation; in short, it may govern every mode of composition in which the poet assumes a character, and speaks and acts in consequence of that character.

To sentiments which spring from character and passion, the lyric poet should unite images productive of sentiment and passion. Objects in repose, or the beauties of still-life, fall not within the province of musical imitation; nor can music take a part in the colouring of language. Our modern lyric poesy is a school for painters, not for musicians. The form of invocation, the distinctions of the strophe, the antistrophe, and chorus, are mere pretensions. To what purpose do we solicit the genius of music, while we abandon, without reserve, the plectrum for the pencil, and cast aside the lyre, as a child doth its rattle, in the moment that we proclaim it to be the object of our preference?

But it is said, that music, by its impressions on one sense, may excite affections similar to those which take their rise from another: and it has been inferred from hence, that the musician can, by a kind of enchantment, *paint* visible objects. To paint by movements would be enchantment indeed; but the wonder ceases when we are made to understand, that music hath no other means of representing a visible object, than by producing in the soul the same movements which we should naturally feel were that object present.[34]

These observations lead us to the necessary distinction of the image from its effect; of its beauty as a visible object, from its energy as a source of pathetic emotions. Thus we draw the line between painting and music: nor does the occasion call for a master-stroke; their separation will be marked in the choice of their objects:

[34]Dict. de Musique, Art. Imitation.

Long, pity, let the nations view
Thy sky-worn robes of tenderest blue,
  And eyes of dewy light.[35]
Deserted at his utmost need
By those his former bounty fed,
On the bare earth expos'd he lies
With not a friend to close his eyes.[36]

If, instead of expressing our own, we describe the feelings of others, and so enter into their condition as to excite a lively sense of their several affections, we retain the spirit of the drama, tho' we abandon the form. The most perfect poem of this kind, in our language, is the Feast of Alexander, by Mr. Dryden. Here, music unites with poetry in the character of a descriptive art; but then the objects of her descriptions are her own impressions.

It was objected by Aristotle to the poets of his time, that they were the principal speakers in their own poems; contrary to the practice of Homer, who well knew, that, while the poet speaks, the imitation or the drama ceases.[37] It is remarkable that this is the very aera from which Plutarch dates the corruption of music. When the poet ceased to write from the movements of the heart, the musician began to sing from the caprice of the imagination.

In proportion as the spirit of expression declines, a taste for description will, of course, prevail; we *express* the agitations and affections of our minds; we *describe* the circumstances and qualities of external objects: the application of measure to either purpose depends on the nature of the subject, or the genius of the writer. A single instance may suffice to set this idea in the clearest light:

When Ajax strives some rock's vast weight to throw,
The line too labours, and the words move slow.[38]

So will they in the expression of a deep and heavy affliction:

And in this harsh world draw they breath in pain.[39]

[35]Collins, Ode to Pity.
[36]Dryden, Alexander's Feast.
[37]De Poet. c. xxiv.
[38]Pope, Essay on Criticism.
[39]Hamlet.

Like parallels may be continued thro' all the examples which have been given of pathetic accords. Now, though the imitations of verse may be applied to the purposes either of expression or of description, it is not the same thing with regard to music, the effects of which are so exquisite, so fitted by nature to move the passions, that we feel ourselves hurt and disappointed, when forced to reconcile our sensations to a simple and unaffecting coincidence of sound or motion.

Again, in descriptive poetry, the imitations often turn on the force of particular words, on the resemblance between the sign and the idea:

Jarring Sound

Th' infernal doors, and on their hinges *grate*
Harsh thunder.[40]

In this, and in every other instance where the resemblance is determined by sound, the characters of Poetry and Music are directly opposed; for, the nature of articulation strictly considered, it will appear, that in poetry, the imitations of harsh and rude sounds must be the most perfect; in music, it is just the reverse. It was for this reason, that our incomparable Milton, in his imitations of musical ideas, threw the force of the imitation, not on the sound, but on the movement:

Save where silence yields

To the night-warbling bird, that now awake
Tunes sweeten his *love-labor'd* song.[41] . . .

These imitations of musical ideas by articulate sounds have much the same effect with the imitations of the force of particular words by musical sounds. Thus, Handel seldom fails to ascend with the word *rise*, and descend with the word *fall*. Purcell goes still farther, and accompanies every idea of *roundness* with an endless *rotation* of notes. But what shall we say to that musician, who disgraces the poet by realizing his metaphors, and, in downright earnest, makes the fields *laugh*, and the vallies *sing*. In music, it is better to have no ideas at all than to have false ones, and it wil be safer to trust to the simple effects of impression than to the idle conceits of a forced imitation.

In our attempts to reduce music into an union with descriptive poetry, we should well to consider, that music can not otherwise imitate any

[40]Paradise Lost.
[41]Paradise Lost.

particular sound, than by becoming the thing it imitates: it hath an equal facility in conforming with simple ideas of motion. What effects can be expected from imitations, in which there is neither ingenuity in the execution nor importance in the object?

Verse on the other hand, considered as motion, falls far short of the promptness and facility of our music; nor can it, with respect to sounds, rise above a distant and vague assimilation: its imitations, therefore, in either case, may be attended with some degree of surprise and pleasure. The misfortune is, that our poets dwell too much on this trifling advantage, and pursue it, to an almost total neglect of the nobler purposes of imitation . . .

Whence is it then, that, in poetry, the most celebrated examples of imitation are such as are merely descriptive?

In imitating the motions of external objects through their various modifications, as, of lightness, heaviness, rapidity,[42] slowness, force, weakness, and the like, the merit of the imitation is decided by a direct comparison with a known and determined object? It would be the same thing with regard to our passions, considered as motions of the soul, were these motions of a nature to be reduced into sensible and determined images. In this case, therefore, we do not judge of the imitation, as in the former, by a direct comparison, but by an instantaneous feeling; with this additional difference, that we are least sensible of the imitation, when most transported by its effects; for, if the poet is successful in touching the springs of passion, our spirits obey the impression, and run into the same movements with those which accompany the sentiment; thus, while we are under the united influence of the natural motion of the passion, and the artificial movement of the verse, we lose sight of the imitation in the simplicity of the union, and

---

[42]A modern critic is of opinion, that the Alexandrine is best calculated to exemplify swiftness, because it most naturally exhibits the act of passing through a long space in a short time. Is it meant, that we pass through the long space of the Alexandrine in as short a time as we should through the shorter space of the pentameter? But this cannot be; for, supposing an equal fluency in the syllables employed in each, their times must be always in the proportion of 12 to 10. That line so often cited as an example of swiftness, sets this matter in the cleared light:

Αυτις επειτα πεδονδε ηυλινδετο λαας αναιες

From whence springs the swiftness in this instance? Is it not from hence, that we pass through a verse of 17 syllables in the same time that we should through a verse of 13? But our Alexandrine can never consist of more or less than 12 syllables. The inference is obvious.

energy of the effect. But in matters of mere description it is not so; in these imitation is professed, and there cannot be a beauty without a manifestation of art. In short, wherever passion is concerned, a coincidence of sound and motion becomes, as it were, the native and proper language of that passion; and our inattention to the art which may be employed on these occasions is so far from contradicting, that it confirms all that has been offered on the origin of verse, and on the natural correspondence between movement and passion.

JOHANN JAKOB ENGEL

Johann Jakob Engel (1741–1802), was one of the central figures of the Berlin *Aufklärung*. Heavily influenced by the French and the English Enlightenment, this cultural milieu had, nevertheless, its own unique characteristics, which were consciously developed since Lessing, Mendelsohn and Krause laid its foundations.

Starting his studies with theology and philosophy, continuing with history and mathematics at the University of Leipzig, Engel became, in 1775, a professor of philosophy and fine arts in the Joachimsthalschen Gymnasium in Berlin. His creative writings gained him immediate acclaim and having been considered a serious connoisseur of the theater as well, Engel was appointed, in 1878, director of the newly founded Berliner Nationaltheater. His experience with opera included the preparation of a libretto for Neeffe's *Der Apotheker* (1771).

In his *Über die musikalische Malerei*, Engel's main concern is with "music imitation"—an issue heavily discussed in the course of the century. The Aristotelian concept of imitation, enlisted by the French as the common denominator for the fine arts, was viewed with suspicion by the English, especially with regard to its applicability to music. While the influence of a Dubos or a Batteux can still be discerned in Engel's essay, his main philosophical and psychological notions derive from Shaftesbury, Burke and Home (Lord Kames), among others. Moreover, his presentation and many of his particular ideas call to mind Webb and Twining, though they do not share their clarity and logical rigor.

Engel relies, ostensibly, on two major streams of thought. The one, which relates music to rhetorics (Bernhard, Kircher, Mattheson), provides the basis for his theory concerning the "destination" of music. Thus, compared to Webb, whose approach is entirely that of an empiricist, Engel's argument concerning the ability of music to move the passions is arrived at deductively. The other, Baumgarten's legacy, which differentiates between scientific and aesthetic knowledge, constitutes the philosophical base for his initial claim. Slightly changing Baumgarten's contention with regard to the main concern of the arts, i.e. the creation of "sensate discourse" (emphasizing the relationship between the object and man's "wishes and wants," rather than the relationship between the object and the perceiver) he states, echoing Krause, that, of all the arts, it is music which is the most aesthetic. Whatever the change, he conceives "imitation" in line with Baumgarten, not as a goal but as an artistic mean. Artistic means, in the final analysis, are determined by the particular medium, content and context of the work of art.

Thus, it is not surprising, that nine years before Twining's two dissertations (*On Poetry as an Imitative Art* and *On the Different Senses of the Word Imitative as Applied to Music by the Antients and by the Moderns*) he arrives at a conceptual scheme with regard to 'painting' which is similar, in interesting points, to Twining's understanding of "imitation" and the way it functions in different genres and artistic forms. Music, accordingly, is the most adequate of arts to "paint" that which concerns the "impressions on the soul." Following a Webb-like psycho-physiological theory,* his "Affektenlehre premises" prevent him, nevertheless, from taking into account some crucial sociological aspects necessary for his argument. Though on the verge of distinguishing between literal and metaphorical ("transcendental" as he calls the latter) "painting," it is the ascription of "naturalness" to tones which halts all attempts to examine "where" and "how" the links between musical ideas and "passionate representations" are actually set in motion. This does not stop Engel from drawing some conclusions on the basis of the philosophical notions which the theory entails. Painting an object, Engel maintains, must resort to but a few, "faint and remote similarities," where the "painting" of feelings may be "expressed" via a multitude of means more akin to the feelings themselves. It is primarily with regard to the latter, argues Engel, that the possibilities of music can be most profitably exploited. Though it lacks the ability to "specify," music has the capacity to render "classes and types of feelings." Engel's distinction between "representation" and "expression" should not be confused with this very distinction made later by Goodman, since Goodman will dispense with resemblances altogether.

---

*Webb's *Observation on the Correspondence between Poetry and Music* was translated into German in 1771.

An "expression," however, can become a "representation"; "what was originally subjective may become objective," argues Engel. Elaborating upon Descartes (*Passions of the soul*), Engel claims that the ideas of an emotion, another's or one's own, may become a "cause for a new emotion," solving thereby the dichotomy between "affect" and "expression." Though "painting" represents the "objective" and "expression" renders the "subjective," the difference between the two is but a matter of "singling out different properties for attention" (as Goodman might have put it). In any case, the inclusion of two contrasting emotions ("heterogenous," in Engel's terminology) in one and the same piece becomes wholly justifiable since effect and affect are frequently part of the very same situation.

Engel's "compositional matrix" is likewise anchored in psychological rather than in purely musical coherence, thereby granting license, though indirectly, to the introduction of "novelties". Indeed, though he provides some explicit rules for composition, he is forced, on the basis of his own contentions, to state that they are liable to be "overruled" by the "true genius." Naturally, the play between the objective and the subjective, between painting that represents and that which expresses, is of a kind that transgresses, by definition, the boundaries the critic is able to envisage. "The relationship between theory and the work of art is such," concludes Engel the poet, critic and philosopher, "that one needs less theory to perfect the works than works to correct the theory."

from Über die Musikalische Malerei[1]

Dearest Friend,

As I see it, the investigative task which you assigned to me can be reduced to the following four questions:

First: What does "painting" mean?

Second: What means for painting does music possess?

Third: Using these means, what is music capable of painting?

Fourth: What should music attempt to paint, what should it refrain from painting?

The answer to these questions, if one intends to be exhaustively thorough, leads here and there to very subtle, almost hair-splitting investigations. I should like to avoid these sophistries, prefacing only what appears to be absolutely necessary, and move on to the practical.

Painting means to delineate an object not only to the mind, using arbitrary, agreed-upon signs, but to make it accessible to sensuous perception, using natural signs. The word: lion produces no more than an image in my mind; the painting of a lion actually presents the visible phenomenon to my eyes. The word: roar has already something pictorial in it; Benda's expression in "Ariadne" constitutes the most complete painting of a roar.

In poetry, however, the word is also used in a different way. A poet is considered the more a painter, the more his presentations turn to the particular, to the individual; the more he fleshes out these presentations with sensuousness and vivacity, by being more specific in his definitions. Language provides him usually only with general notions for the mind, the conversion of these notions into images is left to the imagination of the listener or reader. By more closely circumscribing these notions, the poet assists imagination, stimulating it into perceiving images from a better vantage point, with greater clarity and superior force.

The poet is considered the more a painter, the more he succeeds in achieving a correspondence between the sheer sound of the words and their rhythm and their inner meaning; in other words: the more he invests the sensuous signs representing the object with a resemblance to

---

[1]Text: Johann Jacob Engel, *Schriften*, bd. IV, Berlin 1802, pp. 299-342. The note under asterisk is Engell's note.

the object. In still other words: the more he succeeds in having his arbitrary signs approximate the natural ones.

In music, the first meaning of the word painting does not apply, only the second is of relevance. Tones in music are not arbitrary symbols; nothing that one might think of upon hearing them is predetermined. Their effect is not based upon something that they might be taken to represent, but on the tones themselves and their impressions on our ear. The composer has no generalities to individualize, no intellectual notions to embellish by making them more specific. Yet by means of his tones, as natural symbols, he can awaken images of other, related objects. By using these tones he can try to outline these objects as the painter outlines his objects by using his paints. And then he must do what is done by the poet as painter: he must render his tones in such a way as to be imitative of, and resemble, the object itself as much as possible.

This kind of painting is now either *complete* or *incomplete*. The former presents the *total* phenomenon to our perception, the latter only separate *parts* or *properties* thereof.

Complete painting can take place only where the object itself is audible as well as compatible with measured tone and rhythm.

As regards incomplete painting:

Firstly, the object may be a phenomenon compounded of impressions of various senses, the audible intermingling with the visible, etc. In the imagination, the composer produces the impression of the whole, by imitating the audible. Thus he paints a battle, a thunderstorm, a hurricane.

Secondly, while not comprising any audible components at all, the object may share with the audible tones certain general properties which help imagination to find an easy transition from tone to object.

This is because similarities exist not only between objects pertaining to one single sense only, but also to different senses. Slowness and rapidity, for instance, can be found in a succession of tones as well as in a succession of visible phenomena. I shall call similarities of this type *transcendental* similarities.

It is such transcendental similarities that the composer is after, he paints the swift running of an Atalante—which, of course, only mimicry could fully imitate—by a rapid succession of his tones. If he can combine with this an imitation of the runner's panting, he has at the same time also represented the audible component of the phenomenon: he has painted twice.

This of course multiplies the number of objects paintable by the composer. Due to their transcendental similarity with tones, many objects associated with other senses, especially with that conceptually most fertile, visual sense, are amenable to musical imitation.

At the same time, however, it becomes clear, at least partly, why musical imitation is so ill-defined in general; why, without assistance from the word, it is so difficult to understand the painting composer. Imitation is almost always only incomplete, only partial, dealing only with general properties, whether it is an external, sensuous object, or an internal feeling that is imitated, since feelings, too, are imitated only in general terms. Feelings can be individualized only be a well-defined conception of the object giving rise to them. More about this further below.

To prepare a list here of all trancendental similarities that may serve for such imitation would be as superfluous as it would be impossible. In this respect nature goes into such detail that even the most hair-splitting investigation could hardly follow it. Still, some of those that have pondered the origin of languages, amongst them a noted sect of ancient philosophers,* have produced several ideas which may be of use also for this theory.

It is precisely these philosophers that remind me of the existence of yet another important means for our incomplete painting, the composer also paints, *thirdly*, by imitating neither a part nor a property of the object itself, but the impression made by this object on the soul. It is these means that give musical imitation its widest scope, because now the object no longer needs even those properties that I have called transcendental similarities. Even color now becomes musically paintable, because the impression created by a soft color is similar to the impression made on the soul by a soft tone.

To understand how it is possible to paint these impressions or, indeed, all internal sensations of the soul, why it is precisely this type of painting that music is most adept at and, furthermore, why even this type of musical painting still remains incomplete, we must first provide an answer to our second question above: what means for painting does music possess?

I am putting here whatever I know as I know it, and it will be the task of the expert in the field to correct my ideas if erroneous,and complete them if deficient.

*The Stoics. See Tiedemann's System der Stoischen Philos., Part 1, p. 147ff.

The means for musical painting are thus, according to my knowledge:

First: Choice of *key*. We have hard keys and soft keys.

Second: Choice of the *key note* on which the piece is to be based. The twelve major and minor scales differ from each other in their intervals which give them their specific character. The keys of C major and A flat major differ the most from one another, because the progress of their respective scales differs the most. A characteristic instrumental piece transposed from C major to A flat major would become almost unrecognizable. The same is true of the minor keys.

Third: Melody. It is of great importance whether the tones progress by narrow or wide, by light or heavy intervals, whether in uniformly long, short, or in mixed notes. Also, whether such mixing follows a perceptible order, or is apparently irregular, whether embellishments are simple or elaborate and rich, etc. I doubt whether everything that may be pertinent here can be listed.

Fourth: Movement. This would include uniform or non-uniform, long or short measures, fast or slow, simple or alternating and multivarious movement in different voices, uniform or non-uniform movement, often also movement in opposite directions, etc.

Fifth: Rhythm. Periods and their subdivisions are either long or short, uniform or non-uniform.

Sixth: Harmony, the compounding of simultaneously sounded tones to produce, directly or indirectly, a euphonic effect. Here one may consider: the kind of compounding of simple or manifold, lighter or heavier relations, the kind of progress of these compound relations, which may take place in an infinity of transitions, the sluggishness or swiftness in these transitions, the fullness or emptiness, lucidity or opacity, purity or impurity of harmony, an impurity that is often only apparent, etc.

Seventh: Choice of *voice*. Deep, high, medium voices—different mixtures produce different results.

Eighth: Choice of *instruments* according to their several, very different characters and the way the instruments are blended.

Ninth: Loudness and *softness*, the attaining of different nuances of these by their differing degrees, and the manner in which this is done.

In which way, using these means, the composer is able to paint the inner feelings and emotions of the soul will become clear from the following reflections.

Firstly: All passionate ideas of the soul are inseparably associated with certain corresponding emotions in the nervous system and are fed

131

and reinforced by perceiving these motions. Yet, this corresponding nervous excitation is not produced in the body only when the passionate conception has been evoked first in the soul, these passionate conceptions are also produced in the soul when this related excitation is first produced in the body. The effect is mutual. The same path that leads from the soul to the body leads back from the body to the soul. Yet nothing produces this excitation with such certainty, such might and such diversity as do tones. It is therefore tones that nature preferably uses to evoke the instinctive sympathy between animals of the same kind. The scream of the suffering animal produces in the nervous system of the non-suffering animal a similar excitation that evokes in the soul of the latter a similar feeling, known as compassion. The same holds true also with empathy in joy.

Secondly: The various kinds of passionate representations differ in the abundance and wealth of the several ideas joined therein; in the greater or lesser diversity associated with each kind; in a greater or lesser concurrence of these diversities, resulting in a greater difficulty in grasping the entire conception; in a slower or faster succession of the representations; in narrower or wider steps—intermediate representations are skipped, at times more, at times less; in a greater or lesser uniformity of progression—some representations always proceed slowly, others always rapidly, still others extremely irregularly, sometimes stopping in their course, sometimes continuing with higher speed, etc.

To give only a few examples: The progression of representations of grave contents is slow; the progression of joyous representations of easily grasped content is brisk. Fear works itself through a large number of discordant ideas at high speed, but intermittently; melancholy creeps slowly and haltingly through closely associated ideas.

These remarks make clear:

1) Music is capable of painting or imitating the inner feelings of the soul: It selects tones, the effect of which, on the nervous system, is similar to that of a given feeling; it chooses, for this purpose the instruments and the pitch of the tones, whether high or low. If the tones produced by Franklin's Armonica will irresistibly draw a person of the slightest sensitivity towards melancholy, then the sound of trumpets and the roll of drums will equally irresistbly produce a feeling of joyous exaltation. And if higher tones are more appropriate for all lively, cheerful feelings, and the middle tones for all softer, gentler emotions, it

is the lower tones that best express everything sad, gruesome and lugubrious. Therefore, in the line

Sacri orrori, ombre felici!

Hasse has the first three words descend into every great depths, while placing the last one in a high register.

Infinitely better still does music succeed in painting the emotions by infusing the representations of their corresponding nervous excitations, and especially their succession, by a judicious choice of tone, key, harmony, melody, measure and movement, i.e. with all the above-mentioned analogies to the emotions; by granting harmony more or less splendor or gracefulness, lightness or complexity; by letting melody progress by smaller or larger intervals; by making movement faster or slower, more uniform or less so, etc.

2) It now becomes clear why music is most successful in painting feelings: Here it combines all of its forces, applies all of its means and concentrates the effects of all of them. This will rarely be the case when it paints only the objects that produce the feelings. Objects, mostly, can be hinted at only by a few, faint and remote similarities, whereas feelings are hinted at by a great many very definite ones.

3) It is clear now why even this kind of painting remains incomplete: As already mentioned, a feeling is individualized only by a definite conception of the object producing it. In this respect music is always way behind. It is able, by a joint effort of all its means, to define 'classes,' 'types' of feelings, even if these are already more closely circumscribed. The more specific, the individual, which can be perceived only from the particular nature of the object and the circumstances relating to it, remains undefined, precisely because music is unable to indicate this particular nature as well as these circumstances.

From these last two remarks, which I believe to be valid and convincing, the following two rules can be inferred:

First rule: The musician should paint feelings rather than objects of feelings. He should paint the state to which the soul and body are brought by observing a certain matter or event, rather than the matter or event itself, since each and every art should preferably be used for what it can do best and with the highest degree of perfection. In a thunderstorm episode such as found in various operas, it is therefore better to paint the emotions of the soul during the thunderstorm, rather than the thunderstorm itself which occasions these emotions. Even if this phenomenon appears to offer so much of the audible, the former proceedings will always be more successful than the latter ones. It is for this reason, if anything, that Hiller's thunderstorm episode in the "Jagd" is without doubt superior to Philidor's.

Yet there is still another and, as I believe, even more weighty reason for this rule. Since, strictly speaking, music is made for the emotions, since with music everything acts towards this purpose, the composer, even if intending to paint a mere object, cannot avoid expressing also some feelings which the soul takes up and desires to pursue. Now, due to the composer's striving to imitate a thing or an event, the soul, in a wholly disagreeable way, is almost always driven from emotion to emotion, totally confused in the entire sequence of its conceptions.

Second rule: The composer should not desire to paint a series of emotions which is dependent on another series of events or observations, for the consequences may become incomprehensible or even absurd if one does not simultaneously consider that other series on which the former depends. I shall explain myself in greater detail.

Suppose that the most beautiful of accompanied recitative, say, of a Hasse, or perhaps even better, a duodrama of Benda was performed by the orchestra only, without the singer's or actor's parts. What would you believe to hear in that piece, written as it is in the best of taste and with the soundest of judgments? Most certainly the imagination, run wild, of one delirious with fever. Any why? Clearly, because the sequence of ideas or events, which alone can make the sequence of emotions comprehensible, has been removed from the whole. And will not the same happen when a composer decides, as some have indeed done, to anticipate already in the overture of an opera the entire sequence of emotions which is supposed to be aroused in the audience in the course of the story? I myself at least have always regarded this overture, admired by some, with which Monsigny begins his "Deserteur," as well as that which opens his "Balle Arsene," as rather vulgar.

A symphony, a sonata, any piece of music that is not supported by words or by the mimic arts—the moment it lays claim to be more than a pleasing sound, a charming jumble of tones—must be informed by a single passion, though manifest in a variety of emotions. It must comprise a sequence of emotions such as would develop by themselves, one after another, in a soul fully immersed in this passion, not interfered with from the outside, and unhampered in the free flow of its ideas. If I were permitted to postulate a yet unknown theory concerning the various series of ideas and their laws, I would say that the series of ideas must be no other but the *lyrical*.

I am now arriving at what you primarily expect of me: a determination of the rules of vocal composition. At this point I must first of all distinguish between the vocal part and the accompaniment. Of the former first.

Whatever I have to say on this subject is based on the distinction between *painting* and *expression* which, although established long ago, has not, I am afraid, been made clear enough.

A mere cerebral idea not related to our world of desires, the mere presentation of a matter as such, without the accompanying notion of whether it was good or evil, whether it flattered, or ran counter to, any of our natural inclinations, is not an aesthetic idea suitable for the fine arts. It is not an idea likely to be written down by a true poet, and least of all chosen by him for music. In every truly poetic thought and, even more so, in every musical-poetic thought, two aspects must be distinguishable: the conception regarding the object itself and the conception regarding the relationship between this object and our wishes and wants, whether we hold it in esteem or in contempt, whether we are annoyed or alarmed by it, whether we are delighted or amused by it, afraid of it, or long for it, etc.

In short: in such thoughts one must be able to distinguish between the *objective* and the *subjective*.

To anticipate all confusion and misinterpretation, let me remind you that what was originally subjective may become objective. The idea of an emotion, be it somebody else's or our own, can become the cause for a new emotion—sometimes a different, even opposite emotion. Somebody else's joy may arouse my own anger. I may be saddened to discover in my own self a pleasurable feeling about something my reason would not approve of. In such cases joy and pleasurable feeling are the objective, anger and sadness, the subjective.

In vocal music now, to *paint* means to represent the *objective*, while representing the *subjective* is no longer called painting, but *expressing*.

Basically, to be sure, both fall under our concept, as defined above, of painting. Expression could be explained as the painting of the subjective, of the emotion. Yet I hesitate to say 'emotion,' precisely because that which is emotion, is not always the subjective, that is, the emotion prevailing in the soul that very moment. The subjective, I said before, can become the objective, and now I am saying that it is possible for

135

expression to become painting in a similar way. Namely, when emotion is the object of our emotion, and the musician expresses the object and not that emotion, then it is painting. Or if an object usually produces such and such an emotion, but in the present case has a different, possibly even completely opposite effect, and the composer took the former for the latter than he is not expressing, but painting.

The above, I hope, fully defines and explains the rule which has so often been repeated for the benefit of the composer of vocal music: He should express, not paint.

There is hardly any need to prove this rule, because:

Firstly: If the objective is not in itself subjective, if it is an external matter or event, then, in accordance with one of the above remarks, the vocal composer who prefers to paint rather than express, would labor towards those effects which he is least likely to achieve. And even if the objective was originally subjective, it would be extremely unreasonable to prefer to paint the emotion that is not presently the predominant one, rather than that which now should occupy the singer's entire soul.

Secondly: What else should singing be but the most lively, most sensuous, most passionate speech? And what is it that a passionate man primarily desires to achieve with speech? What is the more important to him? Certainly not to make known the nature of the object that agitates him, but to unburden himself of his passion, to make it known. Towards this end his whole being labors: the sound of his voice, his facial muscles, hand and feet.

Therefore: Only expression attains the aim of vocal music; painting destroys it.

What, however, if occasionally painting and expression coincide? In other words, if at times painting of the objective can stand for the expression of the subjective; nay, if at times the expression of the subjective cannot take place without the painting of the objective?

Since this is so frequently the case, I would rather formulate the above rule in a different way. Instead of saying that the composer of vocal music should not paint but express, one should rather say that the composer of vocal music should be wary of painting against expression. That he has painted is not in itself a mistake; he can and may paint. Painting becomes a mistake only if he paints the wrong subject or at the wrong place.

The insight in this case rests on the difference existing in our feelings which has possibly been too little noticed so far. At the spur of the moment I cannot define this difference any better than as follows: With one kind of feelings, the subjective merges with, loses itself in, the objective. Passion satisfies itself only by embracing the object as fully as possible, the entire soul by resembling the object as much as possible. With another kind of feelings, the subjective and the objective clearly face one another. Passion satisfies itself by transposing the soul into a state diametrically opposed to the nature of the object. As this difference subdivides emotions in a way different from the known classifications, I dare to propose a new term, to enable him to express myself with greater brevity. I shall call the former kind of emotions *homogeneous*, the latter *heterogeneous*.

Examples shall elucidate everything. Admiration of a great or sublime object is a homogeneous emotion. The observing subject adopts the nature and qualities of the observed object as much as possible. The voice becomes full, the chest widens, says Home, when one thinks of great objects. If one thinks of sublime objects, one lifts up one's head, raises one's voice and hands. The subject tries in every way to emulate the object.

With veneration and worship the situation is already different. Here the subject contrasts itself with the object, experiences its weakness, lowliness, smallness and imperfection: the head is bowed, voice and hands are lowered.

Likewise, and even more so, is it with fear. The greatness, the strength that is perceived in the object is directed against the subject: the greater, the stronger the former, the less worthy, the weaker the latter; the fuller, more exalted more magnificent the painting might be, the weaker, meeker and more subdued the expression.

From this emerges the following rule: With homogeneous emotions, painting is expression; with heterogeneous emotions, painting destroys expression.

Still, even where the composer is permitted to paint, he must not do so indiscriminately. I shall list the precautions attached to this rule without bringing proof, because I assume them to be self-evident from the above.

Firstly: An object to be painted may present several musically paintable predicates. The composer must take care to deal only with those that the soul is attuned to in the prevailing context of ideas. With regard to the concept 'sea', for instance, only aspects like danger, depth, the wide expanse may be relevant in a given context. It would be the most obvious mistake against expression, if in such a case one were to paint the gentle beat of the waves. If I remember correctly after so many

137

years, Hasse, in the above-mentioned aria of "Sta Elena," committed such a mistake. The extension he gave, following Italian usage, to the last word in the lines:

Questo è il suol, per cui passai
Tauti regni e tanto mar,

is expressive of a gentle surging, which must have been an unlikely subject of the thoughts of the singing Helena. The whole subject is altogether unsuitable for painting. It is unbelievable to what degree the Italian singsong has destroyed expression, even with our most gifted composers.

Secondly: If in the entire concept the only musically paintable predicate happens to be one that, in the prevailing context, does not draw particular attention, the composer must altogether refrain from descriptive painting, keeping to straightforward recitation.

Thirdly: From the entire series of ideas he must assess the relative importance of each of them separately, how long and with what degree of interest the soul will linger on it. And, where painting becomes expression, the composer must judge the extent to which he may enter into painting. If instead of adhering to the main concept, the concept towards which the whole soul directs itself, around which all other concepts are grouped and in which they all unite, the composer gets hold of one of the secondary concepts and bestows upon it preferential treatment, it may be regarded as a blunder not less serious than misplaced stress, nay, a far more embarrassing blunder, for painting does not slip by as quickly as does a tone.

Fourthly: The most serious offence against expression would be for the composer to paint not ideas, but the words, to suggest an idea which the words proceed to deny and invalidate, or to hold on to the mere image, the metaphor, instead of to the object. Mistakes of this kind need perhaps not be warned against, for whosoever is liable to commit them is anyhow beyond warning.

I intend to add a few remarks, to anticipate possible objections on your part.

Firstly, painting may serve at times as expression where heterogeneous feelings are involved: The object of veneration may be the humility, the gentleness, the submissiveness of a saint, while the object of fear may be the precariousness of the surrounding darkness, a far-away intermittent roar in this darkness. In such cases, the composer has little choice but to select an expression with which he could also paint the object.

Secondly, it may indeed happen that the painting of a secondary aspect, which by right should not be considered, might itself facilitate expression or at least not hinder it. In the aria:

Del Calvario già sorger le cime
Veggo altere di tempio sublime,
E i gran Duci del Re delle sfere
Pellegrini la tomba adorar!

of the oratorio mentioned earlier several times, Hasse has placed such a painting of a secondary aspect, which has not offended, at least, my susceptibilities. He painted the approach of the great army leaders with the aid of a magnificent, march-like phrase which appears quite appropriate to the joyously exalted mood meant to permeate the entire aria. Such apparent transgressions are committed by artists of genius in all arts, and the critic would be wrong to reproach them for it. It would, however, be equally wrong to let genius disregard all rules. True genius remains within the rules anyway, and appears to violate them only because the rules have as yet not been sufficiently defined and delimited. The relationship between theory and the works of art, in most of the arts, is such that one needs less theory to perfect the works than works to correct the theory.

Whatever I have to say about instrumental accompaniment boils down to the fact that here there is far more room for painting than in the vocal part. The best, most expressive composers have therefore, in the accompaniment of their arias, and in particular, of their recitatives not merely continued the expression of the emotion involved, but often also attempted to support and enhance this expression by a representation of the object underlying that emotion. In the well-known aria:

Wenn ich am Rande dieses Lebens
Abgründe sehe, etc.

Graun has introduced a splendid painting of the feared judge, which he has given over to the accompaniment. To have done so in the vocal line would obviously have been a mistake.

However, in the accompaniment, too, painting must represent only essential predicates of the object, which have a positive bearing on the emotions aroused, and must not be so heterogeneous in its expression as to be destructive, rather than supportive, of feeling. Such would be the case, for instance, if an earnest train of thoughts came to be interrupted by a comic painting. A certain modern composer, or rather an otherwise quite excellent composer that has only recently become well-known, has often sinned in this respect. The most disagreeable effect is produced if in an otherwise serious and even exalted piece of music the heart beat is given a pizzicato accompaniment, or the hissing of snakes is imitated by violins.

If in a letter addressed to you it would not appear too unseemly, I would extend the rules established to declamation and pantomime as well, for they are valid, indeed, for all the dynamic arts. In fact, these rules are self-evident, provided one has the slightest inkling of these arts and of the means through which they operate.

With the greatest respect, etc. etc.

LUDWIG JOSEF JOHANN WITTGENSTEIN

Ludwig Josef Johann Wittgenstein (1889–1951 b. Vienna d. Cambridge), one of the most important philosophers of our century, was born to a bourgeois family that occupied a central place in the cultural life of *fin de siècle* Vienna. Devoted to the cultivation of the arts and no less interested in "ideas," for the Wittgensteins, Culture meant, above all, musical culture. Brahms, Mahler and Bruno Walter were among their frequent guests and three of Ludwig's brothers were musicians in their own right (it was for Paul, a gifted pianist who lost his right hand, that Richard Strauss composed his *Paregon zur sinfonia domestica* and Maurice Ravel his *Concerto for the left hand*). Influenced by Schopenhauer's view on music, Ludwig's favorite pastime was reading scores and throughout his life he contemplated the nature of that "transcendental art." His professional training, however, was that of an engineer.

Though professionally more solid than his brothers and sisters, he could not altogether avoid being involved in the ideological upheavals which took place during his maturing years, for they sorely affected his own family. These were the days in which intellectuals and artists came to identify the extreme aestheticism of the last decades of the 19th century with a kind of narcissism—a "pseudo-solution" for contemporary social and spiritual problems. Loos, Kokoshka, Hofmannsthal, Schoenberg and many others, each in his own way, sensed the affectation and the abrasion of that which once was real and authentic. Inspired by Karl Kraus, the "reproaching prophet" of the city for over thirty years, they tried to imbue art with a regained sincerity, always striving towards a meaningful message for society and humanity at large.

A Kantian legacy, transmitted primarily through Schopenhauer and Kierkegaard, nurtured this intellectual milieu. Attacking the issue at its very foundation, young Wittgenstein embarked upon a new attempt, trying to distinguish between the "sayable" and that which we "must be silent" about. While the skepticism of Mautner (a Viennese journalist whose "critique of language" preceded Wittgenstein's treatment of the subject) pointed to language as a fabricated system of metaphors which has little to do with reality, Wittgenstein adopted the more ancient view according to which language represents the "mirror" in which the world is reflected. In the *Tractatus Logico-Philosophicus* he endeavoured to show how the "artificiality" of language is indeed part and parcel of its being a kind of theoretical model constructed as an instrument to interpret and handle reality. For general criteria of the "correctness" of models, Wittgenstein relied on Heinrich Hertz. With regard to coherence pertaining to language, he followed Frege and Russell, developing a logical calculus which was immediately adopted by philosophers and logicians. Indeed, logic, according to Wittgenstein, is the property which language and the world have in common, guaranteeing the isomorphism between them. In the last resort, however, it is empirical observation alone which can distinguish between "correct" and "truthful" sentences. Though necessary for science, neither one constitute what really matters in life.

Distinguishing between the observation of facts and the expression of meaning and values in language is, in fact, the professed point of the *Tractatus*. Since meaning and values are the main concern of human activity, language, according to Wittgenstein, comprises two distinguished levels which must not be confused. While science utilizes logic, poetry, argues Wittgenstein, is the language of paradoxes. The two "cognitive faculties" of Baumgarten are thereby revived, with the difference that that which was "lower," namely, the realm of the aesthetic, is now being treated as transcendental. Indeed, one cannot fail to recognize an "idealistic spell" in Wittgenstein's outlook. "Romantic" is likewise his conclusion: philosophy having reached its end, one should begin to participate in *real* life.

While his *Tractatus* gained more and more admirers in the Viennese Circle, Wittgenstein himself, became increasingly doubtful about the foundation of his entire project. Cognizant of the analytic methods developed by Anglo-Saxon philosophers, it is primarily at Cambridge that most of his mature work was done. Still wishing to "liberate" Man's mind, he now retreated to a more "modest" task, to the "untying of the knots of our thoughts." Aware of the metaphysical aspects of his own system, Wittgenstein felt the need to explore precisely that which

142

relates words to the world. Propositions, Wittgenstein observed, can teach us little about epistemology whereas language in its full scope, complicated and extensive as it is, seems more suggestive. A variety of "language games" seems to lurk under the naive and homogenous surface of language; games such as "dreaming," "commanding," "questioning" etc. that reveal different "forms of life" which they themselves cultivate and structure. Semantics is useless unless it takes into account the different meanings of words as determined by lived contexts. Perception, Wittgenstein stresses, involves, at all times, the formation of judgment, yet understanding is connected to "uses" shared by members of a culture. It is in this context that the whole issue of "understanding music" is raised, integrated into other aphoristic remarks characteristic of Wittgenstein's later works.

For Wittgenstein, understanding music is indeed a particular case of "understanding," or, perhaps, an enlargement of the concept. In most respects, music resembles language. Unlike Hanslick (whose influence on the Viennese was still deeply felt in his youth), Wittgenstein maintained that musical ideas also convey extra-musical meanings which are, at one and the same time, dependent upon contexts and transferable through citations. (Growing up in musical Vienna, Wittgenstein was fully aware of the "extension" or "abrasion" which some of those meanings underwent during the nineteenth century.) In contrast to linguistic understanding, however, "understanding music" does not entail "criteria" for proof, since music is neither related to "uses" in a strict linguistic sense, nor is it liable to be paraphrased and translated. While "form" is undoubtedly most essential to music, feelings, too, in their own way, play an important role. Moreover, understanding music seems to entail the kind of mental process akin, on the whole, to "experience." Inaccessible as it is, this experience is not unlike other psychological states the essence of which is sealed to us forever. Explicating that at which Webb and others only hinted, Wittgenstein explains that shared behavioral signs do not only help recognize an occurrence, say pain, in someone other than oneself, but enable its very identification within one's own consciousness.

"Private language" is a contradiction in terms and music, though a system of "soliloquization" rather than of dialogue, creates the kind of experience unthinkable without a "community of discourse." The experience of music, however, is different from the experience of "pain," since the former, unlike the latter, is not inferred from its own signs but from the "behavioral" signs of the music which produces it. In that

143

sense, maintains Wittgenstein, music resembles other "language games" the rules of which, though neither necessary nor sufficient for playing them or for being identified with them, are "public" and helpful in constituting some measures of "correctness." The language games related to music, it would seem, comprise those outward signs of the experience which, in themselves, are related to internal dynamic structures. Here Wittgenstein distinguishes primarily between "analogies" and music as the "thing in itself." With regard to the former, Wittgenstein calls attention to the role of gesture, rhetoric and other "rhythmical patterns," with full awareness of their tautological implications. According to Wittgenstein, the identification of the isomorphism or correlation is part and parcel of the acquisition of the original structure. What you hear, in other words, is directly related to what you know and what you know is dependent on what you have already learned to hear. Wittgenstein, in this respect, constitutes a perfect link between Schopenhauer and Goodman.

As already noted, the Schopenhauerian "thing in itself," as related to the "Will" was, for Wittgenstein, an important starting point. Though "mythical" contentions are no longer an overt part of his later writings, with regard to music—which for Schopenhauer was on a par with the "Will"—they still burst forth. With music as a "self-pointing system" in context of other language games, however, Wittgenstein is half-way to Goodman's discussion of "notational system" as a particular kind of "world making." In that sense, art and science, for Wittgenstein, has the same status since conventions play in both a most significant role. Still, Wittgenstein emphasizes that conventions, though artificial, are not arbitrary since they entail particular "stories" about human society. Altogether, culture is for the Viennese philosopher a kind of music which crystallizes the "wishes and wants" of its members into untranslatable wholes. Nothing there is natural, neither sufficiently nor necessarily conditioned. As in music, its productions fit into our "world of thoughts and feelings" contributing towards their enrichment.

from Culture and Value¹

Some people think music a primitive art because it has only a few notes and rhythms. But it is only simple on the surface; its substance on the other hand, which makes it possible to interpret this manifest content, has all the infinite complexity that's suggested in the external form of other arts and that music conceals. There is a sense in which it is the most sophisticated art of all.

Pieces of music composed at the piano, on the keyboard, those thought out with pen on paper and those just composed with imagined sounds in the head must all be quite different in character and make quite different kinds of impression.

I am sure Bruckner composed just by imagining the sound of the orchestra in his head, Brahms with pen on paper. Of course this is an oversimplification. But it does highlight *one* feature.

Structure and feeling in music. Feelings accompany our apprehension of a piece of music in the way they accompany the events of our life.

There is definitely a certain sort of kinship between Brahms and Mendelssohn; but I do not mean that shown by the individual passages in Brahm's works which are reminiscent of passages by Mendelssohn, —the kinship I am speaking of could be better expressed by saying that Brahms does with complete rigour what Mendelssohn did only half-rigorously. Or: often Brahms is Mendelssohn without the flaws.

¹Text: Ludwig Wittgenstein, *Culture and Value*, tr. Peter Winch (Oxford: Basil and Blackwell), pp. 8e; 9e; 10e; 12e; 21e; 25e; 28e; 36e; 38e; 39e; 40e; 41e; 47e; 51e; 52e; 55e; 57e; 62e; 69e; 70e; 71e; 73e; 74e; 80e; 81e; 82e; 84e. The following note is Winch's note.
*The time signature is not in the MS. The editor is very grateful to Mr. Fabian Dahlström for professional help in interpreting the written music, which was very hard to read.

That must be the end of a theme which I cannot place. It came into my head today as I was thinking about my philosophical work and saying to myself: "I destroy, I destroy, I destroy—".

The queer resemblance between a philosophical investigation (perhaps especially in mathematics) and an aesthetic one. (E.g. what is bad about this garment, how it should be, etc.)

In the days of silent films all kinds of classical works were played as accompaniments, but not Brahms or Wagner.

Not Brahms, because he is too abstract. I can imagine an exciting scene in a film accompanied by Beethoven's or Schubert's music and might gain some sort of understanding of the music from the film. But this would not help me to understand Brahms's music. Bruckner on the other hand would go with a film.

When I imagine a piece of music, as I do often every day, I always, so I believe, grind my upper and lower teeth together rhythmically. I have noticed this before though I usually do it quite unconsciously. What's more, it's as though the notes I am imagining are produced by this movement. I believe this may be a very common way of imagining music internally. Of course I can imagine music without moving my teeth too, but in that case the notes are much ghostlier, more blurred and less pronounced.

If art serves 'to arouse feelings' is, perhaps, perceiving it with the senses to be included amongst these feelings?

People nowadays think that scientists exist to instruct them, poets, musicians, etc. to give them pleasure. The idea *that these have something to teach them*—that does not occur to them.

'The aim of music: to communicate feelings.'
Connected with this: We may say correctly "his face has the same expression now as previously"—even though measurement yielded different results on the two occasions.
How do we use the words "the same facial expression"?—How do we know that someone is using these words correctly? But do I know that *I* am using them correctly?

146

My style is like bad musical composition.

Counterpoint might present an extraordinarily difficult problem for a composer; the problem namely: what attitude should *I*, given *my* propensities, adopt to counterpoint? He may have hit upon a conventionally acceptable attitude and yet still feel that it is not properly *his*. That it is not clear what counterpoint *ought* to mean to him. (I was thinking of Schubert in this connection; of his wanting to take lessons in counterpoint right at the end of his life. I think his aim may have been not so much just learning more counterpoint as determining where he stood in relation to it.)

Wagner's *motifs* might be called musical prose sentences. And just as there is such a thing as 'rhyming prose', so too these *motifs* can be joined together in melodic form, without their constituting *one* melody. Wagnerian drama too is not drama so much as an assemblage of situations strung together as though on a thread which, for its part, is merely *cleverly* spun and not inspired as the motifs and situations are.

Schubert's tunes can be said to be full of *climaxes*, and this can't be said of Mozart's; Schubert is baroque. You can point to particular places in a tune by Schubert and say: look, that is the point of this tune, this is where the thought comes to a head.

We can apply to the tunes by the various composers the principle: each species of tree is a 'tree' in a different *sense* of the word. That is, don't be misled by the fact that we say all these are tunes. They are stages along a path which leads from something you would not call a tune to something else that you would equally not call a tune. If you just look at the sequences of notes and changes of key all these entities seem to be on the same level. But if you look at the context in which they exist (and hence at their meaning), you will be inclined to say: In this case melody is something quite different from what it is in that one (amongst other things, here it has a different origin and plays a different role).

Once again: what is it to follow a musical phrase with understanding, or to play it with understanding? Don't look inside yourself. Consider rather what makes you say of *someone else* that this is what he is doing. And *what* prompts you to say that *he* is having a particular experience? For that matter, do we actually ever say this? Wouldn't I be more likely to say of someone else that he's having a whole host of experiences?

Perhaps I would say, "He is experiencing the theme intensely"; but consider how this is manifested.

One might again get the idea that experiencing a theme intensely 'consists' in sensations of the movements, etc., with which we accompany it. And that (again) looks a soothing explanation. But do you have any reason to think it true? Such as, for instance, a recollection of this experience? Isn't this theory once again just a picture? In fact, it's not like this: The theory is no more than an attempt to link up the expressive movements with a 'sensation'.

If you ask me: How did I experience the theme?—perhaps I shall answer "As a question" or something of the sort, or I shall whistle it with expression, etc.

"He is experiencing the theme intensely. Something is happening within him as he hears it." *What* exactly?

Doesn't the theme point to anything beyond itself? Oh yes! But this means: the impression it makes on me is connected with things in its environment—for example, with the existence of the German language and its intonation, but that means with the whole range of our language games.

If I say for instance: here it's as though a conclusion were being drawn, here as though someone were expressing agreement, or as though *this* were a reply to what came before,—my understanding of it presupposes my familiarity with conclusions, expressions of agreement, replies.

A theme, no less than a face, wears an expression.

"The repeat is *necessary*." In what respect is it necessary? Well, sing it, and you will see that only the repeat gives it its tremendous power.— Don't we have an impression that a model for this theme already exists in reality and the theme only approaches it, corresponds to it, if this section is repeated? Or am I to utter the inanity: "It just sounds more beautiful with the repeat"? (There you can see by the way what an idiotic role the word "beautiful" plays in aesthetics.) Yet there just *is* no paradigm apart from the theme itself. And yet again there *is* a paradigm apart from the theme: namely, the rhythm of our language, of our thinking and feeling. And the theme, moreover, is a *new* part of our language; it becomes incorporated into it; we learn a new *gesture*.

The theme interacts with language.

148

Sowing ideas is one thing, reaping ideas another.

The last two bars of the "Death and the Maiden" theme, the ⌣; it's possible to understand this at first as an ordinary, conventional figure before coming to understand its deeper expression. I.e. before coming to understand that what is ordinary is here filled with significance.

Irony in music. E.g. in Wagner's "Mastersingers". Incomparably deeper in the Fugato in the first movement of the Ninth. There is something here analogous to the expression of bitter irony in speech.

I could equally well have said: the distorted in music. In the sense in which we speak of features distorted by grief. When Grillparzer says Mozart countenanced only what is "beautiful" in music, I think he means that he did not countenance what is distorted, frightful, that there is nothing corresponding to *this* in his music. I am not saying that is completely true; but even supposing it to be so, it is still a prejudice on Grillparzer's part to think that by rights it ought not to be otherwise. The fact that music since Mozart (and of course especially through Beethoven) has extended the range of its language is to be neither commended nor deplored; rather: *this is how it has changed*. There is something ungrateful about Grillparzer's attitude. Did he want *another* Mozart? Could he imagine what such a being might have composed? Could he have imagined Mozart if he had not known him?

The concept of "the beautiful" has done a lot of mischief in this connection too.

Sometimes a sentence can be understood only if it is read at the *right tempo*. My sentences are all supposed to be read *slowly*.

The 'necessity' with which the second idea succeeds the first. (The overture to "Figaro".) Nothing could be more idiotic than to say that it is *'agreeable'* to hear the one after the other.—All the same, the paradigm according to which everything is *right* is obscure. 'It is the natural development.' We gesture with our hands and are inclined to say: "Of course!"—Or we might compare the transition to a transition like the introduction of a new character in a story for instance, or a poem. *This* is how the piece fits into the world of our thoughts and feelings.

Remember how it was said of Labor's playing: "He is *speaking*." How curious! What was it about this playing that was so strongly reminiscent of speech? And how remarkable that we do not find the similarity with speech incidental, but something important, big!—Music, *some* music at least, makes us want to call it a language; but some music of course doesn't. (Not that this need involve any judgement of value!)

Understanding and explaining a musical phase.—Sometimes the simplest explanation is a gesture; on another occasion it might be a dance step, or words describing a dance.—But isn't understanding the phrase experiencing something whilst we hear it? In that case what part does the explanation play? Are we supposed to think of it as we hear the music? Are we supposed to imagine the dance, or whatever it may be, while we listen? And suppose we do do this—why should *that* be called listening to the music with understanding? If seeing the dance is what is important, it would be better to perform *that* rather than the music. But that is all *mis*understanding.

I give someone an explanation and tell him "It's as though . . . "; then he says "Yes, now I understand it" or "Yes, now I see how it's to be played." It's most important that he didn't have to *accept* the explanation; it's not as though I had, as it were, given him conclusive reasons for thinking that this passage should be compared with that and the other one. I don't, e.g., explain to him that according to things the composer has said this passage is supposed to represent such and such.

If I now ask "So what do I actually experience when I hear this theme and understand what I hear?"—nothing occurs to me by way of reply except trivialities. Images, sensations of movement, recollections and such like.

Perhaps I say, "I respond to it"—but what does that mean? It might mean something like: I gesture in time with the music. And if we point out that for the most part this only happens to a very rudimentary extent, we shall probably get the reply that such rudimentary movements are filled out by images. But suppose we assume all the same that someone accompanies the music with movements in full measure,—to what extent does *that* amount to understanding it? Do I want to say that the movements he makes constitute his understanding, or his kinaesthetic sensations? (How much do I know about these?)—What is true is that in some circumstances I will take the movements he makes as a sign that he understands.

150

But (if I reject images, kinaesthetic sensations, etc. as an explanation), should I say that understanding is simply a specific experience that cannot be analysed any further? Well, that would be tolerable as long as it were not supposed to mean: it is a specific *experiential content*. For in point of fact *these* words make us think of distinctions like those between seeing, hearing and smelling.

So how do we explain to someone what "understanding music" means? By specifying the images, kinaesthetic sensations, etc., experienced by someone who understands? *More likely*, by drawing attention to his expressive movements.—And we really ought to ask what function explanation has here. And what it means to speak of: understanding what it means to understand music. For some would say: to understand that means: to understand music itself. And in that case we should have to ask "Well, can someone be taught to understand music?", for that is the only sort of teaching that could be called explaining music.

There is a certain *expression* proper to the appreciation of music, in listening, playing, and at other times too. Sometimes gestures form part of this expression, but sometimes it will just be a matter of how a man plays, or hums, the piece, now and again of the comparisons he draws and the images with which he as it were illustrates the music. Someone who understands music will listen differently (e.g. with a different expression on his face), he will talk differently, from someone who does not. But he will show that he understands a particular theme not just in manifestations that accompany his hearing or playing that theme but in his understanding for music in general.

Appreciating music is a manifestation of the life of mankind. How should we describe it to someone? Well, I suppose we should first have to describe *music*. Then we could describe how human beings react to it. But is that all we need do, or must we also teach him to understand it for himself? Well, getting him to understand and giving him an explanation that does not achieve this will be "teaching him what understanding is" in *different* senses of that phrase. And again, teaching him to understand poetry or painting may contribute to teaching him what is involved in understanding music.

For me this musical phrase is a gesture. It insinuates itself into my life. I adopt it as my own.

Life's infinite variations are essential to our life. And so too even to the habitual character of life. What we regard as expression *consists* in incalculability. If I knew exactly how he would grimace, move, there would be no facial expression, no gesture.—Is that true though?—I can after all listen again and again to a piece of music that I know (completely) by heart; and it might even be played on a musical box. Its gestures would still be gestures for me, even though I knew all the time what was going to come next. Indeed, I might even keep being surprised. (In a certain sense.)

Bach said that all his achievements were simply the fruit of industry. But industry like that requires humility and an enormous capacity for suffering, hence strength. And someone who, with all this, can also express himself perfectly, simply speaks to us in the language of a great man.

I think it an important and remarkable fact that a musical theme alters its *character* if it is played at (very) different tempi. A transition from quantity to quality.

The temporality of the clock and temporality in music. They are not by any means equivalent concepts.
　　Playing in *strict* tempo does not mean playing according to the metronome. Though it may be that a certain *sort* of music should be played by metronome. (Is the opening theme of the second movement of the 8th Symphony of this sort?)

In Beethoven's music what may be called the expression of irony makes an appearance for the first time. E. g. in the first movement of the Ninth. With him, moreover, it's a terrible irony, the irony of fate perhaps.— Irony reappears with Wagner, but this time transposed into the civic mode.
　　You could no doubt say that both Wagner and Brahms, each in his different way, imitated Beethoven; but what in him was cosmic becomes earthly with them.
　　The same expressions occur in his music, but obeing different laws. In Mozart's or Haydn's music again, fate plays no role of any sort. That is not the *concern* of this music.
　　That ass Tovey says somewhere that this, or something similar, is due to the fact that Mozart had no access to literature of a certain sort. As if it had been proved that the masters' music had been made what it

was solely by books. Certainly, music and books are connected. But if Mozart found no great *tragedy* in what he read, does that mean he did not encounter it in his *life*? And do composers never see anything except through the spectacles of poets?

One and the same theme is different in character in the minor and the major, but it is quite wrong to speak generally about a character belonging to the minor key. (In Schubert the major often sounds sadder than the minor.) And similarly I think it idle and no help in understanding painting to speak of the characters of individual colours. When one speaks like that one actually only has special applications in mind. The fact that green has such and such an effect as the colour of a table cloth, red another, licenses no conclusion about their effect in a picture.

from Philosophical Investigations[1]

Part I

522. If we compare a proposition to a picture, we must think whether we are comparing it to a portrait (a historical representation) or to a genre-picture. And both comparisons have point.

When I look at a genre-picture, it 'tells' me something, even though I don't believe (imagine) for a moment that the people I see in it really exist, or that there have really been people in that situation. But suppose I ask: "*What* does it tell me, then?"

523. I should like to say "What the picture tells me is itself." That is, its telling me something consists in its own structure, in *its* own lines and colours. (What would it mean to say "What this musical theme tells me is itself"?)

524. Don't take it as a matter of course, but as a remarkable fact, that pictures and fictitious narratives give us pleasure, occupy our minds.

("Don't take it as a matter of course" means: find it surprising, as you do some things which disturb you. Then the puzzling aspect of the latter will disappear, by your accepting this fact as you do the other.)

((The transition from patent nonsense to something which is disguised nonsense.))

525. "After he had said this, he left her as he did the day before."— Do I understand this sentence? Do I understand it just as I should if I heard it in the course of a narrative? If it were set down in isolation I should say, I don't know what it's all about. But all the same I should know how this sentence might perhaps be used; I could myself invent a context for it.

(A multitude of familiar paths lead off from these words in every direction.)

526. What does it mean to understand a picture, a drawing? Here too there is understanding and failure to understand. And here too these

[1]Text: Ludwig Wittgenstein, *Philosophical Investigations*, tr. G.E.M. Anscombe, (Oxford: Basil and Blackwell), 1958, pp. 142e–144e; 181e–183e.

expressions may mean various kinds of thing. A picture is perhaps a still-life; but I don't understand one part of it: I cannot see solid objects there, but only patches of colour on the canvas.—Or I see everything as solid but there are objects that I am not acquainted with (they look like implements, but I don't know their use).—Perhaps, however, I am acquainted with the objects, but in another sense do not understand the way they are arranged.

527. Understanding a sentence is much more akin to understanding a theme in music than one may think. What I mean is that understanding a sentence lies nearer than one thinks to what is ordinarily called understanding a musical theme. Why is just *this* the pattern of variation in loudness and tempo? One would like to say "Because I know what it's all about." But what is it all about? I should not be able to say. In order to 'explain' I could only compare it with something else which has the same rhythm (I mean the same pattern). (One says "Don't you see, this is as if a conclusion were being drawn" or "This is as it were a parenthesis", etc. How does one justify such comparisons?—There are very different kinds of justification here.)

528. It would be possible to imagine people who had something not quite unlike a language: a play of sounds, without vocabulary or grammar. ('Speaking with tongues.')

529. "But what would the meaning of the sounds be in such a case?"—What is it in music? Though I don't at all wish to say that this language of a play of sounds would have to be compared to music.

530. There might also be a language in whose use the 'soul' of the words played no part. In which, for example, we had no objection to replacing one word by another arbitrary one of our own invention.

531. We speak of understanding a sentence in the sense in which it can be replaced by another which says the same; but also in the sense in which it cannot be replaced by any other. (Any more than one musical theme can be replaced by another.)

In the one case the thought in the sentence is something common to different sentences; in the other, something that is expressed only by these words in these positions. (Understanding a poem.)

532. Then has "understanding" two different meanings here?—I would rather say that these kinds of use of "understanding" make up its meaning, make up my *concept* of understanding.

For I *want* to apply the word "understanding" to all this.

533. But in the second case how can one explain the expression, transmit one's comprehension? Ask yourself: How does one *lead* anyone to comprehension of a poem or of a theme? The answer to this tells us how meaning is explained here.

534. *Hearing* a word in a particular sense. How queer that there should be such a thing!

Phrased *like this*, emphasized like this, heard in this way, this sentence is the first of a series in which a transition is made to *these* sentences, pictures, actions.

(A multitude of familiar paths lead off from these words in every direction.)

535. What happens when we learn to *feel* the ending of a church mode as an ending?

536. I say: "I can think of this face (which gives an impression of timidity) as courageous too." We do not mean by this that I can imagine someone with this face perhaps saving someone's life (that, of course, is imaginable in connexion with any face). I am speaking rather of an aspect of the face itself. Nor do I mean that I can imagine that this man's face might change so that, in the ordinary sense, it looked courageous; though I may very well mean that there is a quite definite way in which it can change into a courageous face. The reinterpretation of a facial expression can be compared to the reinterpretation of a chord in music, when we hear it as a modulation first into this, then into that key.

Part II

vi

Suppose someone said: every familiar word, in a book for example, actually carries an atmosphere with it in our minds, a 'corona' of lightly indicated uses.—Just as if each figure in a painting were surrounded by delicate shadowy drawings of scenes, as it were in another dimension, and in them we saw the figures in different contexts.—Only let us take this assumption seriously!—Then we see that it is not adequate to explain *intention*.

For if it is like; this, if the possible uses of a word do float before us in half-shades as we say or hear it—this simply goes for *us*. But we communicate with other people without knowing if they have this experience too.

How should we counter someone who told us that with *him* understanding was an inner process?—How should we counter him if he said that with him knowing how to play chess was an inner process?—We should say that when we want to know if he can play chess we aren't interested in anything that goes on inside him.—And if he replies that this is in fact just what we are interested in, that is, we are interested in whether he can play chess—then we shall have to draw his attention to the criteria which would demonstrate his capacity, and on the other hand to the criteria for the 'inner states'.

Even if someone had a particular capacity only when, and only as long as, he had a particular feeling, the feeling would not be the capacity.

The meaning of a word is not the experience one has in hearing or saying it, and the sense of a sentence is not a complex of such experiences.—(How do the meanings of the individual words make up the sense of the sentence "I still haven't seen him yet"?) The sentence is composed of words, and that is enough.

Though—one would like to say—every word has a different character in different contexts, at the same time there is *one* character it always has: a single physiognomy. It looks at us.—But a face in a *painting* looks at us too.

Are you sure that there is a single if-feeling, and not perhaps several? Have you tried saying the word in a great variety of contexts? For example, when it bears the principal stress of the sentence, and when the word next to it does.

Suppose we found a man who, speaking of how words felt to him, told us that "if" and "but" felt the *same*.—Should we have the right to disbelieve him? We might think it strange. "He doesn't play our game at all", one would like to say. Or even: "This is a different type of man."

If he *used* the words "if" and "but" as we do, shouldn't we think he understood them as we do?

One misjudges the psychological interest of the if-feeling if one regards it as the obvious correlate of a meaning; it needs rather to be seen in a different context, in that of the special circumstances in which it occurs.

Does a person never have the if-feeling when he is not uttering the word "if"? Surely it is at least remarkable if this cause alone produces this feeling. And this applies generally to the 'atmosphere' of a word;—why does one regard it so much as a matter of course that only *this* word has this atmosphere?

The if-feeling is not a feeling which accompanies the word "if".

The if-feeling would have to be compared with the special 'feeling' which a musical phrase gives us. (One sometimes describes such a feeling by saying "Here it is as if a conclusion were being drawn", or "I should like to say '*hence* . . . ' ", or "Here I should always like to make a gesture—" and then one makes it.)

But can this feeling be separated from the phrase? And yet it is not the phrase itself, for that can be heard without the feeling.

Is it in this respect like the 'expression' with which the phrase is played?

We say this passage gives us a quite special feeling. We sing it to ourselves, and make a certain movement, and also perhaps have some special sensation. But in a different context we should not recognize these accompaniments—the movement, the sensation—at all. They are quite empty except just when we are singing this passage.

"I sing it with a quite particular expression." This expression is not something that can be separated from the passage. It is a different concept. (A different game.)

The experience is this passage played like *this* (that is, as I am doing it, for instance; a description could only *hint* at it).

Thus the atmosphere that is inseparable from its object—is not an atmosphere.

Closely associated things, things which we *have* associated, seem to fit one another. But what is this seeming to fit? How is their seeming to fit manifested? Perhaps like this: we cannot imagine the man who had this name, this face, this handwriting, not to have produced *these* works, but perhaps quite different ones instead (those of another great man).

We cannot imagine it? Do we try?—

Here is a possibility: I hear that someone is painting a picture "Beethoven writing the ninth symphony". I could easily imagine the kind of thing such a picture would shew us. But suppose someone wanted to represent what Goethe would have looked like writing the ninth symphony? Here I could imagine nothing that would not be embarrassing and ridiculous.

from Zettel[1]

155. A poet's words can pierce us. And that is of course *causally* connected with the use that they have in our life. And it is also connected with the way in which, conformably to this use, we let our thoughts roam up and down in the familiar surroundings of the words.

156. Is there *a* difference of meaning that can be explained and another that does not come out in an explanation?

157. Soulful expression in music—this cannot be recognized by rules. Why can't we imagine that it might be, by other beings?

158. If a theme, a phrase, suddenly means something to you, you don't have to be able to explain it. Just *this* gesture has been made accessible to you.

159. But you do speak of *understanding* music. You understand it, surely, *while* you hear it! Ought we to say this is an experience which accompanies the hearing?

160. The way music speaks. Do not forget that a poem, even though it is composed in the language of information, is not used in the language-game of giving information.

161. Mightn't we imagine a man who, never having had any acquaintance with music, comes to us and hears someone playing a reflective piece of Chopin and is convinced that this is a language and people want to keep the meaning secret from him?

There is a strongly musical element in verbal language. (A sigh, the intonation of voice in a question, in an announcement, in longing; all the innumerable *gestures* made with the voice.)

162. But if I hear a tune with understanding, doesn't something special go on in me—which does not go on if I hear it without understanding? And *what?*—No answer comes; or anything that occurs to me is insipid. I may indeed say: "Now I've understood it," and perhaps talk about it, play it, compare it with others etc. *Signs* of understanding may accompany hearing.

---

[1]Text: Ludwig Wittgenstein, *Zettl*, tr. G.E.M. Anscombe, (Oxford: Basil and Blackwell), 1981, pp. 27e–30e.

163. It is wrong to call understanding a process that accompanies hearing. (Of course its manifestation, expressive playing, cannot be called an accompaniment of hearing either.)

164. For how can it be explained what 'expressive playing' is? Certainly not by anything that accompanies the playing.—What is needed for the explanation? One might say: a culture.—If someone is brought up in a particular culture—and then reacts to music in such-and-such a way, you can teach him the use of the phrase "expressive playing".

165. The understanding of music is neither sensation nor a sum of sensations. Nevertheless it is correct to call it an experience inasmuch as *this* concept of understanding has some kinship with other concepts of experience. You say "I experienced that passage quite differently". But still this expression tells you '*what happened*' only if you are at home in the special conceptual world that belongs to these situations. (Analogy: "I won the match".)

166. *This* floats before my mind as I read. So does something go on in reading . . . ?—This question doesn't get us anywhere.

167. But how can it float before me?—Not in the dimensions you are thinking of.

168. How do I know that someone is enchanted? How does one learn the linguistic expression of enchantment? What does it connect up with? With the expression of bodily sensations? Do we ask someone what he feels in his breast and facial muscles in order to find out whether he is feeling enjoyment?

169. But does that mean that there are not sensations which often return when one is enjoying music? Certainly not.

170. A poem makes an impression on us as we read it. "Do you feel the same way while you read it as when you read something indifferent?"—How have I learnt to answer this question? Perhaps I shall say "Of course not!"—which is as much as to say: *this* takes hold of me, and the other not.

"I experience something different"—And what kind of thing?—I can give no satisfactory answer. For the answer I give is not what is most important.—"But didn't you enjoy it *during* the reading?" Of course—

for the opposite answer would mean: I enjoyed it earlier or later, and I don't want to say that.

But now, surely you remember sensations and images as you read, and they are such as to connect up with the enjoyment, with the impression.—But they got their significance only from the surroundings: through the reading of this poem, from my familiarity with its language, with its metre and with innumerable associations.

You must ask how we learnt the expression "Isn't that glorious!" at all.—No one explained it to us by referring to sensations, images or thoughts that accompany hearing! Nor should we doubt whether he had enjoyed it if he had no account to give of such experiences; though we should, if he shewed that he did not understand certain tie-ups.

171. But isn't understanding shewn e.g. in the expression with which someone reads the poem, sings the tune? Certainly. But what is the experience during the reading? About that you would just have to say: you enjoy and understand it if you hear it well read, or feel it well read in your speech-organs.

172. Understanding a musical phrase may also be called understanding a *language*.

173. I think of a quite short phrase, consisting of only two bars. You say "What a lot that's got in it!" But it is only, so to speak, an optical illusion if you think that what is there goes on as we hear it. ("It all depends *who* says it.") (Only in the stream of thought and life do words have meaning.)

174. What contains the illusion is not *this*: "*Now* I've understood"— followed perhaps by a long explanation of what I have understood.

175. Doesn't the theme point to anything outside itself? Yes, it does! But that means:—it makes an impression on me which is connected with things in its surroundings—e.g. with our language and its intonations; and hence with the whole field of our language-games.

If I say for example: Here it's as if a conclusion were being drawn, here as if something were being confirmed, *this* is like an answer to what was said before,—then my understanding presupposes a familiarity with inferences, with confirmation, with answers.

176. The words "Gottlob! Noch etwas Weniges hat man geflüchtet—

vor den Fingern der Kroaten,"* and the tone and glance that go with them seem indeed to carry within themselves every last *nuance* of the meaning they have. But only because we know them a part of a particular scene. But it would be possible to construct an entirely different scene around these words so as to shew that the special spirit they have resides in the story in which they come.

177. If I hear someone say: "Away!" with a gesture of repulsion, do I have an 'experience' of meaning *here* as I do in the game where I pronounce that to myself meaning it now in one sense, now in another?—For he could also have said "Get away from me!" and then perhaps I'd have experienced the whole phrase in such-and-such a way—but the single word? Perhaps it was the supplementary words that made the impression on me.

178. The peculiar experience of meaning is characterized by the fact that we come out with an explanation and use the past tense: just as if we were explaining the meaning of a word for practical purposes.

*"Heaven be praised! A little slipped—out of the Croat clutches." Schiller, *Wallenstein, Die Piccolomini*, Act I, Scene 2.

SUSANNE K. LANGER*

Langer's *Feeling and Form* comprises an attempt to apply her theory of symbolization developed in *Philosophy in a New Key* to the various arts, endeavoring to clarify their modes of abstraction. Thus music, which previously was considered a symbol of unlogicized mental life, is now being investigated with regard to the ways in which it is organized. "Music makes time audible" declares Langer, the primary illusion of music is its semblance to "lived time." As qualitative duration, Langer argues (following Bergson), it stands in opposition to the sequential organization of clocktime which represents a one-dimensional quantitive contiuum. Combining Hanslick's argument with that of Bergson, Langer maintains that the semblance is made tangible by the movements of the forms which it embodies. As form which is being formed, as sounds which accumulate continuously by the attentive listener into significant wholes, music is apprehended, by definition, through 'tensions', 'progressions' 'resolutions' and the like. In her book Langer contends that the same process also takes place, although the other way round, in the composer. Musical systems and culturally accepted ways of arrangement (which may be considered as the 'language of music') are applied to unique and not yet specified experiences of time—the 'musical matrix'. It is the significant whole which must be the point of departure for the performer, thus enabling the listener to recreate imaginatively that 'virtual time'.*

*See introduction to Langer in Part Five: Sensory Cognition and Unconscious Referentials.

from Feeling and Form[1]

The Image of Time

From the plastic arts, which make space visible in the various modes in which we instinctively conceive and negotiate it, we turn to another great art genus, namely music. At once we are as in a different kingdom. The mirror of the world, the horizon of the human domain, and all tangible realities are gone. Objects become a blur, all sight irrelevant.

Yet the realm of experience, so radically changed, is entirely full. There are forms in it, great and small, forms in motion, sometimes converging to make an impression of complete accomplishment and rest out of their very motions; there is immense agitation, or vast solidity, and again everything is air; all this in a universe of pure *sound*, an audible world, a sonorous beauty taking over the whole of one's consciousness.

Ever since Pythagoras discovered the relation between the pitch of a sound and the vibration rate of the body producing that sound, the analysis of music has centered in physical, physiological and psychological studies of *tones*: their own physical structure and combinability, their somatic effects on men and animals, their reception in human consciousness. Acoustics became a valuable science that made possible not only better conditions of producing and hearing music, but, in the realm of music itself, the tempered scale, and the fixation of a standard pitch.

The objectivity of these gains inspired the hope that, however recalcitrant painting or poetry might be to scientific treatment, music at least could be comprehended and handled under relatively simple natural laws, which might then extend one's understanding, through analogy, to less abstract and less transparent arts. Again and again, therefore, attempts have been made to explain musical invention by the physical complexity of tones themselves, and find the laws and limits of composition on a basis of ratios or mathematical sequences to be exemplified. There is no use discussing the sheer nonsense or the academic oddities to which this hope has given rise, such as the

---

[1]Text: Susanne K. Langer, *Feeling and Form* (New York: Charles Scribner's Sons, 1953), pp. 104–19. The numbered notes are Langer's notes.

Schillinger System of composition,[2] or ther serious and elaborate effort of G.D. Birkhoff[3] to compute the exact degree of beauty in any art work (plastic, poetic and musical) by taking the "aesthetic measure" of its components and integrating these to obtain a quantitative value of judgment.

The only artistically valid and valuable theory I know, based primarily on the composite nature of tone, is Heinrich Schenker's work. But the significance of Schenker will be much more apparent after my own fundamental thesis has been stated, so I shall postpone all comments on his analysis, except one: namely, that its value lies largely in the fact that it always remains analysis, and never pretends to any synthetic function. A work of art is a unit originally, not by synthesis of independent factors. Analysis reveals elements in it, and can go on indefinitely, yielding more and more understanding; but it will never yield a recipe. Because Schenker respects this relation between the theorist and his object, he never treats a masterpiece without reverence, even though his investigations extend to the smallest detail. There is no danger of being "overintellectual" where intellect is playing its proper part.[4]

But the philosophical question: What is music? is not answered even by Schenker, for it cannot be answered by researches into the ingredients out of which musical works are made. Almost all serious inquiry so far has been concerned with the materials of music and the possibilities of their combination. The fact that the tonal proportions were among the first physical laws to be mathematically exprcssed, tested, and systematized, has given music the name of a science, even of a scientific model for cosmology, from ancient times to our own day.[5]

---

[2]See Joseph Schillinger, *The Schillinger System of Musical Composition*, and *The Mathematical Basis of the Arts*.

[3]G.D. Birkhoff, *Aesthetic Measure*. Another "academic oddity" (to speak politely) was my own youthful effort to apply symbolic logic to music; to which I confess, but will not refer by chapter and verse.

[4]Schenker speaks of "synthesis," but not in the sense of a veritable procedure. It is a mystical activity which he attributes to the Archetypal Line, the *Urlinie*, itself, not to the composer. "Diminution is to the Archetypal Line as a man's skeleton to his living flesh. . . . The Archetypal Line leads directly to the synthesis of the whole. It is the synthesis." (*Tonwille*, II, 5.)

[5]See, e.g., Matila C. Ghyka, *Essai sur le rythme*, p. 78: "All this Vitruvian theory of proportions and eurythmics is nothing but a transposition, into the spatial dimension, of the Pythagorean theory of chords, or rather: musical intervals, as we find it reflected in the Timaeus (number as the soul of the world)."

165

The material itself is interesting, and offers a definite, specialized field of inquiry. The order of pitches is continuous, and corresponds to an equally orderly series of vibration rates. Loudness, too, may be expressed in mathematical degrees of an unbroken scale, and reduced to a property of physical vibration. Even timbre—the most definitely qualitative characteristic of tones—is conditioned by the simplicity or complexity of the vibrations that produce the tone. Almost as soon as one proposes to think in strict terms about the phenomenon called "music," the physics of sound presents itself as the natural groundwork for any theory.

But sound, and even tone, as such is not music; music is something made our of sound, usually of definite intonation. Now there is just enough kinship between simple tone-relationships (8ve, 5th, 3rd) and agreeable sensation (consonance) to suggest a system of tonal "stimuli." So the science of acoustics acquired an alter ego, the psychology of music initiated by Carl Stumpf, which begins with the concept of separate auditory perceptions and seeks to build up the tonal musical experience as an emotional response to complex tonal stimuli, reinforced by sensations of contrast, surprise, familiarity, and above all, personal associations. There is, to date, a fairly large literature of psychological findings in this field. But far greater than the body of findings is the faith in the undertaking held mainly by persons who have not themselves gathered or interpreted such data. The program rather than its fulfillment has influenced both musical and unmusical people to think of the art of tone as a process of affective stimulation, and to suppose that musical experience will some day be describable in terms of "nervous vibrations" corresponding to the physical vibrations of sounding instruments.[6]

This ambitious hope rests, of course, on the widely held belief that the proper function of music is to cause a refined sort of sensuous pleasure that in turn evokes a well-timed, variegated succession of feelings.

---

[6] See, for instance, the chapter on music written by Paul Krummreich in L. W. Flaccus' *The Spirit and Substance of Art*, where the author, after asserting that music evokes instinctive reactions, says: "Instincts may be considered a phase of our unconscious life; and the unconscious we can discuss in terms of vibrations." But his discussion is *about* vibrations, never about something else *in terms* of vibrations.

One of the most serious of these hopeful ventures is *La musique et la vie intérieure. Essai d'une histoire psychologique de l'art musical*, by L. Bourguès and A. Denéréaz.

See, further, F. E. Howard: "Is Music an Art or a Science?" *Connecticut Magazine*, VIII, no. 2 (1903), 255–288. There are dozens of other examples.

There is no need of reviewing this "stimulus theory" again after rejecting its credentials for art in general. Suffice it to point out that if music is art, and not an epicure's pleasure, then the study of vibration patterns on sound tracks and encephalographs may tell us astounding things about audition, but not about music, which is the illusion begotten by sounds.

The traditional preoccupation with the ingredients of music has had a somewhat unhappy effect on theoretical study, connoisseurship and criticism, and through criticism on the ideas and attitudes of the general public. It has led people to listen for the wrong things, and suppose that to understand music one must know not simply much music, but much *about* music. Concert-goers try earnestly to recognize chords, and judge key changes, and hear the separate instruments in an ensemble— all technical insights that come of themselves with long familiarity, like the recognition of glazes on pottery or of structural devices in a building—instead of distinguishing *musical elements*, which may be made out of harmonic or melodic material, shifts of range or of tone color, rhythms or dynamic accents or simply changes of volume, and yet be in themselves as audible to a child as to a veteran musician. For the elements of music are not tones of such and such pitch, duration and loudness, nor chords and measured beats; they are, like all artistic elements, something virtual, created only for perception. Eduard Hanslick[7] denoted them rightly: "*tönend bewegte Formen*"—"sounding forms in motion."

Such motion is the essence of music; a motion of forms that are not visible; but are given to the ear instead of the eye. Yet what are these forms? They are not objects in the actual world, like the forms normally revealed by light, because sound, though it is propagated in space, and is variously swallowed or reflected back, i.e. echoed, by the surfaces it encounters, is not sufficiently modified by them to give an impression of their shapes, as light does.[8] Things in a room may affect tone in general,

<hr>

[7] *Vom Musikalisch-Schönen.*
[8] This functional difference between light and sound was observed by Joseph Goddard some 50 years ago. "From a single central source light proceeds continually, which light the surfaces of objects reflect in ways corresponding to their character. . . . Although musical sound is more or less reflected and absorbed as it moves among objects, the result is to modify its general volume and character— as when music is performed in an empty or full room—not to give us impressions of those objects." (*On Beauty and Expression in Music*, pp. 25–27.)

but they do not influence tonal forms specifically, nor obstruct their motions, because forms and motions alike are only seemingly there; they are elements in a purely auditory illusion.

For in all the progressive movements we hear—fast movement or slow, stop, attack, rising melody, widening or closing harmony, crowding chords and flowing figures—there is actually nothing that moves. A word may be in order here to forestall a popular fallacy, namely the supposition that musical motion is actual because strings or pipes and the air around them move. Such motion, however, is not what we perceive. Vibration is minute, very fast, and if it comes to rest sound simply disappears. The movement of tonal forms, on the contrary, is large and directed toward a point of relative rest, which is no less audible than the progression leading to it. In a simple passage like the following:

the three eighth notes progress *upward* to C. Yet actually there is no locomotion. The C is their point of rest; but while it is sustained there is faster vibration than in any other part of the phrase. Musical motion, in short, is something entirely different from physical displacement. It is a semblance, and nothing more.

The last note of the example just given introduces another element that has no prototype in physical dynamics: the element of *sustained rest*. When a progression reaches its point of rest within a piece, the music does not therefore stand still, but moves on. It moves over static harmonies and persistent tones such as pedal points, and silences. Its forward drive may even carry it rhythmically beyond the last sound, as in some of Beethoven's works, e. g. in the finale of opus 9, no. 1, where the last measure is silence:

The elements of music are moving forms of sound; but in their motion nothing is removed. The realm in which tonal entities move is a realm of pure *duration*. Like its elements, however, this duration is not an actual phenomenon. It is not a period—ten minutes or a half hour, some fraction of a day—but is something radically different from the time in which our public and practical life proceeds. It is completely incommensurable with the progress of common affairs. Musical duration is an image of what might be termed "lived" or "experienced" time—the passage of life that we feel as expectations become "now," and "now" turns into unalterable fact. Such passage is measurable only in terms of sensibilities, tensions, and emotions; and it has not merely a different measure, but an altogether different structure from practical or scientific time.

The semblance of this vital, experimental time is the primary illusion of music. All music creates an order of virtual time, in which its sonorous forms move in relation to each other—always and only to each other, for nothing else exists there. Virtual time is as separate from the sequence of actual happenings as virtual space from actual space. In the first place, it is entirely perceptible, through the agency of a single sense—hearing. There is no supplementing of one sort or experience by another. This alone makes it something quite different from our "common-sense" version of time, which is even more composite, heterogeneous, and fragmentary than our similar sense of space. Inward tensions and outward changes, heartbeats and clocks, daylight and routines and weariness furnish various incoherent temporal data, which we coordinate for practical purposes by letting the clock predominate. But music spreads out time for our direct and complete apprehension, by letting our hearing monopolize it—organize, fill, and shape it, all alone. It creates an image of time measured by the motion of forms that seem to give it substance, yet a substance that consists entirely of sound, so it is transitoriness itself. *Music makes time audible, and its form and continuity sensible.*

This theory of music is surprisingly corroborated by the observations of Basil de Selincourt in a short, little-known, but significant essay entitled "Music and Duration," which I have come across quite recently, and found remarkable on several counts, especially for the fact that the author distinguished, clearly and explicitly, between the actual and the virtual, which respect to both space and time. His words, written thirty years ago, may well be quoted here:

169

"Music is one of the forms of duration; it suspends ordinary time, and offers itself as an ideal substitute and equivalent. Nothing is more metaphorical or more forced in music than a suggestion that time is passing while we listen to it, that the development of the themes follows the action in time of some person or persons embodied in them, or that we ourselves change as we listen. . . . The space of which the painter makes use is a translated space, within which all objects are at rest, and though flies may walk about on his canvas, their steps do not measure the distance from one tone to another. . . . The Time of music is similarly an idea time, and if we are less directly aware of it, the reason is that our life and consciousness are more closely conditioned by time than by space. . . . The ideal and the real spatial relations declare their different natures in the simplicity of the contrast which we perceive between them. Music, on the other hand, demands the absorption of the whole of our time-consciousness; our own continuity must be lost in that of the sound to which we listen. . . . Our very life is measured by rhythm: by our breathing, by our heartbeats. These are all irrelevant, their meaning is in abeyance, so long as time is music.

" . . . If we are 'out of time' in listening to music, our state is best explained by the simple consideration that it is as difficult to be in two times at once as in two places. Music uses time as an element of expression; duration is its essence. The beginning and the end of a musical composition are only one if the music has possessed itself of the interval between them and wholly fitted it."[9]

The second radical divergence of virtual time from actual lies in its very structure, its logical pattern, which is not the one-dimensional order we assume for practical purposes (including all historical and scientific purposes). The virtual time created in music is an image of time in a different mode, i.e. appearing to have different terms and relations.

The clock—metaphysically a very problematic instrument—makes a special abstraction from temporal experience, namely *time as pure sequence*, symbolized by a class of ideal events indifferent in themselves, but ranged in an infinite "dense" series by the sole relation of

---

[9]*Music and Letters*, I, no. 4 (1920), 286–293.

Compare also the following passage from "The Composer and His Message," by Roger Sessions (already mentioned in Chapter 4, note 22): "It seems to me that the essential medium of music, the basis of its expressive powers and the element which gives it its unique quality among the arts, is *time*, made living for us through its expressive essence, *movement*."

succession. Conceived under this scheme, time is a one-dimensional continuum, and segments of it may be taken from any extensionless "moment" to any succeeding one, and every actual event may be wholly located within just one segment of the series so as to occupy it completely.

Further descriptions of this ingenious time-concept are not relevant here; suffice it to point out that it is the only adequate scheme we know of for synchronizing practical affairs, dating past events, and constructing some perspective of future ones. It can, moreover, be elaborated to meet the demands of much more precise thought than "common sense." Modern scientific time, which is one coordinate of a many-dimensional structure, is a systematic refinement of "clock-time." But for all its logical virtues, this one-dimensional, infinite succession of moments is an abstraction from direct experiences of time, and it is not the only possible one. Its great intellectual and practical advantages are bought at the price of many interesting phases of our time perception that have to be completely ignored. Consequently we have a great deal of temporal experience—that is, intuitive knowledge of time—that is not recognized as "true" because it is not formalized and presented in any symbolic mode; we have only one way—the way of the clock—to think discursively about time at all.

The underlying principle of clock-time is *change*, which is measured by contrasting two states of an instrument, whether that instrument be the sun in various positions, or the hand on a dial at successive locations, or a parade of monotonous, similar events like ticks or flashes, "counted," i.e. differentiated, by being correlated with a series of distinct numbers. In any case it is the "states," "instants," or whatever we choose to call the terms of the series, that are symbolized, and therefore explicitly conceived, and "change" from one to the other is construed in terms of their differences. "Change" is not itself something represented; it is implicitly given through the contrast of different "states," themselves unchanging.[10]

The time-concept which emerges from such mensuration is something far removed from time as we know it in direct experience, which is

[10]In 1926, Charles Koechlin published an article, "Le temps et la musique" (*La Revue Musicale*, VII, 3, p. 48), wherein I find this passage: "To certain minds, time appears as a resultant of our recollections of a great many states of mind, among which we 'assume' a continued duration that connects them as, given the limits of some measured distance, a path lies between those points. But actually those philosophers admit only the existence of the limits, and deny that of the path."

essentially *passage*, or the sense of transience. Passage is just what we need not take account of in formulating a scientifically useful, i.e. measurable, order of time; and because we can ignore this psychologically prime aspect, clock-time is homogeneous and simple and may be treated as one-dimensional. But the experience of time is anything but simple. It involves more properties than "length," or interval between selected moments; for its passages have also what I can only call, metaphorically, *volume*. Subjectively, a unit of time may be great or small as well as long or short; the slang phrase "a big time" is psychologically more accurate than a "busy," "pleasant," or "exciting" time. It is this voluminousness of the direct experience of passage that makes it, as Bergson observed long ago, indivisible.[11] But even its volume is not simple; for it is filled with its own characteristic forms, as space is filled with material forms, otherwise it could not be observed and appreciated at all. The phenomena that fill time are *tensions*—physical, emotional, or intellectual. Time exists for us because we undergo tensions and their resolutions. Their peculiar building-up, and their ways of breaking or diminishing or merging into longer and greater tensions, make for a vast variety of temporal forms. If we could experience only single, successive organic strains, perhaps subjective time would be one-dimensional like the time ticked off by clocks. But life is always a dense fabric of concurrent tensions, and as each of them is a measure of time, the measurements themselves do not coincide. This causes our temporal experience to fall apart into incommensurate elements which cannot be all perceived together as clear forms. When one is taken as parameter, others become "irrational," out of logical focus, ineffable. Some tensions, therefore, always sink into the background; some drive and some drag, but for perception they give *quality* rather than form to the passage of time, which unfolds in the pattern of the dominant and distinct strains whereby we are measuring it.[12]

[11]In *Matière et Mémoire*, published originally in 1896, he wrote: "All movement, being indeed a passage from one point of rest to another, is absolutely indivisible." (46th ed., Paris, 1946, p. 209.)

[12]Phenomenology attempts to describe in discursive terms this complex experience; and it tries to do so in terms of momentary impressions and actual feelings. The result is a tremendous complication of "states" in which the *sense of passage* is entirely lost in the parade of "moments" (*Augenblicke*, not *Momente*). See, for instance, the article by Philip Merlan, "Time Consciousness in Husserl and Heidegger," *Journal of Phenomenology*, VIII, 1 (September, 1947), 23–53.

The direct experience of passage, as it occurs in each individual life is, of course, something actual, just as actual as the progress of the clock or the speedometer, and like all actuality it is only in part perceived, and its fragmentary data are supplemented by practical knowledge and ideas from other realms of thought altogether. Yet it is the model for the virtual time created in music. There we have its image, completely articulated and pure; every kind of tension transformed into musical tension, every qualitative content into musical quality, every extraneous factor replaced by musical elements. The primary illusion of music is the sonorous image of passage, abstracted from actuality to become free and plastic and entirely perceptible.

Most readers have, undoubtedly, realized long ago that what is here called "subjective time" is the "real time," or "duration," which Henri Bergson attempted to capture and understand. Bergson's dream (one dares not say "concept" in connection with his thought) of *la durée réelle* brings his metaphysics very close to the musical realm—in fact, to the very brink of a philosophy of art. What prevented him from achieving a universal art theory was, essentially, a lack of logical daring; in his horror of a pernicious abstraction, he fled to a realm of no abstraction at all, and having wounded his spirit on the tools of physical science he threw away tools altogether.

Yet his nearness to the problems of art has made him pre-eminently the artists' philosopher. It is a curious fact that Croce and Santayana, who have both produced aesthetic theories, have never had the influence on artistic thought that Bergson still exercises; yet they have said many true things about the arts, whereas Bergson has said many sentimental and amateurish things. [13] But metaphysically he deals with matters that go to the core of all the arts, and especially of music.

His all-important insight is, briefly, that every conceptual form which is supposed to portray time oversimplifies it to the point of leaving out the most interesting aspects of it, namely the characteristic appearances of passage, so that we have a scientific equivalent rather than a conceptual symbol of duration. This criticism throws out a new challenge to the philosopher's powers of logical construction: find us a

---

[13] E.g. the passage in *La perception du changement*: "Without doubt, art causes us to discover in things more qualities and more shades of meaning than we would ordinarily perceive. It broadens our perception, but superficially rather than in depth. It enriches our present, but it does not lead us in any way to transcend the present."

symbolism whereby we can conceive and express our firsthand knowledge of time!

But here the critic himself retires; the challenge was only an oratorical one; his own reply to it is a counsel of despair—namely, that such conception is impossible, its symbolic expression a metaphysical pitfall, because all symbolization is by its very nature a falsification. It is "spatialization," and every traffic with space is a betrayal of our real knowledge of time. [14] Philosophy must give up discursive thought, give up logical conception, and try to grasp intuitively the inward sense of duration.

But it is not the intervention of symbolism as such that balks our understanding of "lived" time; it is the unsuitable and consequently barren structure of the literal symbol. The demand Bergson makes upon philosophy—to set for the dynamic forms of subjective experience— only art can fulfill. Perhaps this explains why he is the artists' philosopher *par excellence*. Croce and Santayana make demands on art that are essentially philosophical; philosophers, therefore, find them interesting, but artists tend to ignore them. Bergson, on the other hand, sets up a task that is impossible to accomplish in the realm of discursive expression, i.e. is beyond the philosopher's pale (and cannot force entrance there by resort to instinct, either), but is exactly the artist's business. Nothing could seem more reasonable to a poet or a musician than Bergson's metaphysical aim; without asking whether it is feasible in philosophy, the artist accepts this aim and subscribes to a philosophy that lays claim to it.

As soon as the expressive symbol, the image of time, is recognized, one can philosophize about its revelations and correct certain Bergsonian errors actually in the light of better knowledge. There has been much astute refutation of Bergson's doctrine, but little constructive criticism, *except from musicians*, who recognized what he was driving at, and with the courage of innocence went straight to the solution, where his philosophical fears confused him. In particular, I have in mind two articles in *La Revue Musicale*, which attacked the chief obstacle to a philosophy of art in Bergson's rich and novel apprehension of time—its radical opposition of space, the repudiation of every property it might share with space. Art can build its illusion in space or in time; metaphysically, we can understand or misunderstand one realm as

[14]See *La pensée et le mouvant*, especially chap. 1; also, for a brief but fundamental presentation, his little *Metaphysics*.

readily as the other; and it is hard to find the interesting characteristics of duration if there be too many things one is determined *not* to find.

The two articles, respectively, are Charles Koechlin's "Le temps et la musique," to which I have already referred,[15] and Gabriel Marcel's slightly earlier "Bergsonisme et musique."[16] Both authors are deeply in sympathy with Bergson's thesis, that the direct intuition of time must be our measure for its philosophical conception, and both realize what Bergson himself never clearly saw—that his "concrete duration," "lived time," is the prototype of "musical time," namely *passage* in its characteristic forms.[17] Furthermore, it is to their intellectual credit that they both distinguish between actual and musical duration, the living reality and the symbol.[18]

Bergson did, indeed, recognize a close relationship between musical time and *la durée pure*, but his idea of thought without symbols would not let him exploit the power of the dynamic image. The desire to exclude all spatial structure led him to deny his "concrete duration" any structure whatever; when he himself uses the simile of musical time, he treats the latter as a completely formless flow, "the successive tones of a melody whereby we let ourselves be cradled." Consequently he misses the most important and novel revelation of music—the fact that time is not a pure succession, but has more than one dimension. His very horror of the scientific abstractions he finds typified in geometry

[15] See footnote, p. 112.

[16] *La Revue Musicale*, VII, 3.

[17] Marcel writes: "It is extremely difficult for the reader of M. Bergson not to suppose—contrary to reason—that a certain philosophy of music is wrapped up in the theory of concrete time. . . . " (*Op. cit.*, p. 221.) And Koechlin: "Heard time comes so close to pure duration that one might say it is the sensation of duration itself." (*Op. cit.*, p. 47.)

[18] Cf. Marcel, *op. cit.*, p. 222: "Concrete duration is not essentially musical. All the more can one say, though only with a turn of phrase . . . of which M. Bergson would heartily disapprove—melodic continuity furnishes an example, an illustration, or pure continuity, given for the philosopher to apprehend directly in a reality both universal and concrete."

Also Koechlin, listing the several concepts of time:

"1. Pure duration, attribute of our deepest consciousness, and seemingly independent of the external world: life unfolding.

2. Psychological time. This is the impression of time that we receive according to the events of life: minutes that seem like centuries, hours that pass too fast. . . .

3. Time measured by mathematical means. . . .

4. And finally, I would speak of musical time. . . . Auditory time is without doubt that which approaches most closely to pure duration. . . . " (*Op. cit.*, p. 46.)

makes him cling to the one-dimensional pure succession of "states," which looks suspiciously like the abstract structure of Newton's one-dimensional time-stream.

But musical time has form and organization, volume and distinguishable parts. In apprehending a melody we are not vaguely billowing along with it. As Marcel observed: "When we speak of the beauty of a melodic line, this aesthetic qualification does not refer to an inward progression, but to a certain object, to a certain non-spatial shape—for which the world of extension can merely furnish a symbolism that we know is inadequate. Gradually, as I pass from tone to tone, a certain *ensemble* emerges, a form is built up, which very surely cannot be reduced to an organized succession of states. . . . It is of the very essence of this form to reveal itself as duration, and yet to transcend, in its own way, the purely temporal order in which it is manifested." To regard musical form and relation as "spatial," as Bergson does, is precisely to miss the real being in music; true musical perception apperceives the form as something dynamic. "But this act of apperception . . . does not in any way resolve itself into that sympathy whereby I am wedded to the phrase and live it. I readily say, it is not an *abandon*, but on the contrary, a sort of mastery." [19]

The frequent references to "musical space" in the technical literature are not purely metaphorical; there are definitely spatial illusions created in music, quite apart from the phenomenon of volume, which is literally spatial, and the fact that movement logically involves space, which may be taking movement too literally. "Tonal space" is a different thing, a genuine semblance of distance and scope. It derives from harmony rather than from either movement or fullness of tone. The reason is, I believe, that harmonic structure gives our hearing an *orientation* in the tonal system, from which we perceive musical elements as holding *places* in an ideal range. [20] But the space of music is never made wholly perceptible, as the fabric of virtual time is; it is really an attribute of musical time, an appearance that serves to develop the temporal realm in more than one dimension. Space, in music, is a *secondary illusion*. But, primary or secondary, it is thoroughly "virtual," i. e. unrelated to the space of actual experience. Ernst Kurth,

[19] Marcel, *op. cit.*, pp. 223–224.
[20] Cf. D.F. Tovey, *Essays in Musical Analysis*, V, 97: Speaking of Handel's modulations he says, "In the Chorus of Darkness . . . they traverse most of harmonic space."

in his *Musikpsychologie*, likens it to "kinetic space,"[21] and in Werner Danckert's *Ursymbole melodischer Gestaltung* it figures as virtual "place."[22] J. Gehring, for his part, speaks of the staggered planes of musical depth.[23] Evidently, the spatial element which all these writers find in music is a plastic space, artistically transformed, yet in no specified visual mode. It is not an importation from actual experience (though Kurth often flirts with sheer associationism), but neither is it the essential substance of the art. It simply arises from the way virtual time unfolds in this or that individual work—arises, and is eclipsed again.

The fact that the primary illusion of one art may appear, like an echo, as a secondary illusion in another, gives us a hint of the basic community of all the arts. As space may suddenly appear in music, time may be involved in visual works. A building, for instance, is the incarnation of a vital space; in symbolizing the feeling of the life that belongs to its precincts, it inevitably shows us time, and in some buildings this element becomes impressively strong. Yet architecture does not create a perceptible totality of time, as it does of space; time is a secondary illusion. The primary illusion always determines the "substance," the real character of an art work, but the possibility of secondary illusions endows it with the richness, elasticity, and wide freedom of creation that make real art so hard to hold in the meshes of theory.

As soon as we regard music as a thoroughgoing symbol, an image of subjective time, the appeal of Bergson's ideas to the artistic mind becomes quite comprehensible; for music presents reality no more directly than philosophical discourse, but it presents a sentient and emotional reality more adequately in a non-discursive image—*globalement*, as the French would say. With this tool it does exactly what he demanded of *la vraie métaphysique*, except one thing: to give a discursive account of itself in the end. That would be eating one's cake

---

[21]See p. 136: "In the light of all these phenomena one might, perhaps, best designate these subjective spatial impressions as 'kinetic space,' since they derive directly from the psychological energies. Only in its marginal manifestations does it [this space] resolve itself into perceptual factors. . . . "

[22]See p. 66: "Like all space in works of art, this [musical space] is nothing less than a cosmic symbol, a representation of Man's 'position,' 'location,' and 'range' in the greater nexus of the world."

[23]Gehring: *Grundprinzipien musikalischer Gestaltung.*

177

and having it too; and for this reason art is neither philosophy nor a substitute for philosophy, but is itself an epistemological datum about which we can philosophize.

The making of the symbol is the musician's entire problem, as it is, indeed, every artist's; and the special difficulties that confront us in dealing with music all spring from the nature of the musical illusion and the creative processes involved in forming and rendering it. Such subordinate issues are: the intervention of a performer between the composer and his audience; the wide range of "interpretations" of any given piece; the value and dangers of virtuosity, the bogey of "mere technique"; the process of "self-expression" attributed now to the composer, now to the performer, or in orchestral works to the conductor; the function of poetic texts; the principle of the "*petit roman*," in default of a text, to inspire or to explain a composition; the opposite idea of "pure music," upheld by the best musicologists and critics, and—paradoxically—the interest of most great composers in opera. All these problems have to be mooted in connection with our present subject. But they are far too complex, too great with implications affecting all the arts, to be passed with a mere bow of recognition. Their solution has to be prepared by a more detailed knowledge of the central theme—*what the musician is making, to what end, and by what means.*

DERYCK VICTOR COOKE

Deryck Victor Cooke (b. Leicester 1919, d. Thornton Heath, 1976), writer and music critic, mainly for the B.B.C. Cooke received his education at Selwyn College, Cambridge. As a writer, he concentrated primarily on 19th-century composers—Mahler, Wagner, Bruckner and Delius, emphasizing their musical semantics.

Opposed to Stravinsky's view, current in the 50's, that "music expresses nothing," Cooke contends that all of the arts, each in its own way, communicate the "subjective" experience of artists. Through a continuous and cumulative process, such experiences, explains Cooke, become part of a culture's artistic tradition, from which artists themselves draw. Feelings, to Cooke, are the *sine qua non* of music, while music itself is a language embracing a vocabulary of unambiguous emotions. That presumably explains why music, the most abstract art, "conveys emotions directly." In *The Language of Music* (1959) Cooke presents an actual "phrasebook."

Cooke's terms become "genuine" within a "man-made" system, that of the tonal period. While musical units are vested with "inherent" power to arouse emotions, they have been ordered, according to Cooke, into "formulae," musical idioms, etc., which over the years have become linked to specific emotions.

The inherent force of musical relationships, Cooke explains, derives from the harmonic series, in which there is a relationship between the position of the notes comprising the series and their emotive qualities. Western European music—its tonal scale and harmony—portrays those qualities. These have remained unaltered over the years, although their particular manifestations have changed over time, and of course, differ from one composer to the next.

Nonetheless, all "new inspirations" are shaped—consciously or

179

not—by a rational musical reservoir, recreating old 'formulae' in a new guise.

Deciphering the language of music (by isolating pitch, time and volume), Cooke concludes that melody, with its different arrangements of the notes of the scale, is its basis. As we read in the following excerpt, Cooke finds 16 specific melodic "motifs" which appear time and again throughout the history of music, each time imparting the same emotive message.

While isolating motifs is essential for the reconstruction of a musical 'vocabulary', according to Cooke, the musical work as a whole is indivisible. Moreover, it does not divide into 'content' and 'form', for structure and expression depend on each other for coherence.

Cooke believes his musical "interpretations" reflect the history of Western man. The major third, with its "joyous uplift" is supposed to reflect the sense of "emancipation" which came in the wake of man's belief in self and self-realization, ushered in by Humanism. The humble submission of Medieval man to God, on the other hand, is correlated with stepwise progressions, while the unrest and disillusion following World War II is reflected in an 'unordered' and 'unartistic' treatment of sounds.

Thus, in his attempt to prove his claim that music is indeed a language of the emotions, Cooke draws not only upon acoustical and musical resources but also upon psychological and ideational ones. While the correlations between some musical phenomena and some cultural attributes, suggested by Cooke, do not enjoy explanatory rigor, the main body of his theory is wholly compatible with more philosophical accounts of the subject. His argument concerning the unambiguity of musical meanings, for example, calls to mind some aspects of Goodman's "notational system", and his contentions concerning "feelings" in some way resemble Susanne Langer's theory. Unlike the hermeneutic approach of a Schweitzer, Cooke is not only concerned with musical idioms but with the composition in its entirety. Moreover, in contrast to that which is based on "resemblances," his contentions are historically derived, pinpointing the process whereby a shared language is created, enabling communication between sender and perceiver. His reconstruction of an actual musical vocabulary concretizes that which may have otherwise been considered vague, creating a link between the history, theory and aesthetic of music.

from The Language of Music[1]

1
What kind of an Art is Music

Although all the arts are essentially autonomous, owing to the different materials and techniques which they employ, there is clearly a kind of bond between them. We speak of the 'architecture' of a symphony, and call architecture, in its turn, 'frozen music'. Again, we say that certain writing has a 'sculptural' quality, and sometimes describe a piece of sculpture as 'a poem in stone'.

Admittedly, much of the phraseology which traffics between the arts is purely *metaphorical*, being concerned only with the *effect* of a work of art. Thus, in calling a statue 'a poem in stone', we merely indicate that its effect on us is of that impalpable kind we normally receive from poetry; we do not make an objective statement about the sculptor's intention or technical procedure. Such a metaphor, while useful for descriptive purposes, cannot help us to gain a deeper understanding of the nature of art.

On the other hand, comparison between one art and another *can* help towards this end, when the comparison is not *metaphorical*, but *analogical*, being concerned with the artist's *intention* and *technical procedure*. Thus, when we speak of the 'architecture' of a fugue, we are making an objective statement that its composer has constructed it by methods analogous to those of the architect—that he has grouped masses of non-representational material (tone instead of stone) into significant form, governed by the principles of proportion, balance, and symmetry; and this throws some light on a particular type of music. In using such analogies, of course, we must keep in mind the differences inherent in the use of different materials.

Analogies of this kind are continually being made between music and the other arts. Besides speaking of the 'architecture' of a piece of music, we use the term 'tone-painting', and we say that composers who are preoccupied with expressing character, mood, and feeling, have a

---

[1]Text: Deryck Cooke, *The Language of Music*, (Oxford: Clarendon Press, 1959), pp. 1–50; 113–167. The numbered notes are Cooke's notes.

leaning towards the 'literary'. And there is no doubt that music can be analogically related to each of these three arts: to architecture, in its quasi-mathematical construction; to painting, in its representation of physical objects; and to literature, in its use of a language to express emotion.

In various periods of musical history, composers have concentrated on one of these three aspects to the partial exclusion of the others. Medieval music was largely architectural in conception: the romantics were much concerned with the literary, the impressionists with the pictorial; modern music has swung back again to the architectural. Yet all three aspects have persisted in all periods: tone-painting and emotionally expressive music date right back to plainsong; and some of the romantics, notably Bruckner and Reger, were nothing if not tonal architects. In a work like Beethoven's Pastoral Symphony, we find all three aspects in a single composition: inspired by a 'literary' idea (the expression of moods and feelings arising out of contact with the countryside), the work is full of tone-painting, and has a perfectly satisfactory 'architectural' design. And in a movement like 'Sind Blitze, sind Donner in Wolken verschwunden?' (Have lightnings and thunders vanished behind the clouds?) in Bach's St. Matthew Passion, the three aspects are actually fused: the whole chorus is at once a piece of musical architecture (imitative polyphony), a tone-painting (of a gathering storm), and a piece of emotional expression (a smouldering and erupting of anger).

Let us now relate music analogically to architecture, painting, and literature, in more detail, and see if this can help us to establish the true nature of music as an art.

We may turn first to the analogy with painting, since this would seem to be the least essential, existing only in the case of a limited number of works, and passages of works. It exists where the composer imitates physical objects in terms of sound, addressed to the ear, as the painter does in terms of light, addressed to the eye. (We need not concern ourselves with painting which does not represent objects, but abstract patterns, since this is rather a case of painting's analogical relationship to music).

There are three ways in which music can represent physical objects. First, by *direct imitation* of something which emits a sound of definite pitch, such as a cuckoo, a shepherd's pipe, or a hunting horn. Here the parallel with painting is almost exact: the painter can represent the visual but not the aural aspect of the object, the composer the aural but not the visual. (In the case of a cuckoo, the composer may even be said to have the advantage, since to anyone but a naturalist it is a purely aural phenomenon!)

The second way is by *approximate imitation* of something which emits a sound of indefinite pitch, such as a thunderstorm, a rippling brook, or rustling branches. Here the composer's representation is inevitably less faithful than the painter's: a painting of a storm strikes the eye as a more or less exact reproduction of the appearance of a storm, but a musical representation of a storm strikes the ear as only an approximate reproduction of the sound of a storm. The definite sounds of music are different from the indefinite sounds of nature: rolls on the timpani do not sound exactly like thunder, nor chromatic scales on the violins exactly like the wind. Nevertheless, even here, the composer has a certain compensatory advantage: he can reproduce the sensation of physical movement which the painter can only suggest.

The third way in which music can represent physical objects is by the *suggestion* or *symbolization* of a purely visual thing, such as lightning, clouds or mountains, using sounds which have an effect on the ear similar to that which the appearance of the object has on the eye. Here music at once approaches closest to painting, and recedes farthest from it. In its attempt to stimulate the visual faculty, it seeks to usurp the very function of painting; but in so far as it lacks the power of direct communication—being unable to represent the object so that it can be immediately identified without recourse to an explanatory title—it is less analogous with painting than when it confines itself the imitation of aural phenomena. Knowing, as we do, that the first of Debussy's Three Nocturnes is entitled *Nuages*, we are persuaded into interpreting the shifting patterns of sound in terms of the visual imagination—shifting patterns of light, such as we experience from the movement of clouds. But if Debussy had not given the Nocturne its title, we should have been uncertain what the composer intended to represent, if anything at all.

(The fact that, in such cases, a title is necessary to set the imagination working, is often taken as proof of illegitimacy of this kind of musical tone-painting. But it is not always realized that even some poems are not fully intelligible without their titles. Take this one by Tennyson:

He clasps the crag with crooked hands;
Close to the sun in lonely lands,
Ring'd with the azure world, he stands.

The wrinkled sea beneath him crawls;
He watches from his mountain walls,
And like a thunderbolt he falls.

One wonders whether, if Tennyson had merely called this poem 'Lines', readers would have realized what it was supposed to be describing. Once the actual title is known, of course, there is nothing ambiguous about the poem at all.)

Frequently, music's three methods of tone-painting are fused, or superimposed on one another, in a single composition. In Beethoven's Pastoral Symphony, for example, the direct imitation of bird-calls (cuckoo and quail) interrupt the approximate imitation of a murmuring brook, while the third bird-call (nightingale) is also approximate; the thunder in the storm movement is approximately imitated, the lightning and rain are suggested, and these are followed by the direct imitation of a shepherd's pipe.

So far, our attention has been strictly confined to the element of imitation; but this, of course, is neither the composer's nor the painter's sole intention. The imitation is only a framework on which each type of artist, using the materials of his own art, superimposes his *vision* of the imitated object, or his *subjective experience* of it. Beethoven's comment on his Pastoral Symphony is apposite here: 'more feeling than tone-painting'.

Now the painter is always free to impose his subjective experience on the basic framework of imitation, by the very nature of his art: the object imitated will still be immediately recognizable even after considerable modification in the interests of subjectivity.[2] But the composer can only impose his subjective experience on his imitation when he is free to choose his own notes to embody the general pattern necessitated by the imitation. Therefore, the power to reproduce sounds from the external world in their exact form is the least valuable part of music's tone-painting equipment, since the composer cannot choose his own notes, but only accept those emitted by the object imitated. Direct imitation is most acceptable when the composer uses it as a single element in a larger whole, weaving it into a web of notes already chosen by him to embody an approximate imitation or a suggestion of that whole. Thus, the cuckoo-calls in Delius's *On Hearing the First Cuckoo in Spring*

---

[2]We are concerned here with painting as it has been known for centuries, not with the revolutionary art of the last fifty years or so.

take their rightful place as a significant detail in the composer's suggestion of the atmosphere of a spring day; and that suggestion already embodies the composer's own subjective experience of spring.

Indirect imitation is more valuable in that it allows the composer considerable latitude to choose exactly what notes he shall use to body forth the general pattern required for the imitation; and by his choice he is able to convey his subjective experience of the object imitated. In most of the songs in Schubert's *Die schöne Müllerin*, for example, the accompaniment indirectly imitates the flowing motion of a brook by regular patterns of quavers or semiquavers; but by embodying the generalized pattern in a different series of notes in each case, Schubert is able to convey the emotional experiences of his young miller (joy, apprehension, jealous fury, etc.) through a subjective vision of the brook. (*Die schöne Müllerin*, in fact, like so much of Schubert's vocal music, works on the principle defined by Ruskin as 'the pathetic fallacy'—the projection by the artist of his own moods into some natural object.)[3]

Suggestion or symbolization of visual phenomena is equally valuable, since it depends wholly on the actual notes used, which must vividly convey the composer's subjective experience of the phenomenon represented, or we shall not recognize it, even when supplied with a title. Thus, Debussy's symbolization of clouds, in *Nuages*, is achieved by shifting patterns of sound; but shifting patterns may be used to symbolize many things: it is the actual notes in which Debussy chose to embody these patterns that convey his subjective vision of clouds.

To sum up: tone-painting is a legitimate, if subsidiary function of music. Its value increases the more it is used as a vehicle for the composer's subjective experience of the object represented; and it is by means of the actual notes chosen by the composer that the experience is conveyed. Here the analogy with painting ends, since there is obviously no connection between the technical organization of notes and that of paint.[4] The composer's way of conveying his subjective experience is a different one from the painters; it resides in the 'literary' aspect of music—its use of a tonal language to express moods and feelings—

[3] *Modern Painters*, Vol. 3, Chap. 12.
[4] Comparisons such as those of piano-writing with black-and-white drawing, or orchestration with colour, and of a certain type of impressionist orchestration with the *pointilliste* technique of painting, are clearly metaphorical, and cannot bring us a deeper understanding of the nature of music.

which will be discussed in the section concerned with the analogy between music and literature.

First, however, it should be said that any piece of tone-painting is of negligible value unless it is integrated into some kind of musical structure; and this brings us to our next section, an examination of the analogy between music and architecture.

The final realization of any work of art is achieved through structure, or form: hence each of the arts can be analogically related to architecture, which is itself the visible embodiment of pure form. The power of large-scale organization which made possible the poetry of Dante, the painting of Michelangelo, and the music of Bach, is obviously analogous to the monumental constructive genius needed in architecture; and it was clearly employed in each of the three cases to produce structures which would satisfy the desire of the aesthetic sense for formal harmony, in the way that architectural forms do.

In the case of music, the analogy would seem to be particularly close, in that, as has been mentioned, both composer and architect group masses of non-representational material (pure sound in time, and stone in space) into significant form, governed by the principles of proportion, balance, and symmetry. At first, our analogy looks to be a simple and conclusive one: music is the audible, as architecture is the visible, embodiment of pure form. Stravinsky adheres to this view of the matter: 'One could not better define the sensation produced by music than by saying that it is identical with the evoked by the contemplation of the interplay of architectural forms.'[5]

But let us look into tha analogy a little more closely. How far can we apply it? To all music, or only to certain kinds of music? It is easy to justify the common application of it to some of the greatest music every written—the contrapuntal masterpieces of the old polyphonic composers, down to and including Bach. In these, the themes are sometimes scarcely more emotionally expressive than bricks or blocks of stone (e.g. those of Bach's 'great' organ fugues in A minor and G minor), and are used simply as raw material capable of being built up into large-scale sound-constructions by means of interwoven lines, various sections being balanced one against another in size, until their combined mass makes possible a final climax, setting a seal on the whole like a tower or a dome. Moreover, the interwoven lines actually 'support' one another in a quasi-mathematical system of stresses and strains. The old polyphonic

[5]*Chronicle of My Life*, translated from the French, p. 93.

composers might truly be regarded as tonal architects, in that, when they wanted to write, say, invertible counterpoint at the twelfth, they had to work according to the following table if the result was to be satisfactory:

1 = 12	7 = 6
2 = 11	8 = 5
3 = 10	9 = 4
4 = 9	10 = 3
5 = 8	11 = 2
6 = 7	12 = 1

What is more, the experience provided by this kind of music is definitely akin to that provided by architecture—the enjoyment of the beauty of pure form. What attracts us is not so much the thematic material as the satisfying way in which it is woven together; not so much, say, the fugue-subject, as the masterly working-out of it in *stretto*, to produce a sonorous climax.

The analogy holds good, of course, for all music that is primarily contrapuntal: for the non-expressive fugal music of later periods (lesser, both in amount and calibre), and for that limited amount of modern music in which non-expressive material is organized contrapuntally by means of quasi-mathematical 'laws' similar to those which governed the old-style polyphony (much *avant-garde* serial music, and the music of Hindemith, for example). In all these cases, the raw material is nothing, the intellectual construction everything, and the impact on the listener almost entirely a formal and aesthetic one. But once we step outside the limited world of polyphony, in which the intellect predominates, the analogy becomes vague and unprofitable, for two reasons. Firstly, the difference in the materials comes to the fore: the musical material of non-polyphonic music is not inexpressive like that of architecture, but is charged with human feeling. Secondly, in the manipulation of such material, purely intellectual techniques are replaced by methods in which the intellect is to some extent at the service of the feelings.

If a theme of the type used in polyphonic music acts very much like a brick or a block of stone (as something of no importance in itself, only useful as raw material to be built into a structure), the thematic material of other types of music—opera, song, symphony—*is* important in itself, being emotionally expressive, as is the material of painting and literature.

The experience derived from a piece of polyphony, like that derived from a piece of architecture, consists mainly of a perception and admiration of its form; but in most cases, the experience derived from a piece of non-polyphonic music, like that derived from a painting or a literary work, is only partly referable to an appreciation of its form: much of it derives from our emotional response to its actual material. A typical contrapuntal point or fugue-subject has no real significance until it takes place in the construction as a whole; but a theme in a sonata, like a hand in a painting or a line in a poem, is already of absorbing emotional interest in itself, even if its full significance is only appreciated when its integration into the overall form is understood. Indeed, in music, as to a greater degree in literature, a work can be outstanding in spite of being cast into a most unsatisfying form: we listen to works like *Boris Godunov* and Delius's Violin Concerto, as we read books like *Tristam Shandy* and *Moby Dick*, not for their formal beauty, but for the fascination of their material.

Actually, in many cases, the thematic material of polyphony is itself expressive, even highly expressive: a few examples are the opening Kyrie of Bach's B minor Mass, several of Purcell's string fantasias, 'For with His Stripes' in *Messiah*, Mozart's C minor Fugue for two pianos and the Quam Olim Abrahae in his Requiem Mass. Indeed, musical material (as it is hoped to show in this book) is by its very nature expressive; though of course its expressiveness can sometimes be extremely slight. Nevertheless, broadly speaking, the architectural analogy holds good for all polyphony, whether expressive or inexpressive, in that the construction is primarily intellectual and the impact primarily formal; and it breaks down outside polyphony because the construction is guided by feeling and the impact is to a considerable extent emotional.

Outside polyphony, in fact, it dwindles to the mere truism that a piece of music, no less than a piece of architecture, must have some kind of shape. Turning away from Bach's polyphony to another type of work by him, the St. Matthew Passion for example, we shall be hard put to it to discover any analogy with architectural construction at all. What small amount of polyphony it does contain is mostly 'free', and all of it is dramatic in conception—a portrayal of the hubbub of a crowd of people; and for the most part the work consists of operatic-type recitative, highly emotional arias of the melody-and-accompaniment kind, and traditional chorales in which the primitive emotions of folk-music are intensified by Bach's extraordinary command of deeply expressive harmony. Again, when we turn to the symphony (classical or romantic) we might just as well (more profitably, in fact) compare its structure to that of a drama, a succession of contrasted events in time following one another by a chain of cause and effect;[6] and an opera, of course, just *is* a sung drama. A work like Debussy's *L'après-midi d'un faune* is constructed (if so tough a word may be used) more like the poem to which it was intended to form a prelude—as a succession of changing moods melting in and out of one another according to the logic of emotion; and a song just *is* a sung poem.

Clearly then, we cannot press the architectural analogy too far (as many are intent on doing at the present juncture of musical history). It has really just as limited an application as the analogy with painting: only a certain type of music, to a certain degree, can legitimately be regarded as pure, quasi-mathematical form. Other music has a different kind of form, and has a wider significance than is imparted to us by its form alone, being expressive of the composer's subjective experience.

So we may say that, except within very closely defined limits, music is neither a representative art, like painting, nor a purely formal art, like architecture. What kind of an art is it, then?

In some way or other, we feel, it conveys to us the subjective experience of composers. But in what way? It is easy to see how the thing is done in painting (by direct but subjective representation of physical objects) and in literature (by direct but subjective description of physical objects, thoughts, characters, and emotions); but how can it be done in music, which can only represent a few physical objects, vaguely suggest a few others, and make no explicit description of anything at all? To try and answer this question, we must turn to a consideration of the analogy between music and literature, and an investigation of the problem of music as language.

But first, a fairly lengthy digression will be necessary, in order to try and settle a vexed point. So far, this book has been persistently begging the question whether music does in fact express composers' subjective experience—a question which everyone once assumed instinctively had an affirmative answer, but which is assumed equally instinctively by many modern musicians to have been answered once and for all in

[6]Bruckner alone of the symphonists found an 'architectural' way of composing his symphonies—balancing masses of melodic harmony one against another; but this is an isolated phenomenon which need not concern us here.

the negative. If we are to establish the right to make any analogy at all between music and literature, the question will have to be reopened, and some reasons sought to support an affirmative answer. Not that we can hope to find any clinching proof; what proof can there be in these matters? In an age which doubts every one of the old intuitive assumptions, there can be no definite answers—not even the new confident negative ones (a fact which may well serve as encouragement at the start). What we may hope to do is to show that there is as much to be said on this side as on that; that the question is still open, whatever the fashionable opinion may be, and that one person's conviction is as good as another's.

It is not the intention here to investigate every theory of music considered as expression; theorists are notoriously limited by abstractions. I propose to deal with the matter in a more concrete way, setting forth the current case against the view of music as expression, in the words of two of our most outstanding present-day composers; and adducing several arguments on the other side—the views of other composers, the view of a poet, the experience of listeners in general, and the practice of composers in general.

First, the negative view, in the words of Stravinsky: 'I consider that music is, by its very nature, powerless to *express* anything at all, whether a feeling, an attitude of mind, a psychological mood, a phenomenon of nature, etc. . . . if, as is nearly always the case, music appears to express something, this is only an illusion, and not a reality.'[7] Obviously, everything depends on what Stravinsky means by 'express': if he means 'express explicitly, as words can', his remark is a truism; if he means 'convey to the listener in any way whatsoever', he is merely offering an expression of opinion, without adducing any proof.

Composers' theories tend to be based on their own artistic needs, and it is evident that Stravinsky, bent as he has been on removing music as far as possible from the romantic aesthetic, would naturally formulate a theory of this kind. It is an extremist theory, the product of an intensely individual composer's mind; but it has been widely accepted, as coming from such an eminent source, and its effect on contemporary aesthetic though has been most harmful. Aaron Copland, himself a disciple of Stravinsky, and a composer who cannot by the wildest stretch of the imagination be called a romantic, has justly described Stravinsky's

[7] Stravinsky, *Chronicle of My Life*, translated from the French, pp. 92–2.

190

attitude in this matter as 'intransigent', saying that 'it may be due to the fact that so many people have tried to read different meanings into so many pieces'. He also adds the following: 'Heaven knows it is difficult enough to say what it is that a piece of music means, to say it finally so that everyone is satisfied with your explanation. But that should not lead one to the other extreme of denying to music the right to be expressive.'[8]

It is worth noting that, until Stravinsky came out with his flat statement to the contrary, everyone naturally assumed that music was expressive. Let us call in another, earlier composer, not an out-and-out romantic of the Wagnerian type, but one firmly grounded in the classical tradition.

Mendelssohn once wrote: 'People usually complain that music is so ambiguous; that it is so doubtful what they ought to think when they hear it; whereas everyone understands words. With me it is entirely the converse. And not only with regard to an entire speech, but also with individual words; these, too, seem to me to be so ambiguous, so vague, and so easily misunderstood in comparison with genuine music, which fills the soul with a thousand things better than words. The thoughts which are expressed to me by a piece of music which I love are not too indefinite to be put into words, but on the contrary too definite. And so I find in every attempt to express such thoughts, that something is right, but at the same time something is unsatisfying in all of them....'[9]

Now when Mendelssohn comes to give examples of *thoughts* (*Gedanken*) which music gives rise to, we find he is using the word in the generalized sense of 'mental activities', and in fact means *feelings*, rather, since he specifically mentions resignation, melancholy, and the praise of God. And those who have found music expressive of anything at all (the majority of mankind) have found it expressive of emotions. Let us here call in another witness, not even a semi-romantic composer this time, but one of the clearest-minded of classical poets.

Dryden, in his 'Song for St. Cecilia's Day', showed that he regarded music as emotionally expressive:

> *The soft complaining flute*
> *In dying notes discovers*
> *The woes of hopeless lovers,*

[8]Aaron Copland, *What to Listen For in Music*, Chap. 2.
[9]Mendelssohn, Letter to Marc André Souchay, Berlin, 5 October 1842.

Whose dirge is whisper'd by the warbling lute.
Sharp violins proclaim
Their jealous pangs and desperation,
Fury, frantic indignation,
Depths of pains, and height of passion
For the fair disdainful dame.

No doubt in Dryden's mind at all! As he said earlier in the same poem: 'What passion cannot Music raise and quell?' And emotional reaction to music has been the experience of listeners everywhere. One has only to read descriptions of musical compositions in programmes or musical biographies, whether in English or any other language, to find the writers limping in their more pedestrian way after Dryden: confident themes, agonizing chords, wistful melodies, ferocious rhythms, jubilant climaxes. . . .

And the composers: what did they themselves think they were doing? Neither Stravinsky nor Mendelssohn tells us, but one of the most classical of all composers has done. Listen to Mozart: 'Now, as for Belmonte's aria in A major—'O wie ängstlich, O wie feurig'—do you know how it is expressed (*ausgedrückt*)?—even the throbbing of his loving heart is indicated (*angezeigt*)—the two violins in octaves. . . . One sees the trembling—the wavering—one sees how his swelling breast heaves—this is expressed (*exprimirt*) by a *crescendo*—one hears the whispering and the sighing—which is expressed (*ausgedrückt*) by the first violins, muted, and a flute in unison'.[10] Nothing could be more definite than that.

Again, here is Schubert, writing home about the reception of his 'Ave Maria' at a private concert: 'They also wondered greatly at my piety, which I have expressed (*ausgedrückt*) in a Hymn to the Holy Virgin, and which, it appears, grips every soul and turns it to devotion. I think this is due to the fact that I never force devotion in myself and never compose hymns or prayers of that kind, unless I am overcome by it unawares; but then it is usually the right and true devotion'.[11]

In any case, it is undeniable (as Chapters 2 and 3 attempt to demonstrate) that composers have consciously or unconsciously used music as a language, from at least 1400 onwards—a language never formulated in a dictionary, because by its very nature it is incapable of such

[10]Mozart, letter to his father, Vienna, 26 September 1781, concerning *The Seraglio*.
[11]Schubert, letter to his father and stepmother, Steyer, 25 (28?) July 1825.

treatment. A few examples may suffice here. A phrase of two notes (the minor sixth of the scale falling to the fifth) is to be found expressing anguish in music by Josquin (*Déploration*); Morley ('Ah, break, alas!'); Bach (Crucifixus in the B minor Mass); Mozart (*Don Giovanni*— Donna Anna's grief at her father's death); Schubert (*The Erl King*— 'my father, my father'); Mussorgsky (*Boris Godunov*—the Simpleton's Lament); Verdi (the end of *La Traviata*); Wagner (the so-called Servitude motive in *The Ring*); Schoenberg (*A Survivor from Warsaw*—'you had been separated from your children'); Stravinsky (*The Rake's Progress*—'In a foolish dream'); Britten (Donne Sonnet 'Oh might these sighs and tears'); and in innumerable other places in the music of these and practically all other composers.[12] Another example is a phrase of 1–3–5–6–5 in the major scale (sometimes with passing notes), used to express a simple, innocent, blessed joy: found in countless plainsong themes and Christmas carols; in Wilbye ('As fair as morn'); Handel (*Messiah*—Pastoral Symphony); Humperdinck (Children's Prayer in *Hansel and Gretel*); Busoni (Easter Hymn in *Doktor Faustus*); Vaughan Williams ('So shalt thou enter in' and 'Holy, holy, holy' in *The Pilgrim's Progress*); and in many other places.[13]

Again, we may note how the tragic subjects of the St. Matthew Passion and *Die Winterreise* forced on Bach and Schubert a heavy (almost too heavy) preponderance of minor keys; while the brighter subjects of the Easter Oratorio and most of *Die schöne Müllerin* turned them inevitably towards the major. Did anyone ever set the Resurrexit of the Mass to slow, soft, minor music? Or the Crucifixus to quick, loud, major strains? Try singing the word 'Crucifixus' to the music of Handel's Hallelujah Chorus, or the word 'Hallelujah' to the music of the Crucifixus in Bach's B minor Mass! Stravinsky himself has complied with the common practice in these matters. In the *Symphony of Psalms*, the first two movements (settings of sombre prayer-psalms) are in E minor and C minor respectively, while the last (a setting of a praise-psalm) moves between E flat major and C major. And his *Oedipus Rex* is mainly in minor keys, his *Rake's Progress* mainly in major ones. Within the orbit of tonality, composers have always been bound by certain expressive laws of the medium, laws which are analogous to those of language.[14]

[12] See Exs. 48, 50, and 62.
[13] See Ex. 64.
[14] The ambiguities of the major-minor opposition (as shown, for example, by the Dead March in *Saul* being in the *major*) are dealt with in Chapter 2.

So we must admit that composers have set out to express emotion, and that listeners have felt it to be present in their music. But we must still consider Stravinsky's opinion that 'if, as is nearly always the case, music appears to express something, this is only an illusion, and not a reality'.

This point of view has been set forth in greater detail by Hindemith in his book *A Composer's World*. His theory is that music does have an emotive effect on the listener, but the apparent emotions are not those of the composer, nor do they arouse the real emotions of the listener; in Stravinsky's words 'this is only an illusion'. Hindemith says: 'Music cannot express the composer's feelings. Let us suppose a composer is writing an extremely funereal piece, which may require three months of intensive work. Is he, during this three-months period, thinking of nothing but funerals? Or can he, in those hours that are not devoted to his work because of his desire to eat and sleep, put his grief on ice, so to speak, and be gay until the moment when he resumes his sombre activity? If he really expressed his feelings accurately during the time of composing and writing, we would be presented with a horrible motley of expressions, among which the grievous part would necessarily occupy but a small space.[15] Later, he continues; 'If the composer himself thinks he is expressing his own feelings, we have to accuse him of lack of observation. Here is what he really does: he knows by experience that certain patterns of tone-setting correspond with certain emotional reactions on the listener's part. Writing these patterns frequently and finding his observations confirmed, in anticipating the listener's reaction he believes himself to be in the same mental situation.'[16]

The naïveté and illogicality of this analysis, coming from a composer of Hindemith's mental stature, is truly regrettable. But we have to remember again that composers write out of their own experience; and we know that Hindemith is, and sees himself as, a superior kind of craftsman, not an 'inspired genius'—that, in fact, he rather derisively denies the existence of inspiration: 'Melodies can, in our time, be constructed rationally. We do not need to believe in benign fairies, bestowing angelic tunes upon their favourites.'[17] Being this kind of composer, he is unable, despite his intellectual insight into musical construction and his laudable concern for music's moral values, to

[15]Hindemith, *A composer's World*, pp. 35–6.
[16]Ibid., p. 36.
[17]Ibid., p. 97.

understand the deep unconscious urges that gave birth to music of the deeply emotive kind—viz., most of the music written between 1400 and the present day.

There seems to be in Hindemith's analysis an almost wilful refusal to understand that an artist has two separate selves: the everyday, conscious self, which is a prey to many passing trivial emotions, and a deep, unconscious, creative self, which is always there to return to, 'inspiration' permitting, and which is apt to intrude itself intermittently, as 'inspiration', during his everyday life. If Hindemith has no personal experience of this, surely he has heard of the fits of 'absent-mindedness' that some great artists have been subject to, when this occurred? Surely he must have some conception of the way in which this unconsciousness creative self persists beneath the distractions of everyday life, concentrated on its all-important realities?[18] When we state that a composer, writing a lengthy piece over a long period, expresses his emotions in it, we really ought not to have to explain that we mean his deep, permanent, significant emotions, not the superficial fleeting ones called forth by trivial pleasures and disappointments.

There is only one way to make clear the superficiality of Hindemith's 'realistic' analysis, and that is to take a concrete example. Let us consider the *Eroica* Symphony, as it came to Beethoven. We know that Beethoven was intoxicated by the libertarian ideals of the French Revolution, and that, at first regarding Napoleon as the hero who would liberate mankind, he conceived the idea of composing a symphony in his honour. Now how would this state of mind function in Beethoven? The heroic, libertarian ideal was (as were 'nature', the 'immortal beloved' and 'fate') the subject of one of his most intense emotions, which was liable to flare up at the slightest provocation (as we know from several anecdotes). And we know that he conceived the symphony to express this burning, persistent emotion, apparently having a vision of the work as a whole, and no doubt being possessed with certain

[18] 'So much in writing depends on the superficiality of one's days. One may be preoccupied with shopping and income-tax returns, but the stream of the unconscious continues to flow undisturbed, solving problems, planning ahead: one sits down sterile and dispirited at the desk, and suddenly the words come as though from the air . . . the work has been done while one slept or shopped or talked with friends.' (Graham Greene, speaking through the character of Maurice Bendrix, the narrator in *The End of the Affair*, Chap. 2.)

musical themes for various parts of it. Now how did these themes originate? Let us take the Funeral March, since Hindemith's example is 'an extremely funereal piece'.

One of the emotions aroused in Beethoven by the heroic, libertarian ideal was, as we know, a deep grief for the unhappy fate that awaited many and many a liberator—that of annihilation. Wherefore he must have felt the compulsion to express this feeling in his symphony, in the natural place: the slow movement would be a Funeral March. Now, the laws of the language of tonality demanded a slow march-tempo, the minor key (relative minor, obviously, C minor, which was the 'tragic' key of Beethoven's great predecessor, Mozart), and a mournful theme. To imagine that these necessities were formulated, one by one, by Beethoven's conscious mind, is ridiculous; they must have crystallized, unconsciously, into the main C minor theme, built around the classical tragic formula of the minor triad. [19] Beethoven's unconscious mind thus embodied his own personal emotion concerning the death of a hero in the time-honoured terms of musical language—but in his own personal way: gradually it stamped on the raw material—the C minor triad—the impress of his own individual emotion so strongly that the resultant theme was 'original' and 'characteristic', and not to be confused with the slow C minor world of Mozart's *Masonic Funeral Music* or Wagner's *Siegfried's Funeral March*, both in the same tradition. (I say 'gradually' since the theme had to be hacked into shape, as was so often the case with Beethoven: the conscious craftsman had to take over, working towards the ideal form of expression envisaged by the creative unconscious.)

Let us compare, for a moment, a similar case in literature: Tennyson, writing his *Ode on the Death of the Duke of Wellington*. The same intense personal emotion (not in any way affected by the fact that, as Poet Laureate, he was obliged to write the Ode, since one has to admit that Tennyson's heart and soul were obviously in the project, whatever one's personal reaction to the subject of the poem); and the same inevitable recourse to certain basic elements of language with time-honoured associations:

Bury the *Great* Duke
With an *empire's lamentation*,

[19] See Ex. 80.

196

Let us *buy* the *Great* Duke
To the noise of the *mourning* of a *mighty nation.*

There is the same heavy stress in the rhythm, the same obsessive repetition, the same unmistakably individual use of well-work language (italicized here), and no doubt there was the same craftsman's struggle to hew the first inspiration into the dimly-apprehended ideal expression.

Now let us remember that, in both cases, the artist must have been disturbed by everyday distractions before the piece was completed; perhaps a visitor to entertain, or a business letter to write. Can it be conceived that the creative current (the be-all and end-all of these two different men's lives) would not be running along unchecked underneath, still concerned with the theme so dear to it? And on the (no doubt impatient) return to the manuscript, would not the old *personal* feeling of grief, concerned with the death of a hero, come flooding back as powerfully as ever, possibly giving a new impetus to continue with another aspect of that obsessive emotion?

Let us admit what is obvious to common sense: that Beethoven used the traditional language of music to express his own personal emotions, and that everyday interruptions did not prevent these emotions from persisting throughout the composition—and beyond it, indeed, for *Egmont* was still to come, and *Coriolan.*

We must now turn to the second part of Hindemith's theory—that concerning the emotional reaction of the listener. He says: 'If music does not express feelings, how then does it affect the listener's emotions? There is no doubt that listeners, performers, and composers alike can be profoundly moved by perceiving, performing, or imagining music, and consequently music must touch on something in their emotional life that brings them into this state of excitation. But if these mental reactions were feelings, they would not change as rapidly as they do, and they would not begin and end precisely with the musical stimulus that aroused them. If we experience a real feeling of grief—that is, grief not caused or released by music—it is not possible to replace it at a moment's notice and without any plausible reason with the feeling of wild gaiety; and gaiety, in turn, cannot be replaced by complacency after a fraction of a second. . . . The reactions which music evokes are not feelings, but they are the images, memories of feelings. . . . We cannot have musical reactions of emotional significance, unless we have once had real feelings, the memory of which is revived by the

197

musical impression. Reactions of a grievous nature can be aroused by music only if a former experience of real grief was stored up in our memory and is now again portrayed in a dream-like fashion. . . . '[20] Again, he says: 'Paintings, poems, sculptures, works of architecture . . . do not—contrary to music—release images of feelings; instead they speak to the real, untransformed, and unmodified feelings.'[21]

It is difficult here to know where to start—there are so many fallacies. Let us return to the *Eroica* Funeral March, and consider the listener's reactions. In the slow, heavy, dragging rhythm, the minor key, and the mournful melody, he will recognize the type of the funeral march, and Beethoven's own individuality of expression, with its indefinable grandeur, will convey that it is a funeral march written by a noble mind in connection with a noble ideal. Will the music awaken 'former experience of real grief, stored-up in the memory, and now portrayed in a dream-like fashion'? Surely nothing of the sort: the listener's capacity for feeling grief (certainly intensified by any strong personal grief he has experienced) will be aroused by the music into feeling (through the distorted medium of his own temperament, admittedly) the personal grief of Beethoven, made incarnate by him in that music. *He will feel as he has never felt before.* (In listening to Chopin's Funeral March, he will experience another quite different personal grief, belonging to a quite different man—a grief more loaded with despair—and again, he will feel as he never felt before.) The listener thus makes direct contact with the mind of a great artist, 'interpreting' his expression of emotion in the same way that he will 'interpret' an emotional letter from a friend: in both cases, mind meets mind, as far as is possible. And if the listener has no capacity for feeling real grief (as opposed to petty chagrin), he will, of course, not really comprehend the Funeral March at all.

Hindemith's two reasons why musical emotions are not 'real' feelings will not hold water. In the first place, emotions called forth by music do *not* 'begin and end with the musical stimulus that aroused them': begin, yes, since a specific emotion cannot be awakened without a stimulus; but end, no, since it is many people's experience that the feelings aroused by a piece of music can persist for days afterwards, without memory of the actual notes that caused them. In the second place, the idea that diverse emotions cannot succeed one another

[20]Ibid., p. 38.
[21]Ibid., p. 49.

198

swiftly is applicable only to placid temperaments: Hindemith himself is no doubt possessed of remarkable equanimity, but more volatile people often find themselves switching suddenly from depression to gaiety with or without external stimulus. And this is found quite commonly in art itself—in literature for example. One has only to consider the violent transitions of mood, from deep gloom to joyous ecstasy, in such a poem as Keat's *Ode to a Nightingale.*

In any case, what is meant by saying that the emotions aroused by the other arts are more 'real' than those of music? In what sense, for instance, is the feeling of grief evoked by the *Ode on the Death of the Duke of Wellington* more 'real' than that evoked by the *Eroica* Funeral March? Surely not that Tennyson exhorts us, in explicit words, to 'bury the Great Duke', whereas Beethoven 'only' expresses the inner feeling of grief on a hero's death? In both cases, the feeling of grief is stimulated by the use of an emotionally affecting language in a particular way. And how far, in both cases, can the grief be said to be 'real'? Not in the sense that one's own grief for a personal loss is real, but in the sense that all great art stimulates our own real emotional capacities to partake vicariously of the artist's experience, as we do of our friends' experiences when they speak to us of them. In one sense, emotion conveyed through music is more real than that conveyed through the other arts—because it is more *pure*, less bound down to a 'local habitation and a name'. The true expressive difference between the arts is that painting conveys feeling through a visual image, and literature through a rationally intelligible statement, but music conveys the naked feeling direct. As the composer felt, so we may hear, and feel: what he saw, or thought, does not interfere.

This brings us to a further difficulty; the supposed vagueness of the emotions expressed in music. Hindemith, like those of whom Mendelssohn spoke, finds music ambiguous. 'One given piece of music may cause remarkably diverse reactions in different listeners. As an illustration of this statement, I like to mention the second movement of Beethoven's Seventh Symphony, which I have found leads some people into a pseudo feeling of profound melancholy, while another group takes it for a kind of scurrilous scherzo, and a third for a subdued kind of pastorale. Each group is justified in judging as it does.'[22]

[22]Ibid., p. 40.

Hindemith is undoubtedly right in his observation that people react in different emotional ways to a given piece of music, but his statement that each reaction is equally justifiable fails to take a simple psychological point into account. Could it not be that some listeners are incapable of understanding the feeling of the music properly?[23] This can even happen in the explicit world of literature: I have seen Edmund in *King Lear* played as a superficially cynical butterfly, and the audience reacted accordingly, with giggles; but a close reading of Shakespeare's text does not justify this conception in the least. Similarly, the great German actor, Gründgens, plays Goethe's Mephistopheles as a self-tormenting fallen angel. And if actors can so distort the emotional make-up of a part, one wonders how many people read, say, Shelley's *Ode to a Skylark* as a pretty and pleasing piece of poetry, or take *Moby Dick* to be merely a stirring sea-story.

The fact is that people can only react to the emotions expressed in a work of art according to their own capacity to feel those emotions. Hindemith describes what too often happens (taking it as a general rule for all listeners): 'The difference in interpretation stems from the difference in memory-images [of emotions] the listeners provide, and the unconscious selection is made on the basis of the sentimental value or the degree of importance each image has: the listener chooses the one which is dearest and closest to his mental disposition, or which represents a most common, most easily accessible feeling.'[24] Such people, whom one knows to exist, are just plainly unmusical: suppose that such a listener's 'memory-image' has no connection with the emotions expressed by the music at all? If someone were to declare the *Eroica* Funeral March to be a sanguine piece, we should unhesitatingly accuse him of being emotionally undeveloped. Such a person would understand *Hamlet* as a tragedy only by virtue of the explicit meaning of the words, and remain utterly oblivious of the dark emotional undertones of the poetry. The truly musical person, with a normal capacity to respond to emotion, immediately apprehends the emotional content of a piece of music to the degree that he can experience it.

Ought we not always to be trying to expand our capacity for

---

[23] The answer is, of course, yes: and this explains why 'tests', in which the reactions of a random collection of individuals are classified and analysed, prove nothing. Sympathetic understanding is a pre-requisite: what would be the use of applying such a test to, say, one of Blake's prophetic books?

[24] Ibid., p. 40.

comprehending what the composer is trying to express, rather than accept the first 'stock response' of our emotions? One is not entirely at the mercy of one's superficial feelings; it is always possible to penetrate deeper. For example, my own (and others') experience of Mozart's major-key music has been: (1) in childhood, pretty music; (2) in adolescence, graceful and elegant, but trivial music; (3) in maturity, graceful and elegant music often shot through with deep and disturbing emotions. Here I would unhesitatingly maintain that in cases 1 and 2, we were not really understanding Mozart at all.

Let us now examine the second movement of Beethoven's Seventh Symphony. It is in the minor, has a heavy monotonous rhythm, and its theme opens with twelve repetitions of the same note, marking that rhythm; also, the movement has a 'trio' section in the major. It should hardly be necessary to point out that these are the emotive elements of the Funeral March. Consider Beethoven's own *Marcia Funebre* in the Piano Sonata in A flat, Op. 26, and that of Chopin in his Sonata in B flat minor. Consider also Schubert's later use of exactly the same rhythm (again to repeated notes) in his 'Death and the Maiden'. The two main differences between the *Allegretto* of the Seventh Symphony and the genuine funeral march is that the rhythm is not dotted, and the tempo is rather quicker. (Much depends on the conductor's tempo, of course; Beethoven is reported to have said he should have marked the movement *Andante*, which would bring it nearer to the real funeral march tempo.) The absolute individuality of the movement is that it is a rather lighter, more gentle type of funeral march: it is, in fact, a restrained elegy, rather than a heavy lament. But a 'scurrilous scherzo'? A 'subdued pastorale'? One is bound to regard anyone who reacts in this way as either superficial, unmusical, or unsympathetic to Beethoven. If anything is needed to clinch the argument, there is that forceful opening and closing minor chord, with the fifth uppermost—one of the most 'tragic' chords in music. Compare the *Marcia Funebre* in the Sonata in A flat, Op. 26, the 'Fate' motive in *The Ring*, the horn chord preceding Rudolph's outcry on Mimi's death, in *La Bohème*, and the opening of 'Sanctus fortis' in *The Dream of Gerontius*: different colours, different registers, different dynamics, different contexts, but the essentially painful connotation is obvious in them all.

This interpretation of the *Allegretto* cannot be dismissed as being out of keeping with the mood of the symphony, since the movement fulfils a musical and 'extra-musical' function similar to that of the Funeral March in the *Eroica*. Of course, no words can ever describe precisely the emotion of this movement, or any other. The emotion is, in Mendelssohn's words, 'too definite' to be transcribed into the ambiguous medium of words. However, the emotion is there, is real; and unless the listener recognizes, consciously or unconsciously, the relationship of the movement to the basic conception of the funeral march, his experience of the music will be false; and once this relationship is pointed out to one who is quite unaware of it, it can revolutionize his whole emotional response to the work, unless he sincerely cannot (or obstinately will not) feel the connection.

Of course, to a more subtle degree, a piece of music does not convey something different to each normally responsive listener. Here is how Aaron Copland puts it: 'Listen . . . to the forty-eight fugue themes of Bach's Well-Tempered Clavichord [sc. Clavier]. Listen to each theme, one after another. You will soon realize that each theme mirrors a different world of feeling. You will also soon realize that the more beautiful a theme seems to you the harder it is to find any word that will describe it to your complete satisfaction. Yes, you will certainly know whether it is a gay theme or a sad one. . . . Now study the sad one a little closer. Try to pin down the exact quality of its sadness. Is it pessimistically or resignedly sad; is it fatefully sad or smilingly sad? Let us suppose that you are fortunate and can describe to your own satisfaction in so many words the exact meaning of your chosen theme. There is still no guarantee that anyone else will be satisfied. Nor need they be. The important thing is that each one feel for himself the specific expressive quality of a theme, or, similarly, of an entire piece of music. And if it is a great work of art, don't expect it to mean exactly the same thing to you each time you return it to.'[25]

Indeed, the same applies in the more explicit field of literature: theidea that there are various layers of feeling and meaning in a poem, say, is a commonplace of literary criticism. Or again, listen to two actors of widely differing temperaments reciting the same poem: it will have quite a different emotional effect in each case. And are we not still arguing as to the precise emotional and intellectual significance of Goethe's *Faust* and Kafka's *The Trial*? Nevertheless, the broad general feeling, in both literature and music, gets over; and some, by intuitive sympathy, get nearer to it than others. *Faust* and Beethoven's Fifth Symphony are felt to be (using the broadest possible terms) 'optimistic', whereas Kafka's *The Trial* and Tchaikovsky's Sixth

[25] Aaron Copland, ibid., Chap. 2.

Symphony are felt to be 'pessimistic', and all four works have many facets to which all react differently, but in the same general way.

But anyone who conceives a quasi-funeral-march movement to be a 'kind of scurrilous scherzo' must be considered emotionally abnormal (or simply unmusical) to a degree.

One final difficulty remains. Is the traditional language of music, to which we have referred, a genuine emotional language, whose terms actually possess the inherent power to awaken certain definite emotions in the listener, or is it a collection of *formulae* attached by habit over a long period to certain verbally explicit emotions in masses, operas, and songs, which produce in the listener a series of conditioned reflexes?

It seems most likely that the answer is simply 'both'. It would be useless to deny that the continuous and consistent use of certain terms of musical language throughout five centuries or more must have conditioned us to accept them without question; and it must have helped to intensify their effect, pinpoint their character, and codify them clearly. But it is difficult to believe that there is no more to it than that. In the first place, one can only wonder how (to quote Hindemith) 'certain patterns of tone-setting' ever came in the first place to 'correspond with certain emotional reactions on the listener's part', unless the correspondences were inherent, as are, for example, those between certain faces that we pull and certain emotions we intend them to express—delight, scorn, or disgust. Again, it seems surprising that throughout five centuries or more all European composers without exception—some of them violently revolutionary in other respects—should have accepted the established connotations of the various terms without demur (see the music examples in Chapters 2 and 3), and that this has proved the only unchanging aspect of music. One might have expected a revolutionary composer to try and cut loose from these connotations—to insist on using, say, the major 1–3–5–6–5 of innocent joy to express some dark and evil emotion; but nothing of this kind has been attempted.[26] In fact, it is possible to discover, as Chapter 2 tries to show, close natural correspondences between the emotive effects of certain notes of the scale and their positions in the acoustic hierarchy known as

[26] Actually, with the advent of atonal and twelve-note music, we have at last witnessed a revolution which implies a total break with the past, a repudiation of even the old terms of musical language, and an attempt to recondition the listener to a new set. Whether it will be successful is not yet clear.

the harmonic series; it seems improbable that the 'strength' of the fifth and the 'joy' of the major third, for example, should not be inherent in their 'basic' positions in the series.

Ultimately, it is for the reader to make up his own mind; in the meantime, the foregoing may perhaps be taken as reasonable support for the view that music is a language of the emotions, and we may proceed to consider in more detail the analogy between music and literature.

The analogy between music and literature, then, is that both make use of a language of sounds for the purpose of expression. But the analogy is only valid on the plane of emotional expression, since abstract intellectual statements such as 'I think, therefore I am' are outside the scope of music, and the power to describe the outside world belongs to the analogy with painting in the case of both arts ('tone-painting' and 'word-painting').

The analogy can best be understood on the primitive level. The most feasible theory of the origin of language is that it began as inarticulate, purely emotional cries of pleasure and pain; and some of these utterances still survive in the two languages—speech and music—which have grown out of them. A groan of 'Ah!' uttered by a character in an opera on a two-note phrase of definite pitch is hardly different from a groan of 'Ah!' uttered by a character in a play at indefinite pitch; the effect is equally emotive in both cases. An example is the wailing of Mime in Scene 3 of *The Rhinegold*: transfer these notes to an instrument, as Wagner does, and one can say that here is a basic term in the emotional vocabulary of music, stemming from a basic term in the emotional vocabulary of speech. It is, in fact, our two-note figure mentioned earlier (flat sixth falling to fifth).[27]

Beyond such simple cases, however, the analogy becomes less close, though still close enough to be fruitful. In literature, the inarticulate cries of primitive man have become elaborated into words, i.e., sounds which possess associations with objects, ideas and feelings—clear, rationally intelligible, but arbitrary associations; whereas in music, they have become elaborated into notes, i.e. sounds which have clear but not rationally intelligible associations, rather inherent associations, with the basic emotions of mankind. Nevertheless, the diverse effects of

[27] See Ex. 62f.

these two different kinds of sounds have a close connection in that they both awaken in the hearer an emotional response; the difference is that a word awakens both an emotional response and a comprehension of its meaning, whereas a note, having no meaning, awakens only an emotional response.[28]

A note? A single note? Certainly. The capacity to react to an isolated musical sound is a testing-point for a listener's emotional apprehension of music. Hindemith's matter-of-fact indifference to music's mysterious emotive power is entirely explained when one reads his flat statement that music cannot exist in a single note: he is completely impervious to the sensual and emotional impact of music's basic material—a single sound of definite pitch. He says: 'The truth is that as single tones they are mere acoustical facts which do not evoke any genuine musical reaction. No musical effect can be obtained unless the tension between at least two different single tones has been perceived.'[29]

Of course, a piece of music cannot be made out of one note; but one note, like one word, can make an immediate artistic-emotional effect, before other notes or words follow. Let us take an example. Browning's poem *Pippa Passes* opens with a little mill-girl springing out of bed, crying 'Day!' This is the *first line* of the poem, and anyone reading it aloud would make a pause before continuing 'Faster and more fast . . . ' In the listener, aware of the situation through the initial stage-direction, the single word calls forth at once an intellectual understanding that dawn has broken, and an emotional response to the ecstatic joy that the young girl feels at her experience of this natural phenomenon. There is poetry here already if not yet a poem.

Now turn to a musical equivalent—Wagner's *Rienzi*. The audience is sitting in the theatre, and the overture beings. A solo trumpet plays the single note A—starting it quietly, holding it, swelling out to a *forte*, and dying away again into silence. This sound is at once beautiful, mysterious, and thrilling—the tone-colour of the trumpet evokes military and heroic associations, the length of the note gives a sense of solemnity, the coming and going of the volume gives a sense of something growing out of nothing and fading whence it came. Not being

[28] Actually, an unknown (foreign) word can awaken a purely emotional response: for example, hearing one foreigner abuse another by a single insulting word, one would react emotionally to the word without understanding its meaning. Here the purely emotional effect of language is isolated.
[29] Ibid., p. 68.

a word, the sound has no intellectual associations, but merely awakens the emotions of awe and wonder, and a subdued expectancy of heroic events to come. There is music here already, if not a piece of music. (The fact that, in this case, the piece of music, when it does come, flagrantly disappoints the expectations aroused by the magical opening need not disturb us here, even if it does in the theatre.)[30]

Hindemith's main point is, of course, correct. A piece of music is made up of aggregations of notes, just as a poem is made up of aggregations of words. And here the analogy with literature breaks down completely in one sense, since there is no connection between the intellectual-emotional organization of words into coherent statements by means of the logic of verbal syntax, and the intellectual-emotional organization of notes into coherent statements by means of the logic of musical syntax. Nevertheless, the analogy is still valid in another sense, for the overall emotional organization of a piece of music is often quite similar to that of a poem or a drama. This can be seen clearly in the case of a song or an opera. Everyone can hear how Schubert, by the use of different types of melody, different rhythms, and subtle tonal modulations, follows the emotional progression of the poem, in such a song as *Gretchen at the Spinning-Wheel*; and, *pace* Hindemith, the conflicting emotions of poem and music follow in swift succession—restless anxiety, joyous ecstasy, a cry of pleasurable pain, restless anxiety—yet the emotions of the one are as 'real' as those of the other. Again, Wagner's musical construction, in such a work as *The Ring*, goes hand in hand with his verbal-dramatic construction; in fact, as is well-known, they were in places conceived as one indissoluble musico-dramatic whole.

But what of 'pure' music—music without words? Not music of the purely 'architectural' type, but music which is clearly intended as the expression of the composer's emotion? A more detailed comparison of the *Eroica* Funeral March and the *Ode on the Death of the Duke of Wellington* will throw some light on this question.

The death of a hero arouses conflicting emotions in the artist who feels such an event deeply: grief at the plain fact of death; a feeling of

[30]Cf. Aaron Copland, *What to Listen For in Music*, Chap. 2: 'You may be sitting in a room reading this book. Imagine one note struck on the piano. Immediately that one note is enough to change the atmosphere of the room—proving that the sound element in music [a few lines earlier he calls it more explicitly 'the sensuous plane'] is a powerful and mysterious agent, which it would be foolish to deride or belittle.'

tender consolation in the thought that death brings peace; joy and triumph at the memory of the great things the hero has done; a fierce, determined courage inspired by his example. (It need hardly be said that, treating a theme like this, an artist feels himself to be the mouthpiece of national or universal emotions.)

Now Tennyson's Ode begins with three brief stanzas expressing a heavy, universalized grief for the hero's death. In a longer fourth stanza, he turns to 'remembering all his greatness in the past . . . great in council and great in war . . . that tower of strength which stood four-square to all the winds that blew'. In a fifth stanza of equal length, more tender feelings emerge: 'Under the cross of gold that shines over city and river, there shall he rest for ever among the wise and the bold'. The sixth and longest stanza is a proud and triumphant paean of praise of the hero's mighty deeds: 'with blare of bugle, clamour of men, roll of cannon and clash of arms'. The seventh and eighth stanzas bring the feeling of courageous determination: 'A people's voice! We are a people yet . . . not once or twice in our rough island-story, the path of duty was the way to glory'. The ninth and last stanza turns to a more serene grief: 'Peace, his triumph will be sung by some yet unmoulded tongue . . . speak no more of his renown, lay your earthly fancies down, and in the vast cathedral leave him. God accept him, Christ receive him.'

This is necessarily a broad general outline of the poem: Tennyson weaves these conflicting emotions in and out of one another in the kaleidoscopic way which words permit. Take for example, the lines:

O peace, it is a day of pain
For one, upon whose hand and heart and brain
Once the weight and fate of Europe hung.
Ours the pain, be his the gain!

It can be seen that three 'real' feelings—grief, admiration, and a sense of triumph—here succeed one another with extreme rapidity; yet there is no sense of what Hindemith, speaking of the way emotions follow one another in music, calls 'their delirious, almost insane manner of appearance'.

Nor is there anything insane in the way in which Beethoven's similar emotions (devoid of any intellectual associations, any 'meaning') succeed one another in the *Eroica* Funeral March. As with Tennyson, the opening section (the Funeral March proper) presents the feeling of heavy, universalized grief, though taking in the tenderer, consoling emotion in the passage in E flat major, and in the momentary appearance of the chord of D flat major, which is immediately contradicted (cf. 'Peace, it is a day of pain'). The second section (the C major trio) moves from joy to triumph, backwards and forwards, and breaks off, for the third section (the re-statement of the first section) to resume the feeling of grief. Here, however, after the first few bars, the mighty fugal passage begins, inverting the E flat 'consolation' theme, and putting it into the minor: this whole section presents the feelings of fierce determination—moving to an inspiriting courage (horns in E flat) and back again, picking up the grievous feeling once more in the resumption of the funeral march proper. After a sudden switch to the tenderer feelings (strings in D flat), the movement ends in hushed grief, with broken references to the opening theme.

Words are poor things, except in the hands of a poet. The emotional adjectives I have used above are only feeble labels to indicate the general feeling of the music. To return to Mendelssohn, words are 'so ambiguous, so vague'; in every attempt to express the emotions of the music in words 'something is right, but something is unsatisfying'. No one, least of all myself, would want to attach verbal labels to the deep feelings aroused during a performance of the *Eroica* Symphony. Nor would I be misunderstood concerning my comparison with Tennyson's Ode: the last thing I would think of when listening to Beethoven's Funeral March is this poem, which obviously expresses the same basic emotions, but through the agency of another man of another race with another attitude towards life, and through another artistic medium. Each says what it has to say in its own way, and there is no such thing as translation or equivalence. My only reason for a comparative verbal analysis of the two works is to endeavour to indicate that music functions very much like poetry in making a coherent and unified statement out of conflicting emotions. Nor am I concerned with the rights and wrongs of Beethoven's and Tennyson's conceptions of a hero, or with comparing the artistic value of the two works: I only chose the instances because of Hindemith's particular reference to 'an extremely funereal piece'.

We have another difficulty to meet here. It is usually objected, when one offers an analysis of the emotions expressed in a musical work, that music has a logic and constructive method of its own, that it ultimately has to stand or fall as a piece of music. With this no one would disagree, and one would hardly bother to make an emotional analysis of a work which one did not already know to be technically excellent. Actually, there is no conflict of ideas here at all. Any artist has to weave the emotions he is expressing into an intellectually and emotionally coherent statement; and emotions woven together in this artistically formal way do not cease to be emotions because they do not float about vaguely as in everyday life; in fact, they become even more 'real' by their isolation and sensitive combination in a great work of art. The great artist makes a supremely 'right' statement of the emotions one feels oneself but cannot organize into a satisfying expression.

Music is no more incapable of being emotionally intelligible because it is bound by the laws of musical construction, than poetry is because it is bound by the laws of verbal grammatical construction. In fact, in both cases, it should be a truism to say that the construction of a work of art is guided both by the feelings and the intellect: the intellect brings craftsmanship to bear on realizing the overall shape which is *felt* before it is intellectually apprehended. Let us turn to the *Eroica* Funeral March once more. We have seen how the C minor tonality and the slow march-rhythm must have crystallized unconsciously in Beethoven as the main theme. Equally unconsciously, the tenderer feelings for the dead hero would give rise to a complex of notes in E flat (the natural key for the end of a first strain beginning in C minor); the feeling of joy would naturally find outlet in brighter complexes of notes in C major (the natural key for the Trio section); and the feelings of triumph in the G major and C major complexes of the trio—the central point, farthest away from the mournful opening and ending. The conscious craftsman in Beethoven would see to it that these unconscious compulsions were realized to the full.

A single example will suffice to show that the laws of musical construction aid rather than impede emotional expression, exactly in the same way as the laws of poetical construction. Both a funeral march and an ode on a dead hero, by the logic of human feeling, will normally move from grief to triumph and back. In Beethoven's case, as we have seen, the triumph was bound by the laws of musical logic to be the G major and C major climaxes, with trumpets and drums, in his C major trio—the central point of the movement; and the result is supremely right and satisfying, formally and emotionally. In Tennyson's case, the laws of language demanded a climax word to form his central point— and the finest word one can use to praise a dead hero in the English language is 'honour'. In the centre of Tennyson's Ode, the following lines appear twice on separate occasions, at a distance roughly proportionate to that between Beethoven's G major and C major climaxes, in so far as such a thing can be measured:

With honour, honour, honour, honour to him,
Eternal honour to his name.

I am not trying to say that these things could not have happened differently—in Chopin's Funeral March the brief moment of triumph is in the first section, in the relative major, and the consolation entirely in the trio, also in the relative major: I am only intent on demonstrating how a musician and a poet have obeyed the laws of their respective arts in a certain natural way, and in each case achieved a tremendous *formal* and *emotional* impact, *which are one and the same thing.*

In this way, one can explain how those who have a feeling for music but no technical knowledge can justifiably be said to 'understand' a piece of music—the form is apprehended as an emotional shape, as it must have originally been conceived by the composer. And one should not need to justify this approach to music (though the present *Zeitgeist* is utterly against it): music can hold up its head as the supreme expression of universal emotions by the great composers, and also be interesting from the point of view of craftsmanship to the technically-minded, in the way that a poem, emotionally absorbed by many readers, may be dissected by a student of poetic technique.

But still, it will be objected, we have not proved any inherent connection between the notes and the emotions they are supposed to express. That is, of course, the task of the rest of the book. At this point, we may sum up the foregoing, before proceeding to our examination of the way in which music functions as a language of the emotions.

The argument of this first part may be stated in brief as follows. Music naturally has its own technical laws, concerned with the organization of notes into coherent forms, but considered as expression, it has three separate aspects, related to the arts of architecture, painting, and literature. (1) The purely 'architectural' aspect is found in a limited number of contrapuntal works built out of material which is not emotionally expressive; though this 'inexpressiveness' is relative, scarcely ever absolute. The appeal of this kind of music is largely to the aesthetic appreciation of the beauty of pure form. (2) The purely 'pictorial' aspect of music is found in a limited number of works, and passages in works, which imitate external objects belonging to the

210

natural world; and it is more valuable when the imitation is so approximate as to leave the composer considerable latitude to choose his own notes to embody his subjective experience of the object imitated. The appeal of this kind of music is through the aural imagination to the visual imagination and thence to the emotions. (3) The 'literary' aspect of music is to be found, to a greater or less extent, in most Western music written betwen 1400 and the present day, since music is, properly speaking, a language of the emotions, akin to speech. The appeal of this music is directly to the emotions and, to be fully appreciated, should be responded to in this way.

The widespread view of music as 'purely music' limits the listener's understanding of the great masterpieces to their purely aural beauty— i.e. to their surface attraction—and to their purely technical construction. This latter is no more (and no less) than the magnificent craftsmanship whereby composers express their emotions coherently: it is forever unintelligible to the layman, except emotionally, and ultimately inexplicable to almost anyone but a potential composer. Music is, in fact, 'extra-musical' in the sense that poetry is 'extra-verbal', since notes, like words, have emotional connotations; it is, let us repeat, the supreme expression of universal emotions, in an entirely personal way, by the great composers.

2

The Elements of Musical Expression

The task facing us is to discover exactly how music functions as a language, to establish the terms of its vocabulary, and to explain how these terms may legitimately be said to express the emotions they appear to.

Beginning with the basic material—notes of definite pitch—we must agree with Hindemith that musical works are built out of the *tensions* between such notes. These tensions can be set up in three dimensions— *ptich*, *time*, and *volume*; and the setting up of such tensions, and the colouring of them by the *characterizing agents* of *tone-colour* and *texture*, constitute the whole apparatus of musical expression.

Let us now distinguish between the various ways in which these dimensions can function, beginning with that of *pitch*. Pitch-tensions can be regarded in two different ways—as *tonal tensions* (what the actual notes of the scale are) and as *intervallic tensions* (in what direction and at what distance the notes are from one another). Three examples will make this clear.

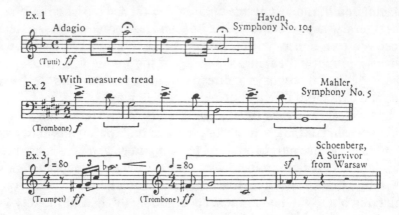

To explain, by using figures to indicate notes of the scale. In Ex. 1, the single tonal tension between 1 and 5 in the key of D is presented as two different intervallic tensions working in opposite directions—rising fifth and falling fourth. In Ex. 2, the single tonal tension between 5 and 1 in G sharp is presented as two different intervallic tensions working in the same direction—falling fifth and falling twelfth. In Ex. 3, the single series of tonal tensions between sharp 4, 5, 1, and flat 6, in the key of C, is presented as two different series of intervallic tensions; (a) rising semitone, rising fourth, rising minor sixth; and (b) rising semitone, falling fifth, rising minor sixth. In each example, there is clearly a similarity of expressive quality due to identical tonal tensions, and a difference of expressive quality due to diverse intervallic tensions. In Ex. 1, the 'launching-off' character of 1–5 is seen in its assertive (rising) and oppressive (falling) aspects. In Ex. 2, the conclusive, clinching power of 5–1 is seen in its oppressive (falling) aspect, but the effect is much emphasized in the second case by adding an octave to its fall. In Ex. 3, the painful effect of sharp–4–5–1–flat–6 is at its most acute when the series of notes is stretched out in ascending order to cover a range of over an octave (we may ignore the rhythmic difference between the two phrases for the moment).

These two kinds of tension, which are the only possible expressive functions of the dimension of pitch, have been disentangled from one another here for the purpose of analysis, but they are in reality always indissolubly united into a single expressive whole. Thus, in Ex. 1, we do not really have 1–5 presented as two different intervals, or two different intervals which are 1–5, so much as (a) 1–5-as-rising-fifth; and (b) 1–5-as-falling-fourth; and each is a single entity in itself.

It should also be mentioned that these two kinds of tension can of course occur not only between notes played successively (melodically) but between notes played simultaneously (harmonically).

The dimension of time functions in a greater variety of ways, as perhaps might be expected.

First of all, music can exist without setting up any strong time-tension at all. Plainsong, for example, uses time not as a dimension in which to set up tension, but as a continuum in which to flow freely. Such fluid, unmeasured rhythm is, properly speaking, outside the scope of this investigation, since we are concerned with the measured music of the harmonic period. However, we may mention the familiar fact that it is just this lack of a measured rhythm which removes plainsong from the human categories of time into those of 'other-worldliness', and gives it its spiritual quality. And occasionally, unmeasured rhythm has been brought back into more recent music, to free it from all trace of purely human expression (Holst's 'other-worldly' *Hymn of Jesus*, for example, and the 'elemental' *melismata* in some of Vaughan William's nature-music). Also, even in music with a measured rhythm, the regular beat can be obliterated by various means— a very slow tempo, syncopation, rubato, etc.— until 'timelessness' is come again (e.g., the opening of Wagner's *Parsifal* or the end of Mahler's *Song of the Earth*).

Turning to measured time, time-tensions are made possible by setting clear fixed points to measure them by; and these points are fixed by having a succession of 'beats', real or implied, spaced out at regular intervals of time, and by making one out of every so many 'strong' by accenting it—drawing on the tension available in the volume-dimension (that of making one note louder than others) to do so. Thus is produced the first expressive function of measured time—*rhythmic accent*—by which one note can be made more important than another. There is of course a sub-category here—that of *syncopation*: the accent is removed from a strong to a weak beat (by means of making the note on the weak beat louder than the note on the strong beat) and the unexpectedness of this procedure gives the note concerned a greater importance than the normally accented note.

213

The regular tensions set up by accent are of two kinds—that between one strong and one weak beat (*duple rhythm*) and one strong and two weak beats (*triple rhythm*). Out of these two basic rhythms all the different 'times' of music are derived: four-four is two twos, six-eight two threes, five-four a two and a three, etc., etc. It is obvious that these two basic kinds of rhythmic tension, and their various combinations and permutations, will all function differently from the expressive point of view, and their effects as part of musical language will have to be analysed.

The only other kind of time-tension besides that of accent is *duration*—notes may be longer or shorter than one another. This tension functions in three ways: as *tempo* (slow-fast), *movement* (even-jerky), and *phrasing* (*staccato-legato*).

The fundamental one is of course *tempo*. It may seem strange to define it as a function of duration, but it is obvious that a slow tempo is created out of beats of long duration, a quick tempo out of beats of short duration. We say of anyone who moves slowly that he 'takes his time'; and when the beats take their time, the tempo is slow. The effect of tempo on the musical expression is obviously of great importance, and will need analysing.

Movement is also extremely important. There is clearly a great expressive difference between an even stream of notes of equal length and a jerky, agitated succession of notes alternately long and short (dotted rhythms).

Phrasing in general is quite as much a product of volume-tensions as of time-tensions; but the *staccato-legato* antithesis belongs mainly to the time-dimension, being a matter of the actual length of a note compared with its rhythmic length. For example, a note that rhythmically lasts the whole of a four-four bar may in fact only be sounding for the first quarter or the first eighth, or it may be sustained right up to the end of the bar. Again, this will make a considerable difference to the expression.

Having begun this section on time by referring to the unmeasured rhythm of the earliest period of our musical history, we may end it by mentioning the highly irregular and broken-up rhythm of much modern music; for just as there is an antithesis between measured and unmeasured rhythm, so there is between regular rhythm (dealt with so far) and irregular. Irregular rhythm is at the opposite pole from unmeasured: it is meticulously measured down to the last fraction of a beat, so as to assure the maximum irregularity, expressing that modern affliction, a high state of nervous tension.

The remaining apparatus of musical expression need not detain us for the moment. As we have already said, *volume* is simply the dimension in which one note can be louder or softer than another; and *tone-colour* and *texture* are characterizing agents, which modify, by 'colour', the tensions set up in the dimensions of pitch, time, and volume.

We are now faced with the problem of disentangling the multifarious interactions of all these elements one upon another. If we are to bring order out of chaos, we must discover which of them is the fundamental one, on which the others merely act (however powerfully) as qualifying influences. Tone-colour and texture we have already admitted to be mere characterizing agents, and volume clearly cannot be regarded as fundamental in any sense (there has first to be a note, before one can consider it is loud or soft). This leaves us with pitch and time: which is fundamental?

Both, one might say. Melody can exist without rhythm (in plainsong), and rhythm without melody (African drum music). But the latter lies outside our experience, whereas plainsong does not; so it is reasonable to assume that, in *our* music, pitch is the fundamental element.

And, ultimately, the fundamental element of the pitch is *tonal tension*, in so far as it can be separated from intervallic tension: for example, '5–1' does mean something vital and all-important apart from its incarnation as a rising fourth or falling fifth; whereas 'a falling fifth' does not mean anything very concrete unless we know whether the tonal tension is, say, 8–4, 7–3, or 5–1. *What the actual notes of the scale are*—this is the basis of the expressive language of music: the subtle and intricate system of relationships which we know as tonality. In this system we shall find the basic terms of music's vocabulary, each of which can be modified in countless ways by intervallic tensions, time-tensions, and volume-tensions, and characterized by tone-colour and texture.

The bed-rock nature of tonal tensions can be seen in this way. A group of four adjacent descending notes, played slowly and quietly, *legato*, to the rhythm 1–2–3–1 in triple time, is a description that means precisely nothing, unless we know exactly what notes they are:

215

But once we make clear the tonal tensions between the notes, by putting, say, a treble or bass clef in front of them, all becomes clear. A treble clef gives 8–7–6–5 in the major scale—and the opening of Dowland's 'Awake, sweet love'; a bass clef gives 8–7–6–5 in the minor scale—and the opening of Bach's 'Come, sweet death' (slightly ornamented):

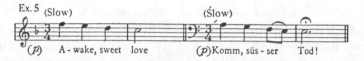

Of course, the qualifying agents do have a kind of general expressive quality of their own. In both phrases in Ex. 5, the slow tempo, the quiet dynamic level, the legato phrasing, and the even rhythm, do combine to produce a general effect of quiet acceptance; but the particular expressive effect in each case is entirely individual, there being all the difference in the world between falling from 8 to 5 via semitone-tone-tone and doing the same thing via tone-tone-semitone.

On the other hand, let us admit that the basic terms of the tonal language have no more than a general significance until brought to life by the action of the qualifying agents. Take, for example, the term 8–7–6–5 in the major scale: its latent power to express a mood of fulfilment can be brought out in quite different ways according to the way in which it is brought to life by the qualifying agents:

The three phrases, from the aforementioned Dowland song, Handel's *Messiah*, and Mahler's First Symphony, are all the same basic term in the system of tonal tensions, and all have the same basic sense of fulfilment, but the qualifying agents make each quite different in its specific effect. In fact, as can be seen, the qualifying agents are really *vitalizing* agents, for they give the basic emotional connotation of any given set of tonal tensions a vivid and entirely individual life of its own.

216

To disentangle and isolate the expressive powers of all the various elements of musical language, it will be necessary to deal with them in the following order. (1) Tonal tensions, because, as we have said, they convey the basic emotional moods, which are brought to life in various ways by the vitalizing agents of pitch, time, and volume. (2) Volume, since this is the simplest of the vitalizing agents in its functioning, working largely independently of time and pitch-as-direction. (3) Time, since this, although much more complex in its working, still functions largely independently of pitch-as-direction. (4) Pitch-as-direction, left till last because its expressive powers very much depend on tonal tensions, volume, and time.

We turn first, then, to an examination of the emotive powers inherent in the various tonal tensions.

The Tonal Tensions

This section brings us to the heart of the problem of musical language, the persistent neglect to tackle which is responsible for the meaninglessness of most attempts to elucidate the 'emotional content' of music, and also for the widespread belief that any such attempts are futile, music being emotionally ambiguous. The simple but amazing fact is that, although certain general directional movements of pitch have occasionally been analysed as 'symbols' (Schweitzer on Bach, for example), no one has evern tried to analyse the expressive qualities inherent in the tonal relationships between the different notes of the scale. No one has seriously got down to the business of discovering, in each particular context, *exactly what the notes of the scale are and what tensions exist between them.*

The expressive basis of the musical language of Western Europe consists of the intricate system of tensional relationships between notes which we call the tonal system: in a given context, it is essential to know whether the important note is, say, the major or minor sixth of the scale. And whence does this system derive? Simply from the vertical structure of music peculiar to Western Europe which we call harmony: there are, of course, 'major' and 'minor' thirds and sixths outside the orbit of Western European harmony, but our investigation is confined to the 'harmonic' period of musical history. And whence does this harmony derive? From the natural phenomenon which we call the harmonic series.

As is well-known, when a note is sounded by vibrating a string, not only does the whole string vibrate, producing the fundamental note which is all that the untrained ear can hear, but the two halves of the string vibrate in their own right at the same time; and so do the thirds, the quarters, the fifths, and so on, producing the rising succession of notes called the harmonic series. Taking the note C below the bass clef as fundamental, the first twenty-four notes of the series are as follows:

(The starred notes are 'out of tune' to our ears.) The fractions of the strings which produce the different notes are obtained by putting a figure 1 over each of the numbers in Ex. 7: note 2 is produced by ½ the string, note 3 by ⅓, etc., etc. A practical demonstration of this natural phenomenon can be made by depressing the damper pedal of a good piano, striking the low C and listening hard; there should be no difficulty in hearing notes 2, 3, 4, and 5—the strings of these notes are set faintly vibrating in sympathy with the halves, thirds, quarters, and fifths of the low C string.

This means that in nature itself, a single note sets up a harmony of its own; and this harmonic series has been the (unconscious) basis of Western European harmony, and the tonal system.

The reader should here be warned that this statement, which was for long regarded as a truism, is being severely challenged by modern theorists, especially those of the twelve-note school. The reason is as follows. Twelve-note music has broken away from the tonal system, producing harmony of acutely dissonant effect; conservative opponents of this music declare that it goes against the 'natural laws of harmony'; twelve-note theorists have retaliated by maintaining the derivation of the tonal system from the harmonic series to be pure illusion, much being made of the practical inaudibility of the harmonic series. The argument is still going on, and the truth will not be found in a hurry. One feels that both sides are misguided, since it is possible for a music based on the harmonic series to give way eventually to a music not based on that series, if that new music can establish its right to exist by achieving new kinds of beauty and significance. Some of man's greatest achievements have been made by going against natural laws; flying, for example, flouts the law of gravity—though only by enlisting the aid of other natural laws. Perhaps twelve-note music will eventually justify its 'naturalness' by discovering another 'natural law' of music on which it is unconsciously based. In the meantime, let us be content to say that it is most unlikely that the close correspondences between the natural harmonic system and the tonal system can be pure coincidence.

These correspondences are as follows. The earliest harmony we know of, that of the Greeks, used only note 2 of the series; i.e. their 'harmony' moved entirely in parallel octaves. This happens naturally, of course, when male and female voices sing the same tune; and the feeling is that they are singing the 'same' notes. Thus is established the naturalness of the octave, which is felt to be the same note as the fundamental, but at a higher pitch; this interval is the span of all the scales of Western music—the modes, the major and minor scales alike.

The earliest recorded attempts at harmony in Western Europe, in the ninth century, at first added only note 3 of the series: *organum*, as this type of harmony was called, moved in parallel fifths and fourths. This too can happen naturally: although most people can hear that note 3 of the series is a 'different' note, unlike note 2 which is 'the same', some people, singing or whistling a tune with others, quite naturally pitch it a fifth above or a fourth below, in blissful ignorance that they are not producing the same notes as the rest. It may well be that the fifth arose in this way, on the 'same note' principle of the octave; but once recognized and exploited as a different note, it opened up the way for harmony. So is established the naturalness of the fifth note of the scale, and the interval of the fifth, which spans the 'halves' of all our scales.

By about the twelfth century, the next different note began to establish its right to a place in harmony—note 5, our major third—and so was established the triad, which was to become the basis of Western European harmony:

Another close correspondence is that notes 8 to 16 in Ex. 7 give us our major scale, with the addition of one extraneous note—note 14, B flat, the *minor* seventh. And in this note is to be found one of the closest and most complex correspondences of all. As will be seen, this is its second appearance in the series; it first occurs an octave lower, as note

219

7, in which capacity it is the next different note after the triad-forming note 5. This B flat may be legitimately described as the parent of the system of key-relationships we call tonality. It works in this way: turning to our scale of C, we can build up, as the composers of *organum* did, seven parallel fifths:

Ex. 9

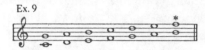

The first six of these seven sounds are all 'firm' and 'stable', the tension between the two notes being the same in each case (the tension between notes 2 and 3 of the harmonic series, which we call the 'perfect fifth'); but the seventh sound is 'unstable', the fifth being imperfect, and not corresponding to any of the simple tensions of the harmonic series. This interval, the diminished fifth, was proscribed by medieval theorists as *diabolus in musica* (the devil in music) because of its 'flawed' sound. And when it was sung, the B was flattened (the procedure was called *musica ficta*) so as to obtain once more the firm sound of the perfect fifth:

Ex. 10

There is clearly a direct connection between this procedure and the fact that the B natural of the harmonic series (note 15) is outbalanced by the B flat (notes 7 and 14, and especially note 7, which can be picked up by a trained ear).

It was, of course, always possible to solve the diminished fifth problem in the opposite way—by sharpening the F:

Ex. 11

Now this too corresponds with a peculiarity of the harmonic series. Note 11 is not really F at all, but between F and F sharp, and slightly nearer to F sharp. This note occurs an octave higher (as note 22), together with a nearly-true F (note 21) and a nearly-true F sharp (note 23); behaving, in fact, rather like the 'out-of-tune' B flat (note 7) which appears an octave higher (note 14), together with a B natural (note 15).

Obviously, the incompatibility of B and F as a harmonic interval derives from the ambiguity surrounding the B flat, B natural, F, and F sharp of the harmonic series; in other words, the 'flaw' in our harmonic system is a result of the 'flaw' in the harmonic series.[31]

Now the medieval composers' treatment of these two ambiguous notes B and F had surprising consequences. Their B flat became the first 'accidental' in Western European music: it turned the Lydian mode (F to F on the white notes of the piano) into our scale of F major, and the Dorian mode (D to D on the white notes) into our scale of D minor. Their F sharp likewise turned the Mixolydian mode (white-note scale G to G) into our G major scale, and the Phrygian mode (white-note scale E to E) into our E minor Scale. Thus, since the white-note scales on C (Ionian mode) and A (Aeolian mode) were already our C major and A minor scales, all the modes eventually became major and minor scales (except for the Locrian—the white-note scale on the fatal note B—which was never used anyway); and so arose our key-system.

Clearly, this system is the product of Western Europe's individual reaction to the 'flaw' in the natural harmonic series: the key-system 'corrects' it.[32] This is further confirmed by the fact that the system of key-relationships is also fundamentally based on the behaviour of the notes B, B flat, F, and F sharp. In C, the flattening of the B takes us into the key of F, as we have said, and we have to make it natural again to return to C:

Ex. 12

Likewise, the sharpening of the F takes us into the key of G, and we have to make it natural again to return to C:

---

[31]This flaw also manifests itself in the fact that to tune a keyboard instrument in pure fifths puts some notes of the chromatic scale badly out of tune to our ears, an 'error' corrected by equal temperament. Looking at it another way, to tune by perfect fifths round the whole cycle of twelve brings us back not to our original note, but to one slightly sharp of it. Expressing it mathematically, we may say that whereas musically we want the equation $\frac{(3/2)^{12}}{128} = 1$, the correct mathematical equation is: $\frac{(3/2)^{12}}{128} = 1.014$.

[32]This musical 'correction' of nature is at one with the overall domination of nature by Western European man since the Renaissance.

Ex. 13

It can be seen that Ex. 13 is the same process as Ex. 12, working the opposite way, a fifth higher. Now the relationship of the keys of F (subdominant) and G (dominant) to the key of C (tonic), is the whole basis of the tonal system of Haydn, Mozart, and Beethoven. And the very behaviour of the notes derives from the harmonic series: note 7 is slightly flat of our B flat, so there is a tension pulling B flat downwards, whereas its offshoot of B natural (note 15) pulls upwards (see Ex. 12); and note 11 is nearer to F sharp than F, hence the tension pulling F sharp upwards, whereas its offshoot of F (note 21) pulls downwards (see Ex. 13). Again, the well-known fact that it is 'easy' to 'fall' into the subdominant, and requires 'effort' to 'rise' into the dominant must be due to the fact that note 7 ('B flat') is a lower, more primary, and more audible note in the harmonic series than note 11 ('F half-sharp'). As Tovey pointed out, if a composer begins by hammering out the note C, you grow more and more certain that it will prove to be, not the key-note of C, but the dominant of F: the 'B flat' of the harmonic series must be responsible.

So, of the twelve notes we use, we have derived from the harmonic series nine: the seven notes of the C major scale, plus a B flat and an F sharp. What of the others? Returning to the harmonic series (Ex. 7), note 13, the note A, is also out of tune, being between A and A flat. If we resolve its ambiguity by treating it as A, it becomes our major sixth; if we treat it as A flat, it becomes our minor sixth. Coupled with the B flat and the B natural (notes 14 and 15), we get the upper part of our melodic minor scale, in its ascending and descending versions, a source of much expressive power in the music of the Elizabethan composers:

Ex. 14

Going up in sequence, the notes were usually natural, coming down usually flat.

Two notes remain unaccounted for—the minor third (E flat) and the minor second (D flat). Neither of these is a 'natural' note: the minor scale does not really belong to either of our two modern scales, but is a survival from the Phrygian mode; and the minor third is a special case, a 'false' harmonic third, to be dealt with later. Both can be derived from the old scales, however: the scale was originally divided into two groups of four notes, called tetrachords, a fifth apart; and by transposing Ex. 14 down a fifth, we get:

Ex. 15

So, although neither E flat nor D flat can be derived from notes 8 to 16 of the harmonic series, we can say that they are justified by analogy. And so we account for the twelve notes of the chromatic scale:

Ex. 16

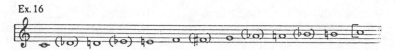

This scale is, of course, to be found in the higher reaches of the harmonic series (between notes 16 and 32, together with other, 'out of tune' notes); but the fact that, as we have seen, certain notes occur much earlier, nearer to audible range, explains their 'basic' quality, and the tensions by which they attract the 'subsidiary' notes to 'resolve' on to them.

Now the tensions between these notes are as follows. C is fixed, the fundamental note, known as the *tonic*. So is G (note 3 in the harmonic series), the fifth note in the scale, known as the *dominant*; though there is a tension pulling it back to C. So is E (note 5 in the harmonic series), the *major third* of the scale; though again there is a tension pulling it back to C. The other notes have tensions pulling them back to these three: D flat and D (the *minor* and *major seconds*) are pulled towards C; F (the *fourth*) is pulled towards E; F sharp (the *sharp fourth*) and A flat and A (the *minor* and *major sixths*) are pulled towards G; B flat (the *minor seventh*) is pulled down to A and thence down to G; B natural (the *major seventh*) is pulled towards the upper C. The note E flat (the *minor third*) is an unusual case: it has a tension pulling it towards E, which was respected for centuries, but it was eventually regarded as fixed, in a way that will be explained when we consider its expressive quality. There is, of course, a tension pulling every note back to the fundamental, C.

We have decided to confine our investigation of the expressive language of music to the Western European 'harmonic' period; and we

223

must now determine the limits of that period. It is easy to fix the latter date, which is, at the time of writing, *now*, since composers such as Britten are still using tonal harmony to good effect, and so of course are the best writers of popular music. If, in the meantime, the twelve-note school and others are devising and using new systems, these have not yet ousted tonality from our everyday experience.

The earlier date is more difficult to settle on. It is generally fixed at about 1600, when the 'figured bass' began to appear: before that, we are often told, composers wrote entirely contrapuntally, deploying their horizontal lines without thinking of the harmonic aspect of the result. Much nonsense has been talked on this subject. For example, the opening of Palestrina's *Stabat Mater* was once described as being actually a piece of pure counterpoint; despite its chordal aspect, it was declared to be a concatenation of horizontal lines:

Ex. 17   Palestrina, c. 1590

Sta - bat   ma - ter do - lo - ro - sa

This opinion will not hold water. What a strange coincidence that Palestrina's flowing lines happened to form by accident a series of chords with a 'key-centre' of D minor! Obviously, the best way of describing the passage is to say that the contrapuntal lines are woven into a harmonic framework. Yet *were* all the lines conceived purely melodically? A definite 'no' is given to this question by the lowest part: whereas the other three move in more or less conjunct motion, as melodies, the lower part functions in the second bar as a harmonic bass, with the same kind of 'unmelodic' rising and falling fifths, creating the roots of triads, that we find in the high harmonic period, say in Mozart's *Marriage of Figaro*:

Ex. 18   Mozart, 1786 (reduced)

Cor - riam tut - ti a fest - eg - giar!

The Palestrina example, and the thousands of others to be found in sixteenth-century music, might be dismissed as mere 'foreshadowings' of the harmonic period, but further examples will take us back across the centuries:

224

Ex. 19, the opening of a motet published in 1503, is clearly 'in F major', and its bass is conceived harmonically as a series of triad-roots. The same may be said of Ex. 20, a 'D minor' passage from a motet written by Dufay to celebrate the signing of a treaty between Pope Eugenius and the Emperor Sigismundus in 1433. Ex. 21, from a Worcester manuscript dating from about 1300, is rather different: clearly 'in F major', it is an example of what is known as 'English descant'—a harmonization of a melody largely as a progression of 'six-three' chords, variety being obtained by moving the bass up and down in fifths or fourths to produce an occasional root-position triad.

The above examples prove conclusively that our harmonic tonal system dates back much further than is generally admitted; its seeds are to be found in the thirteenth century. There is no intention here of denying that much great medieval music, by Pérotin (d. 1235), Machaut (1300–77), and others, was conceived entirely contrapuntally, with vertical clashes between the parts which arose purely out of the horizontal movements of those parts, and which had no harmonic intention at all. What *is* claimed, is that such composers will worked loosely within an implied harmonic and tonal framework, and that this framework was already *implicit* when the first medieval composers, in the ninth century or earlier, literally began to put two notes together as harmony, and immediately encountered the problem of the incompatibility of B and F as a harmonic interval. When they first 'corrected' this 'flaw' with a B flat, or an F sharp, all the modes were destined to become our major and minor keys by the addition of more and more accidentals: the principle of *musica ficta* had already produced B flat, F sharp, E flat, C sharp, and G sharp, *by about 1325*. So we may fix the limits of the harmonic period, not between 1600 and 1900, as is generally done, but between a vague date somewhere in the twelfth or thirteenth century, and a hypothetical date in the twenty-first century, when composers abandon the harmonic conception and the tonal system altogether.

The reasons why theorists have always set the limits at 1600 and 1900 are easy to understand. Before 1600, counterpoint tended to be more independent of the harmonic framework than afterwards, and composers fought hard to preserve the 'white-note' modes against the erosion of *musica ficta*; after 1900, the tonal system seemed to have 'broken down' because some outstanding composers abandoned it altogether for atonal, linear counterpoint. Nevertheless, the harmonic framework was always conditioning early contrapuntal writing, and the tonal system was unavoidable even in modal compositions; and in the twentieth century, the system has still been used to produce fine and original music.

For the practical purposes of our analysis of musical language, owing to the unavailability, unfamiliarity, and occasional unintelligibility of some early music, and to the non-existence of the music of the future, let us take the harmonic period as being roughly between 1400 and the present day; between say:

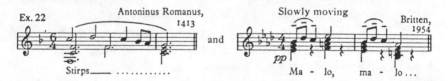

And let us admit that music of the harmonic-tonal kind (in its widest sense, including contrapuntal and modal music), written during these five-hundred-and-fifty years, constitutes nearly the whole of Western Europe's great musical achievement, and is what has most satisfied Western European humanity at large. But let us not deny the possibility that a new kind of music, based on an entirely new system, may arise (may have arisen, indeed), and may achieve equally great things.

[. . .]

226

3

Some Basic Terms of Musical Vocabulary

So far, the attempt to analyse the functioning of musical language has necessitated that most dubious procedure, the breaking down of an indivisible unity into its component parts, which have no genuine separate existence. There are, strictly speaking, no such things as 'the major third', 'quick tempo', 'loud volume', etc., considered apart from the innumerable contexts in which they occur. Every piece of music is a whole, in which the effects of the various well-worn elements interpenetrate and condition one another from note to note, from bar to bar, from movement to movement, in an entirely novel way; in every context, each single element has newly merged its identity into a new overall expression.

Our justification is that this method is the only possible one, and that we are now going to try and put the parts together again with a better idea how they are likely to interfuse with one another for expressive purposes. The first step must be the examination of small-scale examples of the total functioning of musical language—combinations of two or more notes into those short phrases which are the basic terms of musical vocabulary. Once again, though, various uses of these terms will have to be separated from their contexts, and examples will have to be gathered from different periods and different composers, to establish the emotive significance of each term. In fact, as we shall now be dealing, not with single notes, but with melodic patterns, we shall be playing, a little more seriously than usual, the game known as 'twisted tunes'.

This piece of foolery, which crops up from time to time in professional musical circles, has afforded a good deal of harmless amusement in its time, as a radio feature, a parlour game, and a stand-by for anyone planning a musical quiz. It goes like this: having discovered a case of two composers utilizing the same bit of tune, one intrigues people by demonstrating the fact, or by trying to confuse them as to which is which. And there the matter usually ends: few try to puzzle out why such resemblances should be. Why, for exampled, the supreme moments of tragic anguish in Wagner's *Parsifal* and Verdi's *Otello* both found expression in the same triadic phrase—1–3–5–6–5 in the minor system; especially since Verdi was unacquainted with

Parsifal, Wagner died before *Otello* was written, and the two composers'
aims, styles, and methods were utterly different.

From the expressive point of view, of course, the phrase is superbly
right in both cases—a rising minor progression, as we have said,
expresses and outward-going feeling of pain, and our phrases take in
both the tragic minor third and the anguished minor sixth, placing much
emphasis on the latter. Parsifal, after receiving Kundry's soul-seducing
kiss, cries out in agony 'Redeem me, rescue me from guilt-stained
hands!'; Othello, standing by the sleeping Desdemona, looks down at
her, still loving her but determined to kill her, and says nothing. Many
subtle psychological connexions between the two cases might be
established, but as always, the exact situation is irrelevant to the
musical expression, which is concentrated entirely on the painful
emotion of anguish.

But how are we to explain the similarity, or rather the near-identity?
Coincidence? There are an enormous number of them in music. Before
trying to answer the question, let us first assemble our collection of such
'coincidences', as they have occurred throughout the ages. But although
it is necessary to play at 'twisted tunes', a pledge is given that there will
be no 'twisting' of the kind whereby you can prove anything. In giving
examples of, say, 8–7–6–5, anything only approximate like 8–7–6–4,
or 8–7–5–3 will be shunned like the plague. In any case, there are far too
many exact similarities for us to bother with approximations.

Ascending 1–(2)–3–(4)–5 (Major)

We have postulated that to rise in pitch is to express an outgoing
emotion; we know that, purely technically speaking, the tonic is the

point of repose, from which one sets out, and to which one returns; that the dominant is the note of intermediacy, towards which one sets out, and from which one returns; and we have established that the major third is the note which 'looks on the bright side of things', the note of pleasure, of joy. All of which would suggest that to rise from the tonic to the dominant through the major third—or in other words to deploy the major triad as a melodic ascent 1–3–5—is to express an outgoing, active, assertive emotion of joy. Composers have in fact persistetly used the phrase for this very purpose (Ex. 53). We may as well clear up a thorny point at the start. It is not 'twisting' to say that 1–3–5 can materialize in composers' inspiration as 1–2–3–5, 1–3–4–5, or 1–2–3–4–5: Gastoldi and Mozart in Ex. 53h show this clearly, using both simple and ornate forms in the same breath, without changing the basic expressive effect. And it is obviously desirable to exemplify, not only the basic term itself, but the two or three different forms it can take. However, to jumble the different forms together in a block example might awaken suspicions that it had been difficult to find exact examples, and that variants had been dragged in to fill historical gaps. (The opposite is the case—it had been difficult to choose a few examples from the plethora of material.) Wherefore, the four different variants of the basic term have been separated, each with examples in chronological order.

Byrd's 'Blow up the Trumpet' shows the derivation of 1–3–5 from the naturally cheerful sound of a simple trumpet-call; a derivation which probably lies at the root of Purcell's 'O praise God in His Holiness', and is obviously integral to 'The trumpet shall sound' in *Messiah*. The three Mozart examples (Ex. 53 b) show that a composer can use a single term over and over again: there are many examples of this re-use of the same term in the works of every tonal composer. The first is the climax of Belmonte's opening aria in *The Seraglio*: waiting in joyful expectation of seeing his beloved Constanze again after long separation, he prays to Love to 'bring him to his goal'. The second is the orchestral opening of Fiordiligi's aria 'Come scoglio' in *Cos fan tutte*: her fidelity to her lover is 'firm as a rock', she sings with glad confidence. The third is the greeting of the chorus to Tamino and Pamina in *The Magic Flute*, after they have passed through their ordeal triumphantly. In Ex. 53 c, the Berlioz is the Easter Resurrection Chorus in *The Damnation of Faust*; the Liszt part of the *Magnificat*, as the Dante Symphony proceeds to the upper reaches of Purgatory, near to Paradise: the Johann Strauss needs no comment; the 'pop' quotation is the opening of the tune 'Rock around the Clock' which swept the world in 1956—as sung on the record by its exponent Bill Haley, who substituted 1–3–5, with unerring instinct, for the actual tune's less ebullient 1–2–3.

Example 53 d shows 1–3–4–5 in a fifteenth-century *chanson* 'To my lady, kind and fair, I will give a rosary'; a well-known Morley ayre; the chorus of shepherds in Monteverdi's *Orfeo*, calling the nymphs from the mountains to the plains, to join them in dancing; and the music given to the Sons of the Morning in Vaughan Williams's *Job*, at the point where they triumph over Satan (for Satan himself, see the augmented fourths, Ex. 41 n). In Ex. 53 e, we have 1–2–3–5 from 'Every valley shall be exalted' from *Messiah*; 'For he is like a refiner's fire' from the same work (the psalmist may be regarded as expecting the forthcoming purification with a fierce joy—*forte, allegro*); and the phrase sung by Leonora in Beethoven's *Fidelio* when she turns her thoughts from the wickedness of the tyrant who has falsely imprisoned her husband, to express her hope that all will end well—'A many-coloured rainbow shines on me'.

In Ex. 53f, 1–2–3–4–5 is shown in Victoria's anthem telling of the Seraphim singing 'Holy, holy, holy'; two Byrd quotations, which need no comment; and the final chorus ('Praise the Lord') from Debussy's *Martyre de Saint Sébastien*. Ex. 53g, also showing 1–2–3–4–5, consists of the bass duet in Handel's *Israel in Egypt*, expressing a joyful satisfaction in the warlike Jehovah's drowning of the Egyptians in the Red Sea (or a phrase from 'The trumpet shall sound' in *Messiah*); the opening of the Gloria of Beethoven's Mass in D; and the only moment of joy in Stravinsky's *Oedipus Rex*, when Creon relates the words of the oracle—'The God has spoken: avenge Laius, avenge the crime' (joyful satisfaction at having found the reason for the plague which is destroying Thebes, and being able to puruse a line of action which will remove it). In Ex. 53h, the Gastoldi is from *Il Trionfo di Dori*—'Amid the murmuring of crystal foundtains, the nymphs and shepherds sang O happy joyful day'; the Mozart is the serenade which Don Giovanni sings with light-hearted malice to his discarded mistress, Donna Elvira—the light-heartedness is in the music, the malice in the dramatic situation. Ex. 53j—the Gloria from Bach's B minor Mass and the Overture to Handel's St. Cecilia Ode—is included to show how a simple basic term can be expanded into a longer phrase.

The joyful feeling of all the above phrases needs no stressing nor the fact that the feeling is outgoing, i.e. assertive or affirmative in all cases. Naturally the vitalizing agents express the degree and kind of joy: for example, the quiet, calm, assured joy of Berlioz's Resurrection Chorus—*piano* 4/4 *moderato*, even rhythm, *legato*; and the violently animated, vociferous joy of Beethoven's Gloria—*fortissimo*, 3/4 *allegro*, impulsive rhythm, *non-legato*. The effects of the vitalizing agents in these and succeeding examples as analysed in Chapter 2, can be related to the emotional expression by the reader, without fear of error. (For further examples of 1–3–5 major, and its variants, see Ex. 25a, b and j, and Ex. 39a, b and c; the last three are, of course neutralized, saddened in retrospect by the subsequent use of the 'pathetic' 4–3 suspension).

Looking ahead for a moment, does not Ex. 53 show how the opening of the finale of Beethoven's Fifth Symphony can be legitimately said to express triumph? (1–3–5 major, *fortissimo*, *allegro* 4/4, *alla marcia*, with a rhythm of three even hammerblows, played on trumpets, *non-legato*, with a full orchestral texture consisting of the major triad). And can we not say that the opening of Brahms's Second Piano Concerto definitely expresses a serene, romantically dreamy, yet rock-firm feeling of joy? (1–2–3 (432) 3–5 major, *mezzo-piano, allegro non troppo* 4/4, evenly flowing rhythm, played on the 'romantic' horn, unaccompanied).

Ascending 5–1–(2)–3 (Major)

To leap from the dominant up to the tonic, and thence to the major third, with or without the intervening second, is equally expressive of an outgoing emotion of joy. One might say that it is a partial synonym of 1–3–5, as the word 'joy' is a partial synonym of the word 'happiness'. It is not always easy to make a clear distinction between these two terms (see Bach's Gloria, Ex. 53j, in which 5–1–2–3, ornamented, is incorporated into an extended version of 1–2–3–4–5); but in general we may say that 5–1–3, aiming at the major third, is more expressive of joy pure and simple; and 1–3–5, launching farther out from the tonic, more expressive of a sense of exuberance, triumph or aspiration.

Ex. 54a consists of the opening of the Credo from Compère's Mass 'Allez regrets' ('I believe in God the Father Almighty'); the beginning of Byrd's anthem 'Unto the hills mine eyes I lift, my hope shall never fade'; and a well-known 'aubade' madrigal by Morley. In Ex. 54b we have a sixteenth-century chanson 'To the woods I'll go'; the opening of Bach's Cantata No. 31 'The heavens laugh'; and the first phrase of the Resurrexit from his B minor Mass. Ex. 54c shows a phrase from the chorus 'The heavens are telling the glory of God' in *The Creation* (the chorus actually opens with 5–1–2–3, as do several other movements of this work); the *idée fixe* from the Fantastic Symphony, depicting 'the beloved' (the pleasurable feeling towards her, expressed in 5–1–3, with an extra passionate leap from the dominant up to the third, turns to

234

pathos and longing as the melody goes straight on to the 'pathetic' 4–3 suspension, and falls back through two other 'longing' suspensions, 3–2 and 8–7); and the Russian folk-theme which Mussorgsky used for the Coronation Scene in *Boris Godunov*.

Ex. 54d shows Faust's 'O night of love' from Gounod's opera (no 'pathetic' 4–3 suspension here, but the third is harmonized as a dominant thirteenth, resolving on to the second, bringing in the element of pleasurable longing); a phrase from the last of Delius's uncharacteristically heroic and jubilant *Songs of Farewell* (Whitman's poems look forward to death in triumphant mood—'Much, much for thee is yet in store'); and a popular wartime tune, which needs no comment. Ex. 54e is included to demonstrate the near-equivalence of 5–1–3 and 1–3–5, and the fact that they can be telescoped into a single expressive unit: the quotations are the opening of Bach's 'And I expect the resurrection of the dead' from the B minor Mass; the heroic and joyful Sword Motive from *The Ring* (see also the opening of the work, Ex. 25f, from which this motive is clearly derived); and the exultant climax of Britten's setting of Donne's sonnet 'Thou has made me, and shall they work decay?' (up to this point, the song is in E flat minor). Ex. 54f shows how 5–1–3 can be extended into a longer phrase, in quotations from the final triumphant Chorus of Loves from Monteverdi's *L'Incoronazione di Poppea*, and the Resurrexit from Mozart's Mass in C minor. (See also Shostakovich's 'optimism', Ex. 25j, and the Strauss and Britten quotations in Ex. 56j.)

Once again, would it be going too far to find a quiet, peaceful, assured joy in the opening of the Larghetto of Beethoven's Second Symphony? (Ascending 5–1–2–3 major, *piano*, 3/8 *larghetto*, evenly flowing rhythm, *legato*, played by violins as the upper part of a simple harmonic and diatonic string texture.)

Ascending 1–(2)–3–(4)–5 (Minor)

Substituting the minor the for the major third in the 1–3–5 progression, we shall expect to find the resulting phrase expressive of an outgoing feeling of pain—an assertion of sorrow, a complaint, a protest against misfortune—and we shall not be disappointed.

Ex. 55(a)

(b)

(c)

(d)

Ex. 55a quote a fifteenth-century love-lorn madrigal 'I find no peace'; Robert Whyte's anthem 'Behold and see, all ye who pass by, if there be any sorrow like unto my sorrow'; and a madrigal by Byrd, which juxtaposes 1–3–4–5 major and minor ('In fields abroad, where trumpets shrill do sound'—major—'where bodies dead do overspread the ground'—minor). In Ex. 55b, we have Morley's madrigals 'Why sit I here, alas, complaining?', and 'Miraculous love's wounding'; and the phrase 'But Jesus cried again in a loud voice, and gave up the spirit' from Schütz's St. Matthew Passion (note the minor sixth and minor seventh, unable to rise to the tonic—the melody does in fact fall after this phrase). Ex. 55c, from the opening chorus of Bach's St. John Passion 'Lord, our Governor, redeem us through thy holy passion', shows 1–2–3–4–5 in extended, ornamented form. Ex. 55d consists of the opening of the chorus from Mozart's Requiem, 'Lord Jesus Christ, save, we beseech thee, the souls of all thy faithful departed servants from fire everlasting'; and Tamino's terrified cry in *The Magic Flute*, where he enters, pursued by a serpent, 'Help me, or I am lost'.

Ex. 55e shows Schubert's well-known attachment to this phrase, in three quotations from *Die Winterreise*. First, 'Auf dem Flusse'; 'You who once rushed along so gaily, impetuous stream, how still you are now, with never a sound to greet me'—the river is frozen like the lover's heart, now that his sweetheart has deserted him. Second, 'Der stürmische Morgen'; 'How the storm has torn the grey garment of the sky'—the weather, the lover says, is suited to his own mood, in which there's nothing but 'winter cold and wild'. Third, 'Der Wegweiser': 'Why do I seek out the hidden pathways across the snowy crags' (there is only one sign-post that the lover cares for, he says—the one that points to the land from which no one ever came back). In Ex. 55f we see Mahler's 'wayfaring lad' in the same love-lorn frenzy—'I have a red-hot knife in my heart'; Debussy more reticently using the same phrase in setting Baudelaire's words 'Sorrow, give me your hand'; and Don Quixote, in Strauss's tone-poem, beginning to go crazed with thoughts of chivalric heroism, danger and death in defence of the oppressed. Ex. 55g quotes from *Belshazzar's Feast* ('For with violence shall that great city Babylon be destroyed'—a fierce assertion of intended revenge for suffering); Bartók's *Cantata Profana* (the father pleads anxiously with his spell-bound sons to return home to their mother, who is waiting for them; and that pathetic and bitter popular song 'Brother can you spare a dime'—the protest of the out-of-work American war hero. (See also Exs. 32g, 41n (with flattened fifth), 43a, 46b, 51 and 52a and b.)

In view of all this, it would seem that those writers who connect the opening of the slow movement of Schubert's Ninth Symphony with the feeling of *Die Winterreise* are not mistaken (1–2–3–4–5, minor, *piano*, *allegretto* 4/4 dotted rhythm, cellos and basses beneath marching minor triads on upper strings. And should we not understand the opening of Mahler's Second Symphony, then, as a fierce protest against suffering? (1–(7)–1–2–3, 3–(2–3)–4–5, minor, *fortissimo*, 4/4 *allegro*, spasmodic rhythm, marked 'wildly', played low down by cellos and basses beneath a fierce string tremolando on the dominant.)

Ascending 5–1–(2)–3 (Minor)

If the major version of 5–1–3 stresses joy pure and simple, by aiming at the major third, the minor version expresses pure tragedy, by aiming at the minor third. And to move upward *firmly and decisively* from the lower dominant, *via* the tonic, to the minor third, gives a strong feeling of courage, in that it boldly acknowledges the existence of tragedy and springs onward (upward) into the thick of it, as composers have realized.

238

Ex. 56a begins unpromisingly with another love-lorn madrigal, but there is quite definitely something strongly accusing in this particular lover's reproach—try singing the words to 1–3–2–1 or even 1–3–4–5 (both minor), and it will be found that 5–1–2–3 has in fact much more strength of purpose. The example continues with Christ's words 'My God, why has thou forsaken me?'—presented by Schütz in his St. Matthew Passion as a strong protest (we can see this as the moment when Christ becomes a purely human tragic hero, protesting against his fate). The words set to 5–1–2–3 by Purcell are basic to all uses of the phrase: 'In the midst of life we are in death'—the tragic situation firmly acknowledged as the basis of life. In Ex. 56b, we have the brave assertion of the Christian soul in Bach's St. Matthew Passion—'I will watch beside my Lord', reflecting on the fact that the disciples slept when they should have been keeping guard; David's bold scorn of Saul's persecution in Handel's oratorio; and another basic use of the phrase—'As by man came death' from *Messiah*. Ex. 56c shows Electra, in Mozart's *Idomeneo*, fiercely enduring, as a Greek tragic figure should, 'the torments of Orestes and Ajax', after she has finally lost the hero Idamante to her rival Ilia; Schubert's winter-journeyer throwing off his grief for the first and only time in the whole cycle ('When the snow flies in my face, I shake it off again'—the song is entitled 'Muth' (Courage); and the two grenadiers in Schumann's Heine setting, who are willing to face death for their emperor, Napoleon.

In Ex. 56d, we see how Wagner turned to the phrase for the tragic heroes in *The Ring*: first, the opening of the 'Volsung' motive, attached to the brave but long-suffering hero Siegmund; second, the first notes of the phrase attached to him when the Valkyrie comes to announce his death (he sings it to her again and again, first questioningly, then defiantly); third, the beginning of Siegfried's heroic motive, perhaps the supreme example of the phrase (the plunge from the tonic of the major triad to the *minor* third, the buoyant rhythm, and the recoil and leap over the dominant on to the *minor sixth*, normally the note of anguish, but here transfigured into joy by being harmonized by its own major triad—these elements explain to some extent the extraordinarily indomitable character of the theme). Ex. 56e shows that Berlioz was equally dependent on the phrase in his heroic opera *The Trojans* ('cribbing'?—Berlioz didn't know a note of *The Ring* when he wrote his work). First, the ghost of the great Trojan hero, Hector, appears to Aeneas, bidding him set out to Italy and found a new Troy there; second, the tragic heroine Cassandra, during the sacking of Troy, scorns the weaker characters among the Vestal Virgins who wish to yield to the Greeks, being afraid to obey her injunction to commit suicide (she asks them if they really desire a life 'unworthy of noble hearts'). The Mussorgsky quotation is from *Boris Godunov*: the young monk, Grigory, about to leave his cell and become the 'pretender', to take arms against the usurper Boris, militantly apostrophizes his future enemy, saying that his misdeeds are written down in the monastery records and he will one day face the judgement of mankind.

241

Ex. 56f quotes Othello's defiant cry in Verdi's opera, as, supposedly disarmed, he draws an unsuspected dagger and stabs himself—'I have a weapon yet'. The second quotation is from Debussy's *Pelléas*, a work in which one hardly expects to find heroics. But everything is packed with symbolism in this subtle opera, and the words of Pelléas quoted here make an ominous reference to forthcoming disaster, which he feels to be inherent in his own destiny, and which he does nothing to avoid: watching the mysterious ship leaving the harbour for an unknown destination, he says 'We shall have a storm tonight; there has been one every night now for some time'. In Ex. 56g, we find Delius again unusually showing the heroic side of his character in the last of the *Songs of Farewell*—'Now land and life finale and farewell... depart upon thy endless cruise, old Sailor' (it is the minor version of the major 5–1–3 of Ex. 54d—the courageous plunge towards death, as opposed to the joyously triumphant hailing of it). The Stravinsky quotation is from his ballet *Orpheus*; it occurs several times in Orpheus' *Air de Danse*, in which he revolts against the acceptance of Euridice's death. 'Pop numbers' steer clear of heroics, but the fiercely war-like Russian march-tune shows a popular use of the phrase in question (repeated a fourth higher).

Ex. 56h is included to demonstrate that, as with the major triadic phrases, the minor 5–1–3 and 1–3–5 phrases can approach equivalence and merge into a single unit of expression: Cassandra, defying the Greeks in *The Trojans* as she tells them that Aeneas and his men have escaped to Mount Ida, and Wagner's Valkyries, created by Wotan to recruit armies of heroes against expected attacks from enemies, both use 5–1–3 (the 'heroic' element), 1–3–5 (normally the 'protest' element, but here merged by sequence into the 'heroic'), and go over into 1–3–5 in the relative major, into triumphant joy (a feeling common to Cassandra and the Valkyries).

Ex. 56j demonstrates two extensions of the use of 5–1–3. First, from Bach's Cantata No. 56 'I will gladly carry the Cross' (the sharp fourth is set against the minor triad as an accented dissonance—a painful, semitonal one—resolving *upwards*, i.e. *onwards*, to the dominant); and a phrase from Britten's first Donne Sonnet ('Thou'rt like a pilgrim which abroad hath done treason and durst not turne to whence he is fled')—the brave enterprise of a pilgrimage has gone astray and ended in the anguish of fear, i.e. the 5–1–3 phrases goes on to end on the *minor sixth*, which stays unresolved. The Richard Strauss quotation is the theme of that scapegrace hero, Till Eulenspiegel (the minor third of 5–1–2–3 turns slyly upwards to the major third—Till's tragedy is a tragi-comedy); the Britten example shows the use of the same procedure, when Albert Herring, in the opera which bears his name, is mentioned as candidate for the post of May-Queen (May-King)—Albert, too, is a tragi-comical hero.

Pehaps we can now get an idea of the mood of the finale of Brahms's First Piano Concerto. As is well-known, the material of the stormy first movement arose out of Brahms's grief at Schumann's madness and impending death, and over the slow movement he originally wrote the word 'Benedictus', which aptly sums up the serene and blessed feeling of consolation it awakens—see the section on 8–7–6–5 (major). Now, the opening theme of the finale beings 5–1–2–3–(5–1), ascending, minor, *forte*, 2/4 *allegro non troppo, non-legato*, thrusting rhythm, played by the solo pianist (the protagonist in the concerto-drama— Brahms himself at the first performance), without orchestra, but with a strenuous semiquaver accompaniment by the soloist's left hand. The movement is usually described as 'lively' and 'robust', and so it is, but does not the 5–1–3 phrase, shooting on up the minor triad to the upper tonic, deployed in thrusting rhythm, *forte*—does not all this convey the feeling of the grief-stricken youth's courageous, even heroic resolve to leave anguish and consolation, and get on with the business of life—in the midst of which, as Schumann's sudden extinction had made clear to him, we are in death? This interpretation was once suggested to me long ago by a friend; at the time, I could only *feel* he was right, but in view of the persistent 'heroic' use of the minor 5–1–3 phrase, shown in our examples, he would seem to be absolved from the sin of 'reading into the music what isn't there'.

Descending 5–(4)–3–(2)–1 (Major)

If to fall in pitch expresses incoming emotion, to descend from the outlying dominant to the point of repose, the tonic, through the major third, will naturally convey a sense of experiencing joy passively, i.e. accepting or welcoming blessings, relief, consolation, reassurance or fulfilment, together with a feeling of 'having come home'.

Ex. 57 (a)

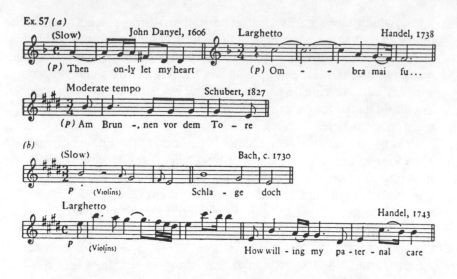

(b)

(c)

(d)

(e)

(f)

Allegro vivace   Mozart, 1787   Fast   ♩.120   Stravinsky, 1927

(f) Già   la   men - sa è pre - par - a - ta   *f* Res - pon - dit   De - us.

Ex. 57a quotes a phrase from John Danyel's ayre 'Grief keep within', at the point where the poet speaks of finding relief, not in shouting his sorrow abroad, but in experiencing it passively: the sorrow of the song resides in the prevailing D minor key—this D major refrain is the moment of consolation. The Handel is the opening vocal phrase of the aria 'Ombra mai fu' from his opera *Xerxes*: the great Persian warrior, at the opening of the opera, is represented as passively enjoying the delights of his garden, apostrophizing his favourite plane-tree with the words 'Never was the shade of a tree so dear to my heart'. The Schubert is the opening vocal phrase of his song 'Der Lindenbaum' in *Die Winterreise*: the jilted lover finds comfort and consolation in his favourite linden-tree, which seems to offer him a 'happy ending' to his sorrows—the peace of death beneath its shade. In Ex. 57b, two composers show, by differing instrumental and vocal forms of the same phrase, that 5–3–1 can appear as 5–4–3–2–1 and even 5–4–3–7–1 (such a radical case as the latter will not be taken as an excuse for any 'twisting' in our examination, though it demonstrates the perfect legitimacy of such twisting, within bounds). In his Cantata No. 53 Bach accepts with joy the comforting thought, for the devout Christian, of the bell striking the last hour of his life on earth; in the second quotation, Samson's father Manoah, in Handel's oratorio, says that if only his blinded son's life is spared, he will gladly comfort and console him in his old age. Ex. 57c shows Palestrina, in his *Missa Brevis*, using the phrase in connexion with the 'Lamb of God', in the way that composers have often employed it to express the receiving of consolation from the gentler manifestations of the Deity; and Bach, in Cantata No. 106, expressing the supreme sense of gratified fulfilment to be drawn from Christ's words 'This day shalt thou be with me in Paradise'.

In Ex. 57d the comforting aspects of the deity as again invoked: by Handel, in *Messiah*, the image of the Good Shepherd tending his sheep; and by Mozart, in his C minor Mass, the image of God the Son, the Lamb of God, the human intermediary (after expressing the appeal to God the Father by ascending 5–6–7–8 in D minor—see Ex. 69). There follows a totally different kind of comforter, the minx Zerlina in

Mozart's *Don Giovanni*, pacifying her jealous lover Masetto. In Ex. 57e, Elgar uses the phrase in the religious context: the dying Gerontius, having sung 'Jesu, Maria, I am near to death' in D minor, with minor sixth, turns to the key of B flat and 5–4–3–2–(3)–1 for the feeling that death means being called home by Jesus and Mary. The two Britten quotations are: first, in *Peter Grimes*, Ellen sits by the sea on the bright Sunday morning following the storm, speaking to the unhappy boy apprentice of the comfort of letting themselves enjoy 'a holiday full of peace and quietness'; second, Lucia, in *The Rape of Lucretia*, sings a vocalise with the other women as they fold the linen (the words of the other parts are significant—'Time treads upon the hands of women; at birth or death their hands must fold clean linen. . . . Home is what man leaves to seek—what is home but women?'—this whole scene represents women as home, the place of repose and comfort to which one returns). (See also Ex. 27b, 31f and 53e.)

In all of the above, the vitalizing agents combine to make the effect of the phrase gentle and tender; but 5–3–1 can be robust, when played *allegro* and *forte*, with strong accent, as Ex. 57f shows. In both cases, the upper tonic is used as a starting point, and the effect is one of final fulfilment. The Mozart is the opening of the last act of *Don Giovanni*, which conveys a remarkable sense of the wheel coming full circle (a critic has recently asked, in a review, 'why is it that this phrase has such a feeling of finality?') The Stravinsky is, like Ex. 53g, from the point in *Oedipus Rex* where Creon announces that the oracle has spoken ('The God has replied')—bringing final relief after much suffering: again, the clinching sense of finality is unmistakable.

Once more extending an interpretation drawn from musico-verbal contexts to a purely musical one, can we perhaps now account for the 'glorious' effect of the broad major theme in the first movement of Carl Nielsen's Fifth Symphony? After some exceedingly grim minor music, declared by the composer to represent 'destructive forces' a G major tune enters, 5–4–3–2–(7)–1, *mf, adagio* 3/4, flowing rhythm, *legato*, played by violas and bassoons, as the upper part of a simple diatonic and harmonic texture: it immediately gives a sense of joyful relief after the turmoil. But the music of the 'destructive forces' returns and grows to a shatteringly brutal climax; and when the G major tune emerges out of it, *fortissimo*, high up on the horns (and violins), supported by a firm texture, and a bass of rushing hemi-demi-semiquavers, its effect is naturally that of an excited welcoming of the relief which has been expectantly striven for, a triumphant acceptance of joyous fulfilment.

246

COOKE

Descending 5–(4)–3–(2)–1 (Minor)

Substituting the minor for the major third in the descending 5–3–1 progression, we have a phrase which has been much used to express an 'incoming' painful emotion, in a context of finality: acceptance of, or yielding to grief; discouragement and depression; passive suffering; and the despair connected with death.

Ex. 58a quotes a famous song attributed to Dunstable; 'O lovely rose, my sweet love, alas, let me not die; alas, must I end my days in weeping, after serving so truly and so loyally?'. The Josquin is the opening of his chanson 'Incessantly I am forced to suffer torment'; the Gesualdo the ending of his madrigal 'Luci serene e chiare', (the lover describes the pangs of hopeless love as 'miraculous'—'one does but does not pass away'). In Ex. 58b, we have the opening of the Qui Tollis from Bach's B minor Mass, which is a deeply sorrowful setting of the prayer 'O Lamb of God that takest away the sins of the world, have mercy upon us'; the opening of the minor verse of Schubert's song 'Der Lindenbaum', in which the lover rejects the consoling thought of dying peacefully beneath the linden-tree (cf. Ex. 57a), saying that he must continue his hopeless journey 'into the deep night'; and the dramatic and despairing cry of Dido in Berlioz's *The Trojans*—'I am going to die'. Ex. 58c consists of the opening of Verdi's Requiem; another symbolic remark from Debussy's *Pelléas et Mélisande*, evoking thoughts of death—'The night falls very quickly'; and Faust's despairing utterance, in Busoni's opera, when he rejects the salvation evoked by the Easter Hymn, and signs the pact with Mephistopheles—hearing the choir sing of the 'quick and the dead', he cries out loudly 'Faust, you are now a dead man'. Ex. 58d shows us the despair of Oedipus in Stravinsky's oratorio—'All is brought to light'; the statement of tragic irrevocability at the end of Britten's *The Rape of Lucretia*—after Lucretia's suicide the question is asked 'Is this all?' and is at first answered in the affirmative; and the despair of Serena in Gershwin's opera *Porgy and Bess*, as she laments that her murdered husband will never come home to her again—'My man's gone now'.

In Ex. 58e, there is a *chanson* by a fifteenth-century Belgian composer—'I used to complain of my lady's falseness',[33] Christ's utterance 'Into thy hands I commend my spirit' from *The Seven Last*

[33]De Lantins seems to have survived his love-lorn grief, since the poem of his song is an acrostic which reads, 'Putain de merde'.

Words by Schütz; and the opening of Delius's *Sea Drift*, where the sense of despair (the work ends with the words 'We two together no more') is infused with nostalgia by the harmonization of the C sharp minor theme with a bass of E major, creating the added sixth of longing. In Ex. 58f, the Wilbye madrigal speaks for itself; the Bach quotations are, first, the final utterance of Christ in the St. John Passion—'It is finished'; second, the farewell to the world of the Christian soul in Cantata No. 82—'World, goodnight'. Ex. 58g quotes the lament of the Princess Xenia, in Mussorgsky's *Boris Godunov*, for her dead lover; the funeral march for Titurel, in Wagner's *Parsifal*, to which the chorus sing 'We bear his body to-day for the last time'; and the theme from the Passacaglia in *Peter Grimes*, which is later connected with the passive suffering of the boy apprentice (note the spotlighted *minor second*, note of hopeless anguish, so appropriate to this pathetically defenceless child).

Ex. 58h brings an extension of the basic term to include a final major seventh, which adds a more bitter feeling to the basic mood. First, a phrase from Wilbye's madrigal 'Despiteful thus unto myself I languish, and in disdain myself from joy I banish'; second, Seneca's friends, in Monteverdi's *L'Incoronazione di Poppea*, lament his decision to take his own life, reminding him poignantly that 'this life is too sweet to reject'; third, the *Arioso dolente* from Beethoven's Piano Sonata in A flat, Op. 110. Ex. 58j continues this variant with the instrumental transformation of the words 'It is finished' in Bach's St. John Passion (cf. Ex. 58f) for the aria following the death of Christ; Micah's injunction to the Israelites to lament Samson's downfall, in Handel's oratorio; and Elijah's despair in Mendelssohn's oratorio—'It is enough; O Lord now take away my life'. Ex. 58k gives examples of one of many other variants of the basic term: a phrase from Gibbon's madrigal 'What is our life?'—which ends with the words 'Only we die in earnest, that's no jest'; and the *lamentoso* opening of the finale in Tchaikovsky's *Pathétique* Symphony. For a further example of the basic term see Samson's despair in Handel's oratorio (Ex. 51); see also Exs. 31f and 65d; for examples of how this term may be relieved of its basic meaning by a lively or a lilting tempo, see Exs. 44a and 45.

The essential feeling of the descending minor 5–3–1 progression is of a passive falling away from the joy of life, in various degrees, the ultimate one being to reject life altogether in favour of death. Wherefore it seems clear, as many have already felt, that the opening theme of Schubert's A minor String Quartet must be taken as a gentle expresion of passive sorrow, of the kind that led to the death-wish of *Die Winterreise* (5–3–1 minor, *pianissimo, allegro ma non troppo* 4/4, smooth rhythm, *legato*, played by the 'expressive' violin over a restless accompaniment, the bass part reiterating a drone of a fifth, in ominous drum-like rhythm.)

Arched 5–3–(2)–1 (Minor)

To rise from the lower dominant over the tonic to the minor third, and fall back to the tonic with or without the intervening second, conveys the feeling of a passionate outburst of painful emotion, which does not protest further, but falls back into acceptance—a flow and ebb of grief. Being neither complete protest nor complete acceptance, it has an effect of restless sorrow.

Ex. 59 (a) (Slow) — Dowland, 1612
(p) When___ the poor crip-ple by the pool did lie
(Moderate tempo) — Bach, 1722
(p) Zer-flies-se,___ mein Her-ze

(b) (Moderate tempo) — Bach, 1729 — (Moderate tempo), — Bach c. 1731
(p) Er bar---me dich___ (f) Ich ha-be ge-nug

(c) Larghetto — Mozart, 1791 — Largo — Verdi, 1873
(p) La-cry-mo-sa... (p) La-cry-mo-sa di-es il-la

(d) Fairly quick — Schubert, 1823 — Moderate tempo — Schubert, 1827
(pp) Ach, es ent-schwin-det mit thau-ig-em Flüg-el (p) Ich hab' an dich ge-dacht

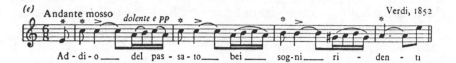

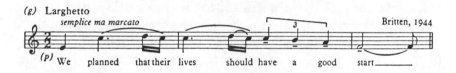

Ex. 59 a shows Dowland 'semper dolens' (to quote his own pun): the ayre tells of the cripple that suffered 'full many, many years' before he was healed by Christ, and ends with the words 'No David, Job, nor cripple in more grief, Christ grant me patience, patience, and my hope's relief'. The Bach is the aria 'Flow, my tears, in floods of weeping' from the St. John Passion. The two further Bach examples in Ex. 59b are the grief-stricken aria 'Have mercy, Lord, on me', from the St. Matthew Passion, and the first vocal phrase from Cantata No. 82, where the Christian soul declares that he is weary of the restless sorrow of this world, and longs for the peace of the next. All three Bach quotations have extremely restless accompaniments. Ex. 59c consists of the two Lachrymosa themes from the Requiems of Mozart and Verdi: in the latter, the slow flowing rhythm removes any 'courageous' effect that the opening 5–1–3 might have in this extended version of the arched 5–3–1.

Schubert was very attached to this phrase, as Ex. 59d shows: first, the melody of the song 'Auf dem Wasser zu singen', which ends with the reflection that life flows away like the waters of a river; second, the closing phrase of the song 'Gute Nacht' in *Die Winterreise*, in which the jilted lover oscillates between despair, wounded pride and continuing love for the faithless girl, eventually writing his name on her door before setting out on his journey, to let her know 'that I have thought of you'; and the opening of the song 'Erstarrung' from the same cycle (in a torment of grief, he 'searches vainly in the snow' for the tracks where he and his beloved used to wander in the springtime). Ex. 59e is one of Violetta's arias in the last act of Verdi's *La Traviata*: ill, and near to death, and restless because she is hoping against hope that her lover will return to her, she bids 'farewell to the past, to the fair smiling dreams', and concludes her aria with 'everything mortal ends in the tomb' (to a variant of the descending 5–3–1 progression).

In Ex. 59f, we see Wagner using the phrase in *The Ring*, for the motive attached to the renunciation of love, the step which must be taken by anyone wishing to forge the ring of absolute power from the Rhinegold: the melody goes straight to the emotional (psychological) point, expressing unhappiness—the fundamental unhappiness of those whose love of power leads them to lose all feeling of love. Mahler, as so often, shows the influence of Schubert, in two phrases from his 'Songs of a Wayfaring Lad': in the first, the rejected lover says that his love's wedding day will be the unhappiest day of his life; in the second, he says goodbye to 'all that he ever loved', before setting out, like Schubert's lover, on a journey in search of death. The Britten quotation (Ex. 59g) shows Ellen, in *Peter Grimes*, meeting the accusations of the villagers that her sympathy for Grimes has helped to bring about the apprentice's death, with a tensely sorrowful plea of good intentions (ending on the anguished minor sixth).

We are led from the above to suppose that the second theme in the first movement of Mozart's G minor String Quintet must be expressive of restless grief, as has frequently been stated: arched 5–3–2–1, repeated, *piano, allegro* 4/4, dotted rhythm, played by the violin over a texture of throbbing quavers (tonic minor triad); after which the theme enlarges on its basic mood, by a passionate leap of a minor ninth from the lower dominant to the minor sixth, note of anguish, and a return down the 'despairing' 5–4–3–2–1).

252

1–(2)–3–(2)–1 (Minor)

To base a theme on the tonic, only moving out as far as the minor third, and returning immediately, is to 'look on the darker side of things' in a context of immobility, neither rising up to protest, nor falling back to accept. Composers have frequently used this progression to express brooding, an obsession with gloomy feelings, a trapped fear, or a sense of inescapable doom, especially when it is repeated over and over.

254

The Josquin madrigal in Ex. 60a is 'Parfons regrets'—'come away, sorrow, and kill my heart, that it may drown itself in woe and weeping'; the Purcell is the sombre opening of his anthem on Psalm 52 ('Hear my prayer, O Lord, and let my crying come unto Thee'); the Debussy is his setting of that grief-obsessed Verlaine poem 'Tears fall in my heart, as rain falls on the town'. In Ex. 60b, we have a phrase from the Dies Irae of Mozart's Requiem Mass—fear of the inescapable Day of Judgment; Don Giovanni suddenly transfixed by fear as the flames of hell flicker about him; and the demons calling to the terrified and praying Marguerite, in the church scene from Gounod's *Faust*. Ex. 60c shows three *bassi ostinati*: that of Chopin's Funeral March; the one that persists for fifty bars while the 'destructive forces' gather power in Nielsen's Fifth Symphony; and the one in Stravinsky's *Oedipus Rex* which supports the chorus as they implore Oedipus to save Thebes from the plague of which it is dying (their melodic line also moves between 1 and 3 for eighteen bars). The Stravinsky in Ex. 60d is from the beginning of the Mourning Chorus for Tom's death, near the end of *The Rake's Progress*; the first Walton (from *Belshazzar's Feast*) is the Israelites' warning to Babylon of its inevitable destruction; the destruction is accomplished (moving on to a major chord). Ex. 60e shows the confined struggle, in Britten's *The Rape of Lucretia*, of the actual rape itself (with its symbolism of the horn trying to close the gap between the tonic and minor third); and the wailing of the 'Doleful Creatures' in Vaughan Williams's *Pilgrim's Progress*.

This latter forms a nice bridge from 1–3–1 to 1–2–3–2–1, using both in conjunction—and to other variants. Ex. 60f consists of two quotations from the Blessed Virgin's Cradle Song by Byrd, in which she is pictured dwelling on the thought of the slaughter of the innocents, which threatens her own child; the beginning of a madrigal by Morley—'In dews of roses, Lycoris thus sat weeping' (the obsessive repetition takes here the familiar form of continuous 'imitation'); and the opening of a Gibbons madrigal which speaks for itself. In Ex. 60g, we have the bass of the opening of the Confutatis Maledictis in Mozart's Requiem Mass (fear of inescapable damnation again); the ending of the first phrase of the theme of Chopin's Funeral March (it has remained on the tonic up to this point); and the opening theme of the first movement of the Sonata in which the Funeral March occurs (Chopin said nothing about this theme at all, but surely we need not talk of 'pure music' now). The 'pop' number is from the Maurice Chevalier film *Ma Pomme*; it is the dirge-like 'Song of the Tramps of Paris'. Ex. 60h brings us the opening of that death-obsessed song 'Der Wegweiser' in *Die Winterreise*; Violetta's agitated, fearful, obsessive plea to her lover's father who has come to ask her to break off their affair—'You don't know what love I have for him'; and the last song of Mahler's 'wayfaring lad'—'the two blue eyes of his faithless sweetheart' have sent him out into the world on his journey to death. (See also Exs. 26, *passim*, 27c and h, 28a and c, and 58d).

It may be advisable at this point to remind the reader that the enormous difference between the various uses of a basic term are accounted for by the vitalizing agents. We are hardly likely to take Morley's shepherd Lycoris (*piano*, lively tempo, lilting rhythm, two sopranos echoing one another) as seriously as Mozart's Don Giovanni (*forte, allegro*, tense, hammering, thrusting rhythm, trombones and strings); but the basic sense of fixation to a painful emotion is common to both. And it is also common to the closing bars of the first movement of Schubert's Unfinished Symphony (1–2–3–1, minor, repeated, *mezzoforte* dying away to *pianissimo, allegro moderato*, 3/4, swaying rhythm, first on top of the rich texture, on violins and violas, then in the bass, on cellos and basses); and to the opening theme of Rachmaninov's Third Piano Concerto.

(5)–6–5 (Major)

The major sixth is often used as a melodic stepping-stone in an ascent from the dominant to the tonic, in which case its expressive identity is merged into an overall pattern with the 'optimistic' major seventh; but its most individual expressive function is its relationship to the dominant in connexion with the major triad beneath. This relationship takes various forms, some of which are shown below.

Ex. 61 (a)

COOKE

257

Ex. 61a shows three cases in which the major sixth is harmonized as the major third of the subdominant chord, and the effect is of a simple assertion of joy, moving up from one major third to another, harmonically speaking, and back again. The first is the 'fa-la-la' refrain from Weelkes's madrigal 'To shorten winter's sadness, see where the nymphs with gladness . . .' (the quotation is a composite top line made up of overlapping parts, and the harmonic counterpoint beneath it is too complex rhythmically to be made clear on one stave); the second and third need no comment.

Ex. 61b demonstrates the simple alteration of 6 and 5 either unaccompanied, or in the triadic context; the effect is similar to the previous case, but there is not so much an assertion of joy as a joyous vibration. The Beethoven is the short, breathless lead-up to the final jubiliant outburst of the finale of the Choral Symphony; the Britten is the music of the church bells on the bright Sunday morning in *The Turn of the Screw*; the Stravinsky is the cheerful, jogging tune of the soldier's violin in *The Soldier's Tale* (the A minor triad scarcely disturbs the G major triadic basis).

In Ex. 61c, we see the sixth functioning as a short anacrusis leading on to the fifth, unaccompanied, or in a triadic context; the effect is practically the same again, that of a joyous vibration, with the faintest touch of longing. The Bach is the opening of the aria 'See, Jesus stretches out his hand towards us' in the St. Matthew Passion. The Mozart is the persistent figure which runs through the scene in which Don Giovanni suggests to Leporello that they should go and console the lady in distress—Donna Elvira: the figure underlines the sense of amusement inherent in the situation. The Schubert is another quotation from 'Der Lindenbaum'—the joy brought to the love-lorn wanderer's heart by the favourite linden-tree.

Ex. 61d shows the effect of leaning on to the sixth, slowly, and falling back again: a sense of joyful serenity, with a slight element of longing, or pleading: the Sanctus from Fauré's Requiem, and the Kyrie in *The Dream of Gerontius*—the loving prayer of the dying man's friends.

The remainder of the examples show the commonest form of the (5)–6–5 progression, concerned with the *appoggiatura* 6–5, producing the effect of a burst of pleasurable longing. Ex. 61e presents Michal's admiring longing for David, in Handel's *Saul*; Don Giovanni's luring call to Donna Elvira (cf. Ex. 61c, which immediately precedes this); and from *La Traviata*, Violetta's last delirious cry 'O joy', when at the moment of her death she feels that she is returning to life (dominant ninth harmony of longing). In Ex. 61f, we have Marguerite's cry of 'He loves me', in Gounod's *Faust* (dominant ninth again); the love-theme from Tchaikovsky's Overture *Romeo and Juliet*; and the opening of Debussy's song *En sourdine*, which tells of two lovers 'mingling their hearts and souls in the evening air'. Ex. 61g quotes the ending of one of Britten's Michelangelo Sonnets, in which the lover expresses his utter dependence on the beloved, comparing his beneficient effect to that of the sun; a recurrent phrase from the *Air de Danse* in Stravinsky's ballet *Orpheus*, expressing Orpheus' longing for the dead Eurydice; and the well-known dance-tune 'Cheek to Cheek' by Irving Berlin, the words of which express an intense attraction towards dancing with the beloved. (See also Exs. 29 and 31, *passim*.)

(5)–6–5 (Minor)

The chief and almost only expressive function of the minor sixth is to act as an *appoggiatura* on to the dominant, giving the effect of a burst of anguish. This is the most widely used of all terms of musical language: one can hardly find a page of 'grief' music by any tonal composer of any period without encountering it several times.

260

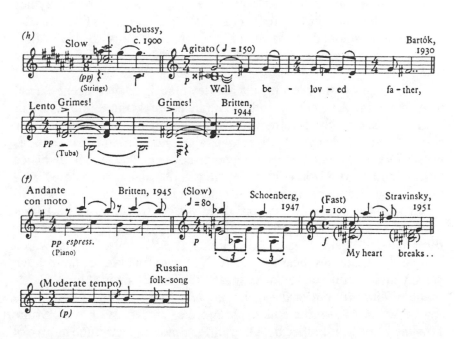

The quotations in Ex. 62a are the opening of a fourteenth-century Belgian *chanson* 'Slave to grief'; the opening of Josquin's *Déploration sur la mort de Ockeghem* (the tenor part uses the plain-song Requiem theme, but converts its rise and fall of a tone to that of a semitone, 5–6–5 in D minor); the lullaby refrain from the aforementioned sorrowful Virgin's Cradle Song by Byrd (3–2 in D minor as 6–5 in A); and, from Schütz's *Resurrection*, the setting of the words 'Mary stood before the grave and wept'. Ex. 62b shows two Mozart examples: the demons threatening Don Giovanni with the words 'any punishment is all too little for your sins' (we hear this statement through the Don's anguished

261

feelings); and the setting of 'how great will be the trembling, when the Judge shall come' in the Requiem Mass. The Beethoven is from *Fidelio*—the introduction to the scene where Florestan lies suffering in the dungeon. In Ex. 62c, the friends of Gerontius, in Elgar's oratorio, hearing him cry out in fear of death and damnation, change their serene prayer of 'Kyrie' (cf. Ex. 61d) to a more urgent and anguished plea for divine aid (note also the quicker tempo and louder dynamics). The Walton is from his setting of 'By the waters of Babylon' in *Belshazzar's Feast*; the Britten from *The Rape of Lucretia*—the morning after the rape, Lucretia cannot bear to look at the flowers brought to her by her servants; the Stravinsky from *The Rake's Progress*—Tom, in the madhouse at the end of the opera, sings remorsefully to Anne 'In a foolish dream, in a gloomy labyrinth, I hunted shadows, disdaining thy true love'.

Ex. 62d quotes the opening of a Morley madrigal; a recurrent phrase from the aria 'Atonement and repentance break the sinful heart in twain' in Bach's St. Matthew Passion; and a phrase from another sorrowful aria in that work—'For love my Saviour will die'. In Ex. 62e, we see Donna Anna's perturbation on discovering the dead body of her father, in Mozart's *Don Giovanni* (the whole scene is permeated with the minor 6–5 *appoggiatura*); a persistent phrase from the last page of Verdi's *La Traviata* (it bursts straight in as a contradiction of Violetta's major 6–5 to the words 'O joy'—cf. Ex. 61e); and the weeping phrase of the timorous Vestal Virgins in Berlioz's *The Trojans*, against which Cassandra addresses them scornfully 'You who tremble', coming down sternly and fatefully on to the minor third. Ex. 62f shows how Wagner made a *leitmotiv* out of the figure, in *The Ring*, in opposition to the joyous major 6–5 of the Rhinegold motive (cf. Ex. 31c); first, Mime howling while he is bullied by Alberich; second, the Servitude motive of the Nibelungs groaning under Alberich's yoke; third, the final, bitter, mournful, 'hating' form of the motive, when it attaches to the evil and self-confessedly unhappy figure of Hagen, in *Götterdämmerung*.

In E. 62g, Mussorgsky is also shown deriving an instrumental term from a vocal one: the wailing of the Simpleton in *Boris Godunov* is taken up as an ostinato for his lament over the future fate of Russia. The extract from the Dies Irae of Verdi's Requiem needs no comment; the other Verdi quotation is Othello's agonized cry to Iago 'You have bound me to the cross!' Ex. 62h shows a characteristically subtle use of

the term by Debussy for the closing page of *Pelléas*: the mingled
serenity and pathos of Mélisande's death is conveyed by a *major* triad
with a *minor 6–5 appoggiatura*. The Bartók is from the *Cantata
Profana*: the eldest of the nine sons, who are turned by a spell into deer,
cries out to his father not to shoot them. The Britten is from *Peter
Grimes*, from the final pathetic scene where Grimes, at the end of his
tether, stumbles about in the darkness in a frenzy, while the far-off
sound of his name being shouted by the pursuing villagers is accompanied by the equally distant, and dismal wail of a fog-horn (tuba, off-
stage, minor 6–5).

The Britten quotation in Ex. 62j is the opening of his Donne Sonnet
'O might these sighs and tears return again into my breast and eyes'; the
Schoenberg occurs in *A Survivor from Warsaw*, at the point where the
narrator says 'you had been separated from your children, from your
wife, your parents, you don't know what happened to them...'. The
Stravinsky, from *The Rake's Progress*, shows the sense of anguished
despair to be obtained from deploying the minor 6–5 as an interval of a
falling minor ninth (note that the phrase opens with arched 5–3–1,
minor, on an F sharp minor triad—the minor 6–5 in C sharp minor is
retrospective). The final quotation is from the popular Russian song
about the 'Black Eyes' by which the lover has been misled and through
which 'the joys of life have vanished for ever'. (See also Exs. 27j; 30 and
31, *passim*; 35b, 41a and f, 48, 49 and 50.)

Having identified this term of musical language, are we not in a
position to understand the moods of the opening pages of Mozart's
Fortieth and Vaughan Williams's Fourth Symphony? The latter, it is
true, gives the impression of beginning with minor 2–1 rather than
minor 6–5, but the terms are partly interchangeable, the former being a
darker version of the latter (see Ex. 35b).

1–2–3–2 (Minor)

This term is actually a fusion of the gloomy relationship between the
tonic and minor third, and (harmonizing the third as a minor sixth of the
dominant) the emotional effect of the minor 6–5 progression. It has
been employed rarely, but these are three outstanding examples which
give it the status of a basic term in musical language.

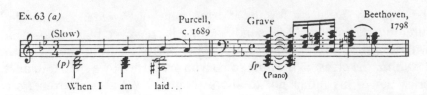

The fact that Beethoven and Tchaikovsky hit on the same phrase to open works which they entitled 'Pathétique', and that Purcell also used the same progression to open Dido's Lament 'When I am laid in earth', in his opera, puts the expressive function of the term in a clear light. To make the restricted movement from the tonic to the 'dark' minor third, and fall back by a harmonic 6–5 *appoggiatura* at a slow tempo, is naturally to express a sense of brooding grief swelling out briefly into a burst of anguish and dying away again; when the phrase is played quickly, and repeated, as in Tchaikovsky's *allegro*, the brooding feeling is replaced by one of agitated obsession. A similar kind of term, substituting for 1–2 the ascending 1–3–5 of protest plus the ascending 5–1–3 of courage, forms the basis of the opening theme of the finale of Mozart's Fortieth Symphony (see Ex. 87f).

1–(2)–(3)–(4)–5–6–5 (Major)

The ascending major 1–3–5 progression, with the 5–6–5 phrase dovetailed on, is another of the most widely-used terms of musical language; it is almost always employed to express the innocence and purity of angels and children, or some natural phenomenon which possesses the same qualities in the eyes of men. That this should be so is hardly surprising, when we consider that the phrase confines itself entirely to the joyful elements of the scale, and being an ascending one, it is consequently an affirmation of maximum joy. It is, in fact, expressive of an absolute happiness that can never be fully experienced in civilized human life but only by savages, children, animals or birds,

or saints or imaginary blessed beings. In expressing the normal
emotions of life, man has to undermine the joy of the major system by
means of the pathetic 4–3 and 8–7 suspensions, or by chromatic
tensions, and at least half the time looks on the darker side with the
minor system: 1–3–5–6–5 in the major system is set aside for states of
pure blessedness.

Ex. 64a and b show the simplest form of the term—1–5–6–5. In Ex.
64a, the first quotation shows the derivation from plainchant ('A boy is
born to us'); the second is an adaptation of the plainchant tune by
Morales for a Christmas motet; the third, the opening of Byrd's

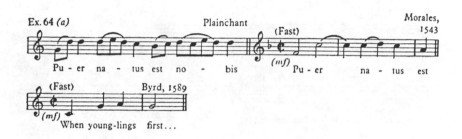

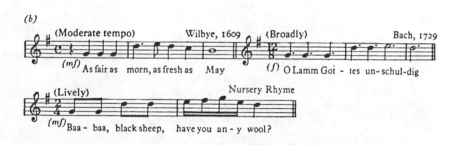

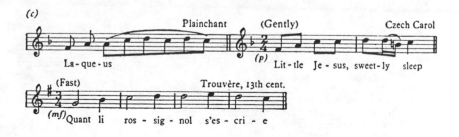

(d)

(e)

(f)

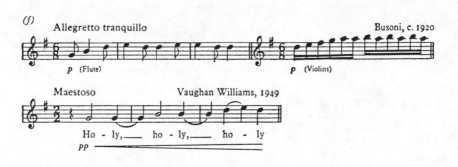

(g)

madrigal on the innocence of youthful love—('When younglings first on Cupid set their eyes . . . they ween he can work them no annoy'). Ex. 64b consists of the opening of Wilbye's madrigal 'As fair as morn' (the connexion between the freshness of morning and innocence is obvious); the chorale which rides with divine purity over the tumultuous human grief of the opening chorus of Bach's St. Matthew Passion—'O Lamb of God, guiltless'; and the children's nursery-tune known the world over (in this country as 'Baa-baa black sheep'). (See also Ex. 97.)

With Ex. 64c, we turn to the 1–3–5–6–5 version, with another plainchant derivation—from the Gradual of the Holy Innocents ('The snare is broken, we are delivered'); a well-known Czech carol (one of the innumerable Christmas carols which open with this phrase); and the song of a thirteenth-century troubadour about the nightingale (another 'innocent' and 'fresh' natural creature). In his chapter on medieval song, in Vol. 2 of *The New Oxford History of Music*, J.A. Westrup draws attention to the widespread use of this figure in the songs of the troubadours, trouvères, minnesingers, and mastersingers, and in the Italian *laudi spirituali*: I have taken the nightingale song and the 'Laqueus' plainchant theme from his article. Ex. 64d brings some variants of the basic pattern: the German chorale 'How brightly shines the morning star'; the opening of Bach's cantata 'Hold in remembrance

Jesus Christ'; the Cum Sancto Spiritu ('With the Holy Ghost') from his Mass in B minor; and the Osanna (the song of the Cherubim and Seraphim) from Mozart's Mass in C minor.

Ex. 64e quotes a theme from Mendelssohn's *Elijah* which needs no comment; and the opening of Wagner's *Parsifal*—the theme of the Holy Grail (the sixth does not fall back to the dominant here, since the theme continues with the phrase connected with the spear that pierced Christ on the Cross, modulating into C minor with the minor 6–5 term and a fall to the minor third—when the opera opens, purity is stained with sin and suffering). The Humperdinck is, of course, the prayer of the children in his opera *Hansel and Gretel*—'When I go to bed at night, fourteen angels stand around me'. In Ex. 64f, the Busoni fragments are from the Easter Chorus in *Doktor Faust*; the Vaughan Williams is the opening of the final chorus of *The Pilgrim's Progress*, sung by voices from the Celestial City. Ex. 64g shows the variant 1–3–4–5–6–5 in another carol; in the theme from Vaughan Williams's *Job*, to which young men and women on earth, after Satan's defeat, play instruments and decorate the altars; and in the theme sung by the Heavenly Beings to Christian, in *The Pilgrim's Progress*, when the tend his wounds after the fight with Apollyon—'So shalt thou enter in the gates of the Celestial City'.

In Ex. 64h, we have the complete form 1–2–3–4–5–6–5: once more the plainchant derivation, in a French 'Alleluia'; the Pastoral Symphony in Handel's *Messiah*; and the lark in Haydn's *Creation*. Ex. 64j shows two further variants: the theme to which the Angel sings to Gerontius of his salvation, in Elgar's oratorio; and the words of Ellen, in *Peter Grimes*, greeting the peace of the bright Sunday morning after the human and elemental turmoil of the storm—in company, significantly, with the innocent boy apprentice.

In 1948, Anthony Alpers gave a radio talk in the Christmas edition of the BBC's Music Magazine, drawing attention to the derivation of many Christmas carols from this term; he reminded his listeners that the fourteenth-century German mystic, Henry Suso, who composed the tune of 'In Dulci Jubilo', said it had been sung to him by the angels, and that the melody was so joyful that he had been drawing into dancing with his heavenly visitors. Alpers made the amusing suggestion that this tune was the 'song the angels sang' at the first Christmas; and indeed, one is inclined to believe that if the angels did appear to the shepherds at the first Christmas, the opening strains of their song may well have been 1–(3)–5–6–5. Alpers also pointed out that the opening violin theme of the finale of Vaughan Williams's Fifth Symphony must naturally be regarded in this light, an opinion with which we are by now disposed to agree.

1–(2)–(3)–(4)–5–6–5 (Minor)

The minor version of the foregoing term, confining itself to the two basic 'grievous' notes of the scale in a triadic context, clearly expresses a powerful assertion of fundamental unhappiness—the 'protest' of 1–3–5 being extended into the 'anguish' of 5–6–5.

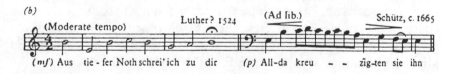

Exs. 65a and b show the simple form 1–5–6–5. Ex. 65a quotes a twelfth-century troubadour song 'He who counsels me to have done with loving does not know how he arouses me, nor what are my grievous sighs'; the opening line of Ockeghem's *chanson* 'Misfortune afflicts me'; and the beginning of Byrd's anthem 'O Lord my God, let flesh and blood thy servant not subdue'. In Ex. 65b, we have the opening of the chorale 'In deepest need I cry to thee'; and from the St. John Passion of Schütz, the setting of the words 'Then they crucified him'. Ex. 65c shows the form 1–3–5–6–5, from the opening of Josquin's motet 'Thou who didst veil thy face and suffer poverty, O Sun of Justice, have mercy on us.' Ex. 65d brings the form 1–3–4–5–6–5: the opening of the Kyrie in a Service by Byrd; and the opening of a madrigal by Giaches Wert (note that 'O unhappy parting' is set to the despairing minor 5–4–3–2–1).

In Ex. 65e, we have Seneca's words in Monteverdi's *L'Incoronazione di Poppea*, as he comes to the point of taking his own life, 'Friends, friends, the hour has come'. Seneca is an equivocal case: he declares that he goes to his death with joy, but he is after all the Stoic philosopher, facing the final misfortune with unbowed head; the stoic emotions function in a tragic context, for which the simple joy of the major system would be inappropriate. In Ex. 65e is also the phrase with which Aida greets Radames as she enters the tomb to die with him, in Verdi's opera.

Ex. 65f quotes two uses of a folk-song common to many countries—the minor version of 'Baa-baa, black sheep' (Ex. 64b)—the original words, in both major and minor cases, being impossible to trace. It is not surprising that the Jewish race, with its tragic past, should have chosen a stern variant of the theme for the Israeli National Anthem (note that the minor sixth is harmonized firmly as the minor third of the subdominant minor chord.) Smetana used a Czech version of the tune as the main theme of his tone-poem portraying the river Vltava, the first part of the cycle *Ma Vlast*, which evokes the heroic-tragic past of his native land. Although to some extent the theme is infused with a legendary-heroic character, the general effect is not in any way tragic in feeling (rather genial in fact), owing to the buoyant rhythm, the flowing semiquaver accompaniment tone-painting the river, and particularly the transformation of 6–5 into 4–3 in the relative major, any suspicion of 4–3 pathos being removed by harmonizing 4 firmly as the tonic of the subdominant major chord of the new key.

For two superb uses of this term in its basic sense, see Ex. 52a and b, and for a 'pop' version, Ex. 27j.

Aaron Copland has drawn attention to an isolated example of the effect of this term (conflated with the minor 5–4–3–2–1) in a piece of 'pure' music: the subject of Bach's E flat minor fugue in Book 1 of the 'Forty-eight'. He says 'To analyse why this theme, consisting only of a few notes, should be so expressive, is impossible'—yet he goes on to try and analyse it: 'Something in the way the theme rises bravely from 1 to 5, rises again from 1 to 4, only to fall back slowly on 1—something also about the shortened rhythmic sense of the second part of the phrase creates an extraordinary feeling of quiet but profound resignation'.[34] Copland's analysis is, of course, hampered by a lack of consideration of the tonal tensions. First, he does not mention that this all happens in the minor scale: the effect of the same procedure in the major scale would be quite different. Second, he does not mention the minor sixth. Thirdly, he does not mention the basic terms 1–5–6–5 or 5–4–3–2–1. Nevertheless, it is clear that he has felt the emotion in the theme exactly.

[34]Aaron Copland, *What to Listen For in Music*, Chap. 2.

The effect of the whole theme is explained as follows. The minor system, soft dynamic, and slow tempo set a quiet, serious mood; and 1–5–6–5, a subdued assertion of the anguish, merges into 5–4–3–2–1, a subdued expression of resigned despair. Thus the final effect, which Copland has felt but been unable to account for, is one of 'quiet but profound resignation'. His pinpointing of the other expressive elements —of the fall from 5 to 1 and the subsequent rise only up as far as 4 (within the overall shape 5–4–3–2–1) and of the rhythmic contraction —shows the endless subtleties of expression to be gained from the inflection of a basic term.

8–7–6–5 (Major)

To fall from the tonic to the dominant, taking in the optimistic major seventh and sixth, is to express an incoming emotion of joy, an acceptance or welcoming of comfort, consolation, or fulfilment. The term is clearly a near-synonym of the major 5–4–3–2–1, with which it often combines into a descending major scale, in the way that the ascending triadic figures 1–3–5 and 5–1–3 combine and intermingle. However, when it is used separately, the fact that it ends on the dominant gives it a more open, continuing feeling towards the future, compared with 5–3–1, which suggests finality.

COOKE

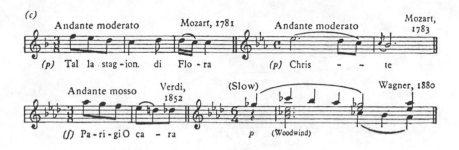

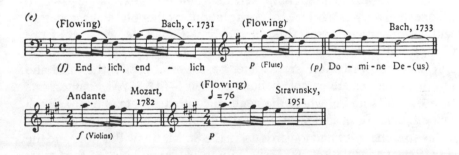

273

In Ex. 66a we see three composers using the term, like 5–4–3–2–1, to invoke the Deity as a bringer of consolation or other blessings, together with an operatic excerpt. First, an early setting of the words 'O Lord God, Lamb of God'; second, a phrase from Dunstable's *Veni sancte spiritus* (the words here are 'Come, bestower of gifts'); the third and fourth quotations are complementary to their 5–(4)–3–2–1 counterparts (see Exs. 57a and c, where the general contexts are explained). Bach made much use of this term, Ex. 66b giving two cases; the aria 'See, Jesus stretches his hand towards us' in the St. Matthew Passion; and the aria 'Sweet consolation, my Jesus comes' in Cantata No. 151. Mozart is represented in Ex. 66c by Idomeneo's song of relief at the end of the opera—'Peace returns to my heart; as in the season of the flowers the trees blossom, so age now flowers in me'; and the Christe Eleison from his Mass in C minor (which follows a Kyrie Eleison based on the minor 1–3–5 progression). The Verdi is from the aria in the last act of *La Traviata*, in which Alfredo tries to console Violetta by saying that they will leave Paris, the scene of all their unhappiness, and live peacefully in the country; the Wagner is the theme of Faith in *Parsifal*, which reveals

274

its true significance at the end of the opera, portraying the descent of the Dove (the Holy Ghost) during the final scene of redemption. Ex. 66d quotes the theme which brings temporary consolation amid the despair of the finale of Tchaikovsky's *Pathétique* Symphony (it is marked 'soothingly and with devotion'); the opening of the love-duet in Debussy's *Pelléas*, in which the lovers welcome the long-awaited relief of being able to avow their passions; and Bianca's complementary phrase to that of Lucia in the linen-folding scene in Britten's *The Rape of Lucretia* (see Ex. 57e for theme and general context). See also Ex. 5 (Dowland).

All the above quotations are slowish in tempo; we now turn to quicker, more animated examples. Ex. 66c shows again Bach's fondness for the term, in the aria 'At last, at last, I am free from my yoke' in Cantata No. 56, and the Domine Deus ('Domine *Fili*') from the B minor Mass. The Mozart is from another of Belmonte's arias in *The Seraglio*, in which he is anticipating the relief of seeing Constanze again after long separation; the Stravinsky from the opening aria of *The Rake's Progress*, in which Anne is enjoying the beauty of spring, and receiving assurance from the thought that 'Love reigns o'er his own'.

Ex. 66f brings louder and weightier versions: the phrase 'Et in terra pax' from the *Gloria in modum tubae* (in the style of the trumpet) by Dufay; the last line of the chorale 'A stronghold sure' which voices the all-embracing sense of fulfilment in the words 'There is nothing on earth like Him' to 8–7–6–5 plus 5–4–3–2–1; and the heartfelt song of thanksgiving for the relief of the rain, in Mendelssohn's *Elijah*. (See also Ex. 6, Handel.)

The remaining examples reveal that this term is employable, in the same sense, as a bass. In Ex. 66g, we see it at work peacefully, in Wilbye's madrigal 'Draw on, sweet night, best friend unto those cares . . .'; actively, in the Easter Hymn which brings temporarily its inherent solace to the tormented Faust, in Berlioz's cantata; and peacefully again, as Anne, in Stravinsky's *The Rake's Progress*, sings her unhappy, demented lover to sleep. In Ex. 66h, its acts firmly as the ground bass for the final duet of Monteverdi's *L'Incoronazione di Poppea*, in which Nero and Poppea, all their worries over, welcome the opportunity to enjoy their love; majestically, in the Sanctus in Bach's B minor Mass; and actively again, in the angel's chorus 'Glory to God' in Handel's *Messiah* (the fulfilment of the long-awaited 'good tidings of great joy').

8–7–6–5 *(Minor)*

To fall from the tonic to the dominant, taking in the 'mournful' minor seventh and 'anguished' minor sixth, is clearly to express an incoming painful emotion, an acceptance of, or yielding to grief; passive suffering; and the despair connected with death. As with the major form, it is a near-synonym of 5–4–3–2–1, and often merges with it, but again, when it is used on its own, it has an open, continuing feeling (never-ending despair) whereas 5–4–3–2–1 suggests finality (death itself).

Ex. 67 *(a)*

(b)

(c)

(d)

276

COOKE

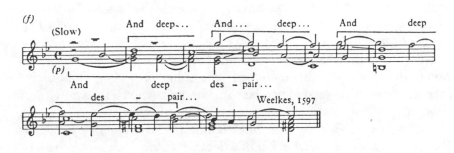

277

The three quotations in Ex. 67 a are: the opening of Ockeghem's *chanson* 'Except only the expectation of death, no hope remains in my weary heart'; a phrase from Obrecht's 'By the waters of Babylon'—'If I forget thee, O Jerusalem, let my right hand forget her cunning'; and Weerbecke's setting of the Tenebrae—'There was darkness over all the land as they crucified Christ of Judea'. Ex. 67 b shows the opening of Josquin's chanson 'Come away, sorrow, and kill my heart, that it may drown itself in woe and weeping'; and the first line of Dowland's famous 'Lachrymae' (note the dovetailing of 8–7–6–5 with the variant of the arched 5–3–1). In Ex. 67 c, we have two cases of the fusing of 8–7–6–5 and 5–(4)–3–(2)–1 into a single expressive unit: Pamina's aria in *The Magic Flute*, 'Ah, I feel it; the joy of love has vanished for ever'; and the opening of Verdi's Requiem. The Tchaikovsky is the minor transformation of the 'consoling' theme in the finale of his *Pathétique* Symphony (see Ex. 66 d) on its second and last appearance, when it falls down and down the minor scale to die out on double-basses. Ex. 67 d is an elaboration of 8–7–6–5—the final theme of *La Bohème*, to which Rudolph sobs out his grief at Mimi's death: this too dovetails into 5–4–3–2–1. Mélisande's death evoked a more rarified version of the phrase from Debussy, and so did Orpheus's grief from Stravinsky (Ex. 67 e): the stage direction in the latter case is 'Orpheus weeps for Euridyce; he stands motionless, with his back to the audience'. See also Exs. 5, 30 a, 32 d, 41 a, 41 g (with flattened fifth).

The superb passage from Weelkes's madrigal 'Ay me, my wonted joys forsake me, and deep despair doth overtake me', demonstrates how 8–7–6–5, by contrapuntal imitation, will function as a bass (notice 5–4–3–2–1 as an inner part). The remaining examples are of such basses.

Ex. 67 g brings us the equivocal Seneca again, from *L'Incoronazione di Poppea*: 'Death is but a brief anguish' he sings, but his philosophy is that death is the end of everything. Blow and Purcell, setting the same poem of lamentation for Queen Mary's death, at approximately the same time, both wove 8–7–6–5 into their otherwise different basses. Ex. 67 h shows the bass of the 'Way of the Cross' aria in Bach's St. Matthew Passion; of the opening remarks of the Statue, coming to claim Don Giovanni for hell, in Mozart's opera; and of the dirge to which Lucretia walks to meet her husband in Britten's opera, in despair at the shattering of their love by the rape. (See also Ex. 46 b).

The Descending Chromatic Scale

To complete our account of the sixteen simplest basic terms of musical language, it is necessary to mention the descending chromatic scale, which is essentially the minor 8–7–6–5 with the intervening semitones filled in, plus or minus the minor 5–4–3–2–1, treated likewise. The effect of filling in the gaps is to make the 'despairing' descent more weary, and to increase the element of pain by every possible chromatic tension. Examples are too long to quote, so a list will be given.

As a melodic line, descending chromatics appear in the following: Giuseppe Caimo's lamenting madrigal of 1564, 'Piangete valli abbandonate' ('Weep, ye forsaken valleys')—8 down to 5, answered by 5 down to 2; Gesualdo's madrigal of 1611 'Moro, lasso' ('I die, weary of my grief')—free chromatics, E sharp, D sharp, D, in D minor; Purcell's Lament for the Death of Queen Mary, on the word 'moerore' (to lament)—8 down to 5; Mozart's *Don Giovanni*, accompanying the deaths of both Don Giovanni and the Commendatore (both 8 down to 5); and Schubert's song 'Der Wegweiser', where the winter-journeyer sings of the signpost pointing out a journey 'from which no-one ever came back' (free chromatics, F, E, E flat, D, D flat, C, in a G minor context). The procedure is used for the dying utterances of Dido, in Berlioz's *The Trojans* (8 down to 2), Valentine, in Gounod's *Faust* (5 down to 1), and Gerontius in Elgar's oratorio (5 down to 2).

As an inner part, a descending chromatic scale from the minor seventh down to the major second ends the Chorus of Mourning for the death of Tom, in Stravinsky's *The Rake's Progress*.

As a bass, the descending chromatic scale is used for the death of Dido, in Purcell's opera, and the Crucifixus of Bach's B minor Mass (both 8 down to 5); during the scene of Mélisande's death, in Debussy's opera (4 down to minor 6); and in the opening chorus of Stravinsky's *Oedipus Rex*, to the words 'Thebes is dying' (5 down to 1).

Such general agreement would suggest that this slow, gradual, painful sinking expresses the feeling of life ebbing away altogether.

There are, of course, many other terms of musical language which we have not considered. For example the phrase in the major system, beginning on various notes, which rises three steps, repeats and accents the last, and falls a fifth, sixth or seventh; which, if we are to accept the instinct of composers, expresses a feeling of passionate love. Consider Christ's words in Bach's St. Matthew Passion 'I shall not drink of this cup until that day when I drink it again with you in my Father's Kingdom': at the words 'until that day', the melody takes the pattern 1–2–3–3–lower 6. Or Zerlina in *Don Giovanni*, who uses exactly the same phrase, on the same notes, but to a quick light rhythm befitting her skittish nature, as she presses Masetto's hand to her heart, singing 'Feel it beating; feel it beating', in the aria 'Vedrai carino'. Or the drawn-out theme in Wagner's *Tristan* (the second theme of the Prelude) connected with the glance of the wounded Tristan into Isolde's eyes, which began the fatal attachment (6–7–8–8–2); or the unmistakably erotic tune of the slow movement of Tchaikovsky's Fifth Symphony, which includes the phrases 3–4–5–5–lower 6, 2–3–4–4–lower 5.

There is also the 'lullaby' phrase which moves between the major third and the dominant: Wilbye's 'Draw on sweet night' (Ex. 66g); the lulling accompaniment of Bach's 'Komm süsser Trost' (Ex. 66b); Schubert's well-known Cradle Song, his song 'Des Baches Wiegenlied' in *Die schöne Müllerin*, his song 'Liebesbotschaft', and his song 'Im Dorfe' in *Die Winterreise*, in which the wanderer envies the villagers sleeping in their beds on that cold night; Brahms's Cradle Song; Tarquin's words as he stands by the sleeping Lucretia's bedside in Britten's opera—'To wake her with a kiss would put Tarquinius asleep awhile'; and the lullaby Anne sings to Tom in Stravinsky's *The Rake's Progress* (Ex. 66g).

But the sixteen terms dealt with above are undoubtedly the really basic ones, and are sufficient for our immediate purpose—an examination of the more far-reaching aspects of the language of music.

NELSON GOODMAN

Nelson Goodman (1906, b. Massachusetts), distinguished philosopher of science, language and the arts, ran an art gallery before launching a career as professor of philosophy. In recent years he has been deeply involved in several projects concerning art and education and has himself produced some multi-media stage-presentations.

Goodman's *Languages of Art* has raised much interest and many debates since its appearance in 1968. Though the book stands on its own, it is better understood against the background of his previous works. Goodman seems to break with the traditional philosophical deliberations on art even when he discusses some of the central aesthetic issues, such as "representation" and "expression." His scope is at the same time narrower, as well as wider, than that which generally prevails in aesthetics; while he ignores questions like "value," he concentrates on the formal aspects that link signs and objects. Accounting for, and only for, objects whose conditions for identification are clear and definite dictates the exclusion of "intentions," for example, without thereby denying their existence. By constructing an "extensional" theory of aesthetics, Goodman attemps to remove the methodological barrier which has separated science and arts since the seventheenth century. Altogether, Goodman applies the rigor and the consistency he managed to achieve elsewhere to issues which were deemed unapproachable from a tight philosophical point of view.

The new alliance between art and science is, however, first and foremost, a consequent of Goodman's conception regarding science. Though "extensional isomorphism" between a theory and the reality to which it relates is, for Goodman, an important criterion for assessing symbolic systems, his approach is neither realistic nor positivistic. Likewise, arguing for the inseparability of observational data from theoretical elements does not stem from some kind of idealism or relativism. Reception and interpretation are interdependent and, though conditioned by pre-conceptions, they are, nevertheless, defined by the actual world. Attributing inevitable and immutable aspects to the nature of human cognition is a misconception, as far as Goodman is concerned, since language is the prime factor in the organization of knowledge, emphasizing cultural, rather than universal aspects.

Thus, while arguing (together with Quine) in favor of a holistic view of science for which deductive inferences are justified by their conformity to valid general rules and, inversely, the rules by their conformity to deductive inferences, Goodman, unlike Quine, anchors both the components as well as the relationship between them in entrenched habits. The rules of deduction, of induction, and of logic are neither analytic nor innate; they are, like the experience for which they account, habits of mind susceptible, though "stubbornly," to revision and change. For Goodman, the structure of the world of presystematic language is simply a "world-structure under one world description," and not "the structure of the world independent of any description." Among the many true descriptions of the world, accordingly, there are the arts, distinguished by their domination of "certain, specific characteristics of symbols." Goodman's explications concerning art not only enrich our understanding of the symbolic system of each of the arts, but his conceptualization of their "languages" also provides a sound base for more rigorous descriptions of the possible combinations and exchanges among them.

Goodman believes that Western music is an example—indeed, the prime example—of a notational system that answers five definitional requirements. Two of the requirements are syntactic, and three of them semantic. Briefly, the symbol scheme of every notational system is notational. It consists of characters ("inscriptions," "marks," "utterances") the essential feature of which is an "abstraction class of character indifference among inscription," i.e., each inscription of a character is a true copy of the character and no mark may belong to more than one character. The syntactic requirements of a notational system are that the characters be *disjoined* and *finitely differentiated*. Disjointness is assured by a classification that counts every difference as a difference of character. Finite differentiation is assured by a scheme of clearly differentiated inscriptions, so that if two characters have an inscription in common, it must be theoretically possible to determine to which of the two characters the inscription belongs.

Symbol systems consist of symbol schemes "correlated with a field of reference." A symbol, however, may or may not denote that to which it refers. A mark is ambiguous if it has different "compliants" at different times, even if it is an inscription of a single character. If "scores" are to be correlated with performances, whatever is denoted by a symbol must comply with it. The three semantic requirements upon notational systems are thus: *unambiguity, disjointness* and *finite differentiation*. Unambiguity pertains to an invariance in compliance relationships; disjointness stipulates that "no two characters have any compliant in common"; and finite differentiation assures the theoretical possibility to determine that a given object does not comply with the first or the second of two characters which have different compliance classes if that object does not comply with both.

As will become apparent from the reading, the above five requirements are not optional, but a must, if a symbol system is to function as a notational system. Standard musical notation, Goodman suggests, is a prime example of a notational system. "Identity of work and of score," says Goodman, "is retained in any series of steps, each of them either from compliant performance to score-inscription to true copy. This is ensured by the fact, and only by the fact, that the language in which a score is written must be notational—must satisfy the five stated requirements." In short, performances of music are not an instance of a musical work, but the end products of the work as defined by its notation. This does not mean that performances do not differ, or may not differ, from each other. In fact, they do because all the aspects that affect the quality of performances are not notational, only those that affect the *identity* of the work are. Developing a notational system like that of music means having arrived at "a real definition of the notion of a musical work," says Goodman. Indeed, the continual struggle to eliminate "ambiguities" which accompanied the early development of *written* music in the West may be viewed, in retrospect, as "stages" in the evolution of a *notational system*. Goodman's analysis, one may argue, conceptualizes one of the major developments in the history of Western music.

In contrast to music, a painting, according to Goodman, is its own beginning and end, lacking a "score," as it were, from which and into which it can be reproduced. (The distinction is developed in Goodman's theory about "autographic" and "allographic" arts.) The point stressed here is the definitiveness of musical works. It should also be added that none of the natural languages, according to Goodman, are notational systems. Discursive languages meet the syntactic requirements but not the semantic ones. It follows that utterances are not the end products of a literary work in the way that performances are the end products of a musical work. Although a literary work may be articulate and "exemplify" or "express" what is articulate, it nevertheless requires "search" in order "to determine precisely what is exemplified or expressed." This is due to the fact that literature is only syntactically articulate but semantically "dense." By definition, then, language leaves something "unsaid" while music says it all, or all it can say.

Despite the fact that scores define musical works, the exemplification or expression of anything beyond the score constitutes reference in a semantically dense system. Representation is relative to different symbol systems, and a scheme is representational insofar as it is dense. Expression, according to Goodman, is no different from exemplification, representation and description insofar as they are types of reference. Resemblance is not necessary for reference and almost anything may stand for anything else. *Denotation*, not imitation, is the core of representation. While expression, like representation, is a species of denotation, it is invariably related to exemplification, and exemplification, in turn, is a mode of symbolization based on "labeling." (The reference to "label" and not to property is crucial for Goodman, the nominalist.) A certain piece or genre of music, for example, may be labeled "sad." That which expresses sadness is metaphorically sad— actually sad, but not literally so—by virtue of "transferred application of some label coextensive with sad." What is expressed is thus "possessed"; the symbol takes on an acquired property. "Establishment of the referential relationship," says Goodman, "is a matter of singling out certain properties for attention, of selecting association with certain other objects. Verbal discourse is not least among the many factors that aid in founding and nurturing such association."

Bearing Goodman in mind, one may argue that the interaction between music and words thus involves a relationship between a fully articulate symbol system and a symbol system that is only syntactically articulate while semantically "dense." The former leaves no room for ambiguity; the latter provides the reference. It is in this sense that music provides an unambiguous statement to that which it cannot even name; once it is linked with a label, it can provide a unique definition.

If mood, disposition and the like are thought to be best expressed by music it is because music is capable of pinning down, incontestably, so to speak, that which is most ambiguous in discursive language. Here lies a clue to Schopenhauer's view of music as an art which men are "content to understand directly" but renounce all claim "to an abstract conception of this direct understanding itself." Assisting in demystifying Schopenhauer, Goodman's systematic theory also helps to fully appreciate the philosophical importance of some of the treatises of the eighteenth century that deal with the relationship between poetry and music. It particularly elucidates Webb's theory of "cxpression" (see Webb) and Twining's treatment of "imitation." Finally, on the basis of Goodman's theory of metaphor and Max Black's theory of "metaphorical interaction" one can better understand some of the "exchanges" between music and the literary arts as well as their historical and theoretical implications.

from Languages of Art[1]

The Theory of Notation

... it is not sufficient to have the whole world at one's disposal—the very infinitude of possibilities cancels out possibilities, as it were, until limitations are discovered.

Roger Sessions*

1. The Primary Function

Concerning notation in the arts there are some questions, often dismissed as mere annoyances, that reach deep into the theory of language and knowledge. Casual speculation on whether a notation for the dance is a legitimate goal, or on why a notation for painting is not, usually stops short of asking what the essential function of a score is, or just what distinguishes a score from a drawing or study or sketch on the one hand and from a verbal description or scenario or script on the other. A score is commonly regarded as a mere tool, no more intrinsic to the finished work than is the sculptor's hammer or the painter's easel. For the score is dispensable after the performance; and music can be composed and learned and played 'by ear', without any score and even by people who cannot read or write any notation. But to take notation as therefore nothing but a practical aid to production is to miss its fundamental theoretical role.

A score, whether or not ever used as a guide for a performance, has as a primary function the authoritative identification of a work from performance to performance. Often scores and notations—and pseudo-scores and pseudo-notations—have such other more exciting functions as facilitating transposition, comprehension, or even composition; but every score, as a score, has the logically prior office of identifying a

---

[1]Text: Nelson Goodman, *Languages of Art* (New York: Bobbs Merrill Co., 1968), pp. 127-221. All of the notes are Goodman's notes.
*"Problems and Issues Facing the Composer Today", in *Problems of Modern Music*, ed. P.H. Lang (New York, W.W. Norton & Co., Inc., 1962), p. 31.

work.[2] From this derive all the requisite theoretical properties of scores and of the notational systems in which they are written. The first step, then, is to look more closely at this primary function.

First, a score must define a work, marking off the performances that belong to the work from those that do not. This is not to say that the score must provide an easy test for deciding whether a given performance belongs to the work or not; after all, the definition of gold as the element with an atomic weight of 197.2 gives me no ready test for telling a gold piece from a brass one. The line drawn need only be theoretically manifest. What is required is that all and only performances that comply with the score be performances of the work.

But that is not all. Most of the definitions we encounter in ordinary discourse and in formal systems fail to satisfy a more stringent demand imposed by the primary duty of a score. While a good definition always unequivocally determines what objects conform to it, a definition is seldom in turn uniquely determined by each of its instances. If I point to an object and ask you what kind of object it is, you may give any of a wide variety of answers, picking out any class to which the object belongs. Accordingly, in passing alternately (and correctly) from an object to a definition—or predicate or other label—the object complies with (e.g., to "table" or some coextensive term), to another object (e.g., a steel table), to another label (e.g., "steel thing") applying to the second object, and to a third object (e.g., an automobile) complying with the second label, we may pass from one object to another such that no label in the series applies to both; and two labels in the series may differ totally in extension, no one object complying with both.

No such latitude can be tolerated in the case of scores. Scores and performances must be so related that in every chain where each step is either from score to compliant performance or from performance to covering score or from one copy of a score to another correct copy of it, all performances belong to the same work and all copies of scores define the same class of performance. Otherwise, the requisite identification of a work from performance to performance would not be guaranteed; we might pass from a performance to another that is not of the same

---

[2]This is by no means true of everything commonly called a score; here, as with most familiar words, systematic use involves a specialization from ordinary use. The reasons for the choice made in this case will already be apparent from the preceding chapter. Obviously what is commonly called but does not by the above criterion qualify as a score is not thereby disparaged but only reclassified (see further V, 2).

work, or from a score to another that determines a different—even an entirely disjoint—class of performances. Not only must a score uniquely determine the class of performances belonging to the work, but the score (as a class of copies or inscriptions that so define the work) must be uniquely determined, given a performance and the notational system.

This double demand is indeed a strong one. Its motivation and consequences, and the results of weakening it in various ways, need to be carefully considered. We may begin by asking what the properties are that scores, and the notational systems in which scores are written, must have in order to meet this basic requirement. Study of that question will call for some inquiry into the nature of languages and into the differences between language and nonlinguistic symbol systems, as well as into the features that distinguish notational systems from other languages, and will mean going into some rather bothersome technical details, but may occasionally expose new aspects of some familiar problems.[3]

2. Syntactic Requirements

The symbol scheme of every notational system is notational, but not every symbol system with a notational scheme is a notational system. What distinguishes the notational systems from the others are certain features of the relationship obtaining between notational scheme and application. "Notation" is commonly used indifferently as short for either "notational scheme" or "notational system", and for brevity I shall often take advantage of this convenient vacillation where the context precludes confusion.

What, first, constitutes a notational scheme? Any symbol scheme consists of characters, usually with modes of combining them to form others. Characters are certain classes of utterances or inscriptions or marks. (I shall use "inscription" to include utterances, and "mark" to include inscriptions; an inscription is any mark—visual, auditory, etc.—that belongs to a character.) Now the essential feature of a character in a notation is that its members may be freely exchanged for

[3]The reader with no background in logic, mathematics, or technical philosophy may well skim or skip the rest of this chapter and rely on gathering from the applications and illustrations in later chapters the principles expounded here.

one another without any syntactical effect; or more literally, since actual marks are seldom moved about and exchanged, that all inscriptions of a given character be syntactically equivalent. In other words, being instances of one character in a notation must constitute a sufficient condition for marks being 'true copies' or replicas[4] of each other, or being spelled the same way. And a true copy of a true copy of ... a true copy of an inscription x must always be a true copy of x. For if the relation of being a true copy is not thus transitive, the basic purpose of a notation is defeated. Requisite separation among characters — and hence among scores — will be lost unless identity is preserved in any chain of true copies.

A necessary condition for a notation, the, is *character-indifference* among the instances of each character. Two marks are character-indifferent if each is an inscription (i.e., belongs to some character) and neither one belongs to any character the other does not. Character-indifference is a typical equivalence-relation: reflexive, symmetric, and transitive. A character in a notation is a most-comprehensive class of character-indifferent inscriptions; that is, a class of marks such that every two are character-indifferent with every member of it. In short, a character in notation is an abstraction class[5] of character-indifference

---

[4] The distinction between a word 'type' and its 'tokens' was stressed by Peirce; see *Collected Papers of Charles Sanders Peirce*, vol. IV, ed. C. Hartshorne and P. Weiss (Cambridge, Mass., Harvard University Press, 1933),p. 423. The type is the universal or class of which marks are instances or members. Although I speak in the present text of a character as a class of marks, this is for me informal parlance admissible only because it can readily be translated into more acceptable language. I prefer (see *SA*, pp. 354–364) to dismiss the type altogether and treat the so-called tokens of a type as *replicas* of one another. An inscription need not be an exact duplicate of another to be a replica, or true copy, of it; indeed, there is in general no degree of similarity that is necessary or sufficient for replicahood. See further examples discussed later in this section.

[5] In the terminology of Rudolf Carnap (*Der Logische Aufbau der Welt* [Berlin, Weltkreis-Verlag, 1928], p. 102; English translation by R.A. George entitled *The Logical Structure of the World and Pseudoproblems in Philosophy* [Berkeley, University of California Press, 1967], p. 119) a *similarity-circle* of a relation R is a class such that (1) every two members form an R-pair, and (2) no nonmember forms an R-pair with every member. Where R, as above, is an equivalence-relation, a similarity-circle of R is called an *abstraction-class* of R. No nonmember of an abstraction-class from an R-pair with any member; for since an equivalence-relation is transitive, a nonmember forming an R-pair with one member would form an R-pair with each member, in violation of condition (2).

among inscriptions. As a result, no mark may belong to more than one character.

That the characters must be *disjoint* may not seem very important or striking; but it is an absolutely essential and, I think, rather remarkable feature of notations. It is essential for reasons already explained. Suppose, for example, that a certain mark (Figure 3) belongs to both the first and the fourth letters of the alphabet. Then either every "*a*" and every "*d*" will be syntactically equivalent with this mark and hence with each other, so that the two letter-classes collapse into one character, or else joint membership in a letter-class will not guarantee syntactical equivalence, so that instances of the same letter may not be true copies of one another. In neither case will the letters qualify as characters in a notation.

Figure 3

The disjointness of the characters is also somewhat surprising since we have in the world not a realm of inscriptions neatly sorted into clearly separate classes but, rather, a bewildering miscellany of marks differing from each other in all ways and degrees. To impose a partitioning into disjoint sets seems a willful even though needful violence. And no matter how characters are specified, there will almost inevitably be many marks for which it will be difficult or even virtually impossible to decide whether or not they belong to a given character. The more delicate and precise the stipulated differentiation between characters (e.g., suppose characters are classes of straight marks differing in length by one-millionth of an inch), the harder it will be to determine whether certain marks belong to one character or another. If, on the other hand, there are wide neutral zones between characters (e.g., suppose that the characters are: the class of straight marks between one and two inches long, the class of straight marks between five and six inches long, etc.), then among the marks that do not belong to any character will be some that are exceedingly difficulty to distinguish from some instances of some character. There is no way of preventing this infiltration at the borders, no way of ensuring that due caution will protect against all mistakes in identifying a mark as belonging or not belonging to a given character. But this trouble is not peculiar to notations; it is a pervasive and inescapable fact of experience. And it by no means precludes establishment of a system of

290

disjoint classes of marks; it only makes hard the determination of the membership of some marks in such classes.

Obviously anyone designing a notation will try to minimize the probability of errors. But this is a technological concern, differing sharply from the theoretical requirement of disjointness. What distinguishes a genuine notation is not how easily correct judgements can be made but what their consequences are. The crucial point here is that for a genuine notation, as contrasted with a nondisjoint classification, marks correctly judged to be joint members of a character will always be true copies of one another. The distinction stands even where correct judgments under a given nondisjoint scheme are relatively easy to make, while those under a given genuine notation are so inordinately difficult as to make it useless.

Yet the difficulty can no longer be dismissed as merely technological when it goes beyond insurmountability in practice and becomes impossibility in principle. So long as the differentiation between characters is finite, no matter how minute, the determination of membership of mark in character will depend upon the acuteness of our perceptions and the sensitivity of the instruments we can devise. But if the differentiation is not finite, if there are two characters such that for some mark no even theoretically workable test could determine that the mark does not belong to both characters, then keeping the characters separate is not just practically but theoretically impossible. Suppose, for example, that only straight marks are concerned, and that marks differing in length by even the smallest fraction of an inch are stipulated to belong to different characters. Then no matter how precisely the length of any mark is measured, there will always be two (indeed, infinitely many) characters, corresponding to different rational numbers, such that the measurement will fail to determine that the mark does not belong to them. For a notational scheme, not only must sameness of spelling be preserved where error is avoided but error must be at least theoretically avoidable.

The second requirement upon a notational scheme, then, is that the characters be *finitely differentiated*, or *articulate*. It runs: *For every two characters K and K' and every mark m that does not actually belong to both, determination either that m does not belong to K or that m does not belong to K' is theoretically possible.* "Theoretically possible" may be interpreted in any reasonable way; whatever the choice, all logically and mathematically grounded impossibility (as in examples given below) will of course be excluded.

291

Finite differentiation neither implies nor is implied by a finite number of characters. On the one hand, a scheme may provide for an infinite number of finitely differentiated characters, as in Arabic fractional notation.[6] On the other hand, a scheme may consist of just two characters that are not finitely differentiated—for example, suppose all marks not longer than one inch belong to one character, and all longer marks belong to the other.

A scheme is syntactically dense if it provides for infinitely many characters so ordered that between each two there is a third. In such a scheme, our second requirement is violated everywhere: no mark can be determined to belong to one rather than to many other characters. But as we have just seen, absence of density does not guarantee finite differentiation; even a completely discontinuous[7] scheme may be undifferentiated throughout. And of course a completely or partially discontinuous scheme may be locally undifferentiated; our second requirement is violated wherever there is even a single mark that does not belong to two characters and yet is such that determination of its nonmembership in at least one of them is theoretically impossible.

The syntactic requirements of disjointness and of finite differentiation are clearly independent of each other. The first but not the second is satisfied by the scheme of classification of straight marks that counts every difference in length, however small, as a difference of character. The second but not the first is satisfied by a scheme where all inscriptions are conspicuously different but some two characters have at least one inscription in common.

None of this should be taken as suggesting that character-indifference—or syntactical equivalence, or being a true copy or a replica of—between marks of any simple function of shape, size, etc. The letter-classes of our alphabet, for example, are established by tradition and habit; and

---

[6]I am speaking here of symbols only, not of numbers or anything else the symbols may stand for. The Arabic fractional numerals are finitely differentiated even though fractional quantities are not. See further section 5 below.

[7]The distinction between density or compactness and continuity—between the rational and the real numbers—need not trouble us much here; for a dense scheme, whether continuous or not, is undifferentiated in the extreme. Since I reserve "discrete" for non-overlapping between individuals, I shall call a scheme that contains no dense subscheme "completely discontinuous" or "discontinuous throughout." "Dense" and "discontinuous" are of course short for "densely ordered" and "discontinuously ordered"; a given set may be dense under one ordering and discontinuous throughout under another (see further note 17 below).

defining them would be as hard as defining such ordinary terms as
"desk" and "table". Plainly, having the same shape, size, etc., is
neither necessary nor sufficient for two marks to belong to the same
letter. A given "a" (Figure 4, left) may be much less like another
(Figure 4, center) than like a given "d" (Figure 4, right) or "o".
Furthermore, two marks of identical shape and size may, as a result of
context, belong to different characters (Figure 5). Indeed, it may even
happen that the one of two marks that looks in isolation more like an "a"
may count as a "d" while the one that looks more like a "d" counts as an
"a" (Figure 6).

$$a \, A \, d$$

Figure 4

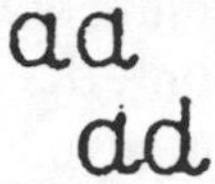

$$a a$$
$$d d$$

Figure 5

$$b a d$$
$$m a n$$

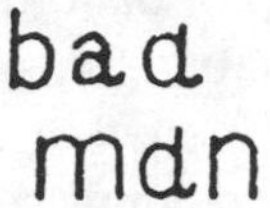

Figure 6

These cases cause no real trouble; for neither of our conditions
demands any specific difference between inscriptions of different
characters, or prohibits use of context in determining membership of a
mark in a character. But what of a mark that, equivocally, reads as
different letters when placed in different contexts at different times?
Disjointness is violated if any mark belongs to two different characters,
whether at the same time or at different times. Thus if the alphabet is to
qualify as a notation, not such enduring marks but, rather, unequivocal
time-slices of them must be taken as members of the characters—that
is, an inscription of letters.[8]

---

[8]In other cases, two simultaneous contexts endow a mark with different readings: for
example, in billboard language, the center mark in

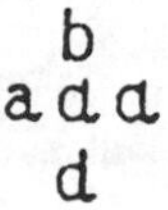

$$b$$
$$a \, d \, a$$
$$d$$

Footnote continued.

When a symbolic scheme is given in use rather than by specific definition, satisfaction of the requirements for a notation has to be judged by observation of practice. If there are alternative, equally good formulations of that practice, the conditions may be satisfied under some but not others among these formulations. But how is the second condition to be interpreted in application to a traditional scheme like the alphabet? That we have no explicit procedure for determining whether a given mark does or does not belong to any given letter hardly means that finite differentiation is lacking. Rather, we adopt a policy of admitting no mark as an inscription of a letter unless or until we can decide that the mark belongs to no other letter. In effect, we impose finite differentiation by excluding the undecidable cases; and the policy must be incorporated in any appropriate specification of the scheme. This does not hold for all schemes; with a dense scheme, the result would be to eliminate all inscriptions. But where membership of only some rather than all marks in each character is undecidable, the policy is normal and is to be assumed for all schemes not given by or plainly calling for a specification that precludes it.

The syntactic requirements of disjointness and finite differentiation are met by our familiar alphabetical, numerical, binary, telegraphic, and basic musical notations, some of them having purely academic interest. On the other hand, we shall see that some schemes recently devised and called notations fail, because they do not meet these minimum demands, to qualify as notations at all. The two requirements are not meant to describe the class of what are ordinarily called notations, but are rather conditions that must be fulfilled if the basic

---

reads down as an instance of one letter and across as an instance of another. Now this equivocal mark is not character-indifferent either with all 'a''s or with all "d''s (for not all exhibit this duplicity); and the mark cannot be counted as both an "a" and a "d" without sacrificing syntactic equivalence among the instances of each of these letters and violating the condition of disjointness. Nor are time-slices of the mark any less equivocal. Rather, this mark, if an inscription at all, is an instance not of any usual letter of the alphabet but of an additional character. Again, consider cases of shifting and of multiple orientation. Where sanctioned changes in orientation make a mark sometimes a "d" and sometimes a "b," unequivocal time-slices rather than the enduring mark qualify as inscriptions in the notation. Where a mark is simultaneously multiply oriented—legitimately subject to different readings from different directions at once—it may belong to a character consisting of all marks having the same multiple orientation and readings.

theoretic purpose of a score is to be served. They will accordingly enable us to draw certain critical distinctions among types of symbol scheme; but I shall come back to this later.

3. Composition of Characters

In most symbol schemes, inscriptions may be combined in certain ways to make other inscriptions. An inscription is *atomic* if it contains no other inscription; otherwise it is *compound*. When a scheme is not newly prescribed but is already before us for description, we have some latitude in what we take as atoms and how we frame the rule of combination. Sometimes the happiest analysis readily makes itself evident; in the usual alphabetical notation, for example, letter-inscriptions (including blanks or spaces separating strings of letters) are best taken as atomic; and sequences of these—ranging from two-letter inscriptions up through entire discourses—as compound. On the other hand, for ordinary musical notation the analysis into atomic inscriptions and modes of combination is more complex and less immediately indicated. The most useful treatment here calls for atoms sorted into categories (note-signs, clef-signs, time-signs, etc.) and for rules that not only make reference to these categories but provide for combination in two dimensions. An intermediate case might be a scheme where the only mode of combination is linear concatenation of atomic inscriptions of a category but where certain sequences are excluded—say on grounds of length or of particular unwanted juxtaposition—as inscriptions in the scheme. In English, for example, not all strings of letters are words. But such exclusion of certain combinations must not be confused with admitting them but giving them no application—a semantic matter I shall come to presently.

In virtually no feasible scheme is every sum of inscriptions an inscription. The component inscriptions must stand to each other in the relationship prescribed by the governing rules of combination. Thus even where unrestricted concatenation is authorized, a sum of scattered inscriptions does not in general constitute an inscription.

A *character* is atomic or compound according as its instances are atomic or compound. The requirements for a notation apply to compound as well as to atomic characters. The character "jup" and the character "j" must be disjoint even though one contains the other. The paradox here is superficial. No inscription of any character may be an

Correlation of a scheme with a field of reference normally involves not merely particular correlation of inscriptions with objects but also correlation of modes of inscription-combination with relationships among objects. For example, left-right succession of letter-inscriptions in sound-English is correlated with temporal succession of sounds. Even where both a compound inscription and components of it have compliants, compliants of the compound may or may not be composed suitably (or at all) of compliants of the components; in sound-English, for example, a compliant of a "ch" is not a sequence of a compliant of a "c" and a compliant of an "h." Where each compliant of a compound inscription is a whole made up of compliants of component inscriptions, and these compliants of components stand in the relation called for by the correlation in question between modes of inscription-combination and certain relationships among objects, the whole inscription is *composite*. Any other nonvacant inscription is *prime*.

All composite inscriptions are compound, but not all (even nonvacant) compound inscriptions are composite. Inversely, all nonvacant atomic inscriptions are prime, but not all prime inscriptions are atomic. "Composite" is the semantic counterpart of the syntactic term "compound", but the semantic term "prime" is only partially parallel to the syntactic term "atomic"; for while no proper part of an atomic inscription is an inscription, parts of a prime inscription may have compliants. The inscription is prime in that compliants of its parts, combined in the specified way, do not make up a compliant of the whole.

This profusion of terminology and technicalities will perhaps be rendered a little more tractable by the tabulation in Figure 8.

A mark that is unequivocally an inscription of a single character is nevertheless *ambiguous* if it has different compliants at different times or in different contexts, whether its several ranges result from different literal or from literal and metaphorical uses. More strictly of course we should say, where the variance is with time, that different time-slices of the mark have different compliance-classes; and where the variance is with simultaneous contexts, that the mark is semantically related in different ways to two or more inscriptions containing it.[12]

[12]Compare the treatment of equivocal marks in section 2 above. Unambiguity can be achieved by dividing up inscriptions, or characters, in certain ways; but then syntactic equivalence will be made to depend upon semantic considerations.

SYNTACTIC CLASSIFICATION

		Inscriptions		Other Marks
		Atomic	Compound	
SEMANTIC CLASSIFICATION	Vacant	*e.g.* a "k" in object-English	*e.g.* a "ktn" (also a "square circle") in object-Eng- lish	Includes ill-formed sequences, fragments of inscriptions, and all other marks not belonging to any character
	Prime	*e.g.* an "o" in sound-English	*e.g.* a "ch" in sound-English	
	Composite	////////	*e.g.* a "bo" in sound-English	

Figure 8

A character is ambiguous if any inscription of it is; but even if every inscription of a character is unambiguous, the character is ambiguous unless all its inscriptions have the same compliance-class. An unambiguous character is vacant, prime, or composite according as its inscriptions are; and the common compliance-class of its inscriptions may be considered the compliance-class of the character. Indeed, since the inscriptions of an unambiguous character are thus semantically as well as syntactically equivalent, we can usually speak of the character and its compliance-class without bothering to distinguish among its several instances.

But since two inscriptions of an ambiguous character may have different compliance-classes, syntactic equivalence implies semantic equivalence in unambiguous systems only. In neither ambiguous nor unambiguous systems does semantic equivalence imply syntactic equivalence. Inscriptions having the same compliance-class may belong to different characters; and different unambiguous characters may have the same compliance-class. Syntactical distinctness is not dissolved by semantic equivalence.

inscription of the other (and, indeed, no "jup" is a "j," and no "j" is a "jup"); but inscriptions of one character may be parts of or otherwise overlap inscriptions of another (as every "jup" has a "j" as part). Even inscriptions of different *atomic* characters may have common parts so long as no such part is an inscription in the scheme; that is, atomic inscriptions need to be discrete relative to the notation in question only, as the "a" and the "e" in Figure 7 are atomic and discrete in a scheme that recognizes no proper part of either as an inscription.[9]

Figure 7

To say that a character is composed of certain others is to be understood as short for saying that each member of the character is composed of inscriptions of certain other characters. Occasionally, however, full and explicit statement pays its way. The character "add" is awkwardly described as consisting of the character "a" followed by the character "d" 'taken twice'—or by the character "d" followed by itself. It is better described as the class of inscriptions each of which consists of an "a" (-inscription) followed by a "d" followed by another "d".

4. Compliance

A symbol system consists of a symbol scheme correlated with a field of reference. Although we have seen (II) that a symbol may nor may not denote what it refers to, I am concerned in this chapter with denotation rather than exemplification. But "denotation" must be taken somewhat more broadly than is usual, to cover a system where scores are correlated with performances complying with them, or words with their pronunciations, as well as a system where words are correlated with what they apply to or name. Partly as a way of keeping this in mind, I shall use "complies with" as interchangeable with "is denoted by,"

---

[9]Technical treatment of discreteness, overlapping, etc., will be found in *SA*, pp. 46–61, 117–118. Note how far astray is the usual idea that the elements of a notation must be discrete. First, *characters* of a notation, as classes, must be disjoint; discreteness is a relation among individuals. Second, *inscriptions* of a notation need not be discrete at all. And finally, even atomic inscriptions of different characters need to be discrete relative to that notation only.

"has as a complaint" as interchangeable with "denotes," and "compliance-class" as interchangeable with "extension."[10] Compliance requires no special conformity; whatever is denoted by a symbol complies with it.

Basically, compliance is with an inscription. In a given system, many things may comply with a single inscription, and the class of these constitutes the compliance-class of the inscription under that system. Of course, the compliance-class normally does not itself comply with the inscription; its members do. An inscription having classes as compliants has a class of classes as its compliance-class.

Convenient illustrations of some technical terms and distinctions may be cited from what I shall for short call *sound-English*, where ordinary English alphabetical notation is correlated with sound-events according to the usual practice of pronunciation, and what I shall call *object-English*, where the correlation is rather with objects (including events, etc.) according to the usual practice of application. The illustration will depend, of course, upon some tacit but obvious arbitrary decisions concerning, and occasionally upon some simplification of, usual practice.[11]

Some inscriptions, even some atomic ones, may have no compliants; in object-English, neither a "ktn" nor a "k" has any compliant. Not only may compound inscriptions happen to be the least units with any compliants but an inscription compounded of inscriptions that have compliants may or may not have compliants; in object-English, though "green" and "horse" have compliants, "green horse" does not. Inscriptions without compliants may be called *vacant*. Vacancy may arise either from a character having been assigned no compliant, or from there being no such compliants as are called for, or from explicit stipulation that the character have no compliant. A vacant inscription belongs as truly to the symbol scheme as does any other, and may be as big and black; its lack is semantic, not syntactic. An object complying with no inscription is unlabeled in the system.

---

[10]This is *not* to say that the extension of a word includes *both* its pronunciations and the objects it applies to; for the extension of a symbol is always relative to a system, and in no normal or useful system is a word correlated with both its pronunciations and its applicata.

[11]Formulation of rules of correlation, like resolution of inscriptions into atoms, is seldom uniquely determined for a given natural language, but depends on how the language is analyzed and described. When we speak of 'a language' we are often speaking elliptically of a language under some such systematic formulation.

5. Semantic Requirements

The first semantic requirement upon notational systems is that they be *unambiguous*; for obviously the basic purpose of a notational system can be served only if the compliance relationship is invariant.[13] Any ambiguous *inscription* must be excluded since it will give conflicting decisions concerning whether some object complies with it. Any ambiguous *character* must be excluded, even if its inscriptions are all unambiguous; for since different inscriptions of it will have different compliants, some inscriptions that count as true copies of each other will have different compliance-classes. In either case, identity of work will not be preserved in every chain of steps from performance to covering score and from score to compliant performance.

Two further semantic requirements upon notational systems parallel but do not follow from the syntactic requirements.

Even though all characters of a symbol system be disjoint classes of unambiguous inscriptions, and all inscriptions of any one character have the same compliance-class, different compliance-classes may intersect in any way. *But in a notational system, the compliance-classes must be disjoint.* For if two different compliance-classes intersect, some inscription will have two compliants such that one belongs to a compliance-class that the other does not; and a chain from compliant to inscription to compliant will thus lead from a member of one compliance-class to something outside that class. For example, in Figure 9, if A and B stand for characters, and A' and B' for their compliance-classes, with A' included in B', then k in A' is also in B' and complies with inscription i, which in turn has as a compliant h, which is not in A'. Where neither of two intersecting compliance-classes is included in the other, a chain from compliant to inscription to compliant to inscription to compliant may connect two objects that do not even belong to any one compliance-class. For example, in Figure 10, h

---

[13] Whether a system is ambiguous will depend not only upon just what marks are taken as its inscriptions and just how these are classified into characters, as we have seen above, but also upon just what correlation between marks and objects is taken as constituting compliance. In sound-English, for example, "c" is naturally regarded as ambiguous since some "c"s are soft and others hard. But we could take "c" as unambiguous, with the soft c-sounds as the compliants of all "c"s—even those in "ct"s. Characters such as "ct" would then be prime. The choice here is between different descriptions of the language. In what follows, I shall often tacitly assume that such decisions have been made in a way that is apparent from the context.

complies with *i*, which in turn has *k* as a compliant; *k* complies also with *j*, which has *m* as another compliant. But *h* and *m* belong to no one compliance-class. Thus any intersection of different compliance-classes defeats the primary purpose of a notational system.

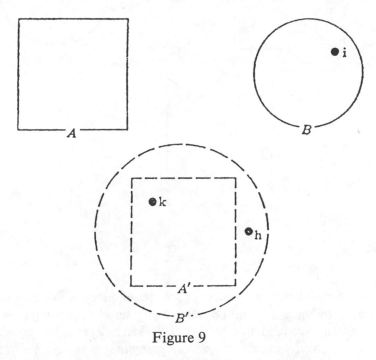

Figure 9

Must different characters, furthermore, have different compliance-classes? That is, must a system be free of redundancy? In a redundant system, some inscription will have a compliant that also complies with a second inscription that is not a true copy of the first.[14] Accordingly, while in every chain of permitted steps every complaint will belong to the same compliance-class, not in every such chain will every inscription belong to the same character. Hence, strictly, redundancy must be proscribed. Yet insofar as preserving identity of character (e.g., of score from copy to copy) is incidental to preserving identity of compliance-class (e.g., of musical work from performance to performance),

[14]Redundancy is the dual of ambiguity. Ambiguity consists of multiplicity of compliance-classes for one character; redundancy consists of multiplicity of characters for one compliance-class. But, of course, with no ambiguity a character may apply to many objects; and with no redundancy an object may comply with many inscriptions.

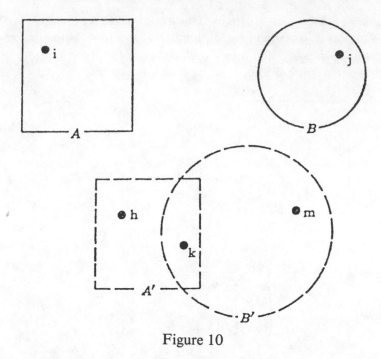

Figure 10

redundancy is harmless. And of course redundancy in a system is easily removed by discarding all but one of any set of coextensive terms. In any case, non-redundancy need not be taken as a separate requirement. We may consider the *disjointness requirement* to stipulate *that no two characters have any compliant in common*; so that not only must every two different compliance-classes in a notational system be disjoint but every two characters must have different compliance-classes. Nevertheless, for two characters to have all as against only some common compliants is often the lesser transgression.

Although each two characters in a purely notational system must be semantically quite separate, compliants of one character may be parts of or properly overlap compliants of another. Semantic disjointness of characters no more implies discreteness of compliants than syntactic disjointness of characters implies discreteness of inscriptions. "State in the U.S." and "county in the U.S.," as applying to certain geographical regions, are semantically disjoint even though every compliant of the one contains several compliants of the other.

The requirement of semantic disjointness rules out most ordinary languages, even if we suppose them freed of ambiguity. For see how

302

much is prohibited. A notational system cannot contain any pair of semantically intersecting terms like "doctor" and "Englishman"; and if the system contains the term "man", for example, it cannot contain the more specific term "Englishman" or the more general term "animal." The characters of a notational system are semantically segregated.

The final requirement for a notational system is *semantic finite differentiation*; that is, *for every two characters K and K' such that their compliance-classes are not identical, and every object h that does not comply with both, determination either that h does not comply with K or that h does not comply with K' must be theoretically possible.* This condition again appreciably narrows the class of systems that qualify as notational. Consider, for example, a system consisting of fully reduced Arabic fractional numerals taking as compliants physical objects according to their weights in fractions of an ounce. The syntactic requirements of disjointness and finite differentiation, and the semantic requirements of unambiguity and disjointness, are met here; but since no limit is set upon significant difference in weight, there will always be many characters such that not even the finest measurement can attest that an object does not comply with them all. Thus the system is not notational.

The particular system just described is semantically dense (that is, provides for an infinite number of characters with compliance-classes so ordered that between each two there is a third), and everywhere violates the fifth condition. But the condition may also be violated everywhere in some systems that are semantically discontinuous throughout—i.e., nowhere semantically dense. In other systems that are semantically discontinuous throughout or in part, violation may be local rather than pervasive. A system for which each reduced Arabic fraction takes as compliants all and only those objects of the indicated weight that are identical with the Cullinan diamond (so that the field of reference consists of but a single object) is still not semantically differentiated. [15] And if a system contains two characters "*a*" and "*b*", and all objects weighing an ounce or less comply with "*a*" while all objects weighing more comply with "*b*", then that system—no matter what other characters and reference-classes it may embrace—lacks semantic differentiation and fails of notationality.

---

[15]Hereafter, I shall often write "differentiated" as short for "finitely differentiated." The convenient alternative term "articulate" will be more often used later in the book.

303

6. Notations

The five stated requirements for a notational system are all negative and general, satisfiable by systems with null or even no characters. These requirements are designed to preclude otherwise inevitable trouble, not to ensure a vocabulary or grammar adequate for a given subject-matter. They are somewhat like a building code that legislates against faults in construction without prescribing the accommodations needed for particular families.

A good many other features that might be thought essential are not covered either. No requirement of a manageably small or even finite set of atomic characters, no requirement of clarity, of legibility, of durability, of maneuverability, of ease of writing or reading, of graphic suggestiveness, of mnemonic efficacy, or of ready duplicability or performability has been imposed. These may be highly desirable properties, and to some degree even necessary for any practicable notation; and the study of such engineering matters could be fascinating and profitable. But none of this has anything to do with the basic theoretical function of notational systems.

Throughout, I have been stressing the nominative or predicative aspect of symbols, not their assertive or imperative or interrogative force, and have taken characters more as predicates or labels than as sentences. This is natural in the present context; for in notational systems the grammatical mood of a character seldom matters much. In sound-English, for example, a string of letters may stand for a certain sequence of sounds; but to add that the string declares that such sound occur in such sequence, or commands that they should, would be quite gratuitous. No one asks whether the string of letters is true or false, and no one says to it "Yes, sir!" or "No, I won't." Offhand, one might guess that absence of grammatical mood is a distinguishing feature of notational systems; but actually it is not. Suppose, for instance, that operators were added to a notational system so that, say, while "vo" stands for a v-sound followed by an o-sound, "†vo" asserts that a v-sound is followed by an o-sound, "!vo" commands that a v-sound be followed by an o-sound, and "?vo" asks whether a v-sound is followed by an o-sound. The system does not thereby cease to be notational. Conversely, object-English deprived of sentences and restricted to phrases does not thereby become notational. The point is that just as tense is irrelevant to languages insofar as they are logical, so mood is irrelevant insofar as they are notational. Mere absence or presence of tense does not make a system logical or unlogical; and mere absence or presence of mood does not make a system notational or non-notational.

I have been further simplifying by speaking usually as if the only predicates involved were one-place predicates of individuals. To cover cases where either many-place predicates or predicates of classes need to be taken into account, without altering the statement of any of our five requirements, about all we need do is to include sequences and classes along with individuals among the 'objects' that may be compliants of characters. [16]

In sum, the properties required of a notational system are unambiguity and syntactic and semantic disjointness and differentiation. These are in no sense merely recommended for a good and useful notation but are features that distinguish notational systems—good or bad—from non-notational systems. All derive from the primary purpose a score must serve; and all are categorically required for any even theoretically workable notational system. A system is notational, then, if and only if all objects complying with inscriptions of a given character belong to the same compliance class and we can, theoretically, determine that each mark belongs to, and each object complies with inscriptions of, at most one particular character.

The five conditions are mutually independent in the usual logical sense that satisfaction or violation of one or more of them does not imply satisfaction or violation of any of the others. And although the conditions were designed to define notational systems, other important types of symbol system are distinguished by violation of certain combinations of these conditions.

The intricate, abstract, and probably trying technical study pursued in the foregoing pages of this chapter has thus provided means for analyzing and for comparing and contrasting in significant ways the varied systems of symbolization used in art, science, and life in general. Before returning to specific questions pertaining to symbolism in the arts, I want to look at some systems from other fields.

---

[16] The way of formulating a nominalistically acceptable version of our five requirements is rather obvious so long as all the predicates involved, whether one-place or many-place, are predicates of individuals; and the nominalist need not allow for ineliminable predicates of classes since he will not construe any admissible language as containing such predicates.

7. Clocks and Counters

Suppose we have a simple pressure gauge with a circular face and a single pointer that moves smoothly clockwise as the pressure increases. If there are no figures or other marks on the face, and every difference in pointer position constitutes a difference in character, the instrument is not using a notation in reporting pressure to us. The requirement of syntactic differentiation is not met; for we can never determine the position of the pointer with absolute precision. And since the semantic ordering—of pressures—is also dense, semantic as well as syntactic differentiation is lacking.

If the dial is graduated by dots into, say, fifty divisions, is the symbol scheme now used notational? That depends upon how the gauge is to be read. If absolute position of the pointer on the face is what counts, the dots being used only as aids in approximate determination of that position, the scheme remains undifferentiated both syntactically and semantically. A notational scheme is indeed present, but the characters (the graduation-dots) of this notation are not the characters (the absolute pointer positions) of the symbol scheme of the gauge. Rather, the dots belong to an auxiliary scheme useful for locating approximately where the pointer is.

On the other hand, suppose the same dial is to be read differently, with each dot taken as marking the center of a region such that any appearance of the pointer within that region counts as an inscription of the same character. This scheme will be notational provided the fifty regions taken are disjoint and separated by some gaps, however small. And the system will be notational provided the ranges of pressure correlated with the fifty characters are also disjoint and separated by gaps, however small.

These are not artificial alternatives. Concrete examples are before us many times a day. Consider an ordinary watch without a second-hand. The hour-hand is normally used only to pick out one of twelve divisions of the half-day. It speaks notationally. So does the minute-hand if used only to pick out one of sixty divisions of the hour; but if the absolute distance of the minute-hand beyond the preceding mark is taken as indicating the absolute time elapsed since that mark was passed, the symbol system is non-notational. Of course, if we set some limit—whether of a half-minute or one second or less—upon the fineness of judgment so to be made, the scheme here too may become notational.

306

On a watch with a second-hand, the minute-hand is read notationally, and the second-hand may be read either way.

But now suppose the field of reference is of a quite different sort, and our instruments report not on pressure or time but upon the number of dimes dropped into a toy bank having a total capacity of fifty dimes. If the count is reported by an Arabic numeral displayed in an aperture, the system is clearly notational. But what if the indicator is rather a pointer as in our pressure gauges? If every position on the circumference is taken as a character, whether or not the dial is graduated, the system—as in the case of the first pressure gauges described above—will be semantically as well as syntactically undifferentiated. Full distinguishability of elements in the field of reference does not of itself guarantee semantic differentiation; indeed, if there is only one object and if determining which of two characters it complies with is theoretically impossible, semantic differentiation is lacking. Incidentally, the counter so read will also be highly inefficient; for we can never tell from it just how many dimes have been deposited, and if each number of dimes is correlated with only one character, infinitely many atomic characters will be vacant. If we take the many positions within a given region as different characters correlated with the same number of dimes, then the system is redundant and so lacks semantic disjointness as well. However, if the counter with a graduated face is so read that there are just fifty syntactically disjoint and differentiated characters, and each is correlated with a different number of dimes, the system will be notational.

8. Analogs and Digits

The pressure gauge first described above is a pure and elementary example of what is called an analog computer. The dime-counter displaying numerals is a simple example of what is called a digital computer; and an ordinary watch, read in the most usual way, combines analog and digital computers. But the difference between analog and digital machines or systems is easier to illustrate than to define, and some current notions about it are mistaken. Plainly, a digital system has nothing special to do with digits, or an analog system with analogy. The characters of a digital system may have objects or events of any kind as their inscriptions; and the compliants under an analog system may be as

307

remote and different as we please from the characters. If one-one correlation between characters and compliance-classes makes a system analog, then digital systems also qualify as analog. Since the misleading traditional terms "analog" and "digital" are unlikely to be discarded, perhaps the best course is to try to dissociate them from analogy and digits and a good deal of loose talk, and distinguish them in terms of density and differentiation—though these are not opposites.

A symbol *scheme* is analog if syntactically dense; a *system* is analog if syntactically and semantically dense. Analog systems are thus both syntactically and semantically undifferentiated in the extreme: for every character there are infinitely many others such that for some mark, we cannot possibly determine that the mark does not belong to all, and such that for some object we cannot possibly determine that the object does not comply with all. A system of this kind is obviously the very antithesis of a notational system. But density, while it implies, is not implied by complete lack of differentiation; and a system is analog only if dense.

A digital scheme, in contrast, is discontinuous throughout; and in a digital system the characters of such a scheme are one-one correlated with compliance-classes of a similarly discontinuous set. But discontinuity, though implied by, does not imply differentiation; for as we have seen, a system with only two characters may be syntactically and semantically undifferentiated throughout. To be digital a system must be not merely discontinuous but *differentiated* throughout, syntactically and semantically. If, as we assume for systems now under discussion, it is also unambiguous and syntactically and semantically disjoint, it will therefore be notational.

Digital computers are sometimes said to be capable of complete precision while analog computers can achieve at best only a good approximation.[17] This is true only insofar as the task of the digital computer is counting while that of the analog computer is registering absolute position in a continuum. The real virtues of digital instruments are those of notational systems: definiteness and repeatability of readings. Analog instruments may offer greater sensitivity and flexibility. With an analog instrument we are not fettered by an arbitrary lower boundary of discrimination; the only limit upon the fineness of our

[17]See, however, the discussion in John von Neumann, "The General and Logical Theory of Automata," in *Cerebral Mechanisms in Behavior*, ed. Lloyd A. Jeffress (New York, John Wiley & Sons, Inc., 1951), pp. 7ff.

readings is the (varying) limit upon our accuracy in determining, say, the position of a pointer. However, once the maximum required fineness of discrimination has been settled, we can construct a digital instrument (if we can construct any instrument) that will give readings that fine. Where the task if gauging or measuring, the analog instrument is likely to play its chief role in the exploratory stages, before units of measurement have been fixed; then a suitably designed digital instrument takes over.

If only thoroughly dense systems are analog, and only thoroughly differentiated ones digital, many systems are of neither type. Some of these are either syntactically or semantically differentiated but not both; and some, although both syntactically and semantically undifferentiated, are yet not both syntactically and semantically dense. When a system is syntactically but not semantically dense, as in the case of our counter with the unmarked dial, the result is commonly but not inevitably (see VI, note 7) either vast waste or vast redundancy: either many vacant characters or huge sets of coextensive characters. When a system is semantically but not syntactically dense, the result may be inadequacy or ambiguity: either some wanted compliance-classes being left nameless or many sharing the same name. In any event, systems of such mongrel types seldom survive long in computer practice; the drive is towards the matching of syntactic with semantic properties that is peculiar to analog and digital systems. If the subject-matter is antecedently atomized, we tend to adopt an articulate symbol scheme and a digital system. Or if we are predisposed to apply an available articulate symbol scheme to a previously undifferentiated field, we try to provide the symbols with differentiated compliance-classes by dividing, combining, deleting; the fractional quantities not registered by our meter tend to be disregarded, and the smallest units it discriminates to be taken as the atomic units of what is measured. Should a prior structuring authoritatively resist such surgery, we may lay aside our articulate symbol scheme and turn to an analog system. Here as elsewhere the development and application of symbol systems is a dynamic process of analysis and organization; and the tensions that arise may be resolved by adjustment on either side of the system until an equilibrium is at least temporarily established.

Apart from computer applications, systems that are neither analog nor digital are common. Consider, for example, the terms "halfway between *a* and *b*," "halfway between *a* and halfway between *a* and *b*," "halfway between *b* and halfway between *a* and *b*," "halfway between *a* and halfway between *a* and halfway between *a* and *b*," and so on without limit. This system is syntactically differentiated but semantically dense; [18] its compliance-classes are the (unit-classes of) points on a line segment. And far from being manufactured to serve as an illustration, the system is part of ordinary English. Everything depends here, of course, upon provision for unlimited compounding of characters out of others. Where, as with a computer, there is a limit to the length of message—e.g., number of decimal places, etc.—that can be produced, no unambiguous system with a notational scheme can have a dense set of compliance-classes. [19]

9. Inductive Translation

Among the many ways a computer may process messages are *deletion* and *supplementation*. The first occurs, for example, where a curve is scanned and the positions of some points on it reported. The second occurs where some points are fed in and a curve or other points on it produced, whether by interpolation or extrapolation. Deletion is often but not always or exclusively involved in translation from analog into digital messages, and supplementation in translation from digital into analog messages. Some important functions of symbols are illustrated in the process of supplementation.

[18]The syntactic ordering of these terms (beginning with one-letter terms alphabetically ordered, proceeding to two-letter terms alphabetically ordered, and so on) is discontinuous throughout, and also the system is syntactically differentiated; yet the ordering of these terms according to the semantic property of left-right position of the compliant points is dense, and the system is semantically undifferentiated throughout. A similar example cited earlier was that of Arabic rational numbers taking as compliants physical objects according to weight in fractions of an ounce; the syntactic ordering here derives from the order of the digits, the semantic from the order of increasing weight. Only because density and discontinuity depend upon ordering can a single system of characters, differently ordered, by syntactically discontinuous throughout and semantically dense, or syntactically dense and semantically discontinuous throughout. Systems of the latter sort cannot, of course, be found among languages, which are—whether natural or notational—always syntactically differentiated; but an example from among nonlinguistic systems has been cited above (section 7) in the system of the ungraduated counter with every point on the circumference constituting a character, and more important examples will be encountered below (VI, 2).

[19]A given computer is always thus limited; but so also, in view of mortality, is a given speaker. The decimal system in general, or the English language, imposes no such limits.

Consider machines designed to receive two or more points and supply others. A crude machine might simply select[20] each point by spinning a wheel or casting dice. The choices cannot be said to be based in any way upon the data; the available evidence is utterly ignored. At the opposite extreme, a machine might be so constructed as to handle straight lines only. Any two points will then determine a line and thereby all points to be interpolated and extrapolated. Far from being ignored, the data dictate all remaining points by dictating the choice of line. If the first machine was a little more than a roulette wheel, the second is a simple calculator like an adding machine.

Now consider a computer capable of handling curves of various types. When the data are compatible with several of these curves, how shall the machine decide? Even if it now resorts to wheel-spinning or dice-throwing, it still differs radically from our first machine; for this one, like the second, chooses among curves rather than points and rejects curves incompatible with the evidence. If a linear order of preference among curves is given and the machine is instructed to choose the remaining curve highest on that scale, chance will not enter at all. Or such a scale may be used merely to weight the odds so that the choice, though made by wheel or dice, will not be purely random. Yet in all these cases, the machine operates independently of what has gone before except for canceling out curves that conflict with the data.[21]

[20]"Selects," "chooses," "decides," etc., in the present context do not imply any deliberation but mean only "gives one among alterative responses". On computers with a random element, see A.M. Turing, "Computing Machinery and Intelligence," *Mind*, vol. 59 (1950), pp. 433–460.

[21]My treatment throughout this section attempts only a simple schematic analysis of the process of supplementation. Variations and elaborations of all sorts may occur. The task may be to choose not one curve but a group of curves; e.g., if the ordinate at only one or a few abscissas is wanted, differences among curves that coincide at these abscissas can be ignored. Or, rather than canceling out curves not fitting the data, the machine may be asked to find among curves meeting some standard of smoothness the curve that comes nearest to fitting the data—though it miss some or even all points. Again, the response called for may not be to select or reject curves but to rate them according to relative probability. Also, the ways of taking cognizance of experience on past problems may be complicated and subtle. And where a scale of preference is involved it may be based upon simplicity of one sort or another, or upon more or different factors; and it may be fixed or variable. Finally, "points" and "curves" may be read more generally as "instances" and "hypotheses." None of this occludes the central issues above discussed.

311

A more sophisticated machine might make more use of the past. Let us suppose data have been fed to a machine, a choice of curve made, additional data supplied, a new choice made accordingly, and so on. The several choices may be regarded as steps in dealing with a single problem having as its cumulative data all those supplied from start to finish. Now the registers are cleared, data again are supplied, and the machine begins work on a new problem. Our present machine may, whenever it thus faces a new problem, look back to its encounters with earlier problems. After eliminating curves incompatible with the present data, it may find earlier problems with sets of data that properly include the present set, and proceed to cancel out every curve that conflicts with any of these more inclusive sets. It thus takes into account not only the immediate evidence, but evidence in past related cases.

Nevertheless, if the machine can handle enough curves, eliminations on the basis of present and past data will always leave a wide choice of alternatives—so wide, indeed, that no prediction concerning remaining points is excluded.[22] No matter for how many values of x the value of y is given, still for every remaining value m of x and every value of n of y, at least one of the curves compatible with the data will pass through m,n. And this will hold true for any more comprehensive sets of data for past problems. Thus the less circumscribed the machine, the more often it must either consult a mandatory fixed scale of preference or resort to chance procedures. The erudite machine has to be either pigheaded or henheaded.

Both faults are corrected in a machine that can acquire habits. Appropriate inertia is required for maximum profit from experience. Suppose a machine to be so designed that in making any choice after its first it consults not only the data for the present and for past related problems but also the record of its own past choices. Among the curves remains after deletions on the basis of all data, it selects or at least favors the one used most often before. And it sticks to a curve once chosen until forced to change by new data. Habit in effect establishes or modifies a preferential weighting; and a unique choice often results.

What I have been speaking of as 'the curves a machine can handle' constitute the inventory of responses it can make. No distinction has been drawn between those curves the machine has initially at its command and those, if any, that it can invent. A machine that can initially respond with straight lines only may be able, when fed three

---

[22]Cf. *FFF*, pp. 72–81.

noncollinear points, to invent some new curve to accommodate these data. But this machine is as well described as one that, among all the curves it can handle, always chooses a straight line until forced by the data to make a different choice. The question what curves are 'there at the start' and what curves the machine 'generates' is thus displaced by the question what curves the machine can handle at all and how it chooses among them.

All these machines perform a task of supplementation, some by sheer guess, some by pure calculation, some by a mixture of the two. Some take no, some minimal, and some very extensive and complex account of the evidence. Those that take account of the evidence operate with curves that relate the given points to the rest. Some such machines can handle very few curves, some many, and some all possible curves in their universes. Certain machines, when confronted with open alternatives after all eliminations on the basis of the evidence, always make a unique choice by applying a preferential scale. Others, lacking such a fully automatic procedure, must sometimes resort to chance. Among these, some do and some do not take account of their past choices, in effect forming habits that perpetuate as far as possible chance decisions once made.

Questions concerning the nature of induction thrust themselves forward here.[23] Does supplementation become induction when account is taken of the evidence? Or not unless the evidence sometimes leaves open alternatives, so that a decision must be made by other means? Or only if for some such decisions a chance procedure is used? Giving an answer is perhaps less important than noting the several significant lines of demarcation. Again, what are the characteristics of the induction performed by human beings? Obviously, we can take account of the evidence in subtle and sophisticated ways. Obviously, also, we can handle any possible curve (or hypothesis). And on the whole we tend to persist in a choice so long as the evidence permits. But are we provided with a completely decisive preferential ordering among these curves, or must we sometimes resort to chance?

Our brief look at some ways of accomplishing message supplementation thus leads directly to the heart of active current controversy in

[23]Cf. Marvin Minsky, "Steps toward Artificial Intelligence," in *Computers and Thought*, ed. E.A. Feigenbaum and J. Feldman (New York, McGraw-Hill Book Co., Inc., 1963), pp. 448–449. This article originally appeared in the special computer issue of the *Proceedings of the Institute of Radio Engineers*, 1961.

epistemology. More to the immediate point of our present inquiry, though, is the disclosure of certain special features of the functioning of symbols not only in overt induction but also in such kindred processes as category detection and pattern perception: first, that evidence takes effect only through application of a general symbol (label or term or hypothesis) having an extension that properly includes the data; second, that the alternatives are primarily such general symbols, divergent in extension, rather than isolated particulars; and third, that pertinent time-and-trouble-saving habits can develop only through use of such symbols. Perhaps, indeed, these are earmarks of cognitive behavior in general.

10. Diagrams, Maps, and Models

Diagrams, whether they occur as the output of recording instruments or as adjuncts to expository texts or as operational guides, are often thought—because of their somewhat pictorial look and their contrast with their mathematical or verbal accompaniments—to be purely analog in type. Some, such as scale drawings for machinery, are indeed analog; but some others, such as diagrams of carbohydrates, are digital; and still others, such as ordinary road maps, are mixed.

The mere presence or absence of letters or figures does not make the difference. What matters with a diagram, as with the face of an instrument, is how we are to read it. For example, if figures on a barogram or seismogram indicate certain points the curve passes through, yet every point on the curve is a character with its own denotation, the diagram is purely analog, or *graphic*. But if the curve on a chart showing annual car production over a decade merely joins the several numbered points to emphasize the trend, the intermediate points on the curve are not characters of the scheme, and the diagram is purely digital. Nor is a diagram without alphabetical or arithmetical characters always analog. Many diagrams in topology, for example, need only have the right number of dots or junctures connected by lines in the right pattern, the size and location of the dots and the length and shape of the lines being irrelevant. Plainly, the dots and lines here function as characters in a notational language; and these diagrams, as well as most diagrams for electrical circuits, are purely digital. The more we are startled by this, because we think of such diagrams as

314

rather schematized pictures, the more strongly we are reminded that the significant distinction between the digital or notational and the non-notational, including the analog, turns not upon some loose notion of analogy or resemblance but upon the grounded technical requirements for a notational language.

While the scientists and philosophers have on the whole taken diagrams for granted, they have been forced to fret at some length about the nature and function of *models*.[24] Few terms are used in popular and scientific discourse more promiscuously than "model". A model is something to be admired or emulated, a pattern, a case in point, a type, a prototype, a specimen, a mock-up, a mathematical description— almost anything from a naked blonde to a quadratic equation—and may bear to what it models almost any relation of symbolization.

In many cases, a model is an exemplar or instance of what it models: the model citizen is a fine example of citizenship, the sculptor's model a sample of the human body, the fashion model a wearer, the model house a sample of the developer's offerings, and the model of a set of axioms is a compliant universe.

In other cases, the roles are reversed: the model denotes, or has as an instance, what it models. The car of a certain model belongs to a certain class. And a mathematical model is a formula that applies to the process or state or object modeled. What is modeled is the particular case that fits the description.

"Model" might well be dispensed with in all these cases in favor of less ambiguous and more informative terms, and reserved for cases where the symbol is neither an instance nor a verbal or mathematical description: the ship model, the miniature bulldozer, the architect's model of a campus, the wood or clay model of an automobile. None of these is a sample—a ship, a bulldozer, a campus, or a car; and none is a description in ordinary or mathematical language. Unlike samples,

---

[24]An exception to the first clause is Clerk Maxwell in the article on diagrams in the eleventh edition of the *Encyclopedia Britannica*, vol. 8 (Cambridge, England, Cambridge University Press, 1910), pp. 146–149. An example of the second clause is Boltzmann in the article on models in the same edition, vol. 18 (1911), pp. 638–640.

these models are denotative; unlike descriptions, they are nonverbal.[25] Models of this sort are in effect diagrams, often in more than two dimensions and with working parts; or in other words, diagrams are flat and static models. Like other diagrams, models may be digital or analog or mixed. Molecular models made of ping-pong balls and chopsticks are digital. A working model of a windmill may be analog. A scale model of a campus, with green papier-mâché for grass, pink cardboard for brick, plastic film for glass, etc., is analog with respect to spatial dimensions but digital with respect to materials. Perhaps the first step toward dispelling a good deal of confused romancing about models is to recognize that they can be treated as diagrams.

But how does a wiring diagram differ significantly, as a symbol, from verbal instructions, a road map from an aerial photograph, a ship model from a sculptural representation? I shall defer all such questions; for my purpose here has not been to study diagrams and models exhaustively but only to illustrate some of the concepts and principles developed in earlier sections.

The questions raised at the beginning of this chapter concerning notation in the arts have not been answered. Indeed, they have hardly been mentioned again. They had to be set aside while we examined some preliminary questions about notations and symbol systems in general. But the connection is less remote than it may seem; for a score, as I conceive it, is a character in a notational language, the compliants of a score are typically performances, and the compliance-class is a work. In the next chapter, I want to consider how some of our results apply to certain questions about the arts, and how some light may be reflected upon some other philosophical problems.

[25]As noted in II, 4, a sample may also take on the denotative role of and become coextensive with a label it exemplifies. The sample house may also function as a denotative model of houses in the development, including itself, and will then also exemplify itself as a label. It differs from the miniature model in the way that "polysyllabic" differs from "monosyllabic". Similarly, literal application of a schema may be a model for metaphorical applications, or may be at once a sample and a denotative model of all the applications. Incidentally, models are not, as sometimes supposed, necessarily metaphorical. Whether application of a model, as of any other label, is metaphorical depends upon whether the application is guided by an antecedently established literal application.

Score, Sketch, and Script

You see no experiment can be repeated exactly. There will always be something different. . . . What it comes to when you say you repeat an experiment is that you repeat all the features of an experiment which a theory determines are relevant. In other words you repeat the experiment as an example of the theory.

Sir George Thomson*

1. Score

A score is a character in a notational system. Even in musical notation not every character is a score, but I count as a score every character that may have compliants. This excludes purely syncategorematic characters, for example, without requiring of a score either that it be a complete composition or that it be actually nonvacant. I have broadened the application of "score" to embrace characters of the sort described in any notational system,[26] not merely in musical notation. Similarly, I often call the compliants of such characters performances where these compliants are not by ordinary usage performed or even events at all; and I often call the compliance-classes works, even when these classes are such—e. g., fortuitous aggregates of natural objects—as not to be works in any usual sense. All this I think may help to keep before us both the cardinal example of music and the more general principles illustrated.

A score, we found, defines a work but is a peculiar and privileged definition, without competitors. A class is uniquely determined by a score, as by an ordinary definition; but a score, unlike an ordinary definition, is also uniquely determined by each member of that class. Given the notational system and a performance of a score, the score is recoverable. Identity of work and of score is retained in any series of steps, each of them either from compliant performance to score-

*In "Some Thoughts on Scientific Method," Lecture of May 2, 1963, printed in *Boston Studies in the Philosophy of Science*, vol. II (New York, Humanities Press, 1965), p. 85.
[26]Not, be it observed, "in any notational *scheme*." The usage here adopted counts only characters of notational *systems* as scores.

inscription, or from score-inscription to compliant performance, or from score-inscription to true copy. This is ensured by the fact, and only by the fact, that the language in which a score is written must be notational—must satisfy the five stated requirements. No inherent partitioning of the subject-matter is presumed; and performances of a work may vary widely and in many respects.

Redundancy, as noted earlier, is a common and minor violation of notationality. The net effect is that in a chain of the sort described, the score-inscriptions may not all be true copies of one another; yet all will be semantically equivalent—all performances will be of the same work. Work-preservation but not score-preservation is ensured; and insofar as work-preservation is paramount, and score-preservation incidental, redundancy is tolerable.

None of our usual natural languages is a notational system. Such *discursive languages* meet the two syntactic requirements but are exempt from the three semantic requirements. Accordingly, a definition or set of coextensive definitions is seldom uniquely determined by a member of the class defined. And as we have seen, ambiguity is not always to blame; a wheelbarrow belongs to many different compliance-classes of object-English—complies, that is, with may extensionally diverse descriptions, such as "wooden object," "wheeled vehicle," etc. In such a language there is no such thing as *the* definition, or set of equivalent definitions, that the given object satisfies. But in a notational system, or even a system that misses notationality only through redundancy, all scores for a given performance are coextensive—have all the same performances as compliants.

2. Music

So far, I have been discussing matters of general theory without examining closely any of the presumably notational systems actually used in the arts. Standard musical notation offers a familiar and at the same time a remarkable case. It is at once complex, serviceable, and—like Arabic numerical notation—common to the users of many different verbal languages. No alternative has gained any currency; and apparently no other culture, such as the Chinese or Indian, has developed any comparably effective musical notation over the centuries. The variety

318

and vitality of recent rebellions against it testify to the authority it has acquired.[27]

Ordinary musical notation has sometimes been thought to owe its origin to the introduction of keyboard instruments, with their separate keys and spaced tones; but the question just when either a true notation or a true keyboard instrument emerged is so elusive that the hypothesis hardly admits of any conclusive historical investigation. And the hypothesis is antecedently implausible; musical notation no more needed to wait upon invention of the clavichord than alphabetical notation is needed to wait upon invention of the typewriter. Development of a notational scheme or system does not depend upon an intrinsic segregation or marks or objects into disjoint and differentiated sets, but is often achieved in the face of virtual continuity in both realms.

In some early mediaeval musical manuscripts, marks were placed higher or lower over syllables or words of a song to indicate pitch.[28] Only later did horizontal lines come to be added. At first these lines may have functioned as mere guides for judging absolute position, like the graduation-marks on a thermometer taken as a analog instrument. When the lines and the spaces between them become characters of the system, with placement of a syllable or note-sign serving only to pick out one of these characters, elements of a genuine notation emerge. However, I am primarily concerned here not with origins or development but with how fully the language of musical scores qualifies as a truly notational system.

That the syntactic requirements are in general met is quite clear. A note-mark may, indeed, be so placed that we are in doubt about whether it belongs to one note-character or another, but in no case does it belong

---

[27] I do not say to its merits, aesthetic or otherwise; see the discussion of this point later in this section.

[28] See the frontispiece to this chapter. According to Carl Parrish, *The Notation of Medieval Music* (New York, W.W. Norton & Co., Inc., 1957), p. 9, this system "is called *diastematic* from the Greek word for 'interval'. In this writing neumes are carefully 'heighted', that is, placed at various distances from an imaginary line representing a given pitch, according to their relationship to that line. Certain schools of neume notation display this feature even in their earliest manuscripts. . . . About the end of the tenth century the imaginary line about which diastematic neumes were placed became a real one. At first it was a dry line scratched on the parchment, an idea probably suggested by the use of the guidelines on which the test was written."

319

to both. Ostensible note-marks do not count as inscriptions in the system unless and until they are determined to belong to one character rather than to any other. Most characters of a musical score, whether numerals or letters or neither, are syntactically disjoint and differentiated. The symbol scheme is thus substantially notational, and the language of scores truly a language. But is this language a notational system? Does it satisfy the semantic requirements?

If we consider piano scores alone, the language is highly redundant since, for example, the same sound-events comply with the characters for *c*-sharp, *d*-flat, *e*-triple-flat, *b*-double-sharp, and so on[29] but redundancy, as we have seen, is not altogether fatal. A more crucial question arises when we consider scores for other instruments as well. In a violin score the characters for *c*-sharp and *d*-flat have no compliants in common.[30] Now if two characters thus have some compliants jointly (in piano scores) and others severally, the two compliance-classes properly intersect, flagrantly violating the requirement of semantic disjointness. What this account misses, though, is that since every performance is on one instrument or another, each of the two characters can be considered a vacant atomic character that combines with different specifications of instrument to form different prime characters. The compliance-classes of the two resultant prime characters occurring in piano scores are identical; the compliance-classes of the two resultant prime characters occurring in violin scores are disjoint. Neither pair nor the pair of atomic vacant characters nor the set of all six characters violates the rule of semantic disjointness by more than the redundancy mentioned.

If we suppose the series of whole note, half-note, quarter-note, eighth-note, etc., to be continued without end, the semantic requirement of finite differentiation will be violated. For then by tying note-signs together we can construct characters for notes differing in duration by less than any given fraction of a beat. Hence no sounding of a note could

[29]I oversimplify here by ignoring features other than pitch, but the central point is unaffected. The redundancy noted above will call for further consideration in another connection.

[30]This may be disputed. I am told that a tone of, say, 333 vibrations per second is accepted for either character. But we may regard such a tone either as actually compliant with both characters or (like the missing of one note) as merely within tolerable limits of deviation in practice. For purposes of illustrating a general point, I choose the latter interpretation here. A more relational notation is still compatible with notationality.

be determined to comply with at most one character. Now of course in any given score or corpus of scores, the number of note-signs, and of flags on any of them, is finite. But there must furthermore be a tacit or express limit on the number of flags permitted by the system at all; otherwise recovery of score from performance will not be even theoretically possible, identity of work from performance to performance will not be ensured, and the primary purpose of a notational system will not be served. Theoretically, any limit would do. Tradition seems to set it for the present at five flags—the 1/128 note.

The main corpus of peculiarly musical characters of the system thus appears on the whole to meet the semantic as well as the syntactic requirements for a notation. The same cannot be said for all the numerical and alphabetical characters that also occur in scores.

First, some compositions are written with a 'figured bass' or 'continuo', allowing performers certain options. Now so long as such scores determine comparatively broad but still mutually disjoint classes of performances,[31] they cause no trouble; what counts is not specificity but separateness. But a system that permits alternative use of figured-bass and specific notation, without rigidly prescribing the choice in every case, materially violates the conditions upon notational systems; for the compliance-classes of some of its characters are properly included in the compliance-classes of other, more general characters. Two score-inscriptions, one in figured-bass and the other in specific notation, even though they will have some common compliant performance, will not thereby be semantically equivalent; and two performances complying with the former may severally comply with two specific scores that have no compliant in common. The comprehensive language of musical scores, insofar as it offers free choice between figured-bass and specific notation, is thus not truly notational. Rather, it comprises two notational subsystems; and the one in use must be designated and adhered to if identification of work from performance to performance is to be ensured.

Much the same can be said concerning the free cadenza. The performer, again, is given wide scope; and scores providing for free cadenzas have compliance-classes that properly include those of other scores with their solo passages all specified note by note. Unless there is

---

[31]The question whether these compliance-classes are in fact disjoint can be answered only by careful examination of the notation in use and some delicate decisions concerning its interpretation.

a way of determining in every case whether a solo passage is to be fully specified or indicated as a free cadenza, we must again recognize that the language of musical scores is not purely notational but divides into notational subsystems.

Trouble of a different sort arises from the verbal notation used for the tempo of a movement. That the words come from ordinary object-language does not of itself matter. "Notational" does not imply "nonverbal"; and not every selection of characters, along with their compliance-classes, from a discursive language violates the conditions for notationality. What matters is whether the borrowed vocabulary meets the semantic requirements. Now just what is the vocabulary of tempo? It contains not only the more common terms like "allegro," "andante," and "adagio," but indefinitely many others like the following, taken from a few programs of chamber music[32]: *presto, allegro vivace, allegro assai, allegro spiritoso, allegro molto, allegro non troppo, allegro moderato, poco allegretto, allegretto quasi-minuetto, minuetto, minuetto con un poco di moto, rondo alla Polacca, andantino mosso, andantino grazioso, fantasia, affetuoso e sostenuto, moderato e amabile.* Apparently almost any words may be used to indicate pace and mood. Even if unambiguity were miraculously preserved, semantic disjointness would not be. And since a tempo may be prescribed as fast, or as slow, or as between fast and slow, or as between fast and between-fast-and-slow, and so on without limit, semantic differentiation goes by the board, too.

Thus the verbal language of tempos is not notational. The tempo words cannot be integral parts of a score insofar as the score serves the function of identifying a work from performance to performance. No departure from the indicated tempo disqualifies a performance as an instance—however wretched—of the work defined by the score. For these tempo specifications cannot be accounted integral parts of the defining score, but are rather auxiliary directions whose observance or nonobservance affects the quality of a performance but not the identity of the work. On the other hand, metronomic specifications of tempo do, under obvious restrictions and under a system universally requiring them, qualify as notational and may be taken as belonging to the score as such.

---

[32]Chosen casually from programs of works played at the Marlboro Music Festival, Marlboro, Vermont, during six weeks in the summer of 1961.

I have been able to discuss here, rather sketchily, only a few salient samples of relevant questions concerning the standard language of musical scores. The results suggest, however, that it comes as near to meeting the theoretical requirements for notationality as might reasonably be expected of any traditional system in constant actual use, and that the excisions and revisions needed to correct any infractions are rather plain and local. After all, one hardly expects chemical purity outside the laboratory.

Since complete compliance with the score is the only requirement for a genuine instance of a work, the most miserable performance without actual mistakes does count as such an instance, while the most brilliant performance with a single wrong note does not. Could we not bring our theoretical vocabulary into better agreement with common practice and common sense by allowing some limited degree of deviation in performances admitted as instances of a work? The practicing musician or composer usually bristles at the idea that a performance with one wrong note is not a performance of the given work at all; and ordinary usage surely sanctions overlooking a few wrong notes. But this is one of those cases where ordinary usage gets us quickly into trouble. The innocent-seeming principle that performance differing by just one note are instances of the same work risks the consequences—in view of the transitivity of identity—that all performances whatsoever are of the same work. If we allow the least deviation, all assurance of work-preservation and score-preservation is lost; for by a series of one-note errors of omission, addition, and modification, we can go all the way from Beethoven's *Fifth Symphony* to *Three Blind Mice*. Thus while a score may leave unspecified many features of a performance, and allow for considerable variation in others within prescribed limits, full compliance with the specifications given is categorically required. This is not to say that the exigencies that dictate our technical discourse need govern our everyday speech. I am no more recommending that in ordinary discourse we refuse to say that a pianist who misses a note has performed a Chopin Polonaise than that we refuse to call a whale a fish, the earth spherical, or a grayish-pink human white.

The overwhelming monopoly long held by standard musical notation has inevitably inspired rebellion and alternative proposals. Composers complain variously that scores in this notation prescribe too few features or too many or the wrong ones, or prescribe the right ones too precisely or not precisely enough. Revolution here as elsewhere may aim at more or at less or at different control of the means of production.

323

One simple system devised by John Cage is roughly as follows (see Figure 11): dots, for single sounds, are placed within a rectangle; across the rectangle, at varying angles and perhaps intersecting, run five straight lines for (severally) frequency, duration, timbre, amplitude, and succession. The significant factors determining the sounds indicated by a dot are the perpendicular distances from the dot to these lines.[33]

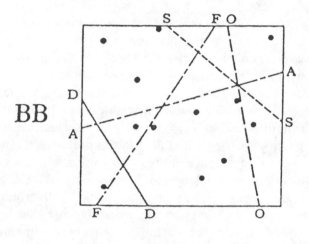

Figure 11

This system is not notational; for without some stipulation of minimal significant units of angle and distance, syntactic differentiation is wanting. So long as no limit is set upon the smallness of the difference in position that makes a difference in character, no measurement can ever determine that any mark belongs to one character rather than to any number of others. Similarly, under this system, no measurement can ever determine that a performance complies with one mark rather than others. Furthermore, depending upon just how the symbols are interpreted, syntactic and semantic disjointness may be lacking. The point is not that a work is less rigidly prescribed than by a standard score; for the character-classes and the compliance-classes of a notational system may be of any size so long as they are disjoint and differentiated. Under the

[33] See *Concert for Piano and Orchestra, Solo for Piano* (New York, Henmar Press, Inc., 1960), p. 53, figure BB. The figure, which has been redrawn, is reproduced here by permission of the publisher.

proposed system there are no disjoint and differentiated characters or compliance-classes, no notation, no language, no scores.

The objection may be raised that the lack of syntactic differentiation here hardly matters if we have the original drawing and photographic means of reproducing it within any desired or consequential degree of accuracy. But however small the inaccuracy of reproduction, a chain of successive reproductions of reproductions can result in departing to any degree from the original. True enough, we can detect significant deviation by direct comparison with the original (if it is available); yet for two significantly different originals there may be a third (or a copy) that does not differ significantly from either. To arrive at a notation here calls not only for a limit upon significant deviation but also for a means of ensuring disjointness of characters.

Now I am by no means pronouncing upon whether adoption of a system like that described might nevertheless be a good idea. I am neither qualified nor called upon to make such a judgment. I am simply pointing out that much more is involved than a mere shift from one notational system to another. Nor am I quibbling about the proper use of such words as "notation," "score," and "work." That matters little more than the proper use of a fork. What does matter is that the system in question furnishes no means of identifying a work from performance to performance or even of a character from mark to mark. Nothing can be determined to be a true copy of Cage's autograph diagram or to be a performance of it. There are only copies *after* and performances *after* that unique object as there are only drawings and paintings after a sketch. The same, of course, may be said of the mediaeval manuscript shown in the frontispiece of this chapter; sometimes revolution is retrogression.

An extreme spirit of *laissez faire* has led some composers to use systems that restrict only slightly the performer's freedom to play what and as he pleases. Such latitude is not incompatible with notationality; even a system with only two characters, one having as compliants all piano performances beginning with a middle *c*, and the other having as compliants all other performances, would be notational—though for this system there could be only two different works. But, of course, systems with characters having wide ranges of application often lack semantic disjointness.

At the opposite extreme, some composers of electronic music, with continuous sound-sources and means of activation, and with the human performer dispensable in favor of mechanical devices, seek to eliminate all latitude in performance and achieve 'exact control'.[34] But except where mere counting is involved, absolutely precise prescription cannot be accomplished by any notational system; differentiation requires gaps that destroy continuity. With a decimal system, for example, absolute precision would require writing out each specification endlessly; stopping at any finite number of decimal places results in some inaccuracy, however slight, that could accumulate in a long enough chain to any amount. For exact control, the symbol system would have to be both syntactically and semantically dense—an analog or graphic system; then any imprecision would arise from mechanical or human errors or limitations rather than from the symbol system. But then, also, we have no notation or scores, and ironically the demand for absolute and inflexible control results in purely autographic works.

Many of the symbol systems developed by modern composers have been described, illustrated, and classified by Erhardt Karkoschka.[35] His classification, differently motivated from ours, recognizes four basic types of system:

(1) Precise Notation (*Präzise Notation*)—where, for example, every note is named.
(2) Range Notation (*Rahmenotation*)—where, for example, only the limits of ranges of notes are set.
(3) Suggestive Notation (*Hinweisende Notation*)—where at most relations of notes, or approximate limits of ranges, are specified.
(4) Musical Graphics.

Obviously, a system of either of the first two kinds may or may not qualify as notational in my terminology. Systems of the third kind seem in general to be non-notational; they include, for example, the usual verbal tempo descriptions. But a system prescribing only relations between notes—such as that one is twice as loud or an octave below the

---

[34]Roger Sessions, in a passage just preceding the paragraph from which the quotation heading Chapter IV is taken, writes that electronic media make possible "the exact control of all musical elements. . . . Every moment of music not only can but must be the result of the minutest calculation, and the composer for the first time has the whole world of sound at his disposal"; then he proceeds to question the musical importance of this approach. Peter Yates, in "The Proof of the Notation," *Arts and Architecture*, vol. 82 (1966), p. 36, points out that "Even a performance by electronic means will vary with the equipment and acoustics".

[35]In *Das Schriftsbild der Neuen Musik* (Celle, Herman Moeck, 1966), pp. 19ff. My discussion of this searching work is brief and inadequate.

preceding note—seems also to belong to the third class and could be notational. The system used for Gregorian chant may have been of this sort. Of his first three classes, Karkoschka writes (p. 80): "A work falls in the three spheres of precise notation, range notation, and suggestive notation if it has the usual coordinate system of space and time as basis, is more sign than sketch, and is essentially linear." The fourth class, musical graphics, apparently consists mainly of analog systems, lacking both syntactic and semantic articulation—that is, of non-notational, nonlinguistic systems that provide diagrams or sketches rather than scores or descriptions.

3. Sketch

Because a painter's sketch, like a composer's score, may be used as a working guide, the crucial difference in their status might go unnoticed. The sketch, unlike the score, is not in a language or notation at all, but in a system without either syntactic or semantic differentation. And while the Cage system described takes certain relationships of dot to line as the only pertinent ones, none among the pictorial properties of a sketch can be dismissed as irrelevant. But in neither case can anything be determined to belong to or to comply with at most one character. Thus, whereas a true score picks out a class of performances that are the equal and only instances of a musical work, a sketch does not determine a class of objects that are the equal and only instances of a work of painting. Unlike the score, the sketch does not define a work, in the strong sense of "define" explained earlier, but rather *is* one.

Now this is not to deny that a notational system might be established such that sketches belong to its characters. Obviously sketches and also paintings can be sorted into disjoint and differentiated classes in any of various ways; and any of a multitude of correlations can be set up. But quite as obviously, to have two realms that can be so sorted and correlated is not yet to have a system. Only when custom or express stipulation actually effects or selects a classification of each realm and a correlation of the two do we have a system. Such a selection has already been made in the case of standard musical notation, but not in the case of sketches. No pictorial respects are distinguished as those in which a sketch must match another to be its equivalent, or a painting match a sketch to be an instance of what the sketch defines. And no magnitude of difference in any respect is set as the threshhold of significance.

Differences of all kinds and degrees, measurable or not, are on equal footing. Hence no classes of sketches are picked out as the characters, and no classes of pictures as the compliance-classes, of a notational system.

In short, the sketch—as a sketch—differs from the score not in functioning as a character in a language of a different kind but in not functioning as a character in a *language* at all.[36] The notational language of musical scores has no parallel in a language (notational or not) of sketches.

4. Painting

That we have ready at hand no notational system for painting does not settle the question whether such a system is possible. Taken at its face value, the question can be answered with an unhesitating but trivial *yes*. For examples of such notational languages are easily constructed. A library-like decimal system assigning a numeral to each painting according to time and place of production would meet all five requirements. Far afield is the objection that no one can tell by inspection, without further information, whether a given painting complies with a given numeral; for likewise no one can tell by inspection, *without further information*, whether a given performance complies with a musical score. One has to be able to interpret the score as one has to be able to interpret the numeral; and to know how to interpret a character is to know what complies with it.

The compliance-classes for the language just described will indeed be unit-classes, so that identification of a work from instance to instance will always be from sole instance to same sole instance, but there are no requirements upon the size of the compliance-classes of a notational system. And the uniqueness of instance in painting is irrelevant here since exactly the same question about the possibility of a notational system arises for etching, and is to be answered in the same way. If impressions are assigned numerals according to the plate printed from, the compliance-class of a numeral will usually have many members. Indeed, nothing precludes taking each plate itself as the unique

---

[36]Of course, nothing prevents a given mark from functioning as an inscription in a notation (or in several different notations) and also as a sketch in a nonlinguistic system (or in several such systems).

inscription of a character having its impressions as its compliants. Hence for painting and etching alike, notational languages are readily devised.

Yet, clearly, this straight-faced answer to the literal question asked misses the main point. For the question of real interest here is whether by means of a notational system the work of painting or etching can be freed of dependence upon a particular author or upon a place or date or means of production. It is theoretically possible to write a score so defining a work of painting or etching that objects produced by others, before or since the usually designated original or originals, and by other means (than, e.g., the 'original' plate) may comply with the score and qualify as equal instances of the work? In short, could institution of a notational system transform painting or etching from an autographic into an allographic art?

Some reasons that have been given for a negative answer are plainly beside the point. That a visual work is more complex and subtle than a musical performance would—even if true—not matter. For a score need not—indeed cannot—specify all aspects of the compliants nor even every degree of difference in any aspect; a score, as in figured-bass or free-cadenza notation, may be summary in the extreme. Nor does the difficulty of making perfect reproductions of a painting have anything to do with confinement of the work to the unique original.[37] The performances of the most specific score are by no means exact duplicates of one another, but vary widely and in many ways. A moderately good copy and the original painting resemble each other more closely than do performances of a Bach suite by Piatigorsky and Casals.

Yet there are constraints. Although a notational system may pick out any set of disjoint and finitely differentiated classes in any realm as compliance-classes not every compliance-class of every such system counts as a work. Standard musical notation might be reinterpreted so that its compliance-classes cut wildly across the standard ones or even contain no musical performances at all. Or a notational system might classify pictures according to size or shape. But in none of these cases does a compliance-class any more constitute a work than the animals in

---

[37]Widespread acceptance of this easy and inapt explanation has inhibited efforts toward real understanding of the matter. Philosophers of art are not immune from the error; see, for example, Joseph Margolis, "The Identity of a Work of Art", *Mind*, vol. 68 (1959), p. 50.

a zoo form a species, or the performances of a musical composition make up a society. Whether the compliance-classes for a system are works (or societies) depends partly upon their relationship to the classes accounted works (or societies) in antecedent practice.

Special care must be taken here. While it would be quite wrong to suppose that a class becomes a work by being assigned a character in a notational system, it would also be quite wrong to suppose that no class is a work unless it has been antecedently considered so. On the one hand, the antecedent classification stands as licence and touchstone for a notational system; only in referece to this classification can there be a charge of material error or a claim of material correctness. On the other hand, the antecedent classification is normally partial and provisional. It submits only sample classes, each only by samples. Adoption of a notational language thus effects a double projection: from the samples of the several classes to the complete classification of the field of reference. This involves a choice among alternatives; and some actual departures from the antecedent classification may be made for the sake of better systematization. In sum, the problem of developing a notational system for an art like music amounted to the problem of arriving at a real definition of the notion of a musical work.

Where a pertinent antecedent classification is lacking or is flouted, a notational language effects only an arbitrary, nominal definition of "work," as if it were a word newly coined. With no prototype, or no recognition of one, there are no material grounds for choosing one systematization rather than any other. But in the case of painting, a work is antecedently identified with (the unit-class of) an individual picture; and in the case of etching, with the class of impressions printed from an individual plate. Now the question is whether by application of a notational system works of painting or etching could legitimately be identified with quite different classes. This would call not just for such minor adjustments as occur in any systematization but for a drastic overhaul that would lump together in each compliance-class many antecedently different works. A notational system effecting such a reclassification may of course be applied at will; but scores in it will not constitute real definitions of works of painting. To repudiate the antecedent classification is to disenable the only authority competent to issue the needed license.

Thus the answer to the significant question about a notational system for painting is *no*. We can devise a notational system that will provide, for works of painting and etching, real definitions that depend upon

330

history of production. We can devise a notational system that will provide purely arbitrary nominal definitions that do not depend upon history of production. But we cannot devise a notational system that will provide, for such works, definitions that are both real (consonant with antecedent practice) and independent of history of production.

In sum, an established art becomes allographic only when the classification of objects or events into works is legitimately projected from an antecedent classification and is fully defined, independently of history of production, in terms of a notational system. Both authority and means are required; a suitable antecedent classifcation provides the one, a suitable notational system the other. Without the means, the authority is unexercised; without the authority, the means are footless.

5. Script

A script, unlike a sketch, is a character in a notational scheme and in a language but, unlike a score, is not in a notational system. The syntactic but not all the semantic requirements are met. "Script" here is thus not confined to cursive inscriptions or to the work of playwrights and film writers. In general, the characters of natural and of most technical languages are scripts; for even if ambiguity is avoided, the compliance-classes of such a language are seldom either disjoint or differentiated from one another.

While most scripts are verbal, notationality obviously does not turn upon the look of marks. We do not arrive at a notational system if we substitute a numeral for each word of English.[38] And we do not sacrifice notationality—although we surely jettison practicality—if we translate standard musical notation into a sublanguage of English in such a way that the vocabulary of admitted words meets our five requirements.

One might suppose that scripts but not scores can assert or denote. But we have already seen that means of effecting assertion (or question or command) can be added to or subtracted from a system without

---

[38]Lexicographical order might be taken as the basis for assigning numerals to words. But if we want to assign a numeral to *every string of letters*, and we place no limit on the length of a string, lexicographical ordering becomes astoundingly complex. However, numerals may be assigned to all such strings on the basis of the different and very simple ordering that begins with lexicographical ordering of all one-letter strings, proceeds to lexicographical ordering of all two-letter strings, and so on. See IV, note 17.

affecting notationality; and the idea that scores do not denote seems no better founded. Offhand, indeed, the relation between a term and what it denotes appears quite different from that between a score and its performances or between a letter and its utterances; but no very clear principle seems to underlie this distinction. The criteria that distinguish notational systems from other languages are in terms of interrelationships among compliance-classes, and provide no good grounds for refusing to say that a character in a language of either sort denotes what complies with it.[39]

Even less can be said for the notion that while we need only know how to recognize a performance of a musical score or an utterance of a phonetic score, we have to understand a script. In both cases, we have to know how to determine what complies with the character. Where a language has few prime characters and fairly simple principles of compliance, so that confident and almost automatic use is acquired rather easily, we tend to regard the language as an instrument we operate. Where the prime characters are many and the principles of compliance are complex, so that interpretation of a character often calls for some deliberation, we tend to speak of having to understand the language. But this difference in complexity, besides being a matter of degree, does not at all coincide with the distinction between notational systems and other languages. For a notational system may have a denumerable infinity of prime characters and an intricate compliance-relation, while a discursive language may have only two characters— say the words "red" and "square", with red things and square things as their compliants.

A script, then, differs from a score not in being verbal or declarative or denotational or in requiring special understanding, but simply in being a character in a language that is either ambiguous or lacks semantic disjointness or differentiation. But this prosaic distinction is more consequential than might appear, both in ways already observed and in its bearing upon some currently touchy philosphical questions.

[39]This is not to say that everything a symbol refers to complies with it; exemplification, though a mode of reference, does not constitute compliance. Also we shall see below (section 7) that the utterances and inscriptions of a language may alternatively, and often happily, be construed as equally instances of visual-auditory characters.

6. Projectibility, Synonymy, Analyticity

To learn and use any language is to resolve problems of projection. On the basis of sample inscriptions of a character we must decide whether other marks, as they appear, belong to that character; and on the basis of sample compliants of a character, we must decide whether other objects comply. Notational and discursive languages are like in this respect.

With discursive languages, further and major projective decisions have to be made. Even after all questions about what marks belong to what characters and about what objects belong to what compliance-classes have been settled, still an object often complies with several characters. In object-English, for example, no object or set of objects complies with just one predicate. All green objects examined to date comply with the character "green object," but all comply equally with "green object examined to date or kangaroo," and with indefinitely many other predicates. Virtually any class that contains all green objects examined to date is the compliance-class of some expression in this language. More generally, the objects in any given selection comply with some English description that has as its other compliants any other given objects. Thus projection from given cases calls for a choice among countless alternatives; and the making of such choices pervades all learning.[40]

Yet no such questions arise when we are using a notational system. Here nothing is a sample of more than one compliance-class; nothing complies with two characters that are not coextensive. So no choice remains except perhaps, where redundancy is permitted, between coextensive labels; projection even from single sample to compliance-class is uniquely determined. What has happened, in effect, is that the decisions have already been taken in adopting the system. We saw earlier that selection and application of a notational system resolves problems of projection of two levels: from partial to complete compli-

---

[40]What constitutes the grounds for choice here is a moot question. Scientists and metaphysicians are wont to posit an ontological difference between 'natural kinds' and other classes. Philosophers often hold that members of a favored class share some real attribute or essence, or bear some absolute resemblance to each other. I think the distinction depends rather upon linguistic habit. For a detailed discussion of the problem of projectibility, see *FFF*.

ance-classes, and from partial to complete set of compliance-classes. Hence so long as we use that system, we are free of the major problems of projectibility.

Of course, part of a performance no more determines the rest than does part of an object. Hearing the first notes of a composition no more tells us what follows than seeing part of an object tells us what lies beyond our view. The difference is that under a notational system one complete performance (whether of a single prime character or of the entire score of a symphony) uniquely determines character and compliance-class, while under a discursive language one complete object or event complying with a character does not uniquely determine character or compliance-class.

Furthermore a notational system, unlike a discursive language, is accordingly untroubled by any distinction in nobility among different ways of classifying an object. An object cannot be assigned by one character of the system to a natural or genuine kind and by another to a random or artificial collection. All labels for an object have the same compliance-class. We cannot, in standard musical notation for example, specify merely that a note is a quarter-note regardless of pitch or merely that it is a middle c regardless of duration. We have no label for all quarter-notes or for all middle c's; detached note-signs and empty staff lines must be taken as vacant characters if notationality is to be preserved. All the properties of a given object that are specifiable in a given notational system are thus coextensive.

The distinction between real and nominal defining still stands, as is illustrated by the difference between writing a score for a work already extant in performance and composing a new work. Once the language is given, a score or class of coextensive scores is in the first case uniquely determined by a performance, and a class of performances is in the second case uniquely determined by a score. But in both cases, all scores for a performance assign it to the same compliance-class: nothing is a performance of more than a single work. Where two works are performed in succession the resultant event, though it contains performances of each of the two, is itself a performance of neither but of the conjoint score.

That all scores for a performance are coextensive does not imply that all are synonymous. Two coextensive characters, c_1 and c_2, are not synonymous unless every two parallel compounds of them are also

334

coextensive. That is, if replacement of c_1 or c_2 by the other in some compound character k_1 yields a character k_2 with an extension different from that of k_1, then c_1 and c_2 may on good grounds be said to differ in meaning.[41] Furthermore, where two terms thus differ in meaning, even coextensive parallel compounds of them may be considered, derivatively, to differ in meaning. We noticed earlier that a c-sharp-sign and a d-flat-sign (equal in indicated duration, etc.) as they occur in piano scores have the same compliance-class of sounds, but that since the effect of adding the natural-sign to these characters is to negate the sharp-sign and the flat-sign alike, the compliance-class for the c-sharp-natural-sign[42] consists of c-sounds and is disjoint from the compliance-class, consisting of d-sounds, for the d-flat-natural-sign. Thus the c-sharp-sign and the d-flat-sign, even though coextensive, are not synonymous; and neither are two scores, even if coextensive, that are parallel compounds of these characters.[43]

[41]The criterion of difference in meaning here employed is that set forth in my papers "On Likeness of Meaning" and "On Some Differences About Meaning" (cited in I, note 19). The *primary* extension of a character consists of what that character denotes. Two characters differ in meaning if they differ in primary extension or in any of their parallel secondary extensions. As applied to natural languages, where there is great freedom in generating compounds, this criterion tends to give the result that every two terms differ in meaning. No such result follows for more restricted languages; and indeed for these the criterion may need to be strengthened by providing further that characters differ in meaning if they are parallel compounds of terms that differ either in primary or in parallel secondary extension.

[42]The characters here in question comprise a note-sign, a sharp-sign or flat-sign (perhaps from the signature), and a natural-sign that neutralizes the sharp-sign or flat-sign. The order of precedence of the note-sign and the sharp-sign or flat-sign makes no difference; but a natural-sign cancels all and only the sharp-signs or flat-signs that precede it and are (immediately or remotely) associated with the note-sign. To modify a c-double-sharp to a c-sharp, we must suffix a natural-sign and then another sharp-sign, so that the unabbreviated result is a c-sharp-sharp-natural-sharp-sign.

[43]All never-performed scores have the same (i.e., no) performances as compliants. They are scores for 'different works' in the oblique sense that pictures of unicorns and pictures of centaurs are pictures of different things. In neither case is there a difference in primary extension. The score for Jones's never-performed Symphony #9 and the score for his never-performed Piano Concerto #3 are strictly just the Jones-Symphony-#9-score and the Jones-Piano-Concerto-#3-score. Replacement of a character in the Jones-Symphony-#9-score will result in the Jones-Symphony-#9-score only if the replaced and replacing characters are coextensive and furthermore, in the way explained above, synonymous.

Wherever there are coextensive nonsynonymous characters, a question may arise concerning principles of preference among them in any given context. Although "rational animal" and "featherless biped" be coextensive, still "All men are rational animals" is said—upon rather obscure grounds—to be analytic, and "All men are featherless bipeds" to be synthetic. How do matters stand in a system that is notational except for containing some coextensive characters? Musicians tell us that in a traditional piano score the usual rules of composition unequivocally decide whether a c-sharp-sign or a d-flat-sign should occur. Although no difference in performance can result, the wrong choice seems to violate a rule of grammatical etiquette comparable to that governing, say, the use in English of the prefixes "un" and "in". Indeed, we might say that using a c-sharp-sign where a d-flat-sign belongs is like saying that such a choice is untolerable (or inbearable).

A more substantive consideration might be found in the relation of a work to its siblings for other instruments. As we have seen, specification of instrument is an integral part of any true score in standard musical notation; and a piano work and the violin version of it, for example, count strictly as different works. Nevertheless, certain violin performances rather than others are accepted as performances of the violin version of the piano work. Let us suppose that for a given piano work the violin performances so recognized have a c-sharp and not a d-flat at a given place. The score for the violin version of the piano work must then have at that place a c-sharp-sign and not a d-flat-sign. This would provide grounds for choosing the c-sharp-sign in the piano score itself; the piano work might be said to have the c-sharp analytically in that in versions of the work for other instruments, where the c-sharp-sign and the d-flat-sign are not coextensive, a c-sharp is mandatory.

How close such a criterion comes to the usual notion of analyticity is hard to say, since that notion is so hopelessly confused. But musical notation seems to offer so much less opportunity than does English for befuddlement over analyticity that some philosophers might do well to stop writing and start composing.

7. Literary Arts

The text of a poem or novel or biography is a character in a notational scheme. As a phonetic character, with utterances as compliants, it belongs to an approximately notational system.[44] As a character with objects as compliants, it belongs to a discursive language.

Since in the latter case the compliance-classes are not disjoint or differentiated, texts are not scores but scripts. If compliance-classes of texts constituted works, then in some cases whether an object belongs to a given work would be theoretically indeterminable, and in some cases an object would be an instance of several works. But obviously works of literature are not compliance-classes of texts. The Civil War is not literature; and two histories of it are different works.

Nor can the work of literature be identified as the class of utterances compliant with the text taken as a phonetic character. For even though the text be a true score, with an exclusive disjoint and differentiated compliance-class, an utterance obviously has no better title to be considered an instance of the work than does an inscription of the text. Utterances are not the end-products as are performances in music. Moreover, the utterances themselves might equally well be considered either as coextensive with inscriptions of the text or as belonging to a converse-phonetic language and having the inscriptions as compliants. Or since compliance is not always asymmetrical, utterances and inscriptions could be considered as having each other as their compliants. Or we might take written and spoken English say, as separate and parallel languages. A character of the one consists of inscriptions, a character of the other consists of utterances, while "character of English" can be taken either way if no restrictions are imposed by the context. But perhaps the simplest course is to consider a character of English to have utterances and inscriptions alike as members. This merely extends in a convenient and appropriate way the practice of counting widely varying marks as members of a single character. Syntactic disjointness— required of a notational scheme and hence of any language, not merely of a notational system—will have to be preserved by refusing to accept any utterance as belonging to two different characters. Just as among certain matching letter-inscriptions some belong to the first letter of the alphabet while some belong to the fourth, so among utterances consisting of a hard-g-sound followed by a long-a-sound followed by a t-sound some will belong to the same character as inscriptions of "gate" while some will belong to the same character as inscriptions of "gait."

---

[44]The approximation will not be very close in English, with its wealth of homonyms, inconstancies, etc., but may be fairly close in a language like Spanish.

A literary work, then, is not the compliance-class of a text but the text or script itself. All and only inscriptions and utterances of the text are instances of the work; and identification of the work from instance to instance is ensured by the fact that the text is a character in a notational scheme—in a vocabulary of syntactically disjoint and differentiated symbols. Even replacement of a character in a text by another synonymous character (if any can be found in a discursive language) yields a different work. Yet the work is the text not as an isolated class of marks and utterances but as a character in a language. The same class as a character in another language is another work, and a translation of a work is not an instance of that work. Both identity of language and syntactic identity within the language are necessary conditions for identity of a literary work.

Obviously I am not concerned with what distinguishes some scripts as 'truly literary' works. Nevertheless, equating a poem with its text may arouse some protest, on the ground that the more immediate or intrinsic properties of classes of inscriptions and utterances hardly coincide with the aesthetically important properties of the poem. But in the first place, defining literary works no more calls for setting forth all their significant aesthetic properties than defining metals calls for setting forth all their significant chemical properties. In the second place, immediacy is a suspect notion and aesthetic relevance a subtle one; and no end of confusion has arisen from association of the two. To identify the literary work with a script is not to isolate and dessicate it but to recognize it as a denotative and expressive symbol that reaches beyond itself along all sorts of short and long referential paths.

We have seen that a musical score is in a notation and defines a work; that a sketch or picture is not in a notation but is itself a work; and that a literary script is both in a notation and is itself a work. Thus in the different arts a work is differently localized. In painting, the work is an individual object; and in etching, a class of objects. In music, the work is the class of performances compliant with a character. In literature, the work is the character itself. And in calligraphy, we may add, the work is an individual inscription. [45]

In the drama, as in music, the work is a compliance-class of performances. The text of a play, however, is a composite of score and

---

[45] The much discussed question whether a work of art is a symbol thus seems to me particularly fruitless. Not only may a work, depending upon the art, be an object or a class of objects or a character in a language or an inscription, but whichever it is may in various ways symbolize other things.

script. The dialogue is in a virtually notational system, with utterances as its compliants. This part of the text is a score; and performances compliant with it constitute the work. The stage directions, descriptions of scenery, etc., are scripts in a language that meets none of the semantic requirements for notationality; and a performance does not uniquely determine such a script or class of coextensive scripts. Given a performance, the dialogue can be univocally transcribed: different correct ways of writing it down will have exactly the same performances as compliants. But this is not true of the rest of the text. A given setting, for example, may comply with extensionally divergent descriptions; and its compliance with some descriptions may be theoretically undecidable. The parts of the text other than the dialogue count not as integral parts of the defining score but as supplementary instructions. In the case of a novel consisting partly or even entirely of dialogue, the text is the work; but the same text taken as the text for a play is or contains the score for a work. The script for a silent film is neither the cinematic work nor a score for it but, though used in producing the film, is otherwise as loosely related to the work as is a verbal description of a painting to the painting itself.

8. Dance

The possibility of a notation for the dance was one of the initial questions that led to our study of notational systems. Because the dance is visual like painting, which has no notation, and yet transient and temporal like music, which has a highly developed standard notation, the answer is not altogether obvious; and ill-grounded negatives and irresponsible affirmatives have been put forth about equally often.

The ill-grounded negatives rest on the argument that the dance, as a visual and mobile art involving the infinitely subtle and varied expressions and three-dimensional motions of one or more highly complex organisms, is far too complicated to be captured by any notation. But, of course, a score need not capture all the subtlety and complexity of a performance. That would be hopeless even in the comparatively simpler art of music, and would always be pointless. The function of a score is to specify the essential properties a performance must have to belong to the work; the stipulations are only of certain aspects and only within certain degrees. All other variations are permitted; and the differences among performances of the same work, even in music, are enormous.

The irresponsible affirmative answers consist of pointing out that a notation can be devised for almost anything. This, of course, is irrelevant. The significant issue is whether in terms of notational language we can provide real definitions that will identify a dance in its several performances, independently of any particular history of production.

For such real definitions to be possible there must, as we have seen, be an antecedent classification of performances into works that is similarly independent of history of production. This classification need not be neat or complete but must serve as a foil, a scaffolding, a springboard, for the development of a full and systematic classification. That the requisite antecedent classification exists for the dance seems clear. Prior to any notation, we make reasonably consistent judgments as to whether performances by different people are instances of the same dance. No theoretical barrier stands in the way of developing a suitable notational system.

Practical feasibility is another matter, not directly in question here. The antecedent classification is so rough and tentative that the decisions to be made are many, intricate, and consequential. And inadvertent violation of one of the syntactic or semantic requirements can easily result in a non-notational language or a system that is no language at all. Bold and intelligent systematization is called for, along with a good deal of care.

Among notations that have been proposed for the dance, the one called *Labanotation*[46] after the inventor, Rudolf Laban, seems deservedly to have gained most recognition. An impressive scheme of analysis and description, it refutes the common belief that continuous complex motion is too recalcitrant a subject-matter for notational articulation, and discredits the dogma that successful systematic description depends in general upon some inherent amenability—some

[46]Laban was working on the matter in Vienna as early as the 1920's. He published *Choreographie* (Jena, Eugen Diederichs, 1926); *Effort*, with F.C. Lawrence (London, MacDonald & Evans, Ltd., 1947); and *Principles of Dance and Movement Notation* (London, MacDonald & Evans, Ltd., 1956). A convenient and well-illustrated exposition by Ann Hutchinson is available in a paperback book, *Labanotation* (Norfolk, Conn., New Directions, 1961), which is cited in the next three footnotes. One of the competing systems has been proposed by Rudolf and Joan Benesh in *An Introduction to Dance Notation* (London, Adam & Charles Black, Ltd., 1956). I leave it as an exercise for the reader to compare the Laban and Benesh systems in the light of the principles set forth in the present book.

native structural neatness—in what is described. Indeed, the development of Laban's language offers us an elaborate and intriguing example of the process that has come to be called "concept formation."

How far, though, does the system meet the theoretical requirements for a notational language? I can answer only tentatively, from an inadequate knowledge of the system. That the characters are syntactically disjoint seems clear. Satisfaction of the requirements of finite differentiation is less easily ascertained; but Laban avoids a good many pitfalls here. For example, one naturally looks for a violation in the directional indications, since if every different angle of a line stands for a different direction, neither the syntactic nor the semantic requirement of differentiation is fulfilled. But in Labanotation, direction of facing is indicated by a "direction pin" in any of eight positions disposed at equal intervals around the full horizontal circle (Figure 12); and a direction halfway between any two proximate directions among these eight is indicated by combining the signs for the two (e.g., as in Figure 13). This device admits of no further iteration to indicate directions between two proximate directions among the sixteen. Elsewhere in the system, differentiation is often achieved just as decisively as here. One is alerted for trouble by such a statement as: "The relative length of the direction symbol shows its time value"; but here, as in music, time is divided into beats, and the least difference in duration provided for in the language is presumably the same as in standard musical notation.[47]

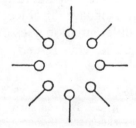

Figure 12

[47]Or less. The least duration indicated by any of the characters actually presented or mentioned in *Labanotation* (p. 52) is one-sixteenth of a beat, probably because at even the slowest normal tempo, that is the shortest time in which a dancer can be expected to execute a distinct and recognizable unit of movement. But so long as a limit is set, just where does not matter.

341

Figure 13

Like standard musical notation, Labanotation provides for more and less specific scoring, and so violates the condition of semantic disjointness. The *ad lib* signs and the explicit license to describe in detail or leave open certain aspects of a movement[48] have much the same effect as do the free-cadenza and figured-bass notations in music. The result is that identity of a work will not be preserved in every chain of alternating steps between scores and performances. The flexibility offered may be welcomed by the choreographer or composer, and does not affect score-to-performance steps; but it leaves the performance-to-score steps insufficiently determined until the specificity of the scoring is stipulated. Labanotation as a whole is a discursive language comprising several notational subsystems; and in some cases, a class of performances may be a work relative to one but not another of these notational systems.

So far, I have been considering only the basic vocabulary. Some of the other symbolism introduced cannot be embraced in any notational system. A prime example is the use of words or pictures to indicate physical objects involved in the dance.[49] If object-words in general are admitted, then semantic disjointness and differentiation are sacrificed and we have a discursive language. If object-sketches in general are admitted, then syntactic differentiation goes by the board, too, and we do not even have a language. One remedy would be to restrict the

[48]For use of the *ad lib* signs, see *Labanotation*, pp. 88, 187. On permitted variance in specificity of scoring, see e.g., pp. 59, 262. In such passages we find, I think, the significance of the introductory statement: "Labanotation allows for any degree of specificity" (p. 6). Read as meaning that the system allows for specification to within any given degree of precision whatsoever, this statement would imply lack of differentiation.

Incidentally, Labanotation seems to be redundant, although whether alternative symbols are actually coextensive is not always clear from the exposition (e.g., see p. 144). We have seen that coextensive characters in music sometimes differ in meaning through entering into parallel compounds that differ in extension; so far I have not discovered any analogue of this in Labanotation.

[49]*Labanotation*, pp. 179–181.

342

admitted words or pictures very severely in appropriate ways. Another, suggested earlier for tempo-words in music and stage directions in the drama, would be to treat these characters not as integral parts of a score at all but as supplementary and nondefinitive. Whether this is fitting depends upon whether (as seems fair enough) a performance employing different objects or even none is an instance of the same dance, just as a performance of *Hamlet* in modern dress and without scenery or accessories is an instance of the same play.

All in all, Labanotation passes the theoretical tests very well—about as well as does ordinary musical notation, and perhaps as well as is compatible with practicality. I am not saying that we have here a good or effective notational system for the dance, that the decisions embodied in it are sound or happy or consistent. Such an appraisal by a layman would be impertinent and worthless. By extensive use, the language may be found unsatisfactory or become traditional enough to acquire authority. If this or another language becomes standard enough, its underlying analysis of movement into factors and particles will prevail; arbitrary decisions will blossom into absolute truth, and expedient units for discourse ripen into the ultimate components of reality—awaiting revolution.

Laban conceived his system as a notation not merely for dance but for human movement in general, and went on to develop and supplement the system as a means for analyzing and classifying all human physical activities. The need for some such system is especially apparent, for example, in industrial engineering and in psychological experimentation. Whether the experimenter or the subject repeats his behavior on a second occasion depends upon the criteria of identity of behavior that are applied; and the problem of formulating such criteria is the problem of developing a notational system. As for nonhuman movement, a zoologist has recently proposed an entertaining and illuminating method of codifying the various gaits of horses.[50]

9. Architecture

The architect's papers are a curious mixture. The specifications are written in ordinary discursive verbal and numerical language. The

[50]See Milton Hildebrand, "Symmetrical Gaits of Horses", *Science*, vol. 150 (1965), pp. 701–708.

renderings made to convey the appearance of the finished building are sketches. But what of the plans?

Because a plan is a drawing, with lines and angles subject to continuous variation, the first guess would be that it is technically a sketch. But on the plan are measurements in words and figures. This suggests that we have here a combination of sketch and script. But I think this again is wrong. In the first place, the drawing is used only to indicate the relative location of elements and measurements. Careful drawing to scale is merely for convenience and elegance; a rough and distorted version, with the same letters and numerals, qualifies as a true copy of the most precisely drafted blueprint, prescribes the constitutive properties as rigorously, and has the same buildings as compliants. In the second place, while the numerals as characters in the unlimited set of fractional numerals are scripts, the numerals admissable in architectural plans are tacitly restricted—e.g., so that measurements are to be given only, say, to the nearest thirty-second of an inch. So long as any such restriction is in force, the admitted part of numerical language does not, like the whole, violate the condition of finite differentiation, but qualifies as notational. Thus although a drawing often counts as a sketch, and a measurement in numerals as a script, the particular selection of drawing and numerals in an architectural plan counts as a digital diagram and as a score.

Architectural plans, like musical scores, may sometimes define works as broader than we usually take them. For the architect's specifications of materials and construction (whether written out separately or on the plans) can no more be considered integral parts of a score than can the composer's verbal specifications of tempo. An architect is free to stipulate that the material of a foundation be stone, or that it be granite, or that it be Rockport seam-faced granite. Given the building, we cannot tell which of these nesting terms occurs in the specifications. The class of buildings picked out by the plans-plus-specifications is narrower than that defined by the plans alone; but the plans-plus-specifications make up a script, not a score. Thus the question whether two buildings are instances of the same work, relative to the architect's total language, is an indeterminate one. Relative to the notational language of plans, it is determinate; but the work is then identified with a more comprehensive class than is customary. However, exact conformity between definition and ordinary practice is never required or to be expected.

We must not be misled by the fact that the compliance-class of a set of plans happens so often to consist of but one building; or by the preeminent interest or value that a given instance of an architectural work may have; or by the emphasis sometimes laid upon immediate supervision, by the architect, of the process of construction. Many a composition is played only once; certain performances of other pieces have exceptional importance; and a building or performance executed under the direction of the designer or composer, while a more personal product and perhaps much better (or much worse) than another building or performance from the same plans or score, is not therefore a more authentic or original instance of the work.

Nevertheless, the work of architecture is not always as surely disengaged from a particular building as is a work of music from a particular performance. The end-product of architecture, unlike that of music, is not ephemeral; and the notational language was developed in response rather to the need for participation of many hands in construction. The language thus has weaker warrant for, and meets more resistance in, overriding the primordial autographic stage of the art. Plainly enough, all houses complying with the plans for Smith-Jones Split-Level #17 are equally instances of that architectural work. But in the case of an earlier architectural tribute to womanhood, the Taj Mahal, we may bridle at considering another building from the same plans and even on the same site to be an instance of the same work rather than a copy. We are not as comfortable about identifying an architectural work with a design rather than a building as we are about identifying a musical work with a composition rather than a performance. In that architecture has a reasonbly appropriate notational system and that some of its works are unmistakably allographic, the art is allographic. But insofar as its notational language has not yet acquired full authority to divorce identity of work in all cases from particular production, architecture is a mixed and transitional case.

In the present chapter I have been applying, chiefly to symbol systems in the arts, principles developed in Chapter IV in response to questions raised in Chapter III. The reader will already have discerned that these principles have some bearing upon problems left unresolved in the first two chapters. I now turn to those problems again and to other unfinished business.

NICHOLAS WOLTERSTORFF

Nicholas Wolterstorff (b. Minnesota, 1932), belongs to a small group of analytical philosophers who addressed themselves, among other things, to questions concerning the arts. Wolterstorff's theories of the arts are primarily contained in his two books, *Works and Worlds of Art* and *Art in Action.*

Wolterstorff's basic assumption in *Works and Worlds of Art* is that works of art, issuing from agents and directed towards receivers, are neither pure aesthetic entities nor exclusively related to the creative artist. Wolterstorff's work constitutes a theoretical attempt to present art from the point of view of pragmatics, i.e. to examine works of art in terms of linguistic behaviour. Concentrating on questions beyond the content of works of art, Wolterstorff is less interested in questions of syntax and structure or, for that matter, in cognitive processes. He tries to inquire, instead, into the ways in which they activate members of the culture. Thus, theories of speech acts, such as those developed by Austin and Searle, interest him more than other theories of art. Altogether Wolterstorff wishes to present a comprehensive system, comprising not only the different phases of Western art but non-Western art as well.

Interested as he is in linguistic behaviour concerning the arts, Wolterstorff is in need of ontology no less than Goodman. However, the role of individuals as well as cultural "intentions" plays a very significant part in his deliberations. Both aspects are manifested in his treatment of "world projection"—a key concept in his theory. Viewing "actions" as ontological entities, Wolterstorff, relying on Alvin Goodman's theory of human action, analyzes different kinds of actions "grammatically," showing how actions generate actions. Wolterstorff distinguishes categorically between actions which *cause* other actions —such as music-making causing delight—and those which may be *counted as* new actions, given a different point of view. The latter,

Wolterstorff argues, is intrinsic to novels, films and certain kinds of pictures. Undergoing the process of "being made," all of them project a world of their own. World projection as "counted as" action, does not only involve conventions—as argued by adherents of the theory of representation—but is conditioned by a complicated arrangement of circumstances and intentions and their acknowledgement by the participants in the action. Avoiding the whole issue of mimesis, Wolterstorff is free to hold that projected worlds are unique and independent of the actual world. Moreover, he is also able to justify the activity of art critics and consumers of art, i.e. those extrapolations which are said to be included in the work though not indicated by it. A work's world, Wolterstorff argues, reminiscent of Leibniz's ontological stance, is a possible world whose indicated state of affairs suggests a whole network of relations, order and structure. Indeed, a projected world, Wolterstorff maintains, though non-occurrent, does exist. In other words, world projection is a mode of selection, not a mode of creation. The artist is not thereby deprived of his creativeness, for it is he who envisages that certain, non-suggested yet possible state of affairs.

Indeed, selection is a prime concept in "bringing about" works of art; it is "selection"—Wolterstorff seems to imply—which accounts for their permanent messages within culture. "Selection" causes a continuity of responses to works of art, which, though heterogenous, are related to each other. As permanent messages, however, the various arts differ one from another in their ways of appearance. While paintings, sculptures and the like, are durable objects, works of music, films and dramas are "occasional works." Their appearance is "occasioned" by performances which may differ one from another. The perceptible artifacts of the various arts do not enjoy similar ontological status. The difference, Wolterstorff will argue, rests, in the final analysis, on the different modes of selection employed by the different arts. Each mode of selection, in turn, involves a distinct set of attitudes and operations for its realization. The following excerpt deals with "occurrence works" exemplifying their case through music.

His starting point is ontological; it rests on the observation that an "occurrence work" constitutes a group whose members are the "work" and its various occurrences. The group is not to be identified with a "set" whose members and their permanent belonging to it is essential within it. Performances, Wolterstorff maintains, are by definition transient; moreover, their actual occurrence is totally irrelevant to the

348

persistence of the work. Their alliance with the work rests on predicates which they and the work hold in common. The model to which they grammatically fit, Wolterstorff suggests, is that of "natural kinds," whose members are related by virtue of exemplifying certain well defined properties. It is impossible for a "kind" to exist whose examples lack the properties associated with it. However, there are kinds— "norm kinds"—which may have properly and improperly formed examples. (A certain animal is a norm kind, while a "colored thing" is not.) Altogether, art works are norm-kinds; a symphony can have correct and incorrect performances.

Wolterstorff's thesis in this respect is similar, as he himself notes, to Peirce's known thesis on the relation "type-token." However, Wolterstorff's distinctions have implications not only for performance but for composing as well. It has already been noted that for a performance to be considered a performance of a certain work means to exemplify certain well-defined properties. It follows that to compose means to select certain properties "as criteria for judging correctness of occurrence." The latter, Wolterstorff maintains, is as applicable to folk music as to traditional Western music (including aleatory music). Since "criteria for correctness" are not always agreed upon with regard to folk music they are replaced by "criteria for incorrectness," as it were. (The difference between "criteria for correctness" and "criteria for incorrectness" may, in fact, prove to be one of the most important factors in distinguishing between written and oral musical traditions as well.) Wolterstorff's analysis regarding the role of the performer is applicable to both, however. His insistence upon the necessity of a significant amount of "adjustment and feedback" in performance deserves special attention. It is in this respect that the difference between music composed for a tape and other music known to us is clearly revealed. From an ontological point of view, the former, Wolterstorff concludes, is closer to painting. In fact, though each of the arts engages its own ontological system it is not applicable throughout it. Moreover, the various modes of operation may "wander" among the arts.

Yet, as demonstrated by Goodman, such wandering is not totally free. It is restricted, to begin with, by the symbols operating (or which are liable to operate) in the particular art. When Wolterstorff attacks Goodman's "zig zag ballet of a notational score," i.e., the endless possibility to move from work to performance and vice versa, he is perhaps right, from a pragmatic point of view. However, having concentrated on a particular phase of Western music, Goodman not only explains why "music needs cognitive mediations for its realization," but also why, unlike drama, it can not have more than one level of mediation, i.e. one kind of occurrence.

In spite of the differences between Goodman and Wolterstorff, the two may be fruitfully combined. Goodman's "ways of worldmaking" may explain what remains unexplored by "selection" and "world projection."

from Works and Worlds of Art[1]

Works

I. Preliminaries

Olivier Messiaen's composition for orchestra, *Et Exspecto Resurrectionem*, has five sections, each of which is a setting of a passage from St John's *Apocalypse*. To say that each is a setting of a passage is to say, I think, that Messiaen used his music to project the very same state of affairs that St John projected with his words. How music can be used to perform such an action is a topic to be taken up later. Here let us ask: what is the work of art that Messiaen composed and which he entitled *Et Exspecto Resurrectionem*? Does it consist just of the sounds he composed? Or does it consist of the sounds along with the world projected?

In the Introduction I said that the concept of work of art that I would use throughout is that of *an instance of one of the major fine arts*. The word 'instance' is a rather ambiguous word, however. In all the arts there are perceptible artefacts; these can always with reason be regarded as instances of the art. Shortly we shall see that, in turn, these perceptible artefacts can in some cases be differentiated into occurrence-works and occurrences thereof. Secondly, when a world is projected with a perceptible artefact, there is the pair whose members are the artefact and the world; and this too can with reason be regarded as an instance of the art. Thirdly, in such arts as poetry, fiction, and drama, the world projected can by itself be regarded, with reason, as an instance of the art. (That is perhaps how we are thinking when we regard ourselves as presented with the same piece of literature that we were presented with on an earlier occasion, even though the perceptible artefact—the text— that we are presented with is only a translation of that with which we were presented earlier and thus not identical with it.)

Which of all these possibilities do I have in mind when I speak of *instances* of the arts? All of them. Different as they are, I shall regard

[1]Text: Nicholas Wolterstorff, *Works and Worlds of Art* (Oxford: Clarendon Press, 1980), pp. 33–105. The numbered notes are Wolterstorff's notes.

entities of all these different sorts as *instances* of the arts. Accordingly, all will be spoken of as *works of art*.

Our project is to explore the projection of worlds by way of artefacts of art. We begin our exploration with an inquiry, in this Part, into the nature of the perceptible artefacts used to perform such projection. Accordingly, in this Part we shall not be inquiring into the nature of works of art generally. We shall not be inquiring into the nature of those projected worlds which are works of art; that inquiry will be inquiring into the nature of those works of art which are artefact-cum-world. The nature of such works will become clear by the end of Part Three. Here, to say it once again, our concern will only be with the nature of those *perceptible artefacts* which are works of art—these perceptible artefacts being what are used in the arts to project worlds. The *text* of the literary work is here our concern; not the world of the literary work, and also not the text-cum-world.

II. *Some Distinctions among Artefacts of Art*

What sort of entity is the musical artefact? The dramatic? The sculptural? The poetic? The cinematic? Are artefacts of art all fundamentally alike in their ontological status? Are any or all of them physical objects? Events? Mental states? Sets? Let us set out toward the answers to these questions by making a rapid survey of the terrain of the arts.

Performing some work of art consists of bring about *a performance* of it—that is to say, it consists of bringing about (in a certain way) an occurrence of that which is performed.[2] Now in several of the arts there is application for the distinction between that which is a performance of something and that which is performed. In music, for example, one can

---

[2] To be wholly precise I should add, 'or bringing about (in a certain way) and occurrence of the artefactual-component of an artefact-cum-world work'. I assume that those works of art which are *worlds* cannot, strictly, be performed. There is nothing to produce an occurrence of. What, then, the telling of a story (which is one species of a world) consists of is something we shall see in Part Four. It probably should be remarked that the phrase 'performance of . . . ' can also be used as true of instances of the *action* of performing something. Using the word in that sense, *the Beaux Arts Trio's performing of Brahms' Trio in C Major, Opus 67 on 17 January 1976*, is a performance. I shall try to avoid using the word in that sense, and confine myself to using it as true of *occurrences* of *entities performed.*

352

distinguish between some performance of *Verklaerte Nacht* and the work performed by bringing about that performance—namely, Arnold Schoenberg's work *Verklaerte Nacht.* Similarly, in dance one can distinguish between some performance of *Swan Lake* and the work performed by bringing about that performance—namely, the ballet *Swan Lake.* So also in drama one can distinguish between some performance of *The American Dream* and the work performed, namely, Edward Albee's work *The American Dream.*

Some persons will be sceptical as to whether, in the cases cited and others of the same sort, we really do have two distinct entities—a performance and that which is performed. But assuming it to be true that the concept of a performance of something and the concept of something performed both have application to the arts, there are two sorts of considerations which force one to the conclusion that that which is performed on a given occasion is distinct from the performance of it.

In the first place, a thing performed and a performance thereof will always diverge in certain of their properties. For example, *having been composed by Schoenberg* is a property of *Verklaerte Nacht* but not of any performance of *Verklaerte Nacht.* On the other hand, *taking place at a certain time and place* is a property of every performance of *Verklaerte Nacht* but not of *Verklaerte Nacht itself.*

A second sort of consideration, one which is actually a specific application of the first, also leads to the conclusion that in certain of the arts one must distinguish between those entities which are performances and those entities which are works performed. This second sort of consideration hinges on applications of the concepts of identity and diversity. That which is performed on one occasion may be identical with that which is performed on another; George Szell, for example, may twice over have conducted a performance of *Verklaerte Nacht.* Thus there may be two distinct performances of one single musical work. But two distinct things cannot each be identical with some one thing. Thus the two distinct performances cannot both be identical with the work performed. But if one of them, call it *A*, was identified with the work performed, then the other, call it *B*, would, by virtue of being a performance of the work performed, be a performance of performance *A*. Not only that, but performance *A* would be capable of being performed on many other occasions as well. Both of these consequences seem impossible.

A performance of a work of art is an occurrence of it (or of the arte-factual component of it). So let us henceforth call a work of art which

353

can be performed, an *occurrence-work*. Let us likewise call a work whose artefactual component can be performed, in case it is an artefact-cum-world work, an *occurrence-work*. Most if not all occurrence-works are universals, in that they can have multiple occurrences. Lastly, let us keep in mind that occurrences of the perceptible artefacts of art are themselves perceptible artefacts of art.

The ontological status of occurrences seems relatively clear. That of occurrence-works, however, is immensely perplexing. Occurrences are events. They take place at a certain time, begin at a certain time, and end at a certain time, last for a certain stretch of time, and have temporal parts in the sense that each occurrence is half over at a certain time, three-quarters over at a certain time, one-eighth over at a certain time, etc. But what sort of entity is an occurrence-work, and in particular, an occurrence-work which is a perceptible artefact? That is something which we shall have to discuss in considerable detail. What should already be clear, though, is that occurrence-works are not events. Thus already we can answer one of our opening questions. The perceptible artefacts of art are not all alike in their ontological status.

In certain of the non-performing arts distinctions similar to the occurrence/occurrence-work distinction have application. Consider for example graphic art prints. Here a commonly applied distinction is that between a particular impression and the work of which it is an impression; between, for example, the tenth impression of *Obedient unto Death* and the print of which it is an impression, namely, George Rouault's *Obedient unto Death*. And consider those cases in which sculpture is produced from a mould. Here a commonly applied distinction is that between a particular casting of, say *The Thinker* and the sculptural work of which it is a casting, namely, Rodin's *The Thinker*. Consider thirdly those cases in the field of architecture in which many different buildings are produced according to one set of specifications. Here a commonly applied distinction is that between a given example of, say, the Tech-Bilt House No. 1 and that of which it is an example, namely, the Tech-Bilt House No. 1.

It may be noticed that an impression of a work of graphic art, a casting of a work of sculptural art, and an example of a work of architectural art, are all enduring physical objects. That is why I have grouped these particular arts together. In order to have a convenient terminology, let us call the works of which there can be impressions, castings, or examples (as well as those works of whose artefactural components there can be such entities), *object-works*. And let us say

354

that impressions, castings, and examples are *objects* of object-works. Thus as a counterpart to the occurrence/occurrence-work distinction we have the object/object-work distinction. As with occurrences, let us remember that those entities which are objects of the perceptible artefacts of art are themselves perceptible artefacts of art.

The considerations which impel us to distinguish between an object-work and those entities which are objects thereof are parallel to those which impel us to distinguish between an occurrence-work and those entities which are occurrences thereof. One consideration is again that of divergence in properties. *Having been pulled through the press last* may be a property of a given impression of Rouault's print *Obedient unto Death*; it is not a property of the print itself. A second consideration is again to be derived from applications of the concept of identity and diversity. There can be two different castings of the same one sculptural work; and neither both of these castings together nor either one singly can be identified with the work. In the case of object-works there is yet a third sort of consideration which may be adduced, hinging on applications of the concepts of existence and non-existence. Any one of the several objects of an object-work can be destroyed without the object-work itself thereby being destroyed. I could, for example, perform the horrifying operation of burning my impression of Rouault's *Obedient unto Death*, but I would not thereby put the print itself out of existence.

The ontological status of the objects of object-works is relatively unproblematic: they are physical objects. Of course plenty of things about the nature of physical objects remain unclear. Yet we know what they are, and it is clear that impressions, castings, and examples are to be numbered among them. But what is an object-work? What is *its* ontological status? That is something which we shall have to discuss in detail.

There remain literary works, films, and paintings to consider. A literary text can be both written down and 'sounded out'. There can be both copies of it and utterances of it. Now a copy is a physical object, whereas an utterance of something is an event. Further, the *copy of* relation seems closely similar to the *example of*, the *impression of*, and the *casting of* relations. Accordingly I shall say that a copy of a literary text is an object of it; and I shall add literary texts (along with the text-cum-world works of which they are the artefactual components) to the group of entities to be called object-works. But since an *utterance* of a literary work is an event, very much like a performance, I shall also include literary texts in the class of things to be called occurrence-works (along with the text-cum-world works of which they are the artefactual components). Thus literary works and literary texts are both occurrence-works and object-works.

Saying this, however, makes one want to look back to see whether we do not have good ground for saying that works of music and drama are also both occurrence-works and object-works. In the case of dramatic works I think it is clear that we must say 'No'. The artefactual component of a dramatic work is a pattern of actions. The actions will in all but the most unusual cases include speech actions. But in all but the most unusual cases they will include other sorts of actions as well. More importantly, that pattern of actions which is the artefactual component of a dramatic work will always include actions of *role-playing*. For these reasons, a reading aloud or a recitation of the script of a drama is not yet a performance of the drama. And a copy of the script for a drama is not a copy of the drama but a copy of the instructions for proper performance thereof. The script may of course be a literary work in its own right. And that work can have both readings aloud and copies. But the artefactual component of the dramatic work is not the script. And a copy of the script is not a copy of the artefactual component. The drama has no copies. All it can have is performances. Dramas are only occurrence-works.

Music presents a somewhat less clear situation. The crucial question is this: does a copy of the score stand to a work of music in a relationship similar enough to that in which a copy stands to a work of literature to justify us in calling a score-copy an object of the work? It seems to me not decisively clear one way or the other. What does seem clear is that a word can be both inscribed and uttered, whereas a sound cannot be inscribed but only sounded. The marks in a copy of a score are not instances of sounds but rather (instances of) instructions for producing sounds. Of course an inscription of some sequence of words can also be treated as instructions for the utterance of that sequence; yet at the same time it is genuinely an instance of those words. Some words, especially those in primitive cultures, are never written down; some, especially those in technical languages, are never sounded out. Yet most words have a dual manifestation. But suppose someone suggests that music should be thought of as being composed of *notes* rather than sounds; and then goes on to argue that notes, like words, can be both sounded out and written down. Obviously this is a suggestion worthy of further investigation. Whether it is true or false is not at once evident. But nothing that is said hereafter will depend essentially on whether it is true or false. So I shall continue to suppose that a work of music (or its artefactual component) consists of sounds.

The film seems to have a dual status similar to that of words. One and the same film may have many prints, a print being a physical object; and it may also have many showings, a showing being an occurrence. Thus a film, like a literary work, has claim to being regarded as both an object-work and an occurrence-work. There is this difference worth noting, though: a showing of a film will always occur by way of the showing of a certain print of the film, whereas the utterance of a literary work need not occur by way of the reading of some copy of the work. One can recite it from memory.

As for paintings, it seems that neither the object/object-work distinction nor the occurrence/occurrence-work distinction has application, nor does it seem that any close counterpart to these distinctions has application. There is of course the distinction between the work and reproductions of the work. But this is a different distinction, as can be seen from the fact that one can also have reproductions of each of the various impressions of a print. What is lacking in painting is any counterpart to the print/impression distinction. All one has is a counterpart to the impression/reproduction distinction. The point may be put by saying that all the impressions of a print are originals, none is a reproduction. The conclusion must be that a painting is a physical object. But more will be said on this matter later in our discussion.

To say that a painting is merely a physical object is not to deny that reproductions of paintings along with reproductions of sculpture are entitled to being called 'works of art' in their own right. So too are films, though for the most part they are 'reproductive' of incidents of role-playing and of visible events and objects. And so too are recordings, though most recordings are 'reproductive' of occurrences of sound. It is interesting to note, however, that in the case of visual art reproductions and sculpture reproductions one again often has application for the print/impression or the work/casting distinction; and that in the case of recordings (records), one can distinguish between the recording on the one hand and the various discs of the recording on the other, and in turn between a given disc on the one hand and various playings of the disc on the other.

We have spoken of the artefacts of art as perceptible; so a word should be said about the relation between our perception of an occurrence-work and our perception of the occurrences thereof, and

357

about the relation between our perception of an object-work and our perception of the objects thereof. It has on occasion been claimed that only occurrences and objects can be perceived, not occurrence-works and object-works.[3] Surely this is a highly paradoxical and implausible claim—that nobody, for example, can hear Bach's *Musical Offering* and that nobody can see the Tech-Bilt House No. 1. The situation seems rather to be that one perceives (i.e., sees, hears, touches, or reads) an occurrence-work or object-work by perceiving an occurrence or object of the work, and that only thus does one perceive the work.[4] In looking at a print one sees two things at once, the print and an impression thereof. In listening to a symphony one hears two things at once, the symphony and a performance thereof. Further, it is of immense importance for the critic to distinghish these two sorts of entities. For the very same predicate may be true of a musical performance and false of the work of which it is a performance.

To simplify our terminology, I shall henceforth call only those artefacts of art which are occurrence-works or object-works, *art works*. And both occurrences of art works and objects of art works will be called *examples* of art works. I shall continue to use 'work of art' to cover both works and their examples, along with such things as paintings which are neither. Perhaps here is also a good place to remark that the fact that the occurrence/occurrence-work distinction or the object/object-work distinction applies to a certain art does not imply that it applies *throughout* that art. There may be works of that art which are neither. Those works of music, for example, which are *total* improvisations (as distinguished from those which are the improvisations on a theme) are neither occurrences of works nor occurrence-works themselves.[5]

[3] C.S. Peirce, *Collected Works of C.S. Peirce* (Harvard Univ. Press: Cambridge, 1933), iv. 537; and C.S. Stevenson, 'On "What Is a Poem?" ' in *Philosophical Review* (July 1957), p. 330.

[4] With this qualification: in the case of the temporal arts one can also perceive the work by perceiving a reproduction of an object or performance of it—though one hasn't then heard it live or seen it live. What I do not admit is that the musician who 'hears' a work by reading the score *really hears* it. He only *imagines* its sounds.

[5] The general drift of the distinctions made above has been acquiring something of a consensus in recent years among those who have concerned themselves with the nature of works of art. See Andrew Harrison, 'Works of Art and other Cultural Objects' in *Proc. of the Aristotelian Society*, lxviii (1967–8), pp. 105–28: Margaret MacDonald, 'Art and Imagination', in *Proc. of the Aristotelian Society*, liii (1952–3), pp. 205–26;

III. Some Untenable Views on the Ontology of Art Works

Let us begin by putting behind us certain common and tempting but none the less untenable views on the nature of art works. In the first place, art works cannot be identified with any physical objects. With what physical object, for example, might a work of music be identified? With the score? But in the case of scores we must also distinguish between the score and a copy thereof—which is just another example of the object/object-work distinction. So with the composer's autograph copy of the score? That the work of music is not to be identified with this physical object is clear from two facts: there may never have been such an object, since many musical works have never been scored; and even if there is or were such an object, it may be destroyed and the work remain in existence. In the case of graphic art the temptation is strong to identify the print with the plate that the artist prepares. But this identification should also be resisted; for the plate may be destroyed without thereby destroying the print. Thus it is in general the case that art works are not to be identified with physical objects.[6]

Are they then to be identified with entities of consciousness—that is, with entities whose existence at a certain time depends on their being an object of some act of consciousness at that time? Here it might be useful to look at the view propounded by R.G. Collingwood, namely, that an art work has the status of a thing imagined. Collingwood says this: 'The work of art proper is something not seen or heard, but something imagined.'[7] And further, 'The business "of an artist proper" ' is 'for example, to make a tune. This tune is already complete and perfect when it exists merely as a tune in his head, that is, an imaginary tune.

Joseph Margolis, *The Language of Art and Art Criticism* (Wayne State Univ. Press: Detroit, 1965), Chap. 4; C.L. Stevenson, 'On "What is a Poem?" ' in *Phil. Review* (July 1957); R. Wellek and A. Warren, *Theory of Literature* (Harcourt, Brace & Co.: New York, 1956), Chap. XII; and Richard Wollheim, *Art and its Objects* (Harper & Row: New York, 1968). Very often writers have borrowed and generalized Peirce's type/token distinction only with reference to words and their written instances. But often all the things which I have labelled occurrence-works and object-works are called types, and all those which I have labelled occurrences or objects of such works are called tokens. Using this terminology our question can be put thus: what is the ontological status of those types which are the artefacts of art?

[6]For a more detailed consideration of the view here rejected, see Wellek and Warren, op. cit.; and R. Wollheim, op. cit.

[7]R.G. Collingwood, op. cit., p. 142.

Next, he may arrange for the tune to be played before an audience. Now there comes into existence a real tune, a collection of noises. But which of these two things is the work of art? Which of them is the music? The answer is implied in what we have already said: the music, the work of art, is not the collection of noises, it is the tune in the composer's head. The noises made by the performers, and heard by the audience, are not the music at all; they are only means by which the audience, if they listen intelligently (not otherwise) can reconstruct for themselves the imaginary tune that existed in the composer's head.'[8]

What does not come through with any clarity in these passage from Collingwood is whether or not he holds that a condition of a tune's existing at a certain time is that it be the object of some act of consciousness occurring at that time—for example, the act of someone's imagining it. Suppose, though, that he does not hold that a tune is an entity of consciousness. Then we are told nothing positive as to the ontological status of art works. Though they cannot be perceived, they can be the object of acts of consciousness other than that of perception while yet existing independently of being the object of any such act. But entities of fundamentally different sorts fit this description: numbers, God, the equator.

Suppose then that Collingwood holds that art works are just entities of consciousness—though of a somewhat special sort, since they are not private to a single consciousness but can be shared among consciousnesses. A number of questions then come at once to mind. When one is 'imagining' the second movement of some quartet and no one else is 'imagining' any part of it, has the first movement then gone out of existence? And when one is 'imagining' the first occurrence of the second theme of the second movement and no one else is 'imagining' any part of it, has the first theme then gone out of existence? In short, does an entire work exist so long as someone is 'imagining' some part of it in the course of 'imagining' the whole? Or does only that fragment which someone is actively 'imagining' exist at the time it is actively imagined? Though the latter interpretation seems most in the spirit of the proposal, the former would seem to be the most charitable interpretation. Even so, it is clear that this view has the consequence that Beethoven's quartets, Rembrandt's prints, and Yeats's poems flit in and out of existence. For at some times these are and at other times

---

[8]Ibid., p. 139.

these are not actually the object of some act of consciousness. But this consequence is surely false. Have not Beethoven's quartets, Rembrandt's prints, and Yeats's poems existed at least ever since their composition?

Let it be noted, though, that it does not follow from the fact that art works are not entities of consciousness that they cannot be composed in one's head. Perhaps musical and literary works can be. We shall have more to say on that later. And perhaps it is the conviction that they can be composed in one's head that has led some people to think of them as entities of consciousness. But from the proposition that an art work can be composed simply by 'imagining' it, without benefit of voice or limb, it does not follow that it depends for its existence (thereafter) on being consciously imagined by someone or other.

Another common but unsatisfactory view which deserves at least brief consideration is that occurrence-works and object-works are *sets* of their examples. The untenability of this suggestion can be seen by noticing that whatever members a set has, it has essentially,[9] whereas an occurrence-work or object-work might always have had different and more or fewer occurrences or objects than it does have; and by noticing that if a set alpha has no members and set beta has no members, then alpha is identical with beta; whereas it is not the case that if art work gamma has no examples and art work delta has no examples, then gamma is identical with delta.

That there is but one null set is of course clear enough. But that a set cannot have had a different membership from what it does have is a fact apt to be confused with related but different facts. The property, *being a member of Carter's cabinet*, is a property shared in common by all and only the members of a certain set; the set, namely, whose members are all and only the members of Carter's cabinet. Let us for convenience's sake name this set, *C*. Now whoever has the property of being a member of Carter's cabinet has it only contingently. Accordingly that set which is *C* might have been such that some of its members lacked this property; indeed, all might have lacked it. Alternatively, persons who are not members of *C* might have had this property. Thus some other set than *C* might have been such that all and only its members have the property of being members of Carter's cabinet. But all of these facts pertaining to what might have been in place of what is are thoroughly

---

[9]For a defence of the view that sets have their memberships essentially, see my *On Universals*, pp. 178–80.

compatible with the fact that *C* has its membership essentially. (See the next Section for a fuller discussion of these points.)

One other oddity of the view that art works are sets of their examples is worth noting. A generally unnoticed, but what I take to be genuine, fact about sets is that in order for some entity at a time *t* to bear to a certain set alpha the relation of being a member of alpha, the entity in question must exist at *t*. Sets cannot have as members entities that there aren't. Now if this is true, then there will be many different pairs of times such that the set of all and only those things which are copies of *Ulysses* at one of the times is distinct from the set of all and only those things which are copies of *Ulysses* at the other time. For, of course, copies of *Ulysses* come into and go out of being. Further, there will never be any such set as the set of all and only those things which are, or will be copies of *Ulysses*. For the destroyed copies are no longer available to be members of any set whatsoever. As copies of *Ulysses* come into and go out of existence, there is a whole flux of sets each of the sort that it has as members all and only those copies of *Ulysses* which exist at some particular time. With which of these, then, are we to identify *Ulysses*? The first? The last? The largest? The smallest? All of the available answers are equally implausible.

Our question remains unanswered: what is the ontological status of art works?

IV. Of Works and Kinds

One striking feature of the relationship between an art work and its examples is the pervasive sharing of predicates between them. Let me explain. Take some logical predicate[10] which in normal usage can be predicated of two distinct things in such a way as to assert something true in both cases. let us say that in such a case those two things *share that predicate*. 'Is in the key of C minor' can be predicated truly of Beethoven's Opus 111 and also of most if not all performances of Beethoven's Opus 111; hence the work and those performances share the predicate. 'Has the figure slightly off-centre to the right' can be predicated truly of Rouault's *Obedient unto Death* and likewise of most if not all impressions of *Obedient unto Death*; hence the predicate is

[10]For the concept of a *logical predicate* see my *On Universals*, Chap. I.

362

shared between work and impressions. 'Has "no" as its third word' can be predicated truly of Yeats's 'Sailing to Byzantium' and also of most if not all copies of 'Sailing to Byzantium'; and so the predicate is shared. If this linguistic fact of the massive sharing of predicates between art works and their examples lies a clue as to the nature of art works.

Not every predicate which can be predicated truly of an art work, or which can be predicated truly of some or even all examples of some art work, is shared between the work and its examples. 'Is a performance' and 'is an occurrence' are never thus shared; nor are 'can be repeatedly performed' and 'can repeatedly occur'. Nor is 'composed by Hindemith' ever thus shared. 'Is thought about by me' is in some cases shared between a certain work and all its examples, in other cases it is shared between a certain work and only some of its examples, while in yet other cases a certain art work shares it with none of its examples. And 'has "no" as its third word' is unshared between the poem 'Sailing to Byzantium' and my particular copy of it, whereas it is shared between the poem and *most* copies of it.

Since the days of Aristotle philosophers have observed that between *natural kinds* and their *examples* there is also a massive sharing of predicates. 'Is an animal' is true of the horse. Likewise it is (or was) true of Bucephalus, and of all other horses. 'Has four feet' is true of the grizzly (*ursus horribilis*). Likewise it is true of the grizzlies in Brookfield Zoo. And so forth, one and on. Thus there is a striking linguistic similarity between art works and natural kinds.

Could it be that the similarity goes deeper than language? Could it be that art works and natural kinds are *ontological* allies? That is the thought that comes to mind. And that is in fact the thesis I shall articulate. To put it more stringently: art works and natural kinds are just two species of kinds. Of course the linguistic facts do not *confirm* this thesis. They only provide a clue. The confirmation must lie in the thesis fitting the ontological facts.

Unfortunately I cannot here presuppose any articulate grasp of the concept of a kind. So I shall myself have to make some general comments on the topic. In making these comments my aim, of course, is not to compose a full treatise on the topic of kinds. Remaining far short of that, I shall limit myself to matters directly relevant to our subsequent discussion. Thus at several points I shall state the assumptions I am making without developing any justification for those assumptions.

I assume in the first place that there is a function f—call it the *associate*-function—mapping properties onto kinds, and such that the

363

value of f for any property *being a k* is the corresponding kind: K. Call K, the *kind-associate* of the property of *being a k*. Thus the property of being a horse has for its kind-associate the kind: Horse. The property of being a chair in this room has for its kind-associate the kind: Chair In This Room. And the property of being red (being a red thing) has for its kind-associate the kind: Red Thing. No doubt what comes first to mind when we think of kinds is natural things—the species, the genera, the phylla, of the botanical and zoological taxonomist. But I see no reason for denying that there is also the kind (type, sort): Chair In This Room. Once we have allowed this, then the assumption above seems plausible.

Is f also a one-to-one mapping of properties into kinds? Well, I dare say we all hold, for any K and any K', that if it is possible that there is something which is an example of K but not of K', or vice versa, then $K \neq K'$.[11] If there can be something which is an example of The Cat but not of The Domestic Cat, or vice versa, then The Cat is not identical with The Domestic Cat. But suppose this were regarded as both a necessary and sufficient condition of kind-identity, thus:

$K = K' \equiv$ it is impossible that there be something which is an example of K and not of K', and vice versa.

Then there would be situations in which two properties would have the same kind as their associate. For consider the property of being a rectangle with sides of equal length, and the property of being a rectangle whose diagonals are at right angles to each other. These, I take it, are distinct properties. The kind-associate of the first is: Rectangle With Sides Of Equal Length. That of the second is: Rectangle Whose Diagonals Are At Right Angles To Each Other. Now it is impossible that there be something which is an example of one of these kinds and not of the other. Accordingly, one the criterion being considered these are identical. And then this one kind is the kind-associate of two distinct properties.

However, I think that the proposed criterion for kind-identity should be rejected. On this criterion, there is just one impossible kind (kind such that it is impossible that there be an example of it); and also just one necessary kind (kind such that it is impossible that there be something which is not an example of it). Now later in our discussion (in Part Three) I shall argue that the best way to construe the nature of

---

[11]This follows from the fact that Leibniz's Law holds in all possible worlds, coupled with the fact that if $x \neq y$ in one possible world, then $x \neq y$ in any possible world.

fictional characters, and fictional entities generally, is to construe them as being kinds. And among fictional entities there are impossible ones, for example, the six characters in Pirandello's *Six Characters in Search of an Author*. A character couldn't possibly walk onto a stage, as Pirandello's six do; though of course an *actor* can. But if there were only one impossible kind, the six characters of Pirandello's play would be one. And that one would in turn be identical with the impossible buildings in the worlds of M.C. Escher's prints. These are consequences to be avoided. Accordingly I shall reject the proposed criterion for identity of kinds; and in its place I shall assume that our associate-function is a one-to-one mapping of properties into kinds.

To get the concept of a kind sharply before us it will be helpful to begin by contrasting kinds with sets. (Some of the points here made about sets will be brief recapitulations of points made in the preceding section.) So consider the property of being a chair in this room. By reference to this property I can specify certain sets; for example, the set of all and only those things which (presently) possess the property. But I can also specify this very same set without reference to this property. If the chairs in this room had names, I could specify the set by listing the chairs by name. Or if the chairs in this room were the only items of furniture in this room, I could specify the set as the set of all and only those things which are (presently) items of furniture in this room. For in specifying the members of a set one uniquely specifies the set. And that in turn is true because of the identity criterion for sets: set A = set B if and only if there is nothing which is a member of the one which is not also a member of the other.

Further, the set of all and only those things which are (presently) chairs in this room retains its membership across time as long as it exists, and necessarily so. No matter whether these chairs do or do not stay forever in this room, as long as that set exists it will have exactly these chairs as members—not others, no more, no fewer. So it is in general. It is impossible for the sets there are to change in their membership across time. More strongly yet: it is impossible for *there to be* a set which changes in its membership across time. The members which a set has at any time in some possible world are those which it has at every time (at which it exists) in that possible world.

Likewise sets retain their membership across possible worlds. The set of chairs (presently) in this room *could not* now have had other or more or fewer members than it does have. It is the set of just exactly those things, and necessarily so. Thus it is in general. All sets have their

365

membership essentially. Indeed, it is impossible for *there to be* a set which does not have its membership essentially. Sets retain their memberships across all possible worlds in which they exist. When we put the point of this paragraph together with the point of the preceding one we get this: it is impossible that there should be a set whose membership at some time in some possible world is different from what it is at that or some other time (at which it exists) in that or some other possible world (in which it exists).

It does not follow, though, that sets exist necessarily. In fact, not all do. There are presently three chairs in this room. Now chairs do not exist necessarily. So suppose that only two of these chairs had never existed. Then the set whose membership consists of exactly these three chairs would not have existed; for a set cannot have some entity as member unless that entity exists. Thus this set exists contingently.

Does it also come into and go out of existence? Certainly. For these three chairs have not always jointly existed, and will not always jointly exist. But there is a set which has these three specific things as members when and only when those three things exist. A set cannot have among its members at a certain time things that don't exist at that time.[12] Or to put it from the other side: an entity x bears to the set A the property of being a member of A only when x exists. And of course if x does not at a certain time have the property of being a member of A, then A at that time does not have the (converse) property of having x as a member. But as we have already seen, sets have their membership invariantly across time, and essentially. So the conclusion must be that some sets become and perish.

What follows is that, though all sets have their membership essentially, it is not in general the case that each of the members of a set is essentially a member thereof. One of these chairs might have existed and not have been a member of the set of all and only the chairs (presently) in this room. For there might have been no such set. But of course it couldn't be that *all three* members of this set should exist at a certain time and this one not be a member of the set at that time.

Though the set of all and only those things which are presently chairs in this room has its membership essentially, it is possible that something

---

[12]In general, I hold that something cannot have a property at a certain time unless it exists at that time. Since this principle will several times over be appealed to in our discussion, let us give it a name. Call it the Principle of Exemplification. For further discussion on the matter, see my 'Can Ontology Do Without Events?'

should be a member of this set and not be a chair in this room. One of the chairs in question might well not have been (presently) in this room. Yet that circumstance, had it obtained, would not have deleted that chair from membership in the set. For once again, the set in question just *is* the set whose members are those very chairs, no matter what property those chairs have or lack (except, of course, the property of belonging to the set and whatever others are entailed by that).

In most of these ways kinds are different from sets. Many of the differences flow from the necessary truth, concerning kinds, that some entity x is an example at t of the kind: K, if and only if x at t has the property of being a k. Or in other words: it's impossible that there be a kind whose examples at a certain time lack at that time the property-associate of the kind. So, for example, it's a necessary truth that something is an example at a certain time of the kind: Chair In This Room, if and only if at that time it has the property of being a chair in this room.

Of course there is variation across time as to what does in fact have the property of being a chair in this room. At some times nothing has it, right now three things have it, at other times other things have it. Thus it varies across time as to what is an example of the kind: Chair In This Room. Furthermore, different things might (presently) have had the property of being a chair in this room than do in fact have it. Thus many kinds do not have their examples essentially. Their exampleships vary across possible worlds as well as across times in our actual world.

Next, suppose once again that the only items of furniture in this room are those three chairs of which I have been speaking. In spite of that, the kind: Item Of Furniture In This Room, would not then be identical with the kind: Chair In This Room. That can easily be seen in this case by noticing that there *could* be something which is an example of the one and not of the other. Rather, the situation would be that these two distinct kinds would coincide in their exampleships at this moment in history. Thus, whereas a listing by name of the three chairs in this room would uniquely specify the set whose members are these three chairs, it would not uniquely specify a kind. In general, specification of the examples of a kind does not uniquely specify the kind.

The kind: Chair In This Room, might exist even if for a time there were no chair in this room. There would then exist that kind, but it would lack for examples. But if that is so, what then is the criterion for the existence of kinds? Well, the kind: K, exists just in case the property of which it is the associate exists. But that just shifts the problem. Under what conditions does a property exist? Without here offering the rationale, the propositions I shall assert with sentences of the form 'The property of *being-f* exists' (alternatively, 'there is the property of *being-f*) are those which are true if and only if either something is-*f* or something is not-*f*.[13] Thus, for example, the property of being a round square exists. For something is not a round square.

With these general comments about kinds as background, we can now move on to formulate some definitions useful in our subsequent

[13] A detailed rationale for this policy can be found in chapters 5 and 7 of my book *On Universals*. However, on two significant points my discussion in the book is deficient.

In the first place, it does not succeed in coping with the Russell Paradox for properties. It is worth seeing why it does not, and how the Paradox can be coped with. In the course of my discussion there I picked out a set of propositions which I called *predicate entailment principles*. These are principles of the form: 'If something is-*f*, then there is such a predicable as *being-f*.' I held that all such principles are true, necessarily true. And the proposition that they are true I called the General Predicate Entailment Principle (General PEP).

To understand what propositions I had in mind we must especially be aware of how 'is-*f*' functions in the formula. It functions as representing predicate expressions, i.e., expressions capable of functioning as logical predicates. I shall not here rehearse the definition offered of 'logical predicate'. What is important to observe, though, is a condition that I attached to something's being a predicate expression. It comes to this: a predicate expression cannot be both true and false at the same time of some one thing. (Here and throughout it must be understood that if some sign 'is-*f*' is used on one occasion with sense *S* and on another occasion with a distinct sense *S*', and if on both occasions it is used as a logical predicate, then the sign used on one occasion is a different *predicate* from that used on the other. Diversity of senses is sufficient for diversity of predicates.)

To see the need for attaching the above cited condition to something's being a predicate expression, let us adapt one of Russell's old examples. Let us say that the expression 'was generally considered to be identical with the author of *Waverley*' is true of what some expression '*α*' denotes just in case the proposition, *that α is identical with the author of 'Waverley'*, was generally thought to be true. And suppose we regarded that expression as a predicate expression. Then by the General Predicate Entailment Principle there is the property of being generally considered to be identical with the author of *Waverley*. Now surely the proposition 'The author of *Waverley* is identical with the author of *Waverley*' was generally considered to be true. Accordingly the expression 'was generally considered to be identical with the author of *Waverley*' was true of the author of *Waverley*. And if it stood for a property, namely, the property of being generally considered to be identical with the author of *Waverley*, the author of *Waverley* would have that property. But now consider the proposition 'Scott is identical with the author of *Waverley*'. Apparently at a certain point in history that was not generally considered to be true. Accordingly, then, the expression 'was generally considered to be identical with the author of *Waverley*' was not true of Scott. And if that

Footnote continued.

discussions. The basic undefined concept will be that of the relation, *being an example of*, it being understood that that which something is an example of is always a kind. (The relation is intransitive, non-symmetrical, and irreflexive.)

First, the concept of a possible kind:

Def. 1: K is a *possible* kind = df it is possible that there should be something which is an example of K.

---

expression is regarded as standing for a property, that of being generally considered to be identical with the author of *Waverley*, Scott would lack that property. However, Scott was in fact identical with the author of *Waverley*. Hence he would both have and lack that property, at the same time. But that is an impossibility. So that expression cannot be regarded as standing for that property. And we can easily forestall the difficulties if, in our general PEP formula, we lay down the condition that only predicate expressions can replace 'is-f', and if we lay down the stipulation that something is a predicate expression only if it cannot be both true and false at the same time of the same thing. Thus 'was generally considered to be identical with the author of *Waverley*', in the sense we have given it above, is not a predicate expression.

And now consider the Russell Paradox for properties. Take, for example, the fact that the property of being a horse does not exemplify itself. It looks as if, on the General PEP, there is then the property of not exemplifying itself. But in fact there is no such property. For let us ask concerning this very property—the property of *not exemplifying itself*—whether it exemplifies itself. If it does exemplify itself, then it does not exemplify itself. And if it does not exemplify itself, then it does. But that is impossible. So there is no such property.

At the time of writing *On Universals* I thought that the condition explained above on what counts as a predicate expression would prevent the General PEP from committing us to there being such a property as that of *not exemplifying itself*. For I thought that the condition attached to something's being a predicate expression would eliminate 'does not exemplify itself' as a candidate for predicatehood. But that was mistaken. For the defect of this expression is not that it can be both true and false of something at a single time. Its defect is rather that *if* it stood for the property of not exemplifying itself, it *would* be both true and false of that property. So we need a *Limited PEP*. Not all propositions of the form 'Something is-f' entail the corresponding propositions of the form 'There is such a thing as *being-f*.' We need to pick out that limited set of those that do. Of course it is not difficult to pick out *a* set all of whose members do. But we want a set such that its members are all and only those in the larger set which entail their correspondents. Is it possible to pick this out?

Well, we have already seen that the decisive peculiarity of the predicate 'does not exemplify itself' is that if it stood for the property of not exemplifying itself, it would itself be both true and false of that property. So, generalizing, let us say that some predicate expression 'is-f' is not a *permissible* predicate expression if it is such that, if it stood for the property of *being-f*, it would be both true and false of that property. Then

369

Correspondingly, the concept of an *impossible* kind:

Def. 2: K is an *impossible* kind = df it is impossible that there should be something which is an example of *K*.

The concept of a possible kind, be it noted, is not the concept of a kind which can *exist*, but of a kind which can have an example; and that of an

_____

the Limited PEP is exactly like the General PEP, except that the expressions which can replace the sign 'is-*f*' are confined to *permissible* predicate expressions. Such predicate expressions as 'does not exemplify itself' and 'lacks the property of exemplifying itself' are not permissible predicate expressions. And in the criterion for the existence of properties offered in the text above we must keep in mind that what replaces the sign 'is-*f*' must always be a permissible predicate expression.

Let it be said, though, that the fact that there is no such property as not exemplifying itself does not imply that we do not say something true when assertively uttering such a sentence as 'The property of being a horse does not exemplify itself.' On the contrary, we can even give an ontological construal of what is claimed. What is claimed is that the property of being a horse *lacks* the property of exemplifying itself. The crux is that we cannot in general say that to lack of property of *being-f* is to have the property of *not-being-f*; and neither can we hold that for every property, *being-f*, there is the complement to that property, namely, *not-being-f*.

I was mistaken on one further matter in *On Universals*. I said that though many sentences of the form 'There is such an entity (predicable) as *f*-ness' can be used to assert propositions which are true if and only if either something is-*f* or something is not-*f*, this insight could not be generalized. My argument was this. Introduce the predicate 'is tove', and give it the same sense as 'has the property last mentioned by John and which is and isn't red'. Now of course there is no such property as being tove. To claim that there is, is to assert a proposition which entails a contradiction. So I said that 'is tove' is true of nothing. I also said, though, that 'is not tove' is true of everything, (and that there is the property of not being tove). But if the criterion cited above were in general acceptable, we would be committed to holding that there is the property of being tove also—an absurdity.

But consider some sentence '*a* is not tove'. This can be used to assert two very different propositions. One is the proposition that there is the property of being tove and *a* lacks it. But that proposition is false, not matter what *a* is. Accordingly, 'is not tove' thus construed is true of nothing, as indeed 'is tove' is true of nothing. But the sentence may also be used to assert that it is not the case that *a* is tove. And that proposition is true. But then 'is not tove' has the same sense as does the predicate, 'it is not the case that . . . is tove' (*not* the same sense as 'lacks the property of being tove'). And *that* predicate can harmlessly be viewed as standing for the property of *being such that it is not the case that it is tove*. There *is* such a property. Likewise there is a complement to it.

And so I think no absurdities follow from my declaration that I shall in general use sentences of the form 'There is such a predictable as *f*-ness' to assert propositions which are true if an only if either something is-*f* or something is not-*f*.

370

impossible kind is not that of a kind which can not exist, but of one which can not have an example. And now for the concept of a necessary kind:

Def. 3: K is a *necessary* kind = df it is impossible that there be something which is *not* an example of K.

We can then introduce the important concept of a property *being essential within* a kind:

Def. 4: (Having) the property P is *essential within* K = df P and K are such that necessarily if something is an example of K then it has P.

It is of crucial importance to notice the difference between a property being essential within a certain kind, and its being a property *of* that kind. The property of *being a physical object* is essential within the kind: Chair In This Room; there couldn't be something which was an example of that kind while lacking that property. But it is not a property *of* that kind. For neither this kind, nor any other is a physical object. Rather, this kind has the property of *having essential within it the property of being a physical object.*

Next, let us introduce the concept of two kinds *coinciding* at a certain time:

Def. 5: K *coincides with* K' at time t = df at t there is nothing which is an example of K which is not also an example of K and vice versa.

Thus, if this room now had only chairs as items of furniture, the kind: Item Of Furniture In This Room, would at present coincide with the kind: Chair In This Room.

Next, we shall need the concept of one kind *including* another:

Def. 6: K *includes* K' = df K and K' are such that necessarily if something is an example of K' then it is an example of K.

Thus the kind: Domestic Cat, includes the kind: Domesticated Siamese Cat.

Given these definitions, we can affirm this truth: if K includes K', and if the property P is essential within K, then P is also essential within K'. And also this: if it is essential to x that it is an example of K, and if the property P is essential within K, then P is an essential property of x.[14]

---

[14]P is an *essential* property of x = df there is no possible world in which x exists and lacks P.

And this: if *P* is essential within *k*, then the property of having-*P*-essential-within-it is an essential property of *K*.

It will also be useful to have the concept of one kind being a *species* of another—*ursus horribilis* being a species of *ursus*, Bachelor being a species of Male Human Being, etc. Now it might be thought that *K* is a species of *K'* just in case *K'* includes *K*. But for one thing, an impossible kind is included within every kind, and accordingly would be a species of every kind—surely an absurdity. (Also a necessary kind includes every kind, and thus would have every kind as a species—also an absurdity.) Further, consider the two kinds: Right-Angled Figure With Equal Length Sides, and Right-Angled Figure Whose Diagonals Are At Right Angles To Each Other. These include each other, and thus would be species of each other. But that too seems not right. For reasons such as these, the concept of a species will have to be defined somewhat more circuitously than might at first be supposed. Let us first say that

Def. 7: *P* is a *conjunctive property of* properties *being-f* and *being-g* = df *being-f* and *being-g* are distinct properties, and *P* = the property of *being-f* & *being-g*.

Then let us formulate the concept of a conjunctive analysis of a property:

Def. 8: The non-null set *α* of properties is a *conjunctive analysis* of *property P* = *df*. The conjunctive property of the members of *α* is identical with *P*.

Later it will be helpful to have the concept of a property being *analytic within* a kind, a concept that can now be explained thus:

Def. 9: Property *P* is *analytic within* kind *K* = df *P* is a member of some conjunctive-analysis of *K*'s property associate (viz., *being a k*).

And lastly, let us define 'species' thus:

Def. 10: *K* is a *species* of *K'* = df Every property which is a member of some conjunctive analysis of *being a k'*. (viz., the property-associate of *K'*) is also a member of some conjunctive analysis of *being a k* (viz., the property-associate of *K'*), but not vice versa.

The kind: Bachelor, is by this criterion a species of the kind: Male Human Being. And notice that it is also included within the kind: Male Human Being. *Being included within* and *being a species of* do not always go hand in glove like this, however. For though an impossible

372

kind is included within every kind, it is certainly not true that it is a species of every kind. And though a necessary kind includes every kind, it is not true that every kind is a species of it. Moreover, consider the kind: Closed Straight-Sided Figure Whose Interior Angles Are All Right Angles, and the kind: Closed Straight-Sided Figure Whose Diagonals Are Of Equal Length And At Right Angles. The latter is included within the former. There couldn't be an example of it which is not an example of the former (and not so vice versa). However, the latter is not a species of the former. For in some conjunctive analysis of the property-associate of the former there will appear the property of having all its interior angles right angles. But that property will not appear in any conjunctive analysis of the property-associate of the latter.

One more concept concerning kinds, of great importance to our subsequent purposes, must be introduced. Many, though no all, kinds are such that it is possible for them to have properly formed and also possible for them to have improperly formed examples. Let us call such kinds, *norm*-kinds. The Lion is obviously a norm-kind. The kind: Red Thing, however, seems not to be. For there can be no such entity as an improperly red thing, a malformedly red thing. So too the kind: Properly Formed Orchid and the kind: Malformed Orchid, are not norm-kinds.

Now in the case of norm-kinds we have application for the concept of some property *being normative within* a certain kind.

Def. 11: The property P is *normative within* the norm-kind $K =$ df K is a norm-kind, and it is impossible that there be something which is a properly-formed example of K and lacks P.

The properties of a species which the botanical or zoological taxonomist cites are, for the most part, properties normative within, but not essential within, the species. (Notice that any property essential within a norm-kind will also be normative within it; but not so vice versa.) [15]

[15] In his article 'The Concept of a Kind' (in *Philosophical Studies*, xxix(1976), pp. 53–61) Michael Loux attempts to pick out from the set of all kinds those which fit the Aristotelian concept of a kind. His proposal is as follows. Suppose that by calling a kind 'extendible' we mean that it could have more examples than it does have. And suppose that by saying that a kind K 'properly includes' a kind K^* we mean that K includes K^* and it is impossible that there be something which is an example of K and not of K^*. Let us then say that a kind K is a 'candidate for an Aristotelian kind' (a 'CA-kind') if and only if (i) K is a possible kind, (ii) K is an extendible kind, and (iii) whatever has the property of being an example of K, has that property essentially. Loux's proposal then
Footnote continued.

Having presented the rudiments of a theory of kinds, my suggestion now is this: occurrence-works and object-works are *kinds*—kinds whose examples are the occurrences or objects of those works. An occurrence-work is an occurrence-kind of a certain sort, an object-work is an object-kind of a certain sort. More specifically, art works are *norm*-kinds. A symphony can have incorrect as well as correct performances. A poem, incorrect as well as correct copies.

The plausibility of this thesis will have to rest in its illuminating power. But at once we can see that it passes muster on the points where the theory that art works are sets failed. Just as an art work might have had different and more or fewer occurrences or objects than it does have, so too the kind: Man, might have had different and more or fewer examples than it does have. If Napoleon had not existed it would not then have been the case that Man did not exist. Rather, Man would then have lacked one of the examples which in fact it had. And secondly, just as there may be two distinct unperformed symphonies, so too there may be two distinct unexemplified kinds—e.g., the Unicorn, and the Hippogriff.

V. A Doctrine of Analogy

We left the phenomenon of the massive sharing of predicates between

---

is that a kind K is an *infima species* if it is a CA-kind such that there is not kind K^* which is a CA-kind and which K properly includes.

Loux himself observes that on Aristotle's view, only men are capable of laughter (risible) and every man has risibility essentially. And so, given other obvious premisses, it turns out that the kind: Object That Is Risible, is an *infima species*. Accordingly, given Aristotle's thoughts about men and their properties, Man, and Object That Is Risible, are *infimae species* that necessarily coincide in their exampleships. Loux suggests that this is quite satisfactory; because, he asserts, these are in fact one and the same kind. And the criterion of kind-identity that he offers is just the one which we earlier considered and rejected. But given the unacceptability of this criterion, and given the criterion which we have put in its place, we get the unsatisfactory result (unsatisfactory certainly to Aristotle) that Man and Object that is Risible are *distinct infimae species* that necessarily coincide in their exampleships.

Further, consider the following: it is impossible (I think) that I or any of my readers be a Pharoah in the Third Dynasty. But then consider the kind: Human Incapable of Being A Pharoah In The Third Dynasty. This is a CA-kind. For it is possible, it is extendible, and it is (I think) essential to each of us who are examples of it that we be examples of it. But this kind is properly including within the kind: Man. Accordingly Man is not an *Infima species*. And that too is out of accord with the results desired.

374

art works and their examples at the point where it had put us on the track of an ontological affinity between art works and natural kinds. We must now return to that phenomenon, since for our subsequent purposes it will be important to spy some of the *pattern* of that sharing, and even more important to determine whether the sharing of a predicate between an art work and some one or more of its examples is normally grounded in the sharing of some *property* for which the predicate stands. If it is, then the predicate is used *univocally*. On the other hand, if the predicate stands for two different properties with some systematic relation between them, then the predicate is used *analogically*. If not even that is true, the predicate is used *equivocally*.

From the start one feels that there is some connection, more than coincidental, between a predicate's being true of the examples of an art work and its being true of the work. Can this feeling be substantiated? What might the connection be?

One of the examples we have already used provides us with evidence for concluding that the following formula will not do: a predicate 'is-f' is true of some art work W if 'is-f' is true of every example of W. For 'is a performance' is true of all examples of many if not all occurrence-works but cannot be true, in its normal sense, of any of these art works themselves.

So suppose that from here on we discard from consideration those predicates which are true of one or more of the examples of some art work but which, in their normal meaning, *cannot* be true of the work itself. (When a predicate used with normal meaning cannot be true of W, it will be said to be *excluded by W*. Likewise when a property cannot be possessed by W, it will be said to be *excluded by W*.) What then of the formula: for any predicate 'is-f' which is not excluded by W, 'is-f' is true of W if 'is-f' is true of every example of W? One objection to this formula is that it is far more constricted in its application that what we were looking for. 'Has a G sharp in its seventh measure' may be true of Bartok's First Quartet even though of many of its performances it is not true. Indeed, it may be true of none of its performances.

A clue to a better formula can be discovered by looking more closely at this example. It is not the case that 'has a G sharp in its seventh measure' is true of Bartok's First Quartet when it is impossible for there to be a *correct* example of Bartok's First which lacks the property of having a G sharp in its seventh measure? And consider another of the examples we have offered. Is it not the case that 'has "no" as its third word" is true of 'Sailing to Byzantium' when it is impossible for there to be a *correct* example of 'Sailing to Byzantium' which lacks the property of having 'no' as its third word?

These examples naturally suggest to us the following formula: for any predicate 'is-*f*' which is not excluded by *W*, if there is some property *being-f* which 'is-*f*' stands for in normal usage and which is such that it is impossible for there to be something which is a correct example of *W* and lack *being-f*, then 'is-*f*' is true of *W*.

But to this general formula as well there are counterexamples. Consider, for instance, the predicate 'is a performance or was highly thought of by Beethoven'. There will be many works from which this predicate (used in its normal sense) will not be excluded. Likewise, it is impossible for there to be something which is a correct *example* of some such work and lack the property of *being either a performance or highly thought of by Beethoven*. For it is impossible for the example to lack the property of being a performance. Yet the predicate in question may very well not be true of the *work*. For the work cannot be a performance, and it may not have been highly thought of by Beethoven. [16]

The essence of difficulty here seems to be that some predicates stand for properties such that it is impossible for there to be something which is an example of *W* at all, correct or incorrect, and lack of property. Now such properties fit exactly our definition of properties *essential within* the kind *W*. If we would eliminate from consideration predicates standing for such properties, then counterexamples of the sort suggested will be forestalled. So given some work *W*, consider any predicate 'is-*f*' which is neither excluded by *W* nor stands for some property essential within *W*. If there is some property *being-f* which 'is-*f*' stands for in normal usage and which is such that something could not be a correct example of *W* and lack *being-f*, then 'is-*f*' is true of *W*. (It should be noticed that the claim here is not *if and only if*, but just *if*.)

If we express this formula by using our concept of a property's *being normative within* a kind, it then comes to this: For any predicate 'is-*f*' which is neither excluded by *W* nor stands for a property essential

---

[16] In general, take a predicate of the form 'is either *A* or anti-*W*', where 'is anti-*W*' represents a predicate such that (i) is excluded by *W* and (ii) when predicated of examples of *W* it stands for a property such that necessarily if something is an example of *W* then it has that property, and where 'is *A*' represents any predicate whatsoever which is not exluded by *W*. Then the 'disjunctive predicate' represented by 'is either *A* or anti-*W*' is itself not excluded by *W* and is itself such that when predicated of some example of *W* it stands for a property such that something would not be a correct example of *W* if it lacked it. Yet obviously the predicate may very well not be true of *W*.

within W, if there is some property *being-f* which 'is-*f*' stands for in a normal usage and which is normative within W, then 'is-*f*' is true of W.

The core feature of this proposal is the suggestion that what is required for something to be a correct example of an art work plays a decisive role in determining what can be predicated truly of the work. Or to put it yet more indefinitely, the core feature is the suggestion that the concept of an art work is initimately connected with the concept of a correct example of the work.

Perhaps if we considered the matter in detail we would find still more pattern to the sharing of predicates between art works and their examples than what we have thus far uncovered. But enough has been discovered for our subsequent purposes. So let us now move from the level of language to the level of ontology and consider whether, when predicates are shared according to the general pattern uncovered, there is also a sharing of properties designated by those predicates.

One is naturally inclined to think that there is. Our dictionaries do not, after all, tell us that a certain word standardly means one thing when truly predicated of an art work and something else when truly predicated of an example of the work. Yet I think that we must in fact come to the conclusion that predicates shared between art works and their examples do not function univocally when the sharing follows the general pattern we have uncovered. For what one means, in correctly predicating 'has "no" as its third word' of some copy of 'Sailing to Byzantium', is that the third work-*occurrence* is 'no'. But when one correctly predicates 'has "no" as its third word' of 'Sailing to Byzantium' itself, one cannot mean this. For the poem does not consist of word-occurrences (and neither does its artefactual component). Similarly, what one means in correctly predicting 'has a G sharp in its seventh meausre' of some performance of Bartok's Fifth is that in its seventh measure there was an *occurrence* of the G sharp pitch. But the quartet itself does not consist of sound-occurrences. So I think it must be admitted that we have not discovered a systematic identity but only a systematic relation between the property designated by some predicate when it is correctly predicated of some art examples and the property designated by that some predicate when truly predicated of the art work. Our conclusion must be that the sharing of predicates between art works and their examples pervasively exhibits *analogical* predication.

The situation is as follows. Suppose that 'is-*f*' is a predicate which can be shared between an art work W and its examples, and suppose further that a property for which 'is-*f*' stands when truly predicated of examples of *W* is *being-f*. Then for those cases in which the sharing of 'is-*f*' fits the general pattern which we formulated, 'is-*f*' when truly predicated of *W* stands for the property of *being such that something cannot be a correct example of it without having the property of being-f*. Or in other words, it stands for the property of *having the property of being-f normative within it*. If *having a G sharp in its seventh measure* is a property that a sound-sequence-occurrence can have, then to predicate 'has a G sharp in its seventh measure' of Bartok's Fifth Quartet is not to claim of Bartok's Fifth that it *has* that property. It is rather to claim that that property is *normative within* Bartok's Fifth.

VI. What Is It to Compose?

I have suggested that an art work is a *kind* whose examples are the occurrences or objects of the work; and more specifically, that it is a norm-kind, capable of having both correct and incorrect examples. Now these schematic suggestions must be worked out in detail. For the sake of convenience I shall conduct the discussion by referring exclusively to music and then, in conclusion, briefly indicate how the points made can be applied in arts other than music.

What must one do to compose a musical work? The beginning of the answer is clear: one must select a certain set of properties which sound-sequence-occurrences can exemplify—the property of being a piano sound of F pitch, the property of being a piano sound of A pitch, etc. [17]

But there's more to it than this. For whenever one selects things, one selects them *as* the ones which are so-and-so. One selects them *for* such-and-such purpose. And in principle the very same things which one selects *as* the ones which are so-and-so or *for* such-and-such purpose can also be selected as, or for, something else. Now merely selecting *as* or *for* something or other is not sufficient for composing. A composer might select a set of sound-sequence-occurrences as ones that he never wants to hear again. He would not then have composed. We must ask, then, what purpose lies behind the composer's selections.

The clue is to be found in our conclusion that a musical work is a norm-kind. The composer selects properties of sounds for the purpose

[17] One can also compose by building and programming a machine, and letting the machine make the actual selections. This qualifying addition should be understood in all that follows.

of their serving as criteria for judging correctness of occurrence. By reference to his selected set, we can judge sound-sequence-occurrences as correct or incorrect. And when we *do* so use his selection, we are using it as he intended. At the end of the composer's activity, sound-sequence-occurrences can be correct or incorrect by reference to that just-selected set of criteria for correctness.

In selecting a set of properties required for correctness, the composer composes a work—that one, namely, which has exactly those properties (plus any other presupposed by them) as normative within it. And any particular sound-sequence-occurrence which is correct by reference to that particular set of requirements for correctness will be a correct occurrence *of* the work composed.

Over the past quarter century analogies to games have played so prominent a part in philosophical discussion that to draw such an analogy once more is to risk ennui or nausea. But the inventing of a game does provide a genuinely illuminating analogy to the composing of a musical work. The inventor of a game selects certain properties which action-sequence-occurrences can exemplify; and therein he makes a game—that one, namely, which has exactly those properties (and any others presupposed by them) as normative within it. Specifically, he selects those properties as a set of criteria for correctness in occurrence.

The work of the taxonomist, though he too deals with norm-kinds, is significantly different from the work of both the composer and the game-inventor. The taxonomist has a certain species in mind and attempts to discover and state some of the properties normative within it. In so doing he makes claims. What he says is true or false of the species in question. You and I, talking now about one of Bartok's works, may do the same. But that is not what Bartok did in composing. In selecting a set of properties as criteria for correctness of occurrence he has not describing a work. He was bringing it about that there was such-and-such a work—the one which has the properties thus selected (and their prerequisites) as normative within it.

To get the nature of composing yet more clearly before us, glance once again at games. The inventor of a game, in addition to selecting a set of properties as criteria for correctness, may also have views as to what a *well-played* occurrence of his game would be like, and views as to how best to win at his game. Such views are matters of judgement and opinion on his part. They are true or false. Accordingly, his holding of such views is fundamentally different from his selection of a set of properties as criteria for correctness of occurrence. For in this latter there is nothing either true or false. His holding of views as to what would constitute a well-played occurrence of his game, or as to the best strategies for winning at his game, has nothing at all to do with his invention of it.

So too, a composer may have views as to what an aesthetically excellent occurrence of his work would be like, and views as to how best to achieve such an occurrence. He may think a certain tempo would give the best performance, or a certain registration on the organ. But if he does not lay these down as requirements for correctness they remain as matters of opinion and judgement on his part. As such, they are true or false. And his holding of such true/false views has nothing to do with his act of composing. Of course it's not always clear, at every point, whether the composer selected a set of criteria for correctness of occurrence or whether he expressed his views as to how correct occurrences of the work composed can also be made aesthetically excellent.

A corollary of this understanding of the nature of composing is that to improvise is not to compose. That corollary is clearly correct. Suppose that someone has improvised on the organ. And suppose that he then goes home and scores a work of such a sort that his improvisation, judged by the requirements for correctness specified in the score, is at all points correct. In spite of that, the composer did not compose his work *in* performing his improvisation. In all likelihood, he did not even compose it *while* improvising. For in all likelihood he did not, during his improvising, finish selecting that particular set of requirements for correctness of occurrence to be found in his score. Suppose, for example, that at a certain point in his improvisation he introduced a bit of rubato, with full consciousness of doing so. In so doing he has not yet decided whether to select rubato at that point as required for correctness of occurrence. One cannot uniquely extract a work from a performance.

I said that in selecting a set of properties as criteria for correctness of occurrence the composer composes a work. And the work composed, I said, is that one which has exactly those properties and their prerequisites as normative within it. The reason for adding 'and their prerequisites' is that it will usually if not always be the case that certain properties which the composer did not select will also be required for correctness— even ones which are not essential within the work. For something cannot have the ones he did select without having others. [18] So, by the definition of 'normative within', those others will also be normative within the work. We can say this: in selecting a set of properties as criteria for correctness of occurrence, the composer has composed that work which requires for correctness in its occurrences all and only those properties that he has thus selected along with whatever others an occurrence would have to have if it had those.

But is it true that there is exactly one such work? And if it *is* true, *why* is it true? *Why* is it true that a musical work is uniquely determined by the properties normative within it? A work, we said, is a norm-kind whose examples are the occurrences of the work. But can there not be a number of distinct norm-kinds which have the same properties normative within them? Let us see.

Suppose that two possible, non-necessary, kinds, *the K* and *the K**, have the same set of properties normative within them. Call that set, kappa. In other words, suppose that though *the K* is not identical with *the K**, yet it is impossible that something should be a correct example of *the K* and lack any of kappa, and also impossible that something should be a correct example of *the K** and lack any of kappa.

That could come about in just one way: some of the properties essential within (and thus normative within) one of the kinds are only normative, not essential, within the other. Is that in fact a real possibility? Can there in fact be a pair of norm-kinds related in that fashion? How about these: The Siamese Cat, and The Properly-Formed Siamese Cat? All the properties normative within the former are essential within the latter, but not vice versa. But of course the latter is not a norm-kind; and our suggestion has been that art works are norm-kinds, capable of having both correct and incorrect examples.

So consider *this* pair of kinds: Performance Of Bartok's Fifth Quartet, and Performance Of Bartok's Fifth Quartet Which Is Correct In Its First Ten Measures. These are clearly distinct kinds. There could be something which is an example of the former and not of the latter. And they are both norm-kinds. Further, they are wholly alike with respect to the set of properties normative within them. However, some

---

[18]Perhaps something could not have some at least of those others without also having some at least of the ones he singled out. So in principle it is possible for the composer to make a different selection of properties and yet to compose the very same work.

of the properties which are merely normative within the former are essential within the latter. And in particular that is true for the property of *being a performance of Bartok's Fifth Quartet which is correct in its first ten measures.* It is for that reason that there can be performances which are examples (incorrect ones of course) of the former which are not examples of the latter.

We seem to have found the refutation of our claim. The work composed, we said, was that work which requires for correctness in its occurrences all and only those properties that the composer has selected as criteria for correctness, along with whatever others an occurrence would have if it had these. Now it seems that in general there will be no one such work. It seems that there will be a number of such works. But if that is really a consequence of our theory, the theory is reduced to absurdity. For surely if there is no ambiguity as to which properties the composer selected, then also there is none as to which work he composed. Are we on the wrong track in our whole theory?

Not at all. But an explanation is in order. The kind: Performance Of Bartok's Fifth Quartet Which Is Correct In Its First Ten Measures, is not the work Bartok composed. The musical work determined by Bartok's selection of properties is one which can be incorrect in its first ten measures as well as in any of its other measures. In general, take the set of properties that some comoser selected as required for correctness of occurrence plus any others presupposed by these. If there is some pair of norm-kinds such that both members have that set of properties normative within them, but such that a member of that set of properties is essential within one of those kinds and not essential within the other, then the former is not the work the composer composed. And the work he did compose is just that norm-kind which, by this test, proves never to have the property of *not being the musical work he composed.* The work he composed is that norm-kind—of all those which have the selected properties and their prerequisites as normative within them— which is maximally generous in the policy of preferring to have an occurrence as *incorrect* example rather than as *no* example at all.

In focusing on composing we must not overlook the fact that there are musical works which were probably never composed. There are works of indigenous folk music such that probably no one ever singled out the requisites properties in the requisite way for composing the work. The work just emerged from performances. But though there may be no one who selected in the requisite way (enough of) the properties normative within the work so as therein to compose it, there will certainly be

382

people who *use* those properties either as guidelines for performing or as criteria for criticizing occurrences with respect to correctness. And given a set of properties thus used, there will be a unique determination of a work which has exactly those properties (and their prerequisites) as normative within it. But it will be the work of those practitioners, not the work of some composer.

In one or the other of these two somewhat different ways—the way of the composer and the way of the practitioners—a work is always a work *of* somebody. Nothing is ever a work of music without, in one or the other of these two ways, being the work of some person or persons. Every musical work can in principle be identified as the so-and-so work of composer *C*, or as the so-and-so work of practitioners *P*.

I have tacitly assumed that the composer can make the selections whereby he composes 'in his head'. Mozart said that he composed whole symphonies in his head. Perhaps he was speaking the truth. But whether or not some composer composes a work entirely 'in his head', normally he indicates for the rest of us what his work is like. And thereupon the work enters into, or becomes available for entering into, human culture. Thereupon the set of properties selected as required for correctness can be used by the rest of us as guidelines for performing. Thereupon the set of properties selected can be used by the rest of us as criteria for criticizing occurrences with respect to correctness. Thereupon the set of properties selected can even be used by the rest of us as guidelines for *imagining* an occurrence. [19] What should be added is that most composers do most of their composing for such functions as these. They have such purposes in mind.

But to understand what the composer *characteristically* does when indicating to us his set of requirements, we must not picture him as completing in his head the selection of that set and then merely *reporting* his selections to us. I now can report what some composed work is like. I can do so by inscribing a score. And if the score is wholly accurate, I would then have spoken truly at all points. By inscribing the score I would have made true claims. But that is not characteristically what the composer does. He might do that. Then by means of his score he would make true/false claims about a work already composed. But more characteristically, he makes his selections *in* putting down his

---

[19] It's possible that the composer might have composed purely conceptual music which, though some of us can imagine what an occurrence would be like, can in fact not be performed because of the limitations of instruments or performers.

inscriptions. Selecting properties is something that one can do in one's head. But also it is something that one can do by inscribing perceptible signs; then one selects by signifying. And that is what the composer *characteristically* does when he scores his work. By inscribing such-and-such signs in such-and-such manner and circumstance he selects a set of properties as required for correctness of occurrence. That is what his inscribing counts as.

Now in selecting by signifying, the composer may make mistakes— not the mistake of falsely reporting what he had already selected, but the mistake of selecting what he did not intend to select. His setting down of various notations may count as his selecting a middle C at a certain point, when he never intended to select middle C. His selection of middle C may have been done inadvertently. He may have misspoken himself and in that way produced an incorrect score. One's use of a notation system acquires a life of its own.

In such cases, what should we take to be the work composed? I have said that the work composed is uniquely determined by the properties selected as required for correctness of occurrence. But that is not, in practice, how our music publishing houses operate. When they receive a score they *correct its mistakes*—changing a C natural to a C sharp in a certain measure, etc. They try to revise the autograph score received from the composer in such a way that it signifies what the composer *would* have signified, had he made no mistakes in his use of the notation. The resultant score is what they regard as specifying the work composed. I shall follow them in that practice. Often one can distinguish between the properties that the composer *did* select, and the properties that he *would* have selected had he used his notation system correctly (if he used one at all). It is the latter that I shall regard as determining the composer's work. For surely we want to take the composer's mistakes for what they are—mistakes, which generosity requires us to correct.

But in following this policy are we not appealing to the composer's intentions? And haven't our twentieth-century critics warned us against ever doing any such thing? Indeed they have. And concerning some appeals to intention, the warning is very much in place. But I am suggesting an appeal to the composer's intentions only in a minimal and innocuous way. I am suggesting that if the composer made mistakes in scoring, then we should regard the work composed as determined by what he *would* have signified had he *not* made any mistakes. And that is no more questionable an appeal to intention than what takes place when

384

a publisher corrects the mistakes in the manuscript that a critic submits. Apart from correcting errors in notation, we appeal to what *in fact* the composer selected when we wish to determine the nature of the work he composed. We do not appeal to what he *intended* to select. We appeal to what he *did* select.

I have described the composer as one who selects, as criteria for correctness of occurrence, a set of properties which sound-occurrences can possess. On hearing this, one is naturally disposed to assume that these are all *acoustic* properties of sounds. But not so. The composer can also lay down as a condition for correctness that the sounds have the property of being produced in such-and-such fashion on such-and-such instruments. Such a property can conveniently be called an *instrumental* property. Composers can and often do include instrumental properties among their selections.

The traditional composer–scorer in the West over the past 200 years offers an interesting blend of properties signified. In part he signifies purely acoustic properties of sounds: the property of *being middle C in pitch*, the property of *being a quarter note long in 4/4 time at andante tempo*, the property of *being forte in volume*, etc. But in addition he tells us, say, that the composition is for violin. He does not go on to tell us how those instruments called 'violins' are to be constructed, nor does he tell us how he wants them played. He *presupposes* the existence of musical instruments of the species: Violin, and of a practice tradition for playing instruments of that species; and he *takes for granted* that some of his readers will know which instruments those are and what that practice tradition is.

One way to depart from this mainline tradition is to make a composition for such-and-such instruments played in such-and-such fashion, but then not to presuppose the existence of such instruments, or of practice traditions for playing them. For example, one might compose a work for prepared piano; and then tell how the piano is to be prepared. Or one might compose a work for ordinary piano but then give instruction for playing it in a non-ordinary way: plucking its strings, rapping its sounding-board. Or one might do as Harry Partch did: invent and construct a new instrument called 'cloud-chamber bowls', devise standard ways of playing it, and then compose a work for that hitherto non-existent instrument.

At a deeper level, however, these various possibilities are only variants on the mainline tradition. The composer follows the tradition in signifying certain purely acoustic properties and then, in addition, making clear to us that the composition is for such-and-such an instrument played in such-and-such a fashion. Whether he remains with the traditional instruments and the conventional practice traditions, or whether he devises new ones, makes no difference when we see that it is possible for the composer to depart from this deeper-lying mainline tradition. He can do so in either of two directions. He can signify no acoustic properties whatsoever, confining himself to telling us that his composition is for such-and-such instruments played in such-and-such a way. John Cage does that with his *Radio Music* (1956). Alternatively, he can confine himself to signifying purely acoustic properties, in no way telling us that the composition is for such-and-such instruments played in such-and-such a way. J.S. Bach did that with his *Art of the Fugue.*

As one might expect, sometimes it's not decisively clear whether the composer has specified that the sounds have certain instrumental properties or whether, instead, he has only specified that the sounds have the acoustic property of *sounding as if they were produced in such-and-such fashion on such-and-such an instrument*—a *mixed-acoustic* property, we might call it. Suppose, for example, that a composer tells us that his work is *for* pipe organ; and that it is clear that he means it to be played in conventional fashion. Then to be a correct occurrence of this composition an occurrence must have the mixed-acoustic property of *sounding as if it were produced by playing a pipe organ in the conventional manner.* But is the instrumental property of *being produced by playing a pipe organ in the conventional manner* also required for correctness?

Until the advent of electronics this particular issue was never concretely presented to anyone. Pipe-organish sounds were produced only by pipe organs. So the answer for traditional composers is not decisively clear. We seem, in fact, to take ambivalent stands on the matter. Almost all of us assume that it is possible to produce a correct performance of one of Bach's works for pipe organ on an electronic organ. Yet I dare say that few of us would regard a sound-sequence-occurrence produced by playing a keyboard to be a correct performance of some work for violin. Perhaps it is the radical difference in means of performance that is decisive for us.

But whatever we decide concerning Bach's works for organ, a knowledge of pipe organs of the sort that Bach was acquainted with, and of the practice traditions that he presupposed, is not the less important; for only by reference to these do we know what is that mixed-acoustic

386

property of *sounding pipe-organish* which is normative within Bach's works for pipe organ. The history of music is inseparable from a history of instruments and of practice traditions for playing them.

Having analysed the nature of composing we can now profitably deal with a question alluded to in Section I of this Part: why can paintings and sculptures not be viewed as single-exampled kinds rather than physical objects, thereby giving us a 'unified theory' of works of art? P.F. Strawson, after saying that 'in a certain sense, paintings and works of sculpture' are types, adds this footnote:

> The mention of paintings and works of sculpture may seem absurd. Are they not particulars? But this is a superficial point. The things the dealers buy and sell are particulars. But it is only because of the empirical deficiencies of reproductive techniques that we identify these with the works of art. Were it not for these deficiencies, the original of a painting would have only the interest which belongs to the original manuscript of a poem. Different people could look at exactly the same painting in different places at the same time, just as different people can listen to exactly the same quartet at different times in the same place. [20]

Strawson's point here is that though, as a matter of fact, in the field of painting it is the particular paintings which are (or, are regarded as) the works of art, this is quite coincidental. If the technology of reproduction were more advanced, there would be kinds which would be (would be regarded as) works of art, and the particular painting which the artist painted would have no more status than that of the first example of the work. In short, if reproductive techniques were more advanced, the situation for painting would be as it already is for graphic art.

About this, several remarks. In the first place, Strawson evidently agrees that *as things are* in the field of painting, it is the particular paintings which are the works of art. So as a matter of fact we cannot form a unified theory of the ontology of art artefacts.

But secondly, Strawson mislocates the reason for this phenomenon. He attributes it to inadequacy of reproductive techniques. But in music we do not demand that the various occurrences of a single work all sound similar to the point of indiscernibility. We allow wide variation. The reason that painting is different is that the painter, in creating his painting, does not select a set of properties as criteria for correctness of

[20]P.F. Strawson, *Individuals* (Methuen & Co.: London, 1959), p. 231.

occurrence. Accordingly, he does not uniquely determine some norm-kind. No requirements for something's being a correct object of something are selected in creating *The Odalisque*. If there were, we could determine whether *The Odalisque* is a correct or incorrect object of the composed art work, just as we can determine whether the author's manuscript copy of his poem is or is not a correct copy. In fact, nothing of the sort can be done for *The Odalisque*.

Of course, one can pick out things which to a certain degree of closeness *resemble* this painting, in one or another respect. There is a kind associated with the property of resembling *The Odalisque* in such-and-such respects to such-and-such a degree. *The Odalisque* is itself an example of the kind. It is not a norm-kind, however; and none of our names of painting are names of such entities.

But *could* we somehow, in the field of painting, compose norm-kinds? Certainly. If, instead of applying paint to canvas, the artist would draw up a set of specifications for paintings, then he would compose a norm-kind. He might also, if he wished, paint a painting in accord with the specifications. But that would be quite incidental. In fact, this phenomenon already exists in the field of painting. One finds it in the 'paint by number' sets for children.

In conclusion it should be noted that our analysis of what it is to compose holds as much for aleatory music, in which chance plays a significant role, as it does for non-aleatory. Chance can play a role in the process of composing. John Cage tells of his idea of letting the specks on the paper one is using determine one's selections. Using chance in this manner does not alter the fact that in composing one selects a set of properties by which to judge correctness of occurrence. More customarily, however, chance is allowed or required to play a role in performance. Composers sometimes stipulate, for example, that sections of the work are to be played in randomly determined sequence. Obviously requirements for correctness still enter in such cases. They enter at two different points. It is required that the *sequence* of sections be randomly determined. And *within* the sections it is required that such-and-such acoustic and instrumental properties occur. So it is for aleatory works in general. Aleatoriness is itself required at certain points if the work is to be performed correctly; all the members of the choir singing on a single pitch, when what is asked is that they make random noise, would result in an incorrect performance. But then secondly, there will always be points where certain definite acoustic or instrumental properties are required if the performance is to be correct.

VII. What Is It to Perform a Musical Work?

Having looked at things from the side of the composer let me now shift focus and look at them from the side of the performer, asking: 'What is it to perform a musical work?' For the sake of clarity I shall remain true to my earlier resolution to use the word 'performance' exclusively for a sound-sequence-occurrence of a certain sort, namely, one brought about by performing; and not to use it for instances (cases) of the *action* of performing.

There can be performances which are not performances of works. In the case of complete improvisation, for example, there is a performance of a *work*. Yet there is a performance—an occurrence of a sound-sequence which is brought about by an instance of the intentional action of performing. However, let us set aside this sort of performance and this sort of instance of performing and concentrate wholly on performance of works.

A point to be kept in mind is that a sound-sequence-occurrence which was not produced by an intentional act of performing may yet have all the acoustic properties normative within some musical work. The wind's blowing through the rocks, someone's doodling on a piano, or an electronic organ's going berserk, might produce a sound-sequence-occurrence which sounds just like a correct performance of 'Greensleeves'. A performance of the work W is something more than an occurrence having all the acoustic properties normative within W.

A more subtle point is this: suppose that someone, not believing that he is performing a work, improvises a sound-sequence-occurrence. And suppose that every acoustic property normative within some work W is one that he by intent exemplified in the occurrence he brought about. He neither knows nor believes that all those properties are normative within some work or other. But they do all happen to be normative within W. Has he then performed W? What he has done is to produce an occurrence which by intent has all the acoustic properties which are in fact normative within some work. But he has not produced an occurrence which by intent has all the properties which he *believes* to be normative within some work. Is the former ever sufficient for performing that work? I am going to assume, in my analysis, that it is not. I am going to assume that one cannot, in that way, inadvertently perform a work. One performs a work only if one *believes* that one is performing a work.

On the other hand, one may perform that which is the such-and-such work of composer C, or the such-and-such work of practitioner P, without knowing that one has done so, and without believing that one has done so—even believing that one has *not* done so. Suppose I believe of some work of J.S. Bach that it was composed by one of his sons. I may none the less perform that work. One's misattribution of a work does not prevent one from performing it. To take account of the fact that one believes to be the work W may not in fact be the work W, I shall henceforth put our question this way: What is it to perform that which one believes to be the work W?

An answer which comes to mind at once is that it consists of producing a sound-sequence-occurrence by (intentionally) following the specifications for correct occurrence that the composer gave in the score associated with that work. But several objections can be raised, to the effect that the following of the score for that which one believes to be the work W is neither sufficient nor necessary for performing that work.

For one thing, one might in every detail follow the specifications for correct occurrence found in (some correct copy of) the score for a work and yet not perform the work. For often the specifications for correct occurrence that composers give in scores are incomplete in ensuring that those who follow them will produce occurrences, let alone correct occurrences, of the work. Scores originated in the Western world in medieval times, when they functioned as devices to remind performers of what they had learned apart from the score. By gradually acquiring greater specificity they gained the function of serving to inform people as to what is required for correct occurrence. But even so, many things go presupposed rather than specified. As we say in our preceding section, the composer often presupposes the existence in his society of certain kinds of instruments and of practice traditions for performing on the specified instruments. Thus it is that a performer might follow all the specifications for correct occurrence given in some (correct copy of) a score and yet fail to perform the associated work. His performance may be too far off target to count as an occurrence of the work.

On the other hand, it is not necessary that one follow *all* the specifications found in a score in order to perform the work associated with that score. Indeed, one can perform some work without *at all* following the specifications for correct occurrence given in the score for that work. For there may at the time be no score, or one may be unaware of it. If Beethoven had completely composed his Opus 111 'in his head' and only scored it later, it would have been possible for him in the interim to have performed the work even though there was as yet no score. That is, it would have been possible for him not merely to produce a sound-sequence-occurrence having the acoustic properties required for something to be a performance of Opus 111, but actually to perform Opus 111. That is of course only a hypothetical case. But in fact the vast bulk of indigenous folk music has always been unscored; so of course one cannot follow the specifications for correct occurrence given in the scores for those works. Yet those works can be performed.

It is true indeed that specification of the properties required for a work's correct occurrence can be communicated to performers by means other than scores, and by people other than composers. The performer of indigenous folk music can be told verbally how some passage must sound. Or the correct rhythm can be stomped out for him by foot. But quite clearly it is no significant improvement over our first thought to say that to perform a work W is to produce a sound-sequence-occurrence by (intentionally) following *whatever* specifications for correct occurrence of W have been given to one. For not only is it not necessary that there *be* any such specifications but also, conversely, in many cases one might follow *all* the specifications ever given to one, those expressed in score notation and otherwise, and still not produce an occurrence of the work. Bartok in his early career set about scoring various Hungarian folk songs. His project did not consist of taking the specifications that the Hungarians were expressing in something other than the Western scoring system and expressing them in score notation. It consisted rather of providing those works, for the first time in their careers, with anything near full specifications of the acoustic properties required for correct occurrence. So it must be said that performing a work W does not consist of intentionally following all the specifications ever given one of properties required for a correct occurrence of W.

The specifications of which we have been speaking are specifications of the *properties* a sound-sequence-occurrence must have if it is to be a correct occurrence of the work in question. Being reminded of this we are naturally led onto the thought that the phenomenon of performing is attached to those properties themselves, not to specifications thereof. I think this is correct. But several complications present themselves on the road to a satisfactory analysis.

In the first place, what a person *believes* to be the properties normative within that work which he believes to be W can be more close or less close to what in fact are those properties. And I take it as true that a person can perform that work even though not all the properties

391

normative within the work (or required by those) are believed to be such by him. He may be uncertain or ignorant or mistaken on some points and yet perform the work. Noah Greenberg and his New York Pro Musica group may very well have performed the medieval work *Play of Herod*, even though by Greenberg's own acknowledgement they were uncertain at many points of the properties normative within the work. On the other hand it is surely true that one's uncertainty, ignorance, or error as to the properties normative within some work can be so severe that in exemplifying what one believes to be those properties one does not perform the work. One performs no work at all.

Secondly, a person can try to exemplify with greater or less exactness what he believes to be the properties normative within that work which he believes to be W. And I take it as true that a person need not try to exemplify *exactly* what he believes to be those properties if he is in fact to perform that work which he believes to be W. Performers, knowing well the properties normative within some work, often deliberately depart from them in the belief that the resulting performance will be better—or sometimes in the knowledge that they are incapable of executing the passage correctly. In spite of that the performer may well have performed the very work from whose normative properties he believed he was departing. On the other hand, one can intentionally depart so far from what one knows or believes to be the properties normative within some work that the result does not count as a performance of that work.

Thirdly, a person can be more successful or less successful in his attempt to exemplify what he believes to be the properties normative within that work which he believes to be W. And I take it as true that a person need not be wholly successful in order to perform that work. He may unintentionally strike what he knows to be the wrong note and yet perform the work. On the other hand, one can fail so abjectly in one's attempt to exemplify what one believes to be the properties normative within some work that one has not performed the work at all—has indeed not succeeded in performing *any* work.

So there are three fundamentally different reasons for the phenomenon of someone producing an incorrect performance of that work which be believes to be W. The performer may be unsuccessful in trying to exemplify what he believes to be the properties normative within that which he believes to be W, the performer may deliberately depart from what he believes to be those properties, and the performer may be uncertain or mistaken or ignorant as to what are those properties.

Likewise there are three fundamentally different reasons for the phenomenon of someone not even producing an incorrect performance of that work which he believes to be W, even though he meant to produce a performance thereof.

Given these complications, how are we to frame a concept of *performing?* Well, first this: in thinking of a *performance* of a work (not just of a *correct* performance) we all operate with the notion of an occurrence of a sound-sequence being closer or less close in its acoustic and instrumental properties to what a *correct* performance of the work would be like. Such relative closeness is by no means merely a matter of the *quantity* of the departures—if indeed departures can be counted. (Suppose one transposes an entire piece into a different key; how many changes is that? One? Or one for each of the sounds played at a different pitch?) It is also a matter of the *scale* of the departures. A reversal of the order of the movements in a quartet would yield a performance farther from a correct performance than would an omission of a quarter note in some rather shapeless transition passage. In a similar way, we operate with the notion of that which one believes to be the properties normative within some work being closer or less close to the properties which are actually normative within that work. These two notions, it seems to me, go into our concept of performing a work.

One or two other complications must still be mentioned. But first let us have before us a preliminary formulation of our analysis. In the light of what I have said so far I suggest this:

One performs that work which one believes to be W if and only if one brings about a sound-sequence-occurrence which comes fairly close to exemplifying the acoustic and instrumental properties normative within that work, and one does so:

(1)   By having beliefs which come fairly close to being correct and complete as to what are the acoustic and instrumental properties normative within the work;

(ii)   by aiming to produce a sound-sequence-occurrence such that for most of the properties about which one has those beliefs, one tries to make the occurrence exemplify them, and for at best a few, one does not try to make it exemplify them; and

(iii)   by coming fairly close to succeeding in that attempt on one's part to produce a sound-sequence-occurrence which, for most of those properties, will exemplify them.

393

And now for some of the additional complications. Suppose, knowing well some musical work, one plays a record (of a recording) of it; and in that way produces a sound-sequence-occurrence. By these preliminary formulations one would have performed the work. Yet of course one has not. What takes place is not a performance, but a *reproduction* of a performance, of the work. So we must exclude the bringing about of sound-sequence-occurrences which are reproductions of occurrences which took place earlier.

Another range of phenomena is somewhat less easily dealt with. Suppose that some musical composition has been put on a player piano roll. And now suppose that one puts one of the rolls on a player piano, and then pumps the piano so that it is played at desired speed and volume. Has one thereby performed the composition? I think that our ordinary concept of *performing* does not yield a decisive 'Yes' or 'No' answer to this question. But now suppose, alternatively, that some composer has composed directly on tape, and that one now puts the tape in one's own tape machine and plays it. Has one thereby performed the composition? In this case it is quite clear that one has *not* done so. Performing disappears from sight for such music. Notice that neither in this case, nor in the player piano case, is the resultant sound-sequence-occurrence a reproduction of another occurrence which took place earlier.

We can visualize an ordered sequence starting from someone performing a composition by playing a piano, through the ambiguous case of someone operating a player piano, on to the case of someone producing an occurrence but not a performance of a composition for tape by putting the tape on a machine, setting the dials, and letting it play. But what is the principle of ordering in this sequence? *This*, I think: as we move along the series, there is less and less *feedback* from what the operator of the instrument *discerns* to be the acoustic properties of the sound-sequence-occurrence produced, to what he actually does with his instrument subsequently; as indeed there is less and less *adjustment* of what he does to his instrument in the light of what he *anticipates* will be the results if he does this or that to his instrument. In the case of the pianist the feedback and adjustment is enormous, of a complexity that defies description, and requiring years of practice. In the case of the operator of the player piano there is some significant feedback and adjustment, mainly pertaining to volume and tempo, though obviously feedback and adjustment have been reduced

394

greatly. In the case of the operator of the tape machine the adjustment and feedback are at a minimum.

If this analysis of the sequence is correct, then what can be said is that one *performs* a musical composition on an instrument only if there is a significant amount of adjustment and feedback which goes into one's production of a sound-sequence-occurrence. In the case of putting on the tape and operating the tape machine, these are comparatively insignificant, though not wholly missing. In the case of playing the piano, these are highly significant. In the case of operating the player piano, they are somewhere in between.

Here then is our completed analysis of what it is to perform:

One performs that work which one believes to be W if and only if one brings about a sound-sequence-occurrence which is not a reproduction of any other occurrence, and which comes fairly close to exemplifying the acoustic and instrumental properties normative within that work which one believes to be W, and one does so:

(i)   by operating the instrument(s) from which the sound is produced in such a way that there is a relatively large amount of *adjustment* in how one handles the instrument(s) in light of what one anticipates will be the acoustic properties of the resultant sound-sequence-occurrence if one does this or that to the instrument, and a relatively large amount of *feedback* from what one discerns to be the acoustic properties of the resultant sound-sequence-occurrences to what one does subsequently with the instrument(s); and

(ii)   by having beliefs which come fairly close to being correct and complete as to what are the acoustic and instrumental properties normative within the work; and

(iii)   by aiming to produce a sound-sequence-occurrence such that, for most of the properties about which one has those beliefs, one tries to make the occurrence exemplify them, and, for at best a few, one does not try to make it exemplify them; and

(iv)   by coming fairly close to succeeding in that attempt on one's part to produce a sound-sequence-occurrence which, for most of those properties, will exemplify them.

When one thus brings about a sound-sequence-occurrence, let us say that one is *guided by* the properties normative within the work that one believes to be S.

One implication of this formulation should be highlighted. Suppose that some pianist has composed a slight variation on some composer's work. And suppose that he now performs his own variant rather than the original. I do not think it true that he has therein also performed the original. And I do not think he would therein have performed the original even if the acoustic and instrumental properties of the sound-sequence-occurrence that he produces are such that *exactly* those properties might be exemplified in a performance of the original work. It is our stipulation (iii) that prevents the undesired result. For suppose, to simplify the case, that there is no misattribution involved. And suppose that the pianist knows fully the properties normative within the original, and also those normative within his own variant. It would not have been his aim to produce a sound-sequence-occurrence exemplifying the acoustic and instrumental properties that he believes to be normative within the original. It would rather have been his aim to produce one exemplifying the acoustic and instrumental properties that he believes to be normative within his variant.

Perhaps it is worth noting that sometimes a performer's goal of producing a performance as aesthetically excellent as possible of the work he is performing may require him to perform the work incorrectly at certain points. The composer perhaps thought otherwise at the time of composition, and possibly continued to do so. That was in part his reason for making those points matters of correctness. But he may just have been mistaken. Correct performances might well be better if something else had been made the correct thing at that point—which is to say, might well have been better if a slightly different work had been composed.

Then, also, the attempt to produce a performance as aesthetically excellent as possible will inevitably require the performer to make decisions on all sorts of matters where correctness is not even at issue. On some of such matters the composer may very well have had an opinion. He may even have expressed it. He may expressly have intended that his work be performed thus and thus because he thought that that would yield the best performances. But once again, he may have been mistaken.

How do we find out which properties the composer has selected for judging correctness in occurrence by? How do we find out which norm-kind he has singled out? How do we find out which properties are normative within the work composed? How do we find out what the work is like that he has composed? It should be evident by now that these four questions, thought distinct, are inextricably related.

We go by the best evidence we have. In the first place we try to discover the relevant parts of the practice tradition that the composer took for granted. Then, secondly, if the composer made, or authorized the making of, a score we begin by trying to find out what the autograph score-copy was like in the relevant respects. But a precise knowledge of the practice tradition may have been lost. And there may never have been a score. Or if there was, we may no longer have the autograph copy nor any reliable evidence as to what it was like in certain relevant respects. Or we may have several differing copies from the composer's hand and not know which he authenticated. Or we may have the original authenticated copy but it may contain what we recognize to be slips on the part of the composer-scorer, and we may find it impossible to determine what a correct copy would be like. Or we may have an original, authenticated, and correct copy but no longer know how to interpret all the symbols. And then there is the peculiar case of Anton Bruckner's symphonies, in which the extent of Bruckner's authorization of his editor's massive revisions is thoroughly obscure. In all such cases and many others we simply have to acknowledge that we are to some extent uncertain as to which properties the composer selected for judging correctness of occurrence by. In being thus ignorant, we are also ignorant as to precisely which norm-kind the composer singled out. And so we are ignorant as to the precise nature of the work he composed. Yet it is clear what we are looking for: the properties that the composer selected for judging correctness of sound-occurrences by. And often, of course, we have very good evidence as to what those properties are.

The situation for those works which are the works of a group—for example, indigenous folk music—is not substantially different. The group in question will use a certain set of properties for judging correctness of occurrence. That then determines the properties normative within the associated work. So that is what we try to discover. Usually a group operates in such matters by acknowledging certain of its members as authorities: a certain group of the old men in a society are acknowledged as knowing how the music should go. So we consult them. And if they differ on some point, then on that point the group has no criterion for correctness. On disputed points they will always agree, though, that everything falling outside a certain rather limited range of possibilities is incorrect. As it were, they have criteria for incorrectness.

Though there may have been disagreement as to how some of the Hungarian folk songs that Bartok scored should go at some points, at no point do they go as the beginning of Penderecki's *Resurrection.*

VII. *What Kind of Kind is a Musical Work?*

A musical work is a norm-kind whose examples, if any, are sound-sequence-occurrences. But now, more specifically, with which of such kinds are musical works to be identified? Sound-sequence-occurrences come in many kinds. Which of these many kinds is identical with Beethoven's Opus 111?

What particularly forces this question on our attention is the distinction made in the preceding section between those sound-sequence-occurrences which are *performances* of some music work *W* and those which, though not performances of *W*, yet possess all the acoustic and instrumental properties necessary for being occurrences of *W* (excluding here from instrumental properties the property of *being a performance*). The question which this distinction brings to mind is this: are the examples of a musical work confined to performances of the work? That is to say, is it the case, for any musical work *W*, that the property of *being a performance of W* is essential within *W*? The wind blowing through the rocks cannot produce a performance of 'Greensleeves'. Might it none the less produce an example of it? Or is that impossible?

Our discussion concerning the nature of performing not only brings this question to mind. It quickly furnishes an answer. When one plays a tape, of a composition for tape, one produces an example of the composition. One does not, though produce a performance; for no one *performs* the composition.[21]

Of course it might not be the case, for *every* musical work *W*, that the property of *being a performance of W* is essential within it, while yet it is the case, for *some* work *W*, that the property of being a performance is essential within it. The phenomenon of the player piano makes this look dubious, however. Consider any work for piano which can be put on player piano rolls. We saw that it is not clear that what one produces,

---

[21]There is also the possibility that the property of *being a performance*, though not essential within works of music, is yet normative within them. However, the existence of compositions for tape surely refutes that view as well. Naturally this still leave open the possibility that this property is normative within *some*, though *not all*, compositions.

when a roll for that work is put in a piano and the piano is pumped, is a performance of the work. Surely, though, it is an example, an occurrence, of the work. After all, one hears the work in hearing the sound-sequence-occurrence produced in that particular playing of it. And in general, it would seem that if one hears work *W* in hearing some particular sound-sequence-occurrence, then that occurrence should be regarded as an occurrence of work *W*.

So it is not necessary, if something is to be an example of Beethoven's Opus 111, that it be a performance—that it be a sound-sequence-occurrence produced by someone performing the work. A possibility to be considered, though, is that it is necessary that the occurrence be produced *either* by someone performing it *or* by someone playing it, as on a player piano or on a record player. So too, of compositions for tape it is obviously not required that their occurrence be produced by performing. Possibly, though, it *is* required that the composition be played by someone who uses an appropriately derived tape. Perhaps it is the case that no example of the work has been produced if all that happens is that some electronic organ goes berserk and produces a sound-sequence-occurrence having all the acoustic properties normative within the composition.

Playing, as we are thinking of it here, involves either the reproduction of a performance (as in the playing of a work by putting on a record), or the use of some appropriately derived artefact in the production of the sounds (as a roll for a player piano, or a copy of the tape that the composer made of a composition for tape). Perhaps what is necessary for a musical work to be exampled is that it be *either* performed *or* played. Let us consider that possibility.

Suppose that something could be an occurrence of a musical work without being either a performance or a playing of the work. How then would we pick out the examples of some work *W*? Well, any sound-sequence-occurrence which has *all* the properties *normative* within *W* will of course be an example of the work. But those would all be correct occurrences. What on this view would be an *incorrect* occurrence? Presumably it would be any sound-sequence-occurrence which still comes fairly close to exemplifying the properties normative within *W*. Thus on this view a property essential within the work would be: *coming fairly close to exemplifying the properties normative within W.*

Our question, then, is whether there is any absurdity in either of these views—the one, the view that essential *within* musical work *W* is the property of *being a sound-sequence-occurrence brought about by*

399

performing or playing W; the other, the view that that property is not essential within the work, but that instead a property essential within the work is that of *coming fairly close to exemplifying the properties normative within* W? Let us call these views, A and B respectively. On A, musical work W is identical with the kind: Sound-Sequence-Occurrence Produced By Performing Or Playing W. On B, musical work W is identical with the kind: Sound-Sequence-Occurrence Coming Fairly Close To One Exemplifying The Properties Normative Within W. Of course, anything which is an example of the former kind will be an example of the latter. Thus the former is included within the latter. And accordingly, the property of *coming fairly close to exemplifying the properties normative within* W is as much essential within the former kind as within the latter.

I see no reason to doubt that there are kinds of these sorts, and that they are indeed distinct. So our question comes down to this: are musical works always of the former kind, the A-view sort, or are some at least of the B-view sort? Let us sharpen the issue by drawing out some of the implications of each view.

On B, an occurrence of 'Greensleeves' might be brought about by the wind whistling through the rocks of Bryce Canyon; and as a corollary, a person might hear 'Greensleeves' without the occurrence that he hears being produced by performing or playing. Furthermore, *in* hearing a performance or a playing (correct or incorrect) of a work W, one could hear an occurrence of a distinct work W^* which is neither a performance nor a playing of W^*. For on B, a given sound-sequence-occurrence may be an example of two (or more) distinct works such that the occurrence is a performance or playing of one work and neither a performance nor playing of the other(s). Thus on B one can hear several distinct musical works in listening to a performance or playing of just one work. On A, however, none of these results obtains. For on A, the only examples of a musical work are performances or playings of that work.

As just remarked, on B it is possible for two distinct works to share some of their examples. Indeed, it is possible for them to share all their examples. This is so because a sound-sequence-occurrence which has enough of the properties required for a correct (or indeed incorrect) occurrence of work W might also have enough to be an occurrence of a distinct work W^*. Counter to what one might expect, however, it is also true on A that two distinct works can share examples. For suppose that one work W is normatively included with another W^*, in the sense that all the properties normative within W^* are also normative within W.

400

Where the one allows some latitude with respect to correctness in a cadenza, let us say, the other does not. Then all performances and playings of the included work W will be performances or playings of the normatively inclusive work W^*. However, it is *only* when one work is normatively included within the other that, on A, two works can share any examples. And in that respect, view A gives different results from view B.

Furthermore, if it be true that a work cannot be performed or played until it has been composed, then on A there can be no occurrence of the work before its composition—that is, before that kind which *is* the work has become a musical work by virtue of the composer's activity. Not so on B, however.

So there are indeed significant differences between the sort of kind which, on A, is to be identified with a work of music and the sort of kind which, on B, is thus to be identified. It would seem, however, that none of the differences we have thus far singled out gives a decisive advantage to either view A or view B. Of course the implications of these two views diverge on more issues than those we have thus far noted. Yet also in those additional, undiscussed divergences I see no *decisive* reason for preferring the one view to the other. The kinds with which these two views propose to identify a given musical work are existent, and are clearly distinct from each other. Yet neither view seems to yield a decisive absurdity.

The situation, I think, is this. When we refer to and speak about what we regard as musical works we do not, with definiteness, pick out entities of either sort as opposed to those of the other. That is no doubt because in most respects entities of these two sorts do not differ.[22] And the points where they do differ are so far on the edge of our normal concerns in the arts that we never have to make up our minds one way or the other as to which of these sorts of entities we intend to be dealing with. It is possible, of course, that future developments in the arts will force us to make up our minds; and it may just be that different developments will force us to move in different directions to cope with different phenomena. But though future developments in music might

---

[22]For example, we think of musical works as capable of existing unperformed—witness the common lament of the contemporary composer that he cannot get his works performed. Likewise we think of them, once they exist, as existing at a certain time whether or not an example is occurring at that time. We do not think of them as existing intermittently. Each of these is a straightforward consequence of *both* A and B.

confront us with works for some of which A is decisively correct and for others of which B is, that does not settle the issue for the mass of musical works now extant. For them, we have no decisive reason for preferring either of A or B to the other.

It does seem to me, though, that on most matters view A provides us with a more *natural* understanding. Neither view yields any decisive absurdities. Yet fewer of A's consequences diverge from the ways in which we normally think of musical works. It's possible, of course, that we are mistaken at crucial junctures in how we normally think of musical works. Yet in the absence of any decisive reason for thinking so, I shall henceforth speak of musical works as if they were all of the kind specified in view A. I shall speak of them as if they were, all of them, kinds of performances or of playings.

What is worth noting here, before we leave the matter, is that if the ontological principles in accord with which we have been conducting our investigations are correct, then no kinds come into or go out of existence. Accordingly, on neither view A nor view B do musical works come into or go out of existence. A kind exists just in case its property-associate exists. And we said that for any property, *being-f*, there is that property if and only if either something is-*f* or something is not-*f*. (We added certain qualifications which need not be repeated here.) Quite obviously a consequence of this is that properties, and so too then *kinds*, do not become or perish. So on both view A and view B, a composer does not bring that which is his work into existence. Musical works exist everlastingly. What the composer does must be understood as consisting in bringing it about that a preexistent kind becomes *a work*—specifically, a *work of his*. To compose is not to bring into existence what one composes. It is to bring it about that something becomes a work. And the composer does that by selecting certain properties as criteria for correctness in occurrence. Though a composer may be eminently creative in this selection, he is not a creator. The only thing a composer normally brings into existence is a copy, a token, of his score. In music, creation is normally token creation.

A final query which comes to mind concerning the nature of those kinds which are works of music is whether they can change with respect to the properties normative or essential within them. Can a work thus change? Or is it in that respect immutable, and is the phenomenon that we might ordinarily describe as a single work changing, actually a temporally successive series of slightly different works? Can a composer change his mind with respect, say, to the instrument assigned to play the theme at a certain point in his composition, and still have the identical work? Can a work of folk music change over time?

The most efficient way to approach this question is to determine whether it is essential to a work W that it have essential or normative *within* it whatever properties it *does* have. For if it is essential to it, then W cannot change in that respect, and cannot have been different from how it is in that respect. On the other hand, if it is not essential, then we will have to consider whether there is something else which prevents it changing.

So suppose that at a certain time t the property P is essential within W. We want to know whether it is possible that at some other time, P may not be essential within W (and whether even at t it is possible for P not to be essential within W). Now to suppose that at t the property P is essential within W, is just to suppose that at t it is impossible that something should be an example of W and lack P. But in general, if a proposition is impossible at any time it is impossible at all times, and necessarily so. Thus, if P is essential within W at *any* time, it is that at all times. Accordingly, those kinds which are works of music are immutable with respect to the properties essential within them, for they cannot be different in this respect from how they are.

What, then, about change with respect to properties normative within musical works? Well, to suppose that at t the property P is normative within W is to suppose that at t it is impossible for there to be something which is a correct example of W and lack P. But once again, if a proposition is impossible at any time it is impossible at all times, and necessarily so. Thus those kinds which are works of music are also immutable with respect to the properties normative within them; for they cannot even in this respect be different from how they are.

IX. Applications to Arts other than Music

In developing our theory as to the nature of the artefacts of art we have used music as our principal example. Let us now briefly consider how the theory applies to arts other than music. It will be helpful to begin by highlighting a few matters concerning music, which thus far in our discussion have received only minor attention.

As already remarked, many occurrences of musical works take place by way of someone playing a record of some recording of one of those works' performances. I put a tape in my tape machine, and there in my living room takes place an occurrence of Mahler's *Symphony of a Thousand*. Now even if the performance recorded was wholly correct, still the occurrence produced by my playing of the tape may be an incorrect example of the work—by virtue of some defect in the equipment used along the way, or by virtue of some defect in how someone used the equipment. So the work's requirements for correctness have independent application to that occurrence which takes place in my living room. But they do not serve to guide me in my production of the occurrence. Accordingly, what takes place in my living room is not—by our analysis of *performance* of a work—a performance of Mahler's symphony. What takes place is only a reproduction of a performance, and so only a *playing* of the work.

We also took notice of the fact that it is possible to compose directly onto magnetic tape, thus producing a tape without recording some sound-sequence-occurrence. In such a case, occurrences of the work are brought about by someone's playing the original tape or a copy derived therefrom. What results from so doing is genuinely an occurrence of the work, though not a performance of it. It too is only a *playing* of the work.

Three things are worth noting about this latter sort of case. In the first place the composer, though certainly he selects properties as required for correctness in occurrence, does not *signify* those properties. He does not use symbols to stand for those properties. Still, he does want his work to be available to the public for producing occurrences. So he produces an artefact such that it and copies derived therefrom can be used in the very process of producing occurrences of the work, without at all serving to give *instructions* for producing such occurrences. And if the (corrected) prototype tape or a copy thereof is used properly in the process of producing an occurrence, then a correct occurrence of the work will ensue.

Secondly, the composer need say nothing, or virtually nothing, as to how to use his tape so as to give rise to a correct occurrence of his work. He can simply presuppose properly functioning tape machines, standard ways of operating those machines, and standard settings for those machines; and the only instruction he need give, even tacitly, is this: Use the tape in a properly functioning machine in the standard way. But these very same instructions for proper use of his production-artefact are given no matter what the composition. Thus the instructions are wholly general, wholly non-specific to any particular composition.

Thirdly, not only are the instructions that the composer gives or presupposes for the use of his tape wholly non-specific to his own particular composition. In the 'practice tradition' for tape machines which he presupposes everything has been made routine. Adjustment and feedback are at a minimum. Great knowledge and skill go into the making of tape machines and the making of the tapes. But the knowledge and skill required for properly using a tape is minimal.

Notice how different it is for scored music of the traditional sort. There too the composer presupposes properly functioning instruments of a certain sort; and there too he presupposes a practice tradition for playing those instruments. But playing the instrument in accord with the practice tradition requires enormous amounts of adjustment and feedback on the part of performers. Secondly, the composer must give detailed instructions specific to his own particular composition as to what those skilled in the practice tradition should do with their instruments so as to give rise to a correct occurrence of the work. Lastly, the artefact that the composer produces—his autograph score—is not a production-artefact. It is not actually used to make sounds of the desired sorts. Violins are so used, and violin bows. But not scores.

All these differences are of course the result of the fact that the artefact which the composer of music for tape makes is not a sequence of symbols giving instructions for producing correct occurrences of his work, but rather an artefact to be used in the production process itself— that, plus the fact that tapes and tape machines are such that whatever variations in sound the composer desires can be achieved by using the machine in the standard way and then building the variations into the tapes themselves.

Cinematic works have both interesting similarities to, and interesting differences from, musical works for tape. Here too there can be both correct and incorrect examples—which shows that once again we are dealing with requirements for correctness. But more specifically, cinematic works are like compositions for tape in that associated with the work is an artefact to be used in the production-process itself. All decisions as to properties normative within the work must ultimately be made by reference to what a showing cannot fail to be like when the (corrected) prototype film is properly used. Further, instructions as to proper use of the relevant instruments—projectors—are wholly non-specific to any particular cinematic work. And the use of those instruments in accord with the 'practice tradition' is wholly routine.

What makes cinematic works interestingly different, though, is that characteristically two different people are responsible for the work.

Two different people select requirements for correctness in occurrence. Further, they make their selections in two very different ways. Let us simplify the situation somewhat by treating cinema as if it were purely visual art.

In the typical case, the process of making a cinematic work begins with a *script* produced by a screen writer. The screen writer selects certain properties of illuminated colour-pattern-sequence-occurrences: and in his script he gives instructions to directors for producing a prototype film (i.e., strip of celluloid) such that, when used in the standard way in properly functioning projectors, showings will ensue which exhibit the properties selected. The director is then the one whose task it is actually to produce a film, thereby to bring a cinematic work into existence. There is no cinematic work, but only a project for one, until someone has brought into existence a strip of celluloid of the appropriate sort. Accordingly, the screen writer must be understood as selecting properties that he *would like to see* become normative within some work. His selections have the nature of proposals. In his selection of properties he does not actually compose a work which *has* those properties as normative within it.

The film that the director produces, like the tape in a musical composition for tape, is a production-artefact. In producing this film the director follows, with more or less fidelity, the instructions of the screen writer. But he himself must make a great many selections of properties as required for correctness in showing. It would be impossible for him not to go beyond the instructions of the screen writer in specificity. Where the screen writer specifies certain colours, the director must select specific shades of those colours.

The result of bringing about a work in this fashion is that there are two sets of criteria for correctness of occurrence—one, the proposals of the screen writer, the other, the actual selections of the director. As we have just seen, the selections of the director will necessarily be more detailed than the proposals of the screen writer. Accordingly, if the director faithfully follows the instructions of the screen writer, the set of correctness-requirements proposed by the writer will be a subset of those selected by the director. But of course they may conflict, with the result that a showing of the film is correct, judged by reference to the director's selections, and incorrect, judged by reference to the writer's proposals.

That does not mean, however, that we have two different cinematic works on our hands. The properties normative within a cinematic work are just those which a showing cannot lack if it is produced by using the corrected authorized prototype film in the standard way in a properly functioning projector. And the director is the one who makes, or supervises the making of that film. He is responsible. In making and supervising the making of the film he may faithfully follow the instructions of the screen writer. But even if he does not, the fact that showings of the work do not fit what the writer proposed does not make them incorrect occurrences of the writer's cinematic work. There is no such work. It is the authorized corrected prototype film, coupled with properly functioning projectors and standard ways of using them, that 'fixes' the work. There can indeed be incorrect occurrences of the work. But those will come about by way of using improperly functioning projectors, or running the film through projectors in other than the standard way, or using defective copies of the prototype film.

Quite obviously this implies that a screen writer's script may be used in the production of many distinct works of cinematic art. It may in fact be *faithfully followed* in the production of many distinct cinematic works. To re-shoot a script is not to bring about a distinct production of the same work. It is to produce a distinct work. The difference between cinematic works and dramatic works on this point should be obvious.

We should take note of one other ontologically significant feature of cinematic works. In very many cases the prototype film is made by having actors play roles and then 'shooting'. But what takes place at a given showing of the cinematic work is *not* an instance of role-playing. A showing of a cinematic work consists not of instances of role-playing but rather of an occurrence of a sequence of illuminated colour-patterns (counting black and white as colours). These colour-patterns may be used to *represent* someone, and may be photographically derived from instances of role-playing. But role-playing itself does not occur there in the cinema. Actors function in the compositional process of bringing a cinematic work into existence. But in occurrences of the work they make no appearance. In drama, by contrast, actors have no function in the compositional process of bringing the work into existence. Rather, they are needed for occurrences of the work.

The fact that role-playing may enter into the making of a film but does not enter into its showing makes the showing of cinematic works quite different from the playing of a tape or record of a recording of some musical performance. A performance which is recorded actually *consists* in an occurrence of certain sounds, and one's playing of a tape or record of a recording of some performance *results* in an occurrence of certain sounds.

In graphic art, too, the artist prepares an artefact—his plate—to be used within the process of producing examples. And the properties normative within the work are whatever properties an impression would have if a sheet of the proper sort of paper were pulled in the proper way through a properly inked and properly functioning press in which the artist's plate served as the printing plate. In this case, however, no *copies* of the production-artefact are permissible; that is to say, the plate that the artist produces is not allowed to serve as the prototype for other plates. And what constitutes the proper sort of paper, being pulled in the proper way, and being properly inked, are by no means determined simply by the 'practice tradition' for printing presses. Rather, quite independently of the production of his plate the artist must determine the kind of paper and ink to be used; and in many cases he must determine just how the impressions are to be pulled. Thus the proper use of his plate is highly specific to the work associated with the plate. Further, there is only a moderate amount of routine in the use of his plate so as to produce correct examples. Especially in the inking of the plate there is considerable room for adjustment and feedback— considerable room for skill. It is interesting to note that graphic art in the twentieth century has, if anything, retreated from routine in the production of impressions. There was more routine in the pulling of Dürer's prints than there is in the pulling of William S. Hayter's prints.

In the respects under discussion architectural works are wholly analogous to musical works; so let us not tarry. The artefact that the architect produces—his architectural drawings—is a set of symbols which indicates many at least of the properties required for correctness in examples. Many others are presupposed as known from the practice tradition within which the architect is working. At the same time, the architectural drawings serve as instructions for the production of correct examples.

Drama deserves more consideration; for it confronts us with phenomena different from any we have yet considered. At the heart of drama lies the phenomenon of role-playing. A dramatic work, on its artefactual side, consists of a sequence of role-playings. And a correct example of it consists of an *occurrence* of that sequence. A dramatic work is composed, then, by someone's selecting a certain set of properties as required for correctness in an occurrence of a sequence of role-playing.

408

Normally the selection of such properties is made, or the properties already selected are signified, by the composition of a script which then not only serves to signify the properties selected but also to give instructions to directors and actors.

Unlike cinematic works, the instructions that the script provides are not instructions for the creation of a production-artefact upon the completion of which the work comes into existence. In the field of drama neither authors nor directors create any production-artefact. (An exception, of sorts, will be mentioned shortly.) And in the field of drama the writer of the script has already brought the dramatic work into existence. Nothing more needs doing for that to take place. Rather, the dramatic script gives instructions for the composition of a *production*. Now a production of a dramatic work can itself have many performances. It is, accordingly, itself an occurrence-kind, as is the dramatic work itself. And it is the director who fixes the requirements for something's being a correct occurrence of his production. So in drama, as in cinema, we have two sets of correctness requirements; one, that of the scriptwriter, the other, that of the director. But the selection by the author is not merely the selection of properties that he *proposes* become normative within some work. He selects them in such a way that thereby·he has *composed* a work within which they *are normative*. Likewise, however, the director selects properties as required for correctness. If the actors stray from his requirements in some perform-ance, then his production has been incorrectly performed.

In the case of a dramatic performance, then, we can best view ourselves as dealing with *two* distinct works, each with its own requirements for correctness. One is the dramatic work, composed by the author. The other is the dramatic-production work, composed by the director.

If the director of a dramatic work has not in all respects followed the instructions of the author, then there is conflict between that work and the production work. Something cannot be a correct example of both. Otherwise the production work will be normatively included within the dramatic work. For the production work will always be much more detailed than the dramatic work. The director must settle all sorts of issues which the dramatist leaves open. The road to a correct performance of the production work is more straight and narrow than is the road to a correct performance of the dramatic work. But in any case, a dramatic performance, being an occurrence of two different works, can be judged with respect to correctness by reference to two different sets of criteria: those of the author's dramatic work, and those of the director's production work.

The authors of dramatic works put into their scripts staging instructions, costuming instructions, casting instructions, etc. Yet in most dramatic works, most of the instructions are specifications of what the actors are to *say* in playing the characters. In effect, the words specified constitute production-artefacts. They are to be used in the process of producing an occurrence of the work. Yet a great deal more is required for the correct performance of a dramatic work than just what results directly from directors and actors following the explicit instructions and uttering the specified words. There is all the rest that the actor must do if he is to 'play his character'. This is to be arrive at by a sensitive consideration of what properties a person would have and what actions he would perform if he uttered (outside of role-playing) such words as the ones specified. *Those* are the properties the actor must represent someone a performing. And a correct dramatic performance must have whatever properties are necessary for such representations to occur, as well as for the explicit instructions of the author to be followed.

Literary works remain. What is new here is that the author, in order to indicate his criteria for correctness, neither offers instructions for producing correct examples nor produces an artefact to be used in the production-process. Rather, he produces a prototype example: an actual copy or actual utterance of the work. If the example is to function as a prototype for the production of other examples we must know which of its properties are to function prototypically and which not. The remarkable thing is that normally this is wholly unambiguous. In most cases it takes virtually no sensitivity whatsoever, given the poet's or the novelist's autograph copy, to know how to go about determining whether something is an accurate replica of the copy, and thus, to determine whether something is a correct copy of his work.

X. The Goodman Alternative

To conclude this Part of our discussion I propose to scrutinize the theory of the nature of art works developed by Nelson Goodman in his *Languages of Art*.[23] Between these two theories, his and mine, there is at many points a head-on clash—or certainly what appears on first

[23]Bobbs-Merrill: New York, 1968.

reading to be a head-on clash. Accordingly, a consideration of the Goodman alternative will serve to highlight the significance of various facets of my own theory.

The most obvious and striking point of contrast between my theory and Goodman's arises on the issue of whether a work of music can have an incorrect performance: Goodman holds that it cannot, I have contended that it can. A good way to get into Goodman's theory as a whole will be to follow the trail that leads him to his conclusion.

A thesis around which very much of Goodman's book pivots is stated in these words:

> A score, whether or not ever used as a guide for a performance, has as a primary function the authoritative identification of a work from performance to performance. [24]

What Goodman has in mind by this thesis is spelled out just a few paragraphs later:

> Scores and performances must be so related that in every chain where each step is either from score to compliant performance or from performance to covering score or from one copy of a score to another correct copy of it, all performances belong to the same work and all copies of scores define the same class of performances. Otherwise, the requisite identification of a work from performance to performance would not be guaranteed; we might pass from a performance to another that is not of the same work, or from a score to another that determines a different—even an entirely disjoint—class of performances. Not only must a score uniquely determine the class of performances belonging to the work, but the score (as a class of copies or inscriptions that so define the work) must be uniquely determined, given a performance and the notational system.
>
> This double demand is indeed a strong one. Its motivation and consequences, and the results of weakening it in various ways, need to be carefully considered. We may begin by asking what the properties are that scores, and the notational systems in which scores are written, must have in order to meet this basic requirement. [25]

What Goodman visualizes here is a zig-zag process from performance to score-copy with which the performance complies, to performance

---

[24]Ibid., p. 128.
[25]Ibid., pp. 129–30. See also p. 178.

complying with the score-copy, to score-copy with which the performance complies, etc., with optional sideways moves from one score-copy to another score-copy, this whole ballet being such that in performing it we never move from a performance of one work to a performance of a distinct work. He then asks what works and scores must be like for this ballet to take place. Concerning scores, his conclusion is that they must be *notational*; and he proceeds to explain what he means by that.

In trying to understand just what it is that Goodman has in mind in posing and answering the above question, it is important to realize, as he himself makes clear, that he is not using 'score' in the usual sense. Many things that we would normally call a score do not fit the concept of a score that he is working with; and conversely, many things that do not fit our ordinary concept of a score do fit his. He defines 'a score' as 'a character in a notational system'.[26] He explicitly says that he has 'broadened the application of "score" to embrace characters of the sort described in any notational system, not merely in musical notation'.[27] And on pp. 179–92 he points out many ways in which what we ordinarily call scores do not satisfy his criterion for being a score. Indeed, what can be said is this: a Goodman-score, in music, is just whatever sort of symbol is necessary for guaranteeing identity-preservation in performing the zig-zag ballet. And so in asking what a score must be like if it is to function in the prescribed way in the identity-preserving zig-zag ballet, Goodman is just asking what a symbol must be like thus to function. Though he thinks we have some symbols that do thus function, the defence of that claim is not at all central in Goodman's discussion. At its centre is just the theoretical question: What would symbols have to be like if they were thus to function?

Now for each score there is the class—possibly empty—of those things that comply with the score. Call that, *the compliance-class* of the score. Goodman's doctrine is that if there is a work associated with a given score, that work will be the compliance-class of the score. That, at least, is how he states his doctrine. He also makes clear, though, that in his view there are no classes, and so no works. There are only performances compliant to scores, not classes of performances compliant to scores. Whenever we use a sentence in which we apparently commit ourselves to classes we are, if not just speaking falsely, then describing in a misleading way a reality devoid of classes. Having said this,

[26]Ibid., p. 177.
[27]Ibid.

however, Goodman proceeds to use the 'vulgar' language of classes without doing anything by way of showing us how to speak better. We as his readers have no choice, then, but to take him as holding that works of music are classes. For there is no other theory to be found in Goodman. He proposes no theory of which his 'class language' can be viewed as a convenient, albeit misleading, expression.

Already in section II of this Part we saw, though, that works of music are not classes; and in our own theory we developed the alternative view that they are *kinds*. It may be helpful briefly to recapitulate the considerations we brought againt the class (set) theory of works of art. For one thing, on this view all works which lack performances would be identical with each other. There would be only one such work, because there is only one null-class. Obviously, though, there are *many* unperformed works. Secondly, a work of music can have had more or fewer or different performances than in fact it does have; it does not have its performances essentially. A set, however, has its membership essentially. And thirdly, given that a set exists only when its members exist, there is no such entity as the set of all and only those things which are ever performances of Beethoven's First. At any given time the expression 'the set of all and only those entities which are (presently) performances of Beethoven's First' will pick out a set. But the set it picks out will vary from time to time, depending on the performances which are taking place at that time. Throughout such flux of sets, however, Beethoven's First endures.

To these objections Goodman might of course reply that when he speaks of works of music he is not using the ordinary concept of *work of music* but is simply applying the phrase 'work of music' to a compliance-class of a notational symbol of a certain sort. If that were the case, then to avoid confusion we would have to speak of 'Goodman-works' as well as of 'Goodman-scores'. However, I know of no passage which suggests that Goodman would in fact take this line of response. To do so would make his enterprise even more hypothetical than alredy it is. We would then not have a theory as to the nature of works of art. We would only have a theory as to what compliance-classes must be like and what symbols must be like if identity is to be preserved in performing the zig-zag ballet.

Goodman's reason for refusing to allow that works of music can have incorrect performances is that, if they could, identity-preservation in performing the zig-zag ballet would no longer be guaranteed. Let us see how he argues the case. 'The constitutive properties demanded of a

413

WORKS AND WORLDS OF ART

performance of the symphony are those *prescribed in* the score,' he says.[28] And then he goes on to say that 'a performance, whatever its interpretative fidelity and independent merit, has or has not all the constitutive properties of a given work, and is or is not strictly a performance of that work, according as it does or does not pass this test.'[29] A bit later he says that 'an incorrect performance, though therefore not strictly an instance of a given quartet at all, may nevertheless . . . be better than a correct performance.'[30] And yet later, 'a score must define a work, marking off the performances that belong to the work from those that do not . . . What is required is that all and only performances that comply with the score be performances of the work.'[31]

Suppose that at this point someone replies that Goodman is simply mistaken in the assumption he is making. There can be, and there are, incorrect performances of musical works. If a theory leads to the denial of this fact, why, then so much the worse for the theory. Goodman knows of course that such an objection will be forthcoming. In a footnote to one of the passages quoted above he says:

> Of course, I am not saying that a correct(ly spelled) performance is correct in any of a number of other usual senses. Nevertheless, the composer or musician is likely to protest indignantly at refusal to accept a performance with a few wrong notes as an instance of a work; and he surely has ordinary usage on his side. But ordinary usage here points the way to disaster for the theory (see V, 2).[32]

The later passage to which Goodman alludes in this footnote then runs as follows:

> Since complete compliance with the score is the only requirement for a genuine instance of a work, the most miserable performance without actual mistakes does count as such an instance, while the most brilliant performance with a single wrong note does not. Could we not bring our theoretical vocabulary into better agreement with common practice and common sense by allowing some limited degree of deviation in perform-

[28]Ibid., p. 117.
[29]Ibid., pp. 117–18.
[30]Ibid., pp. 119–20.
[31]Ibid., p. 128.
[32]Ibid., p. 120 n.

ances admitted as instances of a work? The practising musician or composer usually bristles at the idea that a performance with one wrong note is not a performance of the given work at all; and ordinary usage surely sanctions overlooking a few wrong notes. But this is one of those cases where ordinary usage get us quickly into trouble. The innocent-seeming principle that performances differing by just one note are instances of the same work risks the consequence—in view of the transitivity of identity—that all performances whatsoever are of the same work. If we allow the least deviation, all assurance of work-preservation and score-preservation is lost; for by a series of one-note errors of omission, addition, and modification, we can go all the way from Beethoven's *Fifth Symphony* to *Three Blind Mice*. Thus while a score may leave unspecified many features of a performance, and allow for considerable variation in others within prescribed limits, full compliance with the specifications given is categorically required. This is not to say that the exigencies that dictate our technical discourse need govern our everyday speech. I am no more recommending that in ordinary discourse we refuse to say that a pianist who misses a note has performed a Chopin Polonaise than that we refuse to call the whale a fish, the earth spherical, or a grayish-pink human white.

In those concluding lines Goodman seems to be saying that our customary allowance for incorrect performances is false. In ordinary life this falsehood is best overlooked; it is not only innocent but tolerable. There is no point in eradicating it. There may be some point in keeping it. But in theory, not so.

Why is it that Goodman thinks it false that a work can have incorrect performances? Well, keep in mind the law of the transitivity of identity, says Goodman. In general, if $A = B$ and $B = C$, then $A = C$. Now if we allow incorrect performances to count as performances, then starting at any musical work we could, if we performed the zig-zag long enough, arrive at every other work whatsoever (or at least, at a great many others). The conclusion would have to be then that there is just one work. But that is absurd. So we must allow that works cannot have incorrect performances.

What Goodman is assuming here is that if from work A one could arrive by the zig-zag process at work B, then $A = B$; and if from B one could arrive by that process at C, then $B = C$. And then, with that as background, he reminds us of the implications of the law of the transitivity of identity. But is this is indeed the argument, there is something very peculiar about it. Goodman has been asking what

415

scores and works would have to be like if, in the performance of the zig-zag, we were never to move from one work to another. He observes that scores would have to be notational and that works have to be incapable of having incorrect performances. Let us suppose him to be correct on both counts. It doesn't follow that works *in fact* are incapable of having incorrect performances. All that follows is that, if they are capable of having incorrect performances, the zig-zag won't necessarily keep us within the confines of one single work. If one has laid the correct stipulations on what works and scores must be like if, in following the zig-zag, we are never to move from one work to another, then indeed if we follow the zig-zag from A to B and tolerate only the right kinds of works and scores, A will be identical with B. But that scarcely points to some 'disaster for theory' which ensues if we hold that works can have incorrect performances.

So the crucial question becomes this: is there some necessity in being able to perform the zig-zag in identity-preserving fashion? Is there some absurdity which ensues if we are not able to do this—if we don't have the right kinds of scores around and cannot be dislodged from our common-sense conviction that one can perform a work incorrectly? The whole Goodman theory pivots on the answer to this question.

Strangely, it's not clear that Goodman himself thinks there is any absurdity. For he holds that works may antedate scores; and obviously if some extant work lacks a score it lacks a notational score. Further, he holds that our extant scores are not fully notational, and accordingly that they do not satisfy the requirement. We have already heard him make the latter point. Let us look at a passage in which he makes the former.

Where the works are transitory, as in singing and reciting, or require many persons for their production, as in architecture and symphonic music, a notation may be devised in order to transcend the limitations of time and the individual. This involves establishing a distinction between the constitutive and the contingent properties of a work . . . Of course, the notation does not dictate the distinction arbitrarily, but must follow generally—even though it may amend—lines antecedently drawn by the informal classification of performances into works and by practical decisions as to what is prescribed and what is optional . . .

Where there is a theoretically decisive test for determining that an object has all the constitute properties of the work in question without determining how or by whom the object was produced, there is no requisite history of production and hence no forgery or any given work.

Such a test is provided by a suitable notational system with an articulate set of characters and of relative positions for them . . . Authority for a notation ust be found in an antecedent classification of objects or events into works that cuts across, or admits of a legitimate projection that cuts across, classification by history of production; but definitive identification of works, fully freed from history of production, is achieved only when a notation is established.[33]

Goodman's claim, in short, is that identity-preservation in the zig-zag process is necessary if we are to have 'definitive identification of works fully freed from history of production'. He observes that before the advent of scores this condition was not satisfied; he observes that now, after the advent of scores, it is still not fully satisfied. He agrees, however, that in spite of this past and present lack, musical culture goes on—works get composed, get performed, get listened to. In short, the absurdity ensuing when we do not have the equipment for guaranteeing that the zig-zag ballet will be performed in identity-preserving fashion is mild indeed. Goodman has provided us with no reason for changing our views that works can have incorrect examples.

In fact, in his pursuit of a kind of work and a kind of score which will guarantee the preservation of identity in the performance of the zig-zag ballet. Goodman is pursuing a will-o'-the-wisp. There are no musical works which cannot be performed incorrectly. And also there is no hope of definitively recovering score and work from performance. Consider once again our example of the improvisation. And now suppose that we know *exactly* what the performer has in his arsenal of symbols. Suppose further that his symbolism is fully notational. Can we now unambiguously derive from his performance a work and a score for that work? Certainly not. For we do not yet know what in the performance is to be required. Suppose a trill occurs at a certain point, and suppose that the performer has the symbolic equipment for scoring the trill and doing so notationally. Can we then unambiguously derive a work such that a trill belongs at that point to the work? No, we cannot. For the trill may occur in a correct performance of a work in which the trill is optional. Equally, it

[33]Ibid., p. 122. Cf. pp. 196–7.

417

may occur in a correct performance of a work in which it is required for correctness. But those would be distinct works.[34]

[34]One other consequence of Goodman's theory is worth taking note of. He says that 'the verbal language of tempos is not notational. The tempo words cannot be integral parts of a score insofar as the score serves the function of identifying a work from performance to performance. No departure from the indicated tempo disqualifies a performance as an instance—however wretched—of the work defined by the score' (p. 195). I should have thought that this implication of his theory which Goodman with honesty draws out is in fact false, and thus a refutation of the theory.

PART SEVEN

Conception and Perception

Introduction to Part Seven

The notion that composers—so long as they have something new and original to say—suffer from not being understood is a topos of Romantic musical aesthetics as well as journalism, the latter having trivialized the former. What is important is not whether the condemnation of the public is justified but that it is believed. For a century, music lovers were convinced, at least in Germany, that composers suffer from an uncomprehending environment. One was not ashamed of this but viewed the injustice for which one was responsible as a source of inspiration. 'Tragic necessity' was readily at hand to appease one's conscience.

Although public opinion was represented by the audience, the composer remained principally in the right vis-à-vis that audience—a fact the composer could benefit from, even during his lifetime. Judging music became a kind of trial with numerous hearings. Revisions were possible, however, only because musical works could, so to speak, wait. Whereas, in the eighteenth century, music that was not immediately successful had lost its chance once and for all, in the nineteenth century, largely under the impression of the late Beethoven, when it was respected without necessarily being understood, the curious phenomenon arose whereby works that were not comprehended were given additional chances until they finally established themselves.

In the centuries before the Romantic period, if the work did not meet with approval the first time round, it was not necessarily the music, however significant, which fell victim to the Hegelian "fury of disappearance." There were works—above all in church music—whose purpose consisted in nothing other than their sheer existence, without the listeners being called upon to comprehend the compositional structure or decipher any symbolic content. It was sufficient for music to suit the dignity of the occasion through an obvious artificial manner. The ability to fathom a mass by Ockeghem, rather than merely marveling at it, probably counted in the fifteenth century as an effort both superfluous and futile.

Every attempt to describe the relationship between the conception and perception of musical works seems burdened by the difficulty to establish unequivocally which aspects of the conception are supposed to be apprehended in the first place and who determines which features and facts are "aesthetically constitutive." The dispute over Schoenberg's remark that twelve-tone technique is a private matter for the composer which does not concern the public is a case in point for one is neither compelled to take Schoenberg's self-interpretation at face value, nor are the consequences of accepting the remark less problematic.

The opinion about what "actually" constitutes a musical work is informed by the intention of the composer, what Hegel called the "objectified Spirit" of the work, by the empirically verifiable modes of perception, which one accords equal rights, or by a defined socially representative group whose opinion is supposed to count as adequate. Having abandoned the conviction, which was still largely accepted in the nineteenth century, that the composer's intention is the decisive factor, the predicament of a *Rezeptionsästhetik* ensued which sees no way out from the Scylla of empiricism, which leads to intolerable consequences, and the Charybdis of normative thought, which counts as unscholarly. It would appear that one cannot escape the unreasonable demand of resolving the aesthetic identity of a work into innumerable modes of perception without normatively laying down as adequate certain forms of conception and rejecting others as inadequate.

A simple return to the author's intention is not possible. The composer's self-interpretation has not, as a rule, been handed down, moreover, it does not enjoy a privileged position over other explications. The insight, in other words, that the composer's interpretation forms but the material and not the key to an exegesis—can no longer be overlooked. The composer's intention is therefore, in methodological terms, not identical with the "objectified Spirit" of his work—an "objectified Spirit" that does not, of its own accord, reveal itself as it is, but has to be disclosed through interpretation.

If one allows the systematically and historically founded interpretation to count more than the arbitrary perception of an individual, then one is forced to concede at the same time a greater right to reflective analysis than to aesthetic immediacy. The opposition that such a premise provokes is probably the reason why, an irrationalism gradually gained ground (after the idea of a *unio mystica* between the composer and an ideal listener had declined), which concedes equal rights to innumerable modes of perception by diverse listeners. From the fact of difference an unlimited right to differ derived, in which, however, one can detect a relapse of descriptive science into normative thought.

Schenker's theory of structural levels may illustrate the problem. Whether the basic structure, which Schenker reconstructs, corresponds to the intention of the composer is not ascertainable; Schenker's claim can be neither proven nor refuted. Whether the "middle ground" (not to mention the "background") is fictitious or real as a norm of perception cannot be decided, since one can learn to listen following Schenker, without being certain that one should. The only remaining criterion consists, it seems, in the classicistic maxim that the quality of an interpretation rests on the extent to which it reveals a growing differentiation together with an ever tighter integration of the component parts of a work. It cannot be denied that Schenker's analyses fulfill this criterion to a high degree. However, the scope of the criterion is limited in that it proves to be classicistic and not applicable to manneristic conditions. It would seem that whoever analyzes, judges and apprehends Schoenberg's *Klavierstück* op. 11 no. 3 according to the model of differentiation and integration is off the mark and misses the significance of the eruptive expressivity manifested in that movement.

GOTTFRIED WILHELM LEIBNIZ

Alongside Descartes, Spinoza, Pascal, Newton and Lock, *Gottfried Wilhelm Leibniz* (b. Leipzig 1646, d. Hanover, 1716) is considered— on account of his contributions to mathematics and physics and, altogether, his original philosophical thought—as one of the central figures of his age. Born to a Protestant family, Leibniz began his studies, at the age of 15, in the faculty of law at the university of Leipzig (where his father served as professor before his early death, in 1652).

Already as a student, he attempted to reconcile the prevailing scholastic disciplines and Cartesian philosophy with the Platonic tradition. Like his teacher Erhard Weigel—through whom he became acquainted with Pythagorean and Platonic thought—he, too, wished to reform the various educational systems, turning his back on the academic establishment. In the face of increasing political unrest and drastic changes in traditional ways of thought, Leibniz felt called upon to contribute not only towards a unification of theoretical thinking with practical science, but to the reconciliation between emperors and kings, and the settlement of contradictions in the world of theology as well. His endless projects and enormous correspondence were driven by the fundamental urge to change Europe into a universal community, more just and enlightened, a "city of God" on earth.

Like his contemporaries, Leibniz sought the unification of theoretical thinking with practical science through mathematics. However, "enchanted" by mathematics, as by the music of the Sirens (as he himself admits), Leibniz was among the few who still tried to reveal the essence of existence in a Pythagorean way, by means of numbers. In opposition to Kepler, whose ultimate goal was to reveal the old ties between "chords" and "planets" scientifically, the point of departure for Leibniz was the world as a whole, which by means of those same Pythagorean and Platonic ideas, was musicalized through and through during the Christian millenium. To this harmony, this "Reimung der Dichtung," which was "pre-established" by God, he tried to find a mathematical equivalent. An "infinite calculus," which, if perfected, he believed, could approximate the real design, synchronic and diachronic, of the universal *plenum*. This infinite calculus became, at the same time, an indispensable tool for Leibniz himself, trying, as he did, to bridge between "necessary truths," which are analyzable to their simplest concept, and "contingent truths," known through experience and acquaintance. While "necessary truths" provide the basic for many possible worlds, God chose and realized the best of them, that which could contain together the highest number of "truths." The transition from God as infinite to a world in which everything is finite but unique, he tried to express via a new numerical system: the dyadic system which entails two abstract components—"One" and "Zero." Leibniz does not accept the traditional identification of the "Zero" with "nihilum," instead, he sees the "Zero" as the "confining factor" for every real number. Since the abstract component of "One" becomes, by contrast, "zeroless," the "Oneness" of God is endowed, thereby, with new symbolic significance. Indeed, the different combinations of the binaric pair become, for Leibniz, a more accurate expression for the unification of manifold substances into unique and independent wholes—the ideal monads. Thus a monad—Leibniz's transfiguration of Giordano Bruno's, among others, "individuation"—while striving towards self-realization is, at one and the same time, disconnected from all else and representing everything: disconnected as an effective agent—as dictated by Leibniz's deterministic premises; representing everything—as implied by pre-established "harmonization." The degree of the clarity of the representation of the monad depends on its own perceptive capacity, which though it can be increased, is (except for God) forever limited. Thus man can grasp only partial truths, experiencing the "evil" as an unsolved dissonance, which from God's point of view, enforces the beauty of the whole. Indeed, patience as well as tolerance is part and parcel of Leibniz's system as evidenced in his

426

enlightened treatment of Chinese philosophy and religion. In line with the above, Leibniz sought further perfection for his own system endeavouring to comprehend from the system the many trends of thought which he encountered, using "the best of all possible worlds," as it were, for his model.

The immediate implications of Leibniz's ideas to the arts were fully developed by Baumgarten (See Baumgarten, Introduction and Notes). While the idea of "possible worlds" was applied to the different realms of science and art, the idea of the "monad" served, in music, as a model not only for the initial nucleus of a composition, but also for its potentialities and ultimate realization as an organic whole. These and other related ideas provided, in all likelihood, the intellectual undercurrents for the cultural circle in which Bach was an honorable member, contributing, as they did, to contrapunctal cohesiveness. On the other hand, Leibniz's overall "harmonic" conception lent philosophical support to a music theory (Rameau) which took account of both transformations and interrelationships as part of a "Oneness" enabling "possible worlds." As for Leibniz's famous statement (in a letter to Christoph Goldbach) concerning music as "the hidden arithmetical exercise of a mind, unconscious that it is calculating," though it reflects Leibniz's adherence to an older theory of perception, it suggests something new. Rejecting spirit-theories, á la Ficino, as unscientific, and unwilling to endorse Cartesian skepticism, he maintained that the compatibility and coherence of our perceptions is anchored in a "pre-established harmony" between body and soul, i.e. between mind and the senses. The interaction, Leibniz argues, though it has many forms and levels, constitutes the very process leading to unification. Starting with basic perceptions and ending up with the most abstract conceptions, this process, this "vis activa"* enables us, at the same time, to differentiate between external and internal, between the world and ourselves as conscious beings. In our basic perception, we can indeed isolate the sensational components from their "extension" and "expansion", i.e. our organization of them in time and space. Acknowledging the sensual traces in our most abstract intellectual activities contributes, in fact, to an awareness with regard to the symbolic nature of our thinking.

*See above, in the editors' notes to Baumgarten, where this term of Leibniz appears in the French—"La puissance active."

Leibniz's new outlook is also reflected in his attempt to build a universal language—a project highly favored in his days. While his contemporaries hoped to facilitate communication, Leibniz wished to advance and encourage thought and creativity. By using the dyadic numbers as basic units, he hoped to not only to guarantee logical reasoning and the separation of distinct concepts but to make room for new and unpredicted relationships between them. Since a system securing unambiguity, economy and the possibility for interrelationships was his ultimate goal, no wonder he tried to actually mate it with music proper (see his "Lingua generalis," 1678). This "intuition" of Leibniz is not too far removed from Nelson Goodman's "notational system," though his attempt to invest music with a semantic other than its own contradicts his initial premise. Moreoever, expecting his "music" to evolve into "beautiful and moving songs" stands in contradiction to music's inability to be possessed, at one and the same time, by more than a single meaning. Leibniz also seems to ignore stylistic processes whereby affective contents are created. Nonetheless, Leibniz's ideas concerning perception and knowledge provide the base for the understanding of stylistic processes in cognitive terms. The latter contributed toward a new awareness of the "powers" of music.

from Leibniz Philosophical Papers[1]

On Wisdom

Wisdom is merely the science of happiness or that science which teaches us to achieve happiness.

Happiness is a state of permanent joy. The happy man does not, it is true, feel this joy at every instant, for he sometimes rests from his contemplation, and usually also turns his thoughts to practical affairs. But it is enough that he is in a *state* to feel joy whenever he wishes to think of it and that at other times there is a joyousness in his actions and his nature which arises from this.

Present joy does not make happy if it has no *permanence*; indeed, he is rather unhappy who falls into a long wretchedness for the sake of a brief joy.

Joy is a pleasure which the soul feels in itself. *Pleasure* is the feeling of a perfection or an excellence, whether in ourselves or in something else. For the perfection of other beings also is agreeable, such as understanding, courage, and especially beauty in another human being, or in an animal or even in a lifeless creation, a painting or a work of craftsmanship, as well. For the image of such perfection in others, impressed upon us, causes some of this perfection to be implanted and aroused within ourselves. Thus there is no doubt that he who consorts much with excellent people or things becomes himself more excellent.

Although the perfections of others sometimes displease us—as for example, the understanding or the courage of any enemy, the beauty of a rival, or the luster of another's virtue which overshadows or shames us—this is not because of the perfection itself but because of the circumstance which make it inopportune for us, so that the sweetness of our first perception of this perfection in someone else is exceeded and spoiled by the consequent bitterness of our afterthoughts.

We do not always observe wherein the perfection of pleasing things consists, or what kind of perfection within ourselves they serve, yet our feelings [*Gemüth*] perceive it, even though our understanding does not. We commonly say, 'There is something, I know not what, that pleases

---

[1]Text: *Leibniz Philosophical Papers*, tr. and ed. Leroy E. Loemker (Chicago: University of Chicago Press, 1956) pp. 697–700; 793–798; 873–878; 888–898; 1041–1042; 1053–1055; 1059–1060. The numbered notes are Loemker's notes.

me in the matter.' This we call 'sympathy'. But those who seek the causes of things will usually find a ground for this and understand that there is something at the bottom of the matter which, though unnoticed, really appeals to us.

Music is a beautiful example of this. Everything that emits a sound contains a vibration or transverse motion such as we see in strings; thus everything that emits sounds gives off invisible impulses. When these are not confused,but proceed together in order but with a certain variation, they are pleasing; in the same way, we also notice certain changes from long to short syllables, and a coincidence of rhymes in poetry, which contain a silent music, as it were, and when correctly constructed are pleasant even without being sung. Drum beats, the beat and cadence of the dance, and other motions of this kind in measure and rule derive their pleasurableness from their order, for all order is an aid to the emotions. And a regular though invisible order is found also in the artfully created beats and motions of vibrating strings, pipes, bells, and indeed, even of the air itself, which these bring into uniform motion. Through our hearing, this creates a sympathetic echo in us, to which our animal spirits respond. This is why music is so well adapted to move our minds, even though this main purpose is not usually sufficiently noticed or sought after.

There can be no doubt that even in touch, taste, and smell, sweetness consists in a definite though insensible order and perfection or a fitness, which nature has put there to stimulate us and the animals to that which is otherwise needed, so that the right use of all pleasurable things is really brought about in us, even though these things may give rise to a far greater harm through abuse and intemperance.

I call any elevation of being a *perfection*. Just as illness is a debasement, as it were, and a decline from health, so perfection is something which rises above health. But health itself stands balanced in the middle and lays the foundation for perfection. Now illness comes from an injury to action, as medical men rightly observe. Just so perfection shows itself in great freedom and power of action, since all being consists in a kind of power; and the greater the power, the higher and freer the being.

The greater any power is, moreover, the more there is found in it the many revealed through the one and in the one, in that the one rules many outside of itself and represents them in itself. Now unity in plurality is nothing but harmony [*Übereinstimmung*], and since any particular

430

being agrees with one rather than another being, there flows from this harmony the order from which beauty arises, and beauty awakens love.

Thus we see that happiness, pleasure, love, perfection, being, power, freedom, harmony, order, and beauty are all tied to each other, a truth which is rightly perceived by few.

Now when the soul feels within itself a great harmony, order, freedom, power, or perfection, and hence feels pleasure in this, the result is joy, as these explanations show. Such joy is permanent and cannot deceive, nor can it cause a future unhappiness if it arises from knowledge and is accompanied by a light which kindles an inclination to the good in the will, that is, virtue. But when pleasure and joy are directed toward satisfying the senses rather than the understanding, they can as easily lead us to unhappiness as to bliss, just as a food which tastes good can be unwholesome. So the enjoyment of the senses must be used according to the rules of reason, like a food, medicine, or exercise. But the pleasure which the soul finds in itself through understanding is a present joy such as can conserve our joy for the future as well.

It follows from this that nothing serves our happiness better than the illumination of our understanding and the exercise of our will to act always according to our understanding, and that this illumination is to be sought especially in the knowledge of such things as can bring our understanding ever further into a higher light. For there springs from such knowledge an enduring progress in wisdom and virtue, and therefore also in perfection and joy, the advantage of which remains with the soul even after this life.

A separate discussion would be needed to show what the things are whose knowledge causes so happy a progress. Meanwhile we can say that no one can rise more easily to a higher stage of happiness than can persons of rank, yet that no one finds it more difficult than they actually to achieve this happiness, as Christ himself tells us. The reason is that though they have the power to do much good, they rarely put their minds to it. For having opportunities constantly for sensual indulgence, they grow used to seeking their joys mostly in the pleasures which come from the body. And even when they rise higher, they seek praise and honor from others more than a true satisfaction within themselves. Hence their self-deceit ends when the pleasures of the body are destroyed by illness, and their glory by misfortunes, and they find that they are unhappy. From their youth they have followed the drive of external things for the sake of the pleasure which they found in it, and especially because it is hard, at first, to resist this stream. Thus they have for the most part lost their freedom of mind.

It is a great thing, therefore, when a person of rank can enjoy himself even in illness, misfortune, and disgrace,[2] especially if he can find contentment, not out of necessity because he sees that things must be as they are (this is no more comfort than that of taking a sleeping potion to escape feeling pain), but out of the awakening within himself of a great joy which overcomes these pains and misfortunes.

Such joy, which a person can always create for himself when his mind is well ordered, consists in the perception of pleasure in himself and in the powers of his mind, when a man feels within himself a strong inclination and readiness for the good and the true, and particularly through the profound knowledge which an enlightened understanding provides for us, namely, that we experience the chief source, the course, and the purpose of everything, and the incomprehensible excellence of that Supreme Nature which comprises all things within it. Thus we are lifted above the unknowing, just as if we were looking down from the stars and could see all earthly things under our feet. Then at last we learn that we have reason to find the highest joy in all things that have happened and are yet to happen, but that we must also seek, as far as is in our power, to direct what has not yet happened for the best. For it is one of the eternal laws of nature that we shall enjoy the perfection of things and the pleasure which results from it, only in the measure of our knowledge, our good will, and our contribution to this perfection.

When a person of rank attains this and finds his joy in the actions of his understanding and his virtue, even in the midst of all abundance and honor, I consider him doubly exalted. He is exalted unto himself because of this, his happiness and true joy; he is exalted before others because it is entirely certain that such a person can and will share his light and virtue with many others because of his power and reputation, since such sharing will reflect glory upon himself and so give new light to all those who have the same common purpose of helping each other in

---

[2]Family disasters were striking at the court of Hanover in the early nineties: the deaths of the Princes Frederick August and Karl Philip in battle in 1690; the abortive attempt of Maximilian, the youngest son of Ernest August, to break the newly established law of primogeniture, which failed in 1691; and the notorious Königsmark incident leading to the divorce of George Louis, later George I, king of England, and to the exile of his wife Dorothea, in 1694.

the search for truth, the knowledge of nature, the multiplication of human powers, and the advancement of the common good.

The great happiness of persons who are both exalted in rank and enlightenment as well is therefore apparent, because they can do as much for their happiness as if they had a thousand hands and a thousand lives—indeed, as if they lived a thousand times as long as they do. For only so much of our life is to be valued as truly living as the good we do in it. One who does much good in a short time is thus equal to one who lives a thousand times as long. This is the case with those who can make thousands upon thousands of hands work with them, so that more good can be brought about in a few years, to their supreme glory and enjoyment, than could otherwise be achieved in many hundreds of years.

The beauty of nature is so great, its contemplation is so sweet, and the light and good inclination which arise from these bring such glorious fruitage even in this life that he who has tasted them considers all other delights small by contrast. But when we add that the soul does not perish but that every perfection within her must be preserved to bring forth fruit, then it can be seen in full how the true happiness which arises from wisdom and virtue is incomparably and immeasurably high above all that we may imagine about it.

from On the Radical Organization of Things

. . . And we do in fact observe that everything in the world takes place in accordance with the laws of the eternal truths and not merely geometric but also metaphysical laws; that is, not merely according to material necessities but also according to formal reasons. And not only is this true in general, on the principle which we have just explained—that there should exist a world rather than none and that this world should exist rather than another. (This may be learned in any case from the tendency of possibles toward existence.) But it is true also when we descend to special cases and see the wonderful way in which metaphysical laws of cause, power, and action are present throughout all nature, and how they predominate over the purely geometric laws of matter themselves, as I found to my great admiration when I was explaining the laws of motion. As I have fully explained elsewhere, I was at length compelled to give up the law of the geometric composition of conatuses which I had formerly defended when, as a youth, I was more materialistic.[3]

We therefore have the ultimate reason for the reality of essences as well as existences in one being, which must necessarily be greater, higher, and prior to the world itself, since not only the existing things which compose the world but also all possibilities have their reality through it. But because of the interconnection of all these things, this ultimate reason can be found only in a single source. It is evident, however, that existing things are continuously issuing from this source and are being produced and have been produced by it, since no reason appears why one state of the world should issue from it rather than another, that of yesterday rather than today's. It is clear, too, how God acts not merely physically but freely as well, and how there is in him not only the efficient but the final cause of the world. Thus we have in him the reason not merely for the greatness and power in the world mechanism as already established, but also for the goodness and wisdom exerted in establishing it.

In case anyone may think that this confuses moral perfection or goodness with metaphysical perfection or greatness, and may deny the former while granting the latter, it must be recognized that it follows from what has been said that the world is not only the most perfect naturally or if you prefer, metaphysically—in other words, that that series of things has been produced which actually presents the greatest amount of reality—but also that it is the most perfect morally, because moral perfection is truly natural[4] in minds themselves. Hence the world not only is the most wonderful mechanism but is also, insofar as it consists of minds, the best commonwealth, through which there is conferred on minds as much felicity or joy as possible; it is in this that their natural perfection consists.

You may object, however, that we experience the very opposite of this in the world, for often the very worst things happen to the best; innocent beings, not only beasts but men, are struck down and killed, even tortured. In fact, especially if we consider the government of

---

[3]The allusion is to the *Theory of Abstract Motion* (1671) (No. 8). Leibniz explains his change of opinion in detail in *Specimen Dynamicum*, Part I.

[4]*Physica*. The extension of nature to include human purposes and actions is characteristic of much of Leibniz's writing.

mankind, the world seems rather a kind of confused chaos than something ordained by a supreme wisdom. So it seems at first sight, I admit, but when we look more deeply, the opposite can be established. A priori it is obvious from the principles which I have already given that the highest perfection possible is obtained for all things and therefore also for minds.

And as the jurisconsults say, it is truly unjust to render a judgment without having studied the whole law. We know but a very small part of an eternity stretching out beyond all measure. How tiny is the memory of the few thousand years which history imparts to us! Yet from such slight experience we venture to judge about the immeasurable and the eternal; as if men born and reared in prison or in the underground salt mines of Sarmatia should think that there is no other light in the world but the wretched torch which is scarcely sufficient to guide their steps. If we look at a very beautiful picture but cover up all of it but a tiny spot, what more will appear in it, no matter how closely we study it, indeed, all the more, the more closely we examine it, then a confused mixture of colors without beauty and without art. Yet when the covering is removed and the whole painting is viewed from a position that suits it, we come to understand that what seemed to be a thoughtless smear on the canvas has really been done with the highest artistry by the creator of the work. And what the eyes experience in painting is experienced by the ears in music. Great composers very often mix dissonances with harmonious chords to stimulate the hearer and to sting him, as it were, so that he becomes concerned about the outcome and is all the more pleased when everything is restored to order. Similarly we may enjoy trivial dangers or the experience of evils from the very sense they give us of our own power or our happiness or our fondness for display. Or again, in witnessing performances of rope-dancing or sword-dancing [*sauts périlleux*], we are delighted by the very fears they arouse, and we playfully half-drop children, pretending to be about to throw them away for much the same reason that the ape carried King Christian of Denmark, when he was still a baby dressed in long clothes, to a rooftop and then, while everyone waited in terror, returned him, as if in play, to his cradle. By the same principle it is insipid always to eat sweets; sharp, sour, and even bitter things should be mixed with them to excite the taste. He who has not tasted the bitter does not deserve the sweet; indeed, he will not appreciate it. This is the very law of enjoyment, that pleasure does not run an even course, for this produces aversion and makes us dull, not joyful.

435

But what I have said about a part being disordered without destroying the harmony in the whole must not be interpreted as if there is no reason for the parts or as if it were enough for the world to be perfect as a whole, even though the human race should be wretched and there should be no concern in the universe for justice and no account taken of us, as is held by some people who have not made sound judgments about the totality of things. For we must recognize that just as care is taken in the best-ordered republic that individuals shall fare as well as possible, so the universe would not be perfect enough unless as much care is shown for individuals as is consistent with the universal harmony. No better measure for this matter can be set up that the law of justice itself, which dictates that each one shall take part in the perfection of the universe and his own happiness according to the measure of his own virtue and the degree to which his will is moved toward the common good. And in this very thing is fulfilled what we call the charity and the love of God, in which alone the force and power of the Christian religion also consist, according to the opinion of wise theologians. Nor should it seem remarkable that so much respect should be shown to minds in the universe, since they resemble most closely the image of the supreme Author and are related to him not merely as machines to their maker—as are other beings—but also as citizens to their prince. Moreover, they are to endure as long as the universe itself and in some way to express the whole and concentrate it in themselves, so that it can be said that minds are total-parts.

As for the afflictions, especially of good men, however, we must take it as certain that these lead to their greater good and this this is true not only theologically but also naturally. So a seed sown in the earth suffers before it bears fruit. In general, one may say that though afflictions are temporary evils, they are good in effect, for they are short cuts to greater perfection. So in physics the liquids which ferment slowly also are slower to settle, while those in which there is a stronger disturbance settle more promptly, throwing off impurities with greater force. We may well call this stepping back in order to spring forward with greater force [qu'on recule pour mieux sauter]. These views must therefore be affirmed not merely as gratifying and comforting but also as most true. And in general, I hold that there is nothing truer than happiness and nothing happier and sweeter than truth.

As the crown of the universal beauty and perfection of the works of God, we must also recognize that the entire universe is involved in a perpetual and most free progress, so that it is always advancing toward

436

greater culture. Thus a great part of our earth has now received cultivation and will receive it more and more. And though it is true that some sections occasionally revert into wilderness or are destroyed and sink back again, this must be understood in the same sense in which I have just explained the nature of afflictions, namely, that this very destruction and decline lead to a better result, so that we somehow gain through our very loss.

To the objection which could be offered, moreover, that if this were so, the world should long since have become a paradise, there is an answer near at hand. Although many substances have already attained great perfection, yet because of the infinite divisibility of the continuum, there always remain in the abyss of things parts which are still asleep. These are to be aroused and developed into something greater and better and in a word, to a better culture. And hence progress never comes to an end.

from Correspondence with De Volder

IX
[G., II, 268–71]

Hanover, June 30, 1704

... You continue by saying, "Nevertheless (your argument) does not convince me that a mathematical body has no reality, unless perhaps there is some ambiguity in the word 'reality'. For I conceive of the innumerable properties of such a body with the greatest evidence." To this I reply in two ways. First, it is a necessary inference from my principles that a mathematical body is not real and second, the arguments you urge, for saying that you conceive a body most clearly (as real), do not establish its reality.

As for the first point, it follows from the very fact that a mathematical body cannot be analyzed into primary constituents that it is also not real but something mental and designates nothing but the possibility of parts, not something actual. A mathematical line, namely, is in this respect like arithmetical unity; in both cases the parts are only possible and completely indefinite. A line is no more the aggregate of the lines into which it can be cut than unity is the aggregate of the fractions into which it can be split up. And, as in counting, the number is not a

437

substance without the things counted, so neither is a mathematical body or extension without active and passive entities or motion. But in real things, that is, bodies, the parts are not indefinite—as they are in space, which is a mental thing—but actually specified in a fixed way according to the divisions and subdivisions which nature actually introduces through the varieties of motion. And granted that these divisions proceed to infinity, they are nonetheless all the results of fixed primary constituents or real unities, though infinite in number. Accurately speaking, however, matter is not composed of these constitutive unities but results from them, since matter or extended mass is nothing but a phenomenon grounded in things, like the rainbow or the mock-sun, and all reality belongs only to unities. Phenomena can therefore always be divided into lesser phenomena which could be observed by other, more subtle, animals and we can never arrive at smallest phenomena.[5] Substantial unities are not parts but foundations of phenomena.

I come now to the ground of your objection, esteemed Sir. "I conceive with greatest evidence", you say, "the innumerable properties of a mathematical body." I grant this, in the same sense, that is, in which the properties of number and time are conceived, concepts which are also only orders or relations pertaining to possibility and to the eternal truths of the world, and are then further applicable to actual events. But you add, "I conceive of a mathematical body as existing and inhering in nothing else." This I do not admit, unless we also conceive of time as existing or inhering in nothing. If you regard this mathematical body as *space*, it must be correlated with *time*; if as *extension*, it must be correlated with *duration*. For *space* is nothing but the order of existence of things possible at the same time, while *time* is the order of existence of things possible successively. As a physical body is to space, so the status or series of things is to time. The body and the series of things add to space and time, motion or action and passion, and the principle of motion.[6] For as I have repeatedly reminded you—though you seem to have neglected my reminders—extension is an abstraction from the extended and can no more be considered substance than can number or a multitude, for it expresses nothing but a certain nonsuccessive (i.e.,

---

[5] Here and elsewhere Leibniz has anticipated the criticisms of Berkeley and other empiricists who seek to limit analysis by *minima sensibilia*; for any empirical problem in which we must pass over into causal analysis, analysis is an endless task.

[6] That is, primitive force and its several modes, active and passive.

unlike duration) but simultaneous diffusion or repetition of some particular nature, or what amounts to the same thing, a multitude of things of this same nature which exist together with some order between them; and it is this nature, I say, which is said to be extended or diffused. The notion of extension is thus relative, or extension is the extension of something, just as we say that a multitude or a duration is a multitude, or a duration, of something. But this nature which is said to be diffused, repeated, and continued is that which constitutes a physical body, and it can be found in no other principle but that of acting and enduring, since no other principle is suggested to us by the phenomena. But of what kind this action and passion are, I shall say later. So you see that once we being an analysis of concepts, we always arrive at last at the view which I am urging. It is really not surprising that the Cartesians have failed to understand the nature of corporeal substance and to arrive at true principles, since they consider extension as something absolute, irresolvable, ineffable, or primitive. For trusting their sense perceptions, and perhaps also seeking the applause of men, they were content to stop where their sense perception stopped, even though they also boasted, elsewhere, that they had distinguished sharply between the sensible and the intelligible realms.

"By forces", you say, "I have always meant something nonsubstantial but inhering in substance." And rightly so, if you mean mutable forces. But when force is taken to be the principle of action and passion, which is thus modified by derivative forces or by what is momentary in action, you can understand enough from what I have said that this is involved in the concept of extension itself, which is relative per se, and that by your own analysis of corporeal substance, we must come to this conclusion. This is even more clear, as was shown above, when we consider the analysis of aggregates and of the phenomena in unities and reality.

You add, "I have always considered forces, viewed apart from the foundations from which they spring, as being in the nature of an external denomination." I should prefer to consider derivative forces in relation to their *foundations*, as a figure in relation to extension, that is, as a modification. And you know from my calculus, in which I have demonstrated the true measure of derivative forces a priori, that force multiplied by the time through which it acts equals action and that force is therefore the momentous factor in action but with a relation to the following state. I have often said—and do not remember ever to have deviated from this position—that unless there were some primary active principle in us, there could be no derivative forces and actions in

439

us, since everything accidental or changeable must be a modification of something essential or perpetual and can contain nothing more positive than that which it modifies, since every modification is only a limitation—a figure of that which is varied and a derivative force of that which varies.

You continue, "This foundation which was to be in the thing may perhaps be the same as what you call primitive forces, from which the derivative forces flow." I believe that this is most true, and so it appears that we are agreed on this point.

You add, "But I perceive nothing of these—so feeble is the force of my understanding—except that you assert that all the remaining mutations flow from them." But you do yourself an injury through your excessive modesty, for you understand the matter as far as its nature allows. Would you seek to sense things which can only be understood, to see sounds, to hear colors? You do not in fact disagree with what I have asserted—that mutations flow from them; do you regard it as nothing to know this?

It is important, however, also to consider that this principle of action is most intelligible, because there is something in it analogous to what is in us, namely, perception and appetite. For the nature of things is uniform, and our nature cannot differ infinitely from the other simple substances of which the whole universe consists. Indeed, considering the matter carefully, it may be said that there is nothing in the world except simple substances and, in them, perception and appetite. Matter and motion, however, are not so much substances or things as they are the phenomena of percipient beings, whose reality is located in the harmony of the percipient with himself (at different times) and with other percipient beings.

When Descartes and others say that "there is one substance for all corporeal beings", they mean one similar nature, and do not, I think, intend that all bodies together make one substance. Surely the fact itself shows the world to be an aggregate, like a herd or a machine.

I had said that temporal events follow from particular things. You say that you do not object to this but that it remains to be explained how particulars differ from universals and why temporal events follow from the former and not from the latter. But if I am not mistaken, an essential order of particulars corresponds to the definite parts of time and space, and universals are abstracted from these particulars by the mind.

Last of all, you add, "Particulars act upon each other and are thus subject to change with respect to actions. How this can be explained by substances which do not act upon each other is obscure to me." This seems to be aimed at my opinion about the pre-established harmony between simple substances, which cannot act upon each other. Yet they do produce a change in themselves, and it is necessary for this to happen from your own point of view as well. For you acknowledged above that there is an internal basis for forces or actions, and so we must recognize an internal principle of change. And unless we do, there will be no natural principle of change at all and therefore no natural change. For if the principle of change were external to all and internal to none, there would be none at all, and we should have to turn back with the occasionalists to God as the only agent. It is therefore truly internal to all simple substances, since there is no reason why it should be in one rather than in another, and it consists in the progress of the perceptions of each monad, the entire nature of things containing nothing besides. You see how simple the matter becomes when we have arrived at principles which are manifestly necessary and sufficient, so that it seems not only superfluous but inconsistent and without explanation to add anything further. To go beyond these principles and ask why there is perception and appetite in simple substances is to inquire about something ultramundane, so to speak, and to demand reasons of God why he has willed things to be such as we conceive them to be.

I have been compelled to be more verbose in my answers in order to begin the reasoning by which I establish each point with a repetition of your own words. For I have noted earlier, when we wrote more freely, we almost forgot what had gone before in the progression of the argument and sometimes turned in circles or digressed to other matters, which is sometimes an unintentional sign of impatience. For the rest, our esteemed common friend, John Bernoulli, has written that your health is not of the best; he himself has scarcely recovered from a serious illness. This is a great grief to me, who owe much to your thoughts and expect much fruitage still from them. So I think that you have need fo gaiety, activity, and in brief, a kind of diet adapted to the body; such a diet is the true medicine for chronic illnesses and irregularities, though we often neglect it when pulled away by custom and business.

from On What Is Independent of Sense and of Matter (Letter to Queen Sophia Charlotte of Prussia)

[G., VI, 499–508]

I found the letter truly ingenious and beautiful which was sent some time ago from Paris to Osnabrück, and which I recently read by your order at Hanover. Since it deals with two important questions on which I admit I do not entirely share the opinion of its author—whether there is something in our thoughts which does not come from sense and whether there is something in nature which is not material—I wish I were able to explain myself with the same charm as his, in order to obey Your Majesty's orders and satisfy Your Majesty's curiosity.

To use the analogy of an ancient writer, we use the external senses as a blind man uses his stick, and they help us to know their particular objects, which are colors, sounds, odors, tastes, and tactual qualities. But they do not help us to know what these sensible qualities are or in what they consist. For example, if red is the whirling of certain small globes which, it is claimed, make light; if heat is an eddy of very fine dust; if sound is made in the air as are circles in the water when a stone is thrown in, as some philosophers hold, we at least do not see this, and we cannot even understand how this whirling, these eddies and circles, if they are real, should bring about just the particular perceptions which we have of red, of heat, and of noise. So it can be said that *sensible qualities* are in fact *occult qualities* and that there must be others *more manifest* which could render them understandable. Far from understanding sensible things only, it is just these which we understand the least. And even though we are familiar with them, we do not understand them the better for that, just as a pilot does not understand the nature of the magnetic needle, which turns to the north, better than other men, although he has it constantly before his eyes in the compass, and as a result scarcely even has any more curiosity about it.

I do not deny that many discoveries have been made about the nature of these occult qualities. So, for example, we know what kind of refraction produces blue and yellow and how these two colors mixed produce green. But we still cannot understand as a result how the perception we have of these three colors follows from these causes. Also, we do not have even nominal definitions of such qualities, in order to explain the terms. The purpose of nominal definitions is to give marks sufficient to aid in recognizing things. For example, assayers have marks by which they distinguish gold from all other metals, and even if a man has never even seen gold, these marks could be taught him so that he could recognize it unmistakably should he some day encounter it. But this is not the case with these sensible qualities; no mark for recognizing blue, for example, can be given to one who has never seen it. Thus blue is itself its own mark, and in order that a man may know what blue is, one must of necessity show it to him.

For this reason it is usually said that the *concepts* of these qualities are *clear*, since they serve us in recognizing them, but that these same concepts are not *distinct*, because we cannot distinguish or develop the content included in them. It is an 'I know not what' which we perceive but for which we cannot account. On the other hand, we can make someone else understand what a thing is if we have some kind of description or nominal definition, even though we do not have the thing at hand to show him. We must do justice to the senses, however, by recognizing that besides these occult qualities, they enable us to know other qualities which are more manifest and furnish more distinct concepts. It is these which are ascribed to the *common sense*, because there is no external sense to which they are particularly attached and belong.[7] If is of these that definitions of the terms or words we use can be given. Such is the idea of *numbers*, which is found alike in sounds, colors, and the qualities of touch. It is thus, too, that we perceive the *figures* which are common to colors and to qualities of touch but which we do not observe in sounds. But it is true that in order to conceive numbers and even shapes distinctly and to build sciences from them, we must reach something which sense cannot furnish but which the understanding adds to it.[8]

Since therefore our soul compares the numbers and the shapes of colors, for example, with the numbers and shapes discovered by touch, there must be an *internal sense* where the perceptions of these different external senses are found united. This is called the *imagination*, which

[7]For Leibniz's interpretation of Aristotle's doctrine of the common sense as the "mind itself" in reply to Locke see his *New Essays on Human Understanding*, II. 5.
[8]The selection of number and figures as examples is significant, since Leibniz used them from the beginning as fundamental categories, subforms of quantity and quality, upon which to base and to extend mathematics, particularly geometry and the art of combinations see his *Dissertation on the Art of Combination*.

443

comprises at once the *concepts of particular senses*, which are *clear* but *confused*, and the *concepts of the common sense*, which are clear and distinct.[9] And these clear and distinct ideas which are subject to the imagination are the objects of the *mathematical sciences*, namely, arithmetic and geometry, which are the *pure* mathematical sciences, and their applications to nature, which make up *mixed* mathematics. It is seen also that particular sense qualities are capable of explanation and rationalization only insofar as they have a content common to the objects of several external senses and belong to the internal sense. For whenever one tries to explain sensible qualities distinctly, one always turns back to mathematical ideas, and these ideas always include *magnitude*, or multitude of parts. It is true that the mathematical sciences would not be demonstrative but would consist of a simple induction or observation which could never assure us of the perfect generality of the truths found in it, if something higher, which only the intellect can provide, did not come to the aid of *imagination* and *sense*.

There are thus also objects of another nature, which are not at all included in what we have observed in the objects of either the particular senses or the common sense, and which consequently are also not to be considered objects of the imagination. Besides what is *sensible* and *imaginable*, therefore, there is that which is only *intelligible*, since it is the object of the understanding alone. And such is the object of my thought when I think of myself.

This thought of *myself*, who perceive sensible objects, and of my own action which results from it, adds something to the objects of sense. To think of some color and to consider that I think of it—these two thoughts are very different, just as much as color itself differs from the ego who thinks of it. And since I conceive that there are other beings who also have the right to say 'I', or for whom this can be said, it is by this that I conceive what is called *substance* in general. It is the consideration of myself, also, which provides me with other concepts in *metaphysics*, such as those of cause, effect, action, similarity, etc., and even with those of *logic* and *ethics*. Thus is may be said that there is nothing in the understanding which has not come from the senses, except the understanding itself, or the one who understands.

---

[9]Leibniz's distinction between imagination and sensation itself marks a point of deviation from Locke, since he emphasizes the dependence of the former upon the common sense and therefore its close relation to reflection and understanding.

There are thus three levels of concepts: those which are *sensible* only, which are the objects produced by each sense in particular; those which are at once *sensible and intelligible*, which appertain to the common sense; and those which are *intelligible only*, which belong to the understanding. The first and second together are imaginable, but the third lie beyond the imagination. The second and third are intelligible and distinct, but the first are confused, although they may be clear and recognizable.[10]

Being itself and *truth* are not understood completely through the senses. For it would not at all be impossible for a created being to have long and orderly dreams which resemble our lives, such that everything that it thought it perceived through the senses would be nothing but mere appearances. Something is thus needed beyond the senses, by which to distinguish the true from the apparent. But the truth of the demonstrative sciences is free of such doubts and must even serve to judge the truth of sensible things. For as able ancient and modern philosophers have already well said, even if all that I think I see were only a dream, it would always be true that I who am thinking in my dream would be something and that I should in fact think in many ways for which there must always be a reason.

What the ancient Platonists have said is thus quite true and quite worthy of consideration—that the existence of intelligible things, particularly of the I who think and am called a mind or soul, is incomparably more certain than the existence of sensible things and that it would thus not be impossible, speaking with metaphysical rigor, that there should exist at bottom only intelligible substances, of which sensible things would be only the appearances. Instead, our lack of attention causes us to take sensible things for the only true ones. It is also well to observe that if I should discover some demonstrative truth, mathematical or other, in a dream (and this can in fact be done), it would be just as certain as if I were awake. This shows us that intelligible truth is independent of the truth or existence of sensible and material things outside of us.

[10]At about this time Leibniz was developing his theory of apperception (probably suggested by the reflexive form *s'appercevoir*, which Coste used to translate Locke's *perceive*). Apperception or reflection is the basis of understanding, for without it there would be no perception of the content of perceptions and therefore no ground upon which to discover the universal principles of reason operative in the mind. While memory is the precondition of consciousness for Leibniz, apperception is the essential relation involved in the continuity of consciousness.

This conception of *being* and of *truth* is thus found in the ego and in the understanding rather than in the external senses and the perception of exterior objects.

In the understanding we discover also what it means to affirm, deny, doubt, will, and act. But above all, we find there the *force of the conclusions* in reasoning, which are a part of what is called the *natural light*. For example, by reversing the terms, one can draw from the premise that no wise man is vicious the conclusion that no vicious man is wise. On the other hand, from the premise that every wise man is praiseworthy, one cannot conclude by reversing terms that every praiseworthy man is wise, but only that some praiseworthy men are wise. Although one can always convert particular affirmative propositions, this is impossible with particular negatives. For example, if some wise men are rich, it is necessary also that some rich men are wise. Yet one can say that there are charitable beings who are not just, for this happens when charity is not regular enough, but one cannot infer from this that there are just beings who are not charitable, for charity and the rule of reason are at once included in justice.

It is by this *natural light* that one may recognize also the *axioms* of mathematics; for example, that if the same quantity is taken away from two equals the remainders are equal and likewise that if both sides of a balance are equal neither will sink, a fact which we can foresee without ever having tried it. It is upon such foundations that arithmetic, geometry, mechanics, and the other demonstrative sciences are established, in which it is true that the senses are necessary to have definite ideas of sensible things, and experience is necessary to establish certain facts and even useful in verifying the reasoning involved, by a kind of check, as it were. But the force of the demonstrations depends upon intelligible concepts and truths, for it is these alone which enable us to draw conclusions which are necessary; they even make it possible for us, in the conjectural sciences, to determine demonstratively the degree of probability in certain given assumptions, so that we may choose reasonably, among conflicting appearances, that one whose probability is the greater. But this part of the art of reasoning has not yet been cultivated as much as it ought to be.

To return to *necessary truths*, however, it is universally true that we know them only by this natural light and not at all by sense experiences. For the senses can indeed help us after a fashion to know what is, but they cannot help us to know what *must* be or what cannot be otherwise.

For example, although we can countless times tested the fact that

446

every heavy body falls toward the center of the earth, and is not sustained freely in the air, we are not sure that this is necessary until we have grasped the reason for it. Thus we cannot be sure that the same thing would happen in an altitude a hundred leagues or more higher than we are. There are philosophers who represent the earth as a magnet whose attractive force does not, they think, extend very far, any more than the ordinary magnet attracts a needle some distance away from it. I am not saying that they are right but only that we cannot proceed with much certainty beyond the experiences which we have had, unless we are aided by reason.

It is for this reason that the geometricians have always held that what has only been proved by *induction* or by examples, in geometry or arithmetic, has never been perfectly proved. For example, experience teaches us that the odd numbers when added together continuously in their order produce the square numbers in order, that is, the numbers produced by multiplying a number by itself. Thus 1 and 3 make 4, that is, 2^2; and 1 and 3 and 5 make 9, that is, 3^2; and 1 and 3 and 5 and 7 make 16, or 4^2 and 1 and 3 and 5 and 7 and 9 make 25, or 5^2; and so forth.

However, if one had tried this a hundred thousand times, extending the calculation very far, one might well judge it reasonable that this will always be true, but one could never be absolutely certain of it as long as he does not grasp the demonstrative reason for it which mathematicians long ago discovered. It is on the basis of this uncertainty of induction, pushed a little too far, that an Englishman has recently tried to argue that we can avoid death. For, says he, the following conclusion is not sound: my father, my grandfather, my great-grandfather have died, and so have all the rest whom we know to have lived before us; therefore we too will die. For their death has no influence upon us. The trouble with this argument is that we resemble them a little too much, in that the causes of their death subsist in us as well. For the similarity between us would itself not be sufficient to draw conclusions of complete certainty, without considering the same reasons.

There are in fact *experiments* which succeed countless times in ordinary circumstances, yet instances are found in some extraordinary cases in which the experiment does not succeed. For example, if we have shown a hundred thousand times that iron sinks to the bottom when placed in water, we are still not sure that this must always happen. Without appealing to the miracle of the prophet Elisha, who made iron float, we know than an iron pot can be made so hollow that it floats and can even carry a considerable load besides, as do boats made of copper

447

and of tinplate. Even the abstract sciences like geometry provide cases in which what ordinarily happens does not happen. Ordinarily, for example, we find that two lines which approach each other continuously finally meet, and many people would be quick to swear that it could never happen otherwise. Yet geometry does furnish exceptional lines called *asymptotes* for this reason, that when extended to infinity they approach each other continuously, yet never meet.

This consideration also shows that there is a *light which is born with us*. For since the senses and induction can never teach us truths that are fully universal or absolutely necessary, but only what is and what is found in particular examples, and since we nonetheless know the universal and necessary truths of the sciences—in this we are privileged above the beasts—it follows that we have drawn these truths in part from what is within us. Thus one can lead a child to them by simple questions in the Socratic manner, without telling him anything, and without having him experiment at all about the truth of that which is asked him. This could most easily be carried out in numbers and similar matters.

I agree, however, that in our present state the external senses are necessary for our thinking and that if we had none, we would not think. But what is necessary for something need not therefore make up its essence. The air is necessary for our life, but our life is different from air. The senses furnish us with the matter for reasoning, and we never have thoughts so abstract that something is not mixed with them from sense. But reasoning demands something more than what is sensible.

As for the *second question, whether there are immaterial substances*, one must first explain it in order to answer it. Heretofore matter has been understood to mean that which includes only purely passive and indifferent concepts, such as extension and impenetrability, which need to be given determinate form or activity by something else. Thus when it is said that there are immaterial substances, one means by this that there are substances which include other concepts, namely, perception and the principle of action or of change, which cannot be explained either by extension or by impenetrability. When these beings have feeling, they are called *souls*, and when they are capable of reason, they are called *spirits*. Hence if anyone says that force and perception are essential to matter, he is taking matter for the complete corporeal substance which includes form and matter, or the soul along with the organs. This is the same as if he had said that there are souls everywhere. This could be true, yet not at all contrary to the doctrine of immaterial substances. For this does not require these souls to be free from matter but only to be something more than matter and not produced or destroyed by the change which matter undergoes or subject to dissolution, since they are not composed of parts.

It must also be admitted, however, that there is some *substance separate from matter*. To make this clear, we need only to consider that there is an infinity of possible orders which the totality of matter might have received in place of this particular sequence of changes which it has actually taken on. For it is clear, for example, that the stars could have moved quite differently, since space and time are indifferent to every kind of motion and figure. Hence the reason, or the universal determining cause which makes things be, and make them be as they are rather than otherwise, must of necessity be free of matter. Even the existence of matter depends upon it, since one does not find anything in the concept of matter which carries a reason for its existence with it.

Now this ultimate reason for things which is common to all and universal because of the connection between all the parts of nature is what we call *God*, who must of necessity be an infinite and absolutely perfect substance. I am inclined to believe that all finite immaterial substances—in the opinion of the ancient Church Fathers, even the genii or angels—are joined to organs and accompany matter and even that souls or active forms are found everywhere. And to constitute a complete substance matter cannot dispense with them, since force and action are found everywhere in it. And the laws of force depend upon certain marvelous principles of metaphysics or upon intelligible concepts and cannot be explained by material or mathematical concepts alone or by those which fall within the jurisdiction of the imagination.

Perception, too, cannot be explained by any mechanism, whatever it may be. We can conclude then that there is also something immaterial everywhere in created beings, where this force is accompanied by a fairly distinct perception, and even by that light of which I have spoken above, which makes us resemble God in miniature not only through our knowledge or order but also through the order which we can ourselves impart to the things within our grasp, in imitation of that which God imparts to the universe. It is in this, also, that our *virtue* and perfection consist, as our *felicity* consists in the pleasure which we take in it.

Now whenever we penetrate to the basis of anything, we find there the most beautiful order we can desire, surpassing anything we had expected, as anyone knows who has understood the sciences. We can therefore conclude that it is the same in all the rest and that not only do immaterial substances subsist always but their lives, progress, and changes are controlled to lead to a definite end or better, to approach it more and more, as do the asymptotes. Even though we may sometimes slip back, like curves which descend, the progression must finally prevail and win.

The natural light of reason is insufficient for us to recognize the details, and our experiences are still too limited to discover the laws of this order. Meanwhile the revealed light guides us when we heed it through faith. But there remains room to think that in the future we may know still more by experience itself and that there are spirits who already know more in this way than we.

Meanwhile philosophers and poets, lacking this knowledge, have had recourse to the fictions of metempsychosis or of the Elysian fields in order to provide some ideas which might be popularly appealing. But a consideration of the perfection of things, or what amounts to the same thing, of the sovereign power, wisdom, and goodness of God, who does everything for the best, that is, for the greatest order, is enough to make all reasonable people content and to convince us that our contentment should be the greater in the measure in which we are inclined to follow order and reason.

from Principle of Nature and of Grace

15. For this reason all spirits, whether of men or higher beings [*genies*], enter by virtue of reason and the eternal truths into a kind of society with God and are members of the City of God, that is to say, the most perfect state, formed and governed by the greatest and best of monarchs. Here there is no crime without punishment, no good action without a proportionate reward, and finally, as much virtue and happiness as is possible. And this takes place, not by a dislocation of nature, as if what God has planned for souls could disturb the laws of bodies, but by the very order of natural things itself, by virtue of the harmony pre-established from all time between the realms of nature and of grace, between God as architect and God as monarch, in such a way that nature leads to grace, and grace perfects nature by using it.

16. Thus, though reason cannot teach us the details of the great future, these being reserved for revelation, we can be assured by this

same reason that things are arranged in a way which surpasses our desires. God being also the most perfect, the happiest, and therefore the most lovable of substances, and *true pure love* consisting in the state which causes pleasure to be taken in the perfections and the felicity of the beloved, this love must give us the greatest pleasure of which one is capable, since God is its object.

17. And it is easy to love him as we ought if we know him as I have said. For though God is not visible to our external senses, he is nonetheless most love-worthy and gives great pleasure. We see how much pleasure honors give to men, although they do not consist of qualities which appear to the external senses. Martyrs and fanatics, though the affection of the latter is not well ordered, show what power the pleasure of the spirit has. What is more, even the pleasures of sense are reducible to intellectual pleasures, known confusedly. Music charms us, although its beauty consists only in the agreement of numbers and in the counting, which we do not perceive but which the soul nevertheless continues to carry out, of the beats or vibrations of sounding bodies which coincide at certain intervals. The pleasures which the eye finds in proportions are of the same nature, and those caused by other senses amount to something similar, although we may not be able to explain them so distinctly.

[...]

from the Monadology[11]

1. The *monad* which we are to discuss here is nothing but a simple substance which enters into compounds. *Simple* means without parts. (*Theodicy*, Sec. 10).

2. There must be simple substances, since there are compounds, for the compounded is but a collection or an *aggregate* of simples.

3. But where there are no parts, it is impossible to have either

---

[11]Leibniz's own manuscripts of this work bear no title, but it has been known by this title since Erdmann adopted it in his edition, following the designation of the first published version, a German translation, in 1720.... The references to the *Theodicy* were added by Leibniz in the first revision.

extension, or figure, or divisibility. The monads are the true atoms of nature; in a word, they are the elements of things.

4. We need fear no dissolution in them, and there is no conceivable way in which a simple substance can be destroyed naturally. (*Ibid.*, Sec. 89).

5. For the same reason there is no way in which a simple substance can have a natural beginning, since it cannot be formed by composition.

6. So one can say that monads can only begin or end all at once, that is, they cannot begin except by creation or end except by annihilation. That which is compounded, instead, begins and ends in parts.

7. There is likewise no way of explaining how a monad can be altered or changed internally by any other creature, since nothing can be transposed in it, and we cannot conceive in it, as we can in composite things among whose parts there may be changes, that any internal motion can be excited, directed, increased, or diminished from without. Monads have no windows through which anything could enter or depart. Accidents cannot be detached from substances and march about outside of substances, as the sensible species of the Scholastics once did. So neither substance nor attribute can enter a monad from without.

8. Yet it is necessary for monads to have some qualities; otherwise they would not even be beings. And if simple substances did not differ by their qualities, there would be no way of perceiving any change in things, since what is in the composite can come only from its simple ingredients; and monads, if they were without qualities, could not be distinguished from each other, especially since they do not differ in quantity. Consequently, assuming a plenum, each place would always receive in any motion the equivalent of what it had already had, and one state of things could not be distinguished from another.

9. It is even necessary for each monad to be different from every other. For there are never two things in nature which are perfectly alike and in which it is impossible to find a difference that is internal or founded on an intrinsic denomination.[12]

10. I also take it as agreed that every created being is subject to change, and therefore the created monad also, and further that this change is continuous in each one.

---

[12]... 'Denomination' implies more than 'quality' (in Sec. 8, preceding), for it is a logical term and points to an essence or sufficient reason for changing qualities.

11. It follows from what I have said that the natural changes in monads come from and *internal principle*, since an external cause could not influence [*influer dans*] their interior. (*Ibid.*, Secs. 396 and 400).

12. But besides the principle of change there must be some distinguishing *detail in that which changes*, which constitutes the specific nature and the variety, so to speak, of simple substances.[13]

13. This detail must enfold a multitude in the unity or the simple. For every natural change takes place by degrees—something changes and something remains—and as a result there must be a plurality of affections and of relations in the simple substance, even though it has no parts.

14. The passing state which enfolds and represents a multitude in unity or in the simple substance is merely what is called *perception*. This must be distinguished from apperception or from consciousness, as what follows will make clear. It is in this that the Cartesians made a great mistake, for they disregarded perceptions which are not perceived. It is this, too, which led them to believe that only spirits are monads and that there are no souls in beasts or other entelechies. It led them into the popular confusion of a long stupor with death in a rigorous sense, which made them support the Scholastic prejudice that souls are entirely separate, and even confirmed some ill-balanced minds in a belief in the mortality of the soul.

15. The action of the internal principle which brings about change or the passage from one perception to another can be called *appetition*. It is true that appetite need not always fully attain the whole perception to which it tends, but it always attains some of it and reaches new perceptions.

16. We ourselves experience a multitude in a simple substance when we find that the slightest thought which we perceive enfolds a variety in its object. Hence everyone who recognizes that the soul is a simple

[13]The internal principle in Sec. 11 is clearly the law of the individual series, or the individual concept; the detail in that which changes is the particular value of this law or concept which constitutes the changing qualities of the monad. The dynamic parallels to the two concepts are primary and secondary force. Leibniz now proceeds further to divide the details (or secondary force) into aspects of activity and passivity and, from another point of view, into perceptions and the appetites which impel them. Thus he offers a more popular derivation of the organic structure of the monad than in the more critical Scholastic discussions with such men as De Volder and Des Bosses.

substance should also recognize this multitude in the monad, and Mr. Bayle ought not to find the difficulty in it which he does in his *Dictionary*, in the article on Rorarius.

17. It must be confessed, moreover, that perception and what depends on it are *inexplicable by mechanical reasons*, that is, by figures and motions. If we pretend that there is a machine whose structure enables it to think, feel, and have perception, one could think of it as enlarged yet preserving its same proportions, so that one could enter it as one does a mill. If we did this, we should find nothing within but parts which push upon each other; we should never see anything which would explain a perception. So it is in the simple substance, and not in the composite substance or machine, that perception must be sought. Furthermore, this is the only thing—namely, perceptions and their changes—that can be found in simple substance. It is in this alone that the *internal actions* of simple substances can consist. (*Ibid.*, Preface.)

[...]

26. Memory provides a kind of *consecutiveness* to souls which simulates reason but which must be distinguished from it. Thus we see that when animals have a perception of something which strikes them and of which they have had a similar perception previously, they are led by the representation of their memory to expect whatever was connected with it in this earlier perception and so come to have feelings like those which they had before. When one shows a stick to dogs, for example, they remember the pain it has caused them and whine or run away. (*Ibid.*, Prelim., Sec. 65.)

27. The strong imagination which strikes and moves them comes either from the magnitude or from the number of the perceptions which preceded it. For often one single strong impression produces at once the effect of a long-formed *habit* or of many frequently repeated ordinary perceptions.

[...]

30. It is also by the knowledge of necessary truths and by their abstractions that we rise to *reflective acts*, which enable us to think of what is called *I* and to consider this or that to be in us; it is thus, as we think of ourselves, that we think of being, of substance, of the simple and the compound, of the immaterial, and of God himself, conceiving of that which is limited in us as being without limits in him. These reflective

acts provide us with the principal objects of our reasonings (*Ibid.*, Preface, 4*a*.)

[. . .]

53. Now since there is an infinity of possible universes in the ideas of God, but only one can exist, there must be a sufficient reason for God's choice which determines him to one rather than another. (*Ibid.*, Secs. 8, 10, 44, 173, 196–97, 225, and 414–16.)

54. This reason can be found only in the *fitness* or in the degrees of perfection which these worlds contain, each possible one having a right to claim existence in the measure of the perfection which it enfolds. (*Ibid.*, Secs. 74, 167, 350, 201, 130, 352, 345–46, and 354.)

55. And this is the cause for the existence of the best, which his wisdom causes God to know, his goodness makes him choose, and his power makes him produce. (*Ibid.*, Secs. 8, 78, 80, 84, 119, 204, 206, and 208; Abr. obj. 1, 8.)

56. Now this mutual connection or accommodation of all created things to each other and of each to all the rest causes each simple substance to have relations which express all the others and consequently to be a perpetual living mirror of the universe. (*Ibid.*, Secs. 130 and 360.)

57. Just as the same city viewed from different sides appears to be different and to be, as it were, multiplied in perspectives, so the infinite multitude of simple substances, which seem to be so many different universes, are nevertheless only the perspectives of a single universe according to the different points of view of each monad. (*Ibid.*, Sec. 147.)

58. This is the means of obtaining the greatest variety possible, but with the greatest possible order; that is to say, this is the means of attaining as much perfection as possible. (*Ibid.*, Secs. 120, 124, 241–42, 215, 243, and 275.)

59. It is only this hypothesis, moreover, which I dare say is demonstrated, that exalts the greatness of God as one ought. Mr. Bayle recognized this when he raised objections to it in his *Dictionary* (article Rorarius), where he was even inclined to believe that I ascribed too much to God, more than is possible. Yet he was unable to set forth any reason why this universal harmony, which results in every substance expressing exactly all the others by means of the relations which it has with them, should be impossible.

60. From what I have been saying, furthermore, we may see the a

priori reasons why things could not be otherwise than they are. This is because God has had regard for each part in regulating the whole and in particular for each monad. The nature of the monad being to represent, nothing can keep it from representing only a part of things, though it is true that its representation is merely confused as to the details of the whole universe and can be distinct for a small part of things only, that is, for those which are the nearest or the greatest in relation to each individual monad.[14] Otherwise each monad would be a divinity. It is not in the object but in the modification of their knowledge of the object that the monads are limited. They all move confusedly toward the infinite, toward the whole, but they are limited and distinguished from each other by the degrees of their distinct perceptions.

61. In this respect compound beings are in symbolic agreement with the simple. For everything is a plenum, so that all matter is bound together, and every motion in this plenum has some effect upon distant bodies in proportion to their distance, in such a way that every body not only is affected by those which tough it and somehow feels whatever happens to them is also, by means of them, sensitive to others which adjoin those by which it is immediately touched. It follow that this communication extends to any distance whatever. As a result, every body responds to everything which happens in the universe, so that he who sees all could read in each everything that happens everywhere, and, indeed, even what has happened and will happen, observing in the present all that is removed from it, whether in space or in time. "All things are conspirant", as Hippocrates said.[15] But a soul can read within itself only what it represents distinctly; it cannot all at once develop all that is enfolded within it, for this reaches to infinity.

62. Thus, although each created monad represents the whole universe, it represents more distinctly the body which is particularly affected by it and of which it is the entelechy. And as this body expresses the whole universe by the connection between all matter in the plenum, the soul also represents the whole universe in representing the body which belongs to it in a particular way. (*Ibid.*, Sec. 400.)

---

[14]The relations between monads are not spatial, of course, and therefore do not differ in distance in the phenomenal sense. As Sec. 61 shows, spatial relations are merely symbolic analogies to the ultimate relations of perception. Distance is here a matter of the number of middle terms intervening in the analysis of perceptions.

[15]Leibniz writes σύμπνοια πάντα; he makes the same citation in the *New Essays*, Introduction.

63. The body belonging to a monad which is its entelechy or soul constitutes what may be called a *living being* with that entelechy; with a soul it constitutes an *animal*. Now the body of a living being or an animal is always organic for since every monad is a mirror of the universe in its own way, and the universe is regulated in perfect order, there must also be an order in the being which represents it, that is to say, in the perceptions of the soul and therefore also in the body, according to which the universe is represented in it. (*Ibid.*, Sec. 403.)

64. So each organic body belonging to a living being is a kind of divine machine or natural automaton infinitely surpassing all artificial automata. For a machine made by human art is not a machine in each of its parts; for example, the tooth of a brass wheel has parts or fragments which are not artificial so far as we are concerned, and which do not have the character of a machine, in that they fit the use for which the wheel was intended. But the machines of nature, living bodies, are still machines in their smallest parts, into infinity. It is this that makes the difference between nature and art, that is, between the divine art and ours. (*Ibid.*, Secs. 134, 146, 194, and 403.)

[...]

86. This city of God, this truly universal monarchy, is a moral world within the natural world and is the most exalted and the most divine of all God's works. in it the true glory of God consists, for he would have no glory if his greatness and goodness were not known and admired by spirits. It is also in relation to this divine city that his distinctive goodness is found, whereas his wisdom and power are shown everywhere.

87. As we have established above a perfect harmony between two natural kingdoms, that of efficient and that of final causes, we must also point out here another harmony between the physical kingdom of nature and the moral kingdom of grace, that is to say, between God considered as architect of the machine of the universe and God considered as monarch of the divine city of spirits. (*Ibid.*, Secs. 62, 74, 118, 248, 112, 130, and 247.)

JEAN PHILIPPE RAMEAU

Jean Philippe Rameau (b. Dijon 1683, d. Paris 1764). Little is known of Rameau's musical education except for the fact that at the age of 18 he was sent to Italy by his father, the organist of St. Etienne, to pursue musical studies. Upon his return, he held the post of organist at various cathedrals until he assumed permanent residence in Paris. He is undoubtedly one of the most important musical figures of the 18th century. As theorist he is accredited for having laid the foundations of modern harmonic theory.

Rameau regarded music as a science. Attempting to wed "reason" with "experience" he tried to prove that chords and their progressions were contained in and part of the fixed laws of nature. In his *Traité de l'harmonie* (1722), Rameau presents his theory of harmony, introducing his four basic conceptions concerning music: harmonic generation and chord inversion; the fundamental bass; chords by supposition, and the relation of melody to harmony.

Influenced by Zarlino and Descartes, Rameau sought to deduce from the multitude of harmonic diversity unifying principles which would both provide a frame of reference for existing chords and a generating source for their harmonic construction. Like his predecessors, he believed that all consonances are relationships obtained from the first six numbers—the "senario" (see Zarlino). In addition, the fundamental tone, according to Rameau constitutes a harmonic center, i.e., the foundation and source for the tones related to it. "Sound is to sound as string is to string," says Rameau, quoting Descartes. Moreover, not only do consonances result from one source, but chords and intervals as well. The interrelationships of those are likewise governed by the "fundamental sound." He thus conceives chordal movements in terms of relationships to harmonic centers. In line with Zarlino, the lowest tone, the bass note, carries prime importance for Rameau since all harmonic successions are derived from it. The progression of the bass note, however, depends on the consonant intervals obtained from the first five divisions of the string. The progression of the fundamental bass is not only an outcome of this division but also reflects the hierarchy prevailing among the resultant intervals. While dissonances can be engendered in numerous ways, they depend nonetheless upon consonants as a frame of reference. Melody, on the other hand, derives directly from harmony, for the harmonic intervals generated by the scenario pertain to it as well. Still, Rameau considered a harmony "perfect" if the fundamental served as the bass. While the changed position of the fundamental could not alter its essence, functional harmony thus replaced harmonic diversity. Chords which exceed the span of an octave, like the 9th or 11th chord, though they comprise dissonances are nonetheless related to the basic chord as is the "chord of the seventh".

Altogether, the seemingly disconnected multitude of chords revealed coherence and cohesion provided for by Nature.

In retrospect, it seems that Rameau's theoretical work "recognized" and "legitimized" longstanding practice. Recognition and legitimation may, in the final analysis, be the basic ingredient for innovation. Rameau's categories contain the level of abstraction which, since Aristotle, have proved to carry significance for theoretical thought. In fact, the entire musical system was both simplified and thereby enlarged. An over-awareness of these laws and their systematic application in the compositional process, may, however, cause stalement, as it did, in the case of Rameau the composer. When used too literally in musical analysis it likewise over-emphasizes the stationary at the cost of the unfolding aspect of music. Subsequent theories tried to overcome this drawback; this holds true not only for Schenker, though for him the "unfolding" aspect of music received utmost prominance. Still, introducing a correction of one kind or another into Rameau does not altogether usurp Rameau of the honorable historical place which he rightly deserves.

from Treatise on Harmony[1]

Preface

However much progress music may have made until our time, it appears that the more sensitive the ear has become to the marvelous effects of this art, the less inquisitive the mind has been about its true principles. One might say that reason has lost its rights, while experience has acquired a certain authority.

The surviving writings of the Ancients[2] show us clearly that reason alone enabled them to discover most of the properties of music. Although experience still obliges us to accept the greater part of their rules, we neglect today all the advantages to be derived from the use of reason in favor of purely practical experience.

Even if experience can enlighten us concerning the different properties of music, it alone cannot lead us to discover the principle behind these properties with the precision appropriate to reason. Conclusions drawn from experience are often false, or at least leave us with doubts that only reason can dispel. How, for example, could we prove that our music is more perfect than that of the Ancients, since it no longer appears to produce the same effects they attributed to theirs? Should we answer that the more things become familiar the less they cause surprise, and that the admiration which they can originally inspire degenerates imperceptibly as we accustom ourselves to them, until what we admired becomes at last merely diverting? This would at best imply the equality of our music and not its superiority. But if through the exposition of an evident principle from what we then draw just and certain conclusions, we can show that our music has attained the last degree of perfection and that the Ancients were far from this perfection

---

[1]Text: Jean Philippe Rameau, *Treatise on Harmony*, tr. Ph. Gossett (New York: Dover Publications Inc., 1971), pp. xxxiii–xxxvii; 3–8; 59–82; 139–164; 226–239; 421–444. The numbered notes are Gossett's and Rameau's, as indicated.

[2]Rameau refers to all musicians preceding Zarlino as the Ancients. He does not discriminate between Greek music and plain chant, nor does he show any awareness of medieval or Renaissance polyphony. There are few direct references to Greek theory in this treatise, but in his later writings Rameau cites the Greeks more freely. See, for example, his discussion of tetrachords in *Démonstration du principe de l'harmonie* (Paris, 1750), p. 46. [P.G.]

(refer on this subject to Book II, Chapter 21), we shall know where we stand. We shall better appreciate the force of the preceding claim. Knowing thus the scope of the art, we shall devote ourselves to it more willingly. Persons of taste and outstanding ability in this field will no longer fear a lack of the knowledge necessary for success. In short, the light of reason, dispelling the doubts into which experience can plunge us at any moment, will be the most certain guarantee of success that we can expect in this art.

If modern musicians (i.e., since Zarlino[3]) had attempted to justify their practices, as did the Ancients, they would certainly have put an end to prejudices [of others] unfavorable to them; this might even have led them to give up those prejudices with which they themselves are still obsessed and of which they have great difficulty ridding themselves. Experience is too kind to them. It seduces them, so to speak, making them neglect to study the beauties which it enables them to discover daily. Their knowledge, then, is theirs alone; they do not have the gift of communicating it. Because they do not perceive this at all, they are often more astonished that others do not understand them than they are at their own inability to make themselves understood. This reproach is a bit strong, I admit, but I set it forth, deserving it perhaps myself despite all my efforts. In any case, I wish these reproach could produce on others the effect that it has had on me. It is chiefly to restore noble emulation that once flourished that I have ventured to share with the public my new researches in an art which I have sought to give all its natural simplicity; the mind may thus understand its properties as easily as the ear perceives them.

---

[3]Zarlino was a celebrated author on music who wrote approximately 150 years ago. We find only feeble restatements of his works in later writings on the same subject. [R.]

Gioseffe Zarlino (1517–1590) is the theorist most cited by Rameau throughout this treatise. A student of Adrian Willaert's and choirmaster at St. Mark's in Venice from 1565 to 1590, Zarlino was famed both as a composer and theorist, although it is as a theorist that he has been remembered. His chief works are: the *Istitutioni Harmoniche* (Venice, 1558; revised 1562, 1573); the *Dimostrationi Harmoniche* (Venice, 1571); and the *Sopplimenti musicali* (Venice, 1588). These three works, together with some shorter theological tracts, were published together shortly before his death as *De tutte l'opere del R. M. Gioseffo Zarlino da Chioggia* (Venice, 1589). See Matthew Shirlaw, *The Theory of Harmony* (London, 1917), Chapter 2, for a discussion of those elements of Zarlino's theories pertaining directly to Rameau. Selections from the *Istitutioni* are translated in Oliver Strunk, *Source Readings in Music History* (New York, 1950), pp. 228–261. The *Istitutioni* and *Dimostrationi* are now available in facsimile (Broude Bros., New York). [P.G.]

462

No one man can exhaust materials as profound as this. It is almost inevitable that he will forget something, despite all his pains; but at least his new discoveries, added to those which have already appeared on the same subject, represent so many more paths cleared for those able to go further.

Music is a science which should have definite rules; these rules should be drawn from an evident principle; and this principle cannot really be known to us without the aid of mathematics. Notwithstanding all the experience I may have acquired in music from being associated with it for so long, I must confess that only with the aid of mathematics did my ideas become clear and did light replace a certain obscurity of which I was unaware before. Though I did not know how to distinguish the principle from the rules, the principle soon offered itself to me in a manner convincing in its simplicity. I then recognized that the consequences it revealed constituted so many rules following from this principle. The true sense of these rules, their proper application, their relationships, their sequence (the simplest always introducing the less simple, and so on by degrees), and finally the choice of terms: all this, I say, of which I was ignorant before, developed in my mind with clarity and precision. I could not help thinking that it would be desirable (as someone said to me one day while I was applauding the perfection of our modern music) for the knowledge of musicians of this century to equal the beauties of their compositions. It is not enough to feel the effects of a science or an art. One must also conceptualize these effects in order to render them intelligible. That is the end to which I have principally applied myself in the body of this work, which I have divided into four books.

The First Book contains a summary of the relationship between sounds, consonances, dissonances, and chords in general. The source of harmony is discovered to be a single sound and its most essential properties are explained. We shall see, for example, how the first division of this single sound generates another sound, which is its octave and seems to be identical to the first sound, and how the latter then uses this octave to form all the chords. We shall see that all these chords contain only the source, its third, its fifth, and its seventh, and that all the diversity inherent in these chords derives from the power of the octave. We shall discover several other properties, perhaps less interesting for practice but nonetheless necessary for achieving proficiency. Everything is demonstrated in the simplest manner.

The Second Book concerns both theory and practice. The source is represented by the part called the *bass* in music, to which the epithet *fundamental* is added. All its properties, together with those of the intervals, chords, and modes depending on it alone, are explained. We also speak of everything which may be used to make music perfect in its construction. To this end we recall whenever appropriate the reasoning given in the preceding book, experience, and the authority of the finest authors in this field, though not sparing them when they have erred. As for the new ideas presented here, we shall try to justify them to the learned by reason, to those who follow only their ear by experience, and to those who show too much submission to the rules of their masters by pointing out the errors found there. Finally we shall try to prepare the reader to receive freely the rules set down here and deduced in order and at length in the following books.

The Third Book contains a specific method for learning composition rapidly. The method has already been tested, but since we are rarely persuaded except by our own experience, I shall remain silent about this. I shall content myself with asking those to whom this method is unfamiliar to see the fruits that can be derived from it before opposing it. Those who wish to learn are not concerned about the method used to instruct them, as long as the method succeeds.

No rules have yet been devised to teach composition in all its present perfection. Every skillful man in this field sincerely confesses that he owes all his knowledge to experience alone. When he wishes to share this knowledge with others, he is often forced to add to his lessons this proverb, so familiar to musicians, *Caetera docebit usus.* [4] It is true that certain qualities depend on genius and taste, and for these experience is still more advantageous than even science. But this should not prevent a thorough knowledge from enlightening us when we fear that experience is misleading, even if this knowledge only shows us how to relate to their true source the innovations which experience leads us to produce. Besides, this thorough knowledge activates genius and taste which, without it, would often become useless talent. [5] Therefore I have considered it necessary to search for means to procure more simply and quickly that perfection which has been obtained hitherto only by practical experience. To this end I shall give a reasoned, precise, and

[4] Experience will teach the rest. [P.G.]
[5] Rameau's conception of genius is analyzed by Edward Lowinsky in "Musical Genius—Evolution and origins of a concept," *MQ L*, 321, 476 (1964). [P.G.]

distinct explanation of all harmony through the simple exposition of three intervals, from which are formed two principal chords and the entire progression of the fundamental bass; the latter simultaneously determines the progression of the other parts. Everything else depends on this simple explanation, which you will see can be understood at the very first reading.

The Fourth Book contains the rules of accompaniment, both for the clavecin and for the organ. The position of the hand, the arrangement of the fingers, and everything else useful in acquiring practical facility as rapidly as possible is deduced there.

The basic rules for accompanying on the clavecin can also be used for other similar accompanying instruments.

The last two books have a great deal in common, and will be useful to persons who wish to study either the practice of composition or that of accompaniment. One should also consult Book II, if one wishes to overlook nothing (assuming that I have forgotten nothing). I do not doubt that there are those who could do better than I, however, despite the pains I have taken to let nothing escape me, as my long discourses and repetitions must prove. These defects are due as much to my efforts to make matters clear and intelligible as to the feebleness of my intellect. As for Book I, it will not be of much use in practice. I have placed it at the beginning as proof of everything else contained in this treatise concerning harmony, and one should make whatever use of it one considers appropriate.

As my professional duties have hindered me from seeing this work through the press, I have been obliged to read it again with fresh attention, and I have found some changes and corrections necessary; these will be found in a Supplement at the end.[6] I have placed two Tables at the beginning: one is a Table of Contents, while the other contains an explanation of terms needed for understanding this book, which I herewith dedicate to the public.

The quotations from Zarlino's *Harmonic Institutions* are taken from the edition printed in Venice in 1573.

[...]

---

[6]These changes and corrections have here been incorporated into the body of the text. [P.G.]

Book One: *On the Relationship between Harmonic Ratios and Proportions*

Chapter One

On Music and Sound

Music is the science of sounds; therefore sound is the principal subject of music.

Music is generally divided into harmony and melody, but we shall show in the following that the latter is merely a part of the former and that a knowledge of harmony is sufficient for a complete understanding of all the properties of music.[7]

We shall leave the task of defining sound to physics. In harmony we characterize sound only as grave and acute,[8] without considering either its loudness or its duration. All knowledge of harmony should be founded on the relation of acute sounds to grave ones.

The distance from a low to a high sound is called an *interval,* and from the different distances that may be found between one sound and another, different intervals are formed; their degrees are named after the numbers of arithmetic. Thus, the first degree can only be named after the unit, so that two sounds of the same degree are said to be in unison. Likewise, the second degree is called a second, the 3rd a third, the 4th a fourth, the 5th a fifth, the 6th a sixth, the 7th a seventh, the 8th an octave, etc. The first degree is always assumed to be the lowest, and the others are formed by raising the voice successively according to its natural degrees.[9]

---

[7]An annotation here in the Opéra copy reads: "This paragraph contains a remarkable statement: Harmony and melody are inseparable." [P.G.]

[8]The terms *grave* (grave) and *aigu* (acute) are often used to designate low and high sounds in eighteenth-century music theory, both French and English. We shall normally translate them simply as low and high. [P.G.]

[9]In the *Nouveau système de musique théorique* (Paris, 1726), p. 1, Rameau rephrases this idea as follows: "The intervals, which conform to the natural and successive degrees of our voice, are named after the numbers." Rameau attempts no theoretical justification for this empirical concept of the "natural degrees" of the human voice until his *Génération harmonique* (Paris, 1737). There he incorporates the idea into his general theory. See particularly Chapter 6. [P.G.]

Chapter Two

On the different ways in which the relationship between Sounds can be known to us

In order to understand the relationship between sounds, investigators took a string, stretched so that it could produce a sound, and divided it with movable bridges into several parts. They discovered that all the sounds or intervals that harmonize were contained in the first five divisions of the string, the lengths resulting from these divisions being compared with the original length. [10]

Some have sought an explanation of this relationship in that relationship existing between the numbers indicating the [number of] divisions. Others, having taken the lengths of string resulting from these divisions, have sought an explanation in the relationship between the numbers measuring these different lengths. Still others, having further observed that communication of sound to the ear cannot occur without the participation of the atmosphere, have sought an explanation in the relationship between the numbers indicating the vibrations of these various lengths. We shall not go into the several other ways in which this relationship may be known, such as with strings of different thicknesses, with weights which produce different tensions in the strings, with wind instruments, etc. It was found, in short, that all the consonances[11] were contained in the first six numbers, except for the methods using thicknesses and weights, where the squares of these fundamental numbers had to be used. [12] This has led some to attribute all the power of harmony to that of numbers; it is then only a matter of applying properly the operation on which one chooses to base one's system.

---

[10]An annotation here in the Opéra copy reads: "This is unintelligible." [P.G.]
[11]See the Table of Terms. [R.]
[12]These relationships are summarized in the following equation:

$$f \propto \frac{1}{L}\sqrt{\frac{T}{m}}$$

where f is the frequency, L is the length of the string, T is the tension of the string, and m is the mass per unit length of the string. (See Harry F. Olson, *Musical Engineering*, New York, 1952, p. 74. New edition, Dover Publications, New York, 1967 as *Music, Physics and Engineering*.) Rameau's "thickness" is directly proportional to m; his "weights" are directly proportional to T. [P.G.]

We must remark here that the numbers indicating the divisions of the string or its vibrations follow their natural progression, and that everything is thus based on the rules of arithmetic. The numbers measuring the lengths of string, however, follow a progression which is the inversion of the first progression, thus destroying some of the rules of arithmetic, or at least obliging us to invert them, as we shall see later. [13] Since the choice between these operations does not affect the harmony, we shall use only those in which the numbers follow their natural progression, for everything then becomes much clearer.

Chapter Three

On the origin of Consonances and on their relationships

Sound is to sound as string is to string. Each string contains in itself all other strings shorter than it, but not those which are longer. Therefore, all high sounds are contained in low ones, but low ones, conversely, are not contained in high ones. It is thus evident that we should look for the higher term in the division of the lower; this division should be arithmetic, i.e., into equal parts, etc. [. . .] Let us take AB [Ex. I.1] as the lower term. If I wish to find a higher term so as to form the first of all the consonances, I divide AB in two (this number being the first of all the numbers), as has been done at point C. Thus, AC and AB differ by the first of the consonances, called the octave or diapason. If I wish to find the other consonances immediately following the first, I divide AB into three equal parts. From this, not only one but two higher terms result, i.e., AD and AE; from these, two consonances of the same type are generated, i.e., a twelfth and a fifth. I can further divide the line

---

[13] The mathematical operations used by Rameau in Book I are discussed at length in the Introduction, pp. xv–xxi. [P.G.]

AB into 4, 5, or 6 parts, but no more, since the capacity of the ear extends no further.[14]

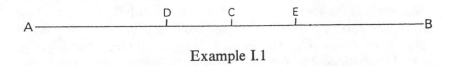

Example I.1

To make this proposition clearer, we shall take seven strings whose [number of] divisions are indicated by numbers. Without inquiring whether they are equal in any other respect we assume that the strings are all tuned at the unison. We then put the numbers in their natural order beside each string, as in the following demonstration [Ex. I.2.]. Each number indicates the equal parts into which the string corresponding to it is divided. Notice that number 7, which cannot give a pleasant interval (as is evident to connoisseurs), has been replaced by number 8; the latter directly follows 7, is twice one of the numbers contained in the *senario*,[15] and forms a triple octave with 1. This does not increase the quantity of numbers put forth, since 6 and 8 give the same interval as 3 and 4, every number always representing the number that is its half.

Remember that in every instance the numbers mark both a division of the unit and of the undivided string, which corresponds to 1.

---

[14]Descartes, *Abrégé de la Musique*, p. 60. [R.] One of René Descartes' (1596–1650) earliest efforts was his *Compendium Musicae* (1618). Though circulated only in manuscript during his lifetime, the *Compendium* was published in Utrecht (1650) shortly after his death. It went through several editions, and was translated into English as early as 1653. Rameau was familiar with the French version, translated from the Latin by Father Nicolas Poisson and published in Paris in 1668 as *Traité de la mechanique, composé par Monsieur Descartes. De plus l'Abrégé de musique du mesme autheur mis en français*. Rameau's citations of Descartes are from this translation. There is a modern English edition available (René Descartes, *Compendium of Music*, translated by Walter Robert, introduction and notes by Charles Kent, American Institute of Musicology, 1961), and we have supplied cross-references to this edition in the form "A.I.M." Our text differs slightly from the text found there, but remember that our text is already based on a translation. A.I.M., pp. 16–17. [P.G.]

[15]The *senario* means simply the first six numbers. Zarlino had used this concept to arrive at ratios for consonant intervals (see the *Istitutioni*, Part I, Chapter 16, edition of 1573). By invoking the *senario*, Rameau follows the pattern of most "natural" theorists; he skirts the problem of the number "7," which does not produce an interval of our tone system. [P.G.]

The order of origin and perfection of these consonances is determined by the order of the numbers. Thus, the octave between 1 and 2, which is generated first, is more perfect than the fifth between 2 and 3. Less perfect again is the fourth between 3 and 4, etc., always following the natural progression of the numbers and admitting the sixths only last.[16]

The names of the notes should make it apparent that the string 1, its octave 2, and its double and triple octaves 4 and 8 yield, so to speak, only a single sound. Furthermore, this arrangement of notes conforming to the order of the numbers and the divisions of the string, gives the most perfect harmony imaginable, as everyone may judge for himself. As for the properties peculiar to each sound or consonance, we shall discuss each of these in a separate article, in order to provide a clearer notion of them.

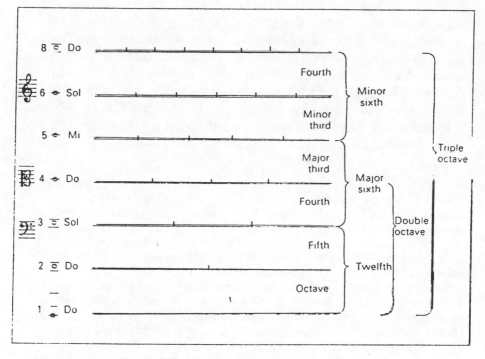

Example I.2

[16] Jacques Chailley has pointed out that this statement is contradictory, for in the order of the numbers 3:5, the major sixth, precedes 4:5 and 5:6, the major and minor thirds. This is only one of many statements by Rameau which are not strictly logical, but must be understood as attempts by him to justify theoretically his musical perceptions. See Jacques Chailley, "Rameau et la Théorie Musicale" in *Jean-Philippe Rameau, 1764–1964* (*La Revue Musicale*, Numéro Spécial No. 260, 1965). [P.G.]

ARTICLE I

On the source of Harmony or the fundamental Sound

We should first assume that the undivided string corresponding to 1 produces a given sound; the properties of this sound must be examined by relating them to those of the single string and even to those of the unit, which is the source of all numbers.

(1) The different divisions are marked on all the strings equal to the first and are determined by the magnitude of the number alongside the strings. These divisions clearly prove that each part of the divided strings arises from the first string, since these parts are contained in that first, unique string. Thus, the sounds which these divided strings produce are generated by the first sound, which is consequently their source and their fundamental.

(2) From the different distances found between this fundamental sound and those it generates by its division, different intervals are formed. The fundamental sound is consequently the source of these intervals.

(3) Finally, from the union of these different intervals, different consonances are formed. The harmony of these consonances can be perfect only if the first sound is formed below them, serving as their base and fundamental, as was seen in the demonstration [Ex. I.2.]. Thus, the first sound remains the source of these consonances and of the harmony they form.

In the following articles, we shall see which sounds are most closely related to this source and what use the source makes of them.

[. . .]

Book Two: *On the Nature and Properties of Chords and on Everything which may be used to make Music perfect*

Chapter One

On the fundamental Sound of Harmony and on its progression

As the nature of the fundamental sound and the role it should play in harmony has already been indicated (Book I, Chapter 3, Article i, page

7), we shall be principally concerned here with determining its progression.

As the part containing the fundamental sound is always the lowest and deepest, we call it the *bass*. Here is what Zarlino says on this subject:[17]

> Just as the earth is the foundation for the other elements, so does the bass have the property of sustaining, establishing, and strengthening the other parts. It is thus taken as the basis and foundation of harmony and is called the bass—the basis and support, so to speak.

After imagining how, if the earth were to disappear, all the beautiful order of nature would fall into ruin, he says:

> In the same way, if the bass were to disappear, the whole piece of music would be filled with dissonance and confusion. [...] Thus, when composing a bass, the composer should make it proceed by movements which are rather slower and more separated, i.e., more spread out, than those of the other parts. In this way the other parts can proceed in conjunct motion, especially the treble, whose property it is to move in this manner, etc.

But if we contrast this clear and accurate definition of the fundamental part of harmony with the rules and examples given by this author, we find everywhere contradictions which leave us in doubt and uncertainty.

Nonetheless, a principle on which everything is founded cannot be established too firmly; to lose sight of it for a moment is to destroy it. Without abandoning the principle that has just been enunciated, then, we shall strengthen it even more by adding to it the principle of the undivided string. The latter contains in its first divisions those consonances which together form a perfect harmony. Thus, when we give a progression to the part representing this undivided string, we can only make it proceed by those consonant intervals obtained from the first divisions of this string. Each sound will consequently harmonize with the sound preceding it. As each can bear in its turn a chord similar to the chord obtained from the first divisions, it will easily represent the undivided string, the source and foundation of the chord. This is what Zarlino means when he says that the bass should proceed by separated intervals, for intervals cannot be consonant unless they are separated.

[17]Zarlino, *Istitutioni Harmoniche*, Part III, Chapter 58, pp. 281–282. [R.]

Although Zarlino also says that the bass should move slowly, he means only in relation to the other parts, which should move diatonically. In this manner the upper parts may make the several movements necessary to pass from one consonance to another, while the bass makes only one. In drawing up our rules, however, we shall first make each part proceed by equal movements [i.e., note against note] for the sake of simplicity and clarity. The octave must be excluded from the progression just determined for the bass since, as long as the bass remains below the other parts, it is irrelevant whether the fundamental sound be several octaves higher or lower. The fifth, however, should be considered the interval best suited to the bass; in fact, we never hear a final cadence or the end of a piece in which this progression is not the primary element. We need only consult on this point those who are at all sensitive to harmony. They can never hear the conclusion of any piece whatsoever without feeling compelled to make the bass proceed by this interval. What we say about the fifth should also be understood to apply to the fourth, which always represents it. Those whose voices are deep enough naturally descend a fifth at endings, while those who cannot do so ascend a fourth. This is clear proof of the power of the octave, which is always present in either of the sounds forming it, and of the relationship between the fourth and the fifth arising from the division of the octave. The fifth is always preferred whenever the voice allows, but nothing is destroyed by substituting the fourth for it. Since the fifth is constructed of two thirds, the bass, in order to hold the listener in an agreeable state of suspense, may be made to proceed by one or several thirds, and consequently by the sixths which represent these thirds. All cadences, however, are reserved for the fifth alone and for the fourth which represents it. Thus, the entire progression of the fundamental bass should involve only these consonances. Dissonance may sometimes oblige us to make the bass ascend only a tone or a semitone. In addition to the fact that this arises from a license introduced by the deceptive cadence, of which we shall speak later, we may note that this ascending (but not descending) tone or semitone is the inversion of the seventh heard between the two sounds forming the tone or semitone. We shall see in Book III, Chapter 11, that, except in the case of the deceptive cadence, the progression of a third and a fourth may be understood here.

If this principle can be maintained everywhere, one should be disposed in its favor. We have not set it forth without having full confidence in it.

Chapter Two

On the Chords appropriate to fundamental Sounds and on their progression

The sounds, or rather the intervals, appropriate to the progression of the fundamental bass should also be found everywhere in the accompanying parts. More caution is required in these parts, however, than in the progression of the bass which is their guide. Briefly, since the perfect chord is the first and only chord formed from the division of the string, it is also the only chord suited to every sound of the fundamental bass. Though the seventh chord cannot be excluded, the third added to a perfect chord to form a seventh chord can certainly be suppressed without thereby changing the perfection of the harmony. The diversity that this chord brings, however, by introducing a certain tartness which simultaneously enhances the sweetness of the perfect chord, makes us desire its presence, not reject it. We must thus place it among the fundamental chords, since it in no way destroys the source which subsists in the lowest sound of the perfect chord.

As for the progression of the upper parts, each of which contains a sound of these chords, Zarlino has already indicated that the progression should be diatonic, this constraint arising from the consonant progression of the fundamental bass. No matter how little we may know about the size of intervals, we feel compelled instinctively to give these upper parts a diatonic progression whence arises an agreeable succession of chords. This occurs without our being obliged to have recourse to any other rule, since nature herself has taken care to lead us to the perfection which befits here. (See below, Chapters 18, 19, and 21; [18] also Book III, Chapters 4 and 6.)

Once we are aware of the progressions appropriate for each part, we are certainly free to give one part the progression suitable for another. We must always be guided, however, by the original arrangement and succession of fundamental chords, especially with regard to the seventh, which the ear accepts only under certain conditions. Its progression must be diatonic from the sound preceding it through the sound following it. Furthermore, these sounds must be consonant, as can be seen in the perfect cadence; from the latter we may even deduce

---

[18]This originally read: "See below, Chapters 19, 20, 24, and 25." Rameau changed this in the Supplement. [P.G.]

where this dissonance should occur in harmony. Of the two sounds in the bass which prepare us for the end of a piece, the second is undoubtedly the principal one, since it is also the sound with which the whole piece began. As the whole piece is based on it, the preceding sound should naturally be distinguished from it by something which renders this preceding sound less perfect. If each of these sounds bore a perfect chord, the mind, not desiring anything more after such a chord, would be uncertain upon which of these two sounds to rest. Dissonance seems needed here in order that its harshness should make the listener desire the rest which follows. Even nature is concerned, for it leads us to choose the third as the sole consonance which may make up for the harshness of the dissonance. The third despite its imperfection becomes the sole object of our desire after a dissonance and gives new charm to the perfect chord. It is for this reason that the rule for resolving dissonances has been established. Those who have not realized that there is only one minor dissonance, however, have been unable to conceive that there is only one consonance for resolving it. This is nonetheless indubitable, as will be seen further on.

Chapter Three

On the nature and properties of the Octave

The octave, which contains all the sounds capable of forming among themselves the fundamental chords, may be added to them in order to heighten the perfection of the chords. Without it, the perfect chord and its derivatives will always subsist, but with it, they become more brilliant, for natural and inverted chords are then heard simultaneously. In four-part pieces we cannot dispense with it, and in five-part pieces it harmonizes perfectly with the sounds of the fundamental seventh chord. In short, it may always be added to chords containing only one minor dissonance. Its progression, which should be diatonic in the upper parts, easily conforms to the rules. In addition, it determines the modulation, as we shall see later.

Chapter Four

On the nature and properties of the Fifth and the Fourth

The fifth is the primary element of all chords; i.e., a chord cannot subsist without either it or the fourth which represents it. We have already discussed the properties of these two intervals in the progression of the bass. As for the other parts, the progression of these intervals is much the same as that of the octave.[19]

Chapter Five

On the Perfect Cadence, in which the nature and properties of all the Intervals are found

The perfect cadence is a certain way of ending a strain which is so satisfying that we desire nothing further after it.

From the first two chapters we should already know something about this cadence, with respect to the progression of the bass (which descends a fifth or ascends a fourth) as well as with respect to the perfect chord and seventh chord of which the cadence is composed. The perfection of this cadence, however, does not end there. We also find that the progression of all intervals in the perfect cadence is determined by the progression of the thirds which are predominant in the chords. The intervals of the octave and the fifth, generated first and consequently having an independent progression, are excluded from this rule.

Though we have regarded the fifth as the primary element of all chords, this quality should also be attributed to the thirds of which the fifth is made up. The octave, after generating the fifth by its division, depends on it for building all chords. The fifth, likewise, after generating the thirds by its division, depends on them for the progression of the other intervals which share the nature and properties of these thirds. Thus, since the major third is naturally lively and gay, everything which is major or augmented will have this property. Since the minor third is naturally tender and sad, everything which is minor or diminished will also have this property. Zarlino says about the progression of these thirds:[20]

---

[19]In other words, notes in the upper parts which form a fifth or a fourth with the bass should follow a diatonic progression. [P.G.]

[20][Zarlino, *Istitutioni*], Part III, Chapter 10, p. 182; Chapter 38, pp. 219–220. [R.] The quotation is from p. 182. In the body of the *Traité*, Rameau quotes an additional sentence at the beginning of this citation: "The extremities of these thirds naturally prefer to move towards the part whose character is closest to their own." This sentence is suppressed by a note in the Supplement. [P.G.]

The major seeks to become major, i.e., to rise, and the minor to fall, [. . .] as is evident to all skillful musicians with true judgement, because the progression occurring in the upper part is the progression of a semitone. This semitone is the salt (if I may thus express myself), the ornament, and the cause of both beautiful harmony and good modulation; modulation without its help would be almost unbearable.

From these two different progressions, we derive the progressions of all intervals that can be characterized as major, augmented, minor, or diminished, and we should accept as a general rule that everything which is major or augmented should rise, while everything which is minor or diminished should fall.

This semitone, to which the progressions of every interval must conform and which Zarlino seems to put forward as a general rule, is in truth the only one which suits major or augmented intervals; minor and diminished intervals may also descend a whole tone, depending on the modulation. It is quite extraordinary that Zarlino, speaking so felicitously of this semitone, should abandon it in places where its effect is most clearly felt. If we recognize that in the perfect system this semitone is found between the octave and the sound which precedes it from below, that this octave is a resting place, and that it can be reached, ascending diatonically, only via this semitone, then we shall see that this sound, which precedes the octave, should have no less a place in harmony than the octave itself, since we must pass by the former in order to reach the latter. Nonetheless, although Zarlino could not avoid saying that "we should ascend from the major third and the major sixth to the octave" (a rule which can follow only from our preceding remarks), he forgets that the tritone should share in this same rule.[21] He speaks of the tritone only in passing and makes no mention of it when speaking of the perfect cadence. He finds the other major or augmented dissonances arising from this major third, which are always formed by the sound which precedes the octave, even less worthy of his attention. He says the least

---

[21]Zarlino, *Istitutioni*, Part III, Chapter 10, p. 182. Rameau does not cite Zarlino accurately here. Zarlino says: "il Ditono & lo Hexachordo maggiore desideranno di farsi maggiori, venendo l'uno alla Quinta & l'altro alla Ottava" (The major third and the major sixth, wishing to become larger [or major], move to the fifth and to the octave, respectively). Thus Zarlino specifies only that the major sixth should ascend to the octave. He does give examples, however, in which the major third also ascends to the octave. [P.G.]

about just those things which could make the progression [of the major dissonances] conform in all respects to the semitone he proposes. We should therefore show his blindness by giving an example of the perfect cadence; here this sound, which precedes the octave, forms a major third from which derive all the major dissonances which should ascend a semitone to the octave.

The first of the two notes forming the perfect cadence in the bass is called the dominant, because it must always precede the final note and therefore dominates it.

The seventh, formed by adding a minor third to the perfect chord of the dominant, forms a dissonance not only with this dominant but also with the major third of this same dominant, so that the major third forms a new dissonance here with regard to the added seventh.[22] This major third is thus the origin of all the major dissonances and this seventh is the origin of all the minor dissonances, without exception.

The note which completes the perfect cadence is called the tonic note, for it is with this note that we begin and end, and it is within its octave that all modulation is determined.

The sound which precedes the octave and forms all the major dissonances is called the leading tone [Fr. *Notte sensible*], because we never hear one of these major dissonances without feeling [Fr. *sentir*] that either the tonic note or its octave should follow immediately. This name is thus eminently suitable for the sound which leads us to that sound which is the center of all modulations [Ex. II.1.]

The two parts of Ex. II.1 are identical except for the progression of the minor dissonance. On the one hand the minor dissonance descends only a semitone, while on the other it descends a tone; the major dissonance always ascends a semitone from the major third to the octave. If the fundamental bass is removed and one of the other parts is put in its place, all the resulting chords will be inversions of the original chords. The harmony will remain good, for even when the fundamental bass is removed, it is always implied. The different dissonances heard because of the different position of these parts will completely follow the progression determined by the original chords. The major will

---

[22]This sentence originally read: "The seventh, formed by adding a minor third to its perfect chord, forms a dissonance not only with it, but also with the major third, so that this third becomes dissonant with regard to this seventh." The expanded form given above is from the Supplement. [P.G.]

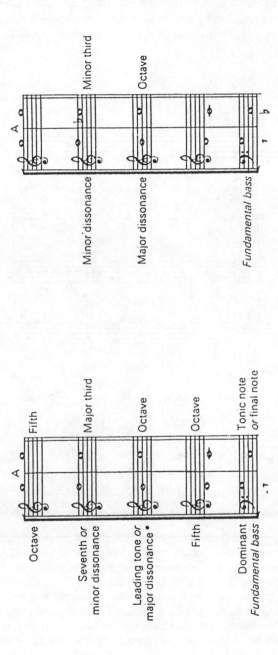

Perfect cadence in the minor mode

Minor third

Octave

Minor dissonance

Major dissonance

Fundamental bass

A

Fifth

Major third

Octave

Octave

Tonic note
or final note

Octave

Seventh *or*
minor dissonance

Leading tone *or*
major dissonance •

Fifth

Dominant
Fundamental bass

• The major dissonance is formed by the major third of the dominant.

Perfect cadence in the major mode

Example II.1

always ascend a semitone to the tonic note or its octave, while the minor will always descend to the major or minor third of this same tonic. Nothing could be clearer, and Zarlino himself proves it in his examples of the false fifth and the tritone.[23] Here he points out the inversion without realizing it.[24] [Ex. II.2.]

Zarlino's example, to which we add the fundamental bass

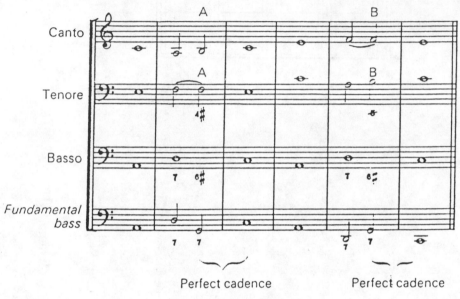

Example II.2

In the upper two parts, the tritone is marked A and the false fifth B. If these are then compared to the part which Zarlino calls *Basso*, we shall find that the tritone forms a major sixth which ascends a semitone to the

[23][Zarlino, *Istitutioni*], Part III, Chapter 61, p. 293. [R.] Zarlino's discussion, of course, centers on those intervals which may follow one another under various conditions. He does not speak of progressions of chords. The figures given in this example and all other examples cited after Zarlino are Rameau's additions. [P.G.]
[24]The figure 6 found in Example 2 should be barred [6], instead of being accompanied by a ♯ [6♯]. This same error is found everywhere I wished to use a chord similar to the one denoted by this figure. In works which authors have had printed until now, however, this distinction is not very common. [R.] This note is from the Supplement. [P.G.]

octave. Finally, if they are compared to our fundamental bass, we shall find that the tritone forms a major third and the false fifth forms a seventh, whose progression conforms to our previous rule. Thus, these different chords always represent the perfect cadence, since their progression does not change and the foundation always subsists, although perhaps by implication. If it did not, the piece of music would be filled with confusion and dissonance. Zarlino believes this in theory, but forgets it in practice.[25] He says that the natural progression of the lowest part in perfect cadences is to descend a fifth,[26] but he gives an example [Ex. II.3 below] in which the upper part ascends from the major third to the octave (A).[27] In another place, while the major third of the dominant ascends, the fifth of this same dominant also descends to the octave (B).[28] While the fifth descends, the third above this fifth, which forms the seventh of the dominant, descends to the third (C).[29] If we assemble these three different examples, we shall find our complete cadence. To this end, we take Zarlino's example of Chapter 52 and add to it the missing parts.[30] [Ex. II.3.]

[25][Zarlino, *Istitutioni*], Part III, Chapter 58, p. 282. [R.]

[26][*Ibid.*, Part III], Chapter 51, p. 251. [R.] This is wishful thinking on Rameau's part. Zarlino does mention a cadence in which the major third moves to an octave or unison while the lower part descends a fifth or ascends a fourth, but Zarlino does not call this a "perfect cadence," nor does he consider the progression to be a "natural" one. [P.G.]

[27][*Ibid.*, Part III], p. 251. [R.] Although Zarlino does not give an example on p. 251 demonstrating various situations in which the major third ascends to the octave, Rameau's A is not strictly equivalent to any of them. [P.G.]

[28]On p. 251 of the *Istitutioni* there is an example in which the major third of the dominant ascends while the fifth of this dominant descends to the octave. Although the progression is similar to Rameau's A and B taken together, these parts are not literally found in Zarlino. [P.G.]

[29][*Ibid.*, Part III], Chapter 52, p. 254, fourteenth and fifteenth measures. [R.] Parts B and C are found together in this example. [P.G.]

[30]The upper part appears to be Rameau's own contribution. There is still another added part in the original text:

Rameau orders this part suppressed in the Supplement. [P.G.]

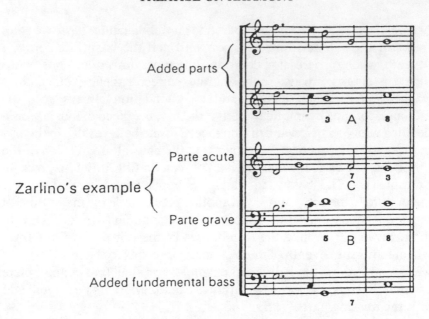

Example II.3

This is not the harmony that Zarlino understood here. He apparently claims that the perfect chord is heard on the second beat of the whole note that forms a fifth with the fundamental bass, because the fourth struck on the first beat of this same whole note is, according to him, more dissonant than consonant. But how could be place a perfect chord on the whole note which ends the cadence after the perfect chord of the other whole note in question? If the minor third of this latter, which forms a seventh with the fundamental bass, descends, what progression should be given to the fifth and to the octave? A skillful man should always figure his bass, especially when his examples are in only two parts, so that these examples can be judged fairly. Otherwise, false conclusions may be drawn from them. Perhaps Zarlino has not figured his basses for fear of pointing out intervals that he himself wishes to ignore and that he wishes to ignore as well. Besides, the perfect chord cannot be heard on each of the last two notes of the part labeled *Grave*. Our first remarks, which were derived from Zarlino's own argument, prove that this would be against the foundation of harmony, since the bass cannot proceed diatonically under perfect chords. Thus, the fourth found in Example 3 should be consonant with regard to the fundamental bass, with which it forms an octave. If it were dissonant, the perfect cadence could no longer occur on the last note and the cadence would then be *irregular.* [Ex. II.4.]

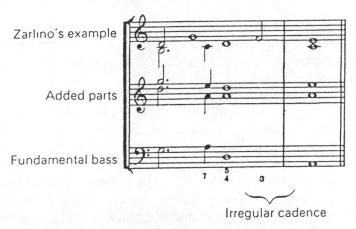

Example II.4

Which of these two cadences did Zarlino wish to use here? Apparently the perfect is meant, since the entire piece is in the key of Do, while this irregular cadence is in that of La or Re. Besides, he does not mention the irregular cadence at all, and it is found in this examples only within a series of chords, where he does not draw attention to it.[31]

It is from Ex. II.1, then, that we should derive all the different methods of using the perfect cadence, whether in two, three, four, or five parts. We choose as many parts as we wish to use together, and place them in any desired order. Those parts found above may be placed below, etc. Only the fundamental bass cannot naturally change its position, although even it is free from constraint as long as good taste guides us. To avoid a perfect conclusion, it may be placed in an upper part, while the bass [*continuo*] proceeds diatonically. Thus, harmony is contained in the two chords proposed: the perfect chord and the seventh chord. All our rules are founded on the natural progression of these two chords.

[31]In fact, Zarlino meant none of these cadences. The example cited by Rameau is part of a rather lengthy piece which illustrates: "How to avoid cadences." In the course of this piece every cadence approached is avoided by leaps, passing tones, sequence, etc. Only at the very end is there a cadence leading from the major sixth to the octave.

Rameau's criticism that Zarlino should have figured his basses is anachronistic, since figured bass was only in its earliest stages during Zarlino's lifetime. [P.G.]

Chapter Six

On the Deceptive Cadence

If we change the progression of one of the sounds in the first chord of a perfect cadence, we shall undoubtedly interrupt the conclusion. From the interruption caused by this change in the progression, the deceptive cadence originates.

This cadence does not differ greatly from the perfect, since they are both composed either of the same chords or of the same fundamental bass. If the chords are the same, the fundamental bass, which in the perfect cadence should descend a fifth, will ascend diatonically. If the fundamental bass is the same in both cadences, the perfect chord which concludes the perfect cadence will become a sixth chord. These changes occur only in consonant sounds, i.e., the fundamental sound, its octave, or its fifth, and not in those which form dissonances. Thus, the major third, the prototype of all major dissonances, will always ascend a semitone, while the seventh, the prototype of all minor dissonances, will descend either a tone or a semitone. This agrees with our rules concerning the progression of dissonances, while changing the foundation of the perfect cadence in only one way [at a time].[32] When the perfect chord no longer subsists, the fundamental bass does not change; when the latter changes, the perfect chord comes to its aid. But in substituting the sixth for the fifth, do we not form a chord derived from the perfect chord? Have we not indicated that the seventh introduces a progression in the bass suited to its interval? Thus, everything continues to subsist even though this last cadence may be admitted only by license, since either the chord is no longer fundamental or the progression of the bass is not generated by the consonances. The liberty which dissonance gives us here alters the perfection [of the cadence], but there is nothing harsh in this alteration. Far from displeasing, it serves only to render the perfection of the perfect cadence still more

[32] In keeping with his notion that this series of chords can be understood in either of two ways, Rameau sometimes selects as the fundamental bass V–I, sometimes V–VI. A similar case of double meaning is set forth in Rameau's theory of "double employment," explained in the *Génération harmonique*, though in the latter case he argues that the ambiguous chord (IV with the added sixth or II⁷) can function in two ways simultaneously, or rather can serve one function at the beginning of the beat and the other at the end. For Rameau's earlier views about this chord, see Book II, Chapter 27, p. 73 below. [P.G.]

agreeable when the latter, after having been temporarily suspended, finally appears. [Ex. II.5].

If these examples are compared with those of the perfect cadence [Ex. II.1], the only difference we shall find is that here the fifth ascends to the sixth in the parts marked A. If parts A of Ex. II.5 are then placed below the fundamental bass, we shall simply find a seventh chord and a perfect chord, in accordance with our initial proposition. The deceptive cadence is most often used in this manner.

All these parts may be inverted and 2, 3, or 4 of the parts may be used separately. Remember that the fundamental bass may be used in the treble only when good taste permits and that the deceptive cadence is perceived only when the fifth is transposed to the sixth; i.e., when the sixth takes the place of the fifth found in the perfect chord which terminates the perfect cadence. All other parts remain the same in both cadences.

Observe that when part A is used as the bass, it is preferable to place the octave of the third in the chord rather than the octave of the bass. This is because the third implies the true fundamental sound, whose replicate cannot be displeasing. In a sequence of perfect harmony, on the other hand, the octave of the third, if preferred to that of the fundamental sound, will be defective. We are not saying that the octave of the bass cannot be used here in place of the octave of the third, but we should first be quite sure of what we are doing. Since this octave hardly ever occurs without introducing gross errors, good judgment is necessary. We should never stray from a principle unless we understand it completely.

Chapter Seven

On the Irregular Cadence[33]

Whereas the perfect cadence ends with a progression from the dominant to the tonic note, the cadence we are discussing here ends on the contrary with a progression from the tonic note to its dominant, or from the fourth note to the tonic. It is therefore called irregular.

There is a new dissonance here which has not yet been discussed, although the majority of skillful musicians use it successfully. It not

---

[33] I have used the revised version of this chapter, as found in the Supplement. It contains all the materials of the original version but in a greatly expanded form. [P.G.]

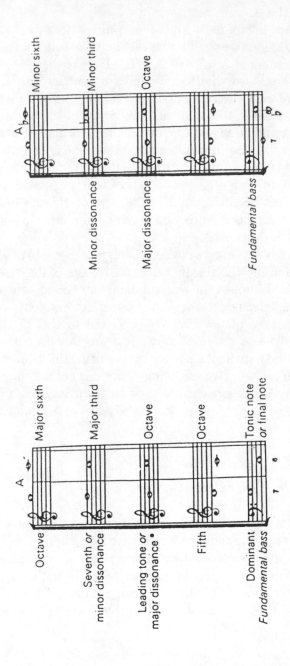

Deceptive cadence in the major mode

Deceptive cadence in the minor mode

• The major dissonance is formed by the major third of the dominant.

Example II.5

only lends a charming diversity to harmony and helps to produce graceful melodies, but is also a great resource for pieces in four or more parts. As a result, we can only praise those who first attempted to use it.

This dissonance is not dissonant with respect to the bass. It is a sixth which is consonant but which forms a dissonance with the fifth of the bass. This dissonance must thus be resolved by ascending, as we shall try to show.

The chord formed by adding a sixth to the perfect chord is called the chord of the large sixth. Although this chord may be derived naturally from the seventh chord,[34] here it should be regarded as original. On all other occasions, however, it should follow the nature and properties of the chord from which it was first derived. [Ex. II.6.]

If we wish the note which begins this cadence to pass for a tonic and that which ends it to pass for a dominant, it is enough to use the major third of the last note. The difference of mode will then be felt only on the first note, which will be, in that case, the tonic and which may bear the major or the minor third.

Masson,[35] who does not discuss this cadence as we do, nonetheless gives and example of it. This example, however, is by inversion and contains chords of whose origin Masson is ignorant. He treats A as a tritone, when it is basically a fourth altered by the power of modulation and, even more important, a sixth with regard to the fundamental bass. [Ex. II.7.]

Zarlino does not mention this cadence at all, and when Masson speaks of it he calls it imperfect.[36] M. de Brossard does the same, using the term irregular only to determine how cadences are employed. "A cadence is called irregular," he says, "when its final note is not one of

---

[34]See Book I, Chapter 8, Article iv. [R.]

[35]Masson, *Nouveau traité de musique*, p. 99. [R.] Charles Masson (?—1705?) was a church musician in Paris, chiefly famed for his book *Nouveau traité des règles pour la composition de la musique* (Paris, 1697). Rameau uses the third edition (Paris, 1705). Example 7 is incompletely cited by Rameau. In Masson, the *G* and *B*♭ of the six-4 chord are resolved in the second half of the measure to *F*♯ and *A*. Rameau's interpretation, then, is highly questionable.

[36]This is untrue. In fact Masson calls the cadence in which the bass descends a fourth or ascends a fifth an "irregular cadence" (p. 24). He does add (pp. 54–55) that "this cadence may be called imperfect, if you will, because the upper part does not finish on the same pitch as the bass," but the generic name for this type of cadence, according to Masson, remains "irregular." [P.G.]

487

Irregular cadence in the major mode

• There is a dissonance of a second between these two parts.

Irregular cadence in the minor mode

† There is a dissonance of a seventh between these two parts.

Example II.6

* Dissonant sixth
† Third

Example II.7

the notes essential to the prevailing mode."[37] We should indicate here: that these notes essential to the mode are the tonic or final note, its third, and its fifth; that since the term irregular is not applied to a type of cadence at all, but only to how various cadences are employed, we are left in doubt as to which of the different cadences to choose and we are led to consider them all as equivalent; that consequently this term does not specify the genre of cadence, but refers instead to the modulation, stating that the modulation is irregular when the cadence strays from notes essential to the initial mode. M. de Brossard, in translating this passage from the Ancients, has apparently not considered that their way of modulating was very different from ours, that their lack of experience imposed great limitations on them, that they applied the term irregular not only to cadences foreign to the original mode but also to the range of the melody, which depends only on the range of the voice, and that in short every piece of their music remained in and concluded in the same mode in which it began (judging, at least, from Zarlino's music). Consequently it was an irregularity with them, not to say an error, to use cadences outside the mode. For us, however, who

[37]M. de Brossard, *Dictionnaire*; see the word *irregolare* [irregular, p. 37]. [R.] For Brossard's use of the term "imperfect," see his article *quinta* (fifth), p. 90, where he says that the fifth "is used to form perfect cadences when it descends and imperfect cadences when it ascends." [P.G.]

are fortunate enough to understand good and correct modulation, it is a sign of perfection to know how to pass appropriately from one mode to another and to know how to introduce thereby new diversity into harmony. The Ancients, once again, understood so little about good modulation that they invented an infinite number of rules in order to make up for the defects of their own modulation. These rules have become useless now, thanks to our fortunate discoveries. If M. de Brossard had remembered here what he himself said about ancient and modern modes, we do not doubt that he would have corrected in some respects the type of cadences he calls irregular.

It might be said that we are arguing only about the name of this cadence, and that we would do well to submit to custom. We might do so if this custom were well established, but practical musicians care so little about the terms of their art that they confuse these terms constantly with utmost unconcern. They even seem to derive pleasure from this, in order to embarrass those who wish to argue with them. Finally, even those who have written about these terms have followed their fancy rather than their reason. For example, if we are to conform to custom, we must believe that Zarlino should guide us rather than anyone who has written after him. Now this author, who speaks almost exclusively of the perfect cadence, calls cadences which are inversions of the perfect *Cadenze fuggite* (this is equivalent to our term deceptive cadence).[38] We call these cadences imperfect in order to remain close to his idea. Calling them deceptive [Fr. *cadence rompue*] would be inappropriate in our language, since this term prepares us for a certain interruption [Fr. *interruption*] of the perfect cadence which is certainly not found in inversions of this cadence, but rather in that cadence which the Moderns call deceptive. Since this author [i.e., Zarlino] gives the name irregular to things which we find quite regular, we must try to apply this term more appropriately. In point of fact, the progression of the cadence being discussed is quite irregular with respect to the perfect cadence. The fundamental bass of the latter should descend a fifth, while the fundamental bass of the former should ascend a fifth. The

---

[38]Zarlino, [*Istitutioni*], Part III, Chapter 52, p. 254. [R.] The term *cadenze fuggite* is equivalent to the term *deceptive cadence* neither literally nor as defined by Zarlino. Literally it means simply an "avoided" cadence, and Zarlino uses it to refer to any avoided cadence, regardless of the technique. It could involve ending on the sixth Mi–Do in the key of Do, but it may also mean moving from Sol–Re to La–Do. Rameau's Ex. II.3 is taken from Zarlino's example of the *cadenze fuggite*. [P.G.]

dissonance formed on the one hand is a seventh, which should be resolved by descending, while the dissonance formed on the other is a sixth, which should be resolved by ascending. In cadences which should be called imperfect, however, the only imperfection is that the fundamental bass is suppressed, transposed, or inverted. Although the terms imperfect and irregular are almost synonymous, the term "imperfect" seems to be closer to "perfect" than is "irregular," or at least so it appears to us.

We have said more than enough about this. Let us pass to something more substantial.

This is a dissonance used by all skillful masters of the art, a dissonance whose effect is not less agreeable to the ear than the dissonance used in the perfect cadence, a dissonance, finally, most useful to us in harmony and melody. So little has been said on this subject, however, that we cannot dispense with adding to experience, which already sanctions the use of this dissonance, all the reasons which may further convince us of the manner in which it should be used.

The different situations in which dissonances occur oblige us to name them differently in order to facilitate their use, but there is basically only one dissonance, from which all the others are derived either directly or indirectly, as we shall see later. This dissonance, which we have already designated at the seventh, is more easily recognized as the interval of a second; this comes to the same thing, since the second is the inversion of the seventh. We cannot resist reaffirming here the admirable order which the harmonic ratios preserve in this situation. After having given us the consonances in the first divisions [of the string], they finally give us this unique dissonance in the division of the major third. All the properties of these divisions end here, with regard to harmony.

Experience shows that no sound can be inserted between two other sounds which together form the interval of a second (we are speaking here only of diatonic sounds appropriate for use in harmony and melody), and consequently that no two sounds can be closer than this interval. If we allow ourselves to speak of these sounds as if they were solids, we might say that they touch each other and collide with each other, for this is certainly similar to the effect they produce on the ear. We customarily say that dissonance disturbs the ear in the same way that badly assorted colors disturb the eye, thus attributing to the senses the effect that the objects which act on them have on one another. For further proof that this idea of the collision of sounds is not simply our invention, we need only look up the literal meaning of the term syncopation, which is principally applied to the use of dissonance. This term is composed of two Greek words: *syn* and *copto*. The first signifies *together* and the other *I hit* or *I collide*. The collision was thus apparent from the very first moment that dissonance was perceived. M. de Brossard tries to prove this in part when he says that " a syncopated note strikes and collides, so to speak, with the natural beats of the measure and with the hand that beats time."[39] Notice, however, that this author speaks only of a secondary cause arising without doubt from the supposed collision of the sounds. The relationship this syncopated note can have with the beats of the measure, etc., arises only because this note, colliding with another (taking notes for sounds here), makes us feel its simultaneous collision with the natural beats of the measure and consequently with the hand that is beating time.

Pursuing this, we shall find that the effect resulting from this so-called collision of sounds has much in common with the collision of solids. Both conform to the following two propositions of Father Pardies:[40]

> *A moving body meeting another body which is at rest gives the body at rest all its motion and remains immobile itself.*
> *A hard body which strikes an immovable body will be reflected together with all its motion.*

The first effect is found, in a sense, in the prepared dissonance, while the second is found in the unprepared dissonance. [Ex. II.8.]

The consonances are contained in the first treble part, while the dissonances are in the second.

The figures indicate the intervals which each treble part forms with the bass, while the lines ╲ , ╱ designate the progression of the dissonance, descending as well as ascending. The notes marked B are prepared dissonances, while those marked F are unprepared dissonances.

In order to judge the effect in question, we need only notice that in Ex. II.8, dissonance B is at rest when consonance A strikes it. Immediately after the collision, the consonance becomes immobile and obliges the dissonance to pass to C. This is effectively the place to which the consonance itself could have passed but can no longer do so, since the

---

[39]M. de Brossard, *Dictionnaire*; see the word *syncope* [syncopation, p. 127]. [R.]
[40]Father Pardies, [*OEuvres*, Lyon, 1709, Book II: *Un Discourse du Mouvement Local*], Proposition XVIII, p. 147; Proposition XXIII, p. 154. [R.]

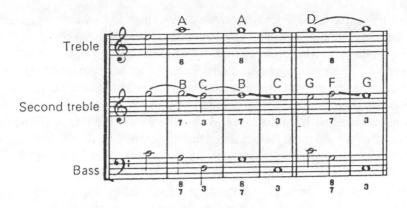

Perfect cadences

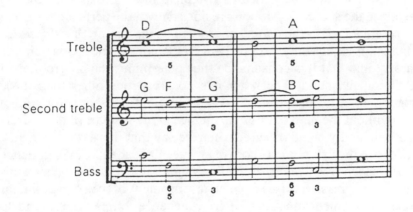

Irregular cadences

Example II.8

dissonance has taken its place. The consonance seems to have given all its motion to the dissonance. Consonance D, however, which seems to be immobile, after having colided with dissonance F obliges it to return to G, from where it started. The dissonance here seems to be reflected with all its motions, after having struck an immovable consonance.

Thus, the progression of the dissonances depends on the consonances closest to them. Furthermore, each of these consonances behaves according to its degree of perfection.

493

In the perfect cadence the octaves A and D, which represent fundamental sounds, compel the sevenths B and F to ascend. In the irregular cadence the fifths D and A, which are less perfect than the octave to the same degree that this cadence is less perfect than the perfect cadence, are operative and compel the sixths F and B to ascend. It is clear than that 7 having collided with 8 must descend, just as 6 having collided with 5 must ascend. Furthermore, the thirds C and G come from all sides to help soften the harshness of the dissonances which they generated, agreeing thus with our remarks of Chapter 2, p. 62.

If one has paid the slightest attention, it should be apparent that the harmony contained in Ex. II.8 is the most perfect that can be used for prepared and unprepared dissonances. We have ignored supplementary sounds which could be added to complete the chords, remembering that, since the source of harmony resides only in the perfect chord, any new sound added to the perfect chord will be dissonant; that the added sound is dissonant only with respect to the consonance to which it is nearer,[41] and that this consonance thus determines the progression of the dissonant sound. The latter has no properties other than those imparted to it by the nearest consonance and consequently cannot move without the help of this consonance, which is part of the source. Thus one hardly could disagree when we say that the sixth which may be added to the first perfect chord of an irregular cadence, as experience shows, must be resolved by ascending, since it is always major here; this irregular progression arises from an arrangement of the sounds similar to that arrangement which in the perfect cadence compels the seventh to be resolved by descending. These two dissonances differ basically from one another only with respect to the nearest consonance (for they both form the interval of a second or a seventh by inversion with the consonance to which they are joined), and both lose their harshness through the consonance by which they were generated, i.e., the third.

It might be said that the progressions of Ex. II.8 are arbitrary with regard to the consonances which precede the unprepared dissonances as well as with regard to consonance C, to which we said consonance A could have passed. We reply that so long as these progressions are good, not to say the best, we should demand nothing more.

The three cadences discussed in the last three chapters contain all the most essential matters of harmony. Not only may all the chords and

[41]See Chapter 14 [*sic*; this should be Chapter 16], Article i, pp. 110–113. [R.]

their progressions be derived from them but, in addition, true modulation originates there. All consonant chords are contained in the perfect chord and all dissonant chords arise from a new sound added to this perfect chord, forming a seventh chord which contains all the dissonant chords. We have just seen that the chord of the large sixth, formed by adding a sixth to the first perfect chord of the irregular cadence, may be reduced to a seventh chord. Those who wish to improve their knowledge should pay close attention to the different properties of these three cadences, since everything we shall say in some way depends on them.

Chapter Eight

On the imitation of Cadences by inversion

To imitate a cadence by inversion, we must ordinarily suppress the fundamental bass and take as bass any other part we consider appropriate. Even the progression of sounds which together form no dissonance, such as the fundamental sound and its fifth, may be diversified in this way (as is explained in Book III), these various parts forming in turn the bass or the treble. We can derive any melody imaginable and diversify the harmony, by placing in the bass a sound contained in the fundamental chord instead of the fundamental sound itself. This leads directly to an inexhaustible succession of melodies and chords from which we may shape a piece of music which constantly stirs the listener by the diversity arising from inversion. Those who have been aware of inversion have not looked into its origin, as their rules and their examples prove; for they give as many different examples and different rules as there are different chords. This one says the seventh is resolved by the third, the fifth, the octave, the sixth; that one says the false fifth is resolved by the third, the fourth, the tritone, the ninth, whether descending, ascending, or standing still. This is how sciences are made obscure. Each part is cited separately when all could be brought together to form a simple and intelligible entity. Though the dissonance of the seventh can be characterized as a false fifth, a second, a ninth, or an eleventh, and can be resolved by different intervals, this arises only from the different progressions of the bass; the latter, by passing to sounds derived from a fundamental chord, gives a different form to the intervals, since the comparison is thus made with derived sounds. The chords, however, remain the same, though arranged differently, and their progression if unchanging. Though the interval changes its appearance, it remains the same when related to the fundamental. The fundamental basses we place below all our examples prove this, and it only remains to make these matters clearer, as we hope to do.

[. . .]

Book Three: *Principles of Composition*

Chapter Eighteen

Observations on establishing Rules, in which the method of composing a Fundamental Bass is taught

ARTICLE I

On establishing Rules

We may judge music only through our hearing, and reason has no authority unless it is in agreement with the ear; yet nothing should be more convincing to us than the union of both in our judgements. We are naturally satisfied by our ear, while the mind is satisfied by reason. Let us judge nothing then except by their mutual agreement.

Experience offers us a large number of chords susceptible of an infinite diversity, in which we shall always lose our way unless we search for the source elsewhere. Experience sows doubts everywhere, and everyone, imagining that his own ear will not mislead him, trusts in himself alone. Reason, on the contrary, presents us with only a single chord whose properties are easy to determine with a little aid from experience. Thus, as long as experience does not contradict what reason authorizes, the latter should prevail. Nothing is more convincing than decisions based on reason, especially when they are drawn from a source as simple as that which reason offers. Let us be ruled then only by reason whenever possible, and let us call experience to its aid only when we desire further confirmation of its proofs.

The earliest musicians—in short, all those interested in theory alone —admitted only the perfect chord as the source. Zarlino, joining practice to theory, speaks of sixth chords and six-four chords, but we

496

already know that these are derived from the same source. It only remains to be seen whether dissonances are also related to this source. Since all dissonances are generated by adding a new sound to the first chord, which always subsists in its full perfection, this is easily tested. Reason alone, therefore, suffices to authorize dissonance and to determine its use. The addition is naturally made either by a rule of three[42] or by a new multiplication of the numbers which gave the first chord, as we observed in Book I, Chapter 7, p. 35. Since the rules of music concern only consonances and usable dissonances, and since these consonances are all contained in the perfect chord and these dissonances are all contained in the same chord with the seventh added, we may conclude that the rules should be founded principally on the first chord and on the chord formed by adding a seventh. If after having established our results on the basis of such a simple and natural source, we follow at every point what has been said and done by those most skillful in composition, always conforming to what our experience leads us to approve, could we then doubt for a moment that this source is the true basis of our rules?

Refer in this connection to what Zarlino says about the fundamental bass, its progression, and the progression it imposes on the other parts, and about the progression of thirds, of consonances in general, and of dissonances. Notice that he forgets those dissonances which we call major; that he does not adequately define the deceptive cadence; that he does not speak at all about the irregular cadence or about the inversion of chords, even though he does teach how to use chords of the sixth, of the seventh, etc.; that he cites without distinction the ninth chord, a chord which we have said is admitted only by supposition; that his modes are without proper foundation (as we shall see in Chapter 21); that consequently his music cannot profit from the perfections of our own; and that, finally, his examples do not agree with his discourse. Examine whether those reasons, from which he draws his explanations, his comparisons, and with them the limits of his knowledge, are reasons or merely words. Then draw your own just conclusions, and you will find in fact that all harmony and all melody must rest on the two chords we have put forward. Even more, they must rest on the lowest sound of

[42]This is the rule by which a fourth term is added to three terms of a proportion. It states that the product of the means of a proposition is equal to the product of the extremes. Rameau invokes this in Book I also, but there he calls it "adding a fourth proportional." [P.G.]

each of these chords, which remains the same in both cases, and on its progression, as we have already said. Listen then to the music of the most skillful masters, examine it, and prove our proposition by means of the fundamental bass, following the explanation we shall give at the close of this chapter. You will find there only the perfect chord and the seventh chord; you will find, I say, only the tonic or its dominant, if you understand the nature of modulation well enough to be able to distinguish all changes of key. Note in addition that the sixth note often takes the place of the dominant, though only in minor keys.

The source of harmony does not subsist merely in the perfect chord or in the seventh chord formed from it. More precisely, it subsists in the lowest sound of these two chords, which is, so to speak, the harmonic center to which all other sounds should be related. This is one of the reasons why we believed it necessary to base our system on the division of a string. This string, which gives the lowest sound, is the source of all those sounds which arise from its division, just as the unit, to which it was compared, is the source of all the numbers.

It is not enough to perceive that all chords and their various properties originate in the perfect chord and the seventh chord. We must notice furthermore that all the properties of these chords depend completely on this harmonic center and on its progression. The intervals of which these chords are constructed are such only with respect to this center, and the center then uses the same intervals for its own progression, which in turn determines the order and progression of the first two chords. The intervals used are the third, the fifth, and the seventh: other intervals used are either inversions of these, such as the sixth, the fourth, and the second; duplications, such as the ninth and the eleventh, etc.; or alterations, such as the tritone, the false fifth, etc. We need not mention the octave here, since we have already shown that it is merely a replicate. This reduction of intervals can be related precisely to the reduction of chords: from inverted intervals are formed inverted chords; from doubled intervals, chords by supposition; and from altered intervals, chords by borrowing. Everything is derived from the first three intervals, from which all the fundamental chords are formed, and everything is related solely to our harmonic center.

This is insufficient, as the ear not only approves these fundamental chords, but, as long as their progression is established by the progression of their lowest and fundamental sound, also finds everything in conformity with this progression pleasing. Whether this fundamental sound be implied, inverted, supposed, or borrowed, reason and the ear

498

are in such good agreement on this point that no exception to it can be found.

How wonderful is this source in its simplicity! So many chords, so many lively melodies, such boundless variety, such beautiful and fitting expressions, such well-rendered feelings! All this flows from two or three intervals arranged by thirds whose source subsists in a single sound. Thus:

Fundamental sound	Third	Fifth	Seventh
1	3	5	7

Our previous remarks should have already been convincing and the rules we shall now establish on the basis of this source will dispel all doubts.

(1) We begin with the consonances, which are all contained in the perfect chord. Since the fundamental bass can proceed only by consonant intervals in this case (see our discussion in Chapters 1 and 2, and in Book III, Chapter 4), it imposes a certain diatonic progression on the upper parts from which almost all rules about these consonances can be derived. If we do not say absolutely all the rules, this is only because dissonance introduces certain liberties. We shall always find the principal rules, however, especially those which the Ancients passed on as unquestionable.

In harmony, for instance, neither two consecutive octaves nor two consecutive fifths are ever found in natural progressions. If, without disturbing the progression of each part, we move each consonance to the one which may follow it, we shall find not only that perfect consonances generally pass to imperfect ones and vice versa, but we shall also find those particular perfect consonances which may follow one another. From this we conclude that, the succession of thirds being unlimited, their progression as well as that of their inversion, the sixths, should be free. It would seem that the fourth, which is the inversion of the fifth, ought to submit to the rule which governs this fifth. Experience, however, which shows that we may tolerate several fourths in succession in a diatonic progression, should outweigh this observation.

As for melody, we know that plain chant uses only diatonic or consonant intervals, and even so the interval of the major sixth is forbidden. Thus our source always subsists here. At the same time, however, let us not impose this rule on complete music, where dissonance has a marvelous effect and modulation alone should be the arbiter. The way we use modulation today permits the musician to employ certain dissonances of great expressive beauty, dissonances which formerly could be used only with difficulty.

(2) Of all the progressions of the bass, the descending fifth is the first and most perfect, since we are fully satisfied only when we hear a final cadence formed from this progression. The fifth appears to return to its source when it passes to one of the sounds of the octave by which it was generated (ascending a fourth being equivalent to descending a fifth). It is certainly for this reason that composers have exploited so fully the properties of this progression, and have derived so many advantages from it. This is further justified because the first progression of the source suffices to set the seal on all our rules, as will be shown below.

The rule requiring the major third to ascend to the octave, while forbidding this progression to the minor third, can arise only from the proposed source, since it is only in such a progression [i.e., the progression of a descending fifth] that the third ascends diatonically to the octave. Beware, however, of applying the rule incorrectly here. There is only one third with respect to the source, and it may not subsist without one of our two fundamental chords. Do not imagine, then, that the thirds of which we are speaking may be related equally to all sounds that inversion permits us to use in the bass. On the contrary, they may be related only to the source. These thirds are thirds only with respect to the source, whether they be found in the perfect chord or in the seventh chord. Another proof of this is that we have to apply this same rule to the sixths, which, occurring only in an inverted chord, follow the properties of the thirds only in so far as they represent these thirds. This may be seen by reducing this inverted chord to one of the two original chords. According to our approach, then, it is unnecessary to mention these sixths, for what we say about the thirds of the fundamental sound should be understood to apply equally to everything which represents these thirds. This will be proved in the dissonances themselves.

(3) The first dissonance is formed by adding a third to the perfect chord, and this third, measured from the fifth of the lowest sound of the chord, should naturally be minor. If this added third then forms a new dissonance with the major third of the lowest sound of this same chord, we see that dissonance is derived from these two thirds, and we are consequently obliged to distinguish two types of dissonance. We call that dissonance which arises from the added minor third minor, and that which arises from the natural major third of the perfect chord major.

500

This is a distinction which has not yet been made but which is nonetheless very reasonable, for by this means we may at once determine the progression of all dissonances. Major dissonances must ascend, while minor dissonances must descend. This rule brooks no exceptions and furthermore proves that fundamental harmony requires only the perfect chord and the seventh chord. All major dissonances may be reduced to the major third of the lowest sound of a seventh chord, while all minor dissonances may be reduced to a seventh. These assumptions raise no difficulties.

Although we have not yet examined the origin of the progression of the minor third, on which we have based the progression of all minor dissonances, the reader may rest assured, judging from what has appeared until now, that we advance nothing false. We are simply waiting for the appropriate moment at which to present our views on this subject.

It might perhaps be objected that both chromaticism and the license which we introduced in the irregular cadence are important exceptions to the preceding rule. We would reply, however, that the sixth added to the perfect chord in the irregular cadence is supernumerary. The harmony would lose none of its perfection without this sixth, the use of which is only a matter of good taste, whereas the harmony would become insipid without the other dissonances. As for chromaticism, by which the major dissonance may descend a semitone instead of ascending, this in no sense destroys our rule. Observe: 1. The sound to which the major dissonance should ascend in this case is understood, when it is not heard in another part. Besides, this sound is none other than the fundamental, which should consequently be found naturally in the bass. 2. The major dissonance is not dissonant in itself, while the minor is. If we suppress the latter, there will no longer be a major dissonance, as experience shows. 3. The major third from which the major dissonance is derived is natural to the perfect chord, and we do not absolutely forbid its remaining on the same degree when we say that it should ascend. 4. As a major dissonance may be formed only from the major third of a dominant-tonic, this dissonance becomes merely accidental with regard to the key which follows immediately. 5. We may consider that this major dissonance remains on the same degree in order to prepare the minor dissonance which follows it. The type of interval does not change at all, as we may see by leaving the bass note, on which this dissonance has been heard, on the same degree. As a result, if it formed a third or a seventh, it would still form a third or a seventh, the difference being only a matter of major and minor, or of augmented and perfect. This difference is also found in the notes marking these intervals, since it is caused simply by adding a flat or a sharp to the same note.

We are sure that skillful men will perceive the power of these proofs, although we have not put them forth fully for fear of tedious repetitions. Besides this, chromaticism is a new genre of harmony which should have its own properties. Although these properties seem to depart from the source, they nonetheless depend on it, as a brief explanation will show.

(4) Since the progression of the upper parts must naturally be diatonic and since the minor third cannot ascend to the octave, the rules absolutely require that this third should remain on the same degree during a part of the final or perfect cadence, so that it may then descend diatonically during the remainder of the cadence, as all connoisseurs can see. Now, this observation may well have brought about the intro- duction of dissonance into harmony and have led to the establishment of rules about it, since as a result of it the minor third, which remains on the same degree, forms a seventh, and then descends to another third. The rule about preparing and resolving the dissonance by a consonance apparently arises from this. It is not unreasonable, then, for us to derive this rule from part of the perfect cadence, rather than from anywhere else, for our purpose is always to comply with generally accepted notions. We see clearly that only the first three progressions of the fundamental bass have been used, i.e., descending a third, a fifth, and a seventh. On these the general rule that the dissonance should always be prepared and resolved has been established, for the seventh may be resolved only in one of these three fundamental progressions. Of these progressions, that of the descending fifth is first. It seems, furthermore, that dissonance owes its origin to the prefect cadence, according to our remarks in Chapter 2. Therefore, all our rules are based upon a single source. We should add that the seventh, from which all minor dissonances arise, may be naturally resolved only by the third in fundamental harmony, as has been said earlier (Chapter 17, Article iv).

These considerations should lead us to conclude that the author of these rules had a thorough knowledge of all the properties of harmony, even though he was guided, it seems, only by the source we are putting forward. Zarlino strives everywhere to prove that the earliest musicians were conscious of only the perfect chord, although he himself did not know all those which we use. Beginning with him each writer had

502

considered only the interval whose properties he seeks, thus giving only vague ideas about the source. This clearly proves that an understanding of inverted chords developed only over a period of time, and that, as this knowledge was dependent on experience alone, the source disappeared and these last chords were regarded as original chords. This has given rise to an infinite number of deviations, exceptions, and ambiguities, with terms, intervals, chords, and their progressions and properties, especially in terms of the modes, all being confused. It seems as if writers took pleasure in making obscure the simplest and most natural science in the world. All men of good sense can perceive this simplicity, whether by means of the old and new rules or by our reduction of these rules to the source. Geometricians have proposed this source in vain. Their limited experience did not permit them to explain themselves as we have done, and the ignorant, lost in the multiplicity of chords generated by this source, suspected that the geometricians themselves were ignorant. How easy it is to make up for this error, however, once we acknowledge the reduction of chords by thirds and the limits of these chords within the octave,[43] both of which we are driven to accept by our own experience. The only original chords will then be the perfect chord and the seventh chord. The first will be the basis for the sixth chord, while the latter will be the basis for the chord of the second. The situation is the same for all those chords called inverted, in which the fundamental sound is implied. This last [i.e., the seventh chord] will then also be the basis of the ninth chord and of the chord of the augmented second. The situation is the same for all chords arising from supposition and borrowing, in which the fundamental sound is supposed or borrowed. This completes all the different types of chords which are generated, as is evident, by the fundamental chords. These latter in turn are generated by the lowest and fundamental sound; it uses to this end its octave, which it had generated first, and from which we derive all consonances and all usable dissonances. We cannot repeat too often truths which theorists have only partially confessed and which the majority of practical musicians have always contested.

(5) It is manifest that the principal and fundamental rules just discussed are derived only from the initial descending progressions of the bass, since it is said there that all dissonances must be prepared. We should indicate, however, that there are exceptions to this rule. It is in

[43] Zarlino prescribes this reduction and these limits in Part III of his *Istitutioni*, Chapter 3, p. 174; Chapter 31, p. 210; and Chapter 66, p. 323. [R.]

fact untrue when the opposite progressions are found [in the bass]. In order to shorten our present discussion, however, we refer the reader to Chapter 13, where this matter is sufficiently explained.

(6) Since the major dissonance arises from the major third natural to the perfect chord, the only precaution that need be taken is to have it ascend a semitone, as is appropriate for this major third. Thus, as the major dissonance need not be prepared, we may say that it is in favor of this major dissonance that the minor dissonance may enjoy this same advantage in certain progressions of the fundamental bass.

(7) The other rules concerning ornamental dissonances, syncopation, etc. may be disregarded here, for they depend on good taste alone, even though they are always derived from our same source.

(8) It might be appropriate to speak here of modulation, which in some ways is at the heart of all our preceding rules. This would enable us to find connections and relationships between everything, thus further establishing the truth of our source, but since this subject requires a good deal of attention if we are to clarify the importance of these connections (which Zarlino and many others have misunderstood), we shall discuss it more fully in Chapters 21, 22, and 23.

(9) Further objections could be raised concerning the supernumerary sounds in chords by supposition and in the irregular cadence, and concerning that sound which borrows its fundamental from the fundamental sound itself, for these sounds are not included in our rules, and seem to demand special rules of their own. We need not to be overly concerned about this, for these sounds should be considered voluntary additions which in no way affect the source. Their use, furthermore, is easily understood, in accordance with the explanations we give in the other books. For a full understanding, we need only add a fundamental bass beneath any piece of music at all, conforming to the following explanation.

ARTICLE II

On how to compose a Fundamental Bass beneath any kind of Music

(1) The harmony is usually perceived only at the beginning of each beat of the measure, although a beat may sometimes be divided into two equal parts. The harmony is then perceived at the beginning of each half of the beat. Now it is at each of these instants that all the parts should

harmonize together and consequently that the fundamental bass should be with them. Notice that many notes can be found during the course of each beat and even at its beginning (although one should be careful about so using them) which are not part of the actual harmony, having been added there only as melodic ornaments.

(2) The fundamental bass cannot subsist unless it is always found below the other parts. It must always form with them a perfect chord or a seventh chord, supernumerary and borrowed sounds being suppressed wherever necessary.

(3) When a ninth chord or a chord of the augmented fifth appears, the fundamental bass should be found a third above the composed bass. When an eleventh chord, called a fourth, or a chord of the augmented seventh appears, the fundamental bass should be found a fifth above the composed bass. The remaining parts then form a seventh chord with this fundamental bass. Remember that the octave of the supernumerary sound of the eleventh should also be regarded as supernumerary, even though in the prescribed arrangement this combination has a pleasing effect.

(4) When a chord by borrowing appears, the dominant must take the place of the sixth note in the fundamental bass. The sixth note always forms an augmented second, or by inversion a diminished seventh, with the major third of this dominant. The rest of the chord will then form a seventh chord with our fundamental bass. We shall speak of this again in Article viii.

(5) We must beware of using an irregular cadence when the added sound might be mistaken for the lowest sound of a seventh chord. In this case, the added sound should be suppressed and only the perfect chord which subsists in the rest of the chord should be heard. We shall speak of this again in Articles viii, ix, and x.

(6) If by chance a chord with both a seventh and a sixth, of the type discussed in Chapter 17, Article v, is found, it need not command our attention. The fundamental bass in such a case must remain on the same degree on which it was previously found.

(7) As this bass is being added at present only as a proof, we need not be concerned about certain errors in its progression, such as two consecutive octaves, etc. These faults occur with the fundamental bass and do not affect the parts already composed at all.

(8) An understanding of modulation is a great asset for this proof. It immediately reveals the key in use and consequently the place a certain note occupies in this key, the chord it should bear, and the fundamental

sound which may be implied, supposed, or borrowed there. It furthermore leads to the recognition that chords by borrowing may appear only in minor keys and that in them the sixth note borrows the fundamental of the dominant-tonic. The fundamental remains in the fundamental bass, however, even when supposition occurs, together with this borrowing. Modulation also leads to a recognition of the fact that an irregular cadence may occur only when a dominant is preceded by its tonic note, or when the latter is preceded by its fourth note. Each of these notes should always be found in the fundamental bass here, bearing a perfect chord: we imagine that the lower sound of the dissonant interval is suppressed from the chord.[44]

(9) To compose this bass properly, we must make it proceed by consonant intervals wherever possible. Exceptions arise only when it is clear that a seventh may be resolved by the fifth or by another seventh or when it may be prepared by the octave. We always assume that the only intervals formed between the parts and the fundamental bass are the third, the fifth, the octave, and the seventh. Since the chords do not always actually contain all the sounds they theoretically should, we must be careful in making the proof, for the foundation of a chord always subsists even though the chord is incomplete. Sometimes taste obliges us to double a sound, instead of using that sound which would complete the chord. When we say that all the parts should form the third, the fifth, etc., with the fundamental bass, we exclude, to reiterate, the supernumerary sound of chords by supposition which should always be found below the fundamental bass, the sound added to the first perfect chord of an irregular cadence, and the sound which borrows its fundamental from the dominant-tonic. These sounds must be suppressed in the proof; we should imagine that they are not even present. Furthermore, the fifth above the second note of a minor key is often false, according to its natural order in the key. It should be considered to be perfect, however, having been altered only by accident.[45] We always assume that this fifth will be found only in a perfect chord or a seventh chord with respect to the fundamental bass. Having done this, then:

[44]He presumably means that in the chord of the added sixth, the sixth should be suppressed. Rameau is once again falling into the trap of his "chord of the added sixth" and is treating the seventh, formed by inverting this chord, as the dissonant interval. [P.G.]

[45]In other words, the fifth is altered by an accidental resulting from the modulation of the key in use. [P.G.]

(10) Notice whether the minor dissonance, which is always a seventh with respect to the fundamental bass, is prepared and resolved properly in the given progressions. Remember that ascending a fourth and descending a fifth are identical with respect to this bass, as are the other intervals having a similar relationship. It is sometimes possible to imply a dissonance which does not appear in the actual work, either to make the progression of the fundamental bass consonant or to suppress all but the appropriate chords above the bass. Thus, we need not censure an author for defects in the progression of this implied dissonance, as long as this dissonance does not appear without the fundamental bass. As for other defects in the progressions between a composed part and this fundamental bass, it is understood that the author does not actually mean to add this part. If these defects occur without the bass, however, then the author has made a mistake. Otherwise, this can not destroy the foundation of the harmony, which should always subsist in the two chords we have proposed. Furthermore, when we perceive that of the two sounds forming the interval of a second or of a seventh the upper sound of the second or the lower of the seventh ascends while the other sound remains on the same degree, then the progression of an irregular cadence will be clearly defined. We must imagine (as we have already said) that the sound which ascends is supernumerary and should never occupy the bass at all. As for the major dissonance, which is always formed by the leading tone or by the major third of a dominant-tonic and is dissonant only when the minor dissonance is joined to it, we must aways be sure, similarly, that it is properly resolved; i.e., by ascending a semitone.

(11) Several things must be said about the resolution of dissonances. 1. Any dissonance which remains on the same degree, but is correctly resolved subsequently, may be considered to be resolved correctly on condition that the same fundamental chord subsists with it. 2. That the ordinary bass may form a minor third with the fundamental need not concern us here. 3. As long as the same fundamental chord subsists, a dissonance may pass to any sound of that chord whatsoever. Later, however, it must normally pass to the sound which should have followed it in the first place. When the major or even the minor dissonance is heard last, however, they can maintain their privilege of being resolved correctly. 4. The major dissonance may be resolved on that consonance which should naturally follow the minor, while the latter may be resolved on that consonance which should naturally follow the former, provided that this occurs in a natural harmony and

that the notes ascend if they originally had to ascend, or descend if they originally had to descend. This conforms to an example given by Zarlino.[46] [Ex. II.51.] 5. In chromaticism, the major dissonance descends a semitone instead of ascending, or it could be considered to remain on the same degree, as we haver already indicated.

Minor dissonance

Major dissonance

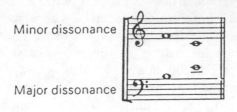

Music to which we may add a bass having all the properties just described will always be good. There may be mistakes in the order of the consonances, in the melody, in the modulation, in the spacing of the notes which prepare, form, and resolve the dissonance, or even in the beats on which this dissonance should be prepared and heard, but there will be no mistakes in relation to the foundation of the harmony. This is most important, for everything else may be handled very easily. Good taste, which dictates most of these rules to us, even obliges us sometimes to set them aside.

This fundamental bass has a very good effect in choral writing, but when we wish it to be heard, the rules must be rigorously observed in all the parts. The basso continuo may nonetheless form several unisons or octaves with the fundamental, especially in chords of $\frac{7}{6}$, chords by supposition, and chords by borrowing, without affecting the fundamental sound.

Since all those who have taken the trouble to lay down the preceding rules have always forgotten to indicate the source behind them, we have believed it necessary to discuss this matter at some length so that the obviousness of this source may clear our minds of doubts and disputes.

[46][Zarlino, *Istitutioni*], Part III, Chapter 30, p. 210. [R.]

Chapter Nineteen

Continuation of the preceding Chapter, in which it appears that Melody arises from Harmony

It would seem at first that harmony arises from melody, since the melodies produced by each voice come together to form the harmony. It is first necessary, however, to find a course for each voice which will permit them all to harmonize well together. No matter what melodic progression is used for each individual part, the voices will join together to form a good harmony only with great difficulty, if indeed at all, unless the progressions are dictated by the rules of harmony. Nonetheless, in order to make this harmonic whole more intelligible, one generally begins by teaching how to write a melodic line. No matter what progress may have been made, however, the ideas developed will disappear as soon as another part has to be added. We are then no longer the master of the melodic line. In looking for the direction a part should take with respect to another part, we often lose sight of the original direction, or at least are obliged to change it. Otherwise, the constraining influence of this first part will not always permit us to give the other parts melodic lines as perfect as we might wish. It is harmony then that guides us, and not melody. Certainly a knowledgeable musician can compose a beautiful melodic line suitable to the harmony, but from where does this happy ability come? May nature be responsible? Doubtless. But if, on the contrary, she has refused her gift, how can he succeed? Only by means of the rules. But from where are these rules derived? This is what we must investigate.

Does the first division of the string offer two sounds from which a melody may be formed? Certainly not, for the man who sings only octaves will not form a very good melodic line. The second and the third divisions of the string, from which harmony is derived, provide us with sounds which are no more suitable to melody, since a melodic line composed only of thirds, fourths, fifths, sixths, and octaves will still not be perfect. Harmony then is generated first, and it is from harmony that the rules of melody must be derived; indeed this is what we do by taking separately the aforementioned harmonic intervals, and forming from them a fundamental progression which is still not a melody. But when these intervals are put together above one of their component sounds, they naturally follow a diatonic course. This course is determined by the progression they follow, when each serves as a foundation for the others. We then derive from these consonant and diatonic progressions all the melody needed. Thus, we have to be acquainted with harmonic intervals before melodic ones, and the only melodic line we can teach a beginner is one consisting of consonant intervals, if indeed these can be called melodic. We shall see furthermore in Chapter 21 that the Ancients derived their modulation from melody alone, whereas it really arises from harmony.

Once this consonant progression is grasped, it is as simple to add three sounds above the sound used as bass as it is to add only one. We explain this as follows: It is possible, and sometimes compulsory, to place a third, a fifth, or an octave above the bass. Now, in order to use any one of them, we must understand them all. When we understand them all, however, it is no more difficult to use them together than separately. Thus, the part which has formed the third will form the fifth when the bass descends a third; this can be explained in no other way. But when in these different progressions of a bass we find the third here, the octave there, and the fifth in the third place, then we must always know how each interval should proceed according to the different progressions of the bass. Thus, without being aware of it, we teach four-part composition while explaining only two-part composition. Since each of the consonances is met alternately, the progression of each individual consonance with respect to the different progressions of the bass should be known. It is thus no more difficult to use them together than separately. It is all the better, for if we cannot distinguish them when they are all together, we need only consider them individually. Thus, by one device or another we can find the means of composing a perfect harmony in four parts from which we can draw all the knowledge necessary to reach perfection. In addition, the explanation which we add keeps us from being misled. We may cite the experience several people have had; knowing no more at first than the value of the notes, after reading our rules twice, they were able to compose a harmony as perfect as could be desired. If the composer gives himself the satisfaction of hearing what he has written, his ear will become formed little by little. [47] Once he becomes sensitive to perfect harmony, to which these introductory studies lead, he may be certain of a success which depends completely on these first principles.

There can be no further doubt that once four parts are familiar to us, we can reduce them to three and to two. Composition in two parts can

[47] It is partly for this reason that we give rules of accompaniment. [R.]

510

give us no knowledge, however, for even if we understood it perfectly, which is almost impossible, there is no fundamental to guide us. Everything that may be taught in this manner is always sterile, whether because our memory is insufficient or because the subject may be covered only with great difficulty. At the end, we are obliged to add the words: *Caetera docebit usus.* If we wish to pass from two to three or to four parts, we find that what has been said is of such little substance that genius and taste as fully developed as that of these great masters would be necessary in order to understand what they wish to teach us. Zarlino says that composition in four parts can hardly be taught on paper, and he leaves four-part writing to the discretion of those composers who can achieve this on the basis of his preceding rules concerning two and three parts.[48] Our opinion is quite the opposite, for as we have said harmony may be taught only in four parts. Everything in harmony may then be found in just two chords (as we have indicated everywhere) and it is very simple to reduce these four parts to three or to two. Zarlino, on the other hand, does not even give a clear definition of these two or three parts, and he claims that he is unable to define four parts. He says this even though he is convinced that a perfect harmony consists of four parts, which he compares to the four elements.[49] In conclusion, we affirm that though it has been impossible to understand fully the rules given until now concerning harmony, the source we have proposed will certainly lead to an understanding which is all-embracing.

Chapter Twenty

On the properties of Chords

Harmony may unquestionably excite different passions in us depending on the chords that are used. There are chords which are sad, languishing, tender, pleasant, gay, and surprising. There are also certain progressions of chords which express the same passions. Although this is beyond my scope, I shall explain it as fully as my experience enables me to do.

Consonant chords can be found everywhere, but they should predominate in cheerful and pompous music. As it is impossible to avoid using dissonant chords there, these chords must arise naturally. The dissonance must be prepared whenever possible, and the most

[48][Zarlino, *Istitutioni*], Part III, Chapter 65, p. 320. [R.]
[49][*Ibid.*], Chapter 58, p. 281. [R.]

exposed parts, i.e., the treble and bass, should always be consonant with one another.

Sweetness and tenderness are sometimes expressed well by prepared minor dissonances.

Tender lamentations sometimes demand dissonances by borrowing and by supposition, minor rather than major. Any major dissonances present should occur in middle parts rather than in the extremes.

Langour and suffering may be expressed well with dissonances by borrowing and especially with chromaticism, of which we shall speak in the following book.

Despair and all passions which lead to fury or strike violently demand all types of unprepared dissonances, with the major dissonances particularly occurring in the treble. In certain expressions of this nature, it is even effective to pass from one key to another by means of an unprepared major dissonance, as long as the ear is not too greatly offended by an overly large disproportion between the two keys. Hence, this must be done discerningly, just like everything else, for to pile up dissonance upon dissonance every time that a dissonance might occur would be a defect infinitely greater than to use only consonances. Dissonance should be employed only with great discretion. Sometimes we should even avoid its use in chords from which it should ordinarily not be separated, suppressing it skillfully when hits harshness is unsuited to the expression, and distributing those consonances which form the rest of the chord through all the parts. We should remember that the seventh, from which all dissonances arise, is only a sound added to the perfect chord, that it consequently does not destroy the fundamental of this chord, and that it may always be suppressed when this is judged appropriate.

Melody has no less expressive force than harmony, but giving definite rules for its use is almost impossible, since good taste plays a greater part in this than anything else. We shall leave to privileged geniuses the pleasure of distinguishing themselves in this domain on which depends almost all the strength of sentiment. We hope that those able men to whom we have said nothing new will not bear us ill-will for having revealed secrets of which they wished perhaps to be the sole trustees. Our little knowledge does not permit us to argue with them about this last degree of perfection, without which the most beautiful harmony may become insipid. In this manner they are always in a position to surpass others. This does not mean that when we know how to arrange appropriately a succession of chords we are unable to derive from it a melody suitable to our subject, as we shall see later, but good taste is always the prime mover here.[50]

In the use of melody, it seems that the Ancients surpassed us, if we may believe what they say. Of this one it is claimed that his melody made Ulysses weep; that one obliged Alexander to take up arms; another made a furious youth soft and human. On all sides, we see the astounding effects of their music. Zarlino comments very sensibly, saying first that the word harmony often signifies only a simple melody to them, and that all these effects arise more from an energetic discourse, whose force is increased by the manner in which they declaim the text while singing, than from melody alone; for their melody could certainly not have profited from all the diversity which the perfect harmony unknown to them procures for us today. Their harmony, Zarlino says further,[51] consisted of a perfect chord above which they sang their different sorts of airs (as with our bagpipes [Fr. *musettes*] or hurdy-gurdies [Fr. *vielles*]); Zarlino called this *Sinfonia*.[52]

A good musician should surrender himself to all the characters he wishes to portray. Like a skillful actor he should take the place of the speaker, believe himself to be at the locations where the different events he wises to depict occur, and participate in these events as do those most involved in them. He must declaim the text well, at least to himself, and must feel when and to what degree the voice should rise or fall, so that he may shape his melody, harmony, modulation, and movement accordingly.

Chapter Twenty-One

On the Modes

Although modern authors have taught that there are only two modes,

---

[50]In French this expression is "le premier moteur," an interesting metaphysical metaphor. [P.G.]

[51][Zarlino, *Istitutioni*], Part III, Chapter 79, p. 356. [R.]

[52]According to Curt Sachs, *Real-Lexikon der musikinstrumente* (Berlin, 1913; reprinted by Dover Publications, New York, 1964), "Symphonie" was simply an alternative name for the hurdy-gurdy, particularly current in Italy during the latter middle ages. All these instruments involve drones above which the singer moves with greater freedom. For a short discussion of these instruments see the article "hurdy-gurdy" by F.W. Galpin in *Grove's Dictionary of Music and Musicians*, fifth edition (London, 1954). Again Rameau could be referring either to the instruments or to the characteristic pieces styled on them. [P.G.]

they have so often been slaves to the rules they have imposed on others, that they have become insensible to everything this fortunate discovery might imply. They speak only of arbitrary chords, and although the mode should be the sole guide, they leave the progression of the chords for us to discover ourselves.

It is well known that what we call a mode consists of the octave of a single sound within which all the sounds that can be used for melodies and chords are to be found. The Ancients considered only the melody, which was an error, for the melody completely depends on the chords fixed by the mode.

We distinguished between two types of modes. They take their names from the major or minor interval formed by the third of the sound which, together with its octave, is the primary element of a mode. Since there are only two thirds, of which one is major and the other minor, we say that there are only two modes, of which one is major and the other minor. It is understood that these words major and minor refer to the third which should accompany the fundamental sound of the mode.

The first mode we perceive is that derived from the perfect diatonic system, in which the octave of Do contains six other notes. The intervals these notes form with the note Do cannot be changed without simultaneously changing the mode. The principal notes of this mode were first derived from the perfect chord built on the note Do: the third was called the mediant and the fifth the dominant. It has been felt in the past that the sixth chord is more suited to the mediant than is the perfect chord, but no one has concluded that in this way the mediant always represents the principal note or tonic, since the sixth chord it should bear is an inversion of the perfect chord built on this tonic note. It has similarly been perceived that the dominant should bear a perfect chord whose third should always be major. Furthermore, the dissonance of the seventh, in which the false fifth is found, is appropriate only to the dominant when it immediately precedes the tonic note, perfect cadences being formed from these two single notes. No one has said, however, that the chords of the false fifth and of the tritone are derived from the seventh chord and that, just as the seventh chord is created only to precede the perfect chord built on the tonic note, all its derivatives should equally precede this perfect chord or its derivatives. This might all have been perceived by experience, without even mentioning the rules. From these observations, the conclusion should have been drawn that in any mode a seventh chord itself or one of its derivatives appears only when it is immediately followed by the perfect chord of the tonic note itself or by one of its derivatives. This would have begun to clarify matters. First of all, we find included in these two chords all the notes of a mode, except the sixth, which, since it has the same nature as the third, is simple to find. In the second place, we discover which chords these notes should bear when they precede the tonic or its mediant. We then have only to find chords suitable for notes which precede the dominant, proceeding as follows: If the perfect chord of a note is preceded by the seventh chord of a note a fifth above, then the dominant, which ordinarily bears a perfect chord and which adds a seventh without destroying its fundamental in any way, must also be preceded by the seventh chord of the note a fifth above it. In order to preserve the mode in use, the third of this last note should always be minor, whether it be considered the seventh of the dominant-tonic or the fourth of the tonic note. The sixth note is now found in this new seventh chord. We may thus judge not only the nature of the intervals which should be within the octave of the tonic note or fundamental note of the mode, but also the chords which the notes of the mode should bear. These chords are derived by inverting the fundamental chords containing these intervals. As for the minor mode, it differs from the major only n that its third and its sixth should be minor, although there are several problems with regard to the sixth which we shall explain in the following book.

By following this principle, we avoid being obliged to say with Masson: "If the bass ascends a semitone, we must use the minor sixth and then the fifth, or two major sixths,"[53] for this distinction refers to different notes in two different modes. As a result, this rules establishes nothing, for it is oblivious to the mode. When he then speaks of ornamental dissonances or dissonances by supposition [see Book III, Chapter 39], Masson cites a large number of dissonances found in chords formed by the consonances which precede or follow these dissonances. Thus, since the consonance and dissonance which meet here are part of the same chord, the dissonance implies nothing further, for it is understood to be part of the chord. We shall ignore many other mistakes of this kind.

When giving rules, we often copy those of others with too much indulgence. As a result, the good statements we make are often contradicted by rules drawn from elsewhere.

[53][Masson, *Nouveau traité*], Chapter 3, pp. 36, 37, and 38. [R.] This is not a direct quotation from Masson, but a summary of the text and examples on these pages. [P.G.]

The Ancients defined the properties of the modes perfectly well, in terms of the different effects they produce and the way in which they control harmony and melody. But the Ancients were always ignorant of their true nature, for the attributed all the power of these modes to melody. They assumed that melody had to be derived from the seven diatonic notes of the perfect system, without distinguishing among them further. As they thought that by using each note of the system as the principal one they would be able to create as many different effects as there are notes in the system, they simultaneously lost sight of what should have been their model. Is this perfect system no longer perfect when it comes to imitating it? Why did the Ancients imitate it with regard to the consonances found in it by adding a flat to the note Si, thus forming the fourth of the note Fa? And why did they then abandon it for the dissonances which precede the tonic note, both ascending and descending? Is there not a tone from Do to Re and a semitone from Do to Si? Yet when they took the note Mi as tonic, they left the semitone between Mi and Fa and the tone between Re and Mi, instead of making this progression conform to the progression of the perfect system by adding a sharp to the notes Fa and Re, just as they added a flat to the note Si. This is how they differentiated between their modes, you will reply. But this is a mistake, as our own experience shows indubitably. By relating this to those remarks of Zarlino which are contrary to his rules, we shall see that his conception of the modes was ill-founded. The bass, he says,[54] is the source, the fundamental, etc., of all the other parts. Its natural progression in perfect cadences is to descend a fifth.[55] Observe that in the examples he gives of these cadences there is always an ascending semitone between the note which precedes the final note and the final note itself. In other examples in which this ascending semitone is found, there is also a voice which descends a tone to this same final note. By assembling the notes which precede the final note from all sides, we shall find that those notes which ascend a semitone are major thirds of the dominant, while whose which descend a tone are fifths of this same dominant. Now, since all perfect conclusions can occur only on a tonic note preceded by its fifth, i.e., its dominant, and since the perfect chord of this dominant can consist only of its fifth and its major third, we see that there is always a tone between this fifth and

[54][Zarlino, *Istitutioni*], Part III, Chapter 58, pp. 281 and 282. [R.]
[55][*Ibid.*], Chapter 51, pp. 251 and 252. [R.] Once again, although Zarlino refers to this cadence, he does not call it either "natural" or "perfect." [P.G.]

the tonic note and a semitone between this major third and the tonic note. Thus no mode can exist in which these properties are not found, for if the natural progression of the bass in a perfect cadence is to descend a fifth, this cadence cannot be heard in other parts without one of these parts ascending a semitone and another of them descending a tone. We may only conclude a piece of music by a perfect cadence on the principal note of a mode; otherwise the spirit will not be satisfied. How absurd it is to propose modes which do not submit to these requirements! From this same principle, Zarlino derived the rule which prohibits the minor third and the minor sixth from ascending to the octave. This proves that the dominant-tonic should always bear a major third and that this third is always a semitone below the octave of the principal note, as in the perfect system between the notes Si and Do. According to the Ancients, however, this semitone is not found at all in the keys of Re, Mi, Sol, or La. It is sufficiently clear then that they were guided only by melody, for had they had any regard for harmony they could not have committed such gross errors. Zarlino, who was more able than his predecessors, could have understood this idea, had he not been so indulgent towards those practices to which he was forced, so to speak, to conform. I am speaking here of ecclesiastical plain chant which had existed for a long time before Zarlino and was very difficult to reform, because of custom or habit, even though it was suitable to harmony only in keys which conform to the perfect system. We thus see only men without taste, full of the rules of the Ancients whose meaning they do not understand, vainly attempting to introduce a good and pleasant harmony beneath this type of chant. Certainly this should be the objective of our nightly labors and work, since music exists only to sing the praises of God; but how unpleasant it must be for a man filled with this truth to be unable to use his full genius for this end. He may place chords beneath melodies, proceeding to the end without fault; but there is quite a difference between a faultless music and a perfect one. The Ancients, too much the slaves of their first discoveries, composed all these chants from melodies provided by the perfect system, thus finishing where they should have begun. They based the rules of harmony on melody, instead of beginning with harmony, which comes first (as the division of the string proves), and basing the rules of melody on harmony, a procedure which would even have led to a type of chant simpler and more flowing than that used in our churches today. Their blindness is further revealed by the fact that they differentiated between authentic or principal modes and plagal or collateral ones.

517

The difference between harmonic and arithmetic proportions became so significant to them that they adapted for the division of the octave a proportion suited only to the division of the fifth. We shall see that the difference between these proportions, which should be applied only to harmony, was applied by the Ancients almost exclusively to melody.

When Zarlino divided the octave by the fourth to obtain a new mode, he merely transposed the place of the sounds forming this octave divided by the fifth, a process we call inversion. Thus, the principal mode, in which the octave is divided by the fifth, and the collateral mode, in which it is divided by the fourth, are one and the same mode. The same note is always the principal or tonic in both modes; its mediant and its dominant are always the same; and the differences which do arise affect only the melody. Here is the example which this author gives.[56] [Ex. II.52.]

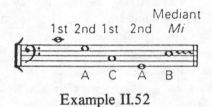

Example II.52

The first note is the principal, the second is its collateral. C indicates that C, Sol–Do, is the tonic note for both modes.[57] Thus, Do has no other mediant than Mi, B, nor any other dominant but Sol, A. The difference between these two modes arises from the melodic line moving from one Do to the other in the principal mode, and from one Sol to the other in the collateral mode. This distinction is quite useless, however, for the melodic line has no other limits besides the range of the voices, as our natural experience teaches us immediately.

When Zarlino divided the firth first by a major third and then by a minor third above the lowest sound, he was unable then to form two modes from them corresponding to the previous ones. Their mediants are different, and consequently so are their sixths; it is this that constitutes all the difference in their modulation, and not the second, the

[56][*Ibid.*], Part IV, Chapter 13, p. 384. [R.] Zarlino does not include the mediant in his diagram. [P.G.]

[57]This nomenclature is a reference to the Guidonian system of hexachords, current even in the Baroque period. See, for example, the discussion by Descartes, A.I.M., pp. 35–42. [P.G.]

518

fourth, the fifth, or the augmented seventh ascending to the octave. These latter intervals never change. Even less is the difference of modulation to be found in the range of a melodic line, for the intervals used above and below the octave do not differ at all from those within the octave. If Zarlino had followed the opinion of Plato, who (as he reports)[58] considered melody to be born of harmony, he would have searched for the fundamentals of modulation in harmony. This would in turn have led him along paths by which he could have achieved the perfection which he believed he had attained, for only from the perfect chord of the tonic note, the perfect chord of its dominant to which a seventh is added whenever appropriate, and the seventh chord of its second note is true modulation, and consequently all the sequence of good harmony and beautiful melody derived. Our preceding rules conform to this principle, which can be maintained everywhere with the same conviction.

Chapter Twenty-Two

On the origin of our liberty to pass from one Mode or from one Key to another

The consonant progression of a fundamental bass bearing only perfect chords can provide us with as many different keys as there are different sounds in the bass. Since the perfect chord alone is appropriate for a tonic note, a key is always established on each of these notes. As a result, from the consonances obtained from the first divisions of the string, we derive not only all the chords, all melody, and all progressions within a given key, but also the progressions to be used when passing from one key to another (as we shall explain in Book III). We need not worry whether the key is major or minor, since we must always be guided by the key we are leaving. Notice that we do not separate the term mode from the term key when a change between major and minor is found on the same tonic note, for we may change the mode from major to minor or from minor to major without changing the tonic or principal note of the mode. For example, when we pass from a gay theme to a sad

---

[58][Zarlino, *Istitutioni*], Part II, Chapter 12, p. 95. [R.] The passages about music from Plato's *Republic* are published in Oliver Strunk, *Source Readings in Music History* (New York, 1950), pp. 4–12. [P.G.]

one, or from a sad to a gay, as occurs in most Chaconnes or Passacaglias or often in two successive airs of the same type, we can say that the key does not change at all, even though the modes changes. If the note Do is the tonic in the major mode, then it is also the tonic in the minor. In order not to confuse these terms, we simply say major key or minor key. The modulation of the key may change only from major to minor or from minor to major. The tonic note, however, may be taken on any of the twenty-four different notes of the chromatic system.[59] This is not to be done randomly during the course of a piece, however, since one we determine that a certain note will be used at the beginning and at the end, we may leave that note only in order to pass to another which is related either to it or to the notes of its chord. We proceed successively in this manner, being obliged to return to our initial note when we wish to conclude, finishing the piece.

Chapter Twenty-Three

On the properties of Modes and Keys[60]

We have already said that there are only two modes, the major and the minor, and each of these modes may be taken on every note of the chromatic system. We may thus say that there are twenty-four keys [Fr. *tons*], because the name tonic [Fr. *ton*] is given to the note which is used as the principal note of a mode.

The major mode follows the nature of the major third, while the minor mode follows that of the minor third. The different arrangement of the semitones found in the octave of each note which can be taken as the principal or tonic note, however, creates certain differences in the modulation of these octaves. It is thus appropriate to explain their properties.

The major mode taken in the octave of the notes Do, Re, or La is suitable for songs of mirth and rejoicing. In the octave of the notes Fa or

[59] It is not certain what Rameau is referring to here. Presumably he is not speaking of enharmonic spelling of pitches, but of the major and minor keys that can be built on any of the twelve chromatic steps of the scale. [P.G.]

[60] Rameau has transposed the position of Chapters 23 and 24 in the Supplement. This chapter, then, was originally Chapter 24, and the present Chapter 24 was originally Chapter 23. [P.G.]

Si ♭ , it is suitable for tempests, furies, and other similar subjects. In the octave of the notes Sol or Mi, it is suitable for both tender and gay songs. Grandeur and magnificence can also be expressed in the octave of the notes Re, La, or Mi.

The minor mode taken in the octaves of the notes Re, Sol, Si, or Mi is suitable for sweetness and tenderness. In the octave of the notes Do or Fa, it is suitable for tenderness and plaints. In the octave of the notes Fa or Si ♭ , it is suitable for mournful songs. The other keys are not in general use, and experience is the surest means by which to learn their properties.

[. . .]

Book Four: *Principles of Accompaniment*

Chapter Ten

On the Basso Continuo

The diatonic progression of the bass, of which we are speaking now, should not be confused with the consonant progression of which we have already given examples using the perfect chord and the seventh chord. These two chords are fundamental. As proof of this, we shall from now on place the bass we call fundamental under our examples. The notes of this fundamental bass will bear only perfect chords and seventh chords, while the notes of the ordinary bass, which we shall call the continuo, will bear chords of all types. All these parts together will form a perfect harmony. This fundamental bass will thus serve as proof for all our compositions, and we shall see that all the different chords used there are derived from a progression which differs from the progression of this fundamental bass only in the sense we have just explained. Chords compared to either bass are always basically the same. Their differences arise only because we are free to place in the bass any note of the fundamental chords. All the notes of the chord taken together, however, will always be the same, and the progression determined for these notes in the fundamental chords will therefore not change.

Chapter Eleven

On the progression of the Bass, which simultaneously determines the progression of the Chords; how we may relate a derived Chord to its Fundamental

The progression of those bass notes which bear consonant chords, i.e., the tonic note, its mediant, and its dominant, is unlimited, as long as the progression is not foreign to the key in use. As we are still dealing with only a single key, however, we cannot go wrong if we use only the notes Do, Re, Mi, Fa, Sol, La, Si.

The progression of those bass notes which bear dissonant chords is limited; these include the dominant, when it bears the seventh chord, and all its derivatives; or rather, these include all notes which bear neither the perfect chord nor one of its derivatives, since once a note bears a dissonant chord it certainly dominates another [note].[61] Thus, it is by relating a chord to its fundamental that we shall indubitably find the chord which should follow, no matter what note is actually found in the bass.

To relate a dissonant chord to its fundamental, we should observe that there are always two notes or two numbers together in such a chord, e.g.,

Fa,	Sol;	Do,	Re;	etc.
3	4	5	6	

This is also found in the seventh chord when we bring the bass note an an octave higher, thus $^{Fa}_7$ $^{Sol}_8$, just as for the second $^{Do}_1$ $^{Re}_2$. When the higher of the two notes or the greater of the two numbers is placed in the fundamental bass, we find that the lower note or the smaller numbers always forms the seventh of the other. These derived chords can thus be reduced to their fundamental division, 1, 3, 5, 7, as indicated in the enumeration on page 223 [Ex. III.30]. If the note Sol is found in the bass after this reduction, then the note Do should certainly follow. If the note Do is not found in the bass at all, then another of the notes in its perfect chord (or in its seventh chord if we are in another key) should certainly be there. Similarly, if the note Re is found in the fundamental

---

[61]Rameau is not taking his "chord of the added sixth" into consideration here. According to his own system, this chord neither derives from the seventh chord nor dominates another note. [P.G.]

bass, the note Sol or one of its derivatives will follow, and so on. Remember that after a seventh chord the fundamental bass should always descend a fifth.

Any bass whose succession does not conform to what we have just set forth must be changed. The correct succession is nonetheless simple to follow, either by means of the chords appropriate to each note of a key, following the different progressions of these notes, or by means of the proof that can be drawn from the fundamental bass, which can bear only the perfect chord or the seventh chord. Any note bearing the last chord should always descend a fifth. Our remarks concerning a bass already composed should also apply to the method of composing a bass. Though this rule suffers some exceptions, such as the deceptive cadence or the irregular cadence, etc., these need not concern us yet.

Before giving an example of the above, we must remember that chords built on notes which in a natural progression lead to notes destined to bear a perfect chord, must always be related to the chord which follows and not to the one which precedes; that a natural progression always leads to that note which should bear a perfect chord; and that this progression normally occurs when going from the tonic to its dominant or from the latter to the former: for as we have said many times, the dominant should always be treated as a tonic note. Thus, if you know the chords which lead to one of these notes in a diatonic progression, you also know the chords which lead to the other. As a result, the following general rules may be given:

(1) All notes which, ascending a tone or a semitone, precede a note bearing the perfect chord should bear the chord of the large sixth or of the false fifth. [Ex. III.31.]

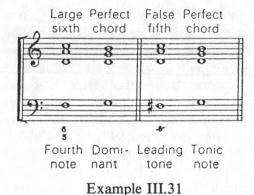

Example III.31

523

Observe that these two chords differ only in the bass, for whether we ascend a tone or a semitone to the note bearing the perfect chord, the chord in the upper parts will always be the same. The composer is thus free to make the bass proceed by a tone or by a semitone, even if he should be in a key in which the semitone is not appropriate; for since the dominant can be treated as a tonic note, it may be approached using all those sounds which naturally precede a tonic note. A sharp may thus be added to the fourth note, as can be seen, making it a leading tone. It is by means of the difference between the progression of a tone and a semitone ascending to the note bearing the perfect chord that we differentiate a dominant and a tonic note. The bass always ascends a tone to the dominant and a semitone to the tonic note. Even if this progression of a semitone is used, thus giving a dominant all the attributes of a tonic note, we may still continue after this dominant (which would then appear to be a tonic note) in the original key, since after a perfect chord we are free to pass wherever we desire.

(2) All notes which, descending, precede a note bearing the perfect chord should bear the chord of the small sixth. [Ex. III.32.]

Second Tonic   Sixth Dominant
note note   note

Example III.32

The guides signify that we may make the bass pass to the mediant of each of the notes which bear perfect chords without changing the foundation of the chords. These mediants will then bear sixth chords.

We cannot differentiate here a second note from a sixth note or a tonic note from a dominant, since the perfect chords borne by the tonic and by the dominant are preceded similarly; thus, we cannot distinguish them in a major key. In a minor key, however, the sixth note descending to the dominant is only a semitone higher, while the second note is always a tone above the tonic. Furthermore, the dominant always bears the major third, while the tonic in minor keys should bear the minor third. That we cannot distinguish a dominant in a major key should not

524

cause embarrassment, however, because we need only treat it as a tonic in such a case, adjusting the chords of the preceding notes to its key. It is simple to judge afterwards whether it is really a tonic or a dominant. [Ex. III.33.]

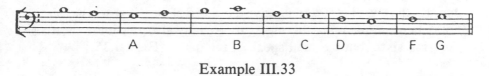

Example III.33

The progression from the first note to note A does not clearly indicate whether note A is a tonic or a dominant. This is immaterial, for the chords would be the same in either progression. It is clear, however, that the progression from A to B is to a tonic note; thus, A is a dominant. If the progression from B to C again raises doubts, note D which follows makes it clear that C is a dominant, just as F makes us recognize this dominant again at G; for in all keys the note immediately below the tonic is separated from it by only a semitone, while there is always a tone between the dominant and the note immediately below it.

Though in a minor key the note below the tonic is separated from it by a tone (when we descend from the tonic note to its dominant or at least to the sixth note), the minor third which the tonic should bear in this case makes the distinction immediately clear, for the dominant should always bear the major third.

(3) All notes found a third above or below the tonic or the dominant should bear sixth chords, when the progression of the bass leads to one of these two notes.[62] [Ex. III.34.]

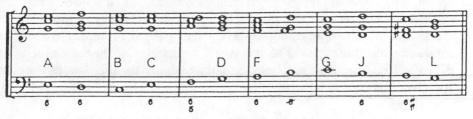

Example III.34

[62]Rameau does not call attention to the parallel fifths in this example. The first chord in measure three in Rameau's original is not the same as the chord he figures in the bass. He figures $\frac{6}{5}$ but notates 7. The former is correct and I have changed the chord accordingly. [P.G.]

The progression of the bass leading to notes B, D, G, and L, at which points the perfect chord should occur, obliges us to give sixth chords to notes A, C, F, and J.

(4) Since the mediant always represents the tonic note, for the sixth chord this mediant should naturally bear is the same as the perfect chord of the tonic note, we must give the chord of the tritone to the fourth note when it descends to this mediant. We may also give it the chord of the large sixth, but we shall speak of this later. [Ex. III.35.]

Example III.35.

Some very useful conclusions may be drawn from these last five examples if we notice the different arrangements possible for the sounds constituting a fundamental chord, depending upon the different progressions of the bass. If the fourth note, ascending to the dominant, bears the chord of the large sixth; if, descending to the mediant which represents the tonic, it bears the chord of the tritone; if the leading tone, ascending to the tonic, bears the chord of the false fifth; and if the second and the sixth notes, descending to the tonic or to the dominant, bear the chord of the small sixth; then it can be seen that these chords are derived from the seventh chords of the notes which dominate those which follow. This will become clearer when we place a fundamental bass below a general example containing everything we have just discussed. Notice here that the leading tone functions as such only when it ascends to the tonic note. When it descends, it should be regarded as simply the mediant of the dominant, taking this latter to be the tonic note so as to avoid mistakes. [Ex. III.36.]

Since the fundamental bass has been placed below the other parts only to demonstrate that, without departing from the natural progression of this bass, the harmony of these other parts consists of the perfect chord and the seventh chord alone, we need not examine whether the rules are rigorously observed between the parts and this fundamental bass. We need only see whether other chords than those figured for each

526

bass are found here. The succession of sounds is related solely to the basso continuo, since we are presently considering a diatonic progression in the bass.

General example of the octave, ascending as well as descending

Example III.36

(1) After having noticed in the basso continuo that the same succession of chords is found from J to L and from B to M, ascending to either the dominant or to the tonic note, and likewise from N to K and from O to U, descending to either the dominant or to the tonic note, we shall realize that everything is related to one of these two notes, for they are the only notes in any key which may naturally bear the perfect chord. Remember that the notes found a third above them are considered to be their mediants when the bass descends from these mediants to either of the two notes. The mediant of the tonic always remains such, however, no matter what course the bass takes. The perfect chord, as we said, may only be preceded by a dissonant chord which dominates it. Thus, we can see that the chords of the small and large sixth, of the false fifth, and of the tritone are the same as the seventh chords of the notes found in the fundamental bass which naturally dominate those notes which follow them. The small sixth of the second note, the false fifth of the leading tone, and the tritone of the

527

fourth note are all derived from the seventh chord of the dominant-tonic D, which is immediately followed by the tonic note. The large sixth of the fourth note and the small sixth of the sixth note are furthermore derived from the seventh chord of the second note A and C, which here dominates the dominant-tonic, by which it is immediately followed. The sixth chord which the mediant, the sixth note, and the leading tone bear is obviously used only because these notes are found a third above or below the tonic and the dominant, to which notes the progression of the bass immediately leads.

(2) It might seem that the sixth note B should bear the chord of the small sixth, thus conforming to the seventh chord borne by the note B in the fundamental bass. We suppress one of the sounds forming the dissonance, however, for several reasons. First, it is dispensable. Second, since the note immediately following in the bass is the leading tone, consequently forming the major dissonance (as we shall presently see), and since no dissonance should be doubled, the chord of the small sixth may not be given to the sixth note in this case; for if it were, the third of this sixth note would have to descend to the same major dissonance. Finally, our rule about using a sixth chord on all notes which precede notes found a third higher or lower bearing a perfect chord continues to hold good.

(3) If in place of the fourth note R in the basso continuo, immediately preceding the dominant L or K, the second note A or C or the sixth note T occurred, we would have to add a sharp to this fourth note as we have done at S, because every note bearing the perfect chord prefers to be preceded by its leading tone. In minor keys, however, where the sixth note always descends a semitone to the dominant, the leading tone of this dominant cannot be heard no matter what note precedes this dominant in the bass; for if the dominant were preceded by its leading tone in the bass, it would become a tonic note and the true key in use would be distinguishable only by means of the notes following this dominant. This can be seen in our example, for the dominant might appear to be a tonic note, its real nature being revealed only by means of the note which follows it. Thus, the chord of the tritone is derived from the seventh chord of this same dominant, found below in the fundamental bass at D.

(4) The diatonic progression of the basso continuo upsets the diatonic progression of the parts at F, G, and H. This cannot be done differently, if we wish to avoid two consecutive octaves or fifths, to

528

return a part to its natural range above the bass, or to utilize all the sounds of which a chord is composed.

The upper parts should follow a diatonic progression only in so far as the bass follows a consonant one; if the latter changes, the former may also change. Besides, it is often appropriate to upset the diatonic order of a part in order to diversify the melody. The order and progression of the parts above the basso continuo may even be changed without making a mistake, but this need not concern us yet.

(5) There are several unprepared sevenths in our example, contradicting our first rule; this is not, however, the place to speak of them. Let us here only try to follow the progression determined for the chords by the order of this octave. We shall see later that after a consonant chord we are free to pass anywhere, as long as the rules of modulation are observed.

(6) We remarked in the preceding book that, whenever it is permissible to have the fundamental bass ascend a tone or a semitone, the progression of a third and a fourth is always implied. This can be seen here between notes Z, Y, and A: note Y is added; the seventh of this note is prepared by the fifth of note Z; and the third prepares the seventh of note A. This does not change the foundation of the chords at all. Notice also that with note Y suppressed, the interval of a tone or a second found between notes Z and A contains the same notes as the seventh between A and X.

Chapter Twelve

Continuation of the Rules drawn from the preceding Example

Remember that when a bass note should bear a seventh chord, the note forming the seventh may always be suppressed, unless it was prepared by a consonance in the preceding chord. If the consonance is major, however, as the third and the sixth may be, it would be preferable to have this third of this sixth ascend a semitone. If the bass note bears only a chord derived from the seventh, you may suppress from the chord that one of these two sounds which forms the dissonance. This sound is simple to recognize, for the two sounds are always joined in the manner indicated in Chapter 11.

The same note may be repeated in the bass as often as good taste permits, with the same chord or different ones, as we gradually come to know how this can be done.

Furthermore, we may pass from one note to another when the chords they bear differ only in name; e.g., we may pass from a seventh chord to the chord of the false fifth built on the note which forms the third of the note on which this seventh was heard. On the note which forms the fifth, we may use the chord of the small sixth, just as we may use the chord of the tritone on the note which forms the seventh. This may be done because all the chords are basically the same chord. The same is true in other similar instances. [Ex. III.37.]

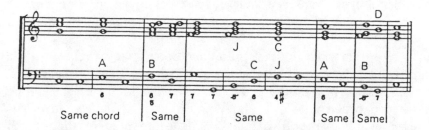

Example III.37

Notes which are a third above those which, immediately after, bear a perfect chord or a seventh chord should normally bear a chord derived from the chord which follows. Thus, at A the sixth chord is derived from the perfect chord which follows, while at B the chord of the large sixth or of the false fifth is derived from the seventh chord which follows.

When the bass notes change their position without the chord itself changing, the upper parts of consonant chords need not be changed. With dissonant chords, however, we must be sure that the four different sounds making up these chords are always heard. This may be done by adding the octave of the note we have left, D, when this note was not already present in the chord built on this same note which had preceded it in the fundamental bass,[63] or by leaving the octave of the present note, J, in order to replace it with the octave of the note we have left, C.

---

[63]This presumably should read "basso continuo," since the pitch Si is not in the fundamental bass. [P.G.]

Chapter Thirteen

On the Perfect Cadence

All conclusions of a strain in which a tonic note is preceded by its dominant are called perfect cadences. This tonic note should always occur on the first beat of a measure, if the conclusion is to be felt; its dominant, which precedes it in this case, should always bear a seventh chord or at least a perfect chord, for the seventh can be implied there. [Ex. III.38.]

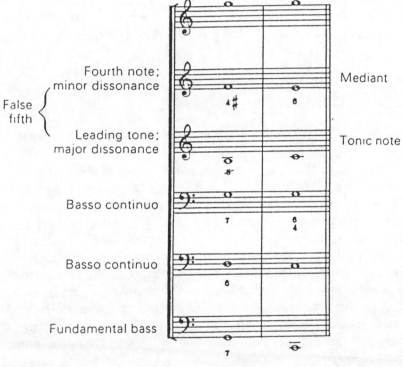

Example III.38

By means of this perfect cadence, we may judge which bass notes should bear perfect chords; for wherever we feel that the strain comes to rest, the perfect chord should certainly be used. This rest is felt not only when the bass has its most natural progression in this cadence, but also when it is formed from sounds which accompany this most natural progression; the arrangement of these other parts may be seen in Ex.

III.38. We have figures each part according to the chord it would bear if it were placed in the bass, remembering that the perfect chord may be heard after the chord of the large sixth, as well as after the chord of the false fifth, so that when we do not depart from the key in use, the strain may rest only on the tonic note or on its dominant. This determines the situation, for no matter what progression is given to the basso continuo, we both feel and know the notes on which the strain may come to rest and the chords which must precede this repose, according to the different progressions of the bass as indicated in each part; for whatever part is chosen as the bass, the others will accompany it in a similar case.

In order to give a clearer idea of all this, we shall examine the power of the leading tone in such instances, how it may be used to distinguish dissonances, and how it obliges us to follow a certain succession of chords.

Chapter Fourteen

On the Leading Tone, and on how all Dissonances are resolved

As soon as the leading tone appears in a dissonant chord, it definitely establishes a conclusion of the strain; it should consequently be followed by the perfect chord of the tonic note or by one of its derivatives. On the other hand, if the leading tone does not appear in a dissonant chord, the conclusion is not established at all, and this dissonant chord should be followed by another dissonant chord, and so on in succession until the leading tone is heard. This then establishes the conclusion or at least an imitation of this conclusion, as for example when the bass falls on the mediant instead of the tonic note. The preceding examples of the seventh prove what we are advancing here, since after the first seventh chord another always follows, until the appearance of the dominant-tonic in which this leading tone is heard.

Remember that, contrary to the rule we have just stated, the perfect chord of the dominant may follow the chord of the large sixth of a fourth note, even though the leading tone does not occur in this last chord; the chord is nonetheless dissonant.

To recognize a leading tone in a dissonant chord, we should remember that either the interval of a false fifth or the interval of a tritone must be found in the chord, whether between the parts or between a part and the bass. Furthermore, these intervals must be formed by the major third and the seventh of the fundamental note of the seventh chord, this note always being the dominant-tonic; otherwise, the rule would be false. Thus, in the key of Do, either the false fifth or the tritone is found between the notes Si and Fa, depending on their different arrangements; one note forms the major third and the other the seventh of Sol, the dominant-tonic. [Ex. III.39.]

Leading tone

Leading tone

Tritone   False fifth

Example III.39

We have just seen the same thing in the example of the perfect cadence; for no matter which part of this cadence is taken as the bass, if the other parts are used to form the chord, then one of these two intervals will always be found there. The difference between these intervals is due only to the different arrangement of the two notes which form them both.

The guides placed after these intervals show their natural progressions, as indicated by the notes in the example of the perfect cadence. From this we should derive a definite rule for the progression of all dissonances, i.e., for resolving them.

Just as we characterized the third as major or minor, we likewise characterize all dissonances as major or minor.

The major dissonances are all those formed by the leading tone; just as the latter should naturally ascend a semitone to the tonic note, as we have just seen in the examples, so should all major dissonances do likewise.

To recognize a major dissonance, knowing the key in use, we need only notice that whenever the note a semitone below the tonic is found in a dissonant chord, it will itself be this major dissonance. Otherwise, by relating a chord to its fundamental, we shall find that this major dissonance will always be formed by the major third of a dominant-tonic bearing a seventh chord. Thus, the major third of a dominant-tonic bearing a seventh chord may be considered to be a major dissonance. Consequently, the leading tone on which the chord of the false fifth is always built, the major sixth of the second note of the key, and the tritone of the fourth note of the key are also major dissonances.

The minor dissonances are all those formed by the note a seventh above the fundamental bass. These dissonances should be resolved by descending diatonically, as are the seventh and the false fifth.

When a major dissonance is not found in a dissonant chord, the minor dissonance will certainly be found there alone. The latter, however, is always found together with the major; this in no way destroys the progression determined for these dissonances.

It is thus that we learn quickly the different ways of resolving dissonances, for these dissonances do not have different progressions. The only difference is in the progression of the bass, where we may use any of the notes in the chord which should naturally be heard. This can always be seen by relating all the chords to their fundamentals.

[. . .]

Chapter Fourteen

Observations on the relations between all the preceding Chords

When the right hand plays a perfect chord, it plays at the same time all the consonant chords, i.e., the sixth chord and the six-four chord. When it plays a seventh chord, it also plays all the dissonant ones, i.e., the chords of the small and of the large sixth, of the false fifth, of the tritone, of the second, of the ninth, of the eleventh or fourth, of the augmented fifth, and of the augmented seventh. There are, however, several particulars that should be discussed.

All dissonant chords may be characterized as major or minor, depending on the third of the note on which the seventh chord is built.

The succession of chords is almost always the same. After a minor dissonance, another minor dissonance normally follows until the major dissonance appears, after which a consonant chord normally follows. Thus, the rule of the sevenths, Chapter 8, shows us how to use several dissonant chords in succession, while the rules of the octave and of the sixths, Chapters 6 and 11, show us how to interweave dissonant chords with consonant ones. Observe the great similarity between the chords found in these different rules. These rules may even be used for chords by supposition. If four fingers are used in these chords by supposition, we need only follow the course of the sevenths until the chord with a major dissonance appears, which determines the conclusion.

534

The progression of these chords will be very easy to play, provided we remember that of the four fingers ordinarily used in the right hand two always descend, while the other two remain stationary; that those fingers which should descend are the highest of they are all arranged by thirds; that, if they are not so arranged, the fingers which should descend are the lower of the two fingers joined together and the finger which is below this one; that if none is found below the two joined together, the highest finger should descend together with the lowest; that the fingers which descend are always the fifth and the seventh of a seventh chord, the seventh and ninth of a ninth chord, or the ninth and the eleventh of an eleventh chord; and that even if only three fingers are used in the right hand, the two fingers playing the preceding intervals must nevertheless descend, while the other remains stationary.

This rule, however, is not general. We are sometimes obliged to make three fingers descend while the upper finger of the two joined together remains stationary or while the lower finger remains stationary, if no others are joined to it. This happens in the deceptive cadence, or in a succession of chords similar to cadence H. It is also possible for the lower finger of the two joined together to descend alone while the other three fingers remain stationary, or for the upper finger to descend alone, if no others are joined to it. This occurs in a succession of chords similar to that in which the bass descends a third, while each note of the progression bears a seventh chord, J. [Ex. IV.35.]

Example IV.35

535

The seventh may be added to the perfect chord of any note, so that a note which appears able to bear only a perfect chord may also bear a seventh chord. This usage depends on the taste and knowledge of the composer.

The succession of chords indicated in this example, under which we have placed several different basses, should be familiar to everyone, even though this succession occurs much less frequently than other ones; but to avoid any surprise, we should be ignorant of nothing. The octave of the bass is seldom added in chords with a major dissonance. It is suitable only for seventh chords and for chords of the small and of the large sixth. We should therefore accustom ourselves to playing these chords in only four parts; i.e., three parts with the right hand, with the bass making the fourth part. Chords by supposition always contain five parts without the octave of the bass, which should never be added.

We forbid adding the octave of the bass to dissonant chords in order to make the accompaniment more regular. Otherwise, we could not avoid using two consecutive octaves or fifths, which are absolutely forbidden in composition. This is why we often double the third or the sixth in a sixth chord, instead of the octave of the bass. It cannot be said that an accompaniment serves only to present all the sounds of a chord and nothing else, but it is always better to strive for perfection. We have therefore placed our chords in such a way that those who are directed by the succession of the chords we have given will avoid almost all mistakes without even having to think about it.

As for the relationship between chords, see the examples we have given in Chapters 5, 8, 11, and 12, together with our discussion in Books II and III. We have still to explain the succession of chords when it is a matter of preparing and resolving dissonances.

Chapter Fifteen

On how to prepare and resolve all Dissonances, from which we shall come to know the Key in use and the Chords which each Note of this Key should bear

We have characterized the dissonant chords as major or minor only with respect to a certain interval found there. Instead of speaking of the chord, then, we shall simply speak of the dissonance.

The preceding rules lead to such great facility in preparing dissonances that accompanists need not know anything more on this subject. For those who wish to pursue it further, however, see our remarks in Books II and III. The rules lead to almost as much facility in resolving dissonances, but for a greater understanding one should know what follows.

Dissonances can be characterized as major or minor. To recognize this distinction, we need only take a seventh chord on a dominant-tonic. The major third of this dominant will form all the major dissonances, and its seventh will form all the minor ones. [Ex. IV.36.]

Minor dissonance
Major dissonance

Example IV.36

ARTICLE I

On the major Dissonance

The major dissonance never appears without the minor, and we need not pay attention to the latter when the former is present. If a chord is dissonant and the major dissonance is not present, however, then the minor dissonance is the essential part of the chord.

To recognize the major dissonance more easily, we should note that it is always formed by the leading tone of the key in use, since this leading tone always forms a major third with the dominant-tonic and since the dissonant chord in which it occurs is always formed from the seventh chord of this dominant-tonic. Either the chord or the leading tone will thus make the key clear, and once you know the key, you know immediately which chord should contain this dissonance and which note should form it, since the leading tone is always a semitone below the tonic note or its octave, double octave, triple octave, etc.

If we begin in a given key, we know its leading tone. If in the course of the piece the key changes, a sharp will always appear as a figure, or added to a figure, or even added directly to a bass note, thus indicating the leading tone explicitly; or else, on the contrary, a flat will be found associated with the leading tone or the sharp of the leading tone will be suppressed, either in the bass or in the chord, thus indicating that what was the leading tone is no longer such. You will thus be obliged to look elsewhere. The key in use can be determined in this way, and as a result, you will know not only the composition or the construction of the chord with a major dissonance, but also that of all the chords in this key, in conformity with the rules of the octave given in Chapter 6. Although a note of a key may sometimes bear a chord which is not the most appropriate in that key (as may be seen in the rules of the sevenths, etc.), it either bears its normal chord immediately after, or else this chord at least occurs on the following note. That the bass does not follow its natural course does not necessarily affect the chords used. If the new sharp which appeared changes again and another sharp occurs, we must then count according to the order of the position of the sharps, always taking the last sharp as the leading tone. This is explained at length in Book III, Chapter 25, Article iii, and the accompanist must possess a perfect knowledge of it.

As for resolving the major dissonance, we need only slide the finger playing it a semitone higher, and we shall never go wrong. Furthermore, the chord in which it occurs is always resolved by the perfect chord of the tonic note, although exceptionally we are sometimes obliged to add a seventh to this perfect chord. [Ex. IV.37.]

The augmented second and its derivatives may be resolved by making the major dissonance ascend alone while the other notes remain stationary, or else by making the minor dissonance descend in the same way. There is an example of this in Book III, Chapter 33 [Ex. III.96, and III.97].

Observe that the notes which bear the chords marked in the preceding example never change their names no matter what the key; the 5 ♯ is found only on the mediant, etc.

This example, which is in a minor key, should serve for all keys in general. The chords of the 5 ♯ and of the 2 ♯ , together with their derivatives, however, do not occur in major keys.

RAMEAU

These two chords are used over the different basses found below. All chords with a major dissonance are found in these basses. It is evident that the major dissonance formed by the leading tone, which is the major third of the dominant-tonic, always ascends a semitone to the tonic note.

The seventh chord of this dominant is naturally resolved by the perfect chord of the tonic note. From this, the succession of the chords found in the other basses is derived.

Here the dominant passes to the mediant, but the chords do not change.

The dominant remains on the same degree, with the same succession of chords.

The fourth note, here bearing the chord of the tritone, passes to the mediant or to the tonic note, with the same succession of chords.

The mediant, here bearing the chord of the augmented fifth, remains on the same degree or passes to the tonic note, without the chords changing.

The second note, bearing the chord of the small sixth, passes to the mediant or to the tonic note, using the same chords.

The tonic note, bearing the chord of the augmented seventh, remains on the same degree so as to bear its perfect chord again.

The leading tone, which always bears the chord of the false fifth, passes to the tonic note or to the mediant, with the same succession of chords.

The sixth note takes the place of the dominant here, and the dominant must therefore be suppressed from the first chord. The sixth note passes to the dominant or to the mediant, with the same succession of chords. To know more fully the successions that the inversion of this chord of the augmented second may cause in the notes of the other basses, one need only place this sixth note in the first chord instead of the dominant. This dominant may then no longer occur in the bass, so long as the sixth note takes its place.

Example IV.37

539

We might also have spoken about the minor dissonance together with the major, since it is always found with the latter. The line conducting the minor dissonance to the follow note makes it clear that it should always descend; we need only take the interval of the false fifth or of the tritone to see this. [Ex. IV.38.]

Example IV.38

These two intervals, which are mutual inversions, are similarly resolved by two other mutually inverted intervals. The major dissonance which always ascends and the minor which always descends are resolved by the third A on the one hand, and by the sixth B on the other. Thus, Fa and Si are resolved by Mi and Do, or, to speak about all keys in general, the leading tone, which forms all the major dissonances, is always resolved by ascending to the tonic note, while the fourth note, which forms all the minor ones when the major dissonances also occurs, is always resolved by descending to the mediant. This can be tested for every key.

ARTICLE II

On the minor Dissonance

All minor dissonances are formed by the seventh, but when the major dissonance is not found with the minor dissonance we may neither determine which note [degree] of the key forms it nor which resolves it, because it is allowable to use a seventh chord on any note of a key. Nevertheless, to recognize the key in use with its aid, we must let the fingers pass in the customary manner from one dissonant chord to another, until the chord with a major dissonance is found. This chord identifies the key. After the chord of the large sixth, however, we may also descend to a consonant chord, which itself defines the key. Such a consonant chord, preceded by the chord of the large sixth, usually occurs only on a certain note of the key, as explained in Chapters 6, 7, 8, and 9. Sometimes after a chord of the large sixth, however, we ascend to a perfect chord which does not define the key. Thus, in the chapter on sevenths the bass ascends in this way to the perfect chord, only to descend immediately a third so as to ascend again in the same manner.[64] The last progression of this sort of bass, however, which always ends on the dominant or on the tonic note preceded by the chord of the false fifth, completely defines the situation.

It is useless to give an example here of how the minor dissonance is resolved, since the preceding example shows this well enough. Observe only that in chords by supposition there are at least two minor dissonances which should always descend, while the the chord of the eleventh, called the fourth, there are three when all the sounds natural to it are present; otherwise, there is only one. Of these three minor dissonances, it is normally enough for the two most harsh, the ninth and the eleventh, to descend, while the seventh remains stationary. In some music we are obliged to do the contrary, but this is less common.

The major dissonances are enumerated in the example we have given of them. The minor dissonances are the second, the false fifth, the seventh, the ninth, and the eleventh, called the fourth. The third of a chord of the small sixth and the fifth of a chord of the large sixth should also be added to this list.

The second must be differentiated from the other minor dissonances, since this dissonance is found in the bass. It is thus the bass which should descend in order to resolve the second.

Of the two fingers joined together in dissonant chords, the lower always forms the minor dissonace. Therefore, in the chord of the second, only the bass may be so joined to form this second. If no fingers are joined at all in other chords, the highest finger will then be playing the minor dissonance and should consequently descend.

The irregular cadence is an exception. Here it is the sixth of a chord of the large sixth which forms the dissonance, and not the fifth. This sixth should thus ascend diatonically, while the fifth remains on the same degree.

---

[64]He is presumably talking about the following progression:

See Chapter 8, Ex. IV.26. [P.G.]

Chapter Sixteen

On Chromaticism

Chromaticism occurs only in minor keys and only on the sixth and seventh notes [degrees] of the key. These notes may be made to proceed by semitones, ascending as well as descending, both in the bass and in the chords.

We have already given some idea of this progression in Chapter 9, Article ii. For further instruction, notice that in this situation the major dissonance, which should naturally ascend a semitone, on the contrary descends a semitone, but always to the flat or natural key [of the keyboard] of that same degree which had formed the major dissonance. Thus, we need only add a note to all consonant chords which normally follow the major dissonance. This added note is the flat we have just mentioned and it is always found immediately below the note which would have been taken to be the tonic after the leading tone which formed the major dissonance. This conforms to our observation in the preceding chapter about adding a seventh to the perfect chord by which the major dissonance is resolved.

Furthermore, chords by borrowing and by supposition often occur in this latter kind of harmony, so that it is difficult not to be misled when the bass is unfigured.[65] [Ex. IV.39.]

The succession of all these chords conforms to our rules.

Though the leading tone descends, the progression between chords A, B, and C and, by inversion, between F and G, conforms basically to the progression of the sevenths. There is also a progression derived from the deceptive cadence, between C and D.[66]

From H to J, the ninth postpones the octave which follows immediately after.

Otherwise, the progression is approximately the same as the progression of the octaves in Chapter 6, except that here we pass from the minor third to the major or from the major to the minor. In addition, we find everywhere notes in chords by supposition or by borrowing which occupy the place of those notes which should be found naturally. Once the fingers become used to these different successions of chords, however, they often anticipate the requisite movements. It is then only

[65] In measure 13 of this example, Rameau has written, Re, Sol, Do for the first chord in the right hand. Presumably Do, Sol, Do is intended. [P.G.]
[66] The fundamental bass of chord D is La. [P.G.]

Example IV.39

necessary to watch for those intervals which may change at any moment from major to minor while descending, or from minor to major while ascending.

We shall not go wrong with regard to the different keys through which we pass in this example, as long as we notice the different leading tones introduced by means of the sharps.

The naturals added to the figures or to the notes serve to return each note to its natural order, thus cancelling the ♯ or the ♭ which had appeared previously. Some people use the ♯ or the ♭ for this purpose, but this is less correct, for a 7 with a ♭ normally indicates a diminished seventh, with a 7 with a ♯ indicates an augmented seventh.

Chapter Seventeen

Recapitulation of the various successions of Chords

We must be fully proficient in the modulation of every key, trying to recognize the key in use by means of every chord we play.

When only consonant chords are used, the key is often uncertain. If it is not clarified by means of the first dissonant chord, this is only because the major dissonance is not present in it. What is lost on the one hand, however, is gained on the other, since the various progressions of the bass indicate which chord should follow the chord being played. We are further aided here by the progression of the minor dissonance, which always seems to descend. Since it is generally only in a progression similar to or derived from the progression of the sevenths given in Chapter 8 that the key becomes uncertain, once the major dissonance which almost always terminates this progression appears, we can find at once what we are looking for. We must both know and be able to play the different successions of chords in order to avoid mistakes. It will therefore not be inappropriate to recapitulate late these matters here.[67] [Ex. IV.40.]

The semicircles ⌢ indicate a dissonance prepared by the preceding consonance. The lines drawn thus — indicate the same thing in chromaticism. There, however, the consonance which prepares the dissonance also forms the major dissonance. The lines drawn thus ＼ or thus ／ indicate the consonance which resolves the dissonance.

The same chords are used for each bass. Since the different successions of chords found in the other basses are determined by the progression of the fundamental bass, however, it is well to warn the reader that the majority of the progressions of these other basses are extravagant for this succession of chords. It is quite rare to find such progressions in a well-composed piece of music. This is especially true of those progressions in the places indicated by the letters D, F, G, H, J, K, L, M, and N. If by chance such a bass should occur, however, one need only observe the following advice.

(1) If we do not care whether there are two consecutive octaves or fifths, we need only add the octave to the first dissonant chord and let the fingers follow their natural course, as in the example.

(2) We may avoid these faults by accompanying each chord in the ordinary manner, i.e., with three fingers in the right hand, by suppressing the octave of these basses in the dissonant chords. If as a result a chord does not fit easily under the fingers, we need only suppress one of the sounds forming the dissonance instead of the octave, thus reducing a dissonant chord to a consonant one. If a seventh chord or a chord of the

---

[67]The chord of the small sixth cannot be distinguished here by means of the figures any more than it can be elsewhere. At least here we can recognize it in the upper part, however, for this part contains all the chords. [R.] This note is from the Supplement. [P.G.]

Example IV.40

Example IV.40. a: Fundamental progression of an ascending 3. The dissonance A cannot be prepared. b: Progression of a descending fifth, as in Chapter 8. b′: Progression of a descending fifth, with chromaticism. c: Progression of a descending 3. The dissonance is resolved by the octave and prepared by the 5. d: Progression of an ascending 2. The dissonance is resolved by the fifth and prepared by the octave. e: The sixth added to the perfect chord C prepared an irregular cadence. It is resolved by ascending to the third. f: Final cadence.

545

small or of the large sixth follows a certain dissonant chord, for example, we may reduce the seventh chord to a perfect chord and the other two chords to simple sixth chords. The chord of the small sixth may also be reduced to a six-four chord and the chord of the large sixth to a perfect chord. This must be determined not only by the natural progression of the fingers, which almost always flow diatonically from one key [of the keyboard] to another, but also on the basis of the rules which say that after a certain chord another should follow, depending on the different progressions of the bass. For example, the perfect chord should follow the chord of the small major sixth, when the bass descends diatonically. If either a seventh chord or a chord of the large sixth then follows the chord of the small sixth in this progression, it may be reduced to a perfect chord, as at M. Since the perfect chord should also follow the chords of the false fifth or of the large sixth when the bass ascends diatonically, we may similarly reduce the chord of the large sixth or the seventh chord when they follow in this progression, again as at M.

Since the six-four chord can follow the chord of the small sixth when the bass descends diatonically and the chord of the large sixth when the bass ascends diatonically, if the chord of the small sixth appears after one of these two other chords in the preceding progression, it may be changed to a six-four chord. This holds as long as the leading tone does not occur in the first chord of the small sixth. If it did occur, it would then be necessary to make the second chord of the small sixth a sixth chord.

Since the sixth chord should naturally follow the chord of the tritone when the bass descends diatonically and the chord of the small major sixth when the bass ascends diatonically, chords of the small or of the large sixth may be changed to sixth chords when they follow chords of the tritone or of the small sixth in this progression, as at N, F, G, H, and R,[68] even though notes F, G, and H of the seventh bass do not follow the progression we have just established. There, however, the fingers will play these chords by habit; the same is true of the chord of the small

[68]I have not found the letter R used in Example 40 at all. The letters N, F, G, and H refer to the various progressions mentioned in the last two paragraphs. There is no one-to-one correspondence between these letters and the progressions, however, for the same letter is used to represent different progressions. [P.G.]

546

sixth which appears after the seventh chord when the bass descends diatonically, as at D in the sixth bass.[69]

(3) If over a diatonic progression of the bass there are two chords in succession which are of the same genre or at least are not prescribed by the natural rule, and if we do not wish to effect the preceding reduction, we must then make the bass and the chords proceed in contrary motion. The chords must descend if the bass ascends and the chords must ascend if the bass descends, as is done at notes P, Q, or P, M, Q. We are assuming that the chord found on note M of the third bass is not reduced to a perfect chord, for the reduction of a chord prohibits the reduction of the following chord, especially over a diatonic progression of the bass.[70] Remember that the contrary motion of which we are speaking does not oblige us to change the position of the lowest finger or that of the highest, whenever one of these fingers plays a note which may be used in the following chord. Over an ascending diatonic progression of the bass, however, we generally find the false fifth or else the large sixth after the seventh, and the seventh after the ninth. This is demonstrated in Ex. IV. 41.

Example IV. 41

The dissonance is simply a sound added to the consonant chord, and it is in this latter alone that the foundation of harmony lies. Thus, since this dissonance is sometimes difficult to include in an accompaniment, we must abandon it when it does not fall naturally under the fingers. We use then only the consonant chord we know should follow and to which we feel will move of their own accord. We assume both that this

[69]The bass does not, however, descend diatonically at D in the sixth bass; in any case, the rule would not apply even if the bass did descend diatonically. Rameau probably meant to write: "if the bass descends a third." The other two places marked D (in the fourth and seventh basses) have the bass remaining stationary, so that the chord of the small sixth of the second note can be transformed into a six-four chord. [P.G.]
[70]Do not be confused by the inclusion of M in this section. Here it refers only to the third bass; its general meaning remains the same as specified in Article ii above. [P.G.]

consonant chord contains only those sounds which should accompany the dissonance and that the practice of all our different examples has been mastered. Thus, the many difficulties which often arise because of mistakes by those who figure the bass may be overcome, and we need pay attention only to the intervals actually used in their music, without bothering about the rest.

The reduction of which we are speaking is not suitable for chords of the second, chords by supposition, chords by borrowing, or really even for seventh chords.

(4) There are two consecutive fifths, B, B, between the parts in the chords [of Ex. IV.40]. These are very difficult to avoid on such occasions, just as they are when the bass ascends to the sixth chord after the perfect chord; this is due to the arrangement of the fingers.

(5) In the eighth and ninth basses, which contain chords by supposition, we must use as many of the sounds which make up each of these chords as possible. We shall never go wrong here if we add the octave of the bass to the chord immediately preceding the chord by supposition, though we should also follow the various rules that have been given.

(6) Notice particularly that when there are several dissonant chords in succession, such as seventh chords or other dissonant chords which though of different genres are not mixed with any consonant chord, the fingers of the right hand always descend until the leading tone appears in one of these chords. Then the fingers, or at least that finger which plays this leading tone, should ascend. [Ex. IV. 42.]

Example IV.42

548

Since the seventh is found in the ninth chords figured in this bass, the sixth should follow it, even though it is not figured and it woud seem that the octave figured after the ninth denotes the perfect chord. The sixth should resolve the seventh here, however, just as the octave resolves the ninth. This requires no thought, for the fingers themselves find it, when we let them descend from one key to another, following their natural progression after all minor dissonances.

Much the same thing occurs when we figure a note which may bear a seventh or a ninth over an ascending diatonic progression of the bass with only a 5, as in Ex. IV.27 of Chapter 9. This same note, figured with a 5 and then with a 6, after which we ascend diatonically, may embarrass the accompanist unless he is forewarned that the dissonances of the seventh and of the ninth which he naturally finds under his fingers will prove very effective together with the perfect chord denoted by the 5. Furthermore, though the chord denoted by the 6 should be influenced by the chord we are already playing, it is determined with even greater certainty by the place the bass note occupies in the key, as indicated in Ex. IV.27 of Chapter 9; there, we may add the ninth to chords which are figured only 7, when this ninth is found under the fingers which played the preceding chord.

(7) Often the same dissonance is used to form another dissonance before it is resolved, as may be seen in Book III, Chapters 12, 15, and 27. Often a note may also bear several different chords in succession, as has appeared in many of our examples. This may further be seen in the technique known as *organ point*. [Ex. IV.43.]

The organ point occurs only as long as the bass note does not change. Thus, it ends at A and begins again immediately.

The harmony of this organ point is in accord with the rules, as the fundamental bass proves. Remember that the sixth note takes the place of the dominant in chords by borrowing and that the fundamental bass should be found above the other bass in chords by supposition.

There is a double supposition at the notes B, for the augmented fifth should naturally be found on the first note, and we cannot avoid giving the chord of the heteroclite eleventh to the second note. Notice, however, that the permanent sound of the bass fades, so to speak, from our attention, which then turns towards the sounds of the chords. If regularity is found in the progression of these chords, then the permanent sound of the bass should no longer be considered to be more than a point, or a zero in terms of the figures. As a result, we are free in such a case to use the sixth together with the seventh. [Ex. IV.44.]

Example IV.43

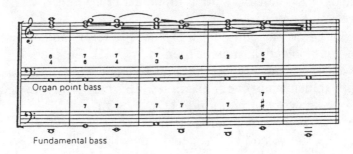

Example IV.44

If we take the chords together with the fundamental bass, cutting out the organ point, we shall find a regular harmony and we should judge the harmony accordingly.

We have indicated another way of using the sixth together with the seventh, in Book II, Chapter 17.

Airs called *Vielle* and *Musette* are in a sense derived from this organ point. By this means, then, the different sorts of basses of this genre can be understood.

We cannot have too great a knowledge of and practical facility with the inversion of chords, or rather with the inversion of the progression of the bass that appears in all our examples, for the difference between chords arises, as our fundamental basses show, only from the different progressions of the bass. Thus, the great similarity between the various progressions of the chords, to which the fingers accustom themselves with a little practice, often prevents a failure of memory. The fingers follow their natural directions; those which strike minor dissonances naturally descend to the neighboring key, and those which strike major dissonances ascend in the same manner. Thus, without actually considering the type of interval involved, since the seventh, the ninth, the eleventh, the false fifth, the third in a chord of the small sixth, and often the fifth in a chord of the large sixth should all descend, the finger which plays one of these intervals moves of its own accord to the next key. In the same way, after the tritone or the augmented second, the finger should ascend. Remember that when two fingers are joined together, the lower should always descend, except in the irregular cadence.

Chapter Eighteen

Rules which are necessary in order to accompany properly

(1) Before placing our hands on the keyboard we should notice the key and mode of the piece to be played; its meter and tempo; any changes or mode, meter, or clef in the course of it; the figures which the notes bear and the sharps and flats associated with them; and the progression of the bass, so that any deficiences in the figuring may be supplemented. In short, we should put into practice all the preceding rules.

(2) The character of the accompaniment should be in keeping with the voices and the air. We should enter into the spirit of the words or of the essential expression of the air, if there are no words. We should proportion the accompaniment to the power of the voices or instruments, so that we do not drown them with too much noise or fail to give them enough support with too little. To this end, we may double with the left hand the chords played with the right (the dissonances must be excluded from this rule), or we may suppress the octaves or even certain dissonances from the chords, depending on the situation.

(3) When the sound of the clavecin or the theorbo beings to fade, we may repeat the same chord, provided that this is done preferably on the first beat of the measure and together with the last syllable of a word. If

the repetition is made in the middle of a word or even in the middle of phrase, it may become difficult to catch the meaning. This may be disregarded for the organ, since there the sounds are sustained.

(4) We must keep our chords in the middle of the keyboard, whenever the bass permits. If we are obliged to change their position, we must make sure that this is done on a single chord, or at least after a consonant chord, never after a dissonant. We are not always able to do this, however, for unexpected changes in the bass may occur; it may sometimes ascend or descend two octaves, depending on the imagination of the composer. In order to transpose a chord from one position to another, we must see or feel whether one of the keys in the chord being played may not also be used in the transposed chord. If this is possible, we must move the lowest finger to this key when the motion is ascending, or the highest finger when the motion is descending, so that the hand is not raised and the transportation is effected in a single movement, one finger taking the place of another. By this means, we are not obliged to look down from the book at all. Remember, furthermore, the manner in which we said chords must be arpeggiated.

As for accompanying without figures, although all our rules touch on this subject, we must add to them the rules of composition. Despite all this, success will be difficult, unless the ear, mind, and fingers anticipate the thorough knowledge [which comes after]. The best training for this is to accustom the ear to good and true harmony through frequent practice of the preceding principles.

Chapter Nineteen

On how to figure a Basso Continuo, and on how to know which Chords each figure denotes

The perfect chord may be figured by any of its three intervals, although it is normally not figured at all, except to distinguish the third by a ♯ when it is major, and by a ♭ when it is minor.

The ♯ alone always indicates the major third, while the ♭ alone indicates the minor third. If these signs are added to other figures, they alter the intervals in question by a semitone with respect to the natural interval.

All chords should be figured by the figure whose name they bear.[71] [Ex. IV.45.]

Chord of the:	Figured by a:
2nd	2
augmented 2nd	2 ♯
11, and 4th	4
tritone	4 or 4 ♯
false 5th	$\bar{5}$ or 5 ♭
augmented 5th	5 ♯
7th	7
diminished 7th	7 ♭
augmented 7th	7 ♯
minor 6th	6 ♭
major 6th	6 ♯
small 6th	6
large 6th	$\frac{6}{5}$
6-4	$\frac{6}{4}$
9th	9

Example IV.45

[71]Rameau adds the following note in the Supplement:

"There are a 4 and a 6 in the example, the first designating the tritone and the other the small sixth, both of which should be crossed by a line. Since the author was not present during the printing of this book and since these varieties of characters are still not used in the printing-house, they were not considered important enough to pay attention to. The barred 6, however, indicates the chord of the small sixth and not the major sixth, as some imagine. We surely should attempt to indicate a complete chord with a single figure, so as to avoid an embarrassing multiplicity of figures. Furthermore, since there are four different chords of the sixth, we should distinguish them as much as possible by using the characters appropriate for each chord. This has rarely been bothered about until now, and the major sixth has been denoted simply by a barred 6, from which it follows that this sixth should be accompanied by the third and the fourth. This is not always correct, however, since in the course of a piece of music we are often obliged to figure a major sixth which is not of this type. It is figured major only with respect to a new transposed modulation, whose necessary sharps are not found beside the clef. Often, the small sixth is even minor. Besides, since usage alone authorizes characters of this sort, the existence of the barred 5 ($\bar{5}$), which denotes the diminished or false fifth, destroys all reason for wanting another figure crossed by a similar line which denotes a major or augmented interval. It would be better to use these new characters to give a true idea of a complete chord than to use them now to indicate a minor interval, now a major one. This is especially true when such an interval may be accompanied in several different ways.

"What we have said in this chapter will serve for the future rather than for the past. In return, however, our rules will provide for the errors of the past." [P.G.]

553

We should add neither a ♯ nor a ♭ to figures indicating intervals which are naturally major or minor in the key in use. When it is necessary to do this, it is preferable to use the ♮ . It is only to the figure which indicates the tritone that it is usual to add a ♯ .

We must add the figure which changes the natural construction of a chord to the figure which normally indicates this chord. [Ex. IV.46.]

All chords in which the major dissonance may occur should be designated by a figure which also indicates the interval of this dissonance.

There are many basso continuos in which this regularity is not observed, so that those who are guided only by the figures may be misled. Those who are guided by our rules, however, will see how necessary these rules are in such a case.

The 11th, called 4th, accompanied by the 2nd instead of by the octave . . . . $\frac{4}{2}$ or $\frac{5}{2}$

The 11th, called 4th, accompanied by the 9th . . . . $\frac{4}{9}$

The 7th accompanied by the false 5th . . . . $\frac{7}{5}$

The tritone accompanied by the minor 3rd . . . . $\frac{4♯}{♭}$

The small 6th accompanied by the false 5th . . . . $\frac{6}{5}$

The augmented 5th accompanied by the 4th . . . . $\frac{5♯}{4}$

The augmented 7th accompanied by the minor 6th . . . . $\frac{7♯}{6,}$

Example IV.46

Some composers place many figures where one would suffice. This confuses matters greatly.

A figure placed beside a note always indicates the chord. If, however, it is placed a little after the note and this note may bear a perfect chord, this is an indication that we must use the perfect chord on the first beat of the note and use on the second, third, or fourth beat, depending on the position of the figure, the chord designated by the figure.

A note worth several beats may bear a different chord on each beat or may sometimes bear the same chord for two beats. When this cannot be easily distinguished by the arrangement of the figures, the ear must decide the matter.

The dot represents the note which precedes it. [Ex. IV.47.]

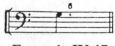

Example IV.47

A figure placed above or below the dot therefore signifies that the chord it represents should occur on that part of the beat represented by this dot.

Chapter Twenty

How to tell which Bass Notes should bear a Chord

We should play a chord at the beginning of each beat of the measure, although the same note may bear the same chord for several beats or several measures.

A note which is worth only one beat may be divided into two beats, and may consequently bear two different chords. We might even divide the beat further, but the chords would then come too rapidly.

In ornamented bases, there are often several notes in each beat, but the chord should be played only on the first note of each beat. The right hand, which strikes a chord on each beat, keeps time, so to speak.

When the tempo is somewhat rapid and a single chord can be used for several consecutive beats, it should not be repeated until we feel that the sound of the instruments has ceased completely, for when the same chord is reiterated too often, it becomes wearisome.

There are some ornamented basses which are often difficult to figure well because the bass notes are not always contained in the chord which should be heard. Our rules are a great help here, for we shall never go wrong if we use those chords which we know should follow naturally. For example, suppose there are several dissonant chords in succession, such as several 7 or 2, over a diatonic progression of the bass, which are not linked by sixth chords as the rule demands. If we assume that each of these dissonant chords is struck at the beginning of each beat, we must then divide each of these beats into two equal parts and use those chords which we know should follow and precede the dissonant chord in question on the first note of the second part of the beat. The fingers often anticipate this on such occasions, if good habits have been formed based on the preceding principles. Since the note beating this chord, which may not be figured or may be figured in a way to which we are unaccustomed, is not always that note which should naturally appear, we must be governed rather by the natural succession of the fingers than by the actual bass note, for this latter could lead us astray. [Ex. IV.48.]

Example IV.48

We know that the chord of the small sixth should precede the seventh chord when the bass descends diatonically, and that the chord of the large sixth or of the false fifth should precede the chord of the second on two bass notes of the same degree. This is true even though these notes are not found at the beginning of the beat in which the chord should be heard, and even though the chord is not figured at all, as at A and D, or is figured in a manner difficult to understand, as at B and C. It is no less necessary, however, to use these chords of the small or of the large sixth here between each [pair] of these seventh chords or chords of the second, according to our rules and following the habit of having one or two fingers descend after the minor dissonance, while the others remain on the same degree. The same is true for other progressions in which similar awkward situations may arise.

We must never leave a sharp or flat which has been used for one chord and may also be used for the next chord, unless this is precisely indicated by a new figure which cancels the sharp or flat. This sharp or flat may be appropriate for the key in use and may thus form false fifths or augmented fifths which are to be preferred in such a case to the perfect fifth, and so on for all the other intervals. The composer should indicate the contrary clearly when his piece demands it; otherwise, only the ear can decide the matter.[72]

End of Book IV

---

[72]Since most of our teachers of music and clavecin find it difficult to overcome their prejudices, we do not hope to capture the favor of everyone. This is why we hope that even those who find it difficult to subscribe to our ideas will kindly inform the public of them; they will thus enable us to give this work all the perfection we wish it to have. [R.] This note is added at the end of the Supplement. [P.G.]

HERMANN HELMHOLTZ

Hermann Helmholtz (b. Potsdam 1821, d. Berlin 1894), renowned primarily for his achievements in medicine, physiology, anatomy and physics, holds an important position in musical thought as well. Taking exception to views widely held in his time, views which primarily placed musical aesthetics within the realm of the metaphysical, Helmholtz set out to discover the connection between the structural-aesthetical aspects of music and their correlary physiological-physical aspects.

The relationship between physiology and physics had begun to occupy Helmholtz in his medical student days. Continuing with explorations in acoustics, in 1858 he presented a first statement on the physical cause of musical harmony. *On the Sensations of Tone* (1862) is the summation of years of acoustical research and experimentation. The book presents both the physical and physiological aspects of acoustics and establishes their role in the construction and perception of musical systems.

Although he believed that aesthetic works are produced by men of genius, Helmholtz maintained that it was necessary to discover the scientific base of artistic processes. As in architecture, where the discovery of technical solutions to physical problems led to distinctive principles of style—such as the horizontal line among the Greeks, the semicircular arch among the Etruscans and the pointed arch in the medieval period—so too the scientific exploration of music will contribute to the understanding of its aesthetics.

Music, more than the other arts, deals with perception anchored in pure sensation, i.e., with physiological properties of stimuli and their consequent psychological perceptions. The construction of musical systems has to take into account the boundary and limits of the variety of tones and their relationships which, Helmholtz believed, were directly influenced by the physiological properties of the sensation of hearing and the physical aspects of the tones themselves.

Acoustical investigations led to the discovery that music prefers to employ "compound tones," i.e., tones which have harmonic upper partial tones, the vibrational numbers of which are integral multiples of the vibrational number of the "prime tone." Compound tones are generated by periodic and uniform motions, producing a uniform and sustained sensation. The physiological construction of the ear, he maintained, influenced this preference, for even "simple tones," if sounded with sufficient intensity, excite sensations of harmonic upper partials in the ear.

Furthermore, the prominence of the octave and the fifth found in the (historically) earliest successions of tones convinced Helmholtz that tonal relationships in the West rest on the degree of identification among tones. Thus, the repetition of the octave not only constitutes the first partial but also provides the basis for the Western division of musical scales. The "natural melodic relationship," i.e., the diatonic scale, was deduced in similar fashion.

Though melodic relationships were recognized first, harmonic relationships played an important part in the expansion of the musical vocabulary in the West. Unlike melodic relationships, the perception of harmonic relationships, consonant or dissonant, is immediate and depends not only on partial tones but on combinational tones as well. Harmonic relationships of the "second degree" can, however, be "connected" to relationships of the "first degree"; in fact, the greater the units involved in the relationships, the richer the musical palette. Moreover, the relationship of chords to one another and to the tonic follows the laws that regulate the relationships of consecutive compound tones. Helmholtz thus suggested a possible connection between the physiological facts of hearing and some aspects of musical aesthetics.

In summary, it may be said that Helmholtz believed that beauty is subject to laws and rules dependent on the nature of human intelligence. Accordingly, regularity, order and design are the main qualities of the work of art. The work must be so arranged, however, as to enable an unconscious perception of its qualities. Though this is already achieved through Helmholtz's "first order" parameters, he insisted on their presence in all other levels of the work as well. Becoming aware of artistic qualities, argued Helmholtz, is not only necessary for the satisfaction of scientific curiosity but contributes directly to the enrichment of the aesthetic experience itself. Implying two divergent

560

emphases in artistic appreciation, Helmholtz comes close to Gombrich's dichotomy between the scientific and the aesthetic. Though Helmholtz may be regarded as a late Pythagorean, his conceptions of culture, on the one hand, and his scientific goals, on the other, reveal that it is the process and not the ingredients that, in the final analysis, he was in search of. It is to the former that he ascribed a "natural" stand in the perception of music, thereby joining the modern paradigm of aesthetic theories.

from On the Sensation of Tone[1]

Esthetical Relations

Let us review the results of the preceding investigation.

Compound tones of a certain class are preferred for all kinds of music, melodic or harmonic; and are almost exclusively employed for the more delicate and artistic development of music: these are the compound tones which have harmonic upper partial tones, that is compound tones in which the higher partial tones have vibrational numbers which are integral multiples of the vibrational number of the lowest partial tone, or prime. For a good musical effect we require a certain moderate degree of force in the five or six lowest partial tones, and a low degree of force in the higher partial tones.

This class of compound tones with harmonic upper partials is objectively distinguished by including all sonorous motions which are generated by a mechanical process that continues to act uniformly, and which consequently produce a uniform and sustained sensation. In the first rank among them stand the compound tones of the human voice, man's first musical instrument in time and value. The compound tones of all wind and bowed instruments belong to this class.

Among the bodies which are made to emit tones by striking, some, as strings, have also harmonic upper partials, and these can be used for artistic music.

The greater number of the rest, as membranes, rods, plates, &c., have inharmonic upper partial tones, and only such of them as have not very strong secondary tones of this kind can be singly and occasionally employed in connection with musical instruments proper.

Although sonorous bodies excited by blows may continue to sound for some time, their tones do not proceed with uniform force, but diminish more or less slowly and die away. Constant power over the intensity of tone, therefore, which is indispensable for expressive performance, can only be attained on instruments of the first kind, which can be maintained in a state of excitement, and which produce only harmonic upper partial tones. On the other hand, bodies excited by blows have a peculiar value for clearly defining the rhythm.

[1]Herman Helmholz, *On the Sensation of Tone*, tr. and ed. by Alexander J. Ellis (New York: Dover Publications, Inc., 1954) pp. 362–371.

A second reason for preferring compound tones with harmonic upper partials is subjective and conditioned by the construction of our ear. In the ear even every simple tone, if sufficiently intense, excites feeble sensations of harmonic upper partials, and each combination of several simple tones generates combinational tones, as I have explained at the end of Chap. VII. (p. 157*d*–159*c*). A single compound tone with irrational partials, when sounded with sufficient force, thus produces the sensation of dissonance, and simple tones acquire in the ear itself something of the nature of composition out of harmonic upper partial tones.

We are justified in assuming that historically all music was developed from song. Afterwards the power of producing similar melodic effects was attained by means of other instruments, which had a quality of tone compounded in a manner resembling that of the human voice. The reason why, even when constructive art was most advanced, the choice of musical instruments was necessarily limited to those which produced compound tones with harmonic upper partials, is clear from the above conditions.

This invariable and peculiar selection of instruments makes us perfectly certain that harmonic upper partials have from all time played an essential part in musical constructions, not merely for harmony, as the second part of this book shews, but also for melody.

Again, we can at any moment convince ourselves of the essential importance of upper partial tones to melody, by the absence of all expression in melodies executed with objectively simple tones, as, for example, those of wide-stopped organ pipes, for which the harmonic upper partials are formed only subjectively and weakly in the ear.

A necessity was always felt for music of all kinds to proceed by certain definite degrees of pitch; but the choice of these degrees was long unsettled. To distinguish small differences of pitch and intonate them with certainty, requires a greater amount of technical musical power and cultivation of ear, than when the intervals are larger. Hence among almost all uncivilised people we find the Semitones neglected, and only the larger intervals retained. For some of the more cultivated nations, as the Chinese and Gaels, a scale of this kind has become established.

It might perhaps have seemed most simple to make all such degrees of pitch of equal amount, that is, equally well distinguishable by our sensations. Such a graduation is possible for all our sensations, as Fechner has shewn in his investigations on psychophysical laws. We find such graduations used for the diversity of musical rhythm, and the astronomers use them in reference to the intensity of light in determining stellar magnitudes. Even in the field of musical pitch, the modern equally tempered chromatic scale presents us with a similar graduation. But although in certain of the less usual Greek scales and in modern Oriental music, cases occur where some particular small intervals have been divided on the principle of equal graduations, yet there seems at no time or place to have been a system of music in which melodies constantly moved in equal degrees of pitch, but smaller and larger intervals have always been mixed in the musical scales in a way that must appear entirely arbitrary and irregular until the relationship of compound tones is taken into consideration.[2]

On the contrary, in all known musical systems the intervals of Octave and Fifth have been decisively emphasised. Their difference is the Fouth, and the difference between this and the Fifth, is the Pythagorean major Tone 8:9, by which (but not by the Fourth or Fifth) the Octave might be approximatively divided.

The sole remnants that I can find in modern music of the endeavour sometimes made in homophonic music to introduce degrees depending on equality of interval and not on relationship of tone, are the chromatic intercalated notes, and the leading note of the key when similarly used. But this is always a Semitone (p. 352c), an interval well known in the series of related tones, which, owing to its smallness, is easily measured by the sensation of its difference, even in places where its tonal relationship is not immediately sensible.

The decisive importance acquired by the Octave and Fifth in all musical scales from the earliest times shews, that the construction of scales must have been originally influenced by another principle, which finally became the sole regulator of every artistic form of a complete scale. This is the principle which we have termed *tonal relationship*.

Relationship in the first degree between two compound tones consists in their each having a partial tone of the same pitch.

In singing, the similarity of two musical tones which stand in the relation of Octave or Fifth to one another, must have been very soon observed. As already remarked, this gives also the Fourth, which has itself a sufficiently perceptible natural relationship to have been remarked independently. To discover the tonal similarity of the major Third and major Sixth, required a finer cultivation of the musical ear,

[2][See, however, App. XX. sect. K.—*Translator*.]

and perhaps also peculiar beauty of voice. Even yet we are easily led by the familiar sharp major Thirds of equal temperament, to endure any major Thirds which are somewhat too sharp, provided they occur melodically and are not sounded together. On the other hand, we must not forget that the rules of Archytas and Abdul Kadir,[3] both of which were applicable to homophonic music only, gave a preference to the natural major Third, although its introduction obliged both musicians to renounce a musical system so theoretically consistent and invested with such high authority as that of Pythagoras.

Hence the principle of tonal relationship did not at all times exclusively determine the construction of the scale, and does not even yet determine it exclusively among all nations. This principle must, therefore, be regarded to some extent as a *freely selected principle of style*, as I have endeavoured to shew in Chapter XIII. But, on the other hand, the art of music in Europe was historically developed from that principle, and on this fact depends the main proof that it was really as important as we have assumed it to be. The preference first given to the *diatonic scale*, and finally the exclusive use of that scale, introduced the principle of tonal relationship in all its integrity into the musical scale. Within the diatonic scale various methods of execution were possible, and these generated the ancient modes, which had equal claims to attention in homophonic song, and hence stood on a level.

But the principle of tonal relationship penetrated far deeper in its harmonic than it did in its melodic form. In melodic sequence the identity of two partial tones is a matter of memory, but when the notes are sounded together the immediate sensible impression of the beats, or else of the undisturbed flow of sound forces itself on the hearer's attention. The liveliness of melodic and harmonic impressions differs in the same way as a recollected image differs from the actual impression made by the original. As an immediate consequence arose that far superior sensibility for the correctness of the intervals which is seen in the harmonic union of tones, and which admitted of being developed into the finest physical methods of measurement.

It must also be remembered that relationship in the second degree can in harmonic music be reduced to audible relationships of the first degree, by a proper selection of the fundamental bass, and that generally more distance relationships can easily be made clearly

[3][For Archytas of Tarentum, about B.C. 400, see p. 262*c*, and for Abdulqadir, see p. 281 note †.—*Translator.*]

audible. By this means, notwithstanding the variety of progression, a much clearer connection of all parts with their origin, the tonic, can be maintained and rendered objectively sensible to the hearer. It cannot be doubted that these are the essential foundations of the great breadth and wealth of expression which modern compositions can attain without losing their artistic unity.

We then saw that the requirements of harmonic music reacted in a peculiar manner on the construction of scales; that properly speaking only one of the old tonal modes (our major mode) could be retained unaltered,[4] and that the rest after undergoing peculiar modifications were fused into our minor mode, which, though most like the ancient mode of the minor Third, can at one time resemble the mode of the minor Sixth, and at another time that of the minor Seventh, but does not perfectly correspond with any one of these.

[4][But see supra, p. 274, note *, scale 1.—*Translator.*]

† *The System of Harmony Dually Developed*, Dorpat and Leipzig, 1866. Herr v. Oettingen, as already observed, p. 308, note §, regards the minor chord as representing the harmonic undertone of its Fifth, and hence as standing in place of a part of its compound tone. He calls it the 'phonic' chord, as opposed to the 'tonic' major chord which stands in place of the upper partials of its root. He proceeds to deduce the formation of the minor system from the relations of the harmonic undertones in a manner precisely analogous to that by which I have deduced the major system from the relations of the upper partial tones. The tonal mode thus constructed is, however, in our language the mode of the minor Sixth (p. 274, note *, scale 7), and the usual minor, a mixed mode. Latterly Dr. Hugo Riemann has given in his adhesion to this view, and in his lately published *Musical Syntaxis* has attempted to examine and establish the consequences of this system by examples from acknowledged composers. The application of this critical method appears to me very commendable, and to be the indispensable condition to advancing in the theory of composition. For the rest this author justifies (p. 54) the assertion I have made in the text by remarking: 'I am sorry to say that I am unable to adduce a single example from the whole of our musical literature, of the carrying out of (v. Oettingen's) pure minor mode harmony even in the simplest manner.' I have not been able to convince myself of the correctness of the fact adduced on p. xiii. and p. 6, that the undertones of a tone strongly struck on the piano sound when the corresponding dampers are raised. Perhaps the author has been deceived by the circumstance that with very resonant instruments (especially older ones) any strong shake, and therefore probably a violent blow on the digitals, will cause some one or several of the deeper strings to sound its note. [The undertones have always each an upper partial tone of the pitch of the note struck; the striking of this note must then sympathetically excite those upper partials of the undertones, and thus reinforce the prime of the note struck, just as striking the undertone sympathetically excites the higher tone itself. Can this have deceived Dr. Riemann?—*Translator.*]

This process of the development of the elements of our modern musical system lasted down to the middle of the last century. It was not until composers ventured to put a minor chord at the close of compositions written in the minor mode, that the musical feeling of European musicians and hearers can be admitted to have become perfectly and surely habituated to the new system. The minor chord was allowed to be a real, although obscure, chord of its tonic.

Whether this admission of the minor chord expressed a feeling for another mode of unifying its three tones, as A. von Oettingen† has assumed,—relying on the fact that the three tones c—e' $\flat$ $+g$ have a common upper partial g'',—must be left to future experience to decide, should it be found practicable to construct long and well-connected musical compositions in *Oettingen's phonic system* (this is the name which he gives to the minor system which he has theoretically developed, and which is essentially different from the historical minor mode). At any rate, the minor mode has historically developed itself as a compromise between different kinds of claims. Thus it is only major triads which can perfectly indicate the compound tone of the tonic; minor chords contain in their Third an element which, although nearly related to the tonic and its Fifth, does not thoroughly fuse with them, and hence in their final cadence they do not so thoroughly agree with the principle of tonality which had ruled the previous development of music. I have endeavoured to make it probable that the peculiar esthetic expression of the minor mode proceeded partly from this cause and partly from the heterogenous combinational tones of the minor chord.

In the last part of my book, I have endeavoured to shew that the construction of scales and of harmonic tissue is a product of artistic invention, and by no means furnished by the natural formation or natural function of our ear, as it has been hitherto most generally asserted. Of course the laws of the natural function of our ear play a great and influential part in this result; these laws are, as it were, the building stones with which the edifice of our musical system has been erected, and the necessity of accurately understanding the nature of these materials in order to understand the construction of the edifice itself, has been clearly shewn by the course of our investigations upon this very subject. But just as people with differently directed tastes can erect extremely different kinds of buildings with the same stones, so also the history of music shews us that the same properties of the human ear could serve as the foundation of very different musical systems. Consequently it seems to me that we cannot doubt, that not merely the

567

composition of perfect musical works of art, but even the construction of our system of scales, keys, chords, in short of all that is usually comprehended in a treatise of Thorough Bass, is the work of artistic invention, and hence must be subject to the laws of artistic beauty. In point of fact, mankind has been at work on the diatonic system for more than 2500 years since the days of Terpander and Pythagoras, and in many cases we are still able to determine that the progressive changes made in the tonal system have been due to the most distinguished composers themselves, partly through their own independent inventions, and partly through the sanction which they gave to the invention of others, by employing them artistically.

The esthetic analysis of complete musical works of art, and the comprehension of the reasons of their beauty, encounter apparently invincible obstacles at almost every point. But in the field of elementary musical art we have now gained so much insight into its internal connection that we are able to bring the results of our investigations to bear on the views which have been formed and in modern times nearly universally accepted respecting the cause and character of artistic beauty in general. It is, in fact, not difficult to discover a close connection and agreement between them; nay, there are probably fewer examples more suitable than the theory of musical scales and harmony, to illustrate the darkest and most difficult points of general esthetics. Hence I feel that I should not be justified in passing over these considerations, more especially as they are closely connected with the theory of sensual perception, and hence with physiology in general.

No doubt is now entertained that beauty is subject to laws and rules dependent on the nature of human intelligence. The difficulty consists in the fact that these laws and rules, on whose fulfilment beauty depends and by which it must be judged, are not consciously present to the mind, either of the artist who creates the work, or the observer who contemplates it. Art works with design, but the work of art ought to have the appearance of being undesigned, and must be judged on that ground. Art creates as imagination pictures, regularly without conscious law, designedly without conscious aim. A work, known and acknowledged as the product of mere intelligence, will never be accepted as a work of art, however perfect be its adaptation to its end. Whenever we see that conscious reflection has acted in the arrangement of the whole, we find it poor.

Man fühlt die Absicht, und man wird verstimmt.
(We feel the purpose, and it jars upon us.)

And yet we require every work of art to be reasonable, and we shew this by subjecting it to a critical examination, and by seeking to enhance our enjoyment and our interest in it by tracing out the suitability, connection, and equilibrium of all its separate parts. The more we succeed in making the harmony and beauty of all its peculiarities clear and distinct, the richer we find it, and we even regard as the principal characteristic of a great work of art that deeper thought, reiterated observation, and continued reflection shew us more and more clearly the reasonableness of all its individual parts. Our endeavour to comprehend the beauty of such a work by critical examination, in which we partly succeed, shews that we assume a certain adaptation to reason in works of art, which may possibly rise to a conscious understanding, although such understanding is neither necessary for the invention nor for the enjoyment of the beautiful. For what is esthetically beautiful is recognised by the immediate judgment of a cultivated taste, which declares it pleasing or displeasing, without any comparison whatever with law or conception.

But that we do not accept delight in the beautiful as something individual, but rather hold it to be in regular accordance with the nature of mind in general, appears by our expecting and requiring from every other healthy human intellect the same homage that we ourselves pay to what we call beautiful. At most we allow that national or individual peculiarities of taste incline to this or that artistic ideal, and are most easily moved by it, precisely in the same way that a certain amount of education and practice in the contemplation of fine works of art is undeniably necessary for penetration into their deeper meaning.

The principal difficulty in pursuing this object, is to understand how regularity can be apprehended by intuition without being consciously felt to exist. And this unconsciouness of regularity is not a mere accident in the effect of the beautiful on our mind, which may indifferently exist or not; it is, on the contrary, most clearly, prominently, and essentially important. For through apprehending everywhere traces of regularity, connection, and order, without being able to grasp the law and plan of the whole, there arises in our mind a feeling that the work of art which are are contemplating is the product of a design which far exceeds anything we can conceive at the moment, and which hence partakes of the character of the illimitable. Remembering the poet's words:

Du gleichst dem Geist, den du begreifst,
(Thou'rt like the spirit thou conceivest).

we feel that those intellectual powers which were at work in the artist, are far above our conscious mental action, and that were it even possible at all, infinite time, meditation, and labour would have been necessary to attain by conscious thought that degree of order, connection, and equilibrium of all parts and all internal relations, which the artist has accomplished under the sole guidance of tact and taste, and which we have in turn to appreciate and comprehend by our own tact and taste, long before we begin a critical analysis of the work.

It is clear that all high appreciation of the artist and his work reposes essentially on this feeling. In the first we honour a genius, a spark of divine creative fire, which far transcends the limits of our intelligent and conscious forecast. And yet the artist is a man as we are, in whom work the same mental powers as in ourselves, only in their own peculair direction, purer, brighter, steadier; and by the greater or less readiness and completeness with which we grasp the artist's language we measure our own share of those powers which produced the wonder.

Herein is manifestly the cause of that moral elevation and feeling of ecstatic satisfaction which is called forth by thorough absorption in genuine and lofty works of art. We learn from them to feel that even in the obscure depths of a healthy and harmoniously developed human mind, which are at least for the present inaccessible to analysis by conscious thought, there slumbers a germ of order that is capable of rich intellectual cultivation, and we learn to recognise and admire in the work of art, though draughted in unimportant material, the picture of a similar arrangement of the universe, governed by law and reason in all its parts. The contemplation of a real work of art awakens our confidence in the originally healthy nature of the human mind, when uncribbed, unobscured, and unfalsified.

But for all this it is an essential condition that the whole extent of the regularity and design of a work of art should *not* be apprehended consciously. It is precisely from that part of its regular subjection to reason, which escapes our conscious apprehension, that a work of art exalts and delights us, and that the chief effects of the artistically beautiful proceed, *not* from the part which we are able fully to analyse.

If we now apply these considerations to the system of musical tones and harmony, we see of course that these are objects belonging to an entirely subordinate and elementary domain, but nevertheless they, too, are slowly matured inventions of the artistic taste of musicians, and consequently they, too, must be governed by the general rules of artistic beauty. Precisely because we are here still treading the lower walks of

570

art, and are not dealing with the expression of deep psychological problems, we are able to discover a comparatively simple and transparent solution of that fundamental enigma of esthetics.

The whole of the last part of this book has explained how musicians gradually discovered the relationships between tones and chords, and how the invention of harmonic music rendered these relationships closer, and clearer, and richer. We have been able to deduce the whole system of rules which constitute Thorough Bass, from an endeavour to introduce a clearly sensible connection into the series of tones which form a piece of music.

A feeling for the melodic relationship of consecutive tones, was first developed, commencing with Octave and Fifth and advancing to the Third. We have taken pains to prove that this feeling of relationship was founded on the perceptions of identical partial tones in the corresponding compound tones. Now these partial tones are of coarse present in the sensations excited in our auditory apparatus, and yet they are not generally the subject of conscious perception as independent sensations. The conscious perception of everyday life is limited to the apprehension of the tone compounded of these partials, as a whole, just as we apprehend the taste of a very compound dish as a whole, without clearly feeling how much of it is due to the salt, or the pepper, or other spices and condiments. A critical examination of our auditory sensations as such was required before we could discover the existence of upper partial tones. Hence the real reason of the melodic relationship of two tones (with the exception of a few more or less clearly expressed conjectures, as, for example, by Rameau and d'Alembert) remained so long undiscovered, or at least was not in any respect clearly and definitely formulated. I believe that I have been able to furnish the required explanation, and hence clearly to exhibit the whole connection of the phenomena. The esthetic problem is thus referred to the common property of all sensual perceptions, namely, the apprehension of compound aggregates of sensations as sensible symbols of simple external objects, without analysing them. In our usual observations on external nature our attention is so thoroughly engaged by external objects that we are entirely unpractised in taking for the subjects of conscious observation, any properties of our sensations themselves, which we do not already know as the sensible expression of some individual external object or event.

After musicians had long been content with the melodic relationship of tones, they began in the middle ages to make use of harmonic relationship as shewn in consonance. The effects of various combinations of tones also depend partly on the identity or difference of two of their different partial tones, but they likewise partly depend on their combinational tones. Whereas, however, in melodic relationship the equality of the upper partial tones can only be perceived by *remembering* the preceding compound tone, in harmonic relationship it is determined by *immediate sensation*, by the presence or absence of beats. Hence in harmonic combinations of tone, tonal relationship is felt with that greater liveliness due to a present sensation as compared with the recollection of a past sensation. The wealth of clearly perceptible relations grows with the number of tones combined. Beats are easy to recognise as such when they occur slowly; but those which characterise dissonances are, almost without exception, very rapid, and are partly covered by sustained tones which do not beat, so that a careful comparison of slower and quicker beats is necessary to gain the conviction that the essence of dissonance consists precisely in rapid beats. Slow beats do not create the feeling of dissonance, which does not arise till the rapidity of the beats confuses the ear and make it unable to distinguish them. In this case also the ear feels the difference between the undisturbed combination of sound in the case of two consonant tones, and the disturbed rough combination resulting from a dissonance. But, as a general rule, the hearer is then perfectly unconscious of the cause to which the disturbance and roughness are due.

The development of harmony gave rise to a much richer opening out of musical art than was previously possible, because the far clearer characterisation of related combinations of tones by means of chords and chordal sequences, allowed of the use of much more distant relationships than were previously available, by modulating into different keys. In this way the means of expression greatly increased as well as the rapidity of the melodic and harmonic transitions which could now be introduced without destroying the musical connection.

As the independent significance of chords came to be appreciated in the fifteenth and sixteenth centuries, a feeling arose for the relationship of chords to one another and to the tonic chord, in accordance with the same law which had long ago unconsciously regulated the relationship of compound tones. The relationship of compound tones depended on the identity of two or more partial tones, that of chords on the identity of two or more notes. For the musician, of course, the law of the relationship of chords and keys is much more intelligible than that of compound tones. He readily hears the identical tones, or seems them in the notes before him. But the unprejudiced and uninstructed hearer is as little conscious of the reason of the connection of a clear and agreeable series of fluent chords, as he is of the reason of a well-connected melody. He is startled by a false cadence and feels its unexpectedness, but is not at all necessarily conscious of the reason of its unexpectedness.

Then, again, we have seen that the reason why a chord in music appears to be the chord of a determinate root, depends as before upon the analysis of a compound tone into its partial tones, that is, as before upon those elements of a sensation which cannot readily become subjects of conscious perception. This relation between chords is of great importance, both in the relation of the tonic chord to the tonic tone, and in the sequence of chords.

The recognition of these resemblances between compound tones and between chords, reminds us of other exactly analogous circumstances which we must have often experienced. We recognise the resemblance between the faces of two near relations, without being at all able to say in what the resemblance consists, especially when age and sex are different, and the coarser outlines of the features consequently present striking differences. And yet notwithstanding these differences—notwithstanding that we are unable to fix upon a single point in the two countenances which is absolutely alike—the resemblance is often so extraordinarily striking and convincing, that we have not a moment's doubt about it. Precisely the same thing occurs in recognising the relationship between two compound tones.

Again, we are often able to assert with perfect certainty, that a passage not previously heard is due to a particular author or composer whose other works we know. Occasionally, but by no means always, individual mannerisms in verbal or musical phrases determine our judgment, but as a rule we are mostly unable to fix upon the exact points of resemblance between the new piece and the known works of the author or composer.

The analogy of these different cases may be even carried farther. When a father and daughter are strikingly alike in some well-marked feature, as the nose or forehead, we observe it at once, and think no more about it. But if the resemblance is so enigmatically concealed that we cannot detect it, we are fascinated, and cannot help continuing to compare their countenances. And if a painter drew two such heads having, say, a somewhat different expression of character combined with a predominant and striking, though indefinable, resemblance, we should undoubtedly value it as one of the principal beauties of his painting. Our admiration would certainly not be due merely to his technical skill; we should rather look upon his painting as evidencing an unusually delicate feeling for the significance of the human countenance, and find in this the artistic justification of his work.

Now the case is similar for musical intervals. The resemblance of an Octave to its root is so great and striking that the dullest ear perceives it; the Octave seems to be almost a pure repetition of the root, as it, in fact, merely repeats a part of the compound tone of its root, without adding anything new. Hence the esthetical effect of an Octave is that of a perfectly simple, but little attractive interval. The most attractive of the intervals, melodically and harmonically, are clearly the Third and Sixths,—the intervals which lie at the very boundary of those that the ear can grasp. The major Third and the major Sixth cannot be properly appreciated unless the first five partial tones are audible. These are present in good musical qualities of tone. The minor Third and the minor Sixth are for the most part justifiable only as inversions of the former intervals. The more complicated intervals in the scale cease to have any direct or easily intelligible relationship. They have no longer the charm of the Thirds.

Moreover, it is by no means a merely external indifferent regularity which the employment of diatonic scales, founded on the relationship of compound tones, has introduced into the tonal material of music, as, for instance, rhythm introduced some such external arrangement into the words of poetry. I have shewn, on the contrary, in Chapter XIV., that this construction of the scale furnished a means of measuring the intervals of their tones, so that the equality of two intervals lying in different sections of the scale would be recognised by immediate sensation. Thus the melodic step of a Fifth is always characterised by having the second partial tone of the second note identical with the third of the first. This produces a definiteness and certainty in the measurement of intervals for our sensation, such as might be looked for in vain in the system of colours, otherwise so similar, or in the estimation of mere differences of intensity in our various sensual perceptions.

Upon this reposes also the characteristic resemblance between the relations of the musical scale and of space, a resemblance which appears to me of vital importance for the peculiar effects of music. It is an essential character of space that at every position within it like bodies can be placed, and the motions can occur. Everything that is possible to happen in one part of space is equally possible in every other part of space and is perceived by us in precisely the same way. This is the case also with the musical scale. Every melodic phrase, every chord, which can be executed at any pitch, can also be executed at any other pitch in such a way that we immediately perceive the characteristic marks of their similarity. On the other hand, also, different voices, executing the same or different melodic phrases, can move at the same time within the compass of the scale, like two bodies in space, and, provided they are consonant in the accented parts of bars, without creating any musical disturbances. Such a close analogy consequently exists in all essential relations between the musical scale and space, that even alteration of pitch has a readily recognised and unmistakable resemblance to motion in space, and is often metaphorically termed the ascending or descending *motion* or *progression* of a part. Hence, again, it becomes possible for motion in music to imitate the peculiar characteristics of motive forces in space, that is, to form an image of the various impulses and forces which lie at the root of motion. And on this, as I believe, essentially depends the power of music to picture emotion.

It is not my intention to deny that music in its initial state and simplest forms may have been originally an artistic imitation of the instinctive modulations of the voice that correspond to various conditions of the feelings. But I cannot think that this is opposed to the above explanation; for a great part of the natural means of vocal expression may be reduced to such facts as the following: its rhythm and accentuation are an immediate expression of the rapidity or force of the corresponding phychical motives—all effort drives the voice up—a desire to make a pleasant impression on another mind leads to selecting a softer, pleasanter quality of tone—and so forth. An endeavour to imitate the involuntary modulations of the voice and make its recitation richer and more expressive, may therefore very possibly have led our ancestors to the discovery of the first means of musical expression, just as the imita- tion of weeping, shouting, or sobbing, and other musical delineations may play a part in even cultivated music, (as in operas), although such modifications of the voice are not confined to the action of free mental motives, but embrace really mechanical and even involuntary muscular contractions. But it is quite clear that every completely developed melody goes far beyond an imitation of nature, even if we include the cases of the most varied alteration of voice under the influence of passion. Nay, the very fact that music introduces progression by fixed degrees both in rhythm and in the scale, renders even an approximately correct representation of nature simply impossible, for most of the passionate affections of the voice are characterised by a gliding transition in pitch. The imitation of nature is thus rendered as imperfect as the imitation of a picture by embroidery on a canvas with separate little squares for each shade of colour. Music, too, departed still further from nature when it introduced the greater compass, the mobility, and the strange qualities of tone belonging to musical instruments, by which the field of attainable musical effects has become so much wider than it was or could be when the human voice alone was employed.

Hence though it is probably correct to say that mankind, in historical development, first learned the means of musical expression from the human voice, it can hardly be denied that these same means of expressing melodic progressions act, in artistically developed music, without the slightest reference to the application made of them in the modulations of the human voice, and have a more general significance than any that can be attributed to innate instinctive cries. That this is the case appears above all in the modern development of instrumental music, which possesses an effective power and artistic justification that need not be gainsaid, although we may not yet be able to explain it in all its details.

HEINRICH SCHENKER

Heinrich Schenker (b. Galicia 1868, d. Vienna 1935), composer, performer, music critic, editor and theorist, is best known for his innovative and controversial theoretical notions concerning the structure of tonal music.

Although he received a formal music education—he studied under Bruckner at the Viennese Conservatory and took a degree at the university—he regarded "schools for composition" as disasters. He believed that real masterpieces are conceived in a "sweep" of genius and do not result from classroom instruction. He himself never taught in an institution but earned his living as a private teacher of theory and piano. He also surrounded himself with a large number of eminent musicians. Some of his students immigrated to America and were responsible, in part, for the influence his thinking had there.

Schenker believed that his ideas related directly to the creative processes manifested in actual compositions. His theory, he declared, is not an extraneous superimposition on music as object, but emerges organically from the music itself in accordance with aural perceptions.

He deplored Rameau's artificial "superimpositions," such as his concept of the 'fundamental bass', and thoroughly rejected any theory of music that did not take into account musical succession, i.e., the "unfolding" nature of music. Schenker demanded that theory address itself to the structural unity and to the continuity of the musical work, for structure and process are organically intertwined.

The primal compositional material, according to Schenker, is the temporal contrapuntal projection of the basic harmony, the *ursatz*. Its transformations create an interaction between "background," "middle-ground," and "foreground," the structural layers of compositions. This process of *auskomponeirung* creates the organic coherence of the musical work, and consequently, of the theory. The *urlinie*, the melodic diatonic structure which spans the upper voice of a composition, itself represents a kind of manifestation of the diatonic chord. In fact, each interacting transformative level represents a kind of "repetition" or "parallelism" of the basic fundamental harmony governing the work as a whole—"always the same, but not the same way" as Schenker liked to say.

It follows that without a knowledge of the general it is impossible to comprehend the specific, while the exploration of the specific leads to a clear understanding of the general. The analytic procedure, however, is one of reduction: the musical surface, the foreground comprising the details, leads to the unveiling of the "middleground" and "background," which contain the deeper and more general compositional patterns. These layers taken together illuminate the *ursatz*, the basic conception from which they emanate. Schenker regarded music structure as a gestalt in which unity and coherence are achieved through interrelation and organic connections, as opposed to the juxtaposition of chords, motives, themes, etc., which "artificially" mold these elements into "form." Schenker was after the kind of analysis that would grow "outward from within," an analysis that would reveal the work as a whole in its particulars and the musical cohesion as self-generated.

The understanding of the structure of compositions, Schenker believed, should be part and parcel not only of musical instruction, but of performance as well. Such musical understanding provides the safeguards for the proper execution of musical works. The totality of a composition, however, could be conceived only spontaneously, through a "sweep" of intuition.

Creativity, Schenker believed, is an intuitive power, derived from Nature and God, a gift possessed by few. Artists, like saints for the church, are few in number. Schenker regarded himself as an artist rather than theorist, repeatedly arguing that "art for everyone is not art," claiming moreover that the genius, who by definition is linked to God, shows his followers a "new way." The unveiling of the relationship between the fundamental structure and the foreground, believed Schenker, provides the kind of religious uplifting of the spirit which reflects the rapport between God and Creation, and Creation and God.

Schenker, as a proponent of Nietzsche, also believed in the cultural supremacy of the German nation and in the supremacy of its music. He ridiculed the French for their "mediocrity" symbolized by Rameau's "enlightenment" and belittled the Italians for their predilection for operatic music. Encountering much criticism and misunderstanding,

Schenker stood firmly by what he believed to be "the essence" of an "eternal order."

The transplantation of Schenker's theory by his faithful disciples into American soil encouraged a new wave of Schenkerian discussion, criticism and application. While Schenkerian analysis, it was admitted, constitutes a "creative act," facilitating a closer touch with the work, divergences among the graphs of the same work nevertheless raise questions concerning the "latitudes of correctness" of its application. Schenkerian analysis was also criticized for its seeming neglect of stylistic uniqueness and, paradoxically, for its neglect of temporal organizations as well, though it addresses itself to the "unfolding" nature of music more profoundly than most other theories. Altogether, while Schenker's system has the appearance of a serious epistemological attempt, its philosophical nature has not been investigated systematically. Given the increased dissemination of Schenkerian analyses and recent developments in generative theories, structualism and other meta-theories of language and knowledge, such an enterprise becomes indispensable indeed.

from Free Composition

The Significance of Fundamental Structure[1]

Section 4: The Significance of the Fundamental Structure for Composition, Instruction, and Performance[2]

Musical coherence can be achieved only through the fundamental structure in the background and its transformations in the middleground and foreground.

It should have been evident long ago that the same principle applies both to a musical organism and to the human body: it grows outward from within. Therefore it would be fruitless as well as incorrect to attempt to draw conclusions about the organism from its epidermis.

The hands, legs, and ears of the human body do not begin to grow after birth; they are present at the time of birth. Similarly, in a composition, a limb which was not somehow born with the middle and background cannot grow to be a diminution. Hugo von Hofmannsthal has found ingenious words for this: "One must conceal the depths. Where? On the surface." And: "No part of the surface of a figure can be formed except from the innermost core outward."

Thus, in the foreground, coherence lies behind the tones, as, in speech, the coherence of thought lies behind the words. Consequently, one can understand that the layman is unable to hear such coherence in music; but this unfortunate situation obtains also at higher levels, among musicians of talent. Even they have not yet learned to hear true coherent relationships. Since most people today lack coherence themselves, they are quite unable to bear the tension of musical coherence.

As a motion through several levels, as a connection between two mentally and spatially separated points, every relationship represents a path which is as real as any we "traverse" with our feet. Therefore, a relationship actually is to be "traversed" in thought—but this must

---

[1]Text: Heinrich Schenker, *Free Composition*, tr. and ed. by Ernest Oster (New York, Longman Inc., 1979), pp. 6–9. The Paragraphs referred to in the text belong to Schenker's *Harmonielehre* (entitled in the English translation as *Harmony*).
[2]Passage (G), omitted here, is supplied in Appendix 4. (Rothgeb)

involve actual time. Even the remarkable improvisatory long-range vision of our great composers, which I once referred to as "aural flight," presupposes, indeed, includes time.[3] And what has become of the concept of time at the present? Technology enables distant parts of the world to be connected at a rate of speed which is approaching the point of frenzy. This has also conditioned our attitude to art. Today one flies over the work of art in the same manner as one flies over villages, cities, palaces, castles, fields, woods, rivers, and lakes. This contradicts not only the historical bases of the work of art but also—more significantly —its coherence, its inner relationships, which demand to be "traversed."[4]

The ability in which all creativity begins—the ability to compose extempore, to improvise fantasies and preludes—lies only in a feeling for the background, middleground, and foreground. Formerly such an ability was regarded as the hallmark of one truly gifted in composition, that which distinguished him from the amateur or the ungifted. Subsequently the rise of the masses made it necessary for the composer to give consideration to the incapabilities of an ever-growing number of musicians. So it would be of greatest importance today to study thoroughly the fantasies, preludes, cadenzas, and similar embellishment which the great composers have left to us. All music instruction, be it public or private, should assign high priority to such study.

Anyone who has seen *sketches* by the great composers must have encountered voice-leading progressions which are far more than brief ideas or mere suggestions. These voice-leading progressions really present structural goals and the paths to them in a manner which could only stem from the far-flung inspiration of a genius. Such a vision, which is based upon the relationship of background, middleground, and foreground, can create a purely musical coherence even, as it were, in flight.[5] Therefore, a thoroughgoing study of the extant sketches of the masters is most necessary. These sketches reveal musical coherence in the process of evolution.

What a deplorably low value is generally placed on music is reflected

---

[3] *Der Tonwille* 5, p. 55. (Schenker)

[4] Passage (H), omitted here, is supplied in Appendix 4. (Rothgeb)

[5] In my work, particularly in the annotated editions (*Erläuterungsausgabe*) of op. 101, 109, 110, and 111, I have often referred to this quality in Beethoven's sketches. (Schenker)

in the fact that sketches by the masters, although long a commercially viable commodity, have been little understood by musicians. The exigencies which the composer encounters as he creates are foreign to these persons; therefore the written records of the composers' successful struggle with such exigencies must necessarily also have a foreign look about them. Under these circumstances Nottebohm's *Beethoveniana*, which Brahms so strongly recommended for publication, had to wait almost a half-century for the printing of its second edition. It is the musicians themselves who abandon their art! How different is the case of the first drafts, fragments, or sketches of great poets and painters—they have always met with a more general and lively appreciation!

Since the musicians up to the present have been unable to perceive the musical coherence in the masterworks, they have been even less able to read the *autographs* of the great composers. These last present the additional difficulty of problems of notation which are highly individual, ever new, and never schematic, but which always correspond to the musical content. *Autograph-study*, a completely new and special field of knowledge, thus goes hand in hand with the theory of musical coherence. The extent to which I have surpassed my few predecessors in this subject—editors, analysts, and the like—is indicated by those works of mine which secure for me the honor of being the true founder of the discipline of autograph-study.[6]

---

[6]In my edition of the Beethoven piano sonatas, the following texts are based upon the autographs: op. 27 no. 2, op. 28, 57, 78, 81a (first movement), 90 (after the manuscript copy by Archduke Rudolph), 101, 109, 110, and 111 (cf. also the *Erläuterungsausgabe*).

In addition, I revised the "Philharmonia" edition of Schubert's Symphony in *B* Minor according to its autograph.

The analytic presentations of Beethoven's Fifth Symphony (Universal Edition), Mozart's Symphony in *G* Minor (*Jahrb. II*), Chopin's Études op. 10 nos. 5 and 6 (*Jahrb. I*), and Schubert's Menuetto in *B* Minor (*Kunstwart*, March 1929) are based upon autographs. In the *Five Graphic Analyses*, the autographs of J.S. Bach's Prelude in *C* (*WTC I*), Haydn's Sonata in *E* ♭ (Hob. 49), and Chopin's Étude op. 10 no. 12 were of the utmost value.

The presentation of the *Eroica* in *Jahrbuch III* relies upon a copy of the manuscript revised by Beethoven.

As a result of a suggestion I made in the preface to my *Erläuterungsausgabe*, which was later orally reinforced in private instruction, Mr. Anthony van Hoboken, a Dutch music enthusiast equipped with the finest musical intelligence, established an archive for *Photogramme von Meisterwerken* and presented it to the *Nationalbibliothek* in Vienna in 1927. This collection has already increased in size to more than 30,000 prints. However, this invaluable treasure is appreciated least of all by the musicians.

Organic coherence also underlies the art of *orchestration* and the treatment of the instruments in *chamber music*. In the masterworks, orchestral colors are not mixed according to whim and applied at random; they are subject to the laws of the whole (cf. *Jahrb. III*, Scherzo of the *Eroica* Symphony). [§ 269]

The *performance* of a musical work of art can be based only upon a perception of that work's organic coherence. Interpretation cannot be acquired through gymnastics or dancing; one can transcend "motive," "theme," "phrase," and "bar line" and achieve true musical punctuation only by comprehending the background, middleground, and foreground. As punctuation in speech transcends syllables and words, so true punctuation in music strives toward more distant goals. This, of course, does not mean that the tones of the fundamental line need be overemphasized, as are the entrances in a poor performance of a fugue. The player who is aware of the coherence of a work will find interpretative means which allow the coherence to be heard. He who performs in this way will take care not to destroy the linear progressions; such destruction would paralyze our participation. Nor will he overestimate the value of the bar line, which indicates neither linear progression nor direction. Consequently, the concept of background, middleground, and foreground is of decisive and practical importance for performance[7] [§ § 252–54, 265, 299].[8]

All previous theory has succeeded in blighting the art of music; it has instilled its own chaos into what is yet an unshakeable organism. It is not the province of theory to provide anything that is totally new or truly its own—yet theory seeks for one new solution after the other, with the emphasis usually upon the "new" and not upon "solution."

Since conventional theory is not able to measure all musical motion in relation to the filling-in of the space of a third, fifth, or octave, it

They gaze at the prints as they would at locks of hair, watches, writing desks and the like, which are shown at exhibits that honor the memory of the great dead. I have often stressed that information of the greatest significance regarding the principles of art, the creation of musical coherence, the individual style of notation, etc., is to be derived from autographs as well as from sketches. (Schenker)

[7]Passage (I), omitted here, is supplied in Appendix 4. (Rothgeb)

[8]Many of Schenker's publications contain beautiful and deeply considered suggestions for performers. See especially the *Erläuterungsausgabe* of the late Beethoven sonatas; also Beethoven's op. 57 in *Der Tonwille 7*, Brahms's Handel Variations in *Der Tonwille 8*, Mozart's *G*-Minor Symphony in *Jahrbuch II*. (Oster)

Footnote continued.

postulates the overtone series and, further, a series of subharmonics as the origin of the major-minor system.[9] But the subdominant, which most definitely forms part of the diatonic system, cannot have its origin in the overtone series. Theory has never departed from this contradictory teaching.

Even up to the present day, theory has not always been able to read foreground *intervals* correctly; one can only recognize them by examining their relation to background and middleground. All too frequently theory has failed to recognize many events in the foreground, simply because it has not understood their origin in the more elemental. Since thoroughbass figures can be understood only in terms of such relations, theory also fails when treating *thoroughbass*. To theory, the figures represent empty, frozen concepts; consequently, musicians of today cannot intelligently realize a continuo part.

But the most baleful error of conventional theory is its recourse to "*keys*" when, in its lack of acquaintance with foreground and middle-ground, it finds no other means of explanation. Often its helplessness is so great that it abandons even this most comfortable means of avoiding difficulties. Nothing is an indicative of the state of theory and analysis as this absurd abundance of "keys." The concept of the "key" as a higher unity in the foreground is completely foreign to theory: it is even capable of designating a single unprolonged chord as a key. To be sure, the great composers spoke of keys in the incorrect sense in their letters and notes. However, when we consider the singularly profound and masterly character of their works, we can certainly disregard their theoretical nomenclature. But we, incapable of such mastery, dare not permit ourselves the luxury of erroneous theories.

It is no wonder, then, that the masterwork remains inaccessible to theory, and that its analyses resemble unsuccessful decipherings of papyrus rolls.

From such theory, who could expect to learn how to improvise, or to develop all the capabilities which lead to the secrets of truly organic and artistic activity?[10]

Music is not only an *object* of theoretical consideration. It is *subject*, just as we ourselves are subject. Even the octave, fifth, and third of the

[9]Bruckner used to teach (following Sechter) that even the sixth tone of the diatonic scale was dissonant and therefore had to be resolved downward. (Schenker)
[10]Passage (J), omitted here, is supplied in Appendix 4. (Rothgeb)

harmonic series are a product of the organic activity of the tone as subject, just as the urges of the human being are organic. Accordingly, the quest for a new form of music is a quest for a homunculus. But nature will endure, indeed, will conquer, in music also; she has revealed herself in the works of the masters and, in this form, she will prevail.

My concepts present, for the first time, a genuine *theory of tonal language.*

Instruction at least in the *linear progressions*, the *primary means of coherence*, is indispensable. Because these progressions are anchored in polyphony, we must first learn to think *contrapuntally*. Even though counterpoint has long existed in the West, it is not yet at home in the mind of Western man. His ear is more apt to disregard counterpoint, to follow the upper voice which is the bearer of the melodic element, just as children rely on the right hand at their first piano lesson. At best, one hears a bass which is inactive; but when the bass goes beyond mere support and undertakes contrapuntal motion, the ear immediately turns back toward the upper voice.

My theory shows that music is a self-contained unity in every respect that gives it its particular life among the arts. I would not presume to say how inspiration comes upon the genius, to declare with any certainty which part of the middleground or foreground first presents itself to his imagination: the ultimate secrets will always remain inaccessible to us [§ § 29, 85].

The greatest disaster for music is the so-called composition school. At best, one might allow music schools to serve as centers where the construction and performance of the instruments would be taught. Without any right, the schools attempt to justify their existence by providing instruction in composition: they even dispense legally binding documents testifying to the results of their instruction. Is not learning to hear the first task, during which time the student might well dispense with composition? Admittedly, to hear correctly and to compose correctly are equally difficult; but no music school can be released from the obligation of teaching to hear correctly. We cannot indulge the student in his favorite objection that he will never be able to reach such a high goal. Do not people devote themselves to many ends, even though they are conscious that they can never attain complete mastery? Are not the masses in the public schools instructed in matters which have no place in everyday life? Therefore, why should they not learn that strange mysteries also lie behind tones? [§ 316] Goethe's words are true: "That which the masses believe is easy to believe"; and, "What the intelligent person knows is difficult to know." It is also true that the fundamental structure amounts to a sort of secret, hidden and unsuspected, a secret which, incidentally, provides music with a kind of natural preservation from destruction by the masses. But, despite all difficulties, the schools ought definitely to give some suggestion of this secret!

Fourth Appendix[1]
Omissions from the Original German Edition

A large portion of the text translated here was already omitted from the second German edition. A few additional passages included here were excised by Ernst Oster in his translation.

These excerpts exhibit all of the difficulties of language alluded to by Oster in his preface. And one particular source of difficulty, the use of metaphor, causes unusually severe problems for translation. Moreover, certain words such as *Wurzel* (root) and *Zusammenhang* (coherence, inner connection) are used repeatedly with subtle changes in meaning or emphasis; in such cases, different English words are used to render a single German word, and there is necessarily some loss of meaning. This is partially compensated by the inclusion in parentheses, where appropriate, of the original German expression. Some especially elliptical passages required a few words of explanation; footnotes have been added for this purpose.

Special thanks are due to Professor Juergen Thym for his careful reading of the manuscript and for his valuable suggestions concerning some unusually problematical passages.

A

Only an artist in language invents words in a way that truly reflects their roots.[2] The masses then transmute the artist's words in countless dialects that vary with landscape, mountain, valley, town, and village. Their ear does not reach down to the root; their memory seldom extends past grandfather. It is the same in music: a mode of thinking based on the roots of tone (*ein Tonwurzelhaftes Denken*) is given only to the genius. The others write fugues, sonatas, symphonies, and so forth, as though in careless dialects whose degenerate condition (*Abfall von der Wurzel*) is plain to see.

---

[1]Text: op. cit., pp. 158–162. Tr. By J. Rothgeb. The numbered notes are the translator's notes.

[2]*Nur ein Sprachschöpfer erfindet Worte wirklich wurzelhaft. Wurzel* (root) and its derivative *wurzelhaft* (rootlike; of or pertaining to a root) are used in various metaphorical senses in this passage and elsewhere.

Nebular spirals solidify and become stars. Music, born from the original irrational state as if from a nebular spiral, and made ever more dense with diminution, grew into a star in the heavens of the spirit. But how strange it is: mankind is more interested in the most distant star in the firmament than in music, the star of the spirit's heaven! May the light of that noble star shine on! It surely is captured and protected in my eyes, but what will happen when my eyes have closed for good?

For the adherent of my doctrines an endless field of study opens up. He sees the ostensibly old creation of our masters anew, as if at the moment of its birth; he feels as the author of the Bible must have felt on being allowed to hail God's creation with the first words of the most blessed wonderment, the most ecstatic tremor.

Although favored by God, the genius is nevertheless removed <from pure art> by the material in which he works. The non-genius, however, is twice removed—by the material, and also by genius itself. The non-genius misses the complexity of genius; the genius appears too simple to him. The non-genius feels himself obliged to transcend the genius.

Only the genius is connected with God, not the people. For this reason it is necessary to strip the masses of their halo.[3]

The geniuses of art are its saints, so to speak. Of course in art, as in the church, the number of saints is very small.

The leveling force to which average people are subject is never imposed upon them by political or, in a broader sense, spiritual dictators; it is, rather, like an infection which passes from one average person to another.

Imitation is no substitute for evolution.

In epochs deprived of genius there is much lamenting of the "irretrievably lost" gift of genius. But did the people ever truly possess this gift? The possession was only illusory, and so is the loss. A history of mankind that tells this truth has yet to be written.

It is said that each generation understands the works of the genius in a different way. I say: *no* generation understands them; but each generation *mis*understands them in a different way.

Those who come and go without having understood the world or themselves revolt mechanically against their forbears in order to gain space for living. They condemn their fathers as reactionary, and

---

[3]*Entgottung der Masse tut daher Not.*

588

consider only themselves the true progressives. It is futile, however, to try to escape from the genius with such a cheap device![4]

B

If I am dedicated in heart and mind to the greatest masters of my art, how can I be considered eccentric or reactionary?

Concerning the law of large numbers: two, four, or eight people can easily be brought together by games, if necessary also by intellectual entertainment. Art can bring together as many as two or three thousand people. But to assemble and entertain 50,000 people—this can be accomplished only by bullfights, cock fights, massacres, pogroms: in short, a brutal ranting and raving, a demented and chaotic outcry. Art is incapable of uniting such large numbers.

It is the same in art as in politics. Just as "freedom" for all is no longer true freedom—it is merely a utopian dream to "reconcile the ideal form of the liberalism, which really wanted only a new selection of elite in place of the obsolete feudal order, with the great experience of society and its great metamorphoses" (Coudenhove-Kalergi)—so "art for everyone is not art" (E.J. Schindler, the painter, in his diary).

High art cannot be attained if it strives to fulfill common ends. But it is not the declining human species that has chosen to allow art to die: on the contrary, art, because misunderstood and unattained, has left the human species behind. But those who have been thus left behind by art call themselves *modern*!

Culture, tradition, the discipline of genius—these terms are all synonymous; they all have to do with the phenomenon of genius. Civilization, however, relinquishes the support of the genius in every respect. When a generation begins to want a new culture, when it attacks tradition and the discipline of genius, it contradicts the true essence of culture.

Just as there are economics conferences which are intended to combat the decline of the world economy, there should be also world conferences for the economies of the spirit, whose duty would be to combat decline in the spiritual domain. In consideration of the petty

---

[4]   *mit solchem billigen Kniff auch dem Genie entlaufen zu wollen!* To invoke "progress" does not compensate for the absence of genius.

jealousy which would inevitably arise, it would be advisable to follow the practice of politics—to have, behind the official politicians of the spiritual, unofficial operatives who understand how to conduct affairs of the spirit securely.

C

Here we shall be concerned only with the way this principle manifests itself in art. Thus, for example, it is not only the historical drama whose special environment must come across to the audience: *every* drama presents a content whose meaning truly reveals itself to the audience only if they perceive the fundamental (*Wurzelhaft*) significance of the inner connections which find expression in it according to background, middleground, and foreground. Whever we lose even the background of a drama, we possess the drama no more, as is the case, for example, with Greek drama.

The background in painting is visible; it requires neither justification nor explanation.

D

Whenever and wherever such heroes are lacking, the masses can never become a true nation (*Volk*). It is only through individuals, and according to the law of origin, development, and present, that the masses can be forged into a nation.

Technological creativity is chiefly concerned with the expansion of man's habitat and spatial existence, or with establishing surface connections between distant points. All such creation yields only surface, only foreground.

E

Included in the elevation of the spirit to the fundamental structure is an uplifting, of an almost religious character, to God and to the geniuses through whom he works—an uplifting, in the literal sense, to the kind of coherence which is found only in God and the geniuses.

Between fundamental structure and foreground there is manifested a rapport much like that ever-present, interactional rapport which connects God to creation and creation to God. Fundamental structure and foreground represent, in terms of this rapport, the celestial and the terrestrial in music.

F

Just as life is an uninterrupted process of energy transformation, so the voice-leading strata represent an energy transformation in the life which originates in the fundamental structure.

G

With limited spiritual vision, composition is no more possible than speech. Certainly both can be undertaken with just such a handicap, but the results will show it.

The most basic necessities of life by themselves foster a certain expansion of the power of thinking. Men must learn how to communicate with each other so that with a joint effort they can wrest from nature, society, and state such benefits as are necessary to survival. This common effort necessarily must be infused with coherence (*Zusammenhang*), even with love; and as a result, a modicum of coherence and a certain degree of love enter into men's spirit and their language.

By contrast, music, as art, has no practical benefit to offer. Thus there is no external stimulus for expansion of the powers of musical creativity and music's artistic means. The expansion of creative vision, then, must spring from within itself, only from the special form of coherence that is proper to it, and the special love intrinsic to it.

Therefore, the person whose tonal sense is not sufficiently mature to bind tones together into linear progressions and to derive from them further linear progressions, clearly lacks musical vision and the love that procreates. Only living love composes, makes possible linear progressions and coherence—not metaphysics, so often invoked in the present time, or the much touted "objectivity"; these, in particular, have neither creativity nor breeding warmth.

H

Just this passion for flying over[5] drives people to revolt against nature. Nature hews to landscapes as rubrics according to which she arranges and attunes her creations. But modern man thinks he can ignore the differentiations of landscapes simply because he is able to fly over them. There is no doubt, however, that nature, like art, will win out. Just as nature will always place elephants and crocodiles, for example, where she can provide their life's necessities, so she will place a Beethoven—if indeed ever again—among the German people!

There is but on grammar of the linear progressions—the one described here in connection with the theory of coherence in music. It sufficed for the masters; therefore those without knowledge or capabilities felt it necessary to seek newer forms of coherence. But I repeat here what I have often said before: the fact that all of the masterworks manifest identical laws of coherence in no way precludes a diversity in essential nature among the masters.[6]

I

Today this is recognized even by the most noted conductors.

J

Until now, all theory had to founder on the foreground, because theory selected and read only from the foreground, using it as the only source of phenomena to be considered.[7] The sorry state of theory, whose arrogance and pretentiousness match its erroneous content, is most accurately characterized by the fact that it labels a true musical hearing process as "musical research" (*Musikforschung*); what is commonly called musical research, however, has nothing to do with

---

[5]*Die Leidenschaft des Ueber-fliegens.*

[6]That is, the masters achieved variety and newness without seeking fundamentally new principles of coherence.

[7]The verb *scheitern* (founder) also means to fail, and it is used in both senses here: first, a theory that looks only at the foreground will not be able to see past it; and secondly, such a theory will be unable even to interpret the foreground correctly.

music. How sad that such a perverse way to thinking finds a place even in Germany, where the greatest music-geniuses practiced their art!

If the Italians object that German music is "philosophical"—perhaps they will also describe by way of thinking as philosophy—we need not pay it any heed; for they use music only for texts and for the folk song, opera, and so forth. Music from the sidestreets and for the sidestreets, so to speak. To be sure, the sun shines on their streets; but if the streets beneath other skies enjoy less sunshine, the music of genius is as sun to those who dwell in them—a sun which illuminates and warms their souls, bathes their chambers in golden light, and even makes the landscape sunny!

Theory today has sunk so low that it hearkens to the mouths of children, accepting their utterances as artistically valid revelations, instead of passing on to children the lessons and principles that have been derived from the masterworks. It even attempts to teach a kind of collective art, and approaches musical creativity, which was, is, and will remain truly the gift of the few, with a purely mechanical way of thinking. Theory courses today have become literally hobby courses for unmusical children.

K

Our era was the first to try to manufacture national musical languages—a political hunger—somewhat in the way that industries are founded on the basis of so-called autarky.

L

At best, the course of culture moves in curves, something like this: <original Fig. 13 follows>.

M

I am aware that with the present discussion I am the first to have recognized and demonstrated in artistic terms the profound difference between Italian and German diminution—that is, between Italian and German music. This difference, however, is not to be interpreted as if the Italian and German types were of equal significance within musical art. On the contrary, one thing should be made explicit: Italian music, always bound to words, must be appraised as merely a preliminary step toward the Germans, just as in previous epochs the period of irrationality, the first contrapuntal attempts, and the first paths of Italian diminution, etc., signified preliminary stages of development, never equally valid states. (May the writers of music history at last recognize this distinction and put it to use in their treatises!) This is in no way negated by the simultaneous existence of such various stages of artistic advancement, of a preliminary stage alongside the most advanced. In nature, different stages of evolution are found not only in succession but also contemporaneously. Isn't the simultaneous existence of the genius and the average person exactly such a contemporaneity? (See Fig. 13.) However, in the last analysis, the standard for judging evolutionary plateaux derives from art as pure idea. Whoever has once perceived the essence of a pure idea—whoever has fathomed its secrets—knows that such an idea remains ever the same, ever indestructible, as an element of an eternal order. Even if, after millenia, such an idea should finally desert mankind and vanish from the foreground of life—that foreground which we like to call chaos—it still partakes of God's cosmos, the background of all creation whence it originated.

Therefore let all men, be they philosophers or not, cease to ruminate on the meaning of life, to lament life's ostensible meaninglessness. How can men hope to stumble upon the true meaning of life when, constrained by mortal organs, they must see immediately the end for each beginning, the fulfillment of each promise, the reward for each good deed, and the punishment for each crime in order to comprehend or even form a notion of the concepts of beginning and end. The "chaos" of the foreground belongs with the universal order of the background; it is one with it. All of the brief time spans of the foreground's chaos fall into the endless time continuum of the universe; let us finally learn humbly to love and honor the chaos for the sake of the cosmos, which is God's own. To partake of the cosmos and its eternal ideas—this alone signifies a life of beauty, true immortality in God.

N

Even the life of pure ideas moves in repetitions, for each of the individual manifestations of such ideas represents a repetition. In the history of humanity we see epochs in which ideas are disseminated and stamp mankind with the mark of evolution; but we also see epochs which, lacking any such working-out of an idea, are destined to be periods of decline.

O

I doubt that the Greeks attained complete clarity regarding the nature of their prosody. If, as I have demonstrated, all systems and scale formations which have been and are taught in the music and theories of various peoples were and are merely self-deceptions, why should I take seriously the Greeks' belief in the correctness of their prosody? Surely an understanding of their poetic meter would have involved first of all the discovery of the natural metric foot, and then how it fitted into a binary or ternary metric scheme. The poetic verse is thus illuminated, so to speak, from two sources at once: the metric foot, whose birthplace is the word, and the schematic meter which runs its course independently. It is the dual illumination which secures the special charm of verse, but at the same time creates an uncertain quality and also leads to insecure theoretical interpretation. Thus in Greek poetic theory it may have been only misunderstandings which led to the establishment of a multiplicity of poetic meters, whose explanation evidently would lie in the aforementioned duality. It is possible that the Greek words were based exclusively on binary and ternary patterns—the binary being the trochee, — ∪ , and the ternary the dactyl, — ∪ ∪ . It is questionable whether the Greek language really made use of an iambus, ∪ —, or of ternary schemes such as ∪ ∪ —, or ∪ — ∪ .

The German language, too, appears to be based on trochaic and dactylic patterns. The illusion of iambuses and other words having metrically weak beginnings evidently has its origin in the use of prefixes; for example, *Geduld* = *dulden, Gewalt* = *walten*, etc. Therefore in German, too, the natural poetic foot of the words often conflicts with a predetermined metric schema. But in any case a mechanical application of the many Greek meters to the German language is not permissible (cf. Marpurg, *Anleitung zur Singe-Composition*, 1758).

P

The phenomenon of form in the foreground can be described in an almost physical-mechanical sense as an energy transformation—a transformation of the forces which flow from the background to the foreground through the structural levels.

Q

In the variation movement of Mozart's A-Major Piano Sonata, K. 331 <300i according to Koechel-Einstein>, the increase of motion from sixteenth-notes to sixteenth-note triplets from Variation 1 to Variation 2 is interrupted by Variations 3 (minor) and 4 (major, with the left hand crossing over); Variation 5 brings thirty-second notes (Adagio), and Variation 6, Allegro, concludes the movement.

from Das Meisterwerk in der Musik[1]

The Organic Aspect of Sonata Form

One of the most difficult problems in human knowlege consists of bringing the general into accord with the specific.[2] In order to grasp the world of phenomena with merely few concepts, we must search for the general, while at the same time explore the ultimate depth of mystery in the specific if we wish to properly comprehend the general, which, in turn, is conveyed by this specific. The task is difficult because the general, regardless how it may be stated, easily tempts people to pursue the path of least resistance and to spare all further effort concerning the specific. Through continued disregard of the specific, however, understanding of the general becomes deprived of intellectuality, as it were; it fails to mature into truth, it does not progress beyond the level of a pattern.

---

[1]Text: Sylvan Sol Kalib, *Essays from the Three Yearbooks "Das Meisterwerk in der Music,"* an annotated translation, Northwestern University, Ph.D. Dissertation (Ann Arbor, UMI Research Press, 1973), Vol. II pp. 224–244; 491–518. The numbered notes are Kalib's notes. Those under asterisk are Schenker's. Many of Kalib's notes (e.g., 3, 4) refer to other essays from *Das Meisterwerk* included in his dissertation.

[2]*Prefatory Note:* In this essay, Schenker discusses and illustrates the contrast between the conventional approach to the sonata form and his own. Whereas the conventional approach to sonata form assumes a general pattern, based on the accepted conception of themes and standard key relationships, etc., Schenker shows the sonata form as taking place through the extemporizing flow of auskomponierung, with the boundaries of sections, and choices of keys being determined by the specific manner in which the urlinie and ursatz are unfolded and distributed. Using examples from the Haydn *Piano Sonata in G Minor*, Op. 54, No. 1, and the Beethoven Piano Sonatas, *Op. 10, No. 2 in F Major, Op. 10, No. 1 in C Minor,* and *Op. 109 in E major,* Schenker points out significant and subtle structural connections which remain unnoticed in the conventional approach to sonata form. As a result of his approach, an original conception of motive and melody emerges, which is brought out in this essay. Also unique is the evidence Schenker brings to support his contention that truly organic sonata composition is created only in extemporization.

In the latter part of the essay, Schenker discusses the importance of an awareness of background connections for performance. Toward the conclusion, he includes a critique on the conventional view of themes, motives, and melody, and nineteenth and twentieth century music whose structure, according to him, are based on that approach to melody.

Thus, it must have been quite simple for conventional theory to have derived common characteristics from the many sonata works. It believed that it had found the ultimate general, and proceeded to transmit the deduced form-conception for practical applications. Conventional theory was so convinced of the correctness of its definition that it dismissed any skepticism even when sonatas that had been composed in accordance with that form-conception had exposed it in the worst possible way.[3] Conventional theory was convinced that it was not its form-conception, but rather the sonata form that was being disposed of. It had simply contented itself prematurely with an inadequate conception before it had developed the talent within itself to be able to absorb the specific in the works of genius. Were this not the case, the understanding of this specific in works of genius would have undoubtedly prevented the establishment of that pattern and would have provided for a more accurate understanding of the general.

* * * *

Conventional theory, to be sure, observed the fact that the tendency toward a three-part form, in which the introduction of a modulation and a contrasting key in the first section, is characteristic of the sonata form. It did not understand it properly, however, in its true meaning. The conception of the sonata form, as conventional theory teaches it till today, lacks of all things, its essential feature—that of the organic aspect, and also fails to show how the organic structure itself is conditioned by the composition of sections out of the unity of the main [or fundamental] chord, i.e., by the horizontalizations of the urlinie and the bass arpeggiation. The talent for such thorough perception of the main chord is a property of geniuses who possess it from Nature.[4] They unfold the main chord into the melodic movement of the urlinie, and at the same time, into a few individual chords which they subsequently split off again and again.[5] Such perception cannot be cultivated in an artificial way, and consequently we say that only extemporaneous invention affords the unity of auskomponierung. Thus the concept of the sonata form would need further clarification in order to express the

---

[3] Schenker is referring to post-Romantic sonatas and symphonies which outwardly exhibit the sonata-allegro pattern, but which fail to connect organically vis-à-vis the sonata-form compositions of the great Classicists in particular.
[4] See *Clarifications*, note 7.
[5] See *The Art of Improvisation*, note 3.

general more accurately: *The whole must be composed in extempore* if it is not to be merely a juxtaposition of individual sections and motives in the sense of a pattern.*

In addition to the many examples of sonatas with which I dealt in the *Tonwille* Booklets and in Yearbook I, in order to prove the decisive extemporaneous characteristic in particular, I wish to add the following example:

The *Haydn Piano Sonata in G minor*, Op. 54, No. 1, composed in 1786 (Part I, No. 4; Collected Edition, No. 44) reveals the following ursatz:[6]

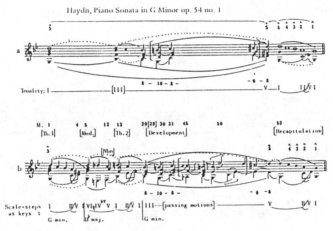

Figure 1

To be sure, Figure 1 b employs the customary designations of sections of the form: First theme, modulation, second theme, development, and recapitulation; nevertheless, it reveals beyond that, the deeper meaning of the movement, since it shows its connection with the first horizontal-izations in the ursatz (Figure 1 a). It is simply insufficient to read off the key changes of the foreground*, as conventional theory does; it is absolutely necessary to know, in addition, which force brings out the key change and guards the unity of the whole.[7] Haydn certainly knew of no theories of form as we know them. The new life which he produced,

---

*Compare Yearbook I, p. 127, where I spoke of the "breath of the sonata."

[6] See the first paragraph of note 4 of *Resumption of Urlinie Considerations*, Yearbook I.

[7] In other words, the source of the organic structure.

was created from the life embodied in his spirit.[8] He was led by the urlinie and the bass arpeggiation with the power of a natural urge, and it is from these that he acquired the ingenious power of tension spanning needed to master the whole as a single unit.[9] But where can one find in conventional theory even a mere trace of such a path toward organic unity? True, it too untiringly proclaims the organic aspect, but only with empty words—in the manner of a pious wish; the fact remains that conventional theory is still unfamiliar with the essence of organic structure in music and is therefore unable to point out the mans which lead to it.

But let us proceed with the diminution of this sonata:

Sonata in G minor   Haydn

[8]Schenker views the organic structure manifest in the great diatonic masterworks as living organisms in the biological sense, as offsprings of the mental creativity of the musical genius, growing from the embryonic state of the background to its ultimate developmental stage of the foreground.

[9]In other words, by sensing intuitively the background ursatz and by possessing the natural ability to create in accordance with that guiding force, his music reveals a structure consisting of multiple, simultaneously-transpiring auskomponierung strata of a single, simple ursatz figure. It is the later strata which extend and increase the tension of the original span and/or arpeggiation which the genius is able to retain mentally throughout the entire compositional process.

The path which captures the master's imagination in the first section is, in short, the following: See Figure 2, Appendix III. From d², hardly sounded on the upbeat, a fourth-leap leads upwards to g² on the downbeat of bar 1. One wonders, will d² or g² be the initiating tone* of the urlinie, $\hat{5}$ or $\hat{8}$?[10] In bars 1–2, despite the high g^2, a sixth-span* d^2–f-sharp[1] is unfolded downwards (see below, Figure 3),[11] which points to d^2 as the $\hat{5}$, for which the neighboring-note turns d^2–e-flat^3–d^2 also testify and which hover above the sixth-span (see Figure 3); but suddenly in bar 3, b-flat^2 rises above g^2, because of which our first supposition becomes open to question, particularly since the third-span b-flat^2–a^2–g^2 is formed in bar 4.[12] The first bass arpeggiation is concluded[13] and we find ourselves still groping in the dark.

In bar 5, the voice leading surprisingly draws the arpeggiation* d^1–g^1–b-flat^1 from the lower register, in which we are able to detect, without further elaboration, an abbreviated repetition of the path reached up to this point.[14] Upper-shifts* are adjoined, which lead ascendingly up to d^3 in bar 8, and this d^3 subsequently descends, beyond the d-flat^3 in bars 9–

---

[10]The reason for the carets above the Arabic numerals is given in *The Art of Improvisation*, note 47.

[11]For further clarity, the portion of the sonata discussed in this essay is reproduced on page 1.

The following illustration shows the descending sixth-span:

[12]The illustration below points out the descending third-span:

[13]The following illustration outlines the first concluded bass arpeggiation:

[14]

The arpeggiation d^2–g^2–b-flat^2 in bars 1–3 is repeated an octave lower in bars 4–5 in abbreviated form.

12, to c^3 in bar 12,[15] and to our greatest astonishment, we finally realize at this point that even though c^3 is not expressly stated, all the content of bars 1–12 was merely a higher-placement* of d^2–d^3, which, instead of pointing to g^2, rather justifies d^2 as a $\hat{5}$,[16] and, in addition, we realize that the one higher-placement [procedure] obviously extends its large arch across all those sections of the form that are designated by conventional theory as the antecedent phrase of the first theme, the consequence, and the modulation*!

This realization is subsequently confirmed in the later course of the voice leading. In bars 12–17, it is an arpeggiation once again which draws from f^2 over b-flat^2 to d^3, which links to the d^3 in bar 8, and only from this point does it descend in bars 17–20 over c^2[17] to b-flat^1 as $\hat{4}$ $\hat{3}$ of the urlinie (B-flat major in the foreground).[18] Thus the second arpeggiation coincides with the second theme of the conventional pattern. But has conventional theory ever considered what service such an arpeggiation performs, how it not only holds the second theme together as a unit, but also, by imitating the first arpeggiation, takes up and carries on the organic structure of the first theme precisely through the parallelism and by the adjustment to the same height (d^3)? Has it ever indicated anywhere such a form of the second theme, or does it not rather require the opposite of it?[19] It follows thenceforth that Haydn could have never written the sonata as he did if he would have had to conform to our conventional theory, which allegedly was to have established the essence of the sonata form.

[15]The following illustration points out, first of all, the upper-shifts:

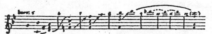

The d^1 of bar 5 is shifted up to c^2 in bar 6 (note the s-shaped slur); the f^1 of bar 6 to f^2 in bar 7; the a^1 of bar 7 to a^2 of the same bar; d^2 of bar 8 to d^3 of the same bar (note the arrows). Thereupon the d^3 of bar 8 descends eventually to the implied c^2 of bar 12.
[16]In other words, the content of bars 1–12 reveals that it has served merely to place up the initiating urlinie $\hat{5}$, d^2, to d^3. See the dotted slur in Appendix III, Figure 2, bars 1–8 (12).
[17]The original German has c^1 instead of c^2 at this point, which is obviously a typographical error.
[18]See the "second arpeggiation" and the larger note heads $^{\hat{4}\,2}_{c}$–$^{\hat{3}}_{b}$-flat^1 in Appendix III, Figure 2.
[19]In other words, instead of an organic viewpoint such as this, the conventional conception of the sonata-allegro pattern implies separately conceived, hence structurally disconnected, themes.

But now the main question. Would it have been possible for Haydn to have carried out both arpeggiations in this manner had he not been guided by an extemporaneous outline? The upbeat had hardly suggested d^2, and already in bar 1 the arpeggiation breaks forth—then must it not have already been established at the very first moment? Where is there a similar power of tension spanning in the work of a non-genius, a similar arpeggiation which stretches across several sections of the form in one large sweep?

If conventional theory possessed knowledge of these connections, it would have to value the arpeggiations as motives of the highest order* (see Yearbook I, p. 64ff, [Eng. p. 87ff], and only then would it also be impelled to speak about the motives of lower order*, as there are: The sixth-span in bars 1–2, the third-span in bars 3–4, the seventh-span d-flat^3–e^2 in bars 10–11, the sixth-span upwards through the 5–6 exchange* in bars 14–17, etc.;[20] the change of diminution[21] in bars 5, 6–8 (this is where the upper-shifts occur), at the second theme beginning with bar 12, etc. Does conventional theory do this? No—for it, all that enters into consideration as motives* are, at best, tonal successions which sooner or later arrive in exact repetitions, as for example, the upbeat triplet and the eighths succession in the first and second quarters of bar 1. On the other hand, it has no idea how to begin explaining the neighboring note turns in these bars (see the brackets in Figure 3), the middle one of which brings the lower neighboring note for the sake of contrast, while the last one even extends into the ensuing neighboring note turn and thus binds both smallest sections of the form;[22] conventional theory knows just as little about the rest of the content, because it is unaware of the repetitions and does not understand the motivic nature of the higher-order sixth-span, d^2–f-sharp^1.[23]

---

[20]See Appendix III, Figure 2.

[21]In other words, a change in the foreground figuration.

[22]The third neighboring-note turn of Figure 3, d^2–e-flat^2–d^2 in bar 2, thus serves to connect the antecedence, which ends on the fourth quarter of bar 2, and the consequence, which begins with the d^2 which concludes the third neightboring-note turn of Figure 3.

[23]In other words, how it inspires the unfolding of the spans which follow, b-flat^2–g^2 in bars 3–4 and d-flat^3–e^2 in bars 10–11.

Figure 3

Conventional theory also fails to recognize the unity of the motive, for example, in the neighboring note formations of bars 5–12 (see Appendix III, Figure 2): The upper-shift, the higher-placement, the seventh-span in these bars make e^2–b-flat^2 [1] in bars 6–8 and d^3–(d-flat^3)–c^3 in bars 8–12 incomprehensible for it,[24] not to speak of the fact that it might also notice the same neighboring note motive in the second theme, where, of course, every two motives, for example, in bar 13, f^2–e-flat^2 and d^2–c^2 are linked to a fourth-span[25] (precisely because of d^2–c^2 in bar 13, Haydn suppresses c^3 in bar 12). The relationship of the fourth-leap d^2–g^2 from the upbeat to the downbeat of bar 1 and at the turn of bars 2/3 to the fourth-leap f^2–b-flat^2 at the turn of bars 12/13 is something it fails to hear; consequently, for conventional theory the fourth-leaps do not as yet constitute any motive.

I believe that I have already made myself amply clear. Nevertheless, I shall restate the conclusion from all this once again: Conventional theory till today has no approach to the organic aspect of the sonata form. The features of the sonata form brought out by conventional

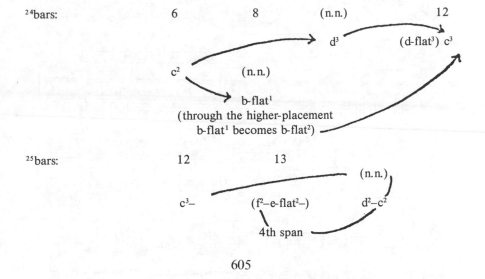

theory give us nothing of its essence; the knowledge of conventional theory is lifeless; likewise stillborn are the works which are the products of its teaching. Stated more succinctly, theory till today has lacked the means to become aware of an understand the extemporaneous characteristic in the composition of the sonata form.

We shall now cite another example, the first section of the Beethoven Piano Sonata, Op. 10, No. 2, First Movement; see Figure 4, Appendix IV.

Conventional theory applies its customary designations even to a content such as this. But in doing so, it describes outwardly and superficially, only the fully developed stage of the composition, and clearly betrays the fact that it has no knowledge of the law of the specific in the developing stages, upon which alone the general definition of the form depends. Yet a more cursory glance at Figure 4h suffices to point out how in this sonata, similarly to the example cited from Haydn, the first theme, the consequence, the modulation, and the second theme are elevated to an organic whole through the force of spans and arpeggiations.[26] Notice the first fifth-span, f^2–g^1,[27] which extends to bar 31: It alone already holds together the first theme, the consequence, the modulation, and the antecedent phrase of the second theme,[28] but as a passage to the middle voice,[29] it gives the initiating tone f^2 to the urlinie

[26] A revised analytical sketch of this Sonata Movement is cited in *Der freie Satz*, Figure 101, 4.
[27] The original German refers to the fith-span as f^2–b^2 instead of f^2–b^1, which is obviously an oversight.
[28] Compare the realization on page 606.
[29] See *law concerning the initiating tone of spans* in the Glossary.

609

(as $\hat{8}$), and therefore the upper voice (see Figure 4i, Appendix IV) links new spans to that f²: The second fifth-span of bar 39 ff which brings the consequence of the second theme, and a third span from bar 47 ff, which finally carries the urlinie tones, $\hat{7}$-$\hat{6}$-$\hat{5}$.

It is precisely the succession of all these spans which creates the connection of sections, the organic structure of the context; it is brought to life through the law concerning the mental retention of the initiating tone.

At this point we can already state: A fifth span such as the first one in bars 1–31 cannot possibly be composed any other way than through extemporization, and as one fifth-span inspires the subsequent spans, we hear with true awe this storm of extemporization as it pours forth, creating, span by span, life and connection!

Add to this the diminutions. What impressive proof they too offer of that control which Nature exerts![30] Individual arpeggiations unfold the chords and connect them[31] (see Figure 4g, Appendix IV); a four-note motive livens the arpeggiations (see the brackets in Figure 4h, Appendix IV); diminutions[32] of it are included within it (in Figure 4i, Appendix IV), and it is even interwoven in the large neighboring-note movement of the development section:[33]

Beethoven, op. 10 no. 2, first movement, development

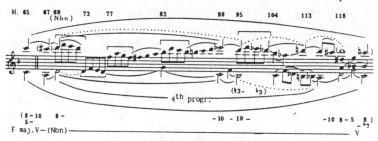

Figure 5

[30]That is to say, Nature controls the unfolding of its chord via the geniuses to whom it has endowed this ability.

[31]a¹–c²–f² (bars 1–12); a¹–c²–e² (bars 12–18); g¹–c²e² (bars 18–27); b¹–d²–f² (bars 31–39).

[32]Here the term diminution is used to signify purely rhythmic diminution, i.e., the reverse procedure of augmentation.

[33]bars: 65 – (69 – 118) – 133

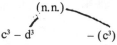

All this, stratum upon stratum, constitutes a world unto itself. Yet this unity can be explained in no other way than through the wonder of extemporization, which creates the whole as one figure!

But does conventional theory make any mention whatsoever of this natural phenomenon of organic structure which we have pointed out here? By its designations of the form, can it determine even the boundaries of the second theme, or the content of the development section?

Has ever a performance of this Sonata succeeded to communicate the wonder of its organic structure to us?[34]

In his Piano Sonata, Op. 10, No. 1, First Movement, Beethoven writes:

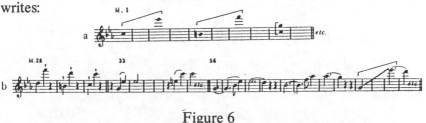

Figure 6

This relationship of all leaps from bar 28 on (see Figure 6b), despite the distinction of staccato, legato, etc., would have to be identifiable at first glance, and yet it can be truly understood only by one who is aware of the source of those leaps from the ones in the first theme (see Figure 6a and compare Yearbook I, page 189 [Eng., page 136], Figure 2),[35]

---

[34]If a performance is to avoid an interpretation based merely on successively presented themes in the foreground sense, it would presume knowledge of the organic structure on the part of the performer.

[35]

In Yearbook I, *Resumption of Urlinie Considerations*, Schenker explains that the above opening bars 1–9 of the Sonata constitute an *ascent** (Anstieg) to the urlinie $\hat{5}$, g^2, in which the notes of the ascent, e-flat^3 (2) and f^3 (2) are themselves reached by the arpeggiating leaps, c^2–e-flat^3 and b^1–f^3 (see the above illustration b). It is these leaps which inspire the later ones in the bars indicated in Schenker's Figure 6b in the present essay. Analytical sketches of the exposition and development sections of this First Movement are given in *Der freie Satz*, Figures 154, 3 and 154, 7. (See the realization on pages 612-613.)

Piano Sonata in C minor, Op. 10, No. 1   Beethoven

that is to say, by one who has grasped the unity of the diminution from the figure of the whole.

Since the unity and synthesis of the whole pours forth from the urlinie and the bass arpeggiation, we see that the diminution in this sonata could not have been developed to this level of unity by the master in any other way than through the wonder of extemporization!

If this were not concealed, as is every wonder, then conventional theory would have grasped long ago more than the few outward characteristics which it applies to each and every content. But if it is not even on the right track regarding the motive formed by the leap, then how could it possibly grasp the organic structure of the whole?

In his *Piano Sonata*, Op. 109, in the development section of the First Movement, Beethoven sets up the following peak points:

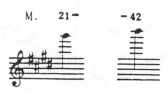

Figure 7

Piano Sonata in E Major, Op. 109 — Beethoven

The manner in which he suddenly abandons g-sharp³ in bar 21 and leaps down to c-sharp² has puzzled everyone. What can this leap, this suddenness, possibly mean?[36] Even if one has succeeded to the point of recognizing a relationship between the two so distantly separated high points, and the single movement through which g-sharp³ is surpassed by b³ (in bar 42), which is to become the initiating tone of the recapitulation (in bar 48)—even then, he would still not have reached the final point of clarification. This emerges rather from the following connection:

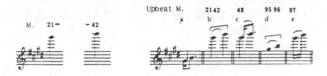

Figure 8

Both tones of the upbeat [to bar 1] are being sought out by the extemporizing imagination of the master in the development section as well as in the coda! He must pursue them. To him they already constitute a motive, the key to a world of unity and connection—but what use has conventional theory of the sonata form for such a wonder? And yet, only through this wonder does the content of this sonata movement emerge!

* * * *

History and experience teach that the talent for extemporization is very rare,* and the situation will indeed be no different in the future. That is why we say, on the other hand, that the sonata form can be fulfilled only by a person—as was true of the old masters—to whom its fulfillment through the organic structure of the whole will be granted through the strength of extemporaneous invention.

Nevertheless, it is possible to visualize this particular natural talent even if one does not possess it himself. We see in cases of lesser talents

---

[36]See the music of the Beethoven *Sonata in E Major*, Op. 109, pages 614-616. Schenker's bar indications in Figures 8d and e should read:

bars:	95	97	98
	g-sharp²–b²		g-sharp³–b³

*Compare Yearbook I, p. 11ff, [Eng. p. 2ff].

at one instrument or another, how so many people, through persistent practice, acquire the ability to execute with ease many notes within a minute. They also develop the ability to provide at the same time utmost exactness of detail in matters such as touch, brightness and darkness, and tempo to individual tones as prescribed by the composer or (more frequently) according to their own personal interpretation. If, however, we imagine a similar type of mastery on the higher plane of musical composition, then we arrive at the picture of a genius-spirit, how it masters all arpeggiations of the many individual chords and all diminutions of the auskomponierung spans while creating mysteriously out of the background of an ursatz.

Of course, merely the ability to picture this process rarely suffices in order for one to be able to follow it.

For the reader or performer, the composition exists as a foreground; but this constitutes only the present, so to speak, taking the word literally from the context of daily life. Just as it is difficult to understand the meaning of a present situation in everyday life if one is unaware of its background, it is equally difficult for the reader or performer to grasp the present [state] of a tonal composition if, at the same time, an awareness of the background is lacking. Just as he is pulled to and fro by the demands of daily life, he is driven no differently by the foreground of the tonal composition. Each change of chord and change of diminution, each chromaticism and neighboring note constitutes a new turn for him, and thus one new detail after another draws him farther away from the background connection.

Precisely today, when mundane, tumultuous everyday life and each momentary hour are valued as the uppermost goal of human existence, instead of people dedicating themselves toward rescuing life from its prevalent chaos, we find that this attitude regarding the present has proven catastrophic even in the approach to the work of genius.[37] But a work of genius is distinguished from everyday life through precisely the extemporaneous outline which gives the whole an unambiguous meaning. It is therefore contradictory to deny the background plan in the work of art for the sake of everyday life and the present, whose ultimate purpose remains concealed to man. Even if we cannot force people to understand such a plan, and even if we must abandon the

[37]In other words people today generally prefer immediate, momentary, and surface pleasures, being oblivious to and disinterested in, background origins and connections —both in daily life and in art music.

unwilling and incapable to bustle about in the foreground as he is accustomed to doing in the chaos of everyday life, we can at least force him to realize the fact that the creation of genius has nothing in common with the unrestricted life which he leads.

* * * *

It merely constitutes borrowing a point of view from everyday life when people search for themes and melodies in the sonata in the same way they pursue enjoyable moments in everyday life. The layman looks toward melody for momentary fulfillment. For him, there would be too little melody, for example, in a fourth-span, fifth-span, or sixth-span even though such spans are—as horizontal prolongations of vertical chord-ideas—nonetheless, also melodies in a broader sense (see *Clarifications*, Figure 3). He demands more auskomponierung, more embellishment. Thus even the layman, thinking of the melody only, of course, senses that the art of music consists of a richer auskomponierung, but his demands for richer auskomponierung are limited by the capacity of his musical intellectuality. An auskomponierung which he is unable to hear structurally is no melody for him; only that which he understands does he call melody!

If conventional theory also shares this lay point of view and likewise searches for themes and melodies in the sonata, understood in the unspecific sense of the layman, then we should not be astonished by the fact that it has still not advanced toward the comprehension of true total melody of a whole[38] or that it is unaware of the figure of the whole,[39] of the diminution stages and their motives. Nor should we be surprised that conventional theory is therefore unaware of the fact that its conceptions of theme, melody, and motive contradict the sonata form.[40]

Melody in the vulgar sense of the layman and theorist comes from the

[38]Schenker uses the expression *Gesamtmelodie eines Ganzen*, translated literally reads the "total melody of a whole," by which he means the overall linear-horizontal unfolding of the chord-idea across all strata of auskomponierung from the background to the foreground. See *melody* in the Glossary. See also *Clarifications*, page 205 (Eng., p. 161).

[39]Compare above, in the essay *Resumption of Urlinie Considerations* (Yearbook II), the section entitled "The Entire Foreground as One Figure," page 40ff (Eng., pp. 216ff).

[40]Because the connection between themes in that sense consists merely of juxtaposition and surface-melodic elements despite possible foreground repetition of motives. Hence the conventional conception of theme and contrasting theme, etc., are contrary to the spirit of the organically-connected sonata.

most elementary, smallest relationships in music. The sonata, however, represents the mastery of the most advanced form by the most highly imaginable musical community in the most highly developed epoch.*[41] Only few geniuses were equal to the demands of organic creation in the sonata form, and what they achieved for organic structure through extemporization was neither learned nor transferable. When the epoch of the masters had passed, there followed "talents" [42] who lacked the gift of improvisation, and who could no longer master the sonata form. Italian opera and its melody deteriorated. Yet at this very time, the ambition of the talented [composers] ventured ever higher goals. They aspired to create sonatas and symphonies of even greater scope than those written by the masters. As a result, the inevitable happened. They aimed at inspiration and melody, and believed they had fulfilled the organic structure of the form when actually they had merely filled their imagined form with melodies and themes. The result was correspondingly deplorable. Instead of producing organic works of art, works were being written which might be compared to a cake batter in which raisins had been added; but even after the cake had been baked, the raisins were still discernible. The sonata, however, is not a cake—it is a tonal mass, comprised of such material in which raisins should not be detectable.*

*See *Der Tonwille*, Booklet 2, pp. 3–6.

[41]Unlike the conventional viewpoint of music history, Schenker considers the period from Bach through Brahms (compare *Clarifications*, note 9) as one period—the era of the great masters, and the zenith period in the history of music as an art. He also considers the musical community of that two-hundred-year period the most highly perceptive and sophisticated in music history in its ability to grasp subtleties in tonal composition and performance (compare above, Yearbook II, *Resumption of Urlinie Considerations*, pages 28–29 [Eng., pp. 196–97]).

[42]Schenker is referring here to the period following Brahms, the post-Romantic period in conventional terms. By the word "talented," Schenker distinguishes between the great masters and composers he evaluates as less gifted. In Yearbook III, *Miscellaneous* (page 108), for example, he speaks of Verdi as "a talent." In other places, Schenker includes the names of Tchaikovsky, Bruckner, R. Strauss, and Reger, etc., as composers of subordinate rank.

*In the interest of clarification, the following comparison is included: The mad rage to bring melodies, as understood by the layman and theorist, into the sonata form is comparable to the madness of certain utopians who seek to apply the morals, customs, and practices of a small group of people to larger states. They overlook the fact, however, that with large masses of people, new requirements and problems must be assumed which do not exist with small groups of people. The same situation exists with the current, increasing desire to revert back to the very first stages of Nature. Culture is being cast aside in favor of Nature because the capability needed in order to meet the highest demands of culture has become extinct.

In addition to the above described situation, a misunderstanding arose which had been caused by Wagner. With his Leitmotif technique, he conformed, to be sure, to a world which had become accustomed to picking out melodies. On the other hand, Wagner was no background-oriented musician, and his overemphasis of the musical foreground which resulted from the needs of the theatre brought an unprecedented heaviness into music as a whole. Suddenly people began to point out a similar type of heaviness in the extemporized work of our masters as well, and an impetuous desire arose to rid themselves of the heaviness in Wagner as well as in the masters. They clamored—for melody!

The failure to understand the extemporized work, however, has exacted its revenge. If one were only capable of hearing the totality, from the totality, how he would rejoice over the brilliance of extemporization in, for example, the last string quartets and symphonies of Beethoven, which overshadows all melody. Beethoven remained—truly till his last breath—to coin a phrase of Hölderlin[43] an emissary of streaming tones, a spokesman for musical tonality, who created all connection with lucidity and with floating ease.

* * * *

So-called melodies, themes, and motives of conventional theory do not lead to sonata form. Of many other possible examples, the above-cited ones have illustrated what should truly be understood by the term diminution motive in the sonata form. Irrespective of peripheral embellishment, the following techniques are required of the diminution motive: auskomponierung, arpeggiations, octave couplings, [all of which occur] through the repetition of authenticated unities of higher connections. See above, for example, the neighboring note turns in Figures 3 and 5, [and the indicated motives] in Figures 4h to 4g in Appendix IV, etc.[44]

Without knowledge of the motive in this sense, however, the expanse and flow of extemporization* cannot be achieved. Yet it is precisely this

---

[43](Johann Christian) Friedrich Hölderlin (1770–1843), German poet.

[44]The higher-order motives in Figure 4h, Appendix IV, are indicated by brackets (bracketed motives are also shown in Figure 5 in addition to the overall neighboring-note turn shown in note 31). In Figure 4g, Appendix IV, the higher-order motive consists of the slurred arpeggiations pointed out in note 29 and the descending spans, f^2–b^1, f^2–b^2, and f^2–c^2.

*See *Der Tonwille*, Booklet 5, pp. 54–57.

ability which creates the organic element in the sonata form. Therefore, a tradition of the sonata form must also be lacking. How could such a tradition have come about if even general awareness as well as general instinct have failed in face of that main characteristic—in face of that extemporaneous characteristic which holds the sections of the form together through spans?*

But precisely because the extemporized outline is inaccessible, the sonata form of the geniuses will remain preserved for all times![45]

---

*The fact that an individual may quote, for example, a motive from one or another movement of a sonata or symphony, and in doing so, support the contention that he knows the work precisely, constitutes anything but a tradition. And the fact that a music lover who, in his youth, had played one or another masterwork, but in later years resists coming back to it while assuring us that he has mastered the work, also offers no evidence of any tradition. Then why the talk about abandoning tradition when there is none to begin with?

[45]Compare below, *The Organic Aspect of the Fugue*, note 94 and *Mozart: Symphony in G Minor*, pages 108–109 (Eng., pp. 325–26).

Rameau or Beethoven[1]? Paralytic Standstill or Ingenious Life in Music?[2]

You may state publicly that the principles followed by me and my father of blessed memory are anti-Rameau.
—C.P.E. Bach in a letter to Kirnberger,[3] appearing in Kirnberger's *Kunst des reinen Satzes (The Art of Pure Composition)*[4] II, 3, 188.

In all histories of music, Rameau's *Traité de l'harmonie* of the year 1722 is cited and extolled as a decisive major achievement in the field of music theory. Its content consists, more or less, of presentations of the new fundamental bass theory and chord inversions, tertian structure of chords and their harmonic relationships.

---

[1]The following essay may be viewed as an outline sketch of the main events in the history of music and viewed by Schenker: that is to say, an outline of the history of the origin, development, acme, decline, and disintegration of German absolute, major-minor oriented great art music.

Schenker opens the essay by enumerating the main innovative features in the theory set forth by Rameau in his *Traité de l'harmonie* of 1722. He then sketches the main events in the history of Western polyphony, from the viewpoint of the development of the art of organically unfolding composition, up to the time of Rameau. He explains the conflict between the horizontally-oriented compositional practice of that time and the vertically-oriented theories of Rameau, and how the latter gradually led to increasing concentration on vertical considerations; how these ultimately led to vertically-oriented and mechanical composition, and to newer vertically-oriented theoretical systems of the twentieth century.

Many of Schenker's negative attitudes are given expression in this essay, all of which relate to his assessment of the decline of diatonic art music as the disintegration of music as an art. Some of his most abusive chauvinistic and antagonistic anti-French remarks occur in this essay. A theme which recurs repeatedly in Schenker's writings and which is given expression in this essay is his belief that the decline of diatonic art music resulted from the lack of its true understanding on the part of lay people as well as musicians. Another theme which appears repeatedly in his writings and which also occurs here is his hope for a renaissance of diatonic art music. In the process of this discussion Schenker outlines his general approach to analysis, and also discusses some of the problems caused him due to the difficulty in communicating his musical concepts. Most interesting is his discussion of his own theory, which he assesses as an art, not a science; he also describes the various functions he feels it can serve.

In conclusion, Schenker decries and debates the contention that diatonic art music stands in contradiction to the spirit of the twentieth century.

Footnotes continued.

However, not a single music historian or music theorist has as yet taken cognizance of the fact that at a time when J. S. Bach and Handel were still alive and Mozart and Beethoven were not even born, through this theory the seeds of death already had penetrated into music theory and indirectly into composition![5]

Ever since counterpoint entered music, the event of which constitutes a gift of the Occident to the peoples of all times, a struggle has existed between the horizontal and vertical directions throughout the history of musical composition. Despite the fact that progress had certainly been made by having advanced from the first contrapuntal attempts in organum, discant, and fauxbourdon to the $\frac{5}{3}$ triad as the most natural arrangement of the vertical element, the purely mechanical exploitation of this law was nevertheless detrimental in the long run to the horizontal.[6] Though this kind of triadic compositional technique was not detrimental to a horizontal design of merely moderate scope and

---

[2]Volume III of *Das Meisterwerk in der Musik* consists of two essays: the one work which follows and the comprehensive study of Beethoven's Symphony No. 3. The first essay deals mainly with the adverse effect Schenker attributes to Rameau's theory on the history of diatonic art music, hence the title *Rameau or Beethoven?* Paralytic Standstill (resulting from the effects of Rameau's theories) or Ingenious Life in Music (resulting from the organic musical life revealed in the analysis of the Beethoven Symphony No. 3 subtitled Beethoven the Hero).

[3]Johann Philipp Kirnberger (1721–1783), theorist; pupil of J.S. Bach.

[4]*Die Kunst des reinen Satzes in der Musik aus sicheren Grundsätzen hergeleitet und mit deutlichen Beispillen versehen (The Art of Pure Composition in Music Derived from Established Principles Illustrated in Distinct Examples)*, two volumes, 1774 and 1779. It is considered Kirnberger's *magnum opus*.

[5]The explanation and development of the viewpoint expressed in this statement forms the essential content of this essay. The ensuing remarks comprise the rationale and foundation of Schenker's view of music history as a whole, i.e., as the rise and decline of the art of absolute diatonic polyphony.

[6]In the compositional technique of the sixteenth century contrapuntal style, the harmonic combinations were determined by the relationship of each note to a cantus firmus note. As such, the harmonies were too many and too frequent for them to be able to achieve expression in the melody at the same time. In other words, the linear formations resulted from harmonic considerations on essentially a note-to-note basis but did not generally represent the unfolding of a particular chord as such. Hence the horizontal element, instead of having the freedom to move within a single chord and thereby increase its content by unfolding that chord, was directly inhibited as a result of the above-described contrapuntal technique. Schenker discusses this subject in his *Harmonielehre (Harmony)* § 88, Note, *Kontrapunkt* I, pp. XXIII–XXIV, and *Der freie Satz*, § 173.

624

simplest diminution (in a situation such as that, it is still practicable even today), the [general] overemphasis of the vertical element had the result of inhibiting both the composer and the listener. The composer became inhibited in the creation of larger horizontal designs, while the listener became limited in the perception of larger connections. Therefore, despite all attempts at expansion of the horizontal element, the excessive emphasis of the vertical was, of necessity, felt as an overweight burden. And even when this problem was approached, as was often the case, by employing familiar sacred or secular songs as subjects of contrapuntal [imitative] compositions, in no way could this obviate the fundamental error involved.*

Monody ensued. Yet despite the retention of contrapuntal [i.e., polyphonic] composition, the new monodic style nevertheless granted prominence to the horizontal element over the vertical, and made it, as the auskomponierung* of the fundamental chord*, the sole carrier of an increased content as well as its connection.[8] This was only made possible, however, by engaging the bass in a particular auskomponierung of the fundamental chord, corresponding to its own essence. This consists of an arpeggiation through its upper-fifth* whereby the arpeggiation could be filled out with more or less passing tones, as if the bass were likewise a horizontally moving voice, a second upper voice below the actual upper voice, as it were.

Then Rameau came along. By tracing all musical activity back to the fundamental bass and its particular movement, Rameau detached super-

---

*Compare my *Harmonielehre*, p. 214 [§ , Note] (1906): "It follows finally and irrefutably, that the principle element in music—even after the introduction and adaptation of the vertical direction—still remains the horizontal line, that is to say, the melody itself. It follows further that in this sense, the vertical direction (corresponding at the same time to the chronology of history also) is a secondary factor.

It is as if the spirit of the harmonic element, in the final analysis, is only called upon to systematically generate broad melodic designs and at the same time, to give order to them."[7]

[7] Stated another way, the horizontal element in music is its uppermost factor. Thus it is the function of the vertical-harmonic element to provide the raw material which is to be unfolded horizontally in time as well as to provide the assumption for orderly connection in the resultant horizontalization at the same time.

[8] That is to say, the new monodic style of early Italian opera was still polyphonic (in that sense, contrapuntal); nevertheless, it found the way of allowing the melody to express the supporting harmony horizontally, and thereby increase its content, and at the same time express its own inner unity provided by the underlying vertical entity at its basis.

positions of tones—which catch the eye and ear of even the layman—out of the flow of horizontal voice leading to which every superposition belongs. In doing so, however, he not only deviated from his predecessors and contempories who followed voice leading through the theory of figured bass, but from the very essence of music itself.[9]

Granted that Rameau was too little aware or was perhaps completely unaware of the extent of the horizontal expanses reached in the works of J.S. Bach and Handel. But surely he had at his disposal ample additional monodic literature from which he could have become aware of what by that time had become an abundant flow of the horizontal element which had been relieved of the preceding vertical-triadic technique. Moreover, he even followed the paths of melody himself.

[9]The following is aimed at illustrating the preceding paragraph:

The upper voice clearly and directly unfolds the fifth, b^1–e^1, of the e minor triad. The bass expresses the arpeggiation of the e chord e–b–e, with the a serving as a partial filling of the fifth space: e–(a)–b (compare *Der freie Satz*, § 186, Figure 66, 2): with the a placed in the low octave, a fifth-space results which is then filled out by passing tones. The middle voices fill out the resultant parallel sixths of the aussensatz, forming a passage comprised essentially of passing chords:

However, the conflicting effect of the d in the last chord of the first bar with the d-sharp in the second chord of the second bar as well as the augmented second in the middle voice of the second bar c–d-sharp in illustration a are avoided in illustration b through the retention of e in the middle voice at the corresponding places. This accounts for the $^6_4$ chord and the suspension resulting in the $^6_5$ formation. The tension for the concluding II $^6_5$ -V-I effect is increased while the dissonant effect of the $^6_4$ chord is decreased through the added suspension of the lower voice in illustration c. Finally the eighths movement involved in the lower voice suspension is prepared by the insertion of the passing tone f-sharp and the neighboring note d-sharp in illustration d.

While the resultant passage is heard as an expression of I-II $^6_5$ -V-I in which the I-II $^6_5$ segment has been prolongated, the fundamental bass theory would show the progression of I V^6 IV^6 VII $^{o4}_2$ VII I $^6_4$ II $^6_5$ V^{8-7} I, which totally obscures the passing nature of the voices which form the chords and consequently the true meaning of the passage.

626

Rameau, however, overlooked the fact that the "voice," as the very being of song and as a concept,[10] was the beginning of all music, and that it consequently represents a succession of tones from Nature and art,[11] not a superposition. The "voice," merely as a movement, lives only within the realm of time, not in the realm of the vertical. *The time-horizontal element of musical movement is consequently*—regardless how we may wish to interpret its laws—*that which alone produces musical content and guarantees its organic connection.*

Furthermore, Rameau overlooked the fact that even in the most modest works of his time, there occurred frequently enough chords which, when considered vertically, formed $\frac{6}{3}$ or $\frac{6}{4}$ combinations or the like, but which could not be inverted according to his principles and traced back to fundamental tones without seriously misinterpreting their horizontally-conceived original meaning; i.e., the musical connection.[12]

Moreover, as to the meaning of the fundamental bass, even from his point of view, Rameau should indeed have asked himself: If in the creation of content, which consists of diminutions and their connection, everything depends upon vertical considerations and their cadences,[13] why did these very cadences themselves not bring about a perpetuum mobile, so to speak, and thereby make the content also a perpetuun mobile? What is it that resists such a perpetuum mobile? Where does

---

[10] In other words, as the basic instrument which conveys the horizontal element in music.

[11] Schenker views music as an art as the artistic adaptation of the chord of Nature— hence a "compromise" between art and Nature. Compare his *Harmonielehre (Harmony)*, § 18, concluding paragraph.

[12] Compare above, note 9.

[13] Conventional theory views each concluding group of chords at the end of a phrase as a cadence. Schenker does not. For example, in the following illustration,

conventional theory would claim three "cadences" in bar 1, II[6] V[7] I; in bar 2, III I $\frac{6}{4}$ V[7] in G major; and in bar 4, II $\frac{6}{5}$ V[7]I. Schenker would say that cadential progressions are *simulated* at those points, that one descending arpeggiation unit, basically g^2–e^1, unites the entire group of bars thereby denying "cadential" status to all three points in question.

the urge to conclude a composition come from altogether? If not from the vertical considerations and their cadences, does it not perhaps come from the form? But where does it come from? From vertical considerations and their cadences? Or does it not rather come from horizontal considerations and the force of the law of the passing tone* which controls them? Instead of viewing the horizontal element, above all, as the content-leading auskomponierung of the fundamental chord, and the vertical element with its first arpeggiation of the fundamental chord and its derivatives as the counterpoint to the horizontal, Rameau deviated at the very outset from horizontal considerations to vertical matters. The possibility thereby arose for the creation of a simpler schematization approach which appealed to his French, less sensitive musical feeling. [14] That is how the sad task fell upon Rameau to lead the musical ear away from voice leading rather than to point out its laws for the first time.

Contemporaries stood up and took note—something new. Moreover, a French innovation! Particularly in Germany, with German subservience to everything French, Rameau's approach was adopted very quickly despite the fact that both J.S. Bach and C.P.E. Bach—one a master of the older, more formal art, and the other a master of the newer, so-called elegant art—rejected this theory; see the accompanying passage above from the letter of Kirnberger.

In his biography of Bach, Volume II, page 604, Spitta[15] writes: "We cannot state with certainty precisely what his (J.S. Bach's) differing view related to, but we must accept the fact that it had to do with the challenging statements also made by Krinberger." Far be it from me to question the great merits of Spitta. But after a century and a half, he still does not know the reason for J.S. Bach's rejection of Rameau. And yet it would have been of greatest value if he would have allotted extensive space to the discussion of this reason since it concerns nothing less than assault by Rameau upon the very heart of our art and the resistance to

[14]Schenker's antagonistic comments against Rameau are obviously extended here to include anti-French feelings as well. This enmity is probably based on the following two factors: (1) Schenker sees in Rameau's theory the ultimate cause in the decline of absolute diatonic polyphony, which from Schenker's point of view (as will be seen below) is the only system capable of effecting organic connection in music. (2) Schenker attributes part of the blame for the decline of absolute diatonic polyphony to what he refers as German subservience to the nations of the "enlightenment" (namely France and her World War I allies); compare above, Let's Do Away With the Phrasing Slur, page 60 and The Organic Aspect of the Fugue, page 95.

[15]See *Resumption of Urlinie Considerations* (Yearbook II), note 22.

this assault by two geniuses, hence a quarrel between mediocrity and genius in music in general, and in this case, between French mediocrity and German genius in music, in particular. (Schweitzer makes no mention of this question at all in his Bach biography. I have good reason to doubt that this omission is due only to the need for the most practical condensation of the material.) One has only to see the Rameauification of the first *Fugue in B minor* and the second *Prelude in A minor* by J.S. Bach, realized in Kirnberger's *Die wahren Grundsätze um Gebrauch der Harmonie [True Principles for the Practice of Harmony]*,[16] (p. 55 ff and page 107 ff), in order to convince oneself of the inapplicability of Rameau's principles. It would have been impossible for J.S. Bach to have conceived even four bars of that Fugue or of that Prelude if, either consciously or unconsciously, instead of the laws which govern the horizontal considerations, the principles of Rameau, stemming from vertical matters had been uppermost in his mind. What good, then, are Rameau's principles if they can be of no service to the composer?

Do I appear to be involved in a political assault when in order to explain thoroughly Rameau's theory I comprehend and designate it, above all, as typical of the French "enlightenment"? It belongs together with the many other concepts of the French "enlightenment" which stem from French mediocrity, but which subsequently affect the mediocrity of other nations as well. And where is there no mediocrity? Those concepts are so characteristic of France's modest capabilities that they alone are sufficient to explain its aggressiveness and greed for conquest. Does not Rameau's inversion concept, in which he found the main expedient for his theory, recur similarly, for example, in the "enlightenment" of the so-called great revolution? What is down is up and what is up is down! cried France's lower class, [in effect], and flattered itself as already being the upper class on the basis of the alleged discovery of human rights in France for the first time. Oh, how the lower class in France, including the superficial encyclopaedist-enlighteners, imagined the progress of human causes! They fancied it as occurring as simply in the cheapest catchword, typical of perennial French mediocrity! As if ever a Guillotine could behead a spirit, particularly a genius! That which is born upper class remains upper class, just as the low class perpetually remains lower class. And all murder and pillage which

---

[16]Johann Philipp Kirnberger. *Die wahren Grundsätze zum Gebrauch der Harmonie (True Principles for the Practice of Harmony)*, 1773. Compare above, note 1.

human beings commit against one another for the sake of overthrowing this Nature-willed rank order remains futile. Genius is Nature-ordained—whoever contests it can settle the matter with Nature—but at the same time it is ordained by people. For without the leadership of genius, humanity would forfeit its life.

Before Rameau, composition and theory constituted a single entity. Both exclusively acknowledged voice leading, not because their laws were already capable of being set forth in words but rather through initially instinctive application.[17] Even the theory of figured bass dealt with voice leading, and adhered to this task so strictly that it did not even permit the concept of inversions. For convincing and methodical reasons, it should not and could not have allowed them.[18]

Since Rameau, however, the paths of composition and theory have completely diverged! Mysteriously liberated from the womb of music—in itself root, trunk, branch, and fruit, which luxuriates in its own growth—musical geniuses appeared in Germany for two centuries.[19] As if there were no false theories all around, as if none at all, they created ever new, ever bolder spans*, diminutions, and forms through the still uncomprehended, albeit inherent principles of music, and thereby brought music to a hitherto unsuspected level of development. Suddenly, an art arose, while disregarding all instructions through eye and concept, proved to be entirely self-generating. And because of the *sense-perceived animated movement of its innate horizontal spans, and because of the fact that it possesses allegorical appeal to the human soul through its movements*, it may very well be considered the most independent and noblest of all the arts.

Through the unbroken chain of those German musical geniuses, Nature expressed its will toward a thunderous growth of musical content.[20] Yet Nature amuses itself with a play of opposing forces—who can say why? It is not at all concerned with the good and bad in man, nor with the beautiful and ugly in him, yet it bestows the laws of growth upon the bad as well as the ugly. In like manner, it allows the mind as well as the body to grow with either beautiful shape or deformity. And thus it was possible that beside the growth of the

[17] See *The Organic Aspect of the Fugue*, note 88.
[18] Presumably because it would have diverted too much attention from horizontal considerations and might have caused too great a concentration on the vertical element.
[19] Bach through Brahms.
[20] That is to say, self-procreating content.

musical art borne by the geniuses, Nature allowed even Rameau's theoretical misconception to grow into the greatest catastrophe. If in the former the most distant voice leading [prolongations] and connections developed, in the latter, [i.e.,] out of Rameau's principles of tertian structure of chords, ever new chordal conceptions developed. Anyone who, in these two centuries, was dependent upon music theory in order to follow the higher art of the geniuses, of necessity, failed in quest of his objectives. That is the extent of the conflict which existed between the masterwork and theory. In the former horizontal considerations predominated, while in the latter the vertical element was uppermost.

Likewise in accordance with the will of Nature—as if art was destined to be led to an impasse—came the paralytic standstill of human mediocrity,[21] as a curse of its perennially-inherent inclination to mechanize its very being.[22]

What is there in the essence and concept of a paralytic standstill which alarms the average person as, let us say, sclerosis frightens the aged?

Instead of creating substance out of the live source of an idea, the average person absorbs ideas handed down to him only mechanically. He upholds them mechanically all his life and even transmits them mechanically. Thus mechanical [acceptance of ideas] spreads throughout human mediocrity like gas. Like a schoolboy who crams his studies instead of absorbing them, the average person since time immemorial, generation after generation, simply parrots the truths and ideas handed down to him, such as the belief in God as a cult, the state as an expedient union, freedom as liberty for licentiousness, love as bisexual pleasure, art as rule and operation, etc. Thus long before the invention of the machine, the soul of the average person was already a kind of machine. Mankind would have perished long ago because of this had not Nature, in its concern for the bare existence of mankind, been intent on sustaining it in animated movement so that Nature would, at the same time, shake the average soul from its own mechanistic tendency. The fact is that the average person remains with that mechanistic tendency as his very last resource. Yet he flees from it a if from an obscure, unbearable nightmare. Be always flees from his mechanized self, but

[21]Compare the Foreword to Yearbook I, last paragraph.
[22]Compare *Resumption of Urlinie Considerations*, (Yearbook I), page 187 (Eng., p. 132).

without being able to escape it. It is a sad illusion, because even when he is jolted as from sleep in revolutions, [new] fashions and the like, the approach from and to himself nevertheless remains intangible. The average person is simply too limited to see through his mechanistic tendency and therefore shifts the blame for his predicament which drives him toward continuous change on the ideas advocated to him from above.

No wonder that the average person has failed in face of the newest and noblest [developments] in the art of music[23]—revelations of *connections, secured through purely musical means.* He has contented himself by merely hearing the music; he has crammed down the uncomprehended connections and has become *benumbed*, naturally in the belief that in reverse contrast to himself, it is the geniuses who were benumbed.

It is true that in the period of vocal counterpoint,[24] one could speak of still immature compositional technique, of an imbalance of the horizontal and the vertical elements. Of necessity, this led to a point of no return, and ultimately to relief through monody.[25] The failure [of the average person] in the face of the art of the geniuses of monody,[26] however, can in no way be excused similarly by any such imbalance in their technique. For contrapuntal [i.e., polyphonic] composition[27]—which remains once and for all immortal to occidental music—there is no other technique, having a correspondingly similar function of content-creation and content-increase, that could fulfill that kind of task even suitably, let alone better. The failure [of the average person] resulted in face of the crushing complexity of connections, yes, in face of connection in music as such. And despite the absolute necessity of such connection, it constitutes for man of chaos something approximating a physical pain. Should connection in music however, be abandoned merely because the average man fails to grasp it?

And now, how did *the paralytic situation in theoretical endeavors* manifest itself at the same time? Since a mechanistic [approach] had

---

[23]Of (absolute) diatonic polyphony, i.e., of Bach through Brahms.

[24]The fifteenth and sixteenth centuries.

[25]See above, page 12 (Eng., pp. 493–94) and note 7.

[26]The great masters of absolute diatonic polyphony (Bach through Brahms).

[27]Schenker's use of the term contrapuntal music does not refer to imitative textures, etc. He means the simultaneous unfolding of the triad in upper, middle, and lower voices— in that sense, counterpointing voices, or simply polyphony. It applies no less to music of foreground homophonic texture. Compare also note 7.

already existed due to the departure from live voice leading in Rameau's principles, one mechanical entity led to another and to still another, etc., as a consequence. Gradually, the seventh, whether a passing tone or a suspension (see [my] *Kontrapunkt* II), and the ninth, whether a suspension or an auxiliary note, were set down as chord constituents, all of which led to the assumption of seventh and ninth chords.[28] Once on this path, there was no hesitation in also recognizing eleventh and thirteenth chords, until finally today, things have gone so far that simply any superposition of tones, regardless how it may have come about, is explained as including distant partials of the overtone series and is likewise taken for a chord.[29] There is no doubt that as a result of all this, Rameau's misconception has reached the uttermost limit, and that the theoretical followers of Rameau have come to a dead end. Paralysis!

[28]For Schenker, seventh and ninth chords are always passing in function: they never function as scaledegrees (stufen). For example, in the following illustration: Chopin, *Mazurka*, Op. 67, No. 2

the sevenths of the seventh chords are understood to arise essentially out of the following chain of suspensions, the possibility of which already exists in strict counterpoint. In the Chopin excerpt, of course, chromatic colorings are added:

The sevenths of the seventh chords could also be explained as passing tones whose starting notes are elided, as follows:

Thus Schenker views *all* seventh and ninth chords, including seemingly unprepared ones, as possessing no less than the implication of a preparation. Compare his *Kontrapunkt* I, pages 366–367 (Figure 423); also *Resumption of Urlinie Considerations* (Yearbook III), page 34, (Eng., pp. 207).

[29]Compare *Resumption of Urlinie Considerations* (Yearbook II), page 34ff (Eng., p. 206ff).

The first to fall victim to the new theory of Rameau was *figured bass.* It is true that the figured bass symbols had to be dropped at a later point in time because the composers, intent on increasing the number of voices, no longer wanted the voices to be left to the discretion of dilettantes, but rather preferred to write them themselves. The theory of figured bass, however, could have still remained as the theory of voice leading. It was therefore a fatal blunder to have exchanged the voice-leading theory of figured bass for Rameau's theory of harmony. Still more catastrophic was the mixture of the two as they are found in figured bass and harmony textbooks, in which neither the one nor the other is given pure expression.* And then came the [inevitable] disaster resulting from the effect of so obtuse a theory upon composition: *the mechanistic approach to theory, of necessity, led to mechanistic composition*! Instead of a musical-organic connection there were only *mechanistic successions*: motives appeared, coming and going as if the composer merely intended "winged" motives from the very beginning.[30] But can be imagine, for example, Goethe or Schiller writing poetry only in "winged words" [familiar quotations] instead of writing from an association of ideas? Chords appeared, coming and going without substantiation by auskomponierung. Truly, the worst cookbook assures better connection in its recipes than Rameau-based compositional theories assure in their formula. In despair, people eventually began to resort to the self-deluding devices. They began to ridicule "tradition," as if through such hardened veins as theirs the living blood of a tradition could circulate. They proclaimed "new progress" and began to dabble in ever new systems. [Entire] cemeteries would sooner rise up before such thoroughly lifeless, obtuse individuals cold ever bring about real progress! Not only did their systems contradict Nature in its main part, the fifth,[31] they also placed themselves at odds with the art of the

---

*C.P.E. Bach's *Generalbasslehre [The Theory of Figured Bass]*, a profound work of a German genius and the only work in musical literature which actually leads toward music as if with magic words, has unfortunately remained a closed book to German musicians. That explains why they were able to devote themselves with such complete abandon to Rameau's theory.

[30] Schenker is probably referring here to composers of the late nineteenth century, such as Bruckner, Reger, Richard Strauss, etc. Compare *The Organic Aspect of Sonata Form*, page 53 (Eng., p. 241), also note 41.

[31] Compare above *Resumption of Urlinie Considerations* (Yearbook II), Concerning the Chord of the Fifth and Dominant (pp. 23–24 [Eng., p. 185ff]), and Schenker's debate against Schönberg which follows on page 30ff (Eng., p. 199ff).

geniuses. That art, however, which is *developed into an organic whole through the connection of background and foreground, is so filled with genuine life, it cannot tolerate the encroachment upon itself by non-living, mechanistic systems of immature musical intellectuals.* Naturally, the countless new systems have the advantage that, as home-made systems, they are unconditionally good for their inventors. From the viewpoint and experience of the obtuse, however, this constitutes the unlimited possibility of producing ever new systems so that anyone's egotism can be satisfied most easily. And yet, if the creators of these mechanistic systems could only imagine the difficulty of the paths needed to make the diatonic system capable of reaching maturity only after centuries, they would undoubtedly drop their trifling and abandon their childish hopes. Perhaps at some future point in time, others would follow them who could muster the strength necessary to convert their systems into live art.

* * * *

Brahms had already once expressed to Mahler the frightening thought of the demise of the tonal art. Mahler, of course, who, in all reverence for Brahms, probably considered himself the more progressive and optimistic composer, was of a different opinion. Already in the Foreword to my *Kontrapunkt* (1910), I spoke of a Pompeii and Herculaneum of the musical art. At that time, however, my words remained isolated and uncomprehended. Today, however, discussion of the decline must have been ever more obvious as the majority of publishers, schools, and journals increasingly undertook upon themselves the task of forcibly putting through the new "progress." However, the incongruity between the expenditure of effort and the new result could not avoid revealing the sad state of music on the whole.

Despite its climate of genius, Germany has forfeited its hitherto uncontested genius-leadership in music. Unparalleled in the history of civilization is the rapid rate at which it relinquished its most sacred wealth of genius, which incidentally was also a source of economic wealth, to its World War enemies. Those enemies, however, will also be Germany's enemies of tomorrow, because they are perennial enemies of genius as such. German musicians have exchanged their wealth of genius for jazz and other exotic types with unequalled shamelessness and undignified readiness. Instead of feeling far more duty bound to guard the genius level of the musical art for the sake of mankind, they have sunk even below the level of primitive peoples. The latter could at least have the excuse of having heretofore only indulged in their musical drives in an animalistic manner.[32] The mere fact that German musicians could find rhythm in jazz, which has as little actual rhythm as a metronome or a railway carriage wheel, is just one more indication of the general paralytic situation vis-à-vis the art of genius; it also proves that German musicians have understood nothing about the two-century-accumulated wealth of [true] musical rhythm, that is to say, art-conforming rhythm.[33] As a result of all this, Germany has become guilty of a grave misdeed, for which it will have to redeem itself in order to avoid becoming the perennial laughing stock of all nations!

* * * *

Only a Christ could awaken the dead. Only the spirit alone could awaken mankind once again toward music of genius which is the only true life in music. This is true because it is the spirit which begets the ever new, [the invention of which constitutes] a reproductive act of an incorporeal nature, as it were, in contrast to a mere mechanistic transcription, which knows no ever new, live procreation.

After two centuries of unqualified loyalty to Rameau, music theory must finally resolve to abandon the way of Rameau and to return to the *theory of the horizontal as the only source of content and connection.* It is not at all my intention to engage in a plea for national defense in a spiritual sense when I say that German musicians, in particular, must finally liberate themselves from the Versailles fetters of that French "enlightenment" if they do not want to permanently forego their musical superiority, and indeed lose their ear for music altogether. This liberation must positively take place, even if the German prefers to be "pacified" by foreign mediocrity than by his own genius.

Then back to voice leading! Very fine, but how? It requires, above all, renewed courage resulting from fresh inspiration in order to awaken an

[32]Compare *Harmonielehre (Harmony)*, § 25.
[33]Schenker explains rhythm in music as resulting from the adjustment of varying numbers of notes between two or more counterpointing voices. He views it as developing this way in each stratum along with the pitches from the background to the foreground, at which level bar lines appear. (See *Der freie Satz*, § 284–300. A beautiful treatment of this viewpoint is found in Chapter of Oswald Jonas's *Das Wesen des Musikalischen Kunstwerks*, recently republished by Universal Editions.) Consequently, he views rhythm in jazz as shallow in the sense that it is formed on a moment-to-moment basis, lacking in depth in terms of background and middleground assumptions.

awareness for the laws of musical connection which have hitherto remained entirely obscure:

Connection is the first thing in music. The principal secret of all connections, however, is a *content, continuously spread out before us in the foreground, only entering into actual connection when it emerges out of a clairvoyantly-perceived connection which is* at the outset *in the depth of a background.* Only the connection of depth from the background to the foreground constitutes connection of breadth in the horizontal direction of the foreground. Only such a connection, even taken biologically, constitutes the actual organic connection, the synthesis of a musical composition, its living breath. Just as the human being, as a living creature, develops in body and mind as from a background to a foreground, from his first existence in his mother's body, from the first cry at the moment of birth, through all years of childhood and maturity till old age, an art-life also develops similarly from background to foreground in the imagination of the genius who clairvoyantly sees into depth and breadth. Even though, on the one hand, the creation of Nature may forever remain a closed book for us, the work of the genius, on the other hand, is only human work whose mysteries, as those of an artistic living organism whish is surely not less organic [than any other] since it possesses form, can and must be closely examined. The clairvoyance for and the creation of connections is, however, only the domain of the genius, in art as well as in all other fields of human endeavor. From this it follows that, above all, the geniuses must be consulted through their works if we are to arrive at the laws of connection which they observed. Who would want to settle for any other kind of light if he could be having the benefit of natural sunlight?

* * * *

In music, the laws of connection provide clarification concerning the procreation and increase of content, concerning the *origin of diminution* and its connections from the *smallest units* to *sections of forms* and *form as a whole.* I have put into words those [laws of connection found in the works] of the geniuses, and in this sense was the first to discover them. In doing so, I have not only given back to the horizontal its innate priority (see above), but I have also revealed the full depth of its essence for the first time.

I point out the primordial state of the horizontal: the *"Urlinie" as the first auskomponierung of the fundamental chord,* within one of the three possible spaces of the same, hence of the third, fifth, or octave, according to the law of the passing tone in steps of seconds descending to the fundamental tone, *counterpointed by the arpeggiation I-V-I of the bass*: by this we are given the *"Ursatz"*. I then pursue the exfoliation, so to speak, of the first horizontal [elements] in *prolongations*, that is to say, derivations, diminutions in the form of spans, couplings*, and neighboring notes, etc. I pursue the ways in which they blossom ever-increasingly, self-expanding into ever new voice-leading strata, [how they are] gathered together in diverse forms all the way to the final unfolding in the *foreground as its climactic peak*, and how they take place at the same time over the contrapuntally-carrying as well as scale-degree-forming unfolding of the bass.

Through all this *is provided and established the connection of the entire content of a musical composition as one unit of background-depth and foreground-breadth.*[34] Within the mystery of such a connection also lies the complete independence of music from the outside world, a self-containment which distinguishes music from all the other arts.

As the first [to discover this], I expressly claim it my achievement, not at all because of vanity, but rather for the benefit of the art, since if, because of false modesty, I were to place myself in the category of those who know everything but really know nothing, I would be belying the truth; though this would detract nothing from the universal essence of the subject itself, it contains enough personal attributes to betray to the curious its true source of origin.

My theory has already found convinced readers, teachers, and listeners the world over. Yes, musicians and authors frequently help themselves to my concepts and terms, without even deeming it necessary to state the name of the one to whom they owe their first information.

I still face, however [the task of completing] the final volume of my *Neue musikalische Theorien und Phantasien [New Musical Theories and Fantasies]*,[35] which will reveal the voice-leading theory in the above-described sense in a strictly systematic presentation. It will thus

---

[34]Compare above, *Resumption of Urlinie Considerations* (Yearbook II), The Whole of the Foreground as One Figure, p. 40ff (Eng., p. 216ff).

[35]Volume III, *Der freie Satz (Free Composition)*, which was subsequently published posthumously in 1935, the year of Schenker's death; a revised edition by Oswald Jonas was published by Universal Edition in 1956.

finally show the picture of free composition as the true expression of the musical art as it lived and breathed in [the works of] our geniuses. The reason I did not bring out this volume sooner, nor shortly designed textbooks for instructional purposes in particular, is linked to the very difficult circumstances of my life. One could hardly deny that my works published to date bear witness to my most ardent zeal and keen sense of responsibility. For it is a fact that the energies of one single individual had to be expended to the utmost in overcoming merely the difficulties caused by publishers and musicians alone. How I would have wanted to accept many an invitation and spoken directly and openly to musicians. At present, however, contrary to the situation in other arts and sciences where common terms and concepts somehow connect the lowest and the highest schools, communication with musicians seems practically impossible due to our entirely different approach to musical hearing and totally different terminology. And these differences separate us to such an extent that for the time being, at least, no understanding can take place without lengthy [preliminary] explanations. (But would I not have deserved long ago a grant by governments and friends of music which would have enabled me to complete more speedily my now-recognized life's work?)

I am very well aware of the fact that my theory, being derived from the practical art of genius, *is itself art, and must remain so*; consequently, it can never become a "science." Far from aspiring to cultivate geniuses, it applies first of all to the practical musician, and at that, only to the most talented among them. Although it is suited to free music theory, music history, music aesthetics, and music philosophy from centuries of misconceptions, it nevertheless applies only to the musicians in those fields of knowledge who possess a trained artistic organ which meets the demands of the art of genius. Since this theory is primarily concerned with auskomponierung and diminution, it pertains to the natural invention on the part of the composer and to the artistic receptivity on the part of the recreator or listener. Because of this, access to it is denied from the outset to all those who have no ear for such pure compositional events.

I proclaimed the new theory from Vienna, the center of Europe, where the paradise of the great musical art was also located. Those who come to Europe from across the ocean, to this very day, rarely make the effort to come to this center. To most newcomers from abroad, Vienna's music makes altogether too rigorous and unpleasant a demand intellectually. They resemble those first-time coastal travellers who prefer getting off at the capitals London, Paris, and Rome, which are nearest the seaports, where they also have the opportunity to indulge in cheaper entertainment of so-called culture. And yet, precisely Vienna, the city of the much abused "Boches" and "Huns," so defrauded politically and tormented by the boldest arrogance of all nations, by all barbarians of mediocrity—precisely Vienna, through my theory, will regain [world] leadership in music for a second time. This time no nation on earth will ever again be able to destroy its leadership against which every political lust of supremacy will be thwarted, even that of the French people, who, totally unoriginal in mind and body and without developing in scope or depth itself, has constantly harassed other European nations both bodily and spiritually, and is now even threatening them with disaster.

Germany has lost a generation in the war which, in resignation to fate, she has had to learn to relinquish. Perhaps she will still have to relinquish another five to ten generations until, finally, the one will come that will find the spiritual strength needed to rise to genius.

Goethe believed one must awaken to the "sense of sight"; how much more is this true of musical hearing? Another present-day German poet wrote: "We ceased to be Germans the moment we no longer experienced our language as something live"; the same applies to German music. Despite all its devotion to economic recovery, and despite the presumptuous, uncultured art-bungling of certain intellectuals such as no other nation would tolerate, it is our hope that the German nation be privileged to safeguard both its languages, the one in words and the one in tones, so that Schiller's creed becomes reality: "Every nation has its day in history, but the day of the German is the harvest of all time."

As if it were not enough that the cruelty of Nature already deprives man of a glimpse into connection, especially into one so naturally characteristic of music, the present-day world outdoes that evil of Nature through an unequalled irresponsibility of its own, which increases its guilt in the doom of music to the utmost. The fashionable catchwords of the so-called new humanism, of the new life, of the new social obligations, etc., with which the true nature of these values has been killed, are even being introduced into music by those confused intellectuals who take the liberty to meddle in music, as well as by musicians who, out of helplessness, allow themselves to be led by these confused intellectuals. These groups are united in believing that the music of genius of the past centuries no longer fits into the world of their new ideals. Hence those who are no longer able to compose, who have never heard music,[36] who have never grasped it in its connections, today simply disclaim the master art. Art of genius is, however, above all, the art of connection. Hence it can only be the connection in the music of genius that is suddenly deemed by those criminal individuals to be in contradiction to humanism, to life, and to social obligations!

Can a connection, however, be it of a natural or artistic type, actually be a hindrance in the fulfillment of ethical obligations?[37] Has ever a prophet, a poet, a statesman, or even the average man in the street, in approaching ethos, done away with connection in language while prophesying, poeticizing, working, or speaking? Then why should music be the only one to allow itself to be robbed of its soul of connection for the sake of ethos? Was a Bach, a Beethoven, a Mozart, or a Brahms, because of the boldly created connections in their works, ever hindered in taking their ethical obligations seriously? Did they not rather, in their creations as well as in their humanism, cultivate and fulfill connections in an exemplary manner? If these adversaries of genius, these natural enemies of connection in music—if only they were true human beings first, if only they were musicians, they would indeed have to be content with the degree of humanism in the great geniuses of music also. But, of course, they themselves have contributed nothing to the ethos of their new ideals. They simply want to give free reign to their own so very mediocre creations, and therefore use the excuse that the geniuses no longer correspond to the supposedly changed, modern ethos.

The fact that those intellectuals and musicians have as yet not at all grasped the art of connections in the masterworks is provable anytime, hence they are surely not called upon to create new connections in music, since for this, knowledge of the previous ones would be the first prerequisite. Hence, it is only a fraud, a fraud on themselves and on others. It would be better, however, if the ill-intentioned would plead guilty and attempt to conform with the musical geniuses in art as well as in humanism in accordance with their modest abilities.

---

[36]Through its auskomponierung process. Compared above in *Resumption of Urlinie Considerations* (Yearbook II) where Schenker states that all connection in music takes place in auskomponierung spans, and "whoever has not heard music in such spans has never heard it at all" (page 11, [Eng., p. 165]).

[37]In other words, in giving artistic expression to the spirit of the times.

ARNOLD SCHOENBERG

Arnold Schoenberg (b. Vienna 1874, d. Los Angeles 1951). One of the most influential and controversial composers of the 20th century, Schoenberg brought the slow but pervasive infiltration of non-functional harmonies and chromatic tones to its culmination; with his "emancipation of the dissonance" theory, he consciously molded and bestowed legitimacy upon a natural process which had begun to take place independently.

Practically an autodidact, apart from the formal instruction he received from his life-long friend and eventual brother-in-law, Alexander Zemlinsky, Schoenberg's approach to composition, reflected also in his teaching methods, was one of continual exploration and independent discovery. Schoenberg's pupils, through all stages of their instruction, were urged to write music relying on their own intuitive resources rather than on ossified academic musical practices. His own development, which was the outcome of continuous musical exploration, was the logical extension of a longstanding tradition. Like all great musicians, he firmly believed that musical ideas should not only serve as structural elements but should contribute to the cohesion of the work as a whole.

Convinced that he was destined to fulfill a mission, he sought to achieve his objectives with the aid of a new conception of music. His "messianic" attitude must be viewed against the background of his time. Neitzsche was promulgating his theory of the Superman, disdaining the average and extolling the "exception." Freud was uncovering the powers of the unconscious, showing man to be more complex than otherwise thought, a theme Kokoschka was portraying visually. Kandinsky was striving for a "pure inwardness," negating subject matter and stressing the psychological aspects of pure color, while Karl Kraus, the writer, saw in fantasy and self-awareness the true source of creativity.

Schoenberg was at home with Mozart, Beethoven and Bach, but was also strongly affected by the musical Vienna of Wagner, Mahler, Bruckner and Strauss. However, he scorned modern composers who, striving to break from tradition, merely added dissonances and "illogical" harmonies, which to his mind, seemed to do no more than to blur a hardly existent, or even non-existent, substance. For, he believed, even in the absence of tonal functionality, structured evaluation of sounds should be based on their functional potentialities. The realization of a musical idea, which is the propelling germinal of a work motive, and above all, comprehensibility, remained foremost in Schoenberg's mind.

While Wagner's musical dramas achieved some kind of unity through their extensive employment of leitmotivs, Schoenberg hailed Brahms for his innovative musical language which successfully condensed a great number of musical ideas in a clear cohesive form. Schoenberg, too, was bent on creating a new musical language; his, however, was supposed to be based on the total emancipation of the dissonance. In his "Opinion or Insight?" he claimed that the development from Beethoven to Wagner, which had already challenged the preponderance of the tonic by the introduction of "vagrant ambiguous" chords, now called for a conscious "final step"—a "deliberate" act of emancipation. While "Opinion or Insight?" dates from 1926, his new approach to tonality can also be found in his *Harmonielehre* of 1911. Dissonances and consonances, according to Schoenberg, do not differ in essence: they are neither discord nor concord. They merely vary in their degree of distance from the fundamental. The further the distance from the fundamental the more difficult it becomes to comprehend dissonances. Given "favorable circumstances," however, such as "expression" or "timbre," their comprehensibility could be ensured. Tonality and "emancipated dissonances" are not ends in themselves; they are but technical resources bringing unity to the perception and conception of music.

Tonality is only one means of musical presentation. Atonality may be legitimately regarded as on the same footing and need not have the negative connotation of anarchy. (Schoenberg, therefore, prefers to talk of "pantonality.") Admittedly, tonality has come to be experienced as though it were some kind of "objective reality" and atonality is still experienced as an intellectual exercise devoid of "shared meanings." This situation, Schoenberg believed, could and must be rectified.

Twelve-Tone Composition originated during the search for a cohesive power that would replace functional harmony as the power relating diverse elements to each other. However, the first pieces Schoenberg composed with the emancipation of the dissonance in mind (1908) still unfolded in accord with an extra-musical stimulus, rather than being guided by a new system. While "inspiration" or "vision" may serve as creative incentives, a purely musical reference was required on which to base "decisions," while also creating the context for the understanding of the art. After years of search, Schoenberg proposed his 12-tone system as a new frame of reference providing the structural differentiations needed to both propel and unite a musical work. In the third selection below, a contemplative essay appended to a practical guide in harmonic technique, Schoenberg reiterates the importance of "functionality" regardless of system.

Based on ideas, music manifests a reasoned unity of musical space. "The unity of musical space," says Schoenberg, "demands an absolute and unitary perception." "Up or down," "forward or backward," are not absolutes; the absolutes are musical configurations, which should be comprehended as multi-directional relations of sounds. Like material objects, which are recognized regardless of position, rows of tones retain their "qualities" regardless of direction, whether retrograde or inversion, or retrograde inversion.

What part in the creative process is to be attributed to feeling and what part to intellect? How is their relative significance to be judged and valued? According to Schoenberg it is impossible to separate the world of feelings from that of the intellect; the true artist, he believed, related equally to both. Just as consonance and dissonance are different points of a continuum, so emotions and intellect complement each other. When the act of composing answers to given requirements, the image of the art work as a whole is spontaneously conceived. Each composition embodies a certain character and conveys a certain mood (see the excerpt from *Fundamentals*) present in the communal musical experience in which composer, performer and listener take part.

Altogether, Schoenberg's compositions and theoretical work, together with the school he founded, may be regarded as one of those few attempts in the history of music which consciously aimed at changing the entire conception of music. However, convincing as his argument in favor of new, non-hierarchical organizations of tones may be, it is not altogether clear whether what he suggested can, in fact, create compatible perceptual dispositions. That Schoenberg's musical language did not become entrenched in our musical culture for more than fifty years after its conception, begs a question. The question seems even more pertinent with regard to his disciples and followers who brought "seriality" to its extreme, applying it also to parameters other than pitch. In contrast to Schoenberg who, breaking with tradition, retained, nonetheless, undefined musical habits, through texture, contour and the like, the break with the next generation was almost total. The difficulty with regard to perception may, perhaps, account for the paradoxical fact that highly sophisticated ways of dealing with sound, frequently result in simple, if not primitive contrasts, notwithstanding the complicated calculations the composers engaged in. One of the apparent reactions towards serial music was that of "aleatory" music, in which the composer tried to reduce to a minimum his own definition of the musical qualities of his work, emphasizing instead, the role of the performer. Both extremes might stem from the same aesthetic outlook, each attempting in its own way to deal with ambiguities as far as perception is concerned (see Eco; also see the Ligeti-Dahlhaus discussion on "Form").

from Style and Idea[1]

Opinion of Insight

Tonal or atonal: by now, the question whether one or the other is justified, admissible, possible, necessary or indispensable, has already taken on a more manageable form—it has become a matter of opinion. This is an advantage, since those confronted by the question can ignore all the objective points on which decisions are based and can follow their own inclination, whim, feelings and the various points to do with self-preservative instinct. If they do so, they know they are covered by a more or less numerous body of other people who share their omission to think, their inclination, whim, feelings or foresight. A party matter.

Parties rely on adherents, whom they recruit with slogans. But these never strike dead-centre, but well to one side, in the space that has to be left for the partisans. For the latter need to develop, to find success. But how are they to do so if their path is laid down by strict laws which come from a foundation of deep insight and show that the Way of the Cross indeed exists, but no cross-roads; and that to have reached a 'parting of the ways' is a sure sign that one has already strayed out of the world of art?

A few of today's composers still find a few tonal triads sufficient, even now (that is part of their private life where, to some extent, anything goes); however, most of them have noted what has been done by the works of Wagner, Strauss, Mahler, Reger, Debussy, Puccini, etc., and they have drawn certain conclusions about harmony, whose outcome is recognizable as the emancipation of the dissonance. But this has placed the tonal centre of gravity in jeopardy (something already perceptible in Wagner), and problems have arisen which are not to be solved by partisan belief, but only through insight. Belief is sweet, and it makes for happiness, but religions themselves develop, since their tendency is to come ever nearer to perfect insight into the Divine Essence. So if belief views the ultimate truth as a variable, why should it be entitled to pronounce judgement, in art, against living certainties?

---

[1]Text: Arnold Schoenberg, *Style and Idea*, ed. by Leonard Stein with translations by Leo Black (Faber and Faber, 1975), pp. 258–264.

Many modern composers believe they are writing tonally if they occasionally introduce a major or minor triad, or a cadence-like turn of phrase, into a series of harmonies that lack, and must lack, any terms of reference. Others hope the use of ostinati and pedal-points will do the same thing for them. Both are acting like believers who buy an indulgence. They betray their God, but remain on good terms with those who call themselves His attorneys. They use accidentals and key-signatures to fit the key that would like to hold sway, as if putting on a Christian-German mantle for loving their neighbour (something they rarely used to wear), to cloak their secret, sinful converse with dissonances. Perhaps this has not much to do with art. But I should like to show why.

Tonality's origin is found—and rightly so—in the laws of sound. But there are other laws that music obeys, apart from these and the laws that result from the combination of time and sound: namely, those governing the workings of our minds. This latter forces us to find a particular kind of layout for those elements that make for cohesion—and to make them come to the fore, often enough and with enough plasticity—so that in the small amount of time granted us by the flow of the events, we can recognize the figures, grasp the way they hang together, and comprehend their meaning. The easiest deviations to grasp are those that can most easily be related back to the underlying tone. These are grasped immediately in cases where their resemblance to it is at a maximum, less immediately where more remote formations can only be felt as logical if one relates them to another, or several others, lying in-between. The farther removed the formations, the greater the deviation, the more intermediaries are needed if one is to work out the connection, and the harder it is to grasp the progression and the sense. So this is the true reason for the marked development of tonality: to make what happens easily comprehensible. *Tonality is not an end in itself, but a means to an end*, and its close accord with nature offers great advantages to those who use it. That is why until our own time composers were always extremely cautious about how the succession of harmonies was arranged, at times even carrying things to the point of using only harmonies whose relationship to the tonic and their 'accessibility' to it (further underlined by convention) was easy to grasp. But the appearance of *vagrant* chords (as I call them in my *Harmonielehre*)—phenomena whose greatest value lies in their ambiguity—so greatly widened the field of events accessible from a tonic, that to an ever increasing extent the tonic could merely be proved, intellectually, to be in command, while it became steadily harder to hear. Or in other words: just as all roads led to Rome, so there is always a road leading back to the point of departure—the tonic; but anyone who went astray in the labyrinth could put the blame on a coloured thread, on which contact between entrance and interior now exclusively depended. Moreover, the proportion of elements pointing to the tonic became ever smaller, as against those pointing away from it; the 'natural preponderance of the tonic' was henceforth out of the question, and the resistance to the music of Wagner and his successors can easily be understood, since he sacrificed the immediate 'accessibility' which still gave a touch of folk-music to Beethoven and Schubert. And yet another element added to its impetus, the tendency towards 'music as expression', which appears with the greatest intensity in Beethoven. Initially limited to elements of performance (tempo, character, variability, etc.), it increasingly used harmony as well—particularly its surprising side—for the same purpose. This led to sudden and surprising modulations, expressive turns of phrase, strange chord-progressions, interesting chords, and later to new hitherto unexploited melodic steps, unusual progressions of intervals and other such things, not to mention the element of rhythm and of variations in articulation, in movements' form, and in the way the smaller thematic components (phrases, motives, etc.) were welded to each other. it is clear that all these tendencies, which exert an eccentric pull, worked against the desire to fix, make sensorily perceptible, and keep effective an harmonic central point, and that the composers who succeeded Wagner were soon obliged to make fast their forms in a way different from that practised until then. (This is the point to mention that the appeal to the 'text' in operas, songs and symphonic poems must be regarded as one attempt at producing cohesion among the heterogeneous elements, and to recall that in my essay, 'The Relationship to the Text', in *Der Blaue Reiter*, 1912, I was perhaps the first to turn away from expressive music—theoretically, for the time being—very soon after my first steps in a new territory where I had still been using expression to the fullest extent, even if unconsciously.)

'The emancipation of the dissonance.' That is to say, it came to be placed on an equal footing with the sounds regarded as consonances (in my *Harmonielehre* the explanation of this lies in the insight that consonance and dissonance differ not as opposites do, but only in point of *degree*; that consonances are the sounds closer to the fundamental, dissonances those farther away; that their comprehensibility is graduated accordingly, since the nearer ones are easier to comprehend than those farther off). This was an unconscious process; it was assumed that the comprehensibility of the dissonance can be ensured, given certain favourable circumstances. In so far as one's aural sense could not, on its own, recognize and comprehend connections and functions, these circumstances had to do with expression and also with something not greatly regarded until then—timbre. At this time impressionism was in full flower, and indeed it used the same extra-musical resources, to the same end, as the classics and romantics had used. Today, one or two masters of that epoch would rather disown the works which most helped the evolutionary process, but their achievement and influence have firmly established for all that, and one is grateful remembering their courage, their strength and the single-mindedness of their youthful ardour.

In the emancipation of the dissonances there was a final step that could be taken, and it has frequently been condemned—a step, as I myself believe, which has excluded consonances from music only for a short period, but one which I have shown to lie along the path followed by the evolution of music, through the works of our greatly revered predecessors. I should now explain this last step as a supplement to remarks made earlier in my *Harmonielehre*; here, as in the earlier part of this article, I am supported by the principles and methods of observation contained in a work entitled 'The Musical Idea and Its Presentation', on which I have long been working.

1. Tonality's function begins to exist if the phenomena that appear can, without exception, be related immediately to a tonic, and if they are arranged so that their accessibility is a matter of sensory perception; or else if one uses the kind of methods that allow those farther away to become accessible.

2. The effect of tonality lies in this: everything that occurs in the harmony is accessible from the tonic, so its internal relationships are given suitable cohesion; and a piece of music so constructed is sure, in advance, of a certain formal effectiveness, whether or not it is constructed with the same logic and cohesion in respect of its other functions.

Tonality is not an end in itself, then; it is one of the technical resources facilitating (but not guaranteeing) unity in the comprehension of tone-progressions.

3. To isolate one or two of the resources which work toward unity if all of them are present, and then to mix them in a purely superficial way, will by no means assist the eventuation of form, but will have merely the

effect of 'style', of veiling the true relationships for reasons of taste. Anyone who wishes to use tonality's cohesive function appropriately can do so with only one end in view: a reliable and effective form. But if one does it merely out of a liking for tonality, ignorant how to use it to its true end, and no other (rather than as a means of creating atmosphere, or to comply with party principles), one commits a grave sin and acts as ludicrously as if one were to paint a marble slab with lacquer. If, even so, a work of that kind is formally effective, it is because of extra-musical influences—performance, character, etc.—some of which are mentioned below.

4. There is no reason in physics or aesthetics that could force a musician to use tonality in order to represent his idea. The only question is whether one can attain formal unity and self-sufficiency without using tonality. The appeal to its origin in nature can be refuted if one recalls that just as tones pull toward triads, and triads toward tonality, gravity pulls us down toward the earth; yet an airplane carries us up away from it. A product can be apparently artificial without being unnatural, for it is based on the laws of nature to just the same degree as are those that seem primary. But I have moreover shown that there is nothing new about the state in which music finds itself when it ceases to seek help from tonality; that, on the contrary, music has been in this state ever since Wagner, and one must simply use a new and strong enough cohesive force to bring all that happens to a common denominator; I have already argued that the 'expressive' musicians and impressionists did exactly that.

5. In my first works in the new style I was particularly guided, in both the details and the whole of the formal construction, by very powerful expressive forces, not to mention a sense of form and logic acquired from tradition and well developed through hard work and conscientiousness. These forms became possible because of a limitation which I had been unconsciously imposing on myself from the very outset—limitation to *short* pieces, something which at the time I explained in my own mind as a reaction against the 'extended' style. Nowadays I know a better explanation: renunciation of traditional means of articulation made the construction of larger forms temporarily impossible, since such forms cannot exist without clear articulation. For the same reason, my only extended works from that time are works with a text, where the words represent the cohesive element.

6. I cannot give a single physical reason justifying the exclusion of consonant chords, but I can give a far more decisive artistic reason. It is

in fact *a question of economy*. My formal sense (and I am immodest enough to hand over to this the exclusive rights of distribution when I compose) tells me that to introduce even a single tonal triad would lead to consequences, and would demand space which is not available within my form. A tonal triad makes claims on what follows, and, retrospectively, on all that has gone before; nobody can ask me to overthrow everything that has gone before, just because a triad has happened by accident and has to be given its due. On this point I prefer if possible to start right and continue in the same way, so far as error is avoidable. Every tone tends to become a tonic. Every triad to become a tonic triad, then the idea could inadvertently be forced aside on to a wrong track; but sense of form and logic have so far saved me. Immediately, in my first attempts, I felt this, and I justified it in my *Harmonielehre* on the grounds, among others, that the consonant chords sound empty and dry alongside those containing many tones. But even standing where I do at the present time, I believe that to use the consonant chords, too, is not out of the question, as soon as someone has found a technical means of either satisfying or paralysing their formal claims.

From the very beginning, this was clear in my mind: tonality's aids to articulation having dropped out, one must find some substitute, so that longer forms can once more be constructed. Length is relative and yet is one of music's dimensions; pieces of music can therefore be either long or short, so short pieces can be only an occasional way out. Starting from that premise, I arrived at twelve-tone composition. Some day I shall explain the paths and detours I followed and the reason why I needed a number of important insights about the musical idea and its presentation before that became possible; but first there are a few problems still to overcome, which I am on the verge of solving.

I still owe an answer (or, surely, I only seem to) to the question whether one is justified in writing tonally or atonally, or whether the one or the other may even be necessary or impossible. First I should like to point out that in my *Harmonielehre* (3rd edition, p. 487), I reject the expression 'atonal'. Nowadays this method of composition is, alas, generally so referred to; if one has to give it a name, I can think of only one which is not a slogan and is therefore unsuitable for a party banner, thank goodness: 'Composition with twelve tones related only to one another.' But as for the question itself: you neither must, may write tonally, nor must you, may you, wrote atonally. Write or don't write, but in any case don't ask, but do what you can. If you can do something pure, you will be able to do it tonally or atonally; but those who think impurely—that is to say, those who do what anyone can—may go ahead and form tonal or atonal parties, and for that matter make a noise about it. They will certainly shout us down, we who give ear to our destiny; and they will surely be heard, soon and in full measure, by those who are in favour of everything ambiguous but against everything genuine. If *we* address ourselves to those people, it is only out of acoustical necessity, since a literally empty concert hall sounds even worse than one full of 'empty people'.

Many of those who went along with me for a time have by now thought better of their atonal aspirations. It is not to these young lions of atonal music, who have now found a more comfortable den in a musical renaissance, that I refer when I say at this point that I have great esteem and respect for many who still adhere to tonality, or who have returned to it. There are true and genuine talents among them, and they have a very important task. The leap from a method of composition that emphasized key to mine was very swift and sudden. For a long time to come, the listener's ear must still be prepared before he finds dissonant sounds a matter of course and can comprehend the processes based on them. It seems to me that such composers' activity is very much the thing to ameliorate this. The idea is timeless, so it can perfectly well wait; but the language must make haste!

from Fundamentals of Musical Composition[1]

Character and Mood

The concept that music expresses something is generally accepted.

However, chess does not tell stories. Mathematics does not evoke emotions. Similarly, from the viewpoint of pure aesthetics, music does not express the extramusical.

But from the viewpoint of psychology, our capacity for mental and emotional associations is as unlimited as our capacity for repudiating them is limited. Thus every ordinary object can provoke musical associations, and, conversely, music can evoke associations with extramusical objects.

Many composers have composed under the urge to express emotional associations. Moreover, programme music goes so far as to narrate entire stories with musical symbols. There also exist a great variety of 'characteristic pieces' expressing every conceivable mood.

There are *Nocturnes, Ballades, Funeral Marches, Romances, Scenes from Childhood, Flower Pieces, Novelettes,* etc., by Chopin and Schumann. There are Beethoven's *Eroica* and *Pastorale* Symphonies; Berlioz's *Roman Carnival*; Tchaikovsky's *Romeo and Juliet,* Strauss's *Thus Spake Zarathustra*; Debussy's *La Mer,* Sibelius's *Swan of Tuonela*; and a multitude of others. Finally, there are songs, choir music, oratorios, operas, melodramas, ballets and motion-picture music.

All these categories are intended to produce not only musical impressions, but also to provoke secondary effects: associations of a definite character.

The term *character*, applied to music, refers not only to the emotion which the piece should produce and the mood in which it was composed, but also the manner in which it must be played. It is fallacious to think that the tempo indications determine character. In classical music, at least, this is not true. There is not one adagio character, but hundreds; not one scherzo character, but thousands. An

---

[1]Text: Arnold Schoenberg, *Fundamentals of Musical Composition*, ed. by Gerald Strang with the collaboration of Leonard Stein (London: Faber and Faber, 1967), pp. 93–96.

adagio is slow; an allegro is fast. This contributes something, but not everything, to the expression of a character.

The type of accompaniment plays an important role in the establishment of character. No player could express the character of a march if the accompaniment were that of a chorale; no one could play a restful adagio melody if the accompaniment were like a torrent.

Old dance forms were characterized by certain rhythms in the accompaniment, which were also reflected in the melody. These rhythmic characteristics are the principal means of distinguishing a mazurka, for example, from a gavotte or a polka. But, in general, rhythmic features help to establish the mood and special character of an individual piece, as well as to provide the structurally necessary internal contrasts.

The concept of difference in character can be clarified by comparison of three movements from Beethoven sonatas which are similar in that they express something 'stormy' or 'passionate' (Op. 27/2–III; Op. 31/2–I; Op. 57–I). The differences in character manifest themselves not only in the thematic material of the openings, but also in the nature of the continuations. Compare the respective subordinate themes: Op. 27/2–III, m. 21 ff.; Op. 31/2–I, m. 41 ff.; Op. 57–I, m. 35 ff.

How little the tempo alone contributes to character will be realized if one compares these three with three others in rapid tempo: the Presto Agitato of Op. 27/2–III with the Allegro Vivace of Op. 31/1–I; or the Allegro of Op. 31/2–I with the Allegro of Op. 31/3–I; or the Assai Allegro of Op. 57–I with the Presto alla Tedesca of Op. 79–I.

But the changes of character within a single movement—even within its smaller sections—are even more important. Apart from the strong contrast between principal subordinate themes in Op. 57–I, there are many other contrasts. Note the sudden change of texture in m. 24, its intensification in m. 28 ff., and its gradual liquidation, m. 31 ff. How dramatic is the change of expression when 'dolce legato', m. 35, replaces the previous hard staccato of the left hand; and when the movement suddenly stops in m. 41. A new and even stronger contrast in texture (m. 51) changes the entire aspect of the rest of this section.

This is not a singular case. All good music consists of many contrasting ideas. An idea achieves distinctness and validity in contrast with others. Heraclitus called contrast 'the principle of development'. Musical thinking is subject to the same dialectic as all other thinking.

Differences of character may have an influence on the structure, but no particular character can be said to demand a particular form.

Though one would scarcely write a waltz in the form of a symphony, Beethoven wrote the first movement of a sonata (Op. 54) 'In tempo d'un Menuetto'; and his Seventh Symphony, because of its character, is commonly called the 'Dance Symphony'. But, in general, light, graceful, simple moods will not require complicated forms nor adventurous elaboration. On the other hand, profound ideas, deeply moving emotions, heroic attitudes, require the bold contrasts and thorough elaboration of more complex forms.

Descriptive music—such as programme music; stage, ballet and moving picture music; melodramas; and even songs—under pressure of strong and sudden contrasts, develops its forms in harmony with those emotions, events and actions which it is supposed to illustrate. In such cases the basic motive itself possesses a descriptive character or mood as illustrated in Ex. 68.

In the second movement of Beethoven's *Pastorale* Symphony (Ex. 68*a*), the sound of the murmuring brook is illustrated by the flowing movement of the accompaniment. Ex. 68*b*, the Magic Fire Music from Wagner's *Die Walküre*, expresses musically the flickering flames. With an equally rich movement, Smetana describes the source of the River Moldau (Ex. 68*c*). Bach's *St. Matthew Passion* is rich in illustrative passages. Among them, particularly striking because it appears in a recitative, is the description of the rending of the curtain (Ex. 68*d*). The swing of the weathervane is depicted in Schubert's *The Weathervane*, and characteristically enough, the trills in m. 4 and 5 represent its creaking (Ex. 68*e*).

In composing even the smallest exercises, the student should never fail to keep in mind a special character. A poem, a story, a play or a moving picture may provide the stimulus to express definite moods. The pieces which he composes should differ widely. Especially fruitful are differences in tempo, rhythm and metre. Such practice will help him to acquire the capacity to produce the manifold types of contrast necessary for larger forms.

Example 68

a) Beethoven, Symphony No. 6 "By the brook"

b) Wagner, *Die Walküre*, Act III, "Magic Fire Music"

from Structural Function of Harmony[1]

Apollonian Evaluation of a Dionysian Epoch

Epochs in which the venture of experimentation enriched the vocabulary of musical expression have always alternated with their counterparts, epochs in which the experiences of the predecessors were either ignored or else abstracted into strict rules which were applied by the following generations. Most of these rules restricted modulations and designed formulae regarding the inclusion and treatment of dissonances.

These restrictions purported to facilitate the understanding of music. In earlier epochs, even more than in our times, the inclusion of a dissonant tone—"foreign" to the harmony—interrupted plain, undeviating understanding. "Whence comes this tone? Whither does it go?"—these questions distracted the mind of a listener, and could even make him forget the basic conditions upon which the continuation of the musical thought depended. Similar disturbances could be caused by the addition of an unexpected chord which was not in accordance with existing conventions. This may have been the reason why, for instance, V–VI in a cadence, instead of V–I, is called a "deceptive" progression. Difficulties of comprehension were once attributed to the minor third. It was at best considered an imperfect consonance, if not a dissonance; accordingly it was considered incapable of producing a definite ending to a work.

Classical music was composed in one of the Apollonian[2] periods, when the application of dissonances and their treatment, as well as the manner and extent of modulation, were governed by rules which had become the second nature of every musician. His musicianship was in question if he failed in this respect, if he were incapable of remaining instinctively within the limits of accepted convention. At this time the harmony was inherent in the melody.

[1]Text: Arnold Schoenberg, *Structural Function of Harmony*, rev. edition, ed. Leonard Stein (New York: W.W. Norton & Company Inc., 1969), pp. 192-196. The numbered notes are Schoenberg's notes.
[2]Nietzsche establishes a contrast between the Apollonian mind, which aims for proportion, moderation, order and harmony and its contrast, the Dionysian, which is passionate, intoxicated, dynamic, expansive, creative, and even destructive.

But the new chords and dissonances of the next epoch, a Dionysian period (provoked by the romantic composers), had barely been digested and catalogued, and the rules for their inclusion had not yet been formulated, when a new progressive movement began even before this last one had settled down. Mahler, Strauss, Debussy and Reger cast new obstacles in the way of the comprehensibility of music. However, their new and more violent dissonances and modulations could still be catalogued and explained with the theoretical tools of the preceding period.

It is different in the contemporary period.

Because of the many attempts to connect the past with the future one might be inclined to call this an Apollonian period. But the fury with which addicts of various schools fight for their theories presents rather a Dionysian aspect.

Many contemporary composers add dissonant tones to simple melodies, expecting thus to produce "modern" sounds. But they overlook the fact that these added dissonant tones may exert unexpected functions. Other composers conceal the tonality of their themes through harmonies which are unrelated to the themes. Semi-contrapuntal imitations—fugatos taking the place of sequences, which were formly used as "fillers-up" in worthless "Kapellmeistermusik"—deepen the confusion in which the meagreness of ideas is lost to sight. Here the harmony is illogical and functionless.

My school, including such men as Alban Berg, Anton Webern and others, does not aim at the establishment of a tonality, yet does not exclude it entirely. The procedure is based upon my theory of "the emancipation of the dissonance." Dissonances, according to this theory, are merely more remote consonances in the series of overtones.[3] Though the resemblance of the more remote overtones to the fundamental tone gradually diminishes, their *comprehensibility* is equal to the *comprehensibility* of the consonances. Thus to the ear of today their sense-interrupting effect has disappeared. Their emancipation is as justified as the emancipation of the minor third was in former times.

For the sake of a more profound logic, the Method of Composing with Twelve Tones derives all configurations [elements of a work] from a basic set (*Grundgestalt*) [tone-row or note series]. The order in this basic set and its three derivatives—contrary motion [inversion],

[3]See Arnold Schoenberg's *Harmonielehre*, p. 495 ff.

retrograde, and retrograde inversion respectively—is, like the motive [in classical music], obligatory for a whole piece. Deviation from this order of tones should normally not occur, in contrast to the treatment of the motive, where variation is indispensable.[4] Nevertheless, variety is not precluded. The tones in the right order may appear either successively in a melody, theme or independent voice, or as an accompaniment consisting of simultaneous sounds (like harmonies).

Evaluation of (quasi-) harmonic progressions in such music is obviously a necessity, though more for the teacher than for the composer. But as such progressions do not derive from roots, harmony is not under discussion and evaluation of structural functions cannot be considered. They are vertical projections of the basic set, or parts of it, and their combination is justified by its logic. This occurred to me even before the introduction of the basic set, when I was composing *Pierrot Lunaire, Die Glückliche Hand* and other works of this period. Tones of the accompaniment often came to my mind like broken chords, successively rather than simultaneously, in the manner of a melody.

There exists no definition of the concepts of *melody* and *melodic* which is better than mere pseudo-aesthetics. Consequently, the composition of melodies depends solely on inspiration, logic, sense of form and musical culture. A composer in the contrapuntal period was in a similar situation with respect to harmony. Rules give only negative advice, that is, what one must *not* do. He, too, therefore, learned what to do only through inspiration. Is then a composer with twelve tones at a greater disadvantage than his predecessors because the evaluation of the chords which he produces has not yet been carried out?

Theory must never precede creation: "And the Lord saw that all was well done."

One day there will be a theory which abstracts rules from these compositions. Certainly, the structural evaluation of these sounds will again be based upon their functional potentialities. But it is improbable that the quality of sharpness or mildness of the dissonances—which, in fact, is nothing more than a gradation according to lesser or greater beauty—is the appropriate foundation for a theory which explores, explains and teaches. From such gradations one cannot deduce

---

[4]Minor changes in the order are admissible if, because of many repetitions, the mind has become acquainted with the basic set. This corresponds to remote variations of a motive in similar circumstances.

principles of construction. Which dissonances should come first? Which later? Should one begin with the sharp ones and end with the mild ones, or vice-versa? Yet the concept of "first" or "later" plays a role in musical construction, and "later" should be the consequence of "first".

Beauty, an undefined concept, is quite useless as a basis for aesthetic discrimination, and so is sentiment. Such a "*Gefühlsaesthetik*" [aesthetic of sentiment] would lead us back to the inadequacy of an obsolete aesthetic which compared sounds to the movement of the stars, and deduced virtues and vices from tone combinations.

This discussion would fail in its main purpose if the damage wreaked by the performer's ignorance of the functions of harmony were to remain undiscussed.

Listening to a concert, I often find myself unexpectedly in a "foreign country", not knowing how I got there; a modulation has occurred which escaped my comprehension. I am sure that this would not have happened to me in former times, when a performer's education did not differ from a composer's.

Great conductors like Nikisch, Mahler and Strauss were aware of the gradual alteration in the texture which precedes a modulation and results in a "change of scenery", the introduction of a contrast. A musician's culture and sense of form is acquired by a thorough education and knowledge. Such a musician will make a modulation lucid by "vitalizing" the appropriate voices. Then the listener will not awake suddenly "as in a foreign country".

Hans Richter, the renowned Wagnerian conductor, was once passing by a studio in the Vienna Opera House, and stopped surprised by the unintelligible sounds he heard from within. A coach who had been engaged for this post, not because of his musical talents, but because of a powerful protector, was accompanying a singer. Furiously Richter opened the door and shouted: "Mr. F—thal, if you plan to continue coaching you must first buy a book on harmony and study it!"

Here was a conductor who believed in harmony and in education.

VICTOR ZUCKERKANDL

Victor Zuckerkandl (b. Vienna, 1896, d. Ascona, Switzerland, 1965), conductor, music theorist and music critic, received his musical education in Vienna where he conducted and taught music theory until he left for America, in 1940. In *Sound and Symbol: Music and the External World* (1956), Zuckerkandl brings a new perspective to the relationship between the subjective and objective worlds of the listener.

Zuckerkandl, who viewed music as a kind of "miracle," wished to go beyond the prevailing physicalistic and psychological interpretations of music by introducing what he called the "third stage." The "third stage" is a spiritual world which represents the interaction between the inner world of the listener and the outer world whence he receives his stimuli.

This merger of the two worlds is possible only because there is a metaphysical component to the material "outer world." Furthermore, the merger of the "within" with the "without" is what constitutes the listener's psyche; the psyche is not a stage antecedent to that fusion.

Music, from the perspective of the "third stage" is, according to Zuckerkandl, an important instrument through which philosophical insights into the world are obtained. In music we both experience the material world and become conscious of ourselves as immaterial beings. Music reveals a concept of space which differs from the physical-geometric one. It reveals an audible, placeless space, one of forces, dynamics, tensions and harmonies—a space experienced. Similarly, time is presented not by the demarcation of successive instances but by their interpenetration, whereby the present also contains both the past and the future.

According to Zuckerkandl, musical tones are perceived as a play of forces presenting specific dynamic qualities and states of activity. Musical form, the "order of tones," is not a mere juxtaposition of bodies of sound, but a representation of the relations generated by the above forces. We hear energy and relations, says Zuckerkandl, not wavelengths and vibrations. The mind perceives these non-physical occurrences, which the physiological processes neither explain nor exhaust. Hearing music, the listener experiences the "reality" of a placeless space of dynamic forces.

To be sure, many of the ingredients of Zuckerkandl's thought have appeared in previous theories concerning music. Yet, there is novelty in his attitude that should not be overlooked. While from Webb and Suzanne Langer via Schopenhauer and others, it was held that music, in one way or another, "mirrors" the dynamics of an inner life, Zuckerkandl insists that music does not reflect psychological states but projects them. Like twentieth-century linguistic theories which regard language as partaking in the very processes of thought, Zuckerkandl calls attention to the cognitive role of music. In any case, real explanations concerning music cannot be achieved, according to Zuckerkandl, solely through "technical analysis." While such analyses may, perhaps, function as compositional manuals, musical analysts labour under a false pretense if they believe to have thereby gained an "understanding of the thing itself." Music theory, in the proper sense, has to take into account other disciplines, including those which try to clarify the meaning of "meaning," the thoughts about and the processes of "thinking" and "creating." As a professional musician, his arguments should have produced more attention; unfortunately, he remained almost alone in his position. In the *Sozietät der musikalische Wissenschaft*, in which Bach was an honorable member, the situation was quite different, as Ursula Kirkandale has shown. "Mere practical musicians" were not admitted, for they were regarded as "incapable of contributing anything to the reception and improvement of music." Thus, while analyzing Bach's *Musical Offering*, one has to bear in mind that treating music in terms of rhetorics was not only considered a scholarly exercise at the time, but a way to account for its "powers" and an efficient way with which to enlist them. By re-examining the "forces," "dynamics" and "tensions" of music, Zuckerkandl not only becomes linked with a glorious past, but joins all those who try to unveil the multi-dimensional aspects of music, aiming at a better understanding of its nature and the way it is conceived and perceived.

664

from Sound and Symbol[1]

The Dynamic Quality of Tone

We begin with a well-known melody of Beethoven's, the theme of the last movement of the Ninth Symphony:

How little of the labor it cost its creator do we hear in this melody! It stands there like the epitome of the self-evident, of the simply and unquestionably valid. What should there be to understand in it beyond the direct auditory experience; what question should it raise? Does it not itself say everything that is to be said about it? The questioning intelligence finds no more points of application here than does the grasping hand on the surface of a crystal ball.

Yet a question must be put if our study is to get under way. A first question is generally a risky step, pregnant with consequences. The step is often taken without much reflection, in obedience to usage, to a traditional schema. Are we always aware how many unexpressed and unadmitted preconceptions such a first question introduces into a study? We think we are still investigating without prejudice, when in reality our thought is set in a definite direction from the very start; the course and the goal are predetermined before the study has really begun.

Four branches of learning provide us with what we may call ready-made questions with which we might begin our study. They are theory of music, acoustics, psychology of music, aesthetics. Let us briefly

[1]Text: Victor Zuckerkandl, *Sound and Symbol*, Princeton University Press, 1956, pp. 11–24; 65–71; 76–87; 117–148; 201–222; 228–242; 267–270; 285–292; 336–348. The numbered notes are Zuckerkandl's notes.

consider what unacknowledged preconceptions we should bring into this study with these four branches of learning.

The musical theorist looks at this subject above all from the viewpoint of the technique of musical composition. This is not the place to say in more detail that "theory of music" is improperly so called; with a few notable exceptions it has been concerned not with understanding music but with making it. It has become chiefly instruction in the practice of composition (generally a superannuated practice, but that is another question); the few scholars who have been concerned with a real theory of music have remained outsiders. To put it in a rather crass comparison: the problems of the musical theorists are the problems of the electrician, not the problems of electricity. What musical theory, in regard to our Beethoven melody, would have to say on the tonal material and its use, on key and time, on phrase and form, would be directed to the interests and needs of a person who wished to acquire a difficult technique. This is in no sense intended as blame or reproach. Doubt begins to enter only when musical theory behaves as if its questions and answers sufficed to attain to understanding the thing itself, its nature, its essence. The inevitable disillusionment of all those who have hoped to gain a deeper insight into music from current musical theory would alone be cause enough not to entrust our investigation to the questions propounded and the orientation adopted by this branch of learning.

Melodies consist of tones. Tones are events in the external world, natural phenomena, parts in the great whole of external nature, to investigate the general laws and connections of which is the task of natural science, especially of physics. Acoustics is the branch of physics that is concerned with tones as natural phenomena. Vibration and frequency, wave and wave forms, medium and manner of propagation, and the special and general natural laws that these phenomena obey—these are the things concerning which acoustics formulates questions. Concerning our Beethoven melody, the acoustician has all sorts of interesting things to say. He can enlighten us concerning that which, in such a melody, is nature or, to put it more accurately, nature as physics knows it, physical nature. But to expect enlightenment from him concerning that in our melody which is not physical nature but art would be tacitly to equate art with physical nature, music with physics.

Nor does the psychologist inquire into music as such. He is predominantly interested in what takes place in the person who hears music. The origin of tone sensations, the functioning of the infinitely complex physical apparatus of ear-nerve-brain, the nature and structure of simple and complex tone sensations, their relations to other sensations, the partly conscious, partly unconscious physiological and psychic reactions that the hearing of tones and music produces in us, our motor responses and, above all, our emotional responses—these and the like constitute the field in which the musical psychologist works. Some of these problems are of great interest; their investigation has yielded valuable insights into the functioning of the human organism and psyche. Yet we must not forget that the psychologist's field lies mainly inside the skin of the living being he is studying; the world of psychology, in the proper sense, is an *inner* world. If we take the questions formulated by psychology as our starting point in a search for insights into the essence of music, we tacitly postulate that the arena of music is the inner world. No musical psychologist believes otherwise. But it is clear that we must guard against making a decision so fraught with consequences *before* we begin our investigation.

(Here an objection may be raised: If music does not belong in the external world, which physics investigates, nor yet in the inner world, which is the subject matter of psychology, where does it belong? That is the very problem. It is obvious how little we are aided by disciplines that implicitly solve this problem merely through their formulation of a first question.)

There still remains the road of traditional aesthetics, of the philosophy of art. One would indeed suppose that the philosopher was just the man to inquire into a thing as such, without preconceptions, to seek out its essence. Actually, however, no other discipline formulates its problems with such a burden of tacit preconceptions as does the traditional philosophy of art. Philosophy has taken up its abode in three houses: Logic and Epistemology is inscribed on the first—here Truth is discussed; Ethics on the second—here the subject is the Good; Aesthetics on the third—here the subject is the Beautiful. In consequence of this tripartite division, which one is obliged to accept at the outset, together with the entire philosophy that stands behind it, music falls under the jurisdiction of the third house and is dealt with in accordance with the basic concepts that obtain there. Ideal of beauty, aesthetic value, judgment of taste, feeling of pleasure and pain—these establish the point of view from which the problem is approached. To inquire into music with the traditional aesthetician means, then, to assume that beauty, aesthetic value, taste, feeling, pleasure-pain, and so forth are the categories in the light of which music must be viewed if it is to be properly understood. This book as it progresses will show, however, that these concepts, rooted in philosophical systems and their require- ments, are not indigenous to the tonal world; the musical experience nowhere suggests them. Under their guidance our questions will forever remain external to the musical phenomenon; our answers will not point to its inner core. Students of aesthetic literature will agree that, in general, thinking about art has produced genuine results to the extent that it has discarded the conceptual framework of traditional aesthetics and has met the artistic phenomenon immediately, with no prepared questions, but, instead, waiting for the phenomenon to suggest the kind of question which should be asked of it and to which it might in turn be willing ultimately to furnish an answer.

Let us now return to our Beethoven melody.

The last sentence sounded insignificant enough, yet something significant was said because the word *melody* was used. Why did we not say simply "succession of tones," or "series of tones," which would have been even more innocuous?

Not every series of tones is a melody. What we hear when a cat runs over the keyboard is a series of tones; presumably it is not a melody. Not because it does not come up to the mark in beauty, in pleasingness, in artistic value—there are ugly, unpleasing, worthless melodies, which are still melodies—but simply because it is nonsense. A melody is a series of tones that makes sense.

Someone talks in a language that we do not know. We hear articulation, vowels and consonants—and nothing more. If we understand the language, we do not hear vowels and consonants but words and sentences. Successions of articulated sounds are words if they have a meaning: *art*, *rat*, *tar* have meaning, they are words; *tra* is nonsense, mere sound. Successions of words are sentences if they express a meaning. It is the meaning that turns vowels and consonants into words, words into sentences. The same is true of tones and melodies. What we hear in melodies is not tones but tone words, tone sentences.

How can tones have meaning? Words have meaning because they relate to things; sentences, because they express something about things. Pictures have meaning if they represent something; symbols, if they betoken something, indicate something. Tones do not relate to things, do not express anything about things, represent nothing, betoken nothing, indicate nothing. What is it, then, that is meaningful in tones, that allows us to distinguish sense from nonsense in successions of tones?

Most people understand the language of tones without further ado; they are capable of hearing successions of tones as melodies, of distinguishing between sense and nonsense in tones. The lack of this ability, so-called tune deafness,[2] is a very rare anomaly. (Tune deafness has nothing to do with lack of musical sense; a person may hear melodies, hear the meaning in tones, and remain completely indifferent.) When a tune-deaf person listens to a melody, he hears tones succeeding one another, he does not hear melody. He hears music as we hear a lecture in a language we do not understand. The tones themselves, the sound, he perceives exactly as the normal person does; he lacks the organ for the *meaning* in the tones. To him our Beethoven melody is a succession of tones, what the cat produces on the keyboard is another succession of tones; the distinction between sense and nonsense, between music and nonmusic, escapes him completely. Were we in a position to demonstrate exactly what it is that the normal person hears in a melody and the tune-deaf person does not hear, we should presumably have isolated the factor that makes tones meaningful and makes music out of successions of tones.

Let us assume that we hear our Beethoven melody in a distorted form, perhaps thus:

The tune-deaf person will likewise hear that something has been changed; if he has good tonal memory—which is not at all incompatible with his anomaly—he will perhaps even be able to point out the places where the changes were made. Yet he will not find that the change has

[2]Cf. Géza Révész, *Introduction to the Psychology of Music*, ch. XVI; also his *Grundlegung der Tonpsychologie.*

much significance. For him the result in both cases is about the same: a series of tones without meaning. To a person who does not understand Italian, it does not matter in the least whether he hears *in questa tomba oscura* or *in tesqua bomta ucsora*. To the Italian it matters a great deal. The first version says something; the second is nonsense. The alterations in our melody are not radical enough to change sense into sheer nonsense; but one certainly need not be a professional to distinguish between the right and the wrong version, in other words, to be aware that one version makes better sense than the other. The change in the tones, then, is heard equally by the normal person and the tune-deaf person; but, in addition, the normal person hears something quite different, something that escapes the tune-deaf person: the change of meaning that goes hand in hand with the change in the tones. Once again we can turn to language for a comparison and for clarification: but and Bill, for example, differ in their vowels, but also, let us say, in the number of legs each possesses—the bull has four, Bill only two. The first difference, the difference in sound, is perceptible to anyone; the second difference, the difference in meaning, is perceptible only to someone who understands English. What is it, then, that changes in a melody when the tones are changed, in the same way as the meaning of a word changes when a sound in it is changed?

That our melody does not proceed to its end in a single nonperiodic sweep, like a long sentence without punctuation, anyone, even the tune-deaf person, will observe without further ado. On the contrary, it is clearly divided into subsections, after every fourth measure, by caesuras—we shall call these subsections *phrases*. (The caesura between the third and fourth phrases is concealed by the anticipation of a tone that is actually not due until the beginning of the next measure.) Of these four phrases, the first and second are very similar, the third is different, and the fourth is the repetition of the second. What would happen if this fourth and last phrase, instead of repeating the second, repeated the first, which sounds almost the same, and the melody ended thus:

Again, even the tune-deaf person would hear the change, but that would be all; he would have no fault to find with it; it would be a matter of indifference to him which phrase ended the melody. The normal person, on the other hand, would react to the change with a determined "No!" Asked why he rejected it, he would explain, more or less: "It's not finished; there's something still to come; you can't end like that." The tune-deaf person will have no notion of what the other is talking about. In order to determine where the hearing of the tune-deaf person differs from that of the normal person, what one hears and the other does not, we must, then, accurately describe what it is that prompts us to accept the one version of the end of the melody and reject the other.

We say, then, that the first phrase of our melody cannot be used as an ending, but the second can. The two phrases are exactly alike until their last measure; it is [♪] in the first phrase, [♪] in the second. If we change the last tone of the first phrase, thus [♪], it can at once be used as an ending. It is, then, the last tone alone that in this case decides between usability and unusability as an ending. We accept [♪] ; we reject [♪] . Why?

Suppose that we hear the tone [♪] , just the single tone, and ask ourselves whether it is a usable concluding tone. The question would have little meaning. Listen to the tone as intensely as we will, we shall discover nothing in it that could either especially qualify it or disqualify it as a concluding tone. The situation is, however, basically changed if we hear the same tone at the end of the first phrase of our melody and then ask ourselves the same question. The tone we hear is the same; everything that we heard before, we hear now. But we hear something more, something new, of which there was not even a trace in the single tone. A new quality has accrued to it—we must call it a dynamic quality. The single tone was simply a tone; the same tone at the end of the phrase in our melody is a *tone that has become active*, a tone in a definite state of activity. We *hear* this state, we hear it clearly and directly, in the tone itself. What we hear in this way we can best designate as a state of disturbed equilibrium, as a tension, a tendency, almost a will. The tone seems to point beyond itself toward release from tension and restoration of equilibrium; it seems to look in a definite direction for the event that will bring about this change; it even seems to demand the event. It is clear that such a tone cannot be used as the concluding tone of a melody.

Let us go through the same process with the other tone, [♪] , and ask the same question. Again we shall not fail to observe that the tone, heard alone, exhibits not the slightest characteristic that could determine its usability or unusability as a concluding note. In this respect the two tones, e and d, are wholly alike. But if now we hear [♪] at the end of

671

our melody, and compare this tone with ♮ at the end of the first phrase, another difference, entirely apart from the difference between the two tones as such, from their difference in pitch, is at once strikingly perceptible: a difference in dynamic quality. Once again we now hear ♮ not simply as a tone but as a tone that has become active—active in an entirely different way from that in which we found ♮ to be active. Instead of the disturbed equilibrium, the tension and dissatisfaction which we registered there, we here receive the impression of perfect equilibrium, of relaxation of tension and satisfaction, we might almost say of self-affirmation. If the other tone pointed beyond itself in a definite direction, if it demanded an event that would restore the state of equilibrium, relax the tension, it now becomes clear that it was precisely the tone ♮ to which it pointed, which it demanded. What takes place here between the two tones is a sort of play of forces, comparable to that between magnetic needle and magnetic pole. The activity of the one is a placing itself in a direction, a pointing toward and striving after a goal; the activity of the other is a dictating of direction, a drawing to itself. The one wants to pass beyond itself, the other wants itself; hence the one cannot be used as the concluding tone of our melody, whereas the other makes a good conclusion.

We now know what distinguishes the hearing of the tune-deaf person from that of the normal person. The tune-deaf person is deaf precisely to the dynamic quality of a tone, to the quality that accrues to a tone in the context of a melody, as part of a musical whole. The result would have been the same, no matter what tone of this or any other melody we had chosen; as we shall see later, there is no tone in music without a specific dynamic quality. If the tune-deaf person is incapable of distinguishing between sense and nonsense in tones, it is because he hears only differences in pitch, not dynamic differences. It is, then, the dynamic quality that permits tones to become the conveyors of meaning; that makes melodies out of successions of tones and music out of acoustical phenomena. The dynamic quality is the properly musical quality of tones.

A tone is a phenomenon of the external world. A physical process, the vibration of air, produces it. We encounter it outside ourselves; our attention, when we listen to it, is directed outward. To be sure, the act of hearing, together with the physiological mechanism that comes into play with it—the mechanism of ear, nerve, central nervous system— belongs to us; what we experience in the act, however, the thing heard, is not in us. The difference between heard and merely imagined tone is unequivocal to the mentally normal person. Science has described in detail what we hear when we hear a tone; has distinguished various properties of tone, such as pitch, intensity, color, volume; and has above all demonstrated the closest correspondence between tone perception and the physical state that corresponds to it. Everything we hear in the tone is, so to speak, prefigured in the physical process, in the length, breadth, shape of the sound wave. If something changes in the tone heard, something must have changed in the physical process. The two stand to each other in the strict relationship of cause and effect.

What we have thus described is tone as everyone hears it, the normal person as well as the tune-deaf person, as every apparatus registers it: the single tone removed from any musical context, tone as an acoustical phenomenon. It is not tone as a musical phenomenon. Precisely the quality that characterizes the tone as an element in a musical context, that makes it a musical phenomenon, its dynamic quality, was absent from our description. And there was reason for its absence. Among the qualities that belong to the tone as an acoustical pheonomenon there is none that is not determined by a particular element of the physical process and only changes, and always changes, if something changes in the physical process. This does not hold for the dynamic quality of tones. Nothing in the physical event corresponds to the tone as a musical event.

Tones can be made visible. The oscilloscope, through electrical processes, transforms vibrations of the air into a picture that appears on an illuminated screen. It is the picture of a wave line. The different tones appear as wave lines of different dimensions and shapes. Everything that characterizes the tone as an acoustical phenomenon is represented in a particular feature of the picture. An experienced observer can accurately read the acoustical qualities of the tone from the outline of the curve. Looking at the picture of the curve, he could accurately represent the tone to himself—pitch, loudness, color, everything. The one thing he could not in any way deduce from the picture is the dynamic state of the tone. Suppose that our Beethoven melody were made visible in this manner, first with the wrong ending, on , and then with the right one, on . The picture would faithfully convey the difference between the two tones and all the characteristics that belong to them as acoustical phenomena; concerning the difference in their state of equilibrium it would show as little as the hands of a clock do concerning the significance of the hours they indicate. There would be no way to draw a conclusion from the picture about the usability or unusability of these tones as concluding tone; the dynamic, the musical difference, does not appear in the curve. If we play the melody on the piano, first in D major, then in C major, the tone D will sound perfectly balanced in the first case, and sharply unbalanced in the second (just like the tone E before). Yet the curve that represents the tone D will be exactly the same in both cases, although the difference between the two D's that we actually hear is hardly less than the difference between standing and falling. While even the slightest difference in the acoustical event instantly appears in a corresponding change in the curve, even the most basic difference in the dynamic state leaves the picture wholly untouched. The dynamic event leaves no trace in the physical process. When we hear a melody, we hear things that have no counterpart in physical nature.

Let us pause for a moment to reflect on what we have said. Since modern science has rid us of any kind of belief in spirits, we no longer doubt that the external world that we perceive is, without any exception, a material world. What we find in it, what our senses permit us to see, hear, feel, are material things and material processes, or at least their direct effects—a color, if you insist, and its basis is a physical process. What our senses show is is a part of the outside world and, as such, belongs in the closed context of physical nature. The nonphysical— thoughts, for example, or feelings, convictions, decisions—exists only in a consciousness, in an inner world, my own or that of some other living creature; it can never be the object of direct sensory perception. Now, however, we say that we hear—that is, perceive in the external world through the sense of hearing—something in the tones of a melody to which nothing in the context of the physical world corresponds. Are not these precisely the words in which one would conventionally characterize an auditory hallucination, a delusion? If one wished, one could call the dynamic quality of tones a hallucination for the very reason that no material process can be co-ordinated with it; but all that this would accomplish would be to leave us faced with the additional difficulty of comprehending the nature and effect of music as the result of vast mass hallucinations, of a mass delusion. No one as yet has seriously proposed this solution. It appears, then, that the very first result of our investigation brings us into sharp conflict with a basic principle of the modern view of the universe: the observation that we hear something in the tones of music which does not fit into the general context of the physical world is irreconcilably opposed to the assertions that our senses are organs for perceiving the physical world and that the world perceived through the senses is physical throughout.

Two theories have been devised to clear this stumbling block from the road: one claims to have discovered the link that after all connects the dynamic qualities of tones to physical processes; the other undertakes to show that in these qualities we are not dealing with processes in the outside world at all. Since this question is of basic importance for the development of our investigation, we must discuss the two theories in greater detail. We shall begin with that which undertakes to demonstrate a physical basis for the dynamic qualities of tones: the Pulse Theory, originally proposed as the theory of tone-rhythms by the psychologist Theodor Lipps.

[. . .]

VI. The Dynamic Symbol

The view here maintained cannot be considered really established so long as we have not disposed of the weightiest argument against it. How do we explain the fact that a Chinese, an Indian, totally unfamiliar with Western music, can no more distinguish between sense and nonsense in our tones than can the tune-deaf person; that he takes the tuning of the orchestra for the beginning of the symphony, has not the most remote idea of what we are talking about when we refer him to the dynamic qualities of tone—but then, years later perhaps, as the result of accumulated experiences and growing familiarity, may reach the point of hearing our music with a comprehension equal to our own? Does not this finding—original incomprehension, comprehension as the result of a process of learning and habituation—seem to justify the associationists and put us in the wrong? If the dynamic qualities were really *in the tones*, then anyone to whom they were pointed out must needs find them there, and immediately, not after long practice, habituation, experience. Perhaps it requires a certain practice to *discover* the outlines of the figures that are hidden in puzzle pictures; but to *see* them, when they are pointed out, requires neither particular practice nor particular experience but simply two good eyes. Thus everyone whose attention is drawn to it hears the difference between high and low, loud and soft, steady and vibrato tones, between the sound of a trumpet and the sound of an oboe—all of them characteristics that are really in the tones and belong

675

to the tones. But when people with good ears and normal minds simply hear *nothing* where we, pointing out certain tones, speak of a distinction between attracting and being attracted, between tension and relaxation, the only conclusion that can possibly be drawn is that the phenomena we cite are not *in* the tones themselves.

This conclusion owes its force simply and solely to the inadequate attention we pay to the little word *in.* It tacitly presupposes that there is only one kind of "being in," of being contained: the material, the physical. Sunspots are *in* the sun, the coffee is *in* the cup, the sugar is *in* the coffee, the chemical element C is *in* the sugar, or sweetness is *in* the sugar, for this kind of "being in" it is true, to be sure, that what one person finds, another must find, and the impersonal measuring instrument must find it too. Whether there are other kinds of "being in," and whether the same conditions of discoverability and demonstrability hold for them as for physical "being in," we do not, at first sight, know at all; one would, rather, tend to deny it. That the dynamic qualities of tone cannot be *in* the tones because no instrument finds them there, because a Chinese or an Indian or indeed an infant, to whom we play our Beethoven melody, will simply hear nothing of a striving of the tone e toward the tone d, however much we may exhort him—the conclusiveness of this dictum rests entirely upon the assumption that physical "being in" is the only possible way of "being in."

It demands no particular subtlety to show how unfounded and indeed arbitrary an assumption this would be. After all, our daily life has made us familiar with various ways of "being in," or being contained. Ideas are in the sentences that we hear or read, and they are certainly not in them physically. Often, for example in a book by a difficult author, the idea is deep in the sentence and hard to extract: a sentence can be understood in various ways, different ideas can be read from it— although, taken physically, it always contains exactly the same letters and groups of letters. We say of a man that there is something sly in his movements; another carries a secret about with him; it is in him, but certainly not physically. The way in which the future organism is contained in the egg can hardly be understood in a purely physical sense. And so on—examples can be multiplied at will.

If we ask ourselves with which of these various kinds of nonmaterial "being in" we have to do in music, the comparison with language will immediately impose itself. Instinctively, when we think of music we think of a language. Like the words of a language, the tones of music are not meaningless sounds and signs; they make sense. We have already

676

emphasized this relationship; we have attempted it, by a comparison with words and their meaning, to make it comprehensible how there can be meaning in the tones of a melody.

Music has often before been interpreted as a language. Since it is of the essence of a language to say something, the question arose: What does music say? The usual answer was: As the words of language have factual meaning, the tones of music have emotional meaning; music is the language of feeling. According to this conception, the musical meaning of our Beethoven melody would lie in its expressing the feeling of joy, with a power far exceeding that of Schiller's poem and of all words. This interpretation cannot be ours. The key to understanding the processes that make the tones of this melody a melody at all, a piece of music, we found not in the relation of the tones to any particular feeling but in the relation of the tone e to the tone d. That the dynamic qualities of tone, in which we recognized the genuine musical element, have nothing to do with the expression of feeling, or with the expression of anything whatsoever, follows from the mere fact that they clearly appear even where absolutely nothing is meant to be expressed or stated, namely, when a scale is played.

Music and language, then, have one thing in common—that tones, like words, have meaning and that the "being in" of the meaning in the word, like that of the musical significance in the tone, is of a nonmaterial nature. But beyond that, the relations that connect the word with its meaning, the tone with its musical significance, are quite different. The word and its meaning are independent things. *Here* is the word—a complex of sounds or signs; *there* is what it means. The two are separable; each exists by itself, the word without the thing, the thing without the word. The same thing is designated in different languages by different words. We can refer to a thing otherwise than through a word—through a symbol, for example, or a sketch. The tone and its meaning, on the other hand, are connected in a far more intimate way. The acoustical event and its musical meaning are in no sense two independent phenomena, existing by themselves. They cannot be imagined separate. To be sure, it is possible to imagine a tone that means nothing, that it is a simple acoustical phenomenon; but it is impossible to imagine the musical meaning of a tone, its dynamic quality, without the tone. The particular state of tension, for example, which we designate by 2 does not exist outside of a tone. What tones mean musically is completely one with them, can only be represented through them, exists only in them. Except in the case of creative language (in the biblical sense of Adam's "naming" things) and of poetic language, where other, more "musical" relations come into play, language always has a finished world of things before it, to which it assigns words; whereas tones must themselves create what they mean. Hence it is possible to translate from one language into another, but not from one music into another—for example, from Western into Chinese music. Hence too the number of words, of the smallest meaning units of language, corresponds roughly to the number of things: languages are rich in words; whereas twelve tones suffice to say everything that has ever been said in our music.

In what sense, then, is the meaning *in* the word? In much the same way as the curve is in the sign ⊘ that warns the motorist of it. Words are signs that refer to particular things; if I understand them, they bring to my knowledge the things they signify. Here we have to deal with three components: the physical sound or written sign, the function of indicating, the thing indicated. Strictly speaking, only the indicating is actually *in* the word, not the thing indicated, the thing meant. Tones too indicate, *point to* something. The meaning of a tone, however, lies not in what it points to but *in the pointing itself*; more precisely, in the different way, in the individual gesture, with which each tone points toward the same place. The meaning is not the thing indicated but the manner of indicating (otherwise all tones would mean the same thing, namely, Î). In words, the indicating is no more than a neutral connecting process between physical sound or written sign and thing signified; in the musical tone the indicating is itself all. In the strictest sense, then, what the tone means is actually and fully contained in the tone itself. Words lead away from themselves; but tones lead into themselves. Words only point toward what they mean, but, beyond that, leave it, so to speak, where it is: the nonmaterial "being in" of the meaning in the word is a mere "being signified." Tones, on the other hand, have completely absorbed their meaning into themselves and discharge it upon the hearer directly in their sound. The nonmaterial "being in" of the meaning in the tone is no mere "being signified"; it is complete, actual presence. The force that gives meaning is in the tone as life is in a face; we see it, we cannot touch it; nonphysical, it is yet one with the physical appearance and cannot appear save through a material medium, which it nevertheless infinitely transcends. When meaning sounds in a musical tone, a nonphysical force intangibly radiates from its physical conveyor.

We find a similar kind of "being in" in the religious symbol. The symbol is the representation of a supermaterial—that is, physically indemonstrable—force in a material form. (We expressly refrain from saying a supersensual or supernatural force, our chief concern being to let music show us that supermaterial is not necessarily also supernatural or supersensual.) The religious symbol is not a sign that merely indicates the divine being to the believer. Rather, the deity is directly present *in* the symbol, is one with it, and is also directly beheld in the symbol by the believer. The believer in the presence of the symbol does not *think* of his god; he does not associate religious *feelings* with the image—association does not enter in at all, otherwise religious experience would be learnable—he apprehends his god in the symbol in a direct perception. He cannot but see him there. Great as the difference between musical tone and religious symbol may be, in this one essential point they are alike: in both, a force that transcends the material is immediately manifested in a material datum. In this very special sense, then, we can speak of the tones of music as *dynamic symbols*. We hear forces in them as the believer sees the divine being in the symbol.

Let us now think back to the objection that the forces cannot be in the tones because many people with normal ears do not hear them there. Do normal eyes suffice to see the god in the symbol? The believer sees him; the unbeliever sees nothing—who is *right?* The believer himself says that the unbeliever can see nothing there. What does disbelief prove against belief? To hear the dynamic qualities of tones requires no particular belief. That they are not physically in the tones, that no instrument would register their presence, is no argument against their existence; it is rather the distinctive character of their existence. To him who opens himself without reservations to symbols, their meaning will gradually become clear of itself. The Chinese who hears mere noise in our music has not yet given the symbols sufficient opportunity to impart to him the significance they contain. But if the opportunity has been present, and still nothing happens, the only conclusion that can be drawn is that, as the result of some obstructive circumstance or other, this one person, although physically his hearing is unimpaired, cannot share in the community of those who hear musically. His musical deafness says neither more nor less against the existence of the dynamic qualities than blindness says against the existence of light, or an absence of metals against the reality of magnetism.

At the beginning of this book we briefly referred to the particular nature of the *audible* in comparison with the data of the other senses. To this we now return.

We do not simply see colors, or light, but colored, illuminated things. We do not touch hardness, smoothness, we do not feel warmth; we touch hard, smooth bodies, feel warm bodies. We do not taste a flavor but a food; do not small an odor but a gas. We do not hear tones but— what?

In seeing, touching, tasting, we reach through the sensation to an object, to a thing. Tone is the only sensation not that of a thing. In the case of color, hardness, odor, we ask, *What* is it that possesses the color, the hardness, the odor? Even in the case of noise we ask, *What* is making it? It is not so with tones. Language makes a very subtle distinction: we say, The leaf is green, the wall is smooth, the honey tastes sweet; but we do not say, The string is g, or the flute sounds d-ish.

Sensations are our answer to the world as given. Seeing, touching, smelling, tasting, we respond to its physicality, its materiality. To what datum of the world do we respond in hearing? Is hearing only a sort of seeing around the corner, seeing in the dark? If noises were all that we heard, hearing could be so interpreted; could be regarded as an auxiliary sense, added to seeing and touching. But there are tones, and there are tones because there is music, not the other way around. Only in tone is that true nature of sound revealed; in the hearing of tones the sense of hearing fulfills its destiny and discovers the side of the world that is its counterpart. Which side is it, since it is *not* the material-factual side? Whatever the answer may be, we know now that the question itself is reasonable; that there is something real to be inquired into in this direction. Because music exists, the tangible and visible cannot be the whole of the given world. The intangible and invisible is itself a part of this world, something we encounter, something to which we respond.

To quote the biologist Jakob von Uexküll: "Where there is a foot, there is also a path; where there is a mouth, there is also nourishment."

VII. The Paradox of Tonal Motion

[. . .]

Musical contexts are *motion* contexts, kinetic contexts. Tones are elements of a musical context because and in so far as they are conveyors of a motion that goes through them and beyond them. When we hear music, what we hear is above all motions.

When motion in music is discussed, we naturally think especially of rhythm. Rhythm seems to us to be the real kinetic element in music. It is the rhythm of a march or of a dance which, as the expression goes, "gets into our legs"; it is the rhythmic power of the performance of a great interpreter which, if the audience were less civilized, would tear them out of their seats. Later we shall discuss the entire complex of rhythmic phenomena; here for the moment we shall leave them out of consideration. Rhythm is not a specifically musical phenomenon. It is the one element which music has in common with other phenomena and processes. The rhythmical instruments in the narrower sense—the percussion instruments, the various drums, cymbals, triangles—are not properly *musical* instruments, since, with the exception of the borderline case of the kettledrum, they produce noises, not tones. But here we are concerned primarily with tones, with the motion that lies in tones as such—with what we called the *ascent* in the opening of the *Marseillaise*. That was prcisely *not* the rhythm, the ever identical rhythm of all marches; it was a motion which, *apart from the rhythm*, we heard in the tones as such. And we must not forget that what *we* call rhythm in music is a comparatively new thing, unknown to antiquity and the Middle Ages. But music has *always* been perceived as motion, entirely independent of whether it possessed rhythm in our sense or not.

It is, in fact, most striking with what uniformity, despite all differences between persons and periods, the idea of motion forced itself upon thinkers and scholars when the question of designating the essential element of music arose.[3] Saint Augustine has little in common with modern experimental psychologists in other respects; but when, in his profound utterances on the subject of music, he describes its nature as *ordered motion*, he and the antique tradition, which he here continues, reach across the millennia to the modern scholars who "hold that, in a study of melody, the focal point must be sought in melodic motion" and to whom "motion appeared to be the essential element."[4] With changing periods, the concept of motion may change its meaning; but nothing changes in the interpretation of music as motion. If in the

[3] The philosophical problem of motion in music is discussed, and sources are quoted, in Kathi Meyer, *Bedeutung und Wesen der Musik.*
[4] Sophie Belaiew-Exemplarsky and Boleslaus Jaworsky, "Die Wirkung des Tonkomplexes bei melodischer Gestaltung."

seventeenth and eighteenth centures all art is held to be imitation, music is held to be the imitation of *the motions of feeling*. If to the earlier Romanticists music stood highest among the arts, it was because they believed that they perceived the mysterious *flow* of life itself in music— here we have a new motion symbol. Hegel speaks of music's task "of echoing the motions of the inmost self," of its power "of penetrating with its motions directly into the inmost seat of all the motions of the soul."[5] The Scientific Age finds its characteristic form of interpreting music as motion: Helmholtz undertakes to refer the effect of music back to its relationship with physical movements.[6] Edmund Gurney, author of a remarkable book, *The Power of Sound*, opposes Helmholtz's view; his musical instinct rejects the attempt to understand music in accordance with the motion of *bodies* but not the use of the concept of motion itself; to him music reveals itself as "ideal motion." Eduard Hanslick's definition of music as "*tönend-bewegte Form*," as "sounding form in motion," is well known. (He was wrong, though, in claiming priority for this idea, as when he wrote: "Though the idea of *motion* appears to us a most far-reaching and important one, it has hitherto been conspicuously disregarded in all enquiries into the nature and action of music."[7] Can it be that his historical knowledge was a imperfect as his artistic judgment?) While Hanslick connected the concept of motion with a shallow and rigid concept of form, we find a far more fruitful linking of the two ideas, form and motion, in the work of the greatest musical theorist of our time, Heinrich Schenker, who understood the musical work of art as a complex kinetic organism.[8] Ernst Kurth, setting out from a different basis and aiming in a different direction, coincides with Schenker in his conclusion that "all musical phenomena rest upon kinetic processes and their inner dynamics."[9] Not only theoreticians, but creative musicians too, are of the same opinion. "Basically, music is not so much sound as motion," writes Roger Sessions in *The Musical*

---

[5] Hegel, *Vorlesungen über die Aesthetik.*
[6] H.L.F. von Helmholtz, *On the Sensations of Tone as a Psychological Basis for the Theory of Music.*
[7] Eduard Hanslick, *The Beautiful in Music*, p. 38.
[8] Heinrich Schenker's principal works are *Neue musikalische Theorien und Phantasien, Der Tonwille*, and *Das Meisterwerk in der Musik*. The most authoritative book in English based on Schenker's theories is Felix Salzer, *Structural Hearing*; cf. also Adele T. Katz, *Challenge to Musical Tradition.*
[9] Ernst Kurth, *Grundlagen des linearen Kontrapunkts* and *Musikpsychologie.*

Experience of Composer, Performer, Listener. To conclude, let us hear a contemporary aesthetician and a contemporary psychologist. "Auditory movement [of a melody]," says Carroll C. Pratt, "as well as visual and kinesthetic, is an immediate fact of direct experience." [10] And in Erwin Straus' *Vom Sinn der Sinne* we read: "The unity of music and motion is primordial, not artificial, not contrived, and not learned."

But it is not only these and similar statements by authoritative thinkers and scholars which we can adduce in support of our contention that music is motion. From a direction whence we should not have expected it, from the side of exact measurement, comes confirmation that we do not deceive ourselves if we interpret the direct musical experience as an experience of motion.

In the first section of this book we spoke of the practical but somewhat crude compromise represented by the tuning of such an instrument as our piano, with its division of the octave into twelve equal half tones. The differences between this compromise, the so-called *equal temperament* and the *just intonation*, which rejects the compromise and which, for instance, a violinist would prefer, are audible to very acute ears, but are so slight that they lie below the threshold of disturbance. Hence the problems involved are of technical and scientific rather than artistic interest. And it was a purely scientific, a psychological problem, in no way connected with the matters that here concern us, which started the experiments we shall now discuss. Their object was to determine if people who sing tend more to equal temperament or to just intonation. To this end, it was only necessary to have the same melody sung by a number of people and to register their tones by a measuring instrument, such as an oscilloscope.

The result of these measurements was highly unexpected. It went so far beyond the limits of the original question as to render it meaningless. What appeared was that the singers sang neither in just intonation nor in equal temperament—they simply sang unimaginably off pitch. And this was equally true of all the singers, trained and untrained, unmusical and highly musical. The scale of measurement employed was as follows: the difference in pitch between two adjacent tones of the tempered chromatic scale was rated as 100,—so that, beginning with c = 0, we get c sharp-d flat = 100, d = 200, d sharp-e flat = 300, e = 400, etc. For every possible pitch, then, between c and c sharp, the instrument shows

[10] Carroll C. Pratt, *The Meaning of Music.*

a particular number between 0 and 100, and so on. According to this scale of measurement, the difference between the tempered and just intonation of a tone lies within the average magnitude of 10. For example: tempered d = 200, pure d = 204; tempered e = 400, pure e = 386. Translated into the language of the measuring instrument, the questions posed by the investigation were, for example: Does the singer at this place tend to produce the tone 300 or the tone 316, at this other place the tone 500 or the tone 493? The answer given by the merciless instrument, from which there was no appeal, was neither 300 nor 316, but 238; neither 500 nor 493, but 586. Tones which lay far closer to the adjacent tone of the chromatic scale than to the tone actually to be sung! Such facts can no longer be discussed in terms of poor intonation; the singers simply sang different notes from those which the text prescribed.[11]

As an answer to the original question, then, the result was valueless. Instead, it brought a very different and much more interesting situation to light. It became evident, that is, that the great discrepancies always appeared where a rise or fall of the melody was clearly marked, and that, in the majority of cases, the *direction* of the discrepancy followed the upward or downward direction of the melody. The impression is inescapable that the movement of the melody seizes upon the tones and carries them with it. (Exceptions to this norm are always to be explained by the particular situation in each case.) Motion establishes itself as a real factor in music by producing tangible, measurable effects.

But the most significant thing about the result of this experiment is the fact that is required the intervention of the measuring instrument to reveal these grotesque distortions of pitch, these false tones. The audience, which included experienced musicians, had not noticed them at all. So long as one is, so to speak, alone with music, so long as there is simply singing on the one side and listening on the other, there is no consciousness that anything is wrong. It is not until physics intervenes, with its measuring instruments, that the false tones are brought to light—to the surprise of the investigators, to the astonishment of the musicians. But what do "wrong" and "false" mean here—where obviously, so long as the approach is purely musical, so long as no measurements are undertaken, everything is right and nothing wrong or false? For what is musically right, musically wrong, the court of last appeal is the ear of the musician, not the physicist's apparatus. If the

[11]Otto Abraham, "Tonometrische Untersuchungen an einem deutschen Volkslied."

same ear, under other circumstances, immediately and unfailingly perceives discrepancies that are mere fractions of those here established, and yet hears nothing wrong here, this means neither more nor less than that right or wrong in music is not a matter of pitch as such but of pitch in relation to the direction of motion. The acoustically wrong tone can be musically right if the deviation is right in the sense of the movement. It cannot, then, be simply tones as such, tones of a predetermined pitch, which we sing or hear in melodies; it is motions represented in tones. Whatever else music may be, one thing it must be: motion.

Thus buttressed by the concurrent testimony of direct experience, of philosophic speculation, and of measurement, we shall now ask ourselves a series of questions that will shake our conviction that music is motion and dispose us to recognize that it was the result of self-deception, of an illusion.

To hear a melody, we said, means to hear a motion. But can one *hear* motion? To see motion, to touch motion, is comprehensible—but to *hear* motion? Certainly we hear the approach and departure of the band playing the *Marseillaise* out in the street. But this—the motion of the musicians and their instruments—is not the motion we have in mind; we mean the motion of the music: the ascent of the melody, for which it is immaterial whether the musicians are marching or sitting down.

Motion always implies something that moves, that is in motion. A bird flies past. A snowflake falls to the ground. To speak of motion makes sense only when something is present that moves. What is it that moves in a melody?

It will be answered: the tones. But is a tone something that can move? What moves is objects, things—and have we not shown that the tones of music are precisely *not* that, are not like things, are not like objects, and have no reference to things and objects? And now are they suddenly to do what only things do—to move?

Something moves—first it is here, then there. This means it is *the same* something, the same thing, which at different moments appears at different places. The thing that remains the same is the indispensable and permanent core of the phenomenon of motion.

What is the permanent core of a tonal motion, the particular something that always remains the same during the course of the motion? To be sure, when we discuss tonal motion we tacitly assume that there actually is such a permanent core of the phenomenon, a real entity "tone" which performs the motion, which, during the course of the melody is to be found first here, then there, and so on. What meaning could the expression "tonal motion" have otherwise? But at every attempt really to grasp this entity "tone," it vanishes in our hands: it is a mere abstraction. We can think it, but we cannot hear it.

Furthermore, motion implies not only something that move but also something that does not move, or moves differently: a background, a frame. The bird flies through the sky; the snowflake falls past the aperture of the window frame. To talk of motion, then, means to talk of two things and their mutual relation. What may this second thing be in a melody? To hear tones means to hear nothing but tones; besides the tones, there is nothing else, no background, no frame, before which they might move.

But do they move at all? Actually, they standstill! In the *Marseillaise*, for example, we hear the first tone 🎵 — it does not move; then comes 🎵 , another static tone; this one is repeated; then comes 🎵 ; and so on. No tone, so long as it sounds, moves from its place. What has happened to the motion? When we said earlier that a thing in motion is now here, now there, now elsewhere, the essence of the matter was certainly not the being here and being elsewhere but what occurred *in between*, the connection, the transition: motion is the process that *conveys* the thing from here to there, in a continuous and never suspended traversal of the interval. If it stops anywhere, the motion is instantly abolished. But in melody we have nothing but this, nothing but stops, a stringing together of static tones, and, between tone and tone, *no* connection, *no* transition, *no* filling up of intervals, nothing. It is the exact opposite of motion. And if we attempt actually to connect tone with tone, to create transitions, to fill up the intervals completely, taking real motion as our model, the result is the familiar screeching glissade of the siren, in which melody and music are destroyed.

In music, then, there is nothing that can move, nothing in relation to which anything can move; there is nothing but tones— and they do not move; indeed, when they actually begin moving, the music vanishes. Under these circumstances, how much sense does it make to speak of music as tonal motion?

For various reasons this question has greatly interested psychologists. We shall briefly summarize the essential points that have been brought forward *against* the argument just outlined.

Certainly tones, if only because they are not things, cannot, like things, occupy positions in space and move from place to place. But to conclude from this that it makes no sense to speak of tonal motion is at least overhasty. Rather, we are here confronted with a phenomenon of motion unique in its kind. Different tones are always also tones of different *pitch*. In fact, among sense perceptions, the distinguishing characteristic of tones is that they differ like two colors, green and blue, *and* like two shades of a single color, light green and dark green; like two tactile sensations, rough and round, *and* like a greater or lesser degree of roughness or roundness. Pitch is a characteristic of such a nature that it both *distinguishes* different tones from one another and at the same time *orders* them in a definite way: tones can be arranged in a series according to pitch as people can be according to height. And this is not an abstract or computed characteristic—as, for example, the vibration numbers of colors are—but a characteristic directly given, perceptible to the senses. Just as normally we do not have to compute and measure in order to determine which of two people standing side by side is the taller and which the shorter, so we do not have to know anything about frequencies and string lengths in order to know at once and unequivocally, to know *by hearing*, which of two tones is the higher and which the lower. Every child to whom the difference is pointed out understands what is meant and can immediately apply the distinction correctly to other cases; whereas the statement that violet is "higher" than blue has little meaning for direct visual experience and does not help one answer other questions, for example, whether blue is higher or lower than green. If, then, tones are not like things, each of which has its particular place in space, every tone nevertheless has its particular pitch, its particular place in tonal space. Differences in tone are always differences in pitch also, and a succession of different tones is always and definitely also a becoming higher or lower, a rise or fall. The quality of motion in music is saved. What we hear as motion in a succession of tones is the rise and fall of the tones in tonal space.

This attempt to save the situation is ephemeral. The counter-argument is that when we speak of a rise and fall of tones as of a real motion, we have simply become victims of a primitive verbal and emotional suggestion.

We say, one tone is higher than another. Why do we use that word "higher" to express the difference? Is there anything *actually* higher about one of the tones than the other? The head of the note is higher on the staff; the singer's larynx is higher in his throat, and often it even draws his whole upper body up with it in a manner unpleasant to behold; the violinist's hand slides up and down (but the cellist's hand slides down and up, the pianist's from side to side); certain bodily sensations of vibration, on the part of the listener, called forth by different tones are supposedly localized at different heights in the body. But in all this we are merely talking about conventional signs in musical notation, about physiological processes connected wit the production and perception of tone—not about tones themselves. Is it possible that, misled by the permanent association of tones with spatial symbols and bodily movements, we have simply carried over the spatial meaning of high and low into our distinguishing of pitches? How else are we to understand the fact that other languages make the same distinction by entirely different words—Greek, for example, by sharp and heavy, English, together with high and low, by sharp and flat? (But in no language would it be said that the fourth floor of a house was sharper than the third, the first flatter than the second.) Let this be clearly understood: it is not intended to deny the presence of the characteristic that permits the arrangement of tones in a series, nor that it is a genuine characteristic of tones, directly perceptible to the ear, not an illusion. What is denied is the *true spatiality* of the characteristic, the assumption that the word *height* in connection with tone is anything more than a metaphor. Suppose that children were taught to distinguish tones not by high and low but by thick and thin, or by light and dark—would anything in these words contradict the phenomena? We are here confronted with a unique characteristic of aural perception, which can only be described metaphorically by words from the realms of the other senses. Talking about the rise and fall of tones is using a metaphor, and nothing more.

The argument over the spatiality of tonal motion fills volumes. It has led to many interesting sidelights, but not to any conclusive result. The negative and affirmative statements remain irreconcilably opposed. Many scholars take a sort of middle position and grant pitch differences a spatiality that, though less than real, is still more than merely metaphorical. The most thorough and conscientious scholar in this field, Karl Stumpf, who was greatly concerned to grant tones real spatiality, thinks that he can say no more than that, in the differentiation of tones by high and low, we have "gradation in an absolute direction." [12] That the gradation is spatial in the direct sense, he could not conclusively show. In general, the closer an investigator is to music, the more he will tend to maintain the genuine spatiality of high and low in tones—very probably on the ground that he sees no other possibility of explaining the compelling impression of motion that music conveys to anyone

[12]Karl Stumpf, *Tonpsychologie.*

musical. But with this the discussion has become a circle. We set out by asking upon what the impression of motion conveyed by a melody is based; the answer was, on the rise and fall of tones in tonal space. Now we ask what justifies us in calling a succession of tones of different pitches a rise and fall; and we answer, the impression of motion conveyed by melodies demands it! In any case, the reality of tonal motion in music, of which wc were so convinced before, had now become wholly problematic.

[. . .]

IX. The Continuity of Tonal Motion

The first stage of the road that we hope will lead us to clarifying the concept of musical motion lie behind us. We have saved tonal motion from being identified with "up" and "down" in tonal space and from being rejected when it appeared that these terms could not be interpreted literally. We are now at the beginning of the second stage, in which a more formidable obstacle remains to be overcome: the problem of the continuity of tonal motion.

We use the term continuous in reference to a process that leads from one state to another in an uninterrupted transition. In contrast, the discontinuous process takes place in jumps; we can find gaps in it. The rise and fall of temperature is a continuous process; in the transition from one degree of heat to another all the intervening degrees of heat are traversed. The transition can be gradual and even, or sudden and uneven; but in no case will it exhibit gaps. We have an example of discontinuity in the process of biological mutation, the appearance of new species or subspecies; this takes place suddenly, at one jump, not as the result of a development that passes through all the intervening stages. The series of all possible tones is continuous—the siren passes through it; the series of overtones is discontinuous.

It is an old article of belief that nature makes no jumps. The principal support of this belief was the conviction that all natural phenomena could be referred back to motions of bodies. For motion, a thing changing place, is obviously a continuous process. One does not get from one place to another without passing through all the intervening places; the motion traverses the space between one place and the other in an uninterrupted transition. The path it follows, the track it leaves behind in space, is an unbroken line—hence the line is the graphic symbol of motion. If a thing changes place without having traversed the interval between its former and latter place uninterruptedly, we have not motion but a miracle.

Not only will a thing in motion from one place to another skip none of the intervening places; it will also halt in none of them. If it did so, the motion would at once be at an end; its contrary, rest, would have appeared. Motion, then, has no gaps and no halts. These are the distinguishing characteristics of its continuity; they belong to it as weight to mass, luminosity to light. Motion without continuity is inconceivable.

How does the case stand with tonal motion?

Let us go back to the melody of our first example:

, etc. What do we hear—a progress advancing in uninterrupted continuity or an alternation of skips and halts, a discontinuous progress? There can be no doubt about the answer: we could not hear the melody as motion if we did not hear it as continuous. Casting about for a graphic symbol for our experience, we will instinctively draw a curve, thus perhaps ⌒⌣ , an unbroken line in any case, such as one would use anywhere to picture a continuous process. Now, does such a line faithfully render what actually occurs in tonal motion?

We know that it does not. Let us look at what takes place in the melody just cited. The tone f sharp sounds: so long as it continues, it does not move from its place, does not change its pitch; it is directly succeeded by the tone g, which, as long as it sounds, shows as little alteration as the preceding tone; in the same manner as the tone A follows; and so on. There is no question of any transitions, whether gradual or sudden; tone stands beside tone without connection. A faithful graphic representation of what takes place would have to look like this (line length signifies duration of the individual tone):

$$— \; {}^{-}{}^{-} \; {}^{-}{}_{-} \; {}_{-}{}_{-} \; {}_{-}{}^{-}{}^{-} \; {}_{\cdot} —$$

Where is the continuously progressing line, the symbol of continuity in motion? Stasis-gap-stasis-gap; our graph is the perfect image of discontinuity. One is at a loss to understand how *this* can ever be heard as a continuous process.

Similar contradictions between acoustical data and musical experiences, which we encountered earlier, were resolved when it appeared that other than acoustical processes, namely, dynamic processes, were the basis of musical experiences. But, this time, such an interpretation does not help, because the dynamic qualities change, so to speak, in step with the tones, in sudden jumps and without transition. So that, whether our question is directed to pitches or to dynamic qualities, the result is the same: it appears that we absurdly apply the term motion to a collection of stases and gaps.

We are, however, familiar with one case in which this very absurdity takes place, in which stases and gaps compose motion: the case of the moving picture. The individual picture in the film shows nothing but stasis. It is a cross section of a train of motion, and between section and section, close together as they may be, there is a gap in the train. But if the film is unrolled before us at the proper rate of speed, the eye supplies the missing transitions, the gaps are filled, the discontinuous series of static pictures becomes a continuous train of motion. Certainly, the continuity that thus appears is not given in the thing itself, it is simply imagined, is an illusion; the motion we see is an illusory motion. Nevertheless, the illusion is not a matter of choice; it is inescapable, it obeys a law, under certain conditions it necessarily occurs. Is not this exactly the same thing that occurs in our melody: the individual tones that do not move from their places, the gaps between tone and tone, and the impression of motion that necessarily follows when the tones pass before us at the correct rate of speed—discontinuity that produces an illusion of continuity? In the last analysis, then, is tonal motion to be interpreted as an illusion after all?

The parallel holds only superficially. The aim and the accomplishment of the film consist in creating an illusion of gaps being filled. The creation of the illusion depends upon the extent of the gaps between the pictures and upon the tempo of their succession; if the gaps are too great, or if the tempo is too slow, the illusion of motion becomes poorer and finally collapses completely, the deception becomes visible. Can one say the like of melody? Does melody perhaps achieve the impression of motion by creating an *illusion* of gradual transitions between tone and tone, of the gaps between pitches being filled? Do we imagine that we hear such transitions, such sliding connections between tone and tone, when we hear melodic motion? All this is out of the question. Does increasing the intervals between pitches, or slowing down the tempo, perhaps influence the perception of motion? Then the illusion must be better, more complete, in the case of our Beethoven melody, with its flowing connection of tones that lie close together, than, for example, in the following fugue theme by Bach, ♪♫♪♩ in which there are great gaps between tones and the tempo is exceedingly slow. Nobody would make such an assumption. Experience teaches that the perception of musical motion is (within reasonable limits) independent of the size of the intervals and the tempo. On the other hand, an actual filling of the gaps between tone and tone, a sirenlike glissading up and down, does not produce the most perfect musical motion but no musical experience at all; it produces mere noise.

The result is even more convincing if, instead of pitches, we consider dynamic qualities. Here there can be no question of filling gaps, of continuous transitions, either actually or as illusion. Is a connecting transition conceivable from the state of attraction to that of being attracted? From the pointing gesture peculiar to the tone $\hat{2}$ to that peculiar to the tone $\hat{3}$? The differences between tonal dynamic qualities are not of the nature of gaps that can be filled by transitions. Melodic and cinematographic motion are incomparable, not only because melody neither achieves nor seeks to produce an illusion of continuous transitions but because among dynamic qualities, upon which the experience of musical motion is based, continuity as uninterrupted transition from one state to another is not even thinkable.

The difference between tonal motion and illusory motion is carried to the extreme in an interesting musical phenomenon: the *rest*. We find rests in music not only at caesuras, not only where a longer or shorter context comes to an end and where, as a result, rests actually mean "interruption"; they also appear within continuous contexts, where they function not as punctuation but as real elements in the context, just like tones themselves. Such a rest does not interrupt the continuing motion of the melody; the motion goes on through it: a void, a nothing, becomes the conveyor of motion. If for example, the theme of another of Bach's fugues begins ♪♫♪♩, the rest does not separate the first two tones from the third (anyone who plays it thus ♪♫♪ talks nonsense with tones); instead, one continuous course of motion runs through tones and rest, ♪♫♪♩. So little is heard motion an illusion, a conjuring up of something where nothing is, that the frank recognition of the fact "nothing" does not cause the slightest break in the experience of motion.

The last way of escape from the dilemma—and one which is often chosen—we have already closed. It is the association and projection theory. For the followers of this theory there is no difficulty; like the dynamic qualities of tone, they hold, the experiences of motion based upon them are the "subjective" product of the listener, "produced representations," inner events released by outer events and projected back into them. To be sure, these authors write of melodies ascending, hovering, descending; but they never fail to tell us that it is only we, the listeners, who ascend, hover, descend, and not the tones. What we call motion here, they say, is a purely psychological phenomenon, and any contradiction to the data of the external world need trouble us as little as that between our dreams of flying and the conditions for flight that we encounter in our waking state.

We need not repeat the arguments against these theories. The attempt to relegate musical phenomena to the subjective realm must come to grief before the facts of tonal motion as it does before the facts of the dynamic qualities of tone.

(This rejection does not refer to theories like that of the psychologist Melchior Palágyi, according to which "perception of motion is bound up with living participation in the motion; without this there could be no perception of a motion."[13] There is an immense difference between saying that in hearing music we inwardly enact the motion of the tones, accomplish it in living participation, and saying that we first generate such a motion in ourselves, as a reaction product to some outside stimulus or other, and then project it outside ourselves. The one statement does not affect the reality of music; the other dissipates it as a phantom.)

There is, then, no escape. Every motion is a continuous process; no succession of tones in music is a continuous process; no succession of tones in music can be in motion. The unassailable logic of this syllogism stands in complete and preclusive opposition to the definition of music as tonal motion. The concept of tonal motion seems finally to be shipwrecked on the problem of continuity.

Philosophical Considerations

Let us think back: How did we reach this point? It was the certainty of direct experience which caused us to refer to music as motion of tones. Musical experiences had to be admitted to the great group of phenomena that we call motion. There were no difficulties, no irreconcilables; on

[13]Palágyi, *Wahrnehmungslehre.*

the contrary, the heard and the seen, tonal motion and material motion, joined for our consciousness in sisterly agreement.

Difficulties began only when reflection entered in. Now contradictions appeared—not between experience and experience but between experience and concept. Our concept of motion, derived from the data of material motion (continued change of place by a thing which remains the same), refused to fit the data of tonal motion. In the case of such a conflict between an experience and a concept authorized by science and generally accepted, we habitually distrust the experience and assume an illusion or an error. This is what has happened in our case. The standard of the generally accepted concept of motion has been applied to the experience of musical motion; since the two could not be reconciled, the assumption of a tonal motion was judged highly problematic if not impossible.

But something essential was overlooked in this. Zeno of Elea had been forgotten. It had been forgotten that there is a *problem* of motion. As a standard, a concept was used that had nothing of the reliability of a standard. The experience of motion in music was held to be highly problematic because it did not correspond to a concept that itself is highly problematic.

Most certainly it did not take music to reveal irresolvable contradictions between reflection and experience in the realm of motion. The difficulty is as old as the search for a conceptual understanding of the universe. The earliest Greek philosophers found themselves faced with it—and did not solve it. "Emancipated thought," writes Oswald Spengler, "was shipwrecked on the problem of motion."[14] Lack of experience in logical training cannot be held responsible for this failure, because two thousand years later such a master of the arts of logic as Leibniz could find no other way of saving the concept of motion except the assumption that the thing in motion is destroyed every instant and created anew by God—an expectation in the face of which one feels inclined to prefer the old Eleatic's solution and hold that the whole universe of motion is an illusion.

Such, then, is the reliability of the standard which it is sought to apply to tonal motion. If tonal motion is problematic, then material motion is certainly not less so. Indeed, it is so on perfectly analogous grounds; it appears that, for reflection, the indigestible kernel in both experiences is the same: continuity.

[14]Spengler, *The Decline of the West*, Vol. I, ch. 1.

A discussion of the problem of continuity, even in outline, would go far beyond the limits of this book as well as the competence of its author. The following is an attempt, with the aid of a simple example, to obtain a view of the central difficulty.

A body in motion traverses a certain distance in a certain time. The velocity of a motion is measured by the length of the distance traversed per time unit. We compare two motions at different velocities, that of an automobile and that of a pedestrian:

Distance traveled in

	1 hr.	1 min.	1 sec.	1/1000 sec.
Automobile	60 km.	1000 m.	16.6 m.	16.6 m.
Pedestrian	6 km.	100 m.	1.66 m.	1.66 m.

However small the time interval, and with it the spatial distance, becomes, the one distance always remains ten times the other: the speed of the car is ten times that of the pedestrian.

Both motions are continuous processes; that is, they stop at no point and skip no point in their course. We may therefore meaningfully ask: What distance does the car traverse in the shortest conceivable time, in an instant? The answer must be, the shortest conceivable distance, the distance from one point of its course to the directly adjacent point. For if the distance were only minutely longer, there would be, between the point where it begins and the point where it ends, at least *one* point, which, for the sake of continuity of the motion, could not be skipped and which the vehicle must needs enter *before* it enters the point that marks the end of the distance—that is, after a time shorter than the shortest conceivable time, which is nonsense. But we arrive at exactly the same answer if we put the same question for the pedestrian: of his motion too it is true that, in the shortest conceivable time, he traverses the shortest conceivable distance. Now the difference has vanished: the automobile and the pedestrian traverse the same distance in the same time; they move with the same speed. Like Achilles and the tortoise, the automobile can never catch up with the pedestrian, to say nothing of passing him.

Thinkers of all ages have been concerned to reconcile this contradiction between irrefutable logic and irrefutable observation. In our context Henri Bergson's attempt is of decisive significance. [15] It began a new epoch in the history of the problem of motion. Following Bergson, we should reason thus:

What do we do when we measure the velocity of moving bodies? We observe, for example, 1:15 P.M.—automobile at point A of the street; 1:16 P.M.—automobile at point B of the street; length of the section of the street between A and B, 1000 meters; elapsed time 1 minute. What has become of the *motion*? We have established a time frame. We have measured a distance. Of the thing in motion we have said nothing except that it is first in one place, then in another. To be in one place, to be in another—is that motion? A moving thing is not in this place and not in that place; it is *on the way* from place to place. To be in motion does not mean to be first here, then there; it means to be on the way from here to there. The basic schema of the process must, in addition to providing for "here" and "there," provide for "on the way"—thus, for example, "place I between I place." As we see, we cannot make up motion out of one thing, two places, and "to be at"; the "between" is lacking, the real, vital element of motion. But in our measurement we were dealing only with "thing," "place," and "to be at"; the being on the way, the transition, precisely what takes place in the "between" and which is the flesh and blood of the process of motion, was omitted.

The measuring process can be schematically represented somewhat like this:

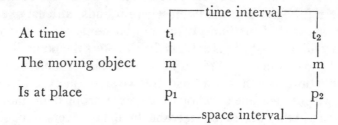

This is still perfectly acceptable—or better, the difficulty has not yet appeared, for the very good reason that the time interval t_1-t_2 is large enough to leave room for a "between" between the corresponding p_1 and p_2. The picture changes, however, when we bring the shortest conceivable length of time into consideration. Now the schema looks like this:

---

[15] The problem of motion is discussed in his *Essai sur les données immédiates de la conscience, Matière et mémoire, Creative Evolution*, and *Durée et simultanéitée*.

shortest conceivable
time interval

| |

t_1 t_2

| |

m m

| |

p_1 p_2

shortest conceivable
space interval

Another point cannot be inserted between p_1 and p_2; otherwise it would not be the shortest conceivable space interval, nor, consequently, would t_1–t_2 be the shortest conceivable time interval. The "between" has vanished. And without a "between" in which it can develop, no motion is possible.

These are not logical tricks, intended to confuse the mind. Things move in space. Space has no gaps. The course the moving thing follows is a line in space, a continuous series of places. Motion thus actually takes place through such shortest conceivable and, so to speak, "betweenless" distances. How are we to understand that motion can develop at all; that space does not nip it in the bud?

The "between" that finally disappears in this measuring process is a "between places," an interspace. But who is to tell us that the "between" from which motion lives is precisely that: an inter*space*? If "place | between | place" is the schema of the process of motion, then the between *cannot* be interspace. Space is a continuous chain of places, and every interspace is likewise to be thought of as continuously filled with places. "Thus "place | between | place" would have to become "place | place | place | place | place"—the image of perpetual stasis, the negation of motion. However, from this it by no means necessarily follows that motion *is* impossible, must be mere illusion; but that it *would be* so if its "between" were nothing but "between places," interspace. Consequently, it *cannot be* inter*space*.

Thus we recognize the error into which Zeno and his successors fell. Without further consideration, they equated the "between" of motion with interspace. They assumed that the process of motion could be entirely comprehended in spatial data; in Bergson's language, they failed to maintain the distinction between motion and its spatial track, the *path* traveled. Now, everything that was true of the spatial path of

697

motion had also to be true of motion itself; nothing might be true of motion that was not also true of its spatial path. The contradictions and paradoxes thus arrived at cannot, however, serve as proof of the intrinsically contradictory character of motion; on the contrary, they merely show that motion *cannot* be entirely comprehended in spatial-local data. It is precisely the essential element of motion which slips through the net of spatial relations—and the more surely, the tighter the net is drawn. If thought perpetually brings us back to a point where it appears that space, as an uninterrupted chain of places, inevitably robs motion of the breath of life, then we can only conclude that motion draws its life elsewhere than from the space of places. If things and places do not suffice to make us understand the process of motion, the this process must in some essential aspect extend beyond the realm of things and places. Rightly understood, what Zeno's paradoxes teach is that the stage on which motion is enacted cannot be—or cannot be only—the space of places. Motion must be something else than things changing place; it must also occur—and perhaps occur essentially—where no more things change their places.

Is all this merely empty playing with ideas? We shall let a psychologist answer the question for us.

Psychological Considerations

The problem of motion is presented to the psychologist in the form of the question, How is motion perceived? How do I see, how do I feel, a motion?

The older psychology sought to understand all psychological phenomena, including sensation and sense perception, after the pattern of physical phenomena, that is, mechanistically and atomistically. A phenomenon was supposed to be understood when, in thought, one had succeeded in reducing it to its elements and reconstructing it from its elements. The phenomenon of seeing a motion was schematically conceived more or less as follows:

To see means to react to light stimuli. The elements of seeing are the individual sensations that are aroused when light rays fall upon cells of the retina. A bundle of light rays stimulates a spot on the retina: I see a thing in a place. The same bundle of light rays successively stimulates adjacent spots on the retina: I see the same thing successively in adjacent places; I see the thing in motion. The same holds for the sense of touch: to feel motion means to feel the same tactile sensation first at one spot on the skin, then successively at adjacent spots on the skin. According to this, perception of motion would be a complex phenomenon, the elements that go to make it up being successive perceptions of the same thing at different places.

The similarity between this way of conceiving motion and the procedure for measuring velocity is obvious. Hence it is not surprising that, in both cases, the same problem arises. The older psychology explains how we see "thing now here," "thing now there"; but it does *not* explain how we see "thing *on the way* from here to there." The transition, the "between," the very core of the process, is again not accounted for in the explanations.

In opposition to the older mechanistic theories, William James maintains the primordiality and immediacy of perception of motion; he saw in it not the result of collocating various elementary data but *one* elementary datum, and indeed, in a certain sense, *the* elementary datum of perception. "We have the feeling of motion," he writes, "given us as a direct and single sensation . . . it [motion] is the most immediate of all our space sensations." [16] He denies that, in order to see or feel motion, we must see or feel a thing first in one place, then in another, and then somehow fill in the transition mentally. In support of his view he cites the following observation:

The skin's sensitivity for localizing a contact is different in different parts of the body. The distance between two contacts that are actually to be felt as contacts *at two different points* must be greater at some parts of the body than at others. If, for example, a fingertip is touched with the points of a pair of calipers set about one centimeter apart, the subject clearly feels two contacts. The same contact on the thigh produces only *one* sensation; the two stimuli flow together; they are too close to each other; the skin at this part of the body is not sensitive enough to separate them locally. This means that two places one centimeter apart here pass as *one* place. But if, on the same spot, the caliper points are moved even at little as one millimeter, motion is immediately and unmistakably perceived. So motion is still registered even when the sense organ is no longer capable of registering differences in place: the perception of motion does not result from the perception of a thing at different places.

[16] William James, "The Perception of Space."

A still more radical departure from the mechanistic view has been achieved by Gestalt psychology. Its principal contribution to the discussion of motion is Max Wertheimer's "Experimentelle Studien über das Sehen von Bewegung." The results of this study are of the most immediate concern for our purpose, the understanding of tonal motion.

The concrete question with which Wertheimer's study deals may be simply formulated as follows: against a dark background, two narrow oblongs that meet at a right angle are alternately illuminated at different rates of speed. What is seen?

The answer is sought and found in a long series of experiments. First of all three "distinct phases" appear. When the rate of speed is slow, that is, when the two oblongs are illuminated at intervals of 1/5 second and more, both are successively seen at rest, first ⎸ , then ⊂⊃ . When the rate of speed is rapid—interval about 1/30 second and less—both oblongs are simultaneously seen at rest, ⌊ . At an intermediate rate of speed—about 1/15 second—one oblong is seen to *turn* from one position to the other, ⌊↘ . This is the case of the moving picture, illusory motion.

Now what happens if we gradually change the speed of the succession from one of these "phases" to another? What takes place in the transition from the middle phase, in which we see a thing in motion, to one of the two extremes, in which we see two things at rest, successively or simultaneously? Since the production of the illusion of motion in the middle phase depends upon the speed of the succession, we should suppose that a change in speed would impair the conditions for the illusion; that the result would be simply a more imperfect, vaguer impression of motion. But something entirely different happens.

If the speed of the succesion is raised a little above the middle stage—the stage favorable to the production of the illusory motion—what appears is not a vague intermediate stage between one thing in motion and two things at rest; we see, with perfect precision, *two things and*, equally precisely, we see *motion*, ⌊↘ . We see the same motion as before, and we see the oblong at the beginning and the oblong at the end as *two different things*. The impression of motion is preserved, but the identity of the moving thing, its remaining the same, ceases! We see motion that, paradoxically, is no longer motion of one and the same thing, motion that does not require that its conveyor remain the same. The thing that emerges from the motion is different from the thing that entered into it.

Let is continue and increase the tempo further. Again the impression of motion is not lessened; but the motion breaks apart in the middle; we get it in two sections, thus, ⌐ . If the tempo is further accelerated these sections become smaller and smaller until finally the two oblongs stand motionless together. If in this intermediate phase we concentrate on one of the two oblongs, we see it perform its section of the motion alone while the other remains at rest, ⌐ . Often we see only one oblong perform its section of the motion; the other has vanished entirely, e.g., ⌐ . In the face of these observations, what becomes of the doctrine that perception of motion is made up of several successive perceptions of a thing at different places; that seeing motion must somehow be understood as a filling of gaps in perception or sensation? In each separate case of these sectional motions, where would be the successive perceptions of the thing at different places; where would be the gaps between them? Each of these sectional motions is based on only *one single* perception of "thing at place"; the motion flows into it or runs out of it. Where the one motion stops, ⌐ , where the other begins, ⌐ , there is nothing in a place, nor is anything seen in a place. If we want to apply the basic schema "place I between I place" here, we should have to drop one or the other of the two cornerstones; what we see here could at best be characterized as "place I between," or "between I place." (If we reverse the procedure and, starting from the intermediate speed, slow down the tempo instead of accelerating it, analogous phenomena result.)

As for the manner in which motion itself appears, the event in the "between," these experiments have clearly shown that "moving is something different from being successively in successive places."[17] The seeing of motion is *not* a seeing of intermediate positions, of a traversal of intermediate places by the moving thing. Even in the case of the complete illusion, when the one oblong is clearly seen first in the starting position, then in the transition, finally in the end position, motion is never motion *of the oblong*. We see motion passing over the background; we do not see a moving thing passing over the background: "The oblong was seen in the first and the final position, motion in between, no intermediate positions, the oblong did not pass through the field, the background remained completely undisturbed, but the motion passes over. . . . I saw a strong motion, but had no impression of objects.

---

[17]Wertheimer, "Experimentelle Studien."

... I saw a strong motion, but had no impression of objects. ... I see motion, not *something* passing by. ... There was simply motion, not referable to an object. ... " Such are the concurring testimonies of the observers. If the time of the flash that illuminates the oblongs is further shortened, the first and final positions are no longer clearly perceived, but the impression of motion remains unimpaired. The actual datum— oblong first in one position, then in another—is now practically not seen; but where there is no datum, in the empty field between the oblongs, something is seen: motion. Now the basic schema "place | between | place" has lost *both* its cornerstones; *only* "between" is seen, pure "between," pure passage. The motion that thus appears cannot be classified as a thing; freed from all connection with things, it bears the same relation to the so-called conveyor of motion as the electric current in the wire bears to the telephone pole.

Nothing would be simpler than to class all these phenomena offhand as optical illusions, than to say that since we see motion where, "in reality," nothing moves, it can only be a matter of our being deceived by our senses. One may adopt this standpoint—if one wants at all costs to block the road to understanding of these things. Certainly one can say it is an illusion when a stick held under water looks bent at the surface; but to say this is only to say something about oneself, about our own narrow perspective, which, out of the whole universe, sees nothing, can see nothing, but the stick; which is unable to conceive that such an image might relate to something else, might contain a statement about something other than the stick. The stick is straight, so the image of it as bent must be an illusion. The image is dumb, it can only present itself; if we attribute false statements to it, something that it does not mean, and then accuse it of leading us astray, it can only persist and wait until we arrive at understanding. Today we know that the image did not refer to the stick but to light; did not way to make a statement about the stick but about the bending of light when it passes from air into water. How long did it not take for us to understand what the eye, in its wonderfully clear and simple way, had since time immemorial been presenting for our understanding! But what do we, with our incorrigible stick-mindedness, do? We boast of what our intellect has accomplished and go on calling the image an illusion.

What, writes Wertheimer, if study of the seeing of illusory motion should further our understanding of the seeing of motion in general— "if, in this way, essential elements could be experimentally isolated, perhaps *the* essential element that is the basis for real seeing of

702

motion?" He carefully compares what takes place when we see illusory motion and when we see real motion. The process is the same in either case: what is true for the seeing of illusory motion also holds true for the seeing of real motion. But this must not be read with a secretly derogatory emphasis on *seeing*, as if we were investigating how motion "merely appears," not what it "really is" (in the current terminology, the "subjective," not the "objective," side of the process). Wertheimer lays the strongest emphasis on the fact that the phenomena which he describes "are of an objective, not a subjective, nature; have the same kind of objective significance as the content of any given color or shape sensation." This means that seeing motion tells us exactly as much about motion as seeing colors does about colors, as seeing shapes does about shapes. If seeing motion is *not* a seeing of things in places, if the process that we see as motion is able to free itself from connection with things and places, appears as a progression neither *in* places nor *through* places, but over them, as a pure passing over, this means that motion *is* such. The definition "transfer of a thing from one place to another" does not embrace it; it is not entirely contained in its spatial track. It reaches beyond the realm of places, transcends it—our schema "place I between I place" does not do it justice; the differences in level would have to be represented, perhaps thus: place I ^{between} place . The flesh and blood of the phenomenon—to use Wertheimer's expression—would, then, have to be sought not on the level of place, of the many places, but on that of the one "between," of the one "passing over."

To see colors, to see shapes, to see motion, does not simply mean to have visual sensations; in all these cases one sees *something*. In the case of colors and shapes this something is always a material thing—it is the pigment on the canvas which is red, it is the crest of the mountain which is jagged—and where we see change, the thing that changes is always present; is the persisting, the static core of the phenomenon. What is the something that we see in these motions which are a pure "passing over," since it is not a material thing? Wertheimer calls it something *purely dynamic*. This is to say that a dynamism detached from everything static, change detached from a thing that changes, is not only conceivable but perceptible. "What should there not be purely dynamic phenomena?" At first blush every seen motion may appear to be motion of a thing: Wertheimer's researches have revealed the core of pure dynamism, of dynamism transcending the material, that motion contains; they have disclosed that every seeing of motion is, essentially,

703

a perceiving of purely dynamic phenomena that transcend the level of things and places.

Musical Considerations

It is not fortuitously that Wertheimer ends his essay with a reference to music—to the "living interval"—as a terrain in which similar studies would lead to similar results. Parallels force themselves upon us at every step. Often we should have only to substitute "tone of a certain pitch" for "thing in place" and we should have a perfectly valid statement concerning heard instead of seen motion. Even more: many statements seem to apply much more naturally, much more easily, to the former than to the latter. Indeed, it seems that a great deal of intellectual effort and laborious experimentation are necessary to isolate from visible motion phenomena that music, heard motion, simply hands us, as it were, on a silver platter.

Let us recall what we said about the elementary experience of musical motion. A series of tones is heard as motion not because the successive tones are of different pitches but because they have different dynamic qualities. The dynamic quality of a tone, we said, is a statement of its incompleteness, its will to completion. To hear a tone as dynamic quality, as a direction, a pointing, means hearing at the same time beyond it, beyond it in the direction of its will, and going toward the expected next tone. Listening to music, then, we are not first *in* one tone, then in the next, and so forth. We are, rather, always *between* the tones, *on the way* from tone to tone; our hearing does not remain with the tone, it reaches through it and beyond it. The usual concept of melodic motion as motion from tone to tone and of the individual step from tone to tone as the bridging of the distance in pitch between two tones (schema "tone I between I tone") does not fit the facts at all. But neither would a schema like this

dynamic quality	between	dynamic quality
↑		↑
tone		tone

do them justice. Dynamic qualities are not stationary, of the nature of fixed pillars, with no bridge between them until one is provided by the connecting transition of the step, they are themselves completely of the nature of a step, of a transition; they are, in other words, dynamic, not static, they are themselves the going on beyond the tone—a passing over, a "between." The schema must be this: $_{\text{tone I tone}}^{\text{between}}$. It is a process on two levels, on one of which, the "lower," there is nothing but the pillars, tones of definite pitch; on the other, the "higher," nothing but the transition, the passing over. And the motion we hear is not at all the "tone I tone" of the lower level; it is the "between" of the upper level, pure betweenness, pure passing over.

But this is where Wertheimer arrives too; the investigation of seen motion and the investigation of heard motion coincide in their end result! Whereas elsewhere we found nothing but contradictions and paradoxes when we tried to understand heard motion after the pattern of seen motion, now suddenly there is helpful agreement. The only difference lies in the fact that, in the motion of things, the core of pure dynamism is well concealed and had to be isolated artifically, whereas in tonal motion hardly anything is perceived but the purely dynamic. The irreconcilability of the phenomena of musical motion with the traditional concept of motion has its parallel in Wertheimer's investigation: the concept of motion to which he was led by his observations is in sharp opposition to the traditional concept. On the other hand, it corresponds beautifully with the facts of tonal motion. Wertheimer's concept of motion is simply the *musical concept of motion*—and the fact that it could be reached from the opposite pole, from seen instead of heard motion, from the motion of things, not the motion of tones, seems to indicate that *all* motion, seen as well as heard, motion of things as well as motion of tones, is, in the last analysis, "of one flesh and blood." Not unjustifiably may we say that musical motion is at the core of every motion; that every experience of motion is, finally, a musical experience.

The position from which we set out is now completely reversed. Instead of doubtfully asking if we had a right to speak of motion in music, since after all there is nothing in music that moves, and no places in which things are, and now we say that it is precisely *because* there are no things and places in music, precisely *because* music has freed itself from all connection with things and places, that the passing over, the "between," the core of motion, can be manifested in absolute purity and immediacy. It is precisely *because* hearing music is a perception of purely dynamic phenomena that the core of the process of motion can be elementally experienced in music, and above all in music. Hearing music means hearing precisely and only the core of motion. Philosophers and aestheticians are wrong when they talk of "ideal" motion, of "abstract" motion, in music. There is nothing ideal or abstract in it. The elimination of thing and place takes away nothing of the reality of motion, of the concreteness of its experience; on the contrary, it reveals its innermost core. *Tonal motion is the most real motion.*

And the problem of continuity? A few pages back, it still seemed impossible to abide by the experience of motion in melody in the face of the fact that the tones from which a melody is constructed do not themselves move at all, that they present a picture of stases and gaps. But now this seems as little paradoxical as the fact that the telephone poles do not run along with the electric current, or that they are poles, with gaps between, not a continuous wall. Certainly, the tones are static, there are gaps between tone and tone; but the motion that we hear in music, the continuous occurrence, does not take place where there are tones and gaps, on the lower level, is not *motion of the tones*, is not "tone | tone," but is "between," is manifested on the upper level. Stasis of the tones and motion of the melody, gaps here and uninterruptedness there, continuity and discontinuity, do not enter into opposition because they concern phenomena on different levels that must be kept apart.

An example to make this clear. The step of a fourth, $\hat{5}$-$\hat{8}$: on the level of tones there are two events, two stases, and a gap; on the level of "between," of passing over, there is one step, one event, one single move. Here there is no question of duality, of gaps. The continuity of the step is not that of an unbroken transition from tone to tone, of a continuous passing through all the "points" between one tone and another; it is the unity and uninterruptedness of the single move, which transforms one dynamic state into another. This unity and uninterruptedness are completely unaffected by the greater or lesser distance of the tones from each other, by the greater or lesser number of intermediate degrees, of intermediate tones, which are "skipped" in the step. As motion, $\hat{5}$-$\hat{8}$ is as perfect, as uninterrupted, as continuous as $\hat{5}$-$\hat{6}$-$\hat{7}$-$\hat{8}$. Nor is the motion $\hat{5}$-$\hat{8}$ to be understood as the sum of the fractional motions $\hat{5}$-$\hat{6}$, $\hat{6}$-$\hat{7}$, $\hat{7}$-$\hat{8}$: a leap is not a sum of steps, and steps are not fractions of a leap. One can subdivide a difference in pitch and reconstruct it from its fractions, but one cannot divide and reconstruct a motion. If the continuity of tonal motion had anything to do with the "lower" level, with differences in pitch, with traversing these intervals, with touching upon intermediate tones, then $\hat{5}$-$\hat{6}$-$\hat{7}$-$\hat{8}$ would necessarily produce a better, more continuous impression of motion than $\hat{5}$-$\hat{8}$. But then, logically, the motion would appear stil better, still more continuous, if the gaps between $\hat{5}$ and $\hat{6}$, $\hat{6}$ and $\hat{7}$, $\hat{7}$ and $\hat{8}$, were to be filled with more and more intermediate tones, until finally, when all intervals were completely filled, a perfect impression of motion would be achieved. The exact opposite is the case: the sirenlike glissade from tone to tone does not give the most perfect impression of motion but no impression of motion at all. Actual continuity on the lower level eliminates the possibility of motion; order becomes chaos, music a mere shriek.

With this shriek, tones show us in exemplary fashion how motion feels when its two-level structure is compressed onto one level, when the upper level is absorbed in the lower, when the "places" swallow up the "between": it is deprived of the breath of life. The siren shriek is the protest of tones against the error into which Zeno of Elea fell when he equated motion with the *path* of motion, "between" with inter*space*, until motion choked to death in his hands. In the realm of tone we hear what is concealed in the realm of things: in the final analysis motion and uninterrupted traversal of intermediate steps have nothing to do with each other; they can certainly not be equated. If motion of things in space actually and necessarily appears as an uninterrupted traversal of intermediate steps, then "uninterrupted traversal of intermediate steps" belongs among the necessary conditions for the existence of things in space, not for the existence of motion. Instead of "Motion is continuous transfer of a thing from one place to another in space," we ought to say: "moving things in space continuously change their place." But then we shall look for the purer, more elemental phenomenon of motion in tones, not in things.

Bergson writes: "There are changes, but there are underneath the change no things which change: change has no need of a support. There are movements, but there is no inert or invariable object which moves: movement does not imply a mobile." To be sure, the eye shows us unaltered things that change their place. But the ear? Hearing a melody is "the clear perception of a movement which is not attached to a mobile, of a change without anything changing. This change is enough, it is the thing itself." We introduce spatial concepts, concepts of "thing in place," into melody if we view it as a succession of individual tones. If we eliminate this false spatialization, "pure change remains, sufficient unto itself, in no way divided, in no way attached to a 'thing' which

changes. . . . Change is the most substantial and durable thing possible."
The inmost being of things is the indivisible continuity of a melody. [18]

The attempt to understand tonal motion in the light of the motion of
things has proved futile. Now it appears that the opposite course is the
more promising: to understand motion in general, including motion of
bodies, in the light of tonal motion. Should he who searches for the
essence of motion perhaps look to music for an answer?

X. The "Third Stage"

Elsewhere in "The Perception of Change," Bergson writes: "Our
personality is precisely that: the continuous melody of our inner life."

Here we pause; a question frames itself. If Bergson, in these thoughts,
connects motion and music, music and human existence, what kind of
motion has he in mind? Is it any longer the outer, perceptible
phenomenon, a phenomenon of the external world, at all? Has not his
attention shifted imperceptibly from outer to inner, from physical to
psychological motion? Has the boundary between the two been
maintained? Does Bergson, when he says "motion," perhaps originally
have in mind the psychological, not the physical?

We do not pose this question here for its own sake, but for the sake of
the remainder that it provides: it points to another question that should
perhaps have been settled earlier.

When, at the beginning of this section, we cited a number of eloquent
witnesses to the immediacy of the experience of motion in music, we
pointed out the fact that, in their testimony, the concept of motion was
used in very different senses—sometimes in the sense of a physical but
also frequently in the sense of a psychological phenomenon, as, for
example, in Hegel's characteristic statement that music "echoes the
motions of the inmost self." [19] For our part, however, throughout this
discussion we have always considered motion as an external phenomenon;
have compared tonal motion only with such phenomena of motion as
we encounter in perception of the external, physical world. Have we
overlooked the fact that the one word "motion" embraces two worlds:

---

[18]Quotations are from Bergson, "The Perception of Change," in *The Creative Mind.*
[19]Hegel, *Vorlesungen über die Aesthetik.*

physical motion and psychological motion? If not, why have we followed only one of the two roads—and perhaps the wrong one?

One thing we shall *not* adduce in justification: that the word "motion" strictly has only one meaning, refers directly only to phenomena of the external world, to bodies in space, and can only be used in reference to phenomena of the psyche by extension, metaphorically. When we speak of images *unrolling* in fantasy, of the *flow* of thought, of *reaching* a decision, we are not speaking in metaphors but directly expressing definite experiences. When William James coined the expression *stream of consciousness*, he was certainly not concerned with finding a striking metaphor but with precisely characterizing a specific fact. There is no doubt that the word "motion" is as native to the inner as to the outer world.

But then it must seem all the more incomprehensible that we did not do the obvious thing and conceive the experience of motion in music above all in the sense of inner, psychological motion—especially in view of the difficulties which we have encountered along our path. That music is incomparably closer to the world of the psyche than to the world of bodies, that it is a pure manifestation of the psychic, are almost commonplaces. And indeed, we should have had an easy time of it if we had looked at musical experiences from the point of view of the phenomena of the inner world instead of doing as we have done. We said that music is motion, and yet we find nothing of things and places in it. But in the psyche too there are neither things nor places; yet it has motion. We said that music is motion, and yet in it there is no thing that moves. Is not the same true of inner motion, the motion of the psyche? The stream of consciousness is not a thing, "consciousness," which "streams," but a streaming in consciousness; feeling is no more motion of a something, the psyche, than is melody the motion of a something, tone. Finally, we said that music is motion, a continuous progression, and yet, objectively, nothing but stases and gaps are given in it, no transitions, no filling of gaps, no passing through intermediate steps. But this is the distinguishing characteristic of what occurs in the psyche. What could be more continuous than the stream of consciousness, and what more discontinuous than the actual data in consciousness, the various contents and states of consciousness that so often succeed one another with no transition, with a complete lack of intermediate stages? The mutual correspondence between the phenomena of the psyche and the phenomena of music could not be more perfect.

   Certainly it would have been easier and simpler to follow the inward course rather than the outward, but it would not have been honest. For one basic fact must not be shirked: music is *not* a phenomenon of the inner world, nor is it something projected from the inner to the outer world; it is a phenomenon of the outer world. It is not felt, it is not imagined, it is not willed—it is perceived. It does not arise from our psyche; it comes to us from the world around us. It is not in our consciousness—or, better, it is there in the same way as, and neither more nor less than, are all other perceived phenomena. The motion we hear—not the passing by of the band but the $\hat{5}$-$\hat{8}$ of the march it is playing—and the motion we see belong, in this respect, on the same plane. Tones move where birds fly and meteors fall; and if the brief that music is motion is to be defended, we must argue it in the court that has proper jurisdiction.

   But under what jurisdiction does music fall? It exhibits the general characteristics of psychological processes, but its stage is not the psyche. It comes from without, but it does not exhibit the general characteristics of what comes from without, body and place. It is distinguished from all psychological phenomena by the way in which it is given, by accuracy, reliability, one might almost say palpability; from all physical phenomena, on the other hand, it is distinguished by the characteristic of impalpability. Thus it rejects the claim which *either* world makes to it, the physical world *and* the world of the psyche; thus it extends beyond *both* of them in the same fashion. Music makes us aware, unmistakably and inescapably, that "beyond the world of things and places" is *not*, as common belief has it, identical with the world of the psyche; nor is "beyond the world of the psyche" identical with the world of things and places. A *third stage* must exist which is neither the world of the psyche nor the world of bodies nor yet a mixture of both, and which stands to the two others in the relation of the general to the particular, of the primary to the derivative. Motion that takes place entirely on this stage is "pure" in the twofold sense that it is bound neither to things and places nor to a stream of consciousness. Such is the motion of tones—motion that has not yet been wedded to a body or a psyche, the purest, most primal form of motion that we know. And if it is true that, in the last analysis, all motion is of one flesh and blood, that at the core of every motion, even the motion of bodies, music lies hidden, then every motion, including the motion of bodies, belongs to the "third stage" perforce of its inmost essence.

710

We recall that at the beginning of this section we asked what it mean to *hear* motion. To see motion, to touch motion, is understandable. But to hear motion? Now, on the contrary, we can ask, What is there in motion which can be seen and touched? Certainly not its core; for that lies beyond body and place, and what has neither body nor place can neither be seen nor touched. But this does not mean that it cannot be perceived at all; can at best be "felt." Instead—music tells us so—*it can be heard*. Compared with seeing and touching, hearing proves to be the faculty that gets at the essence; that pierces to the core of the phenomenon. Instead of asking how we can perceive motion with the ear *too*, we find that the core of the process of motion, what takes place on the "third stage," is *directly* perceptible *only* to the ear. Other senses, whose principal function is to serve orientation on the physical stage, can attain to the perception of the phenomenon of motion in its pure essentiality only under special conditions.

The statement that bodies and their motions in space are, in the last analysis, the only reality is as old as European philosophy. Born in the mind of Democritus, for two thousand years it led a sort of hermetically sealed existence. Then the seal bursts. The advance guard of a new scientific spirit takes up the thread—Hobbes, for example: "The things that really *are* in the world without are *motions* [of bodies]." This passes as materialism, and it is certainly meant as materialism. But in the light of the knowledge to which musical experiences bring us, such statements begin to sound peculiar: they suddenly seem to say exactly the opposite of what they intend to say. If the universe is real as moving bodies are real, if motion of a body is not wholly contained in the physico-spatial world, if the very core of the phenomenon of motion goes beyond the physico-spatial, this means not only that the reality of the universe is *not* exhausted in the physico-spatial, but that precisely its very essence reaches beyond that stage, is transcendent in respect to the visible and tangible—transcendent in the same sense in which a melody is transcendent in respect to tone as acoustical phenomena. It is, so to speak, an internal transcendence; it does not lead away from the phenomenon but into it, to its core. In the first section of this book we discussed the particular way in which dynamic qualities exist in tones and compared it, remotely, with the way in which the divine being is present in the religious symbol. It would seem, then, that, in the same sense, the entire universe would have the nature of a symbol, and that, among all experiences, musical experience might be distinguished by the fact that in it the symbolic nature of the external world would be revealed in direct perception. We *see* the rind, or, under special conditions, *through* the rind, but we *hear* the core of this world.

Those who believe that music provides a source of knowledge of the inner world are certainly not wrong. But the deeper teaching of music concerns the nature not of "psyche" but of "cosmos." The teachers of antiquity, who spoke of the music of the spheres, of the cosmos as a musical order, knew this. A celebrated English physician and scholar, who lived more than three centuries ago, has left us the beautiful statement that melody, *every* melody, is "an Hieroglyphical and shadowed lesson of the whole World and creatures of God."[20] Only a little more than a century ago, Schopenhauer could still write: "A correct, complete, and detailed explanation of music—that is, a full restatement, in terms of concepts, of what music expresses . . . would also be a sufficient restatement and explanation of the world in terms of concepts, or completely in harmony with such a restatement and explanation, and hence the true philosophy."[21] Today we consume music in greater quantities than any previous generation. But we no longer know how to read what stands written. We have forgotten the meaning of the characters.

XII. The Musical Concept of Time

What does it mean to understand a phenomenon, for example, the motion of a star? On the one hand, we have observed facts; they are given, we cannot tamper with them. On the other hand, we have certain concepts, thought constructs, such as time, space, matter, body, force, energy, and so on. The task is so to construct, so to think, these concepts that the observed fact appears to follow from them with logical necessity. In the case of the star, given time, space, etc., as what according to my thought they are, the star *must* perform exactly the movement I observe. If this correspondence of fact and concept has been achieved, the phenomenon has been understood.

[20]Sir Thomas Browne, *Religio Medici.*
[21]Schopenhauer, *The World as Will and Idea.*

712

It is the same with musical phenomena. The observed facts are there; what must the concepts be if understanding is to result? Specifically, in regard to the present problem, what concept of time is required if the phenomena of meter and rhythm are to follow from it with logical necessity? How must I think time if I want to understand musical rhythm?

It appears that the concept of time that would achieve this correspondence of thought and musical fact—the *musical* concept of time—would have to have characteristics that the traditional or *physical* time concept denies to time, just as it would have to lack other characteristics that the traditional time concept attributes to time. The following schematic comparison results:

PHYSICAL TIME CONCEPT	MUSICAL TIME CONCEPT
Time is *order, form* of experience	Time is *content* of experience
Time *measures* events	Time *produces* events
Time is divisible into equal parts	Time knows no equality of parts
Time is perpetual transience	Time knows nothing of transience

Experienced Time

On this point we can be brief; what is essential has been sufficiently stated. Generations of philosophers and psychologists have taught that although an awareness of time goes along with all our sensations, perceptions, feelings, with all possible states and contents of our consciousness, as the order or form of their appearance—namely, succession—in itself time can never be the object of any sensation, perception, or any other kind of experience. Anyone who thought that he could arrive at time by thinking away everything that is *in* time, the moving things, the sense perceptions that crowd upon us, our feelings, all the concrete content of our consciousness, and retaining "only the form," would be in for a rude awakening; with the things that are *in* time, time itself would have slipped through his fingers. What remains of a vessel if one thinks away all matter—hence not only the matter of its contents but also the matter of its body? Something that at best can be thought in pure abstraction. Time, says Leibniz, is idea, not reality.

To whatever else this doctrine may appeal for its support, it is *not* compatible with the facts of music. At first sight it might still seem that our observation concerning the nature of musical rhythm confirmed the

713

thesis of time as pure form. Does not rhythm require tones, hence something material, in order to manifest itself? If the tones disappeared would not all rhythm disappear with them? Must we not, then, admit that here too the concrete content of the experience is not time itself but tone, something that occupies time—that here too time is nothing but the organization, the order, the form, for a content? Certainly time requires matter—in this case the matter of tone—in order to manifest itself; but does that necessarily make it mere form, an abstraction, deny it concrete reality? Light too requires matter to manifest itself; in a space emptied of all matter there would be no light. Yet no one thinks of denying the reality of light as a thing in itself. We clearly distinguish light and illuminated thing as two equally real entities, not as abstract form and concrete content. Certainly time requires the tone in and through which it becomes manifest as rhythm. But it is not true that here only the tones are concrete experiential content, with time an abstract, empty form, only to be apprehended in reflective thought. No—through tones, time becomes concrete experiential content; the experience of musical rhythm is an experience of time made possible through tones. In the unique phenomenon of the musical rest, we have as it were the crucial experiment for our thesis; the rest shows us, with a clarity that leaves nothing to be desired, what happens if tones are not just thought away but actually left out: what remains is not abstract, empty form but a highly concrete experience, the experience of rhythm. There would be no rhythm if time could not be experienced as such, in itself.

Time Producing Events

The idea that effects of any kind could have their basis in time, in the flux of time as such, is, within the limits of the physical time concept, an absurdity. To be sure, snow melts with time, organisms age, the surface of the earth changes its configuration; but these effects appear not *because* time passes but because heat, chemical processes, erosion, and volcanism—forces of things *in* time—are at work. For the natural sciences, "time" is merely another word for the fact that natural processes are susceptible of a certain kind of measurement, measurement by clocks. The second hand of our watch moves 498.7 steps forward while a light ray passes through the space from the sun to the earth: that is all. Basically, natural science stands or falls with the concept of nonactive time. What the law of nature accomplishes is precisely this: it

714

enables me to know *now* what is *not yet*; it abolishes the dividing line between the now and the not-yet; strictly speaking, it destroys time as reality. If I say that in 5100 years this piece of matter will have given off half of its radioactive energy, what I mean is that the continuing activity of the forces now given in this object, *and nothing else*, will produce the prophesied effect after the lapse of the stated amount of time. The actual lapse of time of itself has nothing to do with the matter; it is—to use an expression of Eddington's—a mere formality.[22] Where natural laws hold, there can only be effects *in* time; there can be no effects *of* time.

But music has acquainted us with processes that cannot be comprehended except as effects of time, in the literal sense. This crucial point requires to be elucidated again in greater detail.

What takes place if I correctly answer the question on which beat of a measure a particular tone in a melody falls? Have I, perhaps, in expectation of the question, counted along in time and thus brought together the tone and the count that belong to it; or have I, surprised by the question, repeated the melody in memory, counted the beats afterward in memory? This may occasionally be the method; in difficulties one may fall back on such mechanical devices—for that is what they are. What actually takes place is, as we have seen, a very different process. Hearing music, we oscillate with its metric wave. Each tone falls on a particular phase of this wave; each phase of the wave imparts to the tone that falls on it—and, through the tone, to the auditor—its particular directional impulse. Not because I count "one" to a tone (or because the tone was emphasized by an accent—for often it is not) do I know that I am at the beginning of a measure, but because I feel that, with this tone, I have reached the wave crest and at the same time have been carried beyond it, into a new wave cycle. Because every tone (and every rest) is characterized for my perception by a particular quality, and because in these qualities the place of the tone (or of the rest) on the metric wave is expressed, I am able to hear directly from the tone—and from the rest—in what part of the entire measure I am at the given moment.

The remarkable fact, which we also encounter elsewhere in nature, that a part of a whole is, so to speak, aware of its being a part, of its relation to the whole and its place in the whole, and also imparts this knowledge to the observer—that, consequently, the whole is in some

---

[22]Quoted by Bergson in *Durée et simultanéité*.

manner present in the part—to this fact our thinking seeks to do justice by the *field concept*. A field is the region in which a force is active— active, in accordance with a definite order, differently at every different point of the field. The iron filing feels the effect of the magnet differently according to whether it lies nearer to or farther from the magnet, to the right of it or to the left—in other words, in each instance according to the place it occupies in the magnetic field. What happens in the field depends, among other things, on *where* it happens. The event is marked by the characteristics of the situation obtaining at this point, and only at this point, in relation to the active force; and the observer who is able to read the language of these characteristics will be able from them to read the place of the point in the field. Between the field as a whole and the individual points as its parts, then, there is a relationship of the type described above—the whole being given with and active in the part and the part, as it were, being aware that it is a part and directly announcing its relation to the whole. And wherever we encounter a phenomenon that exhibits this peculiar relation between parts and whole, we may assume that a force, an ordered action of forces, is its basis.

Since the phenomena of meter and rhythm unequivocally exhibit this peculiar relation between parts and whole, we are justified in assuming as their basis an ordered action of forces, a dynamic field. The question remains: What sort of forces are active here?

The answer can only be that they are forces of time. In other cases where we observe an action of forces, we are usually in a position to point out certain things, states of things, processes in things, from which the effects proceed and which appear to us as the agents or sources of the forces in action. But in the case of the rhythmic effects of music, the world of things leaves us completely in the lurch. There simply are no things, no processes in things, as effects *of which* the processes of musical rhythm can be understood. It is not that we know none; it is that none are given. All that is given here is tones of definite durations and a listener. The tones are the element that instigates, provides the possibility; as agents or origin of the forces that produce the rhythm, they are as little in the picture as the listener, whose contribution to the rhythm lies in the fact that he experiences it, not that he produces it. So we are left with only one series of data in which we can seek the source of the phenomena of rhythm: the *durations* of the tones. The answer to the quest, "Of *what* are meter and rhythm the effects," can, then, only be that they are effects of the mere passing of time in the tones, of their temporality. Because tones have duration, because time elapses in them, and for no other reason, we have the rhythm of our music. Only time can be the agent and source of the forces active in meter and rhythm.

When we speak of agents of activity and active forces, we generally think of two clearly separable data; we distinguish between them as between a substance and a function of the same substance, a thing and a quality of a thing. A nail is one thing; the ability of the nail to hold two boards together is another. When a stream carries tree trunks with it, heaves itself against bridge piles, sweeps soil away here, deposits it there, the forces of the flow that work in this way are bound to a flowing something, water, which, instead of flowing, could also stand still and yet remain water, which is able to do many other things too, for example, to nourish animals and plants. In these cases the agent of the action has its own existence, independently of the acting force—in contrast with which it appears as something comparatively stable, lasting, substantial. But it would be a grave error to understand the statement "time is the agent of acting forces" as if it said that first there is time, as a thing by itself, a sort of substance, and then the activity of the forces that manifest themselves in meter and rhythm, as a quality or function, perhaps among others, of this independent datum, the thing "time." Any such notion would go far beyond the result of our investigations. It is precisely the opposite which music has demonstrated for us: the impossibility of separating a thing "time" from the forces that produce rhythm; time was here nothing but the activity of these forces. What we were able to say about this activity was by the same token all that we were able to say about time; agent and acting force merge in each other; no reasonable distinction between them is possible. If we still use the two words, it is not because our observations confronted us with two data, but because *language* forces us to: we speak in sentences and every sentence must at least have a subject and a predicate—that of which something is stated and that which is stated—two terms. In so far as we accept the testimony of music as basic, the existence of time is the same as its activity. We observe an oscillation, an accumulation—and this oscillation, this accumulation, *is* time. There there is something else in addition, a something that oscillates and accumulates—however obvious such an assumption may seem to us, it has nothing to support it except habits of thought and speech. To express it in the simile of the stream: we see tree trunks moved, bridge piles subjected to pressure, soil carried away and deposited—but there is no water, the stream bed is empty.

717

Time Knows No Equality of Parts

The meter of our music, we said, divides the regular flux of time into parts that are all equal. Now what about this equality of parts in time?

That in daily life we divide the flux of time, are able to delimit hours, minutes, seconds in it, and that all these hours, minutes, seconds are equal to each other, is taken as a matter of course, as much as that all centimeters are equally long, all kilograms equally heavy. These are measures, we are a measuring species, and we would not measure if the measures with which we operate changed size in our hands.

But this does not yet explain what it means that all hours are equal in length. We can only compare and find equal what is given simultaneously. Can two hours be given simultaneously? Here we obviously find ourselves in the situation of an imaginary one-dimensional creature whose living space is the line along which it moves and which wants to make statements concerning the equality or inequality of sections of this line. In order to measure and compare these sections, it would have to be able to step out of the line, to look at it from outside. But that is precisely what it cannot do. To step out of time, to look at it from outside — that we cannot. How, then, is it to be understood if we nevertheless maintain that all hours are equal in length?

Within the frame of the physical time concept, the question answers itself. If time as such cannot be perceived, can produce no effects, if there is never anything but phenomena *in* time, never time itself, the question whether we can compare two times with each other has little meaning. The strict scientific definition of time was: "The motion of one body, if it is taken as the measure of the motion of another body, is called time." Hence to compare times means to compare motions of bodies. The equality of hours is the equality of the distances traveled by clock hands; it is in the last analysis an equality of spaces, not of times.

But then what is the meanining of the equality of measures and beats in our music, that equality upon which we so emphatically insist when we train musicians above all to keep good time? It certainly cannot be referred back to space, to the lengths of the paths of moving bodies; for in music we are beyond the realm of bodies and space. Is the equality of measures and beats, then, still a true equality of times, of parts of time?

The meter that arises from the rhythmically arranged succession of tones and conveys itself to the hearer is, as we have seen, experienced as an oscillation, as a wave. Beats are the differently directed wave phases that add up to a full cycle. What is equal here?

The duration of the individual beats, it will be answered—but this answer implies a distinction between what occurs and its duration; it regards the metric wave as a process that takes place *in* time. It tacitly assumes that we are confronted with two data: first, the thing that occurs, the wave; second, a neutral medium, "duration," which underlies the wave as the empty strip of film underlies the pictures that will be taken. Actually we have *not* two data, first the metric wave, or the forces active in the wave, and then a neutral medium "time" or "duration" *in* which the forces work, *in* which the wave pulses; on the contrary, the pulsing of the wave is itself already time, is itself already duration. But with this it has become meaningless to talk of an equality of beats. Where is there place for equality on a wave? Observation has shown us that the elements of meter are not equal stretches of time but differently directed phases. It is not length which makes the beat, but the kinetic impulse. The condition that beat two of a duple meter has to fulfill is not that it must be equal in length to beat one, but that it shall close a cycle. To play in time musically does not mean to play tones that fill equal lengths of time, but tones that give rise to the metric wave.

Is equality perhaps to be found in the succession of measure to measure, of wave to wave? Is not the succession of impulses in each individual measure taken as a whole the faithful repetition of the succession of impulses in every other measure? Yes and no. We have observed how, in music, the succession of measure to measure is never a mere sequence; how, instead, either measure joins with measure to form measure groups in which the equal waves of the individual measures appear as differently directed phases of a wave of higher order. Or how, from measure after measure, from measure group to measure group, a continuous intensification series is built up, in which every measure differs from every other as "more" differs from "less." In neither case is there any room for equality. To talk of an equality of times, or of parts of time, has no reasonable meaning in the realm of meter.

What do we mean, then, when we demand that musicians play in time; demand, that is, that they preserve equality of measures and beats? The poor performer who takes all sorts of liberties with time is censured for the capricious inequality of his measures and beats. By what concept of equality do we measure this inequality? Certainly not by the concept of measurably equal lengths. We have pointed out what happens if the meter of an automaton is substituted for the meter of music: music ceases to exist. It is not the unequal length of the beats which disturbs us in a performance where the time is erratic, but the fact that *they do not give rise to the metric wave*. Variations from absolute mathematical equality do *not* disturb us, if they serve to give the metric wave the form that is musically right. There is no such thing as a musician whose performance does not depart from mathematical equality within certain limits; accurate experiments have given amazing proof of how great such departures can be without even being noticed by the listener (even listeners with a thorough musical training). What, on the other hand, everyone notices instantly, what disturbs everyone, is the departures that do not serve the metric wave but go counter to it. The commandment that is broken in a performance in poor time does not, then, refer to equality in length between intervals of time but to symmetry of mutually complementary wave phases. The so-called equality of time proves to be a rhythmic quality, rhythmic balance.

The picture has undergone a strange reversal. The physical time concept postulated equality of times as something self-evident, but closer examination has shown that this equality had been registered under a false name; it appeared rather as an equality of spaces. The musical time concept rejected equality of times; but, within it, that equality now experiences a sort of rebirth, although in an essentially altered form. The one-dimensional creature to which we referred by way of comparison before, is still unable to see outside of its path; cannot look from without on distances traversed and compare them by measuring them. But it now seems that, under certain circumstances— that is, when its course follows the line of a wave— we can ascribe to it a sort of rhythmic feeling that tells it when phases of its course balance each other. It is though passing through—or let us rather say living through—a phase of its course had established a demand, had created an emptiness, to fill and unfill which is the function of the following phrase: if the emptiness is filled, the brim reached, equilibrium is restored. The two phases do not stand side by side, are not compared and found equal; the sensation is that of a mutual complementing, a mutual interpenetration, a mutual balancing. It is to this sensation, a rhythmic sensation, that our concept of an equality of times reduces itself. The statement already quoted from Alfred Whitehead comes to mind: "We have a primitive perception of equality [of durations] by our perception of rhythm." The expression "equality of times" makes sense only in so far as we take equality to mean rhythmic equivalence. Our definition must be: We call two times *equal* if together they form the "one-two" of a metric wave. If we want information concerning equality of times, it is not from our clocks that we shall get it, but from our music.

Digression I: Repetition in Music

Not until we have recognized that, in the ordinary, literal sense, there is no equality of times, that—to put it in another way—time never repeats itself, are we able to understand how it is that *repetition* plays such an overwhelming role in music.

There are various kinds of repetition in music: the patent, more or less literal repetitions of themes, motifs, melodies, whole complexes, comparatively large sections of a composition; others that, as it were, veil the pattern to be repeated in a just-transparent robe of tone; yet others, more secretive, that represent various degrees of the transformation or development of an original pattern; and finally the most mysterious of all, those which are unknown even to the creating artist himself, which are hidden in the inmost depths of the very tones, whose presence was first pointed out by Heinrich Schenker,[23] and in which the miracles of the organic formation of great masterpieces are revealed. Whereas some of these concealed repetitions are heard only upon increased familiarity with the composition, while others are never heard as repetitions at all (not everything that is repetition is also meant to be heard as such), the patent repetitions are obvious to anyone who has ever listened to a piece of music. Only this kind of repetition, which is part of the immediate experience of music, shall concern us here.

We are so accustomed to repetition in music that we accept it as something self-evident; that we never become aware of what an extraordinary phenomenon it is. A theme, a melody, is a definite statement of tones—and apparently music can never have enough of saying over again what has already been said, not once or twice, but dozens of times; hardly does a section, which consists largely of repetitions, come to an end before the whole story is happily told over again. How is it that a procedure which, in any other form of expression, would produce sheer nonsense proves, in the language of music, to be thoroughly

---

[23]Cf. p. 682, n. 8.

sensible—to such an extent that rehearing what has already been heard is one of the chief sources—for many, *the* chief source—of the pleasure given by music?

Looking for analogous phenomena elsewhere, our first thought is of carpets, tapestries, and other ornamental creations, in which a motif reappears countless times; or of architecture, with its series of like formal members and repetitions of entire extensive formal complexes. The analogy is, however, only superficial; here, in space, the effect does not depend upon the repetition of the individual element as such but upon the *simultaneous presence* of many like elements—in other words, upon the fact that all the repetitions are given us at once, as a whole. The question arises how much pleasure we should take in looking at a carpet if the repeated elements of its pattern were given us not together but successively, if each came before our eyes by itself. More apt is the comparison with the frequent repetitions of groups of words and whole sentences in many epic poems, the repetitions of single verses and entire stanzas in lyrics. But how small this is, how strictly limited, how exceptional and unusual, compared with the role that falls to repetition in the musical context! What should we say if a poet expected us to swallow this:

Say not the struggle, say not the struggle
Naught availeth, naught availeth,
The labor and the wounds are vain,
The labor and the wounds are vain.

The enemy faints not nor faileth,
And as things have been they remain,
The enemy faints not nor faileth,
And as things have been they remain.

If hopes were dupes, fears may be liars;
Your comrades chase e'en now the fliers.
Your comrades chase e'en now the fliers,
Your comrades chase e'en now the fliers.

Say not the struggle naught availeth,
The labor and the wounds are vain,
The labor and the wounds are vain,
The labor and the wounds are vain.

Its musical analogue would be a meaningful construction from beginning to end, and indeed one comparatively poor in repetitions.

Let us examine a few concrete examples of how repetitions actually function in music. First a simple and typical example, a melody by Mozart, the Adagio from the great Piano Fantasy in C minor. The strophe of this melody consists of ten lines of equal length, each of which is divided into two equal hemistichs. The procedure is as follows: the tonal statement of the first line is repeated by the second, except that the end of the second hemistich is differently put; the third line repeats the first note for note, the fourth does the same with the second; the fifth line is new, yet its second hemistich is a repetition of the first; the sixth line repeats the first, with a new variation of the line ending; the seventh is the exact repetition of the second, the eighth the exact repetition of the fifth; the ninth line eactly repeats the sixth; the tenth begins as a repetition of the first, but then loses itself, leading into a new section. We get the following schema:

```
Line 1  ┌───── a ─────┬───── b ─────┐
     2  ┌───── a ─────┬───── b' ────┐
     3  ┌───── a ─────┬───── b ─────┐
     4  ┌───── a ─────┬───── b' ────┐
     5  ┌───── c ─────┬───── c' ────┐
     6  ┌───── a ─────┬───── b" ────┐
     7  ┌───── a ─────┬───── b' ────┐
     8  ┌───── c ─────┬───── c' ────┐
     9  ┌───── a ─────┬───── b" ────┐
    10  ┌───── a ─────┐ ─ ─ ─ ─ ─ ─
```

If we knew nothing about the existence of music, we should not find it easy to imagine a language in which a reasonable statement is 80 per cent repetitions—repetitions of "words" and "sentences," not of "letters."

Let us examine another melody, the Huntsmen's Chorus from Weber's *Freischütz*:

723

Then we get the whole thing over again from the beginning, with a change only in the very last measure. The schema is as follows (each line of the melody extends over four measures):

```
Line 1  ⌐  a  ┬  a  ┬ b ┬ b ┬ b ┬ b ⌐
     2  ⌐  a  ┬  a  ┬ b ┬ b ┬ b ┬ b ⌐
     3  ⌐  c  ┬  c  ┬      d        ⌐
     4  ⌐  a  ┬  a  ┬ b ┬ b ┬ b ┬ b ⌐
     5  ⌐  a  ┬  a  ┬ b ┬ b ┬ b ┬ b ⌐
     6  ⌐  c  ┬  c  ┬      d'       ⌐
```

This is not the aberrant experiment of a composer who wants to see just how far he can carry the principle of repetition without falling into imbecility; it is a completely normal melody, simple as a folk tune and universally popular. It will perhaps be advanced—since we are dealing with a choral piece—that the words contribute the element of variety which is so lacking in the tones. But this is not the case; the melody, it happens, is sung without any text; its linguistic foundation is nothing but the syllable "la" repeated exactly one hundred times—scanty nourishment for our intense hunger for variety.

A really extreme case of repetition looks quite different. One occurs, for example, in a famous passage from the first movement of Beethoven's *Pastoral* Symphony. Schema:

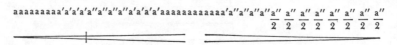

A brief tonal formula, comprising a mere five tones, in three variations —as if I should say: "I gave him apples, apples gave him I, I apples gave him"—repeated thirty-six times in all, followed by eight more repetitions of half the formula. (This $\frac{a''}{2}$, the last two tones of a'', is, in addition, identical with the first two tones of a.) And hardly have we got through it before it begins again, and the whole thing is repeated tone for tone! The sudden change in harmony after the twelfth repetition—indicated in the schema by the vertical line—though, to be sure, it changes what we might call the background against which the statement stands, does not change its content. The increase and decrease in tonal intensity (represented in the schema by the corresponding symbols) and the slight changes in tone color determined by the changing orchestration are equally powerless to detract from the overwhelming monotony of this endless series of repetitions. Regarded purely as the schema of a statement, it is sheer imbecility. How is it possible that, in music, such a thing becomes a meaningful and effective element in the whole of a masterpiece?

What is true of repetition on a small scale is equally true of repetition on a large scale. Innumerable compositions proceed according to a basic plan in accordance with which their often quite extensive first part is first repeated note for note, only to reappear again in a slightly altered version after an interlude that is often very short. Imagine a play of which the first scene should be played twice and which, after the second scene, should be played twice and which, after the second scene, should begin at the beginning again! But the situation is even more paradoxical. In many compositions this interlude follows the pattern of a process of gradual intensification leading to a climax; and what appears at the climax, the event for which we looked with such tension and which actually forms the culmination of the entire development, is nothing but the repetition of the story that we have already heard twice through. What would be sheer idiocy in a narrative, a drama, a poem—this beginning all over again—in music conveys the most powerful effects.

There must, then, be some peculiarity about repetition here. What is it?

The customary interruption attempts to justify repetition by the *lack of objective content* in music. The other arts, it is held, find their objects ready in reality—the visual arts in the visible world, literature in life and thought in general; even architecture is given enough of objective reality in its material and in the practical function of its products. Music, on the other hand, must, like Münchhausen, hold itself in the air by its own pigtail, must give itself its own objective content. Themes, melodies, motifs—these are the "objects" of music; as a painting, for example, "repeats" some objective reality, so a piece of music repeats its particular "objects." The interpretation seems applicable only where repetition is at the same time alteration and transformation, for every artistic representation alters and transforms the objectively given; the representation is never an exact repetition, a duplicate of its reality. But the type of repetition with which we are here concerned, and especially the accumulation of exact repetitions, are not explained by the object theory. What sense would there be to "representing" a given "object" ten times, twenty times, eighty-seven times? Moreover, if we assume that the objective content of a piece of music is the theme destined to be repeated, we leave unanswered the question what the objective content of the theme itself may be. The theme, after all, is already a piece of music.

If the repetitions that we have observed in our examples were really nothing but repetitions, nothing but "the same thing over and over and over . . . " it would be incomprehensible how they could pre-empt so much space in statements intended to be meaningful. From the point of view of the tones, they are precisely this: the same thing again and again and again. . . . But music is not only tone; it is tone and time. Tones may repeat themselves; time cannot repeat itself. It is only because time does not repeat itself that so much repetition is possible here; or, vice versa, that such much repetition does not become meaningless is only to be understood if time does not repeat itself, if there is no equality of times. Measures, beats, groups of measures may be exactly alike so far as tonal content is concerned, but since they must occur at different times they can never be mere repetition; they are necessarily different, as the phases of a wave or the degrees of an intensification are different. The repetition of a tonal statement never simply says the same thing over again; it accomplishes its particular share in the metric process, whether as the fulfillment of a demand for symmetrical complementation or as a link in the chain of intensification. Indeed it would seem that this very equality of tonal contents brings out with especial clarity the inequality of successive measures and groups of measures. If the tones say the same thing again and again, they disappear as the object of attention; they become merely a medium through which the beating of the wave emerges ever more clearly and strongly. The peculiar effect of our example from the *Pastoral* Symphony depends upon this very fact. The more repetition there is, the more clearly and forcefully will time become manifest. We might almost say that if time had its way, tones would never say anything but the same thing; as time projects wave after wave, the tones are to do nothing but to reproduce wave after wave in their material. This is actually the situation which we find in primitive music, where often enough a composition consists of nothing but the endless repetition of one and the same brief tonal formula. Repetition is a sort of natural state of music— and it is not by chance that the extreme example of repetition which we have discussed occurs in a composition whose particular closeness to nature is expressed even in its title. Accordingly, the "exceptional case" would not be repetition but nonrepetition, something new. If the tones say something new, they have of themselves broken through the magic circle of enforced

726

repetition. Every new tonal statement in the course of a composition is, in this sense, made *against* the will of an ever-present urge for repetition, an urge fed by time itself.

It might be asked why, if this is true of music, the same should not be true of all the other arts in which the time flux is an element, hence especially of poetry. After all, the verses of a poem are a temporal sequence and are just as much heard or read at successive times as the phrases of a melody. Why does the use of repetition in poetry reach its possible limits so soon? When a modern poet, Charles Péguy, tries this,

Il allait commencer l'immense événement
Il allait commencer l'immense avènement
Il allait commencer le grand avènement
Il allait commencer le grand gouvernement
Il allait commencer le grand ébranlement
Il allait commencer le grand revêtement
Il allait commencer le grand embarquement
Il allait commencer le grand rechargement
Il allait commencer le nouveau réglement
Il allait commencer le renouvellement . . .

his critic, André Gide, rightfully reproaches him with the illegitimacy of the procedure: it is, he says, repetition for the sake of the hypnotic effect of a litany, repetition as incantation, comparable to the flute playing of the Arab, who tirelessly begins the same melodic phrase over and over again.[24] Language fails in attempting to do what tone is privileged to do. The reason for this would appear to lie in the different capacity of word and tone to act as the medium of time perception. It is conceivable (we shall take up the question later) that tone, in and for itself, quite apart from rhythm, as a result of its basic independence from any relation to the world of objects, clears our sight for the perception of time as such, of time as event. The word has no such virtue. Hence repetition in verbal art is narrowly restricted, even with rhythm making its necessary and obvious contribution. And it occurs almost exclusively in lyrics and epics, the forms of poetry that were originally closely connected with music and still tend toward music. Much the same, furthermore, is true of the dance. The endless repetition of the same succession of motions

[24]Péguy's lines and Gide's criticism are quoted from the latter's introduction to the *Anthologie de la poésie française*, pp. xliv, xlv.

is possible, meaningful, and enjoyable only because the motions are induced and carried by the rhythm of the accompanying music. Dance without music, dancers in silence, always make an impression that is somehow dreary and slightly silly.

In this connection, finally, yet another type of musical repetition appears in a new light: altered repetition—not what is expressed by the technical term "variation," that often far-reaching transformation and recasting of a given tonal entity, but the kind of repetition that leaves the original tonal entity untouched in essentials but here and there supplies alterations that decorate, enrich, and emphasize some of its individual characteristics. In the usual view, these alterations serve the need for variety: the composer has recourse to them if he fears that mere repetition would not be sufficiently interesting. But we have seen that there is no need for such external aids in order to keep interest alive even in the case of note-for-note repetition: time itself takes care of that, time as event, which holds our attention even when, and especially when, the tones of themselves have nothing new to say. Often enough, such slight alterations are mere ornamentation applied more or less externally; but in other cases—as when a master of this kind of repetition like Mozart or Schubert is at work—the effect of a barely perceptible change in the repetition goes far beyond satisfying the need for variety, points toward a source that lies deeper. If a tonal statement can vary within certain limits from its original form and yet remain the same—and that is what happens in this kind of repetition—the possibility is present of having the basic fact of *meter* reflect itself in the tones: the fact that the thing which is constantly repeated is always also something else, a new thing. The tones do not alter for the sake of variety, that is, in order to give the same thing an appearance of being different; on the contrary, because what is apparently the same is basically always different, the tones too do not want always to remain the same. What is expressed in these alterations is, then, in the last analysis, the action of time itself, in which there is no sameness. The will of time that on one occasion is bent upon note-for-note repetition, on another occasion motivates variation from exact repetition.

[. . .]

Digression II: Temporal Gestalt

That we have not lost the firm ground of reality in these considerations is witnessed for us by the simple fact that melodies exist. Only upon the condition that time is thus constituted is the otherwise completely enigmatic process of the hearing of melodies to be comprehended.

A melody is a whole—and a temporal whole, a whole whose parts are given as a sequence, as temporal succession. Such a whole can, in general, be of two kinds. Either it is a sum of parts, which are successively added to one another, and *and-sum*, as it is termed, the result of simple addition; or it is "the whole which is more than the sum of its parts," a *Gestalt*.[25] If ten listeners each hear one tone, the totality of their sensations is an and-sum; if one listener hears ten tones, the totality of his sensations is a *Gestalt*—a melody.

The totalities that are called *Gestalten* are distinguished by the characteristic that in them the individual part does not acquire its meaning from itself (or not exclusively from itself) but receives it from the whole. We know that melodies exhibit this characteristic to an especially pronounced degree: taken by itself, the individual tone is meaningless, mere sound; it is only by entering into relation with other tones, and vice versa, that it acquires musical meaning, becomes a part of the totality "melody." Here there appears to be a contradiction. If the part can acquire its meaning only from the whole, then the whole must in some way be given *before* the parts or at least together with them. How is this to be reconciled with the characteristic feature of the temporal whole, which is always given piecemeal, part after part? The Gestalt psychologists have avoided this problem by applying themselves principally to the investigation of spatial *Gestalten*. In space—where the parts of a whole occur not successively but together, are all present at once—the difficulty did not appear. But once we are committed to dealing with music, we have no recourse but to pose the problem and ask *how a temporal Gestalt is possible.*

Once again, the most natural expedient is to fall back on the function of memory. An individual tone is not a melody; it takes a succession of tones to make a melody. When we hear the second tone of such a

[25]On *and-sum* and *Gestalt*, cf. Max Wertheimer, "Untersuchungen zur Lehre von der Gestalt"; Wolfgang Koehler, *Gestalt Psychology*; and Kurt Koffka, *Principles of Gestalt Psychology.*

succession, the first has not vanished from our consciousness; memory has stored it up, and the tone now present stands beside the tone that, though past, is remembered; it can be related to the former tone, just as two things in space stand beside each other and can be related. The like is true of the third tone in relation to the first and second, and so forth. And even as elsewhere the line between past and present, which we survey retrospectively, is also prolonged toward the future, as coming events are anticipated, foreknown, or foretold, we can in the course of a melody reach beyond the present, actually sounding tone and relate it to tones that, though they do not yet exist, our consciousness anticipates. Temporal *Gestalten* appear possible because the past instant can be held in memory; the future instant can be anticipated in expectation. Although a temporal succession is always given us only part *after* part, in our consciousness part stands *beside* part, remembered part and expected part beside the part immediately given. Between immediate present, stored past, and anticipated future play the relations that make the individual tone a meaningful part of the tonal *Gestalt.*

Plausible as this interpretation sounds, it does not stand up. In the hearing of melodies, nothing is remembered and nothing anticipated. Let us first consider remembering. If it were the remembrance of the past tones which made us understand the present tones of a melody, understanding melodies would be contingent upon remembering them. We know what the situation is. Not one out of a hundred listeners will be capable of singing or playing from memory a melody that he has heard with pleasure—that is, with understanding. Or try breaking off a melody at random and asking listeners what tones, or even what tone, immediately preceded the one they last heard; the majority will be unable to answer. And then try the contrary experiment: let anyone who is capable of it call to mind the immediately preceding tone of a melody that he is hearing. *The instant he does so, he will have lost the thread of the melody.* The hearing of a melody is a hearing *with* the melody, that is, in closest connection with the tone sounding at the moment. It is even a condition of hearing melody that the tone present at the moment should fill consciousness *entirely*, that *nothing* should be remembered, nothing except it or beside it be present in consciousness. The essence of the musical tone, its dynamic quality, lies precisely in its relation to something that itself *is not there*; any turning back of consciousness for the purpose of making past tones present immediately annuls the possibility of musical hearing. Not only, then, is the individual tone in a melody understood in itself, without the slightest regard for whether anything is remembered; it *cannot* be understood *if* something is remembered.

The like holds for the anticipation of coming tones. It is certainly true that in hearing melodies we are always also reaching beyond the tone present at the moment; we are turned toward the coming tone, we listen toward it. This attitude is an expression of the pointing-beyond-itself, the state of incompleteness, of the individual tone—of its demand for completion. But this expectant tension of the present toward the future runs, so to speak, in a different groove from the anticipation of future events on the basis of foreknowledge or forefeeling. The normal process—that, in a state of expectation, one simultaneously imagines the future event which will satisfy the expectation—is foreign to the hearing of melodies and, indeed, is incompatible with it. If we go beyond the present tone in the sense that we imagine the coming tones, toward which we feel that the tension of the present tone is directed, we shall lose the thread of the melody just as we do by making consciousness revert to the preceding tone. Here too, then, it is evident that it cannot be its relation to other tones standing beside it in consciousness which gives the individual tone its meaning as part of the melodic whole. Indeed, the individual tone bears its meaning so exclusively in itself that it can only be understood at all if *no* past or future tone stands beside it in consciousness.

To convince ourselves that our ability to foreknow or forefeel future events has nothing to do with the peculiar relation between present and future that is revealed in music, we have only to think of the effect of surprise that characterizes certain tones in melodies. According to the usual explanation, this effect is based upon the fact that the tone heard is different from the tone expected, with a high degree of certainty, at that moment. Strangely enough, however, this effect is entirely independent of whether one is hearing such a melody for the first time or for the hundredth time; the questionable tone is poignantly heard as a surprise when when one *knows* for certain that it will enter. One may know the slow movement of Mozart's E-flat major Symphony by heart, play it by heart—the done d in the seventh measure of the melody will always be the same startling event. We might almost say that in such a case familiarity, foreknowledge, even intensifies the element of surprise. Here, then, I am expecting, with a high degree of certainty, an event of which I know perfectly well that it will *not* occur; and I am to the highest degree surprised by an event of which I knew in advance that it *would* occur. The paradox reveals that we are here dealing with *two* levels, and that what occurs on the one does not affect the other. One is the stream of events in time, the other the stream of time itself. Our foreknowledge is concerned with the stream of events; our hearing is concerned with the stream of time. So far as I know and represent to myself what is to come, I do not hear; and so far as I hear, I do not know and do not represent to myself what is to come. The expectation that I feel upon hearing a tone in a melody is not directed toward any *event*, toward something future that is become present; it is directed toward futurity, toward what can never become present. It is not expectation *of something*, a feeling whose object is an event in time; it is pure expectation, which has time itself, the eventuation of time, as its object. I can anticipate events in thought or feeling and thus, as the phrase goes, leave the present behind me. But I cannot anticipate time—time already anticipates itself. But the self-anticipation of time can be the subject of an experience. This is precisely what happens when I hear music. Without leaving the present behind me, I experience futurity as that toward which the present is directed and always remains directed. I experience the present as a striving toward a future that it never does more than touch, and that forever draws back from it, a process continually producing tension, continually new. In this way we understand how it is possible in general to experience something foreknown as something new—in concrete terms, to hear familiar melodies again and again with the same enjoyment. Events that I can anticipate in thought are certainly not new when they appear. But time is always new; cannot possibly be anything but new. Heard as a succession of acoustical events, music will soon become boring; heard as the manifestation of time eventuating, it can never bore. The paradox appears at its most acute in the achievement of the performing musician, who attains the heights if he succeeds in performing a work with which he is thoroughly familiar, as if it were the creation of the present moment. In such cases critics commonly say that the familiar work sounded "as if new."

(The processes that we are here attempting to characterize are certainly not confined to music. They must be demonstrable in the other arts in which time appears as a factor. Otherwise, how would it be possible to read an exciting story over and over again with the same tension? If, for example, in rereading Dostoevski's *The Possessed*, I know perfectly well that at the end of the great scene in Varvara

Petrovna's salon, Shatov, who until then has sat silent and unnoticed in a corner, will get up, walk slowly to where Stavrogin is sitting, and hit him in the face with his fist, my foreknowledge does not in the least impair the tension of the previous part of the scene, the part that leads up to the blow. Indeed, it has been said, with good reason, that it is only after the purely objective element of tension, the curiosity to know what is coming, has been disposed of that the other kind of tension and expectation can become manifest. Hence the heightened artistic pleasure one receives from rereading a great story. But what does this mean if not that foreknowledge of events does *not* dissolve the future; that the progress of time from present to future remains the same tense process, even if we know *what* is going to happen. If this were not so, foreknowlege of coming events would actually make the passing of time a "mere formality"; and the physicist, in so far as he wants only to foretell events, is quite justified in operating with just a time concept. However, the simple fact that one can see a play twice with the same tension strikingly demonstrates that time *is* something other than a mere formality, a mere container for successive events.)

Let us summarize: melody is temporal *Gestalt*; temporal *Getalt* presupposes that a temporal whole—a whole whose parts, with the exception of the one part present at the moment, either are no longer there or are not yet there—is given to us in an immediate experience. This is precisely what happens in hearing a melody. The existence of the individual tone in a melody is a being directed toward what no longer exists and what does not yet exist; thus past and future are given with and in the present and are experienced with and in the present; hearing a melody is hearing, having heard, and being about to hear, all at once. But the past is not a part of the future because it is remembered, nor is the future a part of the present because it is foreknown or forefelt. Anyone who thinks back to past tones or anticipates coming tones in imagination ceases to hear melody. The temporal whole with which we are here confronted is, then, certainly not the work of memory and foreknowledge or forefeeling. The simplest temporal *Gestalt*, the melody, shows the erroneousness of the view that the past can be given only as memory, the future only as foreknowledge. If this were so, if the past were, in the fullest sense, *no more* were extinguished, and could only be summoned back to a chimerical existence by virtue of the gift of memory—if the future were, in the fullest sense, *not yet*; if it had existence only in so far as knowledge or feeling enable us to anticipate coming events in imagination—then there could be no melodies. Every melody declares to us that the past can be there without being remembered, the future without being foreknown—that the past is not stored in memory but in time, and that it is not our consciousness which anticipates time but that time anticipates itself. The possibility of music and of every temporal *Gestalt* rests entirely upon the premise of time so constituted, of a time that stores itself and anticipates itself.

Only now are we in a position correctly to understand an essential element of the musical work of art, an element that we have not yet considered: its *form*.

When musicians speak of "form," using the word as a technical term, they refer to the arrangement of the larger sections of which most compositions are made up, as is a novel of chapters, a play of acts and scenes. In the course of the evolution of our musical language, and in the most intimate connection with the forces of tone and meter, certain schemas of arrangement have developed, which continually recur and in which, among other things, repetition plays an outstanding part. This circumstance has led to a widely disseminated misunderstanding of musical forms, and our first task must be to dispose of it. Since there is comparatively little difficulty in recognizing the repetition of a fairly long section as such, it has been thought that the study of forms provided the simplest and shortest approach to understanding musical works of art. That repetitions are not present here for their own sake, any more than they are elsewhere in music, has been overlooked; on the whole, forms have been regarded as stereotyped recipes for repetitions, as predetermined frames into which composers had to fit their ideas—if the repetitions were noted, the forms were understood. The usual "analyses" in the programs of our symphony concerts testify to this unfortunate state of affairs. What should be the acme of any real science of music—the study of the total form of a musical work of art, investigation of the processes that cause this form, in every instance, to manifest itself not as something predetermined from without but as an organic growth from within—has thus degenerated into the emptiest and most barren part of traditional musical theory.

What a melody is on a small scale, the total course of a musical work is on a large scale—a whole that unfolds in time and is so constituted that, though its individual members appear one after another, the whole, in order to be present, does not have to wait for member to be added to member, but is, so to speak, always already there, not factually, as with the spatial *Gestalt*, but as direction, as oriented tension. Let us think of the beginning of a movement from one of Bruckner's symphonies, one of those miracles of audible form. It is not simply "beginning," the start of something; from the first instant we hear in it *what* has begun, *toward what* it is a start: it is as if a great gate had opened upon an immeasurably wide and loft space, through which we now move, not simply step by step, but step by step as one advances through a very wide and lofty space toward a very distant goal. And as the individual parts of this whole, the elements of the total form, unroll before us, that toward which we advance without seeing it becomes, bit by bit, tangible present, until, with the last step, the whole is not *past*, but is *built up*— built up not in our memory (how could a normal memory embrace such a span of event?) but in the perfectly definite dynamic quality of the last step, which is experienced as precisely what it is: the step that brings such a gigantic construction to completion. The incomprehensibility of melody upon any other premise except that of an anticipating and storing time which does not pass away is reproduced here, only at a far higher power. Audible forms are perfect temporal *Gestalten*, creatures of time, as spatial *Gestalten* are creatures of space.

Two structural principles can be distinguished in musical compositions regarded as wholes, together with two corresponding types of musical forms, circular forms and serial forms, or—to use Wölfflin's terms— closed and open forms. The architectonic principle of the one is symmetry, equilibrium, polarity; that of the other is "again and yet again and yet again . . . " ever-increasing intensification. The same twofold nature of time that became apparent in the formation of meter, the will to close every wave cycle and the will to inexhaustible production of wave after wave, manifests itself in the formation of the larger temporal *Gestalten*. We see that, in accordance with their nature, we must refer to the temporal *Gestalten* of music as *rhythmic Gestalten.*

The simple circular forms have a bipartite or tripartite structure. In the binary form, the two parts that balance each other succeed each other immediately:

In the ternary form the dividing line that separates the two symmetrical halves has, so to speak, broadened into a dividing plane:

735

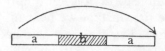

It has become an autonomous part, which now delays the fulfillment of the desire for symmetrical completion. The two parts of the binary form need not necessarily have the same tonal content. It is completely within the possibilities of tonal language to give the two parts, even though their content is different, a relation like that of question and answer, so that the meaning of the form, the symmetrical correspondence, is made apparent. In the ternary form, on the other hand, the third part must in essentials be a repetition of the first, because only thus can it be understood as its symmetrical counterpart across the separating middle part. (Here we see that the contribution of memory—awareness of the repetition—although it represents the necessary condition for understanding the form, is by no means equivalent to this understanding. The point is not that the first part is repeated at the end but that this repetition is a symmetrical fulfillment; establishes an equilibrium which was previously lacking. Memory cannot tell us this.)

We find simple binary and ternary forms in many songs, dances, small compositions of all sorts. With the increase in the dimensions of compositions, the forms extend, grow, as it were, through cell division. The result is the compound binary and ternary circular forms that are characteristic of many larger eighteenth- and nineteenth-century compositions:

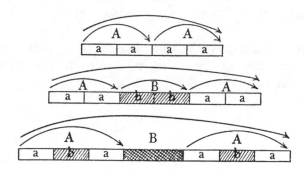

The schema of the serial form is

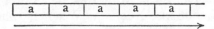

This in intention is an endless succession of form elements. Endless series, which are at the same time endless repetition, are to be found in much primitive music, or in folk ballads that repeat the same melody again and again to the countless stanzas of the poem. Yet this form too harbors powerful artistic possibilities: as repetition of the same tonal content in ever new transformations, as "theme and variations." Serial forms in which every form element has a new content are the natural recourse for many compositions to comparatively long texts, such as the early motets and madrigals. But we find this form in instrumental works too, for example, in many of Bach's clavier and organ fantasies. It appears, carried to the extreme, in an act of a Wagner opera. A great variety of combinations of repetitions with new material is possible in the serial form, as, for example, when, of every two successive sections, one is always the same and the other always new (rondo), or when one strand of the tonal texture keeps repeating the same thing, while another adds ever new things to it (chaconne, passacaglia).

Of particular interest are the forms in which the two structural principles, that of the circle and that of the series, compete with each other: series in which the circle principle finally asserts itself:

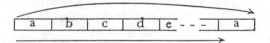

And ternary symmetrical structures that are seized upon by the stream of "yet again":

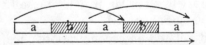

The two forces appear in most intimate interpenetration in the complex form rather misleadingly known as the "sonata form"; it is the form of the majority of the first movements of the great instrumental works of the classical and romantic periods. It was above all Beethoven who recognized the double nature of this form and the possibility it affords for a synthesis of polarity and intensification; his lifelong struggle for this synthesis, one of the chief motifs of his artistic activity, took place for the most part on the terrain of the sonata form.

737

That the great musical forms which we encounter in the works of Bach, Beethoven, Schubert, Bruckner, Wagner, that these gigantic superimposed and opposed blocks of tone, these tonal masses which balance one another or mutually suport and intensify one another, have the character of works of architecture has often been remarked. The phrase, so much quoted, about architecture as frozen music seems to point to a real relation in essence between the two arts. To be sure, if the striking *aperçu* is taken too literally, it ends by misleading us. It conceals the problem instead of explaining it. Temporal architecture cannot be changed into spatial architecture simply by the process of freezing. Frozen time is not space, but nothing, an empty phrase, a round cube. Can we turn the phrase around and say that music is flowing architecture? A building that begins to flow—can it still be called a building? Does not to build mean to set up something firm, based, and enduring against the eternal flux? As builders, we try to rise above our fate of eternal motion and find a stay in the motionless, the enduring, the subsistent. But then must we not regard the art whose sustenance is time, the eternal flux—the art of music—as architecture's most inveterate antagonist? All fundamental opposition to music—an opposition that has become articulate in recent times, setting up its *cave musicam*[26] against the general enthusiasm for music—is rooted in the same concern: that music may hold the threat of chaos; that it may undermine the foundation upon which order rests. Music, so this school of thought maintains, does not build, it dissolves; it does not give us clearly outlined images; on the contrary, it dissipates all outlines and boundaries. Is not structure by its very nature linked with space; is not temporal structure, temporal *Gestalt*, a misleading metaphor? To surrender oneself to music is to give one's soul into the power of the principle that is contrary to all order; is to let oneself be seduced by the "fairest mask of universal chaos."[27]

Behind these and related interpenetrations lies a time-honored dogma—the dogma that order is possible only in the enduring, the immutably fixed, the substantial. Those who subscribe to this dogma must, to be sure, conclude, from the absence of any enduring and substantial elements in music, that it is irreconcilable with order. But

---

[26]Nietzsche's warning, aimed particularly at Richard Wagner's music, in *Human, All Too Human*, Vol. II, foreword.
[27]Erich Wolff and C. Petersen, *Das Schicksal der Musik von der Antike zur Gegenwart.*

what if music presents us with this very thing—the unprecedented spectacle of an order in what is wholly flux, of a building without matter? Music, which can even stamp order upon the flowing, which can even wrest great edifices from the immaterial, is anything but a power incompatible with order, a dissolvent power. Hearing music, we experience a time whose being is no longer a swift flare-up in the passage from one nonexistence to another nonexistence, which reveals itself rather as a self-storing and self-renewal than as a transience, a time whose flux does *not* exclude building. Even more: the miracle of nonspatial building, of a construction that no eye sees, no hand grasps, but that we nevertheless *behold*, descry, envision through hearing— where could it be manifested if not in the pure temporal *Gestalten* of music? Order, liberated from all relation to things, *pure order*, bodiless, detached, and free, not as a mere concept, not as a dream, but as a vision beheld—it is to music that we owe our awareness that such a thing can exist.

XIV. The "Nonspatial Art"

What is a section on space doing in a work of music, the nonspatial art, the time art par excellence?

That the dynamic qualities of tone—the qualities that make music possible at all—are transcendent in respect to the world of space and bodies; that tonal motion cannot be understood as change of place in a tonal space; that time in music can only become an image because tones have freed themselves from every connection with things and the spatial—this, in brief summary, has been what we have so far found in our investigation of the relation between music and space. It is an altogether negative finding. Music seems to have shaken the last grain of the dust of spatiality from its shoes.

Let us try the opposite tack. Let tone and time be given: can we them build up music? Difficulties appear at once. Music puts us in the presence of a series of simple phenomena that seem to presuppose something other than tone and time, in which a third factor, a third component, must participate. And it appears that we cannot even talk about these phenomena except with words that, whether latently or patently, have a *spatial* meaning. Throughout this study we have found ourselves under the necessity of occasionally using spatial language— thus laying ourselves open to the reproach of first gallantly bowing space out of music and then secretly letting it in again through the back door. We shall now cite the most important instances in which we have been guilty of this loose procedure.

Music, we have repeatedly insisted, occurs where the sun rises and sets, where birds fly past, where a shout sounds: outside, outside of myself, not in me. Music that I hear does not arise in me; it encounters me, it come to me—from where? What is the meaning of terms like "outside," "from outside," what is the difference between "within" and "without," if I am not allowed to think of space?

If music were only tone and time—then, if time were thought away, only tone would remain. But something else remains: the chord, the connection of several tones sounding simultaneously. *Where* does this connection occur? If simultaneously sounding tones coalesced into a mixed tone as colors simultaneously projected upon a surface coalesce into a mixed color, then the chord would simply be another tone, as blue-green is another color, and the question would be superfluous. But the tones that make up a chord do not disappear in it; each remains in existence as a separate component of the chord and, in simple cases, can easily be heard in the chord even by untrained ears. What keeps apart simultaneously sounding tones, so that they can jointly form a chord? Simultaneously appearing colors, as we have said, coalesce into a mixed color—unless, that is, they appear in different places, unless *space* keeps them apart. It appears as if the fact of the simultaneity of different tones would in some way bring space, as its indispensable prerequisite, into music.

As the chord arises from the connection of simultaneously sounding tones, the texture of polyphonic music arises from the connection of several voices, or parts, proceeding side by side. Side by side? Pure temporal succession knows nothing of this nature, knows only a "one after the other"; only space makes us aware that there is a "side by side." And how am I to keep apart motions that no space keeps apart? Let us assume that a ballerina is dancing in a circle on a vertically rising platform: in general, we shall clearly distinguish two motions, the vertical rise, the circular motion. But suppose that the thing takes place in darkness, with only a spotlight on the dancer's hand. Now we shall no longer see two motions, the vertical, ↑, and the circular, ◯ , but only one, ⧩ , the ascending spiral; the two motions have coalesced. Can I speak of polyphony as the connection of several simultaneous occurring tonal motions—in the sense in which two lines become not *one* line but a combination of lines—without making any provision for the "space" in which such a phenomena can take place?

In Bach's *St. Matthew Passion* there is a passage that makes a particularly powerful impression on any listener: it is the moment—the only one of its kind in the work—when the choral mass fuses together into a single voice, sings as with one voice:

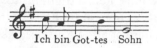

Ich bin Got-tes Sohn

Are they all really singing the same thing? Yes, because the tone is the same, and they all sing it at the same time. No, because the men sing an octave lower than the women. The tone is the same; the time is the same; whence the difference? What is the meaning of "an octave *lower*, an octave *higher*," when the result is still the same tone? To be sure, we distinguish and say that the men sing e, the women sing e'; but what does the symbol ' represent here? An answer involving frequencies is inadmissible; we do not hear vibrating air, we do not hear frequencies, we hear tones. What is it which makes what is the same appear different, what is different appear the same? It would be all very well if we could say that it is as in space, that it is the same object seen in different places, from different distances; or, better yet, as in a hall of mirrors, the many different reflections of the same object. But we cannot say this if music is to be the nonspatial art, the purely temporal art.

The problem, then, must be stated as follows: on the one hand music appears as the art that—in Schopenhauer's words—"is perceived solely in and through time, to the complete exclusion of space"; on the other hand, it is full of phenomena that seem to presuppose a spatial order and that in any case are wholly incomprehensible if space is "completely excluded."

We shall anticipate the result of the following investigation: Schopenhauer is wrong; the world of music is not the nonspatial world it is commonly represented to be; the experience of music is also an experience of space, and indeed a particular experience of space. Tones are not transcendent in repect to space as such but to *the* space in which bodies or objects have locations. Since space is commonly equated with this space—the space of bodies, the totality of all places—the spatiality of music *must* be denied. But then a full understanding of music as well as a full understanding of space have been precluded.

[. . .]

XVI. The Placeless, Flowing Space of Tones

. . . What is the situation with respect to the problem of the *dimensions* of auditory space? We have heard that auditory space "entirely lacks the three-dimensionality of optical space."[28] Then does it make sense to talk about dimensions here at all? More precisely, what is the situation with respect to the *depth* of auditory space?

No one will maintain that the ear is insensible to the perception of spatial depth in general; after all, we are able to distinguish positionally between a nearer and a more distant source of sound, even when the nearer sound is not characterized by greater loudness, when it is a matter of comparing a weak nearby sound with a strong distant sound. This is part of the ear's power to localize sounds. But the perception of differences in the sense of the third dimension, the depth of visual space, is not here under discussion. We are inquiring into the depth of a space that "entirely lacks three-dimensionality," a space for which the distinction "nearer" and "farther" has no more meaning than any other local distinction. Perhaps a brief reference to an auditory anomaly will help us to see the problem more clearly. A functional disturbance has been observed in which the ear, with its faculties otherwise unimpaired, loses that of localization. The person affected by this disturbance hears everything that the normal person hears; but he does not hear from where sound comes, whether from in front or behind, from right or left, from above or below; he hears every sound from everywhere. Auditorily, he is unable to distinguish places in space. Yet he hears space because he hears the sound as coming from without. Our question, then, can be framed as follows: Does the auditory space of such a person possess depth? From all that has so far been said, it is clear that each of us, in a particular situation, functions to all intents and purposes as this person does: namely, when we hear music. In the case of the musical tone, the spatial position of its source is of no importance; compositions that prescribe a particular spatial arrangement for the instruments (at a distance, in the four corners of the hall) by that very fact introduce an element of the theatrical into music—and *theater* comes from a root

---

[28]Géza Révész, "Gibt es einen Hörraum?"

meaning "to see." This is not said derogatorily; only the hopeless pedant would hold that I should lose nothing if the effect of the distant trumpet in Beethoven's *Leonore* Overture escaped me. Apart from such exceptional cases, however, this anomaly puts one at no disadvantage as far as the hearing of music is concerned; the ability to perceive musical tones correctly is entirely unaffected by the ability or inability of the ear to localize sources of sound in visual space. Hence we ask: Does the "without" from which tones encounter us, does the space which we hear in music and which is like the space of the person incapable of localizing sounds—a space in which there is no "there" and "elsewhere," no "nearer" and "farther"—does this space nevertheless have depth?

Let us imagine a spherical creature that drifts back and forth, up and down, in the water, incapable of any motion of its own, and whose only sense organ is its skin. Let this skin be so organized that, although it reacts to a contact by a sensation, it is incapable of localizing this sensation: in other words, the creature is aware that a contact has taken place but is not aware at what place it has been touched. Such an assumption is not fantastic. In an earlier context, reference was made to the variations in the ability of our own skin to localize contacts. If two pencil points 1 centimeter apart touch the fingertip, we feel two contacts; the same stimulus, applied to the back of the hand, we feel as only *one* contact; we cannot tell whether both points, or only one, are actually touching the skin. Simultaneous contacts less than 1 centimeter apart, then, here produce only *one* contact sensation; places less than 1 centimenter apart pass as *one* place. Let us assume that the circumference of our spherical creature is less than 2 centimeters and the localization sensitivity of its skin is the same as that of the back of the human hand. What will such a creature know of space? Generally speaking, it will know space—just as we do—as the without from which things (which, in the case of our creature, means whatever produces contacts, gives rise to tactile sensations) encounter it. But since no two places on its skin are farther than 1 centimeter apart, and since its skin feels places 1 centimeter or less apart as *one* place—and since, furthermore, it has no other sense to fall back on—it will experience all contacts as occurring at the same place; will experience the "without" as an undifferentiated unity, as *one* place. The notions of places in space, of distinctions between places, of distances, would be foreign to it; its space will be a placeless space, comparable in this respect to auditory space.

Has the space of this creature depth? One need only bring to mind the nature of tactile sensations in order to answer this question in the negative. Tactile sensations have no depth; they make no statement concerning the without except in so far as it is in direct contact with the skin. No matter how refined my sense of touch may be, it cannot tell me anything abut the length of the pencil whose point my hand touches, or about the thickness of the wall into which I bump. The space of our hypothetical spherical creature will, then, be perfectly flat. Its experience of space cannot extend beyond its skin; for it, "space," the "without," is like another skin, belonging to another being, and closely and completely surrounding its own. But now let us endow our creature with hearing; let it hear its first tone. Instantly, the most violent revolution will occur in its space. The other skin has burst; the creature's without spreads explosively all around it. The new without, from which the tone encounters it, is no longer the flatness, the enclosure, of the tactile without; in the tone, it encounters the space that the tone fills. Thus for the first time, through a sensation, it reaches beyond its own skin, into a depth; for the first time it feels space, in the full sense, around it.

The step from an unlocalized tactile sensation to an equally unlocalized auditory sensation makes it clear that a placeless space, a space in which there is no distinction between "there" and "elsewhere," between "nearer" and "farther," can nevertheless have depth. Whereas we *feel* the thing in contact with us simply as "there," we *hear* tone as "coming from . . . "—not from any one location *in* space, nor yet from all locations in space, as if space were the inactive vessel through which tone approaches us. No, in tone, space itself—as we put it earlier—is in a unique way directed toward the hearer; is experienced as in motion toward him. In this sensation—"directed from . . . toward . . . "— spatial depth is revealed to the hearer. Depth in auditory space, then, refers not to the distance between my ear and the location in space where a tone is produced, does not refer at all to the space *in* which I encounter tones; it refers to the space I encounter in tones, to the "from . . . " element of the encounter. Depth in auditory space is only another expression for this "coming from . . . " that we sense in every tone. It is as if a swimmer in a river felt, in the pressure of the water against his skin, the whole depth of the extent through which its waters are in motion toward him from its source. One and the same sensation makes us experience auditory space as possessing depth and as flowing.

The term "flowing space" comes from Melchoir Palágyi's notable paper, written about the turn of the century, *Neue Theorie des Raumes und der Zeit*. In it he attempts to show that such a concept of space is a logical necessity. The logical inconsistencies in the classical separation and opposition of static space and flowing time are pointed out. Space without time, he argues, is as unreal as it is unthinkable; time and space do not bear to each other the relation of flux and stasis; to the continuous series of moments in time there does not correspond one space, one static datum, but an equally continuous *series* of spaces, whose totality must be designated as flowing space. Whatever may be argued against these considerations, it is impossible to deny that they point in the same direction in which recent thought on the subject of space has been moving. More and more, modern science is getting us out of the habit of seeing space as the eternally unchanged datum, the inactive vessel in which bodies move and produce and undergo effects. More and more, in the concepts of physicists, space appears as itself entangled in physical event. Space that is less and less distinguishable from the dynamic field that fills it; space that curves; space that expands—to such a space, in any event, the adjective "flowing" is not essentially foreign.

The space of tones, then, is a placeless depth surrounding the hearer or, more properly, directed toward him, moving toward him, from all about. The depth of this space is not the depth that, together with height and width, makes up the three dimensions of visual space. Height, width, depth—there are no such distinctions in auditory space. Here there is only the one "from . . . "—which, if we like, we may call the one dimension of auditory space. Here "from . . . " does not mean "from there or from elsewhere" but "out of depth from all sides"; and "out of depth" is not a direction in space but a (nay, *the*) direction of space. A space that, as a whole, has the direction "out of depth from all sides" *must have a center*, the position toward which it can be thus directed. To be sure, he who sees likewise finds himself, if no objects interfere with vision, in the center of the space he views; but this is a fortuitous situation, and for this reason the space of geometry, derived as it is from visual space, knows nothing of a center. But a being that only heard, that heard only tones, could simply have no idea of a space without a center; such a being can think away its own person, can think of space without a perceiving being, but not of space without a center. The space, that, as a whole, has the distinguishing characteristic "directed from . . . toward . . . " must have a center as necessarily as a circle or a sphere must have a center. And, because of its nature, experience of this space must always be experience out from a center. For him who hears, to perceive

745

space means to be at the point toward which space as a whole is directed, toward which it flows together from all sides. The space experience of him who hears is an experience of space streaming in toward him from all sides.

Only now does the difference between seeing depth and hearing depth become clear. To see depth means to read degrees of nearness and distance from the naturally flat retinal image. The depth that I see is distance, is there where I am not; the eye pushes the without away from me; the step from plane to space, to spatial depth, here has the meaning "away from me." The eye discloses space to me in that it excludes me from it. The ear, on the other hand, discloses space to me in that it lets me participate in it. The depth that I hear is not a being-at-a-distance; it is a coming-from-a-distance. To be sure, in thought and dream I can transport myself out into the distance that I see or that lies beyond my sight; but the distance that I hear comes, as it were, of its own volition toward me, streams into me. Where the eye draws the strict boundary line that divides without from within, world from self, the ear creates a bridge. "Seeing and hearing are distinguished not only by the difference in the physical stimulus, in the functioning organs and their objects, but also, and even more, by the mode of the specific connection between the self and the world."[29] For seeing, there are two poles; for hearing, there is one stream. The space experience of the eye is a disjunctive experience; the space experience of the ear is a participative experience.

Looking back from this point, we recognize the inaccuracy and superficiality of the common classification of music as a purely temporal art. Space speaks from the tones of music; the musical experience is also a space experience, and indeed a very remarkable and special one. The seeming contradiction between this statement and the space transcendence of music, which we so emphatically maintained and so circumstantially demonstrated earlier, is resolved in the fact that tones are transcendent not in relation to space as such but only in relation to the space that the eye sees, that the hand grasps, that geometry thinks and measures. But this means that the space of our practical life and our scientific thinking is not *all* of space. Even where there is nothing to be seen, nothing to be touched, nothing to be measured, where bodies do not move from place to place, there is still space. And it is not empty space; it is space filled to the brim, space "become alive," the space that

[29]Erwin Straus, *Vom Sinn der Sinne.*

tones disclose to us. Far from being unable to testify in matters of space, music makes us understand that we do not learn all that is to be said about space from eye and hand, from geometry, geography, astronomy, physics. The full concept of space must include the experience of the ear, the testimony of music.

XVIII. Space as Place and Space as Force

If we look back over the course that our investigation has followed in this section, we shall not be able to avoid the impression of inadequacy and incompleteness—especially in respect to the question of the order of auditory space. Yet it will not be denied that a certain amount of ground has been gained and consolidated.

1. The nonspatiality of music has been dismissed. Music as purely temporal art, a music that, as Schopenhauer has it, "is perceived in and through time, to the total exclusion of space," does not exist. The musical experience has a spatial component; he who hears music is aware of space.

2. The space experience of the ear in tones and the normal space experience of the eye coincide only in the most general sense: both fulfill the definition of space as the "whence of encounter." But whereas space is given to the eye as that which *is* without, as that which confronts it, where I am not, where things are, and are in places, as multiplicity, as aggregate of places, in which we distinguish somewhere from elsewhere, measure intervals, draw boundaries, divide and put together, the ear knows space only as that which *comes from* without, as that which is directed toward me, streams toward me and into me, as that which is given in no other way than as a boundless indivisible oneness, in which nothing can be divided and nothing measured—as placeless flowing space.

3. The placeless flowing space of our hearing does not represent a primitive stage of our space experience, as might perhaps be concluded from the negative qualification that in it no boundaries can be drawn and no parts distinguished; it is not the as yet unordered space, to create order in which would be the task of the eye and the hand and of the thought they direct. As visual space has its order, which gives the eye the visual arts and thought the art of measurement (geometry), auditory space has its order, which gives the ear the art of music. Without an order of visual space, there would be no architecture and no physics;

but, equally, without an order of auditory space there would be no music. *Order of visual space*, visible-tangible order: order by places, order of "juxtaposition"; relations between positions and magnitudes, quantitative relations; order that governs the course of the motion of bodies from place to place. *Order of auditory space*, audibly spatial order: order by states, order of interpenetration; purely dynamic relations of direction and tension; order that underlies the motion of tones from state to state. Visual space and auditory space: not two different stages but two different types of order in spatiality, two equally ranking, equally justified, equally "right" modes of being of spatiality.

4. Since the eye is man's chief organ of orientation in his biological milieu; since the space experience of the eye (and the hand) becomes knowledge in geometry; since the space concept of geometry has served the science of the motion of bodies, physics, as scaffolding; since physics largely determines modern man's picture of the universe—it is not at all surprising that, in matters of space, we have gone to school to these two sciences; have let geometry and physics tell us *what space is*. Now visual space and geometrical space, to be sure, are not the same: no eye has ever seen a point, a straight line, two parallel lines. But visual space and geometrical space have the same type of order, so that visual space can be understood from geometrical space; can be integrated into it as a special case. The same is also true of the space in which our ear localizes noises. It is *not* true of the space which encounters us in tones, the space of musical experience. The ordering principle of this space is diametrically opposed to that of geometrical space; musical space cannot be integrated into geometrical space. The dogmatic mind that, consciously or unconsciously, clings to the premise that the geometrico-physical space concept is the concept of space as such is consequently unable to admit that music participates in space; it must deny the spatiality of music. For the undogmatic observer, on the other hand, insight into the spatiality of music must destroy the validity of the dogmatist's premise: space and geometrico-physical space do *not* coincide. There are experiences of space that we owe to neither the eye nor the hand; a knowledge of space that is not geometrical knowledge is possible. The limits of the space of things and places are not the limits of space as such. The end of the space in which bodies are in places and move from place to place is not yet the beginning of the nonspatial, the psychic, the spiritual, the supernatural—whatever one chooses to call it. Beyond the space of bodies, there is still space—space that is not therefore any less real, less natural, less "of this world," because in it

748

there is nothing to see, nothing to touch, nothing to measure. It is possible to conceive of spatial events—spatial in the full sense—that leave no trace in the space of things and places. Music is the classic example of such events.

Bergson's *Matière et mémoire* contains the following sentence: "On pourrait... dans une certaine mesure, se dégager de l'espace sans sortir de l'étendue." Literally translated: "One could... in a certain measure, disengage oneself from space without leaving extension." Since Bergson accepted the traditional space concept without criticism (as he did not the traditional time concept), "space" here means "geometrico-physical space." The word "extension," then, presumably stands for a mode of being of spatiality that the traditional space concept does not include. ("Extension," he writes elsewhere, "is not in it [space]; it is the latter that we put in the former.") Translated into our terminology, Bergson's statement would, then, read: "One could, in a certain measure, disengage oneself from geometrico-physical space, from the space of places and bodies, without leaving space as such." This is precisely what happens to us when we hear music—and not "in a certain measure," but in unqualified reality. Far from taking us out of space—as common opinion holds—music discloses to us a mode of being of spatiality that, except through music, is accessible only with difficulty and indirectly. It is the space which, instead of consolidating the boundaries between within and without, obliterates them; space which does not stand over against me but with which I can be one; which permits encounter to be experienced as communication, not as distance; which I must apprehend not as universal place but as universal force.

Thus musical experience demands that our thinking about space be as radically revised as our thinking about time, and we find ourselves confronted by a question similar to that which confronted us in the case of time. Are the two modes of existence of space to which the geometrico-physical and the musical concepts of space refer hermetically sealed from each other, as if there were *two spaces*? Is the *one space*, which presents itself differently from different approaches, from seeing and hearing? Does the space of music have a separate existence of its own? Do the space experiences of the eye and the ear exclude each other? Or do they supplement each other? Do they include each other?

We already know that the space of the eye is *not* closed to the ear. The ear is able to localize noises, that is, to distinguish the places at which bodies are, and to determine, with considerable accuracy, the place at which the physical source of the noise is to be sought. Eye and ear here work together, in the same space. One could call the localizing faculty of the ear its unmusical faculty, but we have pointed out that music by no means regards it as beneath its dignity to make use of this faculty occasionally to achieve particular ends—as, for example, when a particular spatial disposition is prescribed for individual instruments or groups of instruments, perhaps at a distance or at an elevation; or, again, in the case of the so-called antiphonal style of composition, where vocal or instrument choirs, separated in space, sing or play to one another, as it were, in dialogue. Spatial effects of this kind are, in any case, not irreconcilable with the specific effects of auditory space; the ear is capable of both types of space experience. Is the like true of the eye?

Many people like to shut their eyes when they listen to music. Stravinsky roundly expresses his disapproval of the practice. "I have always abominated listening to music with closed eyes, without the eye taking an active part. Seeing the gestures and motions of the different parts of the body that produce music is necessary and essential to grasping it in all its fullness. Those who claim to enjoy music fully only if their eyes are closed do not hear it better than if they eyes were open, but the absence of visual distractions allows them to abandon themselves, under the lulling influence of sounds, to vague reveries—and it is these which they love, far more than music itself."[30] There is something to be said on both sides. It is certainly a valuable idea, pedagogically, to call upon the eye as an auxiliary organ in order to concentration attention upon the kinetic character of music; and it is certainly true that closing the eyes usually serves the ends that Stravinsky so aptly describes. On the other hand, people whose attitude toward "music itself" is above question—Pablo Casals, for example—close their eyes when they play or listen. Certainly we shall not go along with those who claim that closing the eyes, the exclusion of space, is the necessary prerequisite for a pure enjoyment of the spaceless art; for it is not out of space that music seeks to take us but only out of one mode of existence of spatiality—in order to lead us all the more deeply into another. Yet it cannot be denied that the eye is the organ of our most intimate and strongest connection with *the* space that music has left behind; the corporeal things in their places, which we have before us when our eyes are open, may well block our view into the space of which music seeks to make us aware. Thus it

[30]*Stravinsky, an Autobiography.*

750

would be strictly proper to exclude the space experience of the eye temporarily in order to entrust ourselve to the space experience of the ear all the more intimately. The question is only, Is it *necessary* to blind ourselves temporarily in order to be open to the space vision of the ear? Is the eye in this case positively and exclusively a hindrance? Can the eye only see—see things in place? Can the eye perhaps hear too?

For poets, this has never been a question. Shakespeare's lovers "hear with their eyes." Wagner's Tristan, at the highest pitch of expectation, "hears the light"—sight changes into hearing. Dante comes in Hell to a "place dumb of all light"—he hears the absence of light. Goethe speaks of the "whir" of light; light "trumpets." What is referred to in these passages is not so-called synesthesias—auditory sensations produced by visual sensations and accompanying them—it is a real perception through the eyes, but which nevertheless has the characteristics of hearing. Nor is it a matter of poetic imagination; highly sensitive persons have reported strange states that sometimes overtake them when they contemplate a thing (it can be some perfectly insignificant thing); suddenly they seem to lose themselves in the thing; the wall between person seeing and thing seen collapses; at the same time the thing itself loses its contours, expands into the world, seems to contain the whole world in itself, passes into the observer as the whole world, so that the being of the I, of the thing, of the world, coalesce into one. If the random thing I see there before me were suddenly transformed into a tone, the phenomenon would have to be described in much the same way: the limited "there" that enlarges to all space, the without that changes into a coming-from-without, space become alive, become force, directed toward me, streaming into me. Such a seeing may well be called a hearing with the eyes; only, in the case of the eye, this manner of perception is not normal, as it is for the ear: it is the mark of an unusual state, the state of ecstasy.

The observations of many psychologists on the visual sensations of infants, or of blind persons whose sight has been restored by an operation, point in a similar direction. Here the element, characteristic for normal seeing, of the localizing of the visual sensation at a particular place "out there," "where I am not," seems still to be lacking. William James, in his *Psychology*, quotes Condillac: "The first time we see light we are it rather than see it." The boundary between within and without, between the I and the world, is not yet sharply drawn; communication preponderates over distance. The function of the eye that we call its normal function—the perception of things in places—would, accordingly, not

751

be given from the beginning; would rather be the result of a development, whose earlier stages are not so sharply differentiated from hearing as its later ones. May we assume—purely speculatively, or even fancifully— that the early stage, which is quickly passed through in the history of the individual, appeared, in the history of the race, as the distinguishing characteristic of an entire prehistoric epoch—that there was a period in which the normal function of the eye served not only local orientation in space, as it does today, but also a sort of dynamic communication with space, was a seeing of forces rather than of places? In a previous connection we referred to the instinctive performances of many animals, performances that we cannot but call miraculous if we regard them from the point of view of the space of places, but that assume a very different and much more natural complexion if one thinks of them as based on a spatial order of the type of auditory space. May we further assume, even more fancifully, that the case may have been similar with respect to the magical abilities of man, of which the mythologies of remote epochs and of the primitives tell, that they were based upon a direct seeing of space as force, a dynamic communication between within and without, whose last offshoot we should have to recognize in the hearing of tones, in the hearing of space as force? In this case, we should have in music the miraculous echo of a world that once lay open to sight. This ability, in the course of evolution and as life in civilized societies laid other claims upon sight, could have gradually been over- shadowed, until today it appears only exceptionally, at unusual moments. But in this case the space of our hearing, space as force, would be *more primordial* in comparison with the space of our seeing, space as place—and not only in the temporal sense but also in an ontological sense: that of being closer to origins, more in correspondence with the primal nature of the real. Bergson must have had something of the sort in mind when he wrote (we now give in full the sentence quoted in part before): "One could, then, in a certain measure, disengage oneself from space [the space of places and things] without leaving extension [space as such]—*and in this there would be a return to the immediate.*" And elsewhere: "L'étendue précède l'espace"—in our terms: "Space as force precedes space as place."[31]

But now to get back to solid ground. If it remains incontestable that the principal and normal function of the eye for civilized man is orienta-

[31]*Matière et mémoire.*

tion in corporeal space and the seeing of things in their places, it is nevertheless undeniable that the ability of the eye is not exhausted by this activity. We need not at once think of magical abilities; we ourselves, in the course of this investigation, have from time to time had occasion to speak of activities of the eye that go beyond the function of seeing a thing in a place—and go beyond it in a particular direction, which it seems natural to compare with the mode of perception of the ear. Let us recall von Allesch's researches: colors appear to possess dynamic qualities, the eye perceives in them an action of forces;[32] or Wertheimer's study of motion: to see motion does not mean to see a thing first in one place and then in another, is in general not a seeing of "thing in place," but of "pure passing over," the perception of a purely dynamic process.[33] To attain a clearer conception of auditory space, we cited the image of the empty sky: lying on my back and gazing into the empty sky I do not see "thing out there," a blue hemisphere surrounding me; I see boundless space, in which I lose. myself. The strange phenomenon of vertigo, of being drawn by space, might also be mentioned. For Gestalt psychology, seeing in general is primarily a seeing of *Gestalten*, i.e., a direct visual perception of dynamic processes. As Koffka says, both briefly and convincingly: "Visual space is a dynamic event rather than a geometrical pattern."[34]

With this reference to *Gestalt*, we have reached the point at which the ability of the eye to see space as force, so to speak, publicly announces itself: in its encounter with works of visual art. In these, the seeing of forms and colors, like the hearing of tones in a work of music, is a direct perception of acting forces. The individual form or color is no more confined to itself than is the individual tone; none is simply in its place and remains in its place, each points beyond itself, to other forms and colors, each stands to each, in the whole of the work, in a definite relation; indeed, it is only perforce of these relations that the work becomes a whole. They are spatial relations, but not of the kind that the eye otherwise observes in space and that are fully apprehended and described if the mutual positions are determined, the mutual distances measured. What the eye sees here are tensions and countertensions, harmonies and disharmonies: purely dynamic relations. Here the line,

---

[32]Gustav von Allesch, *Die aesthetische Erscheinungsweise der Farben.*
[33]Max Wertheimer, "Experimentelle Studien über das Sehen von Bewegung."
[34]Kurt Koffka, *Principles of Gestalt Psychology.*

the outline, is not only the objective boundary that sets off thing from thing, thing from space; beyond that, it is a sign, a statement, in which a meaning exists, exists symbolically, as musical meaning exists in tones. The space of the picture itself, together with the things represented in it, is not simply set off from the observer; rather it opens itself to him, takes him into itself, passes into him. In another connection we discussed the unique spatial effects of Chinese painting: how a single form, a line, awakens the surrounding void to life, makes it active, makes space as such (supposedly a nothingness to the eye) visible— as space becomes audible through the sounding of a tone. We also mentioned analogous effects of architecture—the making "empty" space visible, almost tangible. But the ability of the eye that lets us perceive such things— how are we to describe it if not as a beholding of forces, of space as force? Might it be conceivable that in our visual arts the mythical ability of the eye to behold the dynamic across the corporeal still survives?

We must at least mention, if only cursorily, an amazing development that belongs in this context: it is that of the dynamization of the space concept in modern physics. Originally, as we have said, physics took over the space concept of geometry, which for its part, drew the logical conclusions from the experiences of the eye and the hand in the space of things and places and put them together in a system. The space concept that physics today returns to geometry (but not without geometry itself having given the cue) has so changed as to be almost unrecognizable. The rigid structure, fixed for all eternity, which served physical phenomena as their absolutely dependable foundation, has become a space that bends one way or another, expands or contracts, in accordance with what physical events seem to require. Statements about space are hardly distinguishable from statements about the dynamic; the line between space and dynamic field becomes blurred like that between matter and energy. The definition of visual space just cited, which comes from Gestalt psychology—"dynamic event rather than geometrical pattern"—could also be applied to the space of modern physics. Philosophy is already drawing conclusions from this development. "All space is process," says Samuel Alexander.[35] Here we have come quite close to the musical space concept—even if we are still at an appreciable distance from it.

[35]*Space, Time, and Deity.*

And now let us briefly summarize our results. Auditory space and visual space are not like two spaces; what we have said of auditory space is not true only of a definite special instance of space, but has a meaning for space in general. To be sure, the musical experience of space is basically different from the normal experience of space by the eye; but this does not make music exist, as it were, in a space of its own, shut off from everything else that encounters us as spatial. No, the space experience of the ear hearing tones is not alien to the eye, as, vice versa, the space experience of the seeing eye is familiar to the ear hearing noises. There is, then, *one* space, *the* space that encounters ear and eye as place and force. A certain difference in rank in the two modes of existence of space is perhaps expressed in the fact that we regard the ability of the ear to localize sources of sound as inferior to its musical ability; whereas, on the contrary, we regard the beholding of space as force in works of painting and architecture as a higher accomplishment than the seeing of things in places.

Finally, it is clear that such a revision of our thought in matters of space cannot remain without consequences for the classical opposition between space and time. We need only think back to the manifestations of time that we have observed in music in order to become aware that, for the person hearing music, time and space are not diametrically opposed principles of being or of order, as they are presented in our traditional thinking and even in Bergson. Above what separates them, the person hearing music recognizes what connects them; even more, his experience forces him to recognize the connecting, rather than the separating, as the essential. He hears time as force and he hears space as force. For him, what keeps the two apart is secondary. This separating element has found expression in the two terms "juxtaposition" and "succession." What remains of it in the musical experience? Our discussion of auditory space centered itself upon a concept of a spatial order that should *not* be understood as juxtaposition; in the space that we hear there simply is no juxtaposition. The situation is not much better in regard to the musical time concept and succession. It is not the series of instant after instant which is essential in music, but the fact that the present instant contains the past instant and the future instant: an interprenetration rather than a succession. The same word by which we distinguished the order of auditory space is, then, also applicable to the order of auditory space is, then, also applicable to the order of auditory time. Space and time: not "juxtaposition" and "succession," but "inter-

755

penetration"—interpenetration of simultaneous occurrence and serial occurrence. The radical separation of the two becomes untenable in the presence of music.

In conclusion, we observe that in the case of "space," as in the case of "time" or "motion," musical experiences illuminate a side of the phenomena that, from the viewpoint and in the thinking of modern man, is normally obscured; but on the other hand, when all is said and done, music, to put it bluntly, has nothing new to tell us. We learn nothing from music that we could not, in principle, learn equally well from other sources; and the concern of the most progressive thinkers of our day is precisely to attain, from other sources, notions such as we have derived from music. This does not represent a weakness in our undertaking; it is, rather, its proper justification. Only thus does it become apparent that, in music, we *experience the world*. Were it otherwise, music would be a special province—something for connoisseurs, even a flight from the world. Its unique significance for our thinking, for our understanding of the world, does not, then, lie in its leading us to otherwise inaccessible insights. But what, elsewhere, can be made accessible only by laborious speculation, and then only uncertainly and insecurely—so that it always remains open to doubt, opposition, and rejection—music brings us patently. In music, what other phenomena conceal itself becomes phenomenon; in music, what is inmost to the world is turned outward.

FRITZ WINCKEL

Fritz Winckel (b. Bregenz, Austria 1907–) a leader in the field of psycho-acoustics related his interests in acoustics to the physical and aesthetic aspects of musical hearing. Interested in the perception of music, Winckel also investigated the ways in which structures of music and language constitute forms of communication, using experimental and electronic music as a basis for his research. His *Music, Sound and Sensation* (1959) attempts to define the relationships among the laws of musical perception—accounting both for the generative mechanism of sound structures and the mechanism of perception—in a "simple, down to earth way" without recourse to "arbitrary interpretations."

Central to his theory are the concepts of perpetual motion and change. Motion and change are germane both to sounds and to the mechanism of perception. Pitch and rhythm are defined within borders of uncertainty rather than being accorded definite quantities. It is the fluctuating character of musical sounds, according to Winckel, that gives music its richness.

Music aesthetics, nonetheless, is based on a "time constant" of sound perception. The boundaries of the tone spectrum, as well as its evaluation and the ability to determine the direction of the source of a sound, are dependent on such a constant. Joos's acoustical investigations set the integration constant of the ear at 50 ms, the time required to become aware of a sensory perception. Here too, however, one must allow for the inability to determine with precision the point of termination of the required time, for the sound pressure impulses at intervals exceeding the "time constant" are not easily differentiated.

Nothing is "independent" or "static" in music, insists Winckel. Though his functional concept of "building blocks," whereby consecutive sounds determine relationships of intervalic tension, is not a new idea, he succeeds in demonstrating that the effect one sound complex has on another also depends on the changes occurring during the intoning of the sound, i.e. on the onset process, the modulation and the decay of the sound. He also attempts to show how dynamic changes influence pitch perception, while changes in tempo and rhythm affect tone color.

In the perception of music, time is subjective. Music, although emitted within an objective time flow, is perceived as a whole, independent of time, says Winckel. The accepted time designations and divisions, the bar lines which segment the ever flowing pulse of time into countable units, only help the listener get his bearings by announcing the approach of oncoming sound events, thereby reducing unnecessary tensions. Indeed, it is the metrical organization of duration which accounts for the perception of the work as a whole, rather than as a succession in time.

Space also plays a part in perception. Not all of the sounds approach the ear directly; some arrive as reflections from walls, furniture, and the like. While reflections may be desirable and contribute to the definition of the sound structure, those exceeding the integration constant of the ear cause an undesirable echo effect. Thus, the perception of a musical work also depends on the acoustics of the room in which it is heard.

Winckel draws sharp distinctions between music as heard, music as represented by a score, and the abstract conception of a work. The score, accordingly, is only a rough approximation of the music's qualities, revealing nothing of the potential effect of the oncoming sounds. The perception of a musical work is richer than its representation in the score, and not necessarily identical with the composer's conception. Many composers, unaware of the importance of the psycho-acoustical aspects of sounds, immerse themselves solely in the functional relationships of a language of notated musical symbols.

Improvements in methods of measurement, claims Winckel, refine the description of the perception process in music, for they contribute greatly to the field of psycho-acoustics in which the dependence of the subjective musical hearing on natural laws becomes evident. The latter serves Winckel as a point of departure for a new aesthetics of music.

Though the field of psycho-acoustics has advanced since Winckel, the merit of his pioneering work goes, undoubtedly, beyond his actual findings. Its importance lies in the very attempt to deal with the "objective" together with the "subjective," and in his attempt to account, within the latter, not only for prime perceptions but for culturally determined aspects as well. Though Bergson's explanation regarding 'wholeness'—the dialectics between linearity and structure

—is more persuasive, Winckel's suggestion concerning the function of the bar-line is interesting. Compared to Winckel's external bar-line however, a more elementary "internal" unit for the organization of duration was suggested by Joseph Holubar in his *Sense of Time* (1969). Holubar suggested the alpha waves, which are constantly produced in the mind, as an objective point of reference, accounting for basic temporal experiences.

Though the abstract conception of a work should not be identified with the process of hearing, nor should the latter be confused with the score, there is more of a connection between them than Winckel cares to admit. It is precisely the score, both Goodman and Wolterstorff will argue, which largely determines the musical qualities to be heard. Controlling the "flow of time" was, in fact, the central problem which medieval notation tried to solve. Nonetheless, while it is true that one may talk about the "correctness" dictated by scores, it seems worthwhile to investigate, in psycho-acoustic terms, the *"constant"* elements which they determine (see Goodman and Wolterstorff).

from Music, Sound and Sensation[1]

The Effect of Music on the listener

> *Music is sounding form in motion.*
> E. Hanslick (1825–1904).

Summary

The investigations discussed in this book have shown that not only music as a whole but also its individual component—sound—is an element exclusively in motion. If one were to permit a single sound to be intoned undisturbed and unmodulated for a certain time and without the addition of other sounds, it would soon be "forgotten" by the psyche and therefore would no longer exist for our consciousness. A continual monotonous hum of a machine in a factory disappears from the consciousness and is noticed again only when it is turned off. The ticking of a clock drops quickly from our consciousness, and will be clearly noticed only at the moment when it stops, because that moment represents a discontinuous transition between two states. A long-held organ point has no independent function; only in conjunction with the upper voices can it accomplish a harmonic modulation. Since in earlier centuries it was not yet customary to enliven a long, steady tone by means of *crescendo*, trills and vibrato, the technique of ornamentation and coloration was extensively employed. Evenness of beat would also lead to rigidity of music. It is the fluctuation in the meter, the agogic molding, which "disturb" the frozen pattern of synchronization and breathe life into the work of art. It is this which creates the inner motion, makes contact with the listener and produces the visible or audible event.

If we examine sounds that occur in nature, we look in vain for sounds which remain even for a short time at the same pitch or are constantly of the same color. For the communication of all beings such sounds would indeed be meaningless, for they contain no information, only a repeti-

[1]Text: Fritz Winckel, *Music, Sound and Sensation* (New York: Dover Publications Inc., 1967), pp. 157–176. The notes under asterisks are Winckel's notes.

tion of the first impulse. A signal forms its characteristics even when only briefly intoned, and even when it is a call for help it is more noticeable when it is interrupted many times (cf. the wobbly tone of the air raid warning siren in Europe as opposed to the constant sound of the allclear siren, the relief). Out of the varied world of animals' voices we select here the song of birds, because it is considered especially musical. If we observe the sounds on oscillograms (Figs. 98 and 99), we see that there is not simply an uninterrupted change in sound formation forming a melody, but, surprisingly enough, the melody is in no way random or without rules, but rather is repeated in fractions of seconds exactly note for note in the same rhythm, as will be seen in the example of the wren. It is also to be noted that a small child in his first years of speaking does not utter lengthy constant sounds, and, as a matter of fact, is unable to do so. The special technique of the physiological functions required here (breath control, training of the muscles of the larynx and of the nervous system) is only acquired after long years of practice. Human *speech* is according to its structure also an uninterrupted series of transients, so that it is not justifiable to speak of speech-"sound" (*Klang*), as unfortunately is still done in the field of phonetics. Normal conversational speech contains on the average four or five syllables/sec, which continually flow one into another and even in these transitions contain information.

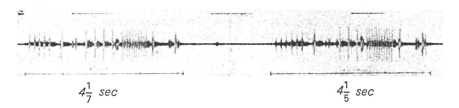

$$4\tfrac{1}{7} \; sec \qquad\qquad 4\tfrac{1}{5} \; sec$$

Fig. 98. Song of a wren.
Demonstration of the rhythm by the sound pressure recording.

Fig. 99. Song of a nighthawk.
Pitch recording on the sonagraph.

761

How are we going to define *singing* as opposed to speaking in terms of our investigation? Singing is the development of utterances of speech into a cultivated sound through the extension of the vowels in time, mostly on a higher pitch level. The vowels can predominate over the consonants to the point where one has a pure *vocalise*. According to the style and character of the vocal music, all intermediate stages from *parlando* and recitative to aria and chorale occur. The more song develops in the direction of vocalization the lower is the information content of a composition. The expression content must therefore be increased in equal measure, which is achieved, for example, by larger intervallic leaps in the melody. This means greater unsteadiness in the transitions and more abrupt changes in the color registers of sound, psychologically an increase of tension. In addition, we have a more intensive modulation of the sustained vowel intonation, rhythmic changes and so forth. How difficult it is to satisfy the ear by sufficient density of events may be seen in a quotation from Helmholtz: "Monophonic song does not appeal to us any more, it seems empty and incomplete. On the other hand, we are satisfied even if only the twanging of a guitar adds the fundamental chords of the key and indicates the harmonic relationships of the tones."

How our aesthetic feeling prescribes the resolution of a "straight tone," of a strict periodic series, into an elastic configuration—a more plastic remolding of the rigid framework of tones arranged according to the rules of harmony and counterpoint—this can be seen objectively in the photography of music or speech through apparatus that register tone series, e.g., the oscillograph, level recorder and sonagraph. The latter, which is also known as the Visible Speech process, shows the time flow of a sound phenomenon as a transient. The frequency scale—in the limited area of 85 to 12,000 cps—is entered on the verticals, the spectral lines varying lengths being replaced by dots of varying blackness (see Figs. 38 and 50).

On a piece of paper stretched over a rotating drum head, lines for frequency areas with a width of 300 cps are inscribed for the time flow of speech or music of 2.4 sec duration with an electronically activated writing tool. Also necessary is an electric filter component which switches, from line to line, a further 300 cps band filter (Fig. 100).

The very prominent black bands which occur in a sonagram are identified as especially strong partials in the spectral construction of the sound, that is, as formants (see p. 13). The lowest band, as fundamental, shows the movement of the melody; the second and third are of particular significance as the color-determining formants. One sees that there are no straight lines, that is, no absolutely stationary sounds. Uninterrupted changing of speech progression and music flow is characteristic, obtaining even in the smallest time intervals, where the actual forming of the substance for purposes of information occurs.

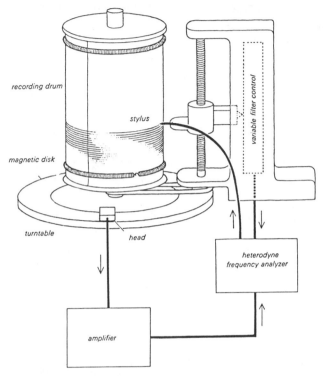

Fig. 100. Sound spectrograph (sonagraph).
A sound of 2.4 sec duration is transferred to the magnetic disk and then repeatedly sampled as the disk rotates with the recording drug. The stylus passes a spark to the drum, etching the recording paper.

From studying the Visible Speech diagrams, we see how the transients achieve full aesthetic effect at a critical optimum, but in excess or insufficiency reveal deficiencies in the voice sound.

The movement of sound in music—clearly seen in the sonagram—is physically a time, frequency and amplitude modulation whose limits are known to us today with respect to its musical aesthetic value. These phenomena are shown theoretically in the onset transients and in practice in the attack and further in the frequency modulation of

763

vibrato, tremolo, trills and other figuration, the amplitude modulation in *crescendo* and in the dynamic expression and so forth. Frequently frequency and amplitude modulation are combined. Changes in sound achieved in this way influence the tone color in countless variations, as already established.

In sound emission the written note value never corresponds accurately to an exactly defined vibration frequency, but rather to a *"frequency band"* of vibrations, where the written note simply indicates the average pitch. Our note-head symbolism is far from showing the actual relationships in music. Apart from the fact that the frequency band depends on the resonance width of the sound emitter (musical instrument), one attempts in performance to widen the band through modulation effects, such as vibrato or trills. A certain amount of spectral energy, a lowest-level stimulation quantum, is therefore important for hearing. This cannot be covered by a single sine wave, since for physiological reasons the amplitudes can assume only limited values.

The concept of a frequency bandwidth for the single note value corresponds to the principle of uncertainty better than the concept of a single vibration of a certain pitch does, since a tone cannot be precisely determined physically for frequency and duration simultaneously (see p. 49f.). An attempt to do this would lead to a blocking of the nerves as a result of fatigue.

In addition, the pitch differentiation sense in the ear is not so well developed that it can determine a pitch exactly. Intonation fluctuations within certain bounds are not noticed. In the purely theoretical considerations up till now the demands of pure intonation have been overestimated. The different tuning system are only slightly different from each other as far as hearing is concerned. *Tempered tuning* proves to be much more stable in practical musical performance than pure intonation, for instance, because unintentional distuning, such as bad intonation, faults in the instruments and so forth, is more disturbing in pure than in tempered tuning, which permits a certain area of fluctuation. The maintenance of this fluctuation area is important for the performance of music, since it creates an inner modulation which supports the sound (combination tones and beats). Of course, it then becomes very critical, since a slight exaggeration is immediately recognized as bad intonation.

From the aesthetic standpoint it might be feared that the distuning would lead to sound dimming, to impurity of sound, to noise. However, further researches have shown how important the dimming and the noise are. In painting, too, we know the principle of covering colors, making them intentionally "impure" by mixing in order to provide differentiated tones within one basic color, even to make the entire picture behind a veil so that it appears as if seen through smoke, which is what Leonardo da Vinci referred to with the term *sfumato*. The painter's "complex sound" thus becomes richer in information.

In music, too, intonation and color formation obey similar aesthetic laws of deviation from strict harmony and perfect form. It is becoming more clear to us now that noise is an important as are consonants between vowels. It is physically unavoidable, but its use in practical music extends beyond the minimum. Noises are present in the continual transients; they can profile or smear the sound picture, and thereby give music the power of communication.

Thus we come closer to the question: What actually is the communicative power of music? What is its effect on the listener? In a way, music is a double language. First, there is the series of tones, irrespective of the formation of intervals or melody, rather like series of syllables in speech, likewise disregarding speech melody. This experiment was made with the help of the synthetic speech generator Vocoder (monotonous speech). Then, there is something quite different, namely the tone simply a fixed signal, without further information content of other parameters, and the tone relationship conceived mathematically, for instance in the Pythagorean sense. That is the other language, controlled by *logos*, but not the subject of this book. Thus there are a Pythagorean and a poetical principle alongside one another (W. Gurlitt); in the course of history, each has from time to time been dominant. This is also related to the development of musical instruments; for the tones of a dulcimer and of a guitar do not have the same rich and variable structural content as, for example, syllables of speech. With increasing cultivation of instrumental sound and, the collaboration of instruments in the orchestra, the sound language has gained the upper hand.

Eggebrecht points out that from the end of the *ars nova* around 1420 up to the appearance of "atonal" music after 1900, the dominance of the tone as signal declines in favor of color of the tone, finally becoming completely lost (17).

There is still another point of view to discuss, which pertains to the nature of music. We have already seen that the feeling of formal order which we receive in listening to music does not stem from an all-embracing harmony of the artistic work in a strict mathematical sense.

On the contrary, because of the stationary character of the highest principle of order, which is rooted in a contrast between the proportions of small integers, it leads to the concept of infinity, a harmony of the spheres, which the senses can no longer grasp and—if an approximation were possible—would then exclude our participation.

At the root of the phenomenon of harmony lies the strict periodicity of every progression. It is precisely this which must be avoided in music, as experience shows. Thus we have seen that the quite elementary entity, the sine wave, does not exist for us (p. 24f.), and that the pure intervals of the triad of simple tones do not evoke a musical experience, but on the contrary actually require a stimulating component—at least the 7th partial—in order for a vital and satisfying triad to be formed.

Thus we come even closer to the goal of the harmonic ideal, but we can never attain it since it would then elude our consciousness. We have seen further that the strictly periodic partition of time leads to rigidity of sound impression, that strictly periodic vibrato and the corresponding tremolo and trill coming from a tone generator are unbearable, and even that the series of reflections of sound from the walls of rooms which combine to form reverberation must not be periodic, therefore that even the architecture of the room in which music is to be heard must be constructed in accordance with acoustical and musical principles. Experiments with synthesized music have established the truth of this. Periodic organization would impose a rigid law on a work of art from outside which would make human creative power illusory or would be prejudicial to its operation.

When a musical revelation is called "divine," a very human god is meant, one who speaks to us in the idiom of fluctuating human nature, for only in terms of these same sounds, related to us, can the soul be reached by means of the senses. The "harmony of infinity" will never reach our senses, and only similes can give us an idea of it.

Of what type are the fluctuations, that is, the deviations of periodicity, with which we have become acquainted in the diagrams, registration strips, mathematical and physical deductions? We have indeed established an admissible fluctuation breadth, but we have not as yet found laws.

We find a hint in an electroacoustical experiment. If one cuts the amplitude of the vibration curves of a spoken sound in a process which turns it into a rectangular curve, the understandability is thereby scarcely impaired. Accordingly, the distances cut between the zero line and the sides of the vibration curve are important for the information content(Figs. 101 and 102). The case is similar when the original curve (*a*) is subjected to a process of mathematical differentiation (*c*), the peak clipping process according to Licklider, referred to by Laey and Saxe (49).

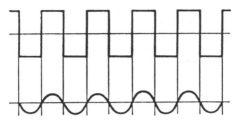

Fig. 101. Repeated peak clipping and amplification of a sine wave produce a rectangular wave.
The original zero crossings of the horizontal axis are preserved.

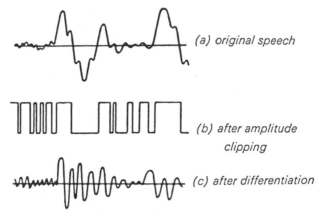

(a) original speech

(b) after amplitude
clipping

(c) after differentiation

Fig. 102. Repeated clipping (*b*) and differentiation (*c*) of speech curves (*a*).

The information transmitted by such vibrations—regardless whether it is semantic or aesthetic in nature—is given not through periodic but through irregularly distributed zero crossings of the curves (Fig. 102). In this rhythm, impulses are transmitted through the nerves to our perception organs. Stress and accent, or the emotional content transmitted by them, are given in the non-periodic time division.

The perception of small fluctuations in a determined series, as the characteristic phenomenon of semantic development, agrees with the basic tendencies of our nervous system and its time constants. A diagram of the impulse transmission in the network of the nerve fibres is given, for instance, with the help of Figure 64, but it must be recognized that we are concerned here with a very simplified presentation of a basic framework of relationships, and moreover the finer modulatory behavior could not be taken into consideration since it still has been too little investigated.

In any case, we know that impulses are not only sent forth through electrochemical transformation, connected with the nerve fibres, but also exist in the form of electrical fields, which go beyond the limits of the individual neurons and influence their excitability positively or negatively. Thus a second level of nervous activity exists, which exerts an influence on the numerous cross contacts of the fibres running toward the center. From this is derived a fine scale of excitability states, which is further influenced by the hormone regulation of the synapses in the transmission network of the nerves. Thus man's whole state of being is interrelated, through the circulation of the blood and the hormone system (analogue system), with the signaling system (digital) leading to perception. Accordingly, the impulse series, as an image of the acoustical environment, is modified by fluctuations which are caused by other environmental influences and individual conditions.

There are tiny deviations from periodicity which have significant effects, as mentioned before. They are subject to a statistical behavior and thus express the multitude of individual possibilities. They elude exact classical mathematical analysis. More success is obtained with statistical mathematics. Nevertheless, we can construct only a formal scheme, a framework for our work of art, but sensations are not fully explained by causal connections. "Cette irrégularité donne précisément cette richesse," says Pablo Casals. "Tout est irrégulier et différent, mais combien magnifique est l'harmonie de toutes ces choses."

It has been proved physicomathematically that every attack of sound is accompanied by noise, and the more suddenly it appears the more noise is present. A composer unconsciously makes use of this; in the Baroque period, for instance, the hard attack of the harpsichord strings supplied energy to the cantilena being accompanied; in other words, a function of disturbance leads to an enlivening. After the disappearance of the harpsichord and especially in the classical symphony, the kettledrum with its broad noise spectrum assumed more importance and gradually an increasing number of noise instruments came into play until exaggeration finally led to exclusively noise compositions (e.g., the noise compositions of Edgar Varèse and the toccata for percussion instruments by Chávez).

768

In a certain sense there is also a perception of noise involved in *dissonance*. When two tones of a interval or their overtones or combination tones are too close together, a sort of audible friction effect results; in other words, the conglomeration of tones which are too close together (tone cluster in modern music) is to be viewed as an energy enrichment, and thereby as a spectral concentration. Besides, very low lying difference tones, because of the significance of the low frequency transients, attract the attention of the listener.

Observed aesthetically, a musical work (of any period!) represents a thought-out distribution of "good sound" and noise—an analogue to vowels and consonants—in which the statistical distribution may fall either in favor of the "good sound" or of the noise. Accordingly, one can consider the musical work more as a sound painting or more as speech (message). The differentiation of the acoustical complex in the one or the other direction occurs psychically in the sphere of hearing. Ontogenetically, the sound perception appears to be primary; the apprehension of melody as a collective concept for pitch differentiation, linear development and, further, perception of form are secondary.

If one investigates the onset transients of different sounds in general, one can establish that, seen mathematically, they represent a natural phenomenon in any case but that this process can be extended by the mechanical onset time of the sound generator as well as by the onset behavior of the room in which the sound is intoned—and finally that it can be modified further by the characteristic attack of the player as well as by the attack or operation noise of the instrument. In addition, the ear's perception must be taken in to consideration; it, too, "attacks" with a certain time constant (Fig. 72). But if one ignores the fact that the onset is theoretically infinite and lasts quite long even in practice (at least one second if nothing but the onset reverberation of the room is considered), then one can limit the significant changes of the sound complex during the formation of the sound to 1/10 sec.

Fig. 103. J.S. Bach, *Brandenburg Concerto* No. 5.

With a view to these observations, one finds in inspecting musical literature that very frequently two tones occur at least 1/10 sec apart, for instance in Bach's fifth *Brandenburg Concerto* (Fig. 103), where the thirty-second notes occur 8/100 sec, that is, barely 1/10 sec apart. If the simple notes of a melody are arranged in a slow tempo, it is necessary to add one or more parts *punctus contra punctum* to get an energetic saturation in the nervous system, in this way arousing attention for the perception of the music. Notes of longer duration have to be contrasted by florid effects in other parts. In Occidental music the added parts to a *cantus firmus* have the functions of linear counterpoint, influencing the harmonic progressions or emphasizing the rhythm by accents. A distinct measure for richness in music patterns is given by information theory. If this requirement of a desired disturbance function is not satisfied, the held tone usually will be modulated dynamically or by vibrato; the performer follows his feelings in this more or less unconsciously. If even this is not the case, as in Figure 105, the sustained unison sound serves to increase the contrast of the following abruptly cut-off dissonant chord; the long rest is required for the process of psychic assimilation. During this time the dissonant sound complex is stored as it decays by the reverberation of the room. There is no such thing as an absolute silence in music. A composer should be aware of this when he prescribes a *fermata*. We see through more exact observance of the level diagrams of sustained tones that this is not a strictly peridic event. The loudness fluctuates by more than 10 db, as Figure 105 shows.

Fig. 104. C.P.E. Bach, *Allegro.*

The significance of the rest is greater in non-tonal music, because the expressiveness with which every sound combination is charged requires a subsequent interval for psychical assimilation. Figure 106 presents a complete piece of music with a high information content, insofar as its performance is at all possible considering the low sound level called for and the basic background noise of the room. The range covered is only the bass range from 41 to 349 cps—a range in which distinctness of pitch is reduced (see Fig. 76).

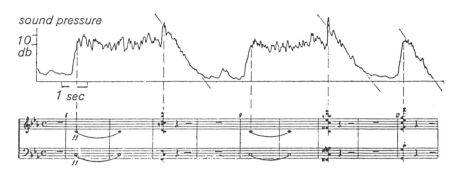

Fig. 105. Beethoven, *Coriolan Overture*.
Above: the reverberation process.

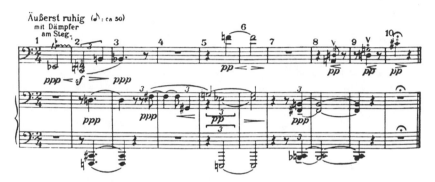

Fig. 106. Webern, the third piece from *Drei kleine Stücke*, Op. 11,
for cello and piano (Universal Edition).

Another musical example (Fig. 107) shows how a certain fundamental noise with dominant character below the strings—tympani *pianissimo* for 35 measures—influences the atmosphere of the sound space. It is much less than a whisper or forest murmur, as in Richard Wagner's *Siegfried*, for instance. The *pianissimo* of the strings, as the usable signal, is scarcely heard above the noise background, as the communications engineer would say; the engineer, conversely, attempts to lower the noise so much that a high usable signal is obtained. We must remember that we can never achieve absolute quiet, for even "holding one's breath" at suspenseful moments does not exclude the accidental presense of some room noise. In concert halls a value of about 40 phons is to be given for this.

A further example shows how the entire sound mass of an orchestra with choruses can be crammed together into a "gray" blending for the

Fig. 107. Bruckner, Fourth Symphony in E-flat Major.

listener, often unconsciously. This can be occasionally heard in Bach's B Minor Mass, and can even be clearly proved if one cuts short test pieces out of a magnetic tape recording. It is grandiose how Bach then employs a bright, gleaming trumpet over these masses of sound.

In this connection the question may occur how one differentiates the individual parts of an orchestra with the ear if they are distributed over a wide frequency area and, together with all their overtones, produce a complete spectral filling-out of the frequency scale which would have to be perceived as a noise. If all the instruments were to play constant tones of different pitches but of one certain duration, this effect of gray blending would be generated. But since every instrument has its own characteristic onset transients and, so to say, lives its private life for the duration of its sounding, the inner ear can, through analysis, already identify it, unless fatigue sets in because of the sounding of too many instruments (masking, see p. 145; blending, see p. 71).

Let us keep in mind that the stationary sound value, as it would occur if it were reproduced as it is in the score, practically never reaches the ear, for music is *constantly in motion.* The transients described in this book provide another tone color than that of a stationary value. Anyone can test this out by playing a rapid piece with 64th notes on a string or wind instrument first in a normal tempo and ten extremely slowly, so that every note is held. The tone color is changed slightly. Thus it is not the tempo or the changed rhythm alone which causes the different impression. One can say, conversely, that the changes in tempo give the transients more or less opportunity to have an effect and therefore change the tone color. Thus the rhythm at any given moment indirectly produces the nuances of the tone color!

772

The basic difference in the techniques of two conductors may lie in such relationships (see p. 47). Sharp attacks and quick tempi make music noisier. The layman appropriately calls such a performance "dizzying" or "intoxicating."[2] The composer who is able to hear such differences contrasts very active passages with very sustained phrases (Fig. 108). Even the piano can be used for register differentiation, and this can be achieved in the composition itself, i.e., apart from the pianist's use of touch. On the other hand, the pianist can consciously or unconsciously influence the sound picture, for instance through a delayed attack by the right hand as compared with the left. The attack as a whole is thereby lengthened, and this may have a disturbing effect on the listener. These disjoint attacks are used in a positive sense by the composer in arpeggio passages and also in simple grace notes, especially in passages where this forming element is in the foreground as opposed to the sound element, i.e., where the communicative power is to be greater. This is particularly clear in the case of song, in which the music should have an immediate speaking effect through the woods. An agitated, expressive statement does not begin soberly and precisely at a prescribed pitch, but is an outcry, in which the pitch glides upward, or a falling-off of tension, a groan, in which the pitch glides downward.[3] The human voice expresses all states of excitation with gliding series of tones, that is, with a considerable gradient of frequency change, which is related to the sudden muscular tension of the glottis. For want of a more suitable notation, Franz Schubert marked such expressions of

Fig. 108. Beethoven, Sonata, Op. 10, No. 2.

[2][The German adjective used here (*berauschend*) is linguistically related to the German word for noise (*Geräusch*).]

[3][The prefixes *auf-* and *ab-* of the German words *Aufschrei* and *Abspannen* here translated as "outcry" and "falling-off tension" convey the notion of a movement upward and downward, respectively.]

feeling in his songs with grace notes, which in this case glide into the main note (Fig. 109) The Trautonium (the electronic instrument invented by Trautwein) reproduces such excited expressions with gripping reality (see, for example, its outcries in Honegger's *Jeanne d'Arc au bûcher*). From this viewpoint it is understandable why a feature like Caruso's typical moan at the end of a phrase is perceived as exciting, although it is a noise and against the rules of vocal training, or why a vocal smearing, of course within bounds, is sometimes felt to be not unpleasant. We could list here numerous examples from the performance of music, but the reader is now able himself to point out interesting cases. The essential point is not to be prejudiced by the written page of music and to rely entirely on the *ear as the sole authority and court of appeal.* Then, by a growing refinement in one's listening ability, one will constantly make new discoveries which can be explained very naturally without entering into complicated explanations or metaphysical interpretations. Music, too, is down to earth: all sounds are generated by concrete vibration forms the laws of which are quite well known today.

Fig. 109. Schubert, *Winterreise* ("Der greise Kopf").

The increasing exactitude of musical performance has been brought about through the microphone. It is the sensitivity of this "electronic ear" and thus the preference for the primary sound with considerable suppression of the secondary influences, namely the room reverberation, which has the effect of a beneficient adjustment of unclean performance. This more accurate listening by means of electronic amplification has doubtless been a good education for better achievements in the area of music, but in its development toward absolute exactitude—toward the ideal form—a work of sound of nearly mathematical abstraction has come into being, for we miss something of man's far from perfect behavior, the fluctuations in his mind, in other words his deficiencies of various kind. The extent to which the "fluctuation width" is necessary for the hearing proces should have been established in this book. In this sense we can also understand why the ideal form of a Greek Venus is often not as gripping as a statue of Käthe Kollwitz, for example, if we ignore absolute artistic evaluation for the moment.

Music which is being heard must be evaluated differently than the abstract notation of the score. Herein lies the failure of so many composers, who do not take the effects conditioned by the listener as their point of departure, but have become involved in the external function relationships of a language of symbols in musical notation. Contemporary scientific investigation and the derived experimentation in the area of art will lead to a healthy clarification and refinement of the various opinions and, it is hoped, will provide the stimulus for new creative accomplishments.

FORM

The discussion about "form" that was held at the Darmstädter Internationale Ferienkurse für Neue Musik confronted an issue which no one knew, at the time, whether it still existed or was worth keeping alive. The dispute as to whether form represents a fundamental aesthetic category or a mere possibility that one can either take up or abandon did not end with what was said publicly in 1965. In retrospect it seems that the "subterranean" effects were, if anything, the decisive ones. The lectures by *György Ligeti* and *Carl Dahlhaus* and the latter's concluding remarks, should give, at least in rough outline, an idea of the discussion's substance.

The extreme manifestations of the concept of form, which one could call metaphysical and didactic, were disqualified *a priori*. That the "prima materia" is a pure abstraction, that nothing exists without having form, is a philosophical truth which appeared incontestable but, in terms of music theory, inconsequential. On the other hand, in view of the New Music after 1945 or 1950, there was no one so narrow-minded as to insist on the concept of form that underpinned the *Formenlehre* established in the nineteenth century by Adolf Bernhard Marx.

The influence of John Cage, whose appearance in Darmstadt in 1958 swept across the European avant-garde like a natural disaster, was still undiminished in 1965. Nevertheless, a change in musical thinking was being paved, in "cluster composition," which had achieved a breakthrough in 1961 with the première of Ligeti's *Atmosphères*, that would ultimately make the problem of form relevant again.

Initially, however, it seemed that the "stationary" clusters, albeit moving in themselves, in which Ligeti transformed experiences of electronic music into instrumental music had to lead to a destruction of musical form no less than the "chance" operations which Cage used in order to sever the threads between acoustic events, thus making their

777

"pure nature" perceivable. The one *modus operandi* tended, at least superficially, just as much towards the amorphous, even programatically so, as the other.

However, the "microstructures" that lay concealed in Ligeti's clusters—sometimes, for example, complicated canons—contained the possibility of latent processes becoming manifest. Allowing the inside, composed as it was with almost pedantic scrupulousness, gradually to emerge into the open was, in fact, the path Ligeti took during the next decade. Confronting the problem of form, which in the 1950s seemed obsolete, became unavoidable again. What Ligeti had to say about this in Darmstadt in 1965 was typical and representative of the phase in which the avant-garde no longer adopted methods from the serial music of the immediately preceding decade but struggled, instead, with inherited unsolved problems.

Ligeti defended the conception of an individual form, for which he pleaded, in various ways. A mode of composition that presupposed an overall formal plan, claimed Ligeti, had to be separated from serial mechanics which took as its starting-point the determination of the individual part and largely removed the whole from the composer's control. Ligeti was forced to resist, however, the tendency merely to sketch form "globally," in rough outlines, leaving the details to, so called, "aleatoric" improvisation.

If—as a consequence of the implications of "cluster composition"— recourse to the traditional aesthetic maxim, whereby the whole must be grounded in the composition of the parts and, conversely, the function of the parts should result from the peculiarity of the whole, became the problem of how the thoroughly individual form, postulated by Ligeti, could be apprehended as form at all, remained, for the time being, unresolved. A listener can, as he could before, perceive with sufficient clarity similarities, divergencies and contrasts, in the various dimensions or parameters of a musical work. In other words, he can perceive connections, segmentations and mediations. Nonetheless, without the support of some notions concerning form, whose validity goes beyond the individual artifact, it is extremely difficult to retain an overview. Listening to a particular passage, one can never be sure whether the density of events, the relative pitch level, the dominance of a certain interval or that of a prominent rhythmic pattern, the curve of intensity or the mixture of timbres, will prove to be essential in the next section, be it in the formal function of a similarity or a contrast.

In other words: the Darmstädt discussion concerning form, which was held from the point of view of conception—it could scarcely be any different at a composers' symposium—really requires a supplementary discourse on "Form in New Music" as a category of perception. Were a composer to reflect on the psychology of the impact and comprehensibility of his works and were he to draw consequences from his reflections, he would only do harm to himself. Yet, psychologists of music cannot escape taking seriously the problems of New Music, free of prejudice, guided by the premises of the matter at hand, rather than by preconceived concepts of a particular scientific trend.

GYORGY LIGETI

Form[1]

I

"Musical form" can be investigated and described from various points of view.

A quite general approach leads first of all to the formulation: "Form is the relation of the parts to one another and to the whole." This definition is readily applied, not only in the theory of musical form but also in other contexts where form is under discussion, and is admittedly valid and true, yet it says very little about the real essence of musical form. Descriptions of schemata such as "A-B-A," "sonata" and "rondo" belong to this perspective as does also the description of how the whole and its parts are articulated, down to the smallest segments and fractions of segments. With more recent types of music for which traditional formal schemata are no longer valid, general description is concentrated on the proportions of the whole and its parts, thereby recording but not interpreting.

With a more sophisticated approach, it becomes apparent that musical form is more than the mere relation of the parts to one another and to the whole. Syntactic aspects are accorded a primary role in the understanding of form: within the musical process each phase and individual aspect possess characteristics by means of which the process is determined; status and within the totality, connection or non-

[1]Text: György Ligeti, "Form," *Form in der Neuen Musik*, ed. E. Thomas (Mainz: Darmstädter Beitrage zur Neuen Musik x, 1966), pp. 23–25.

connection, similarity and contrast of individual features produce a system of relationships which provokes the appearance of progression or rest, an "expansion in time." The concept "musical form" thus refers to aspects connected with the type of effect the parts have within the whole as well as to aspects connected with the relationship of those parts; to that extent, the category of function is more decisive than that of mere segmentation.

If one approaches the concept of "musical form" via the more comprehensive concept of "form," then a further aspect emerges: that of an analogy with space. "Form" is originally an abstraction from spatial configurations, from the proportions of objects being extended in space. Applied to nonspatial areas—the form of poetry or music—"form" is an abstraction of an abstraction. Corresponding to the provenance of the concept, spatial aspects cling to forms that unfold in time. This is corroborated by time and space always being linked with each other in our imagination and thoughts: where one of the two categories is primarily at hand, the other immediately appears by association. When we imagine or listen to music, where the acoustic process is primarily temporal, imaginary spatial connections come about on several levels. Initially on the associative level, whereby changes of pitch (the word itself at once refers to a spatial analogy) evokes the vertical dimension, staying on the same pitch the horizontal dimension, while changes in dynamics and tone colour, for instance the differences between an open and muted sound, create the impression of near and far, in general of depth of space: musical shapes and events are imagined by us as though they took up position in the imaginary space which they themselves fabricate. Secondly, imaginary spatial connotations come about on the level of further abstraction, whereby several types of "spaces" can be thought up. Thus we speak of a "harmonic space," of an abstraction of the associatively arisen pitch-space, whereby it is not the pitches as such that fabricate the space but their harmonic relations to one another. The syntactic relations of the musical aspects are also transposed by our imagination into an implied space, whereby the individual aspects —elements, shapes, segments, parts etc.—have the effect of places or objects, the complete progression of musical events thus appearing as it were as architecture in space.[2] This goes not only for "static" musical

[2]Cf. T.W. Adorno, "Anweisungen zum Hören Neuer Musik", in: *Der getreue Korrepetitor* (Frankfurt, 1963), pp. 95-96.

forms in which the analogy to space arises directly through the musical events appearing to stand still, but in general for every kind of music, even that which progresses in a developmental fashion; for, by involuntarily comparing each new aspect that enters our consciousness with those aspects already experienced, and by drawing conclusions from this comparison about what is to come, we pass through the construction of the music as if it were present in its entirety. It is the interaction of association, abstraction, remembrance and prognosis which elicits in the first place the nexus of relations that makes the conception of musical form possible.

It is possible, from the approach described here, to demonstrate the difference between music as such and musical form: "music" would thus be the purely temporal process, "musical form," conversely, the abstraction of the same temporal process, in which the relations within the process are no longer temporal but present themselves as spatial; musical form arises only when one retrospectively views music's course in time as "space."

A retrospective view means history. The historical aspect, however, relates not only to the form of the individual musical work but also to formal connections that develop between the individual works. The function of a work's segments can really not be explained from the inner musical connections of the work in question: characteristics of individual aspects as well as the connections of these aspects only have a point in relation to the more general characteristics and schemes of connections that arise from the totality of works within a stylistic area or a tradition; individual aspects can only be recognized as such when similarities between, or deviations from, the historically developed types are brought to bear. The historical factor is therefore significant both in the syntactic as well as the space-analogy approach to musical form; musical syntax is transformed by and through history; the implied space of the formal frame of reference includes not only the aspects of the individual work but also those of the past: "present" in musical form are the past aspects both of the music just passed through and of all music previously experienced. The real time in which music happens—a time that appears in musical form as imaginary space—is not the only temporal level of the work: at every moment an imaginary time is at work, as it were a time of higher potency, produced by the compressing of events against the real temporal process of the individual work. This imaginary time becomes, for its part, abstracted to "space": history, as stored and recalled time, is already imaginary-cum-spatial.

The historical function within musical form can be demonstrated in particular using types from the same tradition.

An example:

It is characteristic for the formal segments of a classical sonata that, because of their historically developed qualities, they can reveal in which particular phase the formal process happens to be: themes, bridge passages, development, retransition to the recapitulation, and coda are not only identifiable through their position within the large-scale form but above all through how each of them behaves musically in its own particular way, whereby the behaviour in each case can be exactly described by means of harmonic, modulatory, rhythmic-motivic and, in part, dynamic features. As soon as the types of classical sonata that have become a historical convention appear in the musical context of Romanticism they suffer a change in their formal significance (one can see it the other way round: the change in significance gives rise to the changed context in the first place); yet this change is not comprehensive: the new significance arises ultimately from a shift of emphasis vis-à-vis the old meaning, which is at the same time retained.

One of the classical types of coda, the gesture of closure—resulting harmonically from the repeated affirmation of the tonic, rhythmically from a "composed-out" pause, dynamically and instrumentally from a fortissimo orchestral tutti shining forth in the brightest light and heightened, particularly at the end of overtures and finale movements of symphonies, to become positively festive—was further expanded and, as it were, overloaded in overtures and symphonies of the Romantic period; the zenith of this type is to be found above all in the coda apotheoses of Bruckner, such as in the close of the Seventh Symphony's outer movements. The change of function that has occurred as compared with the classical tutti coda can be clearly recognized here: the composed-out pauses are no longer a mere affirmation of closure but are also static layers of sound, which may have retained the earlier effect of affirmation but which no longer affirmatively maintain "now it is finished"; instead, by enlarging the concluding gesture into something oversized, they postpone it and transfer it into a state of suspension, so it appears that the closure itself could last forever. Such a coda only acquires this meaning when its shift of meaning is registered in confrontation with the significance accumulated from its predecessors: if it were viewed merely as a segment of an individual work, its meaning would not be wholly non-existent, but it would be considerably dwindled; the complete meaning arises by bringing to bear the whole tradition of formal significance, by tracing connections from the manifest musical configuration to subliminally related configurations which resound as history.

The example described here—which stands for countless others—admits conclusions about two aspects of musical form.

First, it sheds light on the concept of "meaning" in relation to musical form, in general to music *per se*. Musical meaning that makes musical contexts appear, in several respects, analogous to language is fundamentally different from verbal meaning[3]: musical meaning is not related directly to anything conceptual and consequently has merely an "either-or" substratum as far as semantics are concerned. Music simulates meanings which, however, slip away into nothing as soon as one tries to pin them down to unequivocal semantic ground. Musical aspects acquire meaning only by referring to other musical aspects: it is not the meanings themselves but the shifts and changes in meaning that are ascertainable. The aspect of music analogous to language is even more limited by the fact that musical syntax is considerable more flexible and ephemeral than that of language: although it is partly justified to see music as a syntactic system, this system is pervaded by gaps and internal inconsistencies; and, furthermore, it is not at all self-contained but, principally in the direction of history, is open to every transformation. The system of music therefore scarcely satisfies the requirements of a self-contained, consistently constructed system, and attempts to describe music and musical form with criteria of logic or mathematics are extremely questionable.[4] The system of music indeed has logical aspects, yet they result from appearances just as the semantic aspects do: music can make assertions, yet no criteria of unconditional rightness or truth can be said to apply here. Musical meaning and musical logic relate to actual meaning and actual logic like dreams to reality.

Secondly, from the example, the peculiarity of formal function is shown to be fully comprehensible not simply within the individual work

[3]Cf. T.W. Adorno, "Fragment über Musik und Sprache" (1956), in: *Quasi una fantasia* (Frankfurt, 1963), pp. 9–16.
[4]This of course does not pertain to those areas of composition or those methods that *per se* have a logical, arithmethical or mathematical basis; with these—and only with these—methods a corresponding exact description is thoroughly appropriate, so long as the boundaries within which logic, arithmetic and mathematics themselves are applied are not over-stepped.

but only within historical interconnection. This leads to the conclusion that musical form is a category that points beyond the individual phenomenon of music: each aspect of a work is, on one level, an element in the frame of reference within the individual form, yet, on a higher level, it is an element in a more comprehensive historical frame of reference.

The historical aspect of musical form has been investigated and demonstrated principally by T.W. Adorno; above all, his Mahler book should be referred to as—in many of its parts—the most significant contribution to a "historical theory of form."[5]

The historical approach to form is all the more essential in that there is in music no actual material—in the original sense of the word—that would, in the compositional process, be "formed"; tones, sonorities, etc., the acoustic substratum, cannot be seen as material for music in the sense that stone and wood are material of sculpture. The process of "forming" in music refers rather to relations mediated by contexts of tones and sonorities; what is formed in music is, in itself, already "form" and not material. The system of musical form and its change in history can, by analogy, be seen as an immense net which drags itself through the ages: individual composers latch on to this or that place of the giant net, creating new tangles and knots which are then further knotted, unknotted or differently woven by the next one. Places occur where there is no continuation but where the net is torn into: one then ties further knots with new threads following a new pattern, seemingly independent of the previous structure of the net. Yet viewing it at a great distance, one sees almost transparent tangles of thread which imperceptibly cover the tears: even what is seemingly without tradition has a secret connection to what has been.

II

Today we find ourselves directly after such a tear in the historical process. The principal aspects of form—the relation of the parts to the whole, the analogy to space, historical interconnection—remain as such valid, yet the nature of this validity is essentially different from the way in which the same principles manifested themselves within the

[5]Frankfurt, 1960.

tonal tradition, even within the tradition of New Music that was in itself no longer tonal but still thought in syntax analogous to tonality. This does not mean that in the most recent musical phase the "secret threads" to tradition were not present; on the contrary, the more this phase could be surveyed in its entirety, the more visible did the connections with the past become. A reservation must however be introduced here: the "ahistorical" compositional movement which to a large extent has its origin in Schillinger's theoretical reflections cannot be done justice to with the criteria of musical form. This in no way means that the criteria of form have in themselves become invalid, only that Schillinger's compositional conception and in particular Cage's conception, which follows on from Schillinger, do not even claim to generate form. On the other hand, this in itself a-formal music—through objective formal principles at work independently of the compositional intention—created form as it were despite itself, in that, by going through time and affected by time, it became history and itself brought forth a new tradition. One may ask whether the appropriation of certain aspects of Schillinger's and Cage's conceptions by the European avant-garde was adequate or inadequate, thinking as the latter does automatically in connections and, in its gesture of traditionlessness, nevertheless influenced by tradition: the use of certain partial aspects of a formal conception within a compositional thought aimed at coherence, that is, at form, projects in retrospect form into something conceived of, in itself, as formless. The Cage circle's a-syntactic music is similar to isolating language. Connections between the individual components are evaded, and the music acquires connecting features in the dimension in which, unintendedly, history arises from the music's intended ahistoricity.

In general terms, that is, by taking together the more prominent features of serial and static music manipulating chance and music that lies "beyond" the serial,[6] the following main differences are apparent between the nature of this music's form and musical form in the earlier tradition:

1. There are no longer any established formal schemata; each individual work is forced, by virtue of the historical constellation, to display

[6]The expression "beyond the serial" was coined by G.M. Koenig; as a slogan it seems more appropriate than any other to describe those types of music that are not composed serially but which, while storing up the entire serial experience, radically avoid resorting in any way to out-of-date traditional types.

a unique overall form adequate only to that work. "Unique forms," however, acquire in retrospect, through history, a common characteristics which, albeit not in a similarly fixed construction to that in the tonal phrase, turn the most varied individual formal realizations into members of a generic family of forms.

2. Rhythmic articulation—even that of the form's large-scale rhythm —became independent of every metrically pulsating basis. This led, on the one hand, to possibilities of differentiation in articulation that earlier could not have been foreseen, as well as, on the other hand, by virtue of all too advanced differentiation turning into something indifferent, to the formally constructive power of articulation itself becoming weakened.

3. There is no longer a generally valid syntax, one that, despite its variants, nevertheless forms a more or less coherent system, such as there was in music composed tonally, partially tonally or even with twelve-note rows. Syntax in the sense of direct connection has largely been eradicated; there is syntax in the sense of different possible systems of coherence, yet they are partial solutions, comparable to individual forms. True, with the "generic family of forms" common connections do arise between the individual syntactic systems, yet these connections are all too weak and ephemeral to establish a binding, general syntax. (To complain about this situation would be inappropriate: nothing can justify why an established syntax would necessarily be more adequate than a splitting-up into partial syntactic systems. Universal validity is not a criterion of art.) A borderline case among the different possible syntactic solutions is Cage's method of negating all syntax.

4. The individualization of syntax was accompanied by another change of function. Formal function in the sense of tonal tradition no longer exists; formal segments that more or less unequivocally mark the phrases of form through historical connection are unthinkable in a formal structure that no longer adheres to established schemata and explicit models of connection. This is not to say, however, that the concept of function is meaningless for present-day types of form, it is only the nature of function that has changed in being no longer fixed within the formal structure but flexible and relative. Different types of structure and motion, different possibilities of distributing sonorities, sound objects, sound layers, sound patterns, contrasting and mediating shapes, fragmenting and blending elements, constructive and decomposing elements—all these and more serve as functionally constitutive elements of form; what unequivocally demarcates and indicates direction is simply not present. Thus the position of a formal segment within the

whole is not binding for the function of that segment, and the function, conversely, is not bound to any one position: functional types articulate the form and establish coherence, yet the overall form is, in itself, usually directionless and non-developmental, and the individual components of the form are, in their function and position, interchangeable.

The four characteristics described here developed in close causal connection with one another: the disappearance of formal schemata was ultimately determined by the dissolution of tonality (the temporary restoration of the schemata by twelve-note technique proved, in the absence of a tonal substratum, to be all too short-lived); with the decline of schemata and, in particular, with the equality of compositional elements resulting from the demolition of tonal hierarchy, the possibility of a universally valid syntax also declined; the vectorial character of formal function vanished on account of the dissolution of directional tonal harmony and syntax as well as the disappearance of formal schemata; the basic metrical types of articulation were dissolved by the demolition of harmonic and formal hierarchy etc.—the causal connections of the transformation can be reversed at will according to the chicken-and-egg principle: each individual aspect of the transformation is both cause and effect within the described process.

Since function is particularly crucial in order for musical form to come into being, the question arises as to the extent to which the far-reaching change in the nature of formal function has affected form itself.

If one approaches today's music with the traditional criteria of form, then one will be led to think that this music is in general "formless": the absence of direction-indicating function makes it difficult for anyone expecting a signpost to apprehend formal architecture. If, on the other hand, one approaches the same music without expecting that function to mean direction and signposting within the architecture, then one comes across a whole series of architectural possibilities that are no less discernible than traditional formal constructions; the possibilities range from, as it were, single-room, huge empty buildings to subterraneously winding labyrinths and settlements scattered across a wide expanse.

While the vectorial character of formal function vanished, the coherence-establishing character—even in the historical dimension—remained intact. There scarcely exist any longer meanings and changes of meaning analogous to language in the sense that they were described using the example of a segment from classical form, for the aspect of similarity to language was largely debilitated along with music's general tendency to become static. On the other hand, an arsenal of types came together in due course, such as: aperiodic jumps to and fro in wide intervals, followed by sudden inertia and then a resumption of the jumping movements; unbroken, fixed layers of sound usually built up like clusters; sound objects that are deposited as it were individually into the space of the form; certain colour combinations, such as tender and bustling percussion immersed in sounds of vibraphones and bells. These types have made so extensive an impression that they have become all but as familiar as a perfect cadence. The instilled types acquired, with time, the appearance of universal validity, so that changes in character became observable as additions to, or deviations from, what is generally the case: through the back door, as it were, either-or meanings and rudimentary similarities to language crept into musical contexts originally conceived as anti-linguistic and anti-semantic.

It is at this point that the problem of today's music can be shown most clearly; the internal contradiction between intended and resulting form. While no universally valid established formal schemata and syntactic systems exist, musical types paradoxically tend to become fixed historically: instead of the coherence-establishing systems themselves, it is the *same* types resulting from *different* such systems that become the established thing.[7] The consequence of this paradoxical situation is a possible widespread but misguided belief that today's musical language is as similarly fixed as traditional tonal music was for centuries and that the task remaining consists in nothing other than enriching and further cultivating the musical language already arrived at.

In the fact that with a great variety of syntax there exists a considerably smaller variety of musical types can be sought one of the reasons why so many pieces are similar to one another, like one egg to the next one, and why a new academicism appears to develop almost faster than the academicism of earlier epochs.

---

[7]Cf. H. Brün, "Against Plausibility", in: *Perspectives of New Music*, Vol. 2 No. 1, pp. 43–4: " . . . this view seems to embody a growing suspicion that whatever compositional methods may be employed, the formation of really new patterns is becoming increasingly less possible. By now, even widely divergent methods of organizing musical elements seem to produce very similar musical results, and the semantic value of such similarity overshadows in its power of communication the differences among dissimilar methods of origination."

III

How and why have we arrived at the paradoxical situation described above?

The reasons are most probably to be sought in the loosening of the connection between compositional process and the resulting sensual appearance of music. Although the resulting music displays throughout internal connections—has, that is, syntax—this syntax does not always necessarily coincide with the system of connections that informed the compositional process. By virtue of the compositional process being divided into preformation (of elements and connections) and "actual" composition, in some cases into three parts—preformation, production of the score and compositional-cum-interpretational realization—partitions sprang up as it were between composition and result. The separation of the processes of ordering and manipulating caused a situation in which it could no longer be guaranteed that what one had at one's disposal could be fully manipulated and that what was manipulated could be fully resolved in the resulting music; disposition and manipulation were, on the one hand, conceived of as independent activities; and one tended, on the other hand, to organize individual phases of the compositional process so that they were perfectly self-contained—so perfectly, in fact, that the result could not be adequately accommodated, precisely on account of that perfection, into the next phase of work. Furthermore, in the various phases, compositional work was done in which the character of the hoped-for music was either only summarily anticipated or even not at all. It was not so much musical connections that were composed as connections restricted to the music on the page. The compositional process together with the score and the resulting music became as it were hermetic towards each other. This problem was recognized and demonstrated very early on by Adorno.[8] Metzger rightly criticized Adorno's somewhat hasty generalizations,[9] since in the works that were crucial for the situation then—above all in compositions by Stockhausen and Boulez—the said discrepancy between composing and what was composed proved rather to be a side issue: thanks to compositional potency and concentration, and despite the division of

[8] In: "Das Altern der Neuen Musik" (1954), published in: *Dissonanzen* (Göttingen, 1956).
[9] In: "Das Altern der Philosophie der Neuen Musik," published in: *Die Reihe*, No. 4 (Vienna, 1958).

the work process, there were still sufficient supplies of power available which held together meaningfully what was composed in order that the resulting sound could appear as music of a high formal standard. Meanwhile it is not to be denied that, although the impression arises in these works of a wealth of connections, these connections—as a consequence of the said lack of identity with the relations created during composition—were not free of a hint of "malgré lui." The high formal standard resulted partly from the wealth of what was invested in terms of composition, hidden as it were beneath the mirrored surface of the music and shining through it in a veiled fashion. It is admittedly often the case that with music of a high standard "secret" constructions support the dome of the form—Machaut, Ockeghem, Bach and Webern could be drawn on as examples—and that every kind of paper-music has its justification if the level of the resulting acoustic impression is assured by the level of what is on the paper: something unheard, only sensed, can contribute more to the aura of high art than all-too-superficial compositional handicraft. The justification of paper-music only disappears when the construction remains excluded from the aura of the actual sound and the music produced is left over, as it were, as a by-product of the compositional work process. It would appear in the course of the development and dissemination of serial, statistical and chance-manipulating working methods, as well in as those lying "beyond" serialism, that this internal discrepancy has become ever bigger, apart from in a few main works: in 1954 Adorno's criticism was valid only with reservation; yet it was all the more relevant as a prognosis for later developments, for the situation around 1960.

With the generalization of the serial method—that is, with the transfer of dispositions once applied to a repertoire of elements to more global, even abstract categories, such as general musical characteristics, structural constellations and types of distribution and motion—and with the incorporation of aleatoric manipulations with the general serial procedure, the crux of the situation—the division of the phases of the work process—was by no means eliminated. There was, it is true, a shift of emphasis within the division of the work process, but it was more in the direction of preformation gaining the upper hand to such an extent that it tended to absorb into itself the "actual" composition: what remained of the latter was merged with interpretation. This meant that compositional intention together with the creation of connections increasingly concentrated on generalized preformation and receded ever further from the acoustic "second" composer, the interpreter, in greater or lesser independence from the "first" composer. The division of labour that initially manifested itself within the compositional process consequently became transferred to separate people. The handing over of the result to the interpreter, ultimately the further division of the work process among a number of interpreters who passed on the composed music from hand to hand (like in the game where a message is whispered from ear to ear, ending with the final result scarcely corresponding to the original), or between a number of simultaneous yet not necessarily mutually dependent interpreters—all this created a situation in which music and thus musical form became to a high degree unintentional and structurally indifferent, despite working methods that were in principle antithetical.

Serial music and music produced by the manipulation of change thus became largely identical in terms of the final result—something that only increased the already-mentioned paucity of types: paucity, that is, in relation to the diversity of methods.

On this aspect it has to be remarked that the antithesis "determinate-indeterminate" was not as decisive as the unintended similarity of the apparently atagonistic methods. The similarity consisted from the start in the two methods working with *directives*: the serial method with directives concerning the preformation of determined orderings and operations, the chance method with directives for certain manipulations with things pre-musical or extra-musical—Cage's dice, coins or celestial atlases are no less preformation programmes than the exact plans of the serial composers, for with orderings of numbers and with distribution patterns of elements it is not the indeterminacy of the ordering or distribution that is decisive for the fate of what is prepared but the fact that orderings and distributions—of whatever nature—are accepted *at all* as binding for the starting-point of the compositional process. *Every* kind of method working with general preformation—whatever directives may be applied— produces on the level of music as sound, apart from the isolation of individual aspects, connections that were not intended by the method in question but nonetheless appear in what results.

Here can be found the origin of the "malgré lui" connections and "malgré lui" forms. In the horizontal dimension of musical structure this means that, apart from the shifting of musical meaning from the totality or larger formal sections to unlinked individual components, certain coherences of meaning unintentionally appear in succession and work against the isolation of individual aspects; in the vertical dimension, however, that events originally conceived independently of one another, which are incongruent but manipulated in the result towards simultaneity, produce chance constellations which lend the simultaneity an "either-or" meaning. The interaction of the two dimensions and the apparent connections inherent in them ultimately give rise, with what is in itself primarily unconnected, to the phantasm of a frame of reference and, as a consequence, musical form.[10]

IV

A question related to the issues outlined here is whether, with forms described as polyvalent or mobile, the musical form is really the mobile factor or whether the mobility pertains rather to another level than the one on which musical form is established.

Polyvalency and mobility logically result from the tendency towards isolation of individual aspects: what is not linked contains the possibility of being exchangeable in its position. (The independence of the formal function of individual aspects and formal segments from their position and the non-vectorial character of function are aspects that belong in this context.) There already exists an interchangeability of components in late Webern; though with him this interchangeability is not actually realizable but merely contained in the structure as a possibility: the mobility is so to speak composed-out, in that the individual segments, which stand in an inverse or retrograde relation to one another, appear interchangeable, whereas in reality they are firmly slotted into the structure in a coglike fashion. With the increasing isolation of individual aspects—as a result of compositional methods working with more generalized preformation—real interchangeability was soon apparent as a consequence. There, however, the levels changed on which mobility occurs: precisely because with Webern the mobility was only potential, existing on the level of appearances, it became a characteristic of the form; with its being shifted to the level of the real (as opposed to the abstract level of form) interchangeability became a characteristic of what was committed to paper, part of the text of the music to be realized. There resulted numerous possible interpretations of this text;

[10]Cf. G. Ligeti, "Wandlungen der musikalischen Form" (1958), published in *Die Reihe*, No. 7 (Vienna, 1960), pp. 9–10.

but the individual interpretations no longer revealed any mobility in the resulting music: the written text can mean "either-or," not so the musical form, however; as soon as it is produced through performed music it is an unequivocal variant of an equivocal text—the mobility of the text itself remained outside the sphere of the resulting music.

The problem of polyvalency and mobility essentially goes back to the different characteristics of primarily spatial configurations and primarily temporal events as well as to a widespread tendency not to separate sufficiently clearly from each other these fundamentally different areas, that is, to apply principles valid for one area also in another, without having critically tested the legitimacy of this transfer.

A sculpture is a primarily spatial configuration. A moving sculpture— for instance, a mobile by Calder—incorporates however the dimension of time into the primarily spatial configuration. The form of the mobile is thus not merely an abstraction of its spatial configuration but also embraces the changes of the spatial configuration in time. The situation in music is reversed: here form is the product of an imaginary spatialization of the temporal process—with the mobile sculpture it is a product of the "temporalization" of spatial objects. Music as a primarily temporal process is already, in itself, motion (completely static types of music are merely a borderline case). Thus there is no analogy in music to a mobile sculpture; to reintroduce motion into motion does not signify a transformation: the result would again be motion. Since music contains mobility within, as something belonging primarily to the musical process itself and actually producing it, and since this mobility, as something spatialized, enters into musical form and determines it, musical form cannot be conceived of as mobile: mobility is inherent to the form; the form *itself* is not mobile. Various musical realizations of a polyvalent text, produced one after the other, relate to one another like different snapshots of a Calderian mobile.[11]

From all this can be explained why realized music is indifferent to the distinction of whether it is derived from an unequivocal or equivocal text and whether it is taken from a text or improvised: the equivocality of the text is not preserved in the appearance of the music.

[11]Cf. Ligeti, Ibid., p. 17.

V

The consequences of this lead in two opposite directions.

On the one hand, "do-it-yourself" composition—as a consequence of its inherent qualities—has a tendency to move away from the area of sound towards that of pure action; music, as something unintended and hypothetical, becomes the concomitant of the action and merges with these to become a kind of (absolutely anti-Wagnerian) Gesamtkunstwerk.

On the other hand, by virtue of a shift in the starting-point of compositional method, it becomes possible again to dispose over form as something intentional. This means that connections within the compositional process largely correspond to connections that appear in the music composed; at the same time, it means doing without disposition and manipulation with directives proposed in advance: what is primarily given is not the compositional procedure but the conception of the form's totality, the imagination of the music as sound. The method, whichever applied, adapts to the anticipated musical result and is drawn up in concordance with the formal demands of this result. Such a compositional procedure is both bound and free: what is free is the vision of the resulting form; the respective method, however, is bound to the demands of the formal ideas as already set down. Such a method can work with a close dovetailing of formal connections, not unlike the serial method; it is just that the starting-point lies in the opposite direction. The primacy of formal imagination means, in consequence, that the hardened types of the newest music can be avoided, since unintentional matter no longer creeps in: the idea can exclude in advance every unwanted pattern. This would be consistent with the unestablished nature of today's compositional situation, since through the abolition of all kinds of preformation the musical imagination can freely devote itself to what is unfixed and unassured. It is only possible to avoid induration and ossification and thus the new academicism by continually thinking up something new: neither sticking with what has already been achieved nor a "return to" is possible without deceiving oneself that terra firma exists when it in fact never does.

CARL DAHLHAUS

Form[1]

I

The urge to define, grasp and contain appears to be as ineradicable as the opposing urge to dissolve and break out. Definitions have a calming as well as a restricting effect; one seeks support from them while at the same time regarding them with suspicion.

What is musical form, if it is meaningful to speak both of sonata form and of statistical form? I fear the answer is: nothing but a word on the one hand, and, on the other, a confused mass of facts, whereby it is not at all certain whether they can be subsumed under a single concept.

The expression 'form' is as respectable as it is ambiguous, and is therefore serviceable as a catchword. Catchwords are defined less by their content than by their function. And it is noticeable that in literature form tends to be a critical catchword, yet in music an affirmative one. Whoever declares support for literary formalism may entertain the hope of being counted among the avant garde; an apologist of musical form, however, provokes the suspicion that he is trying to lay down norms for compositional practice. If literary formalism represents the critical antithesis of attempts to assert the primacy of content, then the aesthetics of musical content are dead and buried. Formalism is the aesthetic morality that is taken for granted; yet as soon as clearly defined forms, rather than form in general, are discussed, formalism is suspected of wanting to incarcerate music in schematic patterns.

[1]Text: Carl Dahlhaus, "Form," *Form in der Neuen Musik*, ed. E. Thomas (Mainz: Darmstädter Beitrage zur Neuen Musik, 1966), pp. 41–49; 71–75.

The critical function that formalism performs in literature has fallen in music to the concern with material. Yet matter and form are correlative concepts; the one is empty without the other. The concept of material as propounded by Adorno means preformed material. It is only formally defined matter or materially defined form—*materia secunda* or *forma secunda* (to use the language of scholasticism)—that has a real existence. One can, for example, view a drawn line from four different angles: as traces of lead, as an ornament, as a sine curve or as the image of a snake. But it is impossible to apprehend the line as pure matter beyond all forms of contemplation (and even viewing it as traces of lead is a form of contemplation).

Pure matter is a mystical category. Grasping it may be a goal that one may approach by means of, to use the language of mysticism, 'deformation' and 'de-becoming,' yet without reaching it. Mysticism and art, however, are mutually exclusive. Mystical 'deformation'—the attempt to break out of the forms of contemplation felt to be a prison—is completely at odds with the intention of making form perceivable. And however inappropriate it might be to judge using aesthetic criteria mystical tendencies that take their cue from acoustical facts or productions, it is nonetheless crucial to emphasize that music as art is incompatible with mysticism.

II

Form, according to Aristotle, is relative. In contrast to individual notes, the motif represents a form, as does the period in relation to the motifs and the movement in relation to the periods. And the conditions of formal concision are different on each level. A theory of form that neglects as indifferent or accidental the scale on which a formal component is effective is fancifully misguided.

Thus the statement, for example, that form is large-scale rhythm is a metaphor that should not be taken literally; it is of no use as a principle of a theory of form. The concept of rhythmic correspondence does not extend beyond the scope of the period. An antecedent and a consequent can just—and by no means always—be perceived as analogous to a weak and a strong beat, as rhythmically corresponding parts; correspondence between longer sections has to be justified thematically. The false assumption that form is large-scale rhythm has the consequence that sections comprising hundreds of bars are seen as corresponding bars, though thematic connections are either lacking or only vaguely implied. The mere exactness or similarity of the continuation is supposed to be sufficient to justify a connection that corresponds to the relation of the antecedent and consequent. The model of the period is blindly applied to stretches that are too long to be discernible as periods.

If it is thus sometimes difficult in the case of earlier music to avoid mistakes about the scale on which a formal principle is effective, then the possibilities for confusion have, in recent years, become boundless. Let it suffice to demonstrate this with a single example: that of statistical formation.

The procedure of describing a section or a group by the vertical or horizontal density of events is not unambiguous. In principle, all polyphonic music can be viewed from the point of view of density, and it is not clear where statistics are meaningful and where they are not. On the other hand, statistical concepts would be the most meagre of all imaginable categories, if vertical and horizontal density were to represent nothing more than the remainder of differentiation after the levelling-out of harmonic and rhythmic details. One would have to enquire, then, after the conditions under which statistical definitions could be effective without there having to be a loss of concision as far as detail is concerned. And one of the conditions would appear to be clarity in distinguishing between differences of scale.

Statistical categories are the more general ones and thus relate to fairly long stretches. If, however, the horizontal density of notes is to be, on the one hand, perceivable as a group feature and, on the other, compatible with the concision of rhythmic details, then there must be no doubt as to the approximate length of sections that are supposed to count as groups; an extreme change of scale in the course of a piece would make for confusion. What is a detail and what is a group must be as unmistakable as the difference in earlier music between motif and period. The clarity of statistical formation and the stability of formal scale are mutually supportive. The comprehensibility of a group resides in the forcefulness of statistical formation; as does, conversely, the perceptibility of statistical formation in expectations of the length of groups.

On the other hand, it is not futile to remind oneself how in earlier music the individual characteristics (the melodic, rhythmic and harmonic details) and the more general statistical features (average pitch level, vertical density and dynamic level) were distinguished from one another. The pitch level was less a melodic than a timbral, instrumental aspect; the harmonic-tonal function of a chord was dependent on the vertical density, that is, the number of notes; and a *sforzato* that performed a rhythmic function, such as accentuating a syncopation, was possible at different dynamic levels. The principle behind the distinction is clear. The details are independent of the statistically ascertainable features, since they are defined by categories other than merely high and low or loud and soft: melody by the character of intervals, harmony by tonal functions, and dynamics by rhythmic functions.

The premisses of earlier music—tonal harmony and metrical rhythm—cannot be restored. That, however, the special conditions of distinguishing detail from statistical formation are inoperative does not mean that the principle is dead and buried. The idea of basing individual characteristics on categories that extend beyond features to which statistical formation adheres retains its significance, even if the means with which it was realised are spent and have to be replaced by others.

III

If one is going to nominate a feature common to recent compositional tendencies, even the superficially divergent ones, then one would have to speak of a fear of things becoming fixed, the mistrust of consolidation. It is significant that the difference between consolidation and objectification —a difference that is decisive, however small it may seem—is seldom mentioned, if it is mentioned at all. The dialectic at work in the categories is reduced to an indiscriminate mistrust of everything fixed and complete. What is real or realised is felt to be—to put it bluntly—a betrayal of what is possible.

The objection is levelled against the clearly defined musical work. The expression 'work' is beginning to sound empty. The emphasis is supposed to be placed on the creation of music, not on the result; musical listening, it is argued, is the reconstruction of the process of composition, not the apprehension of a given artifact. "The work of art," wrote Paul Klee, "is first and foremost genesis. It is never experienced as a product."

The concepts of form coined by Stockhausen—'pointillist form,' 'group form' and 'statistical form'—also refer primarily to the creation, not the existence, of music. Stockhausen makes a distinction between form and formation; and the expression 'pointillist form' is an abbreviation for 'pointillist form-genesis.'

No one would wish to contradict the requirement that musical form has to be grasped in performance as the process of interaction between the individual components of a work. And in view of the popular misconception that musical forms are patterns filled out with varying content, the polemical assertion that the genesis is decisive, not the final product, is entirely justified.

However, the antithesis of genesis and product, as formulated by Paul Klee, becomes precarious as soon as it falls into the hands of epigones and no longer functions as criticism but as dogmatism. The mistrust of patterns and the endeavour to draw formal categories into the performance of music and understand them in that context turns into a tendency to disparage form as an artefact and a result, and ultimately to reject it as superfluous and as an impediment. Anyone who emphasizes the performance of music and neglects the interaction between formation and form, genesis and result is moving towards the abolition of formal categories.

One would not include Stockhausen among those who despise form; yet the concepts 'pointillist' and 'statistical,' although they were introduced as formal categories, do not refer to form but to compositional technique. They describe the structure of individual sections, not how they cohere. A complex of notes can be defined as 'pointillist' or 'statistical'; to say as much of a relation between two sections would be meaningless. The concepts 'pointillist' and 'statistical' say little or nothing about form, the relation of parts to one another and to the whole.

To object that the difference between compositional technique and form has been transcended and rendered inoperative in the newest music, and to say that anyone who insists upon the difference is applying an obsolete standard, would be futile. Decrees are not enough to eliminate and render ineffective the difference between structure and function, between the composition and the coherence of parts. The difference remains, whether or not one is inclined to talk about it. However, vocabularies that contain the word form, although they may describe nothing more than compositional technique, are misleading with regard to the fact that the problem of form, or of musical coherence, which they have seemingly solved, has not even been posed.

IV

The concept of parameter is a fetish to which theory clings all the more stubbornly, the more clearly experience reveals the dubious nature of its usefulness. One might accept that an expression for the physical correlative of a sound quality is applied to the sound quality itself, if the correlation were complete; but it is not. Timbre is a sound quality, but not a parameter, since it does not fulfil the condition of being variable independently of the other parameters.

It is not certain whether the other sound qualities signified by the expression parameter are suitable as the starting-point for the development of formal categories. The concept of parameter is tangential to the accustomed categories; and, although tradition may be a weak authority, it is by no means futile to remind oneself of the difference.

The difference is concealed by efforts to bring the categories melody, rhythm and dynamics into line with the idea that music is made up of parameters. Melody is supposed to be definable as an arrangement of pitches, rhythm as that of note values, dynamics as the gradation of degrees of loudness. However, the reduction of the traditional categories to sound qualities is arbitrary. For melody implies rhythm, and rhythm implies aspects of dynamics. Whereas a parameter is a simple quality strictly separated from the other parameters, melody and rhythm are complex matters or forms of perception that merge into one another.

What is simple, the individual parameter, is abstract; a sound quality, separated from the other ones, has no real existence. Only what is complex is concrete, the note as the embodiment of its features. And the analysis of serial music, if it is facts of perception that are to be described, must itself form concepts that describe what is concrete. The term 'pointillist' is characteristic, defining notes as individuals, not as relative positions in three or four rows.

Even when the parameters are individually and separately subject to the serial principle, a group of notes is nonetheless perceived as something that results from the interaction of sound qualities. This fact makes it seem reasonable to investigate the relations between parameters. It scarcely needs to be mentioned that parameters are qualities that fit only reluctantly into a common scheme that is the same for all of them; the primitive kind of parallelism which attempted to subject dynamics or articulation to the same conditions as pitch is a thing of the past. Boulez has observed: "One should no longer have any illusions about our perceptional ability to trace different acoustical phenomena such as pitch and duration back to common patterns." However, bearing in mind the unequal behaviour of the parameters is only an initial and basic precondition for an analysis of the relationships between sound qualities. In traditional music, a description of interactions is a retrospective procedure, an attempt to explain complexes that present themselves to our immediate perception as complete and undissected. Thus, in the idea of rhythm, for example, relations between the duration and dynamics are included which one seldom has to (nor needs to) become conscious of to listen in an adequate manner. It is precisely one of the functions of the traditional categories to make the compound appear as an undivided unity. Categories are forms of contemplation, and they regulate perception. And the concept of rhythm, which combines duration with aspects of dynamic gradation, represents the exact equivalent of a way of listening.

It is probably impossible to restore unaltered the complex categories which relate several parameters. Analytical thinking, the correlative to composition with separate parameters, cannot be revoked. Thus it is all the more necessary to become aware of the interaction of the sound qualities. They can neither be ignored, nor are they, as in tradition, self-evidencies implicit in the categories of musical listening which do not require explication. There is no alternative but, in an analytical context, to solve problems concerning the interaction of parameters which in earlier music were solved without being thought of as problems.

Schoenberg wrote in 1926: "Real thought, the musical idea, the immutable, is determined by the relationship between the pitches and the division of time. Everything else, on the other hand—dynamics, clarity, effect etc.—is really only a means of presentation serving to make the idea comprehensible, and can be changed." To dismiss the distinction Schoenberg makes as being the expression of an outmoded state of compositional technique would be blind presumption, for it could very well be that the hierarchy of sound qualities of which Schoenberg speaks, the priority of pitch and duration, is a fact which one has to take into account and not a mere assumption which one can ignore. The most obvious differences are those between pitch and timbre. Whereas in the case of pitches the relative quality—the interval character—is of decisive, and the absolute quality of minor, significance, the opposite is true in the case of timbre, which is perceived primarily as an absolute quality.

Relationships between tone colours—degrees of similarity and difference—can only be defined in vague terms; and the idea of transposing the relationship between two tone colours would border on the fictitious. Duration and dynamics occupy the middleground between pitch and timbre—from the point of view of concision and transposability of relationships. Duration is nearer to pitch, dynamics nearer to timbre. Thus it is not an empty assertion to say that sound qualities form a hierarchy.

It is not difficult to sketch some of the consequences for a theory of form that emerge as a result. Degrees of loudness and timbres, however much they may be graded, are restricted to elementary, rudimentary formal connections. They are either similar or different and antithetical, and nothing else. Other categories appear not to be accessible to subordinate, peripheral sound qualities. It is scarcely conceivable that something could be composed which concisely and unambiguously performs the function of a continuation or a complement merely by making use of timbres and degrees of loudness. Yet no one is safe from mistaking the limits of his imagination for those of reality, least of all the theoretician.

V

Banal matters, and they in particular, are also sometimes forgotten or ignored. The spread of an analytical technique that Boulez has deservedly called 'book-keeping' compels one to recall the fact that formal categories are not reducible to features that are present in the score and, conversely, that it is not sufficient to register characteristics of a composition in order to arrive at formal concepts by summarising and generalisation. 'Inductive method' is not infrequently a synonym for thoughtlessness.

Thus, for instance, the features on which the division of a period into an antecedent and a consequent are based are not always the same. The harmonic outline can be decisive, but so can the melodic connection or the rhythmic correspondence of the halves; and components that in one case are constitutive diminish in importance in another or are omitted altogether. It is not possible, then, to reduce the concept of the period to fixed characteristics that recur in each and every case. And, conversely, it is improbable or even impossible that the method of registering features would ever have led one to formulate a concept such as that of the period.

Formal concepts are regulative concepts. They mark points of view from which notes or groups of notes are supposed to be brought together and related. They are not derivable from the mere accumulation of perceptual data. If anything, it is the other way round: perception depends on formal categories. In Schoenberg's Piano Piece Op. 11, No. 1, for example, it is not immaterial whether bars 9–11, a variant of bars 1–3, are understood as the conclusion of the first, or the beginning of a second period. There are interactions between the division (the form) and the melodic connections (the content). On the one hand, the motivic connections establish one of the prerequisites of the formal functions; on the other hand, the motivic connections that are emphasized depend on the formal function. If the modified return of the main thematic idea in bars 9–11 is understood as the beginning of a second period, then the alterations of the melody come under the concept of variation. They appear as the augmentation and inversion of intervals: the minor third B–G sharp and the minor second G sharp–G are expanded in bars 9–10 to a major third F sharp–D and a major second D–C; and the falling semitone F–E is inverted in bar 11 to become a rising semitone A–B flat. If, on the other hand, one views bars 9–11 as the conclusion of a tripartite period, the features which make the third phrase appear as a complement and consequence of the first two, bars 1–8, come to the fore. The rising semitone is then less a mere variant of the descending one than a complementary 'answer'; and the sequence F sharp–D–C in bars 9–10 is understood not only as an extension of B–G sharp–G but also as a transposition of E–C–B flat, the beginning of the second phrase. The motivic connections are a prerequisite as well as a function—a dependent variable—of the formal categories that determine musical listening.

The expression 'period' describes a pattern, a model; more precisely, since the eighteenth century it has been so closely associated with a particular pattern that it has become unusable in any other context. But because the model is incompatible with the conditions of contemporary composition does not mean that the general concept it represents is a thing of the past. The category of complementation on which the period pattern is based is not tied to any particular version of it. It is still relevant independently of the preconditions of compositional technique.

Yet in a strict sense one can only speak of a formal category in music when it is neither so general as the category of complementation nor when it has the task of disguising metaphorically the description of one particular case. A use of metaphor which plunders the arsenal of scientific terminology is merely the reverse of 'book-keeping'.

What one ought to be looking for are categories which a listener must have at his disposal in order to understand the relationship between two sections as being one of complementation; regulative categories, which mark points of view from which individual features fit together as meaningful constructs. A theory of form remains unfounded if it cannot find support in intermediate categories which mediate between blind facts and empty universals, categories which neither hover in the rarified air of abstraction nor amount to no more than pigeonholing the registering of features. The category 'period' may be taken to be paradigmatic. Whether the concept 'group' can perform a similar function, or whether a group is defined by nothing more than the fact that a sound quality or compositional feature is sustained during a section, appears to be an open question.

VI

The attempt to develop concepts of form that go beyond definitions of compositional technique is impeded by the idea that dodecaphony is incompatible with categories such as theme and development, transition and countersubject. The claim that Schoenberg's method of forcibly combining twelve-note composition and developmental form is in itself contradictory, and the result inconsistent, has become a *topos* it is not necessary to talk about because it is supposed to be self-evident. It would appear, however, that the arguments on which the objections to Schoenberg are founded are themselves based on a misunderstanding, namely, on the confusion of abstract relationships and concrete forms.

A theme is a melodic shape, a real structure. But the sequence of pitches—that is, also the row which regulates it—is a dependent component which has no real existence without rhythm and dynamics. It is only together with an arrangement of durations and a gradation of degrees of dynamics that a sequence of pitches becomes a musical phenomenon.

However, if a sequence of pitches is already an abstraction, then a row is one to an even greater degree. It consists in nothing but the relationships linking basic set, inversion, retrograde and retrograde inversion. The name 'basic set' is misleading, for the initial shape in which a row appears is no more important than later ones. The name suggests that we should treat basic set and row as equivalents, thereby confusing the means of representation with what is being represented. The basic set is just one form of the row among others. What can be notated is a particular interval, a major third, for instance. The concept of a row, however, refers to the abstract factor which is common to the major third, the minor sixth and the major tenth, both upwards and downwards—to a feature for which there is neither a name nor a sign.

The meaning of the serial principle is distorted by talking about exposition and derivations of the row. A row relates to the individual forms, by means of which it is represented, as the formula $n/n+1$ does to the ratios $1{:}2$, $2{:}3$, $3{:}4$ etc. And it is just as nonsensical to describe particular forms of a row as derivations of a basic set as it is to maintain that the ratios $2{:}3$ and $3{:}4$ are derivations of $1{:}2$. A row is nothing but an embodiment of relationships.

If one thinks of the row as an abstraction, then the assertion that dodecaphony and developmental form are incompatible becomes questionable. Categories such as theme and continuation, complement and contrast, transition and countersubject are not affected by the serial principle; dodecaphony neither suggests nor justifies them, neither precludes them nor divests them of meaning. Form is independent of the serial principle in the same way as the syntax of a language is independent of phonological rules. One can change the one system without tampering with the other; in the case of categories such as conditional or final clause it is irrelevant whether the pitch at which a syllable is spoken registers a difference in the meaning of the words or not. Categories of musical form refer to things that are real, to melodic-rhythmic forms, not to abstract components. Nor does the generalisation of the serial of the serial principle to cover all parameters affect the difference between syntax and phonology. It is not the arrangement of rows but the musical forms resulting from the interaction of pitch sequence, rhythm and dynamics that comprise the substance of form. The serial principle is neutral; it does not establish form, but it does not preclude it either.

Schoenberg understood form as coherence. He only partly realised his intention to write a theory of musical coherence. One suspects that a repeat attempt under conditions that make it still more difficult would similarly remain a fragment. Yet difficulties constitute a provocation, or at least they should do.

Concluding Remarks

I

To expect a discussion about musical form to produce definitions and prescriptions would be naive. It is by no means certain what form in music is, and an attempt to formulate rules would provoke nothing but derision. Even the premiss on which the discussion was based, the assertion that the newest music had encountered difficulties that one would have to understand as formal problems, did not pass unchallenged. Some composers seem convinced that form is something self-evident which does not need talking about. Nothing that appears, they argue, is without form; in order to be perceivable a thing or a process must present itself in a form. Thus they conclude that it is absurd to speak of formlessness.

Yet the universal concept of form that embraces everything in existence is not a topic of music theory. That is not what was meant, and was only used to deny the existence of the problem at hand. Even debris has a form; but it is not the object of discussion between architects.

On the other hand, nothing would be more erroneous than to assert that it is only compositional practice that has lost its bearings. Theory is in no less of a predicament. The concept of form itself—and not just the creation of forms—has become a problem.

This concept of form derives from nineteenth-century formal theory, and the traces of its origins are still in evidence. A historical digression is thus unavoidable. Anyone who wishes to get away from the past, instead of merely denying its existence, must first become aware of it.

The concept of form that was developed on the basis of the model of the song, the rondo and the sonata rests on two principles which have become doubtful in the twentieth century, yet which were so much taken for granted in the nineteenth century that they did not need to be explicitly described and were thus not recognised as problems. The first premiss was the distinction between content and form. It was not intended as a division; no one denied that content and form constituted a whole. Yet one regarded the indivisibility on the lines of the unity of soul and body. The form was considered to be the shell surrounding the content, and the theory of form a parallel to anatomy; the soul was consigned to aesthetics, the theology of art religion.

One can only do justice to the theory of form if one recognises that it was thought of as a complement to aesthetics. Musical poetics, a coherent and unified theory of the creation of musical forms, did not exist; it was divided into aesthetics and theory of form.

The double meaning of the concept of the theme is a typical example, whereas in formal terms a theme was considered to be a complex of motifs, in aesthetic terms it was seen as the expression of a content. The elaboration of a theme was thought of as the development of the motifs on the one hand, and of an explication of the contents on the other. A theme was a character, as it were, who had to be taken through changing situations in order to show the stuff he was made of.

The second principle of the theory of form was the idea that a musical form belonged primarily to a genre and was only secondarily an individual. No one denied that an individual is not only an example of a genre, but also a person. Yet the soul was the concern of aesthetics. In the theory of form the features common to musical works counted as essential, whereas the distinguishing ones were regarded as being inessential. The theory of form was a description of genres. True, the theory of form repeated the universals debate; whether a genre was an idea *ante rem*, an essence *in re* or an abstraction *post rem* remained uncertain. That, however, concepts of form were concepts of genre appeared to be beyond dispute. Whatever did not belong to a genre counted as 'formless'; musical malformations were analogous to the monsters of zoology.

Both principles—the distinction between content and form as well as the explanation of forms as genres—have been abandoned in the twentieth century, and it would be anachronistic to adhere to them. Traditional theory of form and its correlative, the aesthetics of content, are dead and buried. Yet the decline has left behind problems that cannot be solved by not talking about them.

First, a theory of the new and newest music would have to attempt to develop musical poetics which are not split into theory of form and aesthetics. And secondly, it would have to establish the possibility of appraising musical forms without invoking concepts of genre. As long as one understood forms in terms of genre it was not difficult to justify the assertion that a work was formless; the criticism may have been narrow-minded, but it was not unfounded. If, however, a work is an individual without genre, then the judgment seems to be based on nothing. Nonetheless, no one doubts that one can distinguish between successful and unsuccessful forms; and the difference that exists must also be explainable.

II

The erosion of the concept of form upheld by the theory of form led to the concept of structure acquiring a significance that one can describe, without exaggeration, as a hyperfunction. 'Structure' has become an in-word. However, in-words sometimes serve no other purpose than to conceal difficulties; they are ideology, false consciousness, in verbal form.

The concept of structure occupies a position midway between categories that are clearly distinguished in traditional music theory: between 'form' and 'compositional technique.' And the mediating character, which permits a *quid pro quo*, leads one to draw false conclusions. Under the cover of the ambiguity of the concept the error thrives that it is sufficient to solve difficulties in compositional technique in order at the same time to solve formal ones. The problem concealed by using the term 'structure' as an in-word is the problem of form. No one denies that it would be unnatural to keep form and structure firmly apart. That, however, it is impossible to break something down into pieces does not mean that a distinction is nonsensical. And it is perhaps not unfruitful, by analysing verbal usage, to call to mind some of the differences between form and structure.

First, the term 'structure' suggests details, connections in a small space; the word 'form', on the other hand, the outline of the whole, relations over wide stretches. Form is a relative concept; a motif is the form of its notes, a theme the form of the motifs. Yet the level to which the concept of form primarily refers is that of the whole movement.

Secondly, the expression 'structure' can be related to abstract components, to pitches or time values separated from the remaining sound qualities. It is reasonable to speak of the structure of a series of pitches, although a series of pitches without duration or dynamics has no real, perceivable existence, for it is a mere abstraction. What is meant by the term 'form,' on the other hand, is a concrete musical shape in which pitch, duration, dynamics and timbre interact. One automatically hesitates to ascribe a form to an abstract sequence of pitches; a row is a structure, but not a form.

Thirdly, structure tends to be a technical concept, which suggests the genesis of a work, the process of production, whereas form is an aesthetic category which refers to the result, the audible shape. A structure need not be perceivable; the method need not be apparent from the result. The idea of an inaudible musical form would be a contradiction in terms. Structure is the aspect of the work directed at the composer, form that which is directed at the listener.

If one accepts as adequate the analysis of the use of the word, then the fact that the term 'structure' has become an in-word in the last fifteen years appears symptomatic. The emphasis placed on the term is characteristic of the thing it signifies: a compositional structure that seeks to attain self-awareness in the concept of structure.

First, attention was focused more on details, not on the form of the whole. Secondly, a network of connections was created from the abstract components of music, the parameters of pitch, duration, dynamics and timbre, but often the concrete melodic-rhythmic forms, the result of the interaction between individual sound qualities, were left to chance, although they alone are the object of musical perception. Thirdly, there was a tendency to neglect the result in favour of the process of creation; caught up in the problems of method, one treated the product almost with contempt, as if it were a side-product of composition and not its goals.

In contrast, it transpired in the discussion about form that it was the point of the congress to draw attention to the concept of form as a counter-principle to that of structure. If we are talking about form, then we should—generally speaking—remember the trivial fact that it is nonsensical to sacrifice the outline of the whole to the structure of the details, the concrete musical shape to the preparation of abstract components, and the result to the method.

III

Next to structure, 'open form' appeared to be the central point around which the discussion revolved. Yet in order to be able to talk about the matter one must analyse the word and distinguish between several meanings of the expression 'open form'. For the arguments brought forward either for or against 'open form' sometimes pertained to matters that, apart from the name, had little or nothing in common.

By 'open forms' one understood, first, pieces in which individual sections are fixed and unalterable, yet where the sequence of the sections is variable and left to the performer. The variability is, however, aesthetically fictitious. For the listener it does not exist; he does not relate the version he is hearing to other possible ones the performer could have chosen, but did not choose. What is a variable form on paper is fixed in performance; and, insofar as form is a category that refers to the perceivable result and not to the method, 'open form' is not 'open.'

In the case of a second method described by Earle Brown the composer limits himself to providing materials the arrangement of which is variable. Not only the arrangement of the sections is alterable but also the structure of details. One can, without the expression being meant polemically, speak of a 'building-block principle.' If the preformed materials were motifs, then the variable interweaving would be comparable with traditional motivic work, with the difference that the work is not the job of the composer but of the performer. The method appears to be based on the intention to restore the game quality of music. What is supposed to be decisive is not the complete work as a law and an obligation to which performer and listener submit, but the activity of musicmaking. The ultimate consequence would be the assertion that the evolution from musical activity to producing works, from *praxis* to *poiesis*, has been misguided. Yet it is difficult to accept this view.

According to a third version, the concept of 'open form' means that the division or articulation of a musical shape is a matter for the listener. Mauricio Kagel characterised structure as a passive aspect and articulation as an active one; and he appeared to be thinking of the activity of the listener who is supposed to impose order upon a structure presented to him. However, the procedure has certain drawbacks.

On the one hand, a lack of concise rhythmic articulation provokes a relapse into primitive forms of reaction on the part of the listener. Rhythmic structures that are not clearly articulated are related to a regular beat pattern and perceived as incoherent syncopations.

On the other hand, musical form, coherence on a large scale, is endangered or even negated by the ambiguity of articulation. A single section may be articulated in different ways, all of which are meaningful. Yet it is improbable, even if not impossible, that a large number of sections will form a coherent whole if the articulation of the individual sections, on which the connection between the sections depends, is left to the listener.

If form is clearly articulated, then an error on the part of the listener will be corrected by the continuation. Anyone who mistakes a consequent clause for an antecedent one will be made aware of his error by the break in musical syntax which becomes apparent in the transition to the next section. If he clings to the misunderstanding, then the form disintegrates; the music becomes incomprehensible. If, however, all possible articulations are equally correct, then the form, which is not present in the object, can also not be established by the subject. The formal imagination of the listener is not enough when it comes to larger contexts. If form is to be heard it must also be composed.

IV

The tendency towards 'open form' is a protest against the fixed patterns of which the theory of form is accused. The embodiment of what composers take particular exception to is the A–B–A formula, ternary form, which a century ago was considered to be the origin and foundation of all musical forms. Yet it seems on the one hand that an injustice is being done to the fixed patterns, and that, on the other hand, there is a renewed tendency towards the abstract (which was criticised in the case of the theory of form) in compositional procedures, albeit in a new guise.

Abstract patterns are not the goal but rather the starting-point of music analysis. They perform a heuristic, not a normative function. In its immediate, abstract form, a formula such as A–B–B–A says little or nothing about the music which one is attempting to describe. In order to become significant it has to be interpreted. Only the individual case will reveal whether the opening sections A–B belong together, and whether the closing sections B–A are to be understood as the inversion of A–B, or whether the return of A constitutes the formal framework into which section B and its repetition are inserted. The pattern is not a representation of the form but an instrument towards its understanding; and one can only pass judgement on tools on the basis of the use one makes of them. *Musique informelle* strives away from the abstractness of the pattern, from form as formula, yet it falls victim to a second abstractness which is just as empty as the first. The symptom of extreme *musique informelle* is the heterogeneous nature of the details from which a musical shape is constructed. Disconnected matter stands side by side in sharp contrast. Yet the more heterogeneous two events are, the more abstrct is the connection that exists between them. The interval of a fifth and the noise of a machine are linked by nothing except the common feature of being acoustical data. The designation 'acoustical data' is the most abstract definition in music one can think of.

It would appear to be the goal of *musique informelle* to draw undivided attention to the isolated detail, to the individual musical

813

moment. What is acoustically given is supposed to appear in the pure present, without links to the past or the future. However, the possibility of severing completely the connection between individual musical moments is doubtful. The connection is not eliminated, but simply becomes ever more tenuous and abstract.

In contrast, musical form consists in a balance between detail and context, between the heterogeneous and the homogeneous. If the juxta-position of fifth and machine noise is an example of heterogeneity, then the metrical framework of the eight-bar period appears as the paradigm of homogeneity: beats, bars and groups of bars are subjected to the same law of alternation between strong and weak.

Anyone who speaks of balance arouses suspicion of having classicist inclinations. But the point of a discussion about form is less to defend certain positions than to reach agreement about concepts. One does not need to want form—and form is balance. Yet if it is not form one wants, then it is not form one should talk about.